1001
PROGRAMMING
RESOURCES

By Edward J. Renehan, Jr.

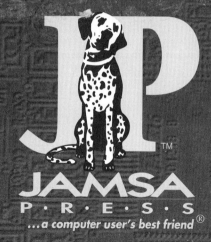

JAMSA
P·R·E·S·S
...a computer user's best friend®

Published by
Jamsa Press
2975 S. Rainbow Blvd., Suite I
Las Vegas, NV 89102
U.S.A.

For information about the translation or distribution of any Jamsa Press book, please write to Jamsa Press at the address listed above.

1001 Programming Resources

Printed in the United States of America.
98765432

ISBN 1-884133-50-9

Publisher
  Debbie Jamsa

Director of Publishing Operations
  Janet Lawrie

Composition
  Nelson Yee

Cover Design
  Marianne Helm

Proofers
  Heather Grigg
  Rosemary Pasco
  Jeanne Smith

Technical Advisor
  Phil Schmauder

Copy Editors
  Heather Grigg
  Rosemary Pasco

Indexer
  John Bianchi

Cover Photograph
  O'Gara/Bissell

Production Manager
  Rick Pearson

Table of Contents

98-771

III

IV

INTRODUCTION

THE CONVERSION

My programmer friend scoffed when I told him what I was up to. "Sure Ed," he aid. "Great idea. Here, have another beer."

"What don't you like about it?" I asked. We were sitting on the aft-end of a sloop moored in Wickford Harbor, near my home in Rhode Island. It was a lazy day. We had time to shoot-the-bull.

"There's nothing for you to work with," said Chris. "There's nothing left for programmers and other turbo-geeks on the World Wide Web. And, even if there is stuff out there, you can't find it amid everything else. There is so much junk! All the new cyber-immigrants have brought their garbage along with them and dumped it along the electronic roadside. They've literally trashed the digital wilderness. There's so much useless, dated, bad information floating around in cyberspace that you can spend your life trying to ferret out the small bits of useful, current, good information."

"Tell me more," I said. Chris took another tug on his beer, sighed, and started talking. I'm sure it seems to him that he is always having to educate me.

"The Internet used to be just a bunch of scientists sending each other notes. It was their land. They were the Indians. (Excuse me, did I say 'Indians'? I mean 'Native Americans.') They were on the Internet from the very beginning. They roughed-out the first perilous trails. They communicated with packets of cyber smoke-signals that seem primitive to us today."

"Then, us hackers came along. We were the trappers and cowboys. And inadvertently, by settling the wilderness and making the place a bit more habitable through our innovations, we created an infrastructure that allowed less-technically-astute people to come after us and squeeze us out. We settled the country and made it safe for the amateurs: the pioneers. Now they've all arrived: the preachers and pornographers, the accountants and stock-brokers, the corporations and the outlaws. And like I said, they've brought their junk with them."

"So how does the junk get in your way?" I asked. "After all, unlike the American west, geography on the Internet is truly limitless. There is and always will be plenty of room for everybody."

"Yes," said Chris. "But how do you find yourself and get your bearings in that limitless geography? If you don't know where you are, if you can't find your way to the next watering-hole, you're dead. The only maps we have are Web search engines; and they are less than optimal when you consider all the new-pioneer trash an engine has to wade through before providing responses to queries. I look up 'game programming' and I get CBS sports broadcast schedules along with details on game-protection programs in Yosemite. I have to do some heavy scrolling to find something with a title that even looks like it might address my need, and even then I am often disappointed. The link is either old and goes nowhere or it is old and goes to dated information. And then, once again, I'm stranded."

I tugged on my beer. I was about to win the debate. Chris was providing my argument. He was defining the book's purpose himself, without much help from me.

"That's what I want to do," I said.

"What's that?"

VI

"I want to provide a map. a reliable map to the watering holes. I want to help programmers find their way home on the vast expanse of the Web."

"There are still places for them in cyberspace. I want to provide pointers to those places: pointers to a whole bunch of informationally-rich, current, and useful information-watering-holes."

"These are places that the programmers and systems developers might find anyway, eventually, but will find much faster (and perhaps before supplies run out) with the help of a good map."

Chris' eyes lit up. He suddenly "got it." He had undergone a conversion.

"Hey man," he said. "You do that and you'll have yourself a book."

"OK, cowboy. That's what I'm going to do."

THE MANY TYPES OF WATERING HOLES

Various watering-holes differ in the nature of the sustenance they provide. Look up any old, antique pioneer map of the American west. You'll find that the watering-holes are not only clearly marked, but also color-coded.

The different color codes indicate practical, geological, seasonal and medicinal differences. One watering-hole might hold an abundance, another something less than an abundance. One watering-hole might dry up in winter, another in summer. One might be safe for cattle but not for humans. And another might be poison for all. One might be in the public domain and available free to all comers; another might be the property of a pistol-packing hermit. One watering-hold might be spring-fed, another stream-fed. Both provide fresh water, but the latter offers not only the chance of a drink, but the option of sticking to the stream, following it on its course.

In mapping the programmer-oriented watering-holes of the Internet, I have done away with sites that are poison. In other words, I have simply not included those sites which are past their season, or which are so skimpy with their resources so as not to be useful. What remains are the essential sites, the essential watering-holes. And these can be divided up into resources offering any or all of five distinct characteristics.

WHAT MAKES A GOOD WATERING HOLE?

As I have mentioned, there are five key characteristics which, alone or in any combination, go to qualify a Web site as a worthwhile watering-hole. The presence of any single one of these characteristics is good enough, in my estimation, to define a site as a recommended destination for programmers and system developers seeking sustenance on the cyber-prairies and deserts of the World Wide Web. These characteristics are present in sites which are:

STRONG CONTENT

Informationally Rich—Who can dispute the usefulness of a Web site that provides a wealth and depth of useful, timely, and constantly-refreshed technical information (white papers and so on)?

COVERS DETAILS

Esoterically Essential—Who can doubt the value of a site that provides otherwise undocumented hints or tips designed to help one solve rare and exotic programming problems addressed nowhere else in the literature?

OPEN TO ALL

Open To All—Who needs to deal with pistol-packing squatters? Who needs gatekeepers and ticket-punchers on the frontier? Not us!

FREE SOFTWARE

Free Software Trading Posts—Who can doubt the need to take on provisions once in a while? And who can dispute the value of a site where those supplies (in the form of Java applets, software demos, compilers and other goodies) are available for free?

EXCELLENT REFERENCES

Stream-Fed—Finally, who can question the safety and efficiency of a stream-fed watering hole, such as a site offering many related links to speed and help you on your journey in search of essential programming information?

As you shall see, for every site listed in this book I have provided an icon key to indicate precisely which of the above characteristics, singly or in combination, the site has been found to contain. Without possessing at least one of these characteristics, a site quite-simply will not be found here. Our map takes us to places that are worth getting to, and nowhere else.

HOME ON THE RANGE

Your home on the range is the place you start from when exploring the Web. Many readers of this book will probably already have access to the World Wide Web via a corporate connection or a pre-established account with an on-line service. (Many of today's on-line services even allow members to create their own home-page on the Web, thus making them very real homes "on the range.")

For those readers who are not as yet connected to the Web, the good people at Jamsa Press have arranged with several major Internet providers and on-line services to offer readers of *1001 Programming Resources* some excellent deals. In fact, they have set it up so that you can get, in some cases, free access time to the Internet. In other cases, you get significantly reduced start-up costs. Either way, we are talking about some very good deals.

The process could not be easier. Use the software provided on the accompanying CD-ROM to connect to the Web and to great deals for Web access. The CD-ROM includes software for various providers and services, each of which offers different levels of Web support and access. None of them are the right option for everyone. But at least one is bound to be the right option for you. Test drive the various providers and services courtesy of the special offers you'll find described on the disc, then choose the service that you think best suits your needs.

USING THE CD-ROM VERSION OF THIS BOOK

In addition to Internet connection software for Windows 95 and Windows 3.1, the CD-ROM that accompanies this book includes a fully searchable electronic version of the book itself. Using the CD, you can read the electronic book much like you would this one. You can read sequentially, moving from one site to the next. Or you can search for specific topics using fast and easy search-software that is built into the electronic edition. The links in the Windows 95 version of the CD-ROM's electronic book are clickable. If you are connected to the Web when you run the CD, you can click on a URL in the electronic-book and go directly to the actual desired page on the Web.

To start the CD-ROM under Windows 95 all you need to is insert the CD into your drive. Windows 95 will, in turn, automatically display the "cover" of the electronic version of the book.

To start the CD-ROM using Windows 3.1, perform these simple steps:

1. Place the CD-ROM in your drive.

2. Under Windows 3.1, select the Program Manager file menu and choose Run. Windows will display the Run dialog box.

3.   Within the Run dialog box, type the command D:\SETUP, replacing the drive letter D with the drive letter that corresponds to your CD-ROM drive. For example, if your CD-ROM drive is E, you would type E:\SETUP.

4.   Choose OK. The SETUP program will install the necessary files onto your hard drive, in the process creating a *1001 Programming Resources* icon.

5.   Click on the icon. Hereafter, whenever you want to use the electronic version of the book, simply put the CD into the drive and click this icon.

A WORD ABOUT TREES

Books, at least for the moment, are primarily printed on paper. Paper, of course, comes from trees. And trees, of course, come from forests. Worldwide, our forests are being devastated. In South America, a section of rain forest equivalent to the size of ten city blocks is burned off every minute. And 96,000 acres are burned off every day. In fact, more than 55% of the world's tropical rain forests have been wiped out in the scope of the last twenty years. Through the Rain Forest Action Network's Protect-an-Acre Program, I am subsidizing the protection of an acre of rain-forest for every ten thousand copies of this book printed, thereby protecting at least two trees for every one felled for production of this book. For more information on the Rain Forest Action Network's Protect-an-Acre Program, access the Web site addressed as *http://www.ran.org* or write to them at 450 Sansome Street, Suite 700, San Francisco, CA 94111. You may also send them e-mail requesting more information at *ran-info@ran.org*.

Asta la vista,

Edward J. Renehan, Jr.

Wickford, North Kingstown, Rhode Island

ejren@earthlink.net

http://members.aol.com/EJRen/EJRen.html

AMERICAN ASSOCIATION FOR ARTIFICIAL INTELLIGENCE

http://www.aaai.org/

If you are looking for "research quality" high-tech discussions on all aspects of Artificial Intelligence (AI), from agents to neural nets and more, take time now to visit the AI industry's Web-based watering hole. The American Association for Artificial Intelligence (AAAI) launched its Web site in March 1995, and since that time it has developed into a rich resource. For starters, the site contains complete details on each of the organization's many conferences, symposiums, workshops, scholarships, fellowships, and publications. Among the latter are none other than the internationally acclaimed *AI Magazine*, the annual *AI Directory*, and many technical reports, proceedings, and complete books published jointly by the AAAI in cooperation with MIT Press.

Figure 1.1 Home page of the AAAI.

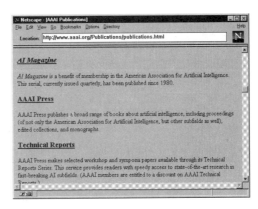

Figure 1.2 AAAI publications.

ARTIFICIAL INTELLIGENCE RESOURCES ON THE INTERNET

http://ai.iit.nrc.ca/ai_top.html

Best described as a cornucopia of AI-based topics, the folks at the Institute for Information Technology (and their friends at the Canadian Society for the Computational Studies of Intelligence) have created this splendid site. You will find links to hundreds of AI-related Internet resources including archives for newsgroups and mailing-lists, AI bibliographies, and information on conferences, journals, lists of frequently asked questions, researcher home pages, employment opportunities, software repositories and directories, AI WAIS servers, and more. You can search for AI organizations by specialty or by geographical region. The same goes for AI research firms and laboratories. If you bookmark just one AI site, this cyber-crossroads of AI information on the Internet is the one you want.

Figure 2.1 AI resources on the Internet.

Figure 2.2 Also available in French.

3

ARTIFICIAL INTELLIGENCE VIDEOS

http://www.uvc.com/us/ArtificialIntelligence.index.html

Are you thinking about having the guys and gals from the AI lab over for a Friday night "get together" but you're not sure how to keep them entertained? Well, check out these videos on artificial intelligence created by leading researchers in the field. Among your choices are Karen Sparck Jones of Cambridge University discussing the art of "Finding Information Wood in the Natural Language Trees," Barbara Grosz of Harvard explaining collaborative plans and dialogue participation, Ruzena Bajcsy of the University of Pennsylvania lecturing on the topic of cooperative agents (machine and human), and Stanford's Edward A. Feigenbaum ruminating on the "tiger in a cage" that a knowledge-system can sometimes be. Each video is at least one hour in length.

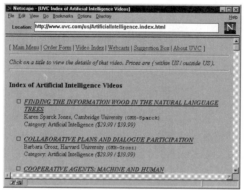

Figure 3.1 AI video information.

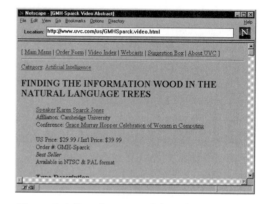

Figure 3.2 Details on one of the videos.

4

ASSOCIATION FOR UNCERTAINTY IN ARTIFICIAL INTELLIGENCE

http://www.auai.org/

Can't make up your mind which AI site to visit first? The Association for Uncertainty in Artificial Intelligence is a non-profit organization whose main purpose is run the annual Conference on Uncertainty in Artificial Intelligence (UAI)—which they have run every year since 1985. Uncertainty is the science of fostering machine reasoning via fuzzy logic, a logic system built by that machine through trial and error. The Association also maintains a great mailing list for discussion of topics related to the representation and management of uncertain information. To subscribe, send mail to: *Majordomo@Maillist.cs.orst.edu.* In the body of your e-mail message, type the text: *subscribe [your e-mail address]* (for example, subscribe BillC@whitehouse.gov).

Figure 4.1 The Association's home page.

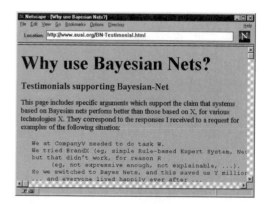

Figure 4.2 An on-line tutorial from AUAI.

Austrian Research Institute for Artificial Intelligence

http://www.ai.univie.ac.at/

One of the most exciting applications of AI research relates to the field of medicine. Maintained by the Department of Medical Cybernetics and Artificial Intelligence at the University of Vienna (IMKAI) and the Austrian Research Institute for Artificial Intelligence (OFAI), this impressive Web site includes a number of valuable AI software packages for medical diagnosis (which you can download using FTP), including software designed to diagnose cardiac arrhythmia from symbolic descriptions of electrocardiograms, an Incremental Diagnostic Algorithm (IDA) for model-based diagnosis (when models are represented by constraint logic programs), and a robust toolbox for simulating artificial neural networks in C or C++ with graphical interfaces for X-Windows and Windows.

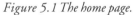

Figure 5.1 The home page.

Figure 5.2 Details on OFAI.

C++ Machine Learning Library (Free Download!)

http://www.sgi.com/Technololgy/mlc

Machine learning is, quite simply, the science of enabling machines to learn from trial and error via fuzzy logic and neural networks. The Machine Learning Library in C++ (MLC++) is a library of C++ classes for supervised machine learning. The MLC++ utilities were created using this library. The library is public domain and was originally created at Stanford University. Silicon Graphics is now making the library, the utilities, the documentation, the source code, and even a great MLC++ tree visualizer available for free download on their Web site. More than just a collection of existing algorithms, MLC++ is an attempt to extract the commonalities of machine learning algorithms and decompose them for a unified view that is simple, coherent, and extensible.

Figure 6.1 Silicon Graphics' MLC++ page.

Figure 6.2 MLC++ documentation.

UNIVERSITY OF CHICAGO AI LAB

http://www.cs.uchicago.edu/html/groups/ai/

In the not too distant future, the folks at the AI lab of the University of Chicago envision creating machines that interact with and learn from their environment in much the same way as living creatures do now. With this thought in mind, we should not be surprised that the Lab's researchers are developing these machines by deriving inspiration from and emulating biological nervous systems. Using this neuromorphic approach, the Lab's researchers are developing and integrating for machine visual, auditory, tactile, and olfactory systems. Tune into the Web site for all the fascinating details. In short, these folks are making "fuzzy sciences" real.

Figure 7.1 AI at Chicago.

Figure 7.2 Projects at the lab.

Figure 7.3 The Animate Agent Project.

CARNEGIE MELLON ROBOTICS INSTITUTE

http://www.ri.cmu.edu/

The Robotics Institute of Carnegie Mellon University (CMU) was established in 1979 to conduct fundamental research in robotics technologies relevant to industrial and societal tasks and to facilitate the adoption of the results of that research in everyday work environments. One fun project from the standpoint of the Web-surfer is *Xavier*, which allows you to control a mobile robot via the Web from the comfort of your desktop computer. You are also free to noodle around with *Dante II*, a tethered walking robot developed at CMU, and other such toys, as well as browse reports concerning ongoing research at the Institute. The folks at CMU do a fantastic job of making complex technologies not just interesting, but understandable to all.

Figure 8.1 The Robotics Institute Web site.

Figure 8.2 Have fun with Xavier.

AI CAFÉ C/C++ CGI HTML HTTP JAVA J++ PERL VBSCRIPT VRML WIN32 WINSOCK 1100110100101111001101110011010101000110011100100101

COGNITIVE ROBOTICS GROUP/UNIVERSITY OF TORONTO

http://www.cs.utoronto.ca/~cogrobo/

The Cognitive Robotics Group of the University of Toronto is charged with endowing robotic or software agents with subtle, high-level cognitive functions that involve reasoning such as goals, perceptions, actions, the mental states of other agents, and collaborative task execution. In this connection, the group has developed a logic programming language for agents called GOLOG (alGOl in LOGic) which enables the agents to represent and "reason out" the prerequisites and effects of actions, perceptions and other knowledge-producing actions, natural events, and actions by other agents. Visit the Web site for much more on this fascinating research, including dozens of original papers.

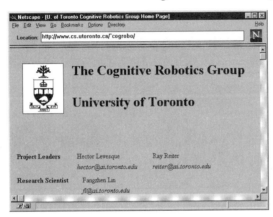

Figure 9 The Cognitive Robotics Group Web site.

AI CAFÉ C/C++ CGI HTML HTTP JAVA J++ PERL VBSCRIPT VRML WIN32 WINSOCK 1100110100101111001101110011010101000110011100100101

COMPUTATIONAL INTELLIGENCE RESEARCH GROUP

http://www.spd.louisville.edu/~ci/index.html

The AI folks at the University of Louisville are applying neural networks for process control, state identification, and prediction. Neural networks are mathematical models that are loosely patterned after the workings of the human brain. They consist of highly interconnected, interactive data processing units called neurons. Just like our human neural networks, these neurons can identify objects and predict their actions. In addition, they are using computational-intelligence techniques for identification of semiconductor manufacturing processes and microelectronic circuit testing. Neural-network researchers should check out the lab's efforts to use fuzzy approaches for rule extraction from data for linguistic description. In addition, take time to examine the lab's ongoing research toward optimizing neural-network architectures through perturbation, pruning, and improved learning/scaling approaches. This state-of-the-art research lab is run by Dr. Jacek M. Zurada. Intriguing.

Figure 10.1 The Research Group Web site.

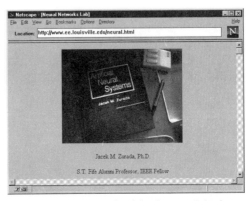

Figure 10.2 A recent book by the group's leader.

DISTRIBUTED ARTIFICIAL INTELLIGENCE LABORATORY

http://dis.cs.umass.edu/dis.html

With Intranets, the Web, and multiprocessor-based systems pulling the world closer together, the folks at MIT are thinking of better ways to farm out work—primarily though the use of distributed agents. The Distributed Artificial Intelligence Lab at the University of Massachusetts investigates the problems that arise when multiple agents (including computational agents and humans) interact to solve interrelated problems such as multi-agent coordination, organization, and negotiation. The Lab also investigates the design of sophisticated individual control mechanisms for sensor interpretation, acoustic signal understanding, real-time scheduling, and resource-constrained scheduling. Current research projects address, among other things, control issues in parallel knowledge-based systems. If you want a glance at the future of computing, this site is a good place to start.

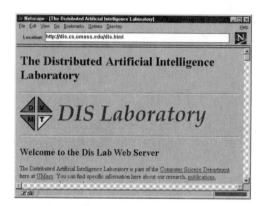

Figure 11.1 The laboratory Web site.

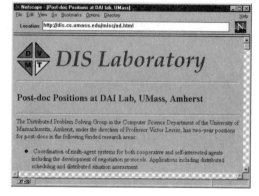

Figure 11.2 Post-Doc positions available.

DISTRIBUTED ARTIFICIAL INTELLIGENCE RESEARCH GROUP

http://www.elec.qmw.ac.uk/dai/

Affiliated with the Queen Mary and Westfield College of the University of London, the Distributed Artificial Intelligence (DAI) Research Group is headed by Dr. Nick Jennings. The lab focuses on conflicts in multi-agent systems, modeling cooperative intelligence agents, and negotiation through argumentation. Of particular interest here is the work to develop ADEPT, an Advanced Decision Environment for Process Tasks, as well as ARCHON (Architecture for Cooperative Heterogeneous On-line systems), the largest European project to date in the area of DAI. ARCHON has, in fact, lead to a general purpose architecture, software framework, and methodology which has been used to support DAI systems in a number of real-world domains.

Figure 12.1 The Group's Web site.

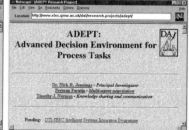

Figure 12.2 Information on ADEPT.

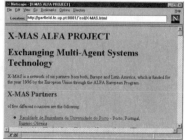

Figure 12.3 Information on X-Mas.

EXPERT SYSTEM FREEWARE

http://knight3.cit.ics.saitama-u.ac.jp/ai/expert.html

Sure, AI theory is great, but I want to "test drive" some of these concepts. If you feel the same way, visit this site and download free software, including *Babylon* (a complete expert system development environment), *Clips* (a C-language integrated production system), and *ES* (a public-domain expert system). In addition, you can download such programs as *ESIE* and *Logic-Line* (an expert system shell and AI retrieval/correlation tool), *EXPERT* (an expert system written in ADA), *FRulekit* (a frame-based RETE production system), and *HUGIN*. If that's not enough, try out *LES* (a learning expert system), *MIKE* (a portable expert system teaching package), *OPS5* (a RETE-based expert system shell), and *PROTEST* (a Prolog expert system building tool). You want AI software . . . you got it.

Figure 13.1 Free downloads.   *Figure 13.2 Details on BABYLON.*   *Figure 13.3 Details on CLIPS.*

HARVARD ROBOTICS LAB

http://hrl.harvard.edu

OK, so maybe your football team always beat Harvard. However, you don't want to take them on in a game of robotics. The Harvard Robotics Lab emphasizes work on computational vision, neural networks, tactile sensing, motion control, and VLSI (very large scale integration) systems. At this Web site, you'll find an extensive HTML library of papers that address such topics as hybrid models for motion control systems, differential equations and matrix inequalities in isospectral families, dynamical systems and their associated automata, pattern generation and the control of non-holonomic systems, the dynamics of kinetic chains, and more. The research at Harvard always seems to stretch the edge of the envelope and signal what is coming to other labs soon.

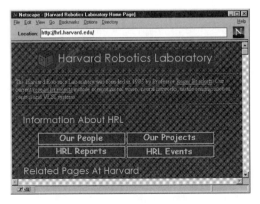 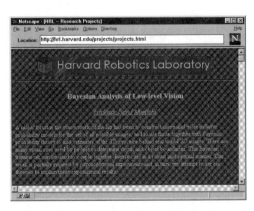

Figure 14.1 Harvard Robotics Lab home page.   *Figure 14.2 Bayesian analysis at Harvard.*

INTERNATIONAL JOINT CONFERENCE ON AI

http://ijcai.org

If you really want to understand where AI is going in both the short and long term, you need to follow the research that comes out of the International Joint Conference on AI (IJCAI). Begun in 1969, this bi-annual event is the main international gathering of AI researchers. The conference is held jointly by IJCAI and the national AI societies of the host countries. The 15th conference, which is upcoming, will be held at Nagoya, Japan from August 23 through August 29, 1997, and will be sponsored jointly by IJCAI and the Japanese Society for Artificial Intelligence (*http://www.robocup.org/jsai/jsai-e.html*). The IJCAI Web site includes complete details on the conference, including calls for papers and videos, as well as proposals for tutorials, workshops, and panels.

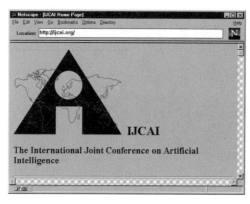

Figure 15.1 IJCAI home page.

Figure 15.2 The Japan conference.

IOWA STATE ARTIFICIAL INTELLIGENCE RESEARCH LABORATORY

http://www.cs.iastate.edu/~honavar/aigroup.html

If you thought the only thing happening in Iowa is corn, think again. At the Iowa State AI research lab, you will also find late-breaking work in the fields of machine learning and perception, parallel and distributed computing, and spatial and temporal knowledge representation. Directed by Dr. Vasant Honavar, the Artificial Intelligence Research Laboratory at Iowa State uses this rich Web site to present its latest and ongoing research in the fields of artificial neural networks, cognitive and neural modeling, constructive learning patterns for pattern classification, evolutionary design of neural architectures, intelligent multimedia information systems, and intelligent diagnosis systems.

Figure 16.1 Iowa State AI Web site.

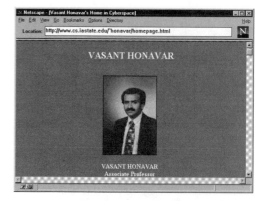

Figure 16.2 The lab's director.

JOURNAL OF ARTIFICIAL INTELLIGENCE RESEARCH

http://www.cs.washington.edu/research/jair/home.html

Published by Morgan Kaufman, the *Journal of Artificial Intelligence Research* (JAIR) is, as its Web site tells us, "a refereed journal, covering all areas of Artificial Intelligence, which is distributed free of charge over the Internet." To find the articles you need, you can browse complete Tables of Contents (with abstracts) going back as far as 1993. You can also search the full text of all JAIR articles going back to 1993, or ferret out research by way of the handy author index (complete with easy, hyperlinked "Ask the Author" e-mail addresses). After you find an article you want to read, you may download it either as a PostScript file or as a compressed PostScript file, as you please and free of charge. Cool!

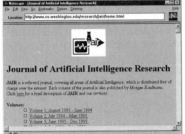
Figure 17.1 The JAIR Web site.

Figure 17.2 Ask the Author.

Figure 17.3 Full-text search of JAIR.

JOURNAL OF EXPERIMENTAL & THEORETICAL ARTIFICIAL INTELLIGENCE

http://turing.paccs.binghamton.edu/jetai

Edited by Eric Dietrich and published by Taylor & Francis, the *Journal of Experimental and Theoretical Artificial Intelligence* (JETAI) addresses all aspects of cutting-edge research into artificial intelligence. The journal's emphasis is on problem solving, perception, learning, knowledge-representation, and neural system modeling, in the realms of both the test lab and the abstract. The Web site contains Tables of Contents, abstracts and editorials, author guidelines, and an invitation to request, via e-mail, a free trial issue of the Journal. There is also a small, but carefully chosen, assembly of links to other useful AI sites on the Web.

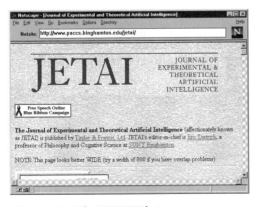
Figure 18.1 The JETAI Web site.

Figure 18.2 The publisher of JETAI.

AI Cafe C/C++ CGI HTML HTTP Java J++ Perl VBScript VRML Win32 Winsock

KQML Discussion & Free Software

http://www.cs.umbc.edu/kqml

What is Knowledge Query & Manipulation Language (KQML)? Put as simply as possible, it is a part of the ARPA (Advanced Research Projects Agency) Knowledge Sharing Effort. To be more precise, KQML contributes to the development of large-scale, shareable knowledge-bases by providing a message format and message-handling protocol to support run-time knowledge sharing among agents. At KQML's official Web site, you can access free downloadable copies of the KQML compiler, several very cool test applications, and even the draft KQML specification document (which is available in both PostScript and HTML formats). If you are thinking about writing Intranet- or Web-based applications that share information, you should first check out KQML.

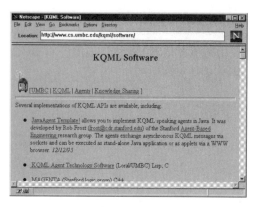

Figure 19.1 KQML software download.

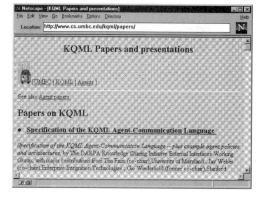

Figure 19.2 Papers on KQML.

AI Cafe C/C++ CGI HTML HTTP Java J++ Perl VBScript VRML Win32 Winsock

MIT Artificial Intelligence Laboratory Web Site

http://www.ai.mit.edu

At the MIT AI Lab, you'll find information on the latest groundbreaking AI research those nutty professors and students at Kenmore Square are conducting, including the crazy post-docs who have dubbed themselves "the Zoo." Get the scoop on what's happening with Boston-baked robotics, machine-vision, learning systems, and intelligent information access. Come to this site for details on the Pendulum Reversible Computing Project, which aims to build a CPU that will be capable of "totally reversible" operation at all levels from the high-level language down to the circuits! You might also check up on Scheme Underground, a project to develop a new, highly portable programming environment for Unix, the Web, and wearable computers. Nutty? No. Cool? Definitely.

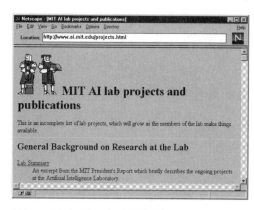

Figure 20.1 AI at the MIT Web site.

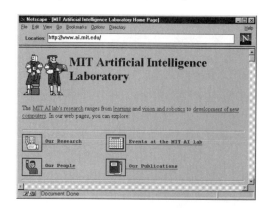

Figure 20.2 Lab projects and publications.

NESTOR, INC.

http://www.nestor.com

When it comes to applying AI technology, few do it better than Nestor, Inc. You can find Nestor's patented neural network technology in over 3,000 businesses worldwide. Organizations as diverse as the Internal Revenue Service and Mellon Bank have used Nestor neural network solutions to enhance their computer systems and security. Nestor's Ni1000 Recognition Accelerator Embedded Neural Network Chip is at the heart of numerous high-speed pattern-recognition applications in use around the world today. At this site, you'll find complete information on Nestor, its products, its pricing, its personnel, and its ongoing research and development projects. You'll also find information on job openings at Nestor which, by the way, is located in Providence, Rhode Island (just down the road from me).

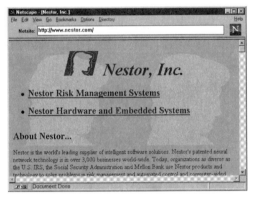

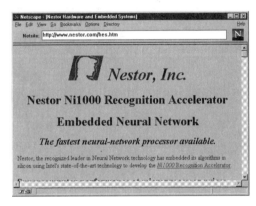

Figure 21.1 The Nestor Web site.   *Figure 21.2 Details on Nestor products.*

NEURAL APPLICATIONS CORPORATION

http://www.neural.com

Neural Applications Corporation is a leader in the field of developing neural networks for science and industry. Their Intelligent Arc Furnace (IAF) Controller has revolutionized steel-making, just as their Aegis Development System is revolutionizing other industries. At this site, you can learn about the company's many programs and products, as well as employment opportunities. As a bonus, you may also download a free copy of their new *NetProphet* software. This stock tracking and prediction software has been judged in the Top 1% and as number 3 in the Top 10 by the Java Applet Rating Service (*http://www.jars.com*) for June 1996.

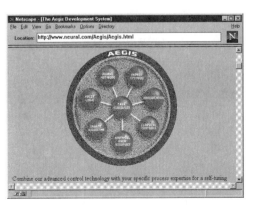

Figure 22.1 The Neural Web site.   *Figure 22.2 The Aegis Development System.*

NEURAL NETWORK SHAREWARE LINKS

http://www.emsl.pnl.gov:2080/docs/cie/neural/systems/shareware.html

If you are looking for AI software, check out this site. You will find links to free downloads for dozens of popular shareware neural network software packages for UNIX, DOS, the Macintosh, and other platforms. The shareware includes *Aspirin/MIGRAINES*, *Backprop-1.4* (a biological simulator), *Biosim*, *Brain Neural Network Simulator*, *FuNeGen*, *Fuzzy ARTmap*, *GENESIS*, *Hyperplane Animator*, *LVQ PAK* (Learning Vector Quantizer), *Mactivation*, *Matrix Backpropagation*, *Necognitron*, *NeuralShell*, *NeurDS*, *NevProp*, *NNMODEL*, *PDP Code*, *PDP++ Software*, *PlaNet*, *Pygmalion*, *SESAME*, *SOM PAK*, *Spike and Neurallog*, *UCLA-SFINX*, *WinNN*, and *Xerion*. Additonal pieces of shareware demonstrate adaptive resonance theory, optimal linear associated memory, recurrant back propagation, Hopfield Networks, and other common AI algorithms. Just to name a few. Awesome.

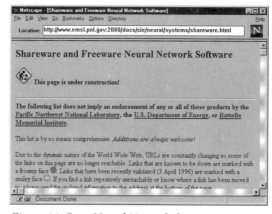

Figure 23 Great Neural Network shareware.

NEURALITY: THE NEURAL NETWORKS META-SITE

http://www.icenet.it/icenet/neurality/home_uk.html

This site is loaded with free AI stuff. Download *DamNet*, a neural net that knows how to design arch dams. Or would you prefer *NeuroTetris*, the great freeware neural network version of the famous game? Of course, you might want to try *Neuro Fractals* (for generating neural networks that recognize and plot fractals), or the more-practical *Cop-Net* (a neural network that filters noisy and "bad" data). Let's see. What else is here? You'll find a great HTML tutorial introducing the fundamentals of neural nets, pointers to the Web sites of just about every major neural network organization around the globe, and an outstanding set of links to *even more* great free neural network software. Cool.

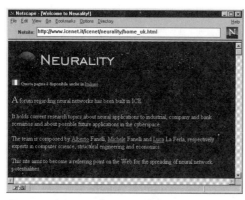

Figure 24.1 Neurality in English.

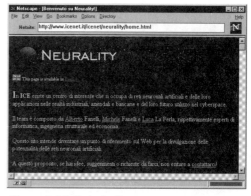

Figure 24.2 Or in Italian.

NEURALWARE, INC.

http://www.neuralware.com/

NeuralWare offers software solutions based in neural network technology. A wide range of industries use NeuralWare's solutions for such operations as power generation, pulp and paper manufacture, chemical processing, aquaculture, medicine, finance, and more. NeuralWare specializes in developing proprietary software designed to learn trends from existing data where the trends are otherwise very subtle or difficult to determine by other methods. As you thread your way through the NeuralWare Web site, you can learn about the software solutions they have to offer, what references they have to offer, and even what jobs they have to offer. It's real-world AI.

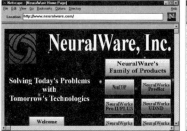

Figure 25.1 NeuralWare's Web site.   *Figure 25.2 NeuralWorks software.*   *Figure 25.3 Free demos.*

NEURONET: NEURAL NETWORK SITES AROUND THE WEB

http://www.neuronet.ph.kcl.ac.uk/neuronet/places.html

Wow! Featuring hundreds of invaluable links, this site should be the number one stop on the Web for anyone interested in ferreting out information on neural networks. The site has links to every major lab, every major researcher, and every shred of free downloadable software. You'll find links to the Carnegie Mellon Computer Vision Lab, *Neuron Digest* Magazine, the Aston Neural Network Labs List, the UCSD Neuro Web, the Neural Computing Center at Keio University, the SVR (Speech, Vision & Robotics) Group at Cambridge University, the Neural Nets Groups at the University of Limburg (Netherlands), the NeuroGeek Page, the Institute of Electrical and Electronics Engineers (IEEE) Neural Networks Council, and much, much more. Start here.

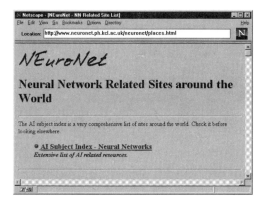

Figure 26.1 The NEuroNet Web site.   *Figure 26.2 One of many links.*

OUTSIDER'S GUIDE TO ARTIFICIAL INTELLIGENCE

http://www.mcs.net/~jorn/html/ai.html

Maintained by Jorn Barger, this site offers a skeptical view of AI for non-specialists. The site includes sections on the prehistory of AI, the LISP language, natural language processing, expert systems, and Cyc (from enCYClopedia, a ten-year project whose goal was to create a system which could speak and understand ordinary language and detect violations of common sense as easily as humans). You will also find coverage of an obscure sub-specialty called "story-representation," which Webmaster Barger believes will be the key to future successes in AI. The irreverent tone of this extended tutorial is quite refreshing, while the information is sound and the conclusions lucid. Come in from the cold and treat yourself to the *Outsider's Guide to Artificial Intelligence*. You'll be glad you did.

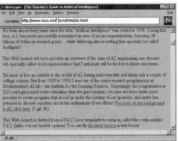 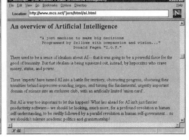 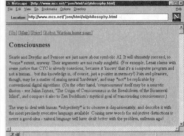

Figure 27.1 A page from the Outsider. *Figure 27.2 And another page.* *Figure 27.3 And another.*

SIGART

http://sigart.acm.org/

SIGART is the ACM's Special Interest Group on Artificial Intelligence. (And ACM, of course, stands for the Association for Computing Machinery which you can reach at *http://www.acm.org*.) ACM is the world's leading society of computer science professionals, fonded in 1946. At the SIGART site, you will find complete information on SIGART and its officers, as well as details on SIGART locals, SIGART-supported conferences and workshops, the SIGART Bulletin, and more. Sponsored conferences include international conferences on autonomous agents, intelligent user interfaces, and information and knowledge management. You'll also find information on AI scholarships and fellowships, job postings, and timely announcements of interest to the AI community.

  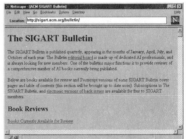

Figure 28.1 SIGART's Web site. *Figure 28.2 ACM - The Mothership.* *Figure 28.3 The SIGART Bulletin.*

SILICON GRAPHICS APPLICATIONS & NEURAL NETWORKS

http://www.sgi.com/Products/

Come to this Web site for information about and developer support for the *MATLAB Neural Network Toolbox*, *Neural Network Processor (NNP)*, *NeuralWorks Professional II/PLUS*, *Robotic Control*, and *Tsar*. Each of these products is, of course, a powerful combination of tools for the design, training, and simulation of neural networks. And, each supports a wide range of network architectures with an unlimited number of processing elements and interconnections (up to operating system constraints). You'll also find add-on utility libraries, comprehensive on-line documentation, developer-program enrollment information, and much more.

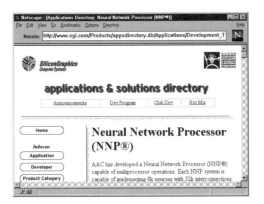

Figure 29.1 Neural Network Processor.

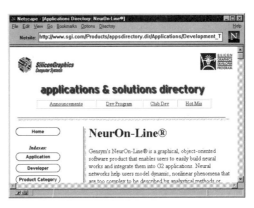

Figure 29.2 NeurOn-Line.

SIMON FRASER UNIVERSITY ARTIFICIAL INTELLIGENCE RESEARCH

http://fas.sfu.ca/cs/research/groups/AI.html

What does NAFTA have to do with AI? Possibly nothing, but the AI research at Canada's Simon Fraser University embraces computational vision, intelligent (expert) systems, knowledge representation, learning and reasoning, and natural language processing. This research is conducted within Simon Fraser's Intelligent Systems Lab, Natural Language Lab, Intelligent Software Group, and Case Based Reasoning Group. Bill Havens, the director of the Intelligent Systems Lab, is currently involved in major research surrounding intelligent scheduling and intelligent graphical user interfaces. In addition, a key priority at the Natural Language Lab is the development of natural language interfaces for databases.

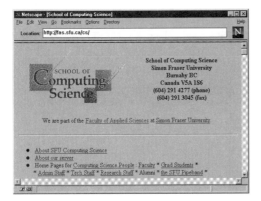

Figure 30.1 AI at SFU.

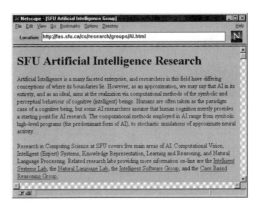

Figure 30.2 Computer science at SFU.

THE SOAR PROJECT (FREE SOFTWARE DOWNLOAD)

http://www.isi.edu/soar/soar.html

Soar is a research project in artificial intelligence based on a general cognitive architecture proposed as a model of human cognition. For those interested in programming Soar, this site includes a preliminary HTML version of the Soar User's Manual, Version 6, Edition 1. Additionally, there is a link that enables a free download of Soar 6, which is public-domain software. Currently supported versions are implemented in C, although there is also an older LISP version for those interested. Although Soar for Windows/PC is designed to run on UNIX platforms, you will find versions for the Mac. A Soar Development Environment that provides an Emacs interface to the Soar program is also yours to download.

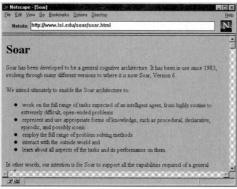

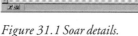

Figure 31.1 Soar details.

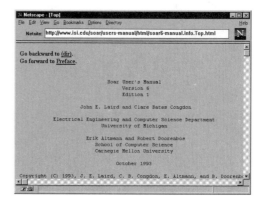

Figure 31.2 The Soar Manual.

SRI INTERNATIONAL: ARTIFICIAL INTELLIGENCE CENTER

http://www.ai.sri.com/

SRI International, formerly known as the Stanford Research Institute, is a nonprofit corporation which performs a spectrum of problem-oriented research. SRI's Artificial Intelligence Center (AIC), founded in 1966, is widely regarded as one of the world's most important centers of AI research and development. The three main areas of research are natural language, perception, and representation and reasoning. Within natural language processing, the center's emphasis is on multimedia/multimodal interfaces, spoken language systems, and written language systems. In the perception area, the focus is on 3-D modeling and interpretation, analysis of range images, image matching, and autonomous navigation. Finally, with regard to representation and reasoning, AIC devotes its attention to generative planning, fuzzy control, reactive planning/control, and evidential reasoning. Cool stuff.

Figure 32.1 The SRI-AI Web site.

Figure 32.2 All about SRI.

TOP SCHOOLS IN *AI*

http://mx.nsu.ru/FAQ/F-ai-general/Q4-1.html

At this site, you will find balanced comparisons of programs at all the best schools for AI research. The best of the best schools in AI are generally acknowledged. The list is quite predictable. In no particular order, it goes as follows: Carnegie Mellon, Georgia Tech, Johns Hopkins, UC-Berkeley, MIT, Imperial College, Rutgers, Stanford, Northwestern, SUNY-Buffalo, University of Edinburgh, and Yale. Each school has its strengths and weaknesses. And this measured, thoughtful site goes a long way toward identifying and comparing the relative strengths and weaknesses of the various schools at the top of the AI food chain. In all, you will find this a very useful (and uncompromisingly fair) document.

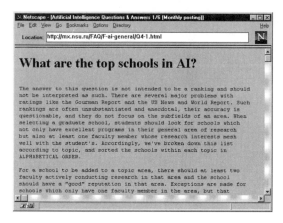

Figure 33 Addressing a key position.

UNIVERSAL PROBLEM SOLVERS, INC.

http://pages.prodigy.com/upso/

Universal Problem Solvers, Inc. kindly invites you to download free demo copies of three cutting-edge, Windows-based, pattern-recognition tools: *TDL* (Trans-Dimensional Learning), *fSC-Net* (Fuzzy Symbolic/Connectionist Network), and *MPIL* (Multi-Pass Instance-Based Learning). The neatest of these is probably *TDL*, which makes it possible to incrementally learn various pattern recognition tasks within a single coherent neural-network structure. The software *fSC-Net* is also extremely cool, since it utilizes a hybrid structure in which symbolic, as well as Connectionist features, are exploited, while at the same time incorporating both fuzzy logic and a pruning mechanism.

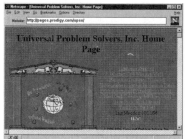

Figure 34.1 Problem Solvers.   *Figure 34.2 UPSO software products.*   *Figure 34.3 All about MPIL.*

35

UNIVERSITY OF CALIFORNIA, DAVIS, AI LABORATORY

http://phobos.cs.ucdavis.edu:8001/

Visit this elegantly executed Web site to get details concerning ongoing research in both performance and simulation models of intelligence. Current performance projects at the lab include: high-performance game-playing, search-and-constraint satisfaction algorithms, automated breath analysis, machine learning, and discovery of heuristics. Current simulation projects focus on simulating human cognition through the comprehension and generation of natural language text. Further research addresses intelligent information filtering, intelligent agents, and artificial life/genetic programming.

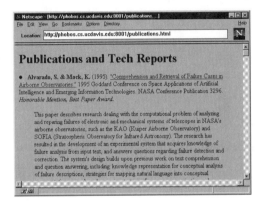

Figure 35.1 AI at UC Davis.

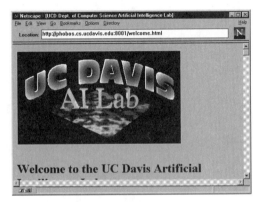

Figure 35.2 Faculty publications.

36

UNIVERSITY OF EDINBURGH DEPT. OF ARTIFICIAL INTELLIGENCE

http://www.dai.ed.ac.uk/research/

One of the most important AI labs in Europe is located in the ancient city of Edinburgh, Scotland. Come to this fascinating collection of Web pages to discover the latest news on advanced, groundbreaking research in mathematical reasoning, machine vision, mobile robots, natural language processing, and evolutionary algorithms. Of particular interest is the work of Dr. Graeme Ritchie in the construction of integrated user interfaces using natural language for input and output to extract information from knowledge bases, and the mathematical study of the properties (such as complexity) of linguistic notations and rule systems.

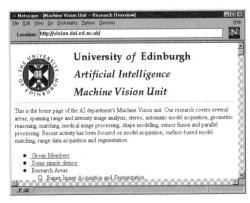

Figure 36.1 AI at Edinburgh.

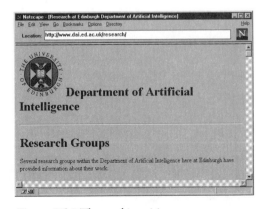

Figure 36.2 The machine vision group.

AI CAFE C/C++ CGI HTML HTTP JAVA J++ PERL VBSCRIPT VRML WIN32 WINSOCK 1100110100101111001101110011010101000110011001001001

THE ART OF ASSEMBLY LANGUAGE PROGRAMMING

http://cs.ucr.edu/~rhyde/aoatoc.html

Packed with sample programs, this great hypertext tutorial covers all aspects of PC assembly language, including data representation, Boolean algebra, system organization, memory layout and access, variables and data structures, the 8086 Instruction set, the UCR Standard Library, MASM directives, arithmetic and logical operations, control structures, and procedures and functions. The tutorial also explains advanced topics such as lexical nesting, static links, displays, unit activation, address binding, accessing non-local variables using static links, passing variables at different lexical levels as parameters, passing parameters as parameters to another procedure, and more. The site also details floating point arithmetic, strings and character sets, pattern matching, interrupts, traps, exceptions, and even the Zen of resident programs!

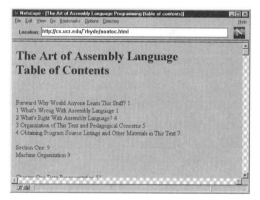

Figure 37.1 A great tutorial.

Figure 37.2 Variables and data structures.

AI CAFE C/C++ CGI HTML HTTP JAVA J++ PERL VBSCRIPT VRML WIN32 WINSOCK 1100110100101111001101110011010101000110011001001001

ASM EDIT V1.82, FREE DOWNLOAD

http://www.inf.tu-dresden.de/~ok3/asmedit.html

For all you "assembler freaks" out there, check out *ASM Edit*, a shareware, DOS-based assembler IDE (integrated development environment). The program's development environment integrates such features as an editor, on-line help, easy linkage with external assemblers, linkers and debuggers, and more. Although the software is DOS-based, it works with Windows, Windows 95, Windows NT, and OS/2. You can use the environment for syntax coloring, disassembly of short code pieces, file conversion between DOS and UNIX, and memory management that enables editing of files up to 256Mb. The on-line help includes assembler mnemonics from 8088 up to 80686, a complete description of FPU opcodes and MMX opcodes, a large interrupt list, and more. And remember, it's free!

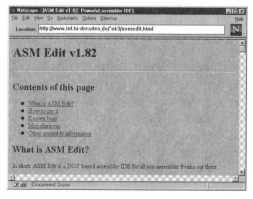

Figure 38.1 ASM Edit Web site.

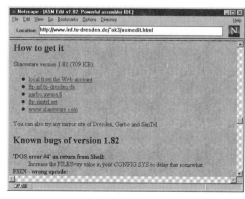

Figure 38.2 How to get the software.

DIGITAL'S ASSEMBLY LANGUAGE PROGRAMMER'S GUIDE

http://sawyer.wustl.edu/du4-docs/AA-PS31D-TET1_html/TITLE.html

This hypertext manual details assembly language programming for Digital's UNIX system. You will find specifics about syntax rules, short cuts to writing assembly programs, and more. The manual includes in-depth explanations of architecture-based programming considerations, lexical conventions, standard and floating-point instruction sets, assembler directives, object files, symbol tables, program loading and dynamic linking, 32-bit considerations, basic machine definition, and more. The tutorial also includes working examples of the leaf and non-leaf procedures for local variables, and discussion of programming considerations such as calling conventions, developing code for procedure calls, and memory allocation.

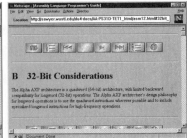

Figure 39.1 The official word.   *Figure 39.2 Assembler directives.*   *Figure 39.3 32-bit information.*

FABER'S 80x86 ASSEMBLY LINKS

http://www.fys.ruu.nl/~faber/Amain.html

James Faber is a programmer in the Netherlands who has taken it upon himself to put together what is probably the very best collection of x86 assembly-language links on the Web. At his site, you'll find a handy "Beginners Corner" together with frequently asked questions, home-grown tutorials on how to create terminate-and-stay resident programs (TSR), and how to run Windows without a graphics user interface. Of course, Faber has included links to dozens of great software archives, Web pages, newsgroups, and other assembly-language programmer resources, which include a direct-link to Microsoft's Plug-and-Play BIOS specification, and more.

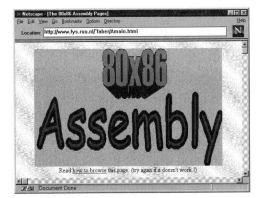
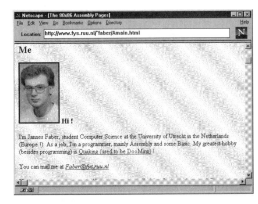

Figure 40.1 Assembly Links page.   *Figure 40.2 Your host.*

AI CAFE C/C++ CGI HTML HTTP JAVA J++ PERL VBSCRIPT VRML WIN32 WINSOCK 110011010010111100110111001101010100011001100100101

FREE SOFTWARE FROM ASSEMBLY LANGUAGE CENTRAL

http://www.ibilce.unesp.br/courseware/asm/default.htm

If you are looking for some great assembly-language tools with which you can get up and running quickly, this is a must-visit site. This great collection of links includes not only lists of frequently asked questions (FAQs) and tutorials, but also great compilers, software, and documentation available for free downloading. You will find such software as the Motorola 6802 Simulator (including the Pascal source), the Motorola 6802/6809 assembler, linker, and documentation, along with the 6802/6809 C compiler for generating ASM source code. You will also find 68000 simulators, as well as Matthew Brandt's great C compiler, and a fantastic 8086 to 68000 source code converter!

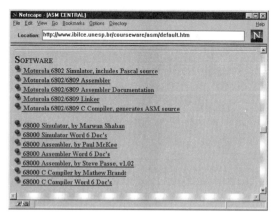

Figure 41 Take your pick.

AI CAFE C/C++ CGI HTML HTTP JAVA J++ PERL VBSCRIPT VRML WIN32 WINSOCK 110011010010111100110111001101010100011001100100101

GENERAL SOFTWARE, INC.

http://www.halcyon.com/general/

Sure, it supposed to be all ones and zeros, but the folks who build ROMable code or use logic analyzers see things differently than most of us. General Software employs many such engineers. Their products include *Embedded BIOS 3.1* (BIOS for x86-based hand-held and embedded systems), *Embedded DOS 6-XL* (DOS compatible, real-time x86 based operating system), *Embedded DOS-ROM* (a full-featured ROMable drop-in replacement operating system), *Embedded LAN* (a real-time embedded network operating system), the *Snooper* and *Ether Probe*, two Ethernet protocol analyzers, and *CodeProbe* (a software analyzer for asynchronous applications). Visit this great Web page for free demos and source files, as well as frequently asked questions and press releases about General Software products.

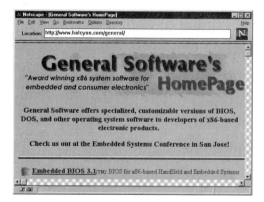

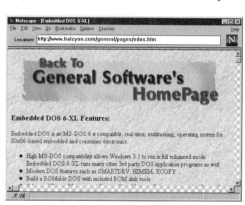

Figure 42.1 General Software's home page.   *Figure 42.2 Embedded DOS.*

Heath's x86 Assembly Page for Beginners

http://www.wfu.edu/~holcojh5/asm/x86asm.html

This highly useful page, which incorporates an easy to use tutorial, is the ideal place for a beginning assembly-language programmer to begin his or her explorations. The site builds its discussion from the ground up, addressing such fundamental questions as "What is assembly language?" and "What is it good for?" You will also find a good set of links, an excellent collection of frequently asked questions, and some robust programming examples that are not only highly illustrative, but ideal for cutting and pasting into your own assembly language efforts. All told, there is probably no better place on the Web for the beginning assembly language programmer. Period.

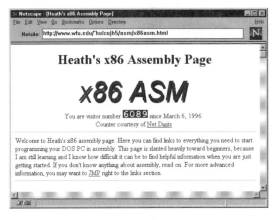

Figure 43 Heath's x86 page.

Intel Secrets: What Intel Doesn't Want You to Know

http://www.x86.org

Maintained by Robert Collins, who is a senior design engineer in Dallas, this fantastic Web site is where all the secrets (all the bugs Intel doesn't want you to know about) reside. Collins' list of frequently asked questions include such chatter as the following: Why are you disclosing Intel trade secrets? Why do you hate Intel? Why do you think Intel is conspiring to hide details of their architecture? Why do you think Intel engineers are so incompetent? The site is a great repository for notes on undocumented processor behavior gathered from programmers and engineers in "the field." So, for all the latest undocumented P6 opcodes and other goodies, check out *Intel Secrets: What Intel Doesn't Want You to Know*. Why does he hate Intel?

Figure 44.1 The Intel Secrets Web site.

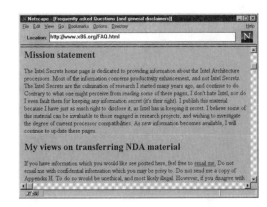

Figure 44.2 Mission statement.

INTERRUPT LIST FROM RALPH BROWN

http://www-cgi.cs.cmu.edu/afs/cs.cmu.edu/user/ralf/pub/WWW/files.html

If you've been around programming circles for a few years, you may know that Ralph Brown is the keeper (and creator) of the industry's best documentation on PC interrupts. Although you may not give Ralph the credit, you have undoubtedly taken advantage of his well-known lists. At this site, you will find a list of interrupt description files you can download. You will also find programming libraries, including *SPAWNO* (a swapping replacement for the C run-time library's spawn functions), *AMISLIB* (a MASM function library for writing self-highloading, removable terminate-and-stay-resident programs), and more. If you have questions about PC interrupts, visit this site.

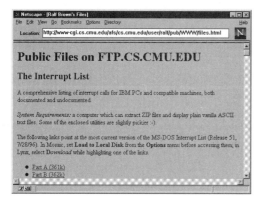

Figure 45.1 Ralph Brown's great list.

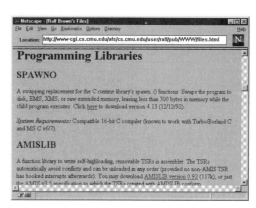

Figure 45.2 Programming libraries.

MIKE'S ASM TUTOR

http://www.cyberbeach.net/~mbabcock/Programming/asmtut1.htm

This site's creator, Mike Babcock, shares a lot of great, fundamental advice for current and would be assembly-language programmers. "Plan a lot," he says. His other rules are that you use "deep thinking" optimization only where you need maximum speed, write "generic routines" that perform many tasks, keep your code "clean" by using "dirty tricks" only when absolutely necessary, and know when it's time to break the rules and when it's not. In assembly-language programming, as in life, some choices are never easy. Mike, of course, also offers somewhat less philosophical musings on topics that include the nature of registers and basic ASM syntax. Take time to visit this site. Your programs will be better off for your visit.

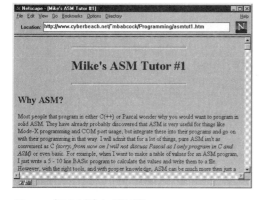

Figure 46.1 Mike's ASM Tutor.

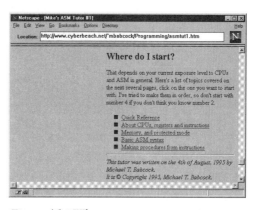

Figure 46.2 Where to start.

MORE ASSEMBLER SOFTWARE

http://www.dlc.fi/~arzie/programming/

At this Web site, you will find download access to *Gema* (an assembler that uses Motorola syntax), *Desa* (disassemble for *Gema*), and the *Magic Assembler* (which you can use to create boot sectors). You will also find the *Hacker's View* for DOS and OS/2, a great sector-level disk editor, and *Assembler Laboratory 1.0* for TASM, MASM, and A86. You also get access to fantastic protected-mode software that includes a simple 386 operating system kernel with drivers, 32-bit executables, a small sample protected-mode operating-system kernel, and even a sample protected-mode multitasking sound system! You will want to check all these items out. After all, the price is right!

Figure 47 A few of your choices.

NASM: THE NETWIDE ASSEMBLER PROJECT

http://www.dcs.warwick.ac.uk/~jules/nasm1.html

What happens when a large group of assembler code-heads get together on the Internet, intent on designing the ideal assembler? They design it. Then, they make the assembler available to you and me. This new assembler removes the necessity for red-tape assembler directives, and allows the programmer to turn off the assembler's "intelligent" behavior using command-line switches. The assembler is highly portable, designed in a modular format, features a highly-structured macro processor that allows for structured programming constructs, and supports object-oriented programming. Check it out.

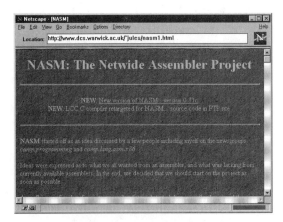

Figure 48 The Netwide Assembler Project.

PHOAKS OF ALT.LANG.ASM

http://weblab.research.att.com/phoaks/alt/lang/asm/contributors/http---udgftp.cencar.udg.mx-ingles-tutor-Assembler.html0.html

Normally, I would not subject either myself or you to a URL of this length and complexity. However, the page is too cool, and the information too good, to pass up. *PHOAKS* stands for People Helping One Another Know Stuff. These particular folks are all associated with the assembly-language tutorial effort of the ASM. The links this site supplies are extremely useful, extremely esoteric, and extremely obscure. This is a rich nook (or cranny) of the Web that is loaded with links to similarly rich information sources for the non-casual browser in search of excellent information and tips with regard to 8086 assembly language programming.

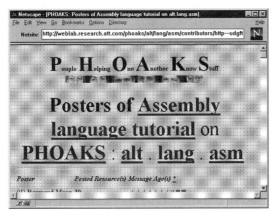

Figure 49 Time to meet the PHOAKS.

PLUG & PLAY BIOS SPECIFICATION

http://www.microsoft.com/msdn/library/specs/BIO10A.HTM

As you may know, plug-and-play is a new technology that allows users to install (plug) a new hardware card into their systems and immediately use (play) the card without having to manually set switches or jumpers on the card so that it does not conflict with another card's settings. The Plug & Play BIOS Specification defines the functionality a PC's system BIOS must include to support plug-and-play operations. The specification details BIOS resource management, run-time configuration, and event management. This on-line reference is a fundamental resource for system programmers who are writing plug-and-play applications.

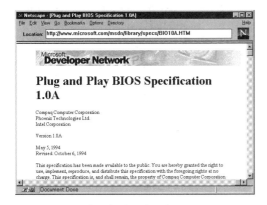

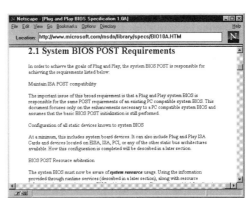

Figure 50.1 Plug & Play details.   *Figure 50.2 POST requirements.*

PROTECTED MODE: A TUTORIAL BY ROBERT COLLINS

http://www.x86.org/articles/pmbasics/

The scarcity of good documentation and tutorials on the topic of protected-mode programming is no secret. In an effort to fill that gap, Robert Collins first taught himself all there is to know about protected-mode programming and now, full of good will, he has set himself the task of educating you in the same way, for free. At this Web site, you will discover all the voodoo that occurs in relation to memory segmentation, interrupts, and device drivers when you try to port DOS applications to protected mode. You will also find solutions to virtually every potential problem, and answers to every question. Thank you, Robert.

Figure 51.1 Only the basics.

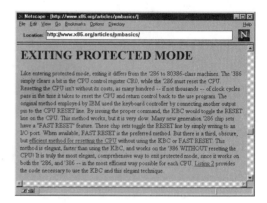

Figure 51.2 Exiting protected mode.

PROTECTED MODE OPERATION OF THE INTEL ARCHITECTURE

http://www.intel.com/embedded/news/esc_ia.htm

Steve Gorman provides a good, politically-correct overview of protected-mode operation with Intel chips. He covers descriptors, descriptor tables, selectors, protection, type checking, limit checking, privilege levels, the paging unit, multitasking, interrupts, and virtual-86 mode, as well as the art of addressing memory. Gorman's discussion of privilege levels includes all the details on call rates, RET instruction processing, protected instructions and, of course, I/O privilege-level sensitive instructions. The tutorial is clear and to the point, and the illustrations and examples are well-done. Check it out.

Figure 52.1 An overview.

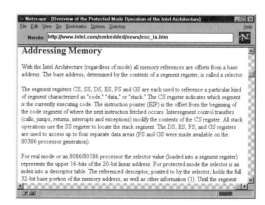

Figure 52.2 Addressing memory.

PUBLIC DOMAIN NASM FILES

http://www.thepoint.net/~jkracht/pdnasm.htm

If you are looking for assemblers, low-level programming tools, and lots of sample assembly-language source code, you have found the right place. This site features awesome downloads that include the A86 macro assembler, the D86 debugger, and the *XLIB* library which simplifies protected-mode programming under DOS. You will also encounter *ASM32* for 32-bit assembly-language programming with the *CauseWay DOS* extender, the *Magic Assembler Simple 8086* assembler, the *ASM Edit* easy-to-use assembler editor (with syntax coloring), and WALK32 (a complete application and DLL development kit and linker for MASM that supports Windows NT or Windows 95). In addition, you'll find the programmer's IDE for Windows (which creates an integrated development environment for C and assembly language programs) and Skeleton for Windows 95. Good stuff!

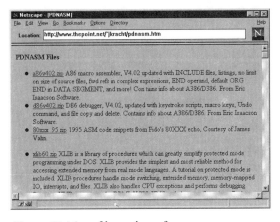

Figure 53 Many files to choose from.

BOB RICH'S ASSEMBLY LANGUAGE GOODIES

http://www.lexitech.com/bobrich

Looking for yet another rich set of resources? Check out the some of the fastest text-mode animations "in the world," which were created using assembly language. Browse a list of links that will provide you access to virtually every assembler on the Internet (for the full family of Intel processors). And, surf an equally complete list of links to assembly-language instruction programs. At this site, you will learn how to master the Zen of using MODE_X's ultra fast graphics in game programs, become skilled at creating IBM touchscreen information system routines, and more. You will even get a set of Intel assembly-language libraries, complete with helper applications that are ready to go.

Figure 54.1 Bob Rich's goodies.

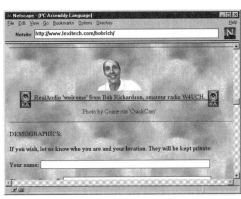

Figure 54.2 Bob himself!

SEARCHABLE ASSEMBLY LANGUAGE TUTORIAL

http://udgftp.cencar.udg.mx/ingles/tutor/Assembler.html

Unlike the other excellent 8086 assembly language tutorials I've discovered on the Web, this one has the added bonus of a robust search facility that lets you perform a keyword search throughout the entire tutorial document—so you can zero in on the information you need directly, without having to browse the table of contents. This hypertext tutorial covers everything from the basics to interrupts, file management, macros, procedures, and more. The programming examples are numerous and elegant. And, as a bonus, you'll find great supporting documentation available as a free download, a useful bibliography, and even an interlinked on-line computing dictionary.

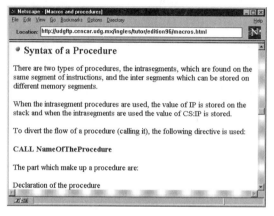

Figure 55 Syntax of a procedure.

SOURCE CODE FROM JOE COFFLAN

http://onyx.idbsu.edu/~jcofflan/

In the spirit of the Web, assembly-language programmer extraordinaire, Joe Cofflan, has not only assembled a great "assembly-language search engine," but he also has posted his and other people's source code on the Web for you to download and put to use. Among the goodies Joe has posted are a useful DOS path extender, code for using the Microsoft Real Time Compression Server, some very simple code for debugging a 4 bit parallel connection, and more. You will also find code for serial port I/O, floating-point I/O, numeric-console I/O, character-console I/O, and more. The source code is plentiful and useful.

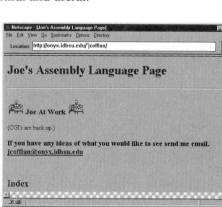

Figure 56.1 Joe's Assembly page.

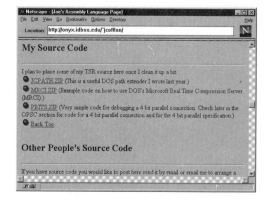

Figure 56.2 Some code options.

TMiOSDGL REVISION 2

http://cnit2.uniyar.ac.ru/user/BobbyZ/

Too-Much-in-One-So-Don't-Get-Lost (the TMiOSDGL site) is billed on its home page as the best x86 CPU/FPU detection library available. Fortunately, the library is available for free, complete with full source code for C, Pascal, and assembler. According to its hype, TMiOSDGL outperforms all freeware detectors, as well as all commercial programs, including *Quarterdeck's Manifest, Touchstone's CheckIt,* and *Symantec's Norton SysInfo* from The Norton Utilities. TMiOSDGL version 1 was popular, but revision 2 is even better and was rewritten "from the ground up" to incorporate over 25 CPUs and over 15 FPUs—all reliably detected. Perhaps the best things in life *are* free.

Figure 57 All about TMiOSDGL.

x86 ASSEMBLY LANGUAGE FAQ

http://www2.dgsys.com/~raymoon/x86faqs.html

Maintained by Raymond Moon, this complete and regularly-updated list of frequently asked x86 assembly-language questions includes information of interest to all x86 assembly-language programmers, as well as specific data of particular interest to those working with Microsoft *MASM*, Borland *TASM*, and the shareware A86 assembler and the D86 debugger. However, the scope and content of this list of frequently asked questions (FAQs) go beyond merely answering frequently asked questions. In this spirit, Moon includes numerous pointers to "assembly language treasure troves that are hidden out on the Internet." This FAQ list is not only of use to novices, but to seasoned assembly language programmers as well.

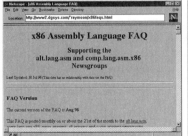

Figure 58.1 A great FAQ.   *Figure 58.2 Some sample topics.*   *Figure 58.3 Questions and answers.*

ANSI C++ Working Paper

http://www.ugcs.caltech.edu/~jlm/C++draft

Over the past few years, C++ has become the most widely used programming language in the world. Programmers write applications ranging from the *Netscape Navigator* to Windows 95 in C++. At this site, you will find the complete draft proposed International Standard for C++. The paper addresses every element of the language: lexical conventions, standard conversions, expressions, statements, declarations, classes, member-access control, special member functions, exception handling, preprocessor directives, strings, iterators, and so on. Anything you might want to know about C++ you will find at this site. A must-read document.

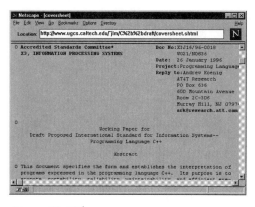

Figure 59.1 The cover page.

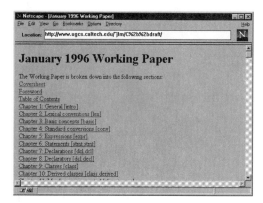

Figure 59.2 The table of contents.

ASK THE MFC PRO AT INQUIRY.COM

http://www.inquiry.com/techtips/mfc_pro/

The Microsoft Foundation Classes (better known as the MFC) are a collection of C++ classes that programmers use to perform key operations such as window control, dialog box processing, and so on. At Inquiry.com, that's right, Inquiry.com, you'll find answers to all your questions with regard to Microsoft Foundation Classes. This site gears the material toward developers at all levels—beginners, intermediates, and gurus alike. *Inquiry.com* invites you to ask questions of the site's resident experts, or to contribute your own expertise in the discussion forums. You can also thumb (or search) through the site's great database of more than 130,000 articles from major computer publications. The MFC Pro will provide you with a solid foundation in C++ class operations.

Figure 60.1 Go ahead and ask.

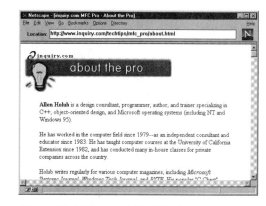

Figure 60.2 The pro, Allen Holub.

BENCH++: *A SUITE OF* C++ *BENCHMARKS*

http://paul.rutgers.edu/~orost/bench_plus_plus.html

Benchmarks are programs users run to measure their system, software, or hardware performance. Joe Orost and Barbara Ryder designed this suite of benchmark programs to measure the performance of code generated by C++ and to test individual language features. Unlike most other benchmark suites, *Bench++* measures the performance of code generated by a compiler, rather than hardware performance. The suite includes tests for traditional benchmarks (Dhrystone, Whetstone, Hennessy), applications (*Tracker, Orbit, Kalman,* and *Centroid*), and language features (if-then-else, method calls, exceptions, and so on). If you are serious about writing professional quality, high performance C++ programs, put these benchmarks to use and pay attention to their results.

Figure 61.1 Bench++ home page.

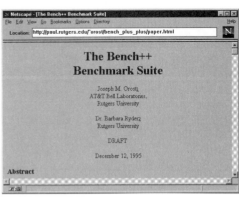

Figure 61.2 Complete doc right on-line.

BORLAND C++ *AND* OWL *INTERNET RESOURCES*

http://www.r2m.com/windev/OWL.html

The Borland Object Windows Library is a collection of routines that programmers use to implement common operations such as window control, dialog box operations, and so on. In general, Borland's OWL is functionally equivalent to the Microsoft Foundation Classes (MFC). At this site, you'll find essential and esoteric OWL information including, for example, a tutorial on how to get *DirectX2* to work with Borland C++ Version 5.0 (no easy feat!). You'll also find direct links to the latest patches for Borland C++ 5.0, a fantastic list of frequently asked questions, as well as information on great Borland C++ developer mailing lists and links to software archives. Of special interest is the "unofficial" and "otherwise undocumented" Borland hints and tips, including bugs and bug-fix information you simply will not find anywhere else on the planet. Go for it.

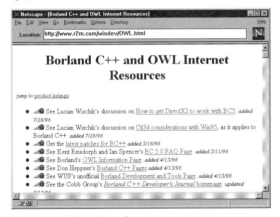

Figure 62 A long list of options.

BORLAND C++ INFORMATION CENTER (OFFICIAL)

http://netserv.borland.com/techsupport/borlandcpp/

Borland brings some impressive support to the C++ party via their nicely designed Web page. At this site, you'll find an invaluable product information library packed with white papers and downloadable files, technical support for current and previous versions of the compiler, and more. You'll also find the Borland-sponsored C++ Discussion Forum, as well as downloadable patches for all versions of Borland's C++ compiler. Finally, you will encounter links to relevant newsgroups, mailing lists, and FTP archives, along with the official connection for Borland C++ bug submission, inspection, and publication. All told, this should be the first stop for anyone seeking information on Borland C++ or any related Borland product.

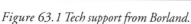

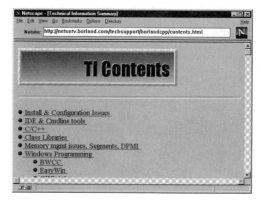

Figure 63.1 Tech support from Borland.

Figure 63.2 Gobs of tech information.

CGI/C++ CLASS LIBRARY

http://sweetbay.will.uiuc.edu/cgi%2b%2b/

CGI, or the common gate interface, is a specification program designed to exchange data between servers and browsers. Courtesy of Dragos Manolescu, this C++ library provides functions that decode data encoded according to CGI specifications using Standard Template Library (STL) containers. Dragos, you should understand, is in favor of exceptions. Even though he makes code larger and slower, he favors using them with relation to CGI. "Unless it is dead slow, one does not care too much about the execution speed of a CGI program," he writes, "because the network delay is unpredictable (and sometimes long) anyway." Quite right, Dragos. If you write Web-based programs, this is a must-visit site.

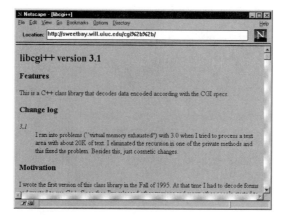

Figure 64 The class library.

CODING CONVENTION FOR C++

http://www.cs.princeton.edu/~dwallach/CPlusPlusStyle.html

Keep in mind that the idea is to make it easier for us to read each other's source code. Thus, we'd all benefit by following the few guidelines this site enumerates. If you focus on creating readable code, you may find many of the guidelines fundamental, and often predictable: All variable and constant identifiers should begin with a lowercase letter. Static data members should always begin with *their* (for example, *theirTotal*). With regard to classes, you should declare them in the following order: public member functions, protected member functions, private member functions, protected data members, and private data members. Come to this informative Web page to glean all the rules and guidelines. You have little to lose and readable code to gain.

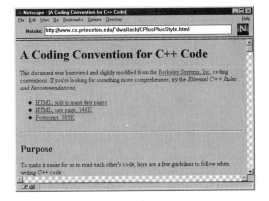

Figure 65.1 The coding convention.   *Figure 65.2 Control structures.*

C PROGRAMMING TUTORIAL FROM NEW ZEALAND

http://www.cit.ac.nz/smac/cprogram/

Trying to understand C programming? You will find all the specifics at this site: string and character handling, data validation, arrays, functions, assignment operators, structures, files, pointers, linked lists, dynamic memory allocation, enumerated data types, system calls—*the works!* You name it. You'll also find great downloadable software aids, including the noted *Small C* compiler for DOS and *C Flow* (which shows the flow of C programs), *C Check* (which checks C programs for errors), *C Lint* (which also checks C programs for type errors), *C Indent* (which automatically indents C programs correctly), and the old but reliable *Turbo C tutor*, which shows you how to use the old war-horse, *Turbo C*, to write C programs efficiently and elegantly.

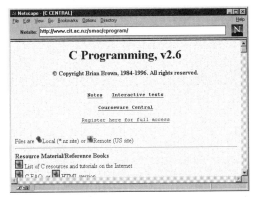

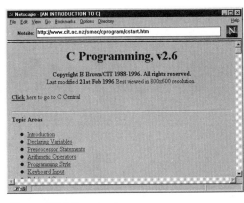

Figure 66.1 Web site for the tutorial.   *Figure 66.2 Some topic areas.*

67

CC++ PROGRAMMING

http://www.compbio.caltech.edu/ccpp/

Want to understand the future of C++ programming? Check out CC++, a parallel-programming language based on the sequential C++ programming language. The extensions in CC++ enable programmers to construct reliable parallel libraries that integrate a range of parallel-programming paradigms such as task parallel and data parallel programming styles. The CC++ parallel-programming extensions incorporate the fundamental ideas from compositional programming: synchronization variables and parallel composition. With CC++, you can use compositional programming methods while maintaining the ability to execute existing C and C++ programs *without modification.* Come to this Web site for full documentation *and* the compiler. Cool.

Figure 67.1 The CC++ Web site.

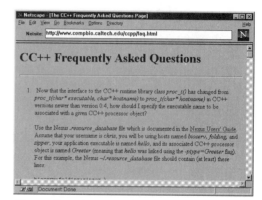

Figure 67.2 A great FAQ.

68

C++ PROGRAMMING FOR SCIENTISTS

http://math.nist.gov/pozo/class.html

Scientists used to make extensive use of the FORTRAN programming language to create a wide range of applications. Today, however, many scientists are jumping onto the C/C++ bandwagon. This site consists of lecture notes and programming samples for a course on C++ programming for scientists, written by Roldan Pozo and Karin Remington. The course starts with an explanation of ANSI C and then quickly moves on to show how C++ is a "better" C. It then considers C++ classes and objects, the role of objects in scientific computing, the ideas of inheritance and polymorphism, and more. The code included here embraces the *LAPACK++* linear algebra package, the *SparseLib++* package for matrix computations, the *IML++* iterative methods library, and the *MV++* matrix/vector library. This is essential stuff for all involved with object-oriented scientific computing.

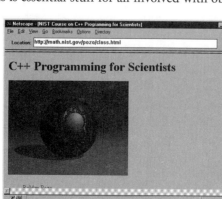

Figure 68.1 C++ Programming for Scientists.

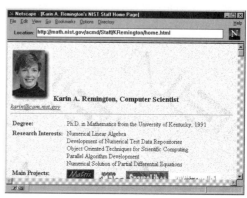

Figure 68.2 One of your instructors.

C/C++ USERS JOURNAL

http://www.cuj.com/

Through the *C/C++ Users Journal*, you can share the insights of the most recognized C/C++ experts in the world. At the Web site, you can access free sample articles in HTML format, as well as view the contents of the current edition of the Journal. When I visited the page, I found a wonderful article available, written by Marc Marini, explaining how to use inheritance to produce non-uniform-distribution generators from a common uniform distribution base class. The site also includes late-breaking development tool information and links, job opportunities in the C/C++ programming field, the Web Master's favorite C/C++ source code links, and much, much more. Check out the *C/C++ Users Journal* on-line. It's an outstanding source of technical solutions.

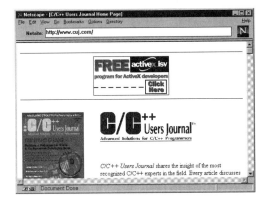

Figure 69.1 The C/C++ Users Journal home page.

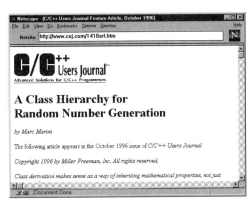

Figure 69.2 A sample article.

C++ VIRTUAL LIBRARY

http://info.desy.de/user/projects/C++.html

This impressive list of links includes a complete HTML edition of the draft C++ standard. It also includes documents and sources on C++ and OOP, a customizable environment for Emacs editors, virtual courses and tutorials, newsgroups, and newsletters. You will also find C++ software and libraries available for free download, conferences and seminars that feature C++ and object-oriented programming, lists of frequently asked questions, reviews of C++ tools and products, and much more, including hotlinks to consultant Web pages. If you bookmark just one C++ page on the Web, this should be the one. From this site, you can get to any site on the Internet that is of interest to C++ programmers. Oh yeah, if you are looking for employment, you'll find a detailed listing of available jobs.

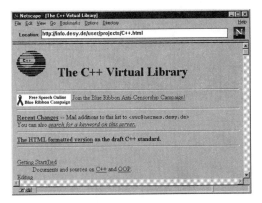

Figure 70.1 The C++ Virtual Library.

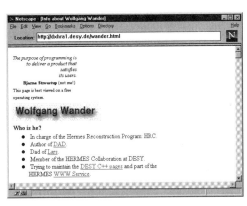

Figure 70.2 Your host.

71 C++ Windows Developer Directory: Free Advertising!

http://www.r2m.com/windev/consultants.html

Looking for a consultant? Looking for consulting clients? In either case, start at this site. If you are a professional consultant, you may list yourself and your services on this page for free. Send e-mail to *rmashlan@r2m.com* for more information. If you are looking for a consultant, there is absolutely no better place on the Web to find one. This site provides dozens of listings of the best and the brightest in C++ Windows programming around the country and around the world. Of course, along with the listings that detail specialties and previous clients, you also get direct links to the consultants' own Web sites. Couldn't be easier. Let your fingers do the walking.

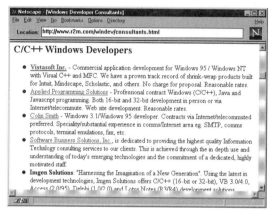

Figure 71 Imagine your link here.

72 The Cocoon Utilities

http://www.cs.umn.edu/~kotula/cocoon/cocoon.htm

Written by Jeffrey Kotula of the University of Minnesota, the *Cocoon Utilities* process C++ *include* files and produce a net of Web pages that document the libraries, classes, and global functions and types that the files contain. The Cocoon relies on a small set of simple formatting conventions in the header files. Use of these conventions does not interfere with most formatting preferences and does not obfuscate the code. Nevertheless, Cocoon organizes the information in C or C++ header files into liberally cross-linked hypertext documents affording all the most important navigational aids. In doing so, it provides a wonderful service.

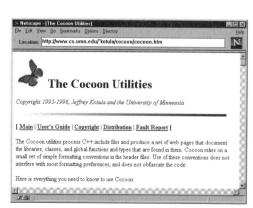

Figure 72.1 Cocoon Web sites.

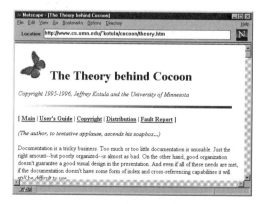

Figure 72.2 The theory behind it all.

FREE C++ APPLICATIONS & LIBRARIES

http://info.desy.de/user/projects/C++/Projects.html

If you are like most C/C++ programmers, you are probably in search of code, code, and more code. At this site you will find dozens of great applications and libraries available for free download. Among other things, you will encounter an object-oriented simulation package written in C++, a library of C++ routines which lets you draw high-quality PostScript Feynman diagrams (by writing a short C++ program to describe the diagram), an object-oriented C++ library that facilitates the development of applications with a graphical user interface, a set of C++ class libraries with high-level abstractions for implementing interactive programs, a C++ library for sparse-matrix computations, a powerful portable C++ GUI tool kit for Motif, and even a C++ object-oriented framework for the solution of partial differential equations! A source-code gold mine.

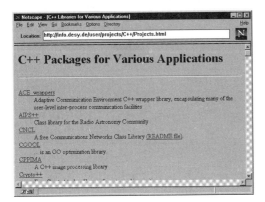

Figure 73.1 Take your pick.

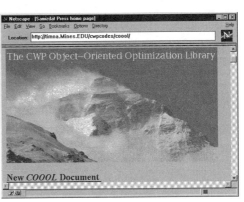

Figure 73.2 Just one of your choices.

FREE VISUAL C++ 4.0 (AND 4.2) ON-LINE TUTORIAL

http://www.iftech.com/classes/vc4mfc/vc4mfc0.htm

Experienced MFC programmers will tell you that the Microsoft Foundation Classes and the AppWizard's automated code development are the best thing since sliced bread. Programmers new to Visual C++, however, may question such a statement. At this site, you will find an excellent hypertext on-line tutorial adapted from the book by Marshall Brain, *Visual C++: Developing Professional Applications in Windows 95 and Windows NT Using MFC*. The tutorial's goal is to help you gain an understanding of the fundamental concepts that make MFC programs work under Visual C++. This on-line tutorial, along with the book it is derived from, are meant to leap over this wall, and do so very well.

Figure 74.1 The opening page.

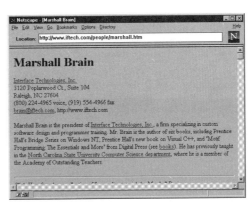

Figure 74.2 The author.

From the Ground Up: A Guide to C++

http://tqd.advanced.org/3074

This site bills itself as the world's first free, fully interactive tutorial to C++. It is absolutely great. How many times have you skipped through parts of a tutorial, only to have the parts you missed come back to haunt you later in the game? This tutorial will know when you skip ahead, and it will try to adapt what it does to make sure you don't miss out. By the way, people who already have a decent knowledge of Pascal will gain the most from this tutorial. It is fun, filled with light humor and concise, efficient code examples. And, like so many very excellent things on the Web, it is free. So, if you want to get up to speed on C++ fast, there is really no reason at all not to give this a shot. Is there?

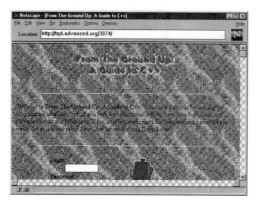

Figure 75.1 From the ground up.

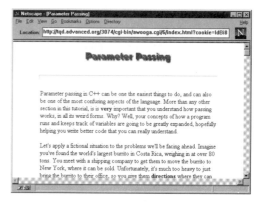

Figure 75.2 Parameter passing.

Great Circle: Memory Management for C++

http://www.geodesic.com/GreatCircle/

One of the primary challenges C++ programmers face as their programs increase in complexity is efficient memory management. Luckily, at this site you will learn that Great Circle offers an appealing library of memory management routines. Link these to your C/C++ programs and memory leaks disappear, as do premature frees (a program's errant release of memory that is in use). Best yet, to put these routines to work, you don't have to change a line of code, and you don't have to sacrifice an ounce of performance. Heck, Great Circle even offers you a leak-free guarantee. The underlying technology is called, believe it or not, "garbage collection." The reviews, I should tell you, are superlative. From *Information Week,* to *BYTE Magazine* to *Datapro,* the software gets great marks.

Figure 76.1 Great Circle Web sites.

Figure 76.2 The guarantee.

AI CAFÉ C/C++ CGI HTML HTTP JAVA J++ PERL VBSCRIPT VRML WIN32 WINSOCK 110011010010111100110110011010100011001100100101

INSIDE MICROSOFT VISUAL C++/FREE ISSUE

http://www.cobb.com/mcd/index.htm

A neat feature of the Cobb Group's *Inside Microsoft Visual C++* is that their articles truly look inside the software. When you visit this site, you not only get a free issue (using an interactive request form), you can also search the contents of back issues of this popular newsletter. And you can access the full on-line text of terrific selected articles, including such esoteric topics as how to upgrade C-style structures to make light use of member functions while leaving data "public," how to detect whether a user has modified the field on a *CFormView* or *CRecordView* (and how to prevent the *CFormView* or *CRecordView* from closing without saving the changes), and how to make any control completely fill any view's area in its frame, regardless of how the user sizes the frame. This is all very cool.

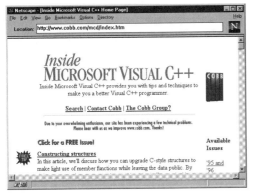

Figure 77.1 The Inside Microsoft home page.

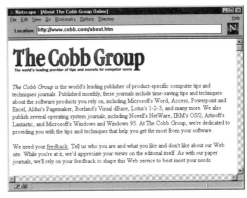

Figure 77.2 About the Cobb Group.

AI CAFÉ C/C++ CGI HTML HTTP JAVA J++ PERL VBSCRIPT VRML WIN32 WINSOCK 110011010010111100110110011010100011001100100101

INTERNET WISDOM: WINDOWS MFC PROGRAMMING

http://www.kudonet.com/~ixfwin/winprog_faqs/wpw_mfc_index.html

Sure, programmers are problem solvers. They like to dig and dig until they uncover solutions. However, using the findings of those that have gone before them makes more sense. One of the best ways for programmers to share their findings is within a newsgroup. At this site, you will find a great collection of Internet newsgroup postings, sorted by topic and thread, that relate to Visual C++ and MFC programming. For example, you will learn the subtleties of minimizing and restoring windows, how to disable the ESC key from closing a dialog box, and how to understand the "black magic" of update-edit controls. Best yet, this information is just the tip of the iceberg. You'll discover lots at this site. Delve deeply.

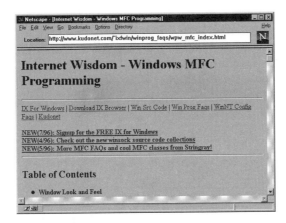

Figure 78 Internet Wisdom.

AI CAFE C/C++ CGI HTML HTTP JAVA J++ PERL VBSCRIPT VRML WIN32 WINSOCK

JON'S DIRECTORY OF C++ RESOURCES (MOSTLY FOR EUROPEANS)

http://www.cs.bham.ac.uk/~jdm/cpp.html

Maintained by John Morris-Smith of the University of Birmingham, this British-grown directory of C++ resources provides a list of C++ resources *indexed by geographic region.* Why? "Often for European (C++) users," writes Jon, "Web searches reveal a majority of useful sites which are in the USA; unfortunately, the sometimes slow connection over the pond can lead to frustration." This directory is, he writes, "an attempt to put a stop to the rising blood pressure of European C++ users." The resources are grouped in two categories. The first is "UK and Europe." The second is "Outside of Europe" and embraces, of course, the rest of the world. Thank you, Dr. Morris-Smith!

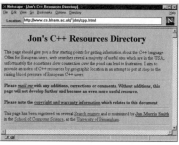

Figure 79.1 A European slant.

Figure 79.2 Your host.

Figure 79.3 A few options.

AI CAFE C/C++ CGI HTML HTTP JAVA J++ PERL VBSCRIPT VRML WIN32 WINSOCK

LOGISCOPE C FOR WINDOWS: A FREE DEMO FROM VERILOG

http://www.verilogusa.com/home.htm

In their struggle to finish or later fix code, programmer's often don't take time to take a close look at their program's processing and interrelationships. At this site, however, you will find several valuable tools you should put to immediate use. Treat yourself to a free download of the demo version of *Logiscope C* for Windows 95 and Windows NT, the outstanding software solution for reverse engineering and test- and C-code checking. The product supports most major compilers. The downloadable demo includes the *WinViewer*, a graphical browser able to show the structure of a C application (the program's call tree) as well as the logical structure of each C function. *WinViewer* can also provide more than 50 metrics, Kiviat graphs and histograms, and test coverage results. Valuable!

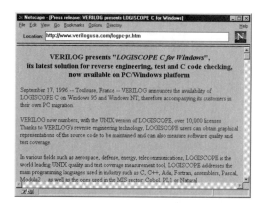

Figure 80.1 A press release.

Figure 80.2 Brought to you by Verilog.

MFC PROFESSIONAL

http://www.visionx.com/mfcpro/

Geared to the information needs of the professional programmer using Visual C++ and the Microsoft Foundation Classes, this site is packed with information. You'll find weekly tips, discussion groups, a database of MFC professionals (feel free to add yourself), archived threads, help-wanted notices, shareware/free archives, source code, tips for newbies, product listings and reviews, and so on. This slightly irreverent site is run by Mike Lorenz with the help of several other cool people, and is "not affiliated in any way with Microsoft, Bill Gates, Bill's wife, Bill's pedicurist, Bill's wife's pedicurist, or anyone who looks like a pedicurist."

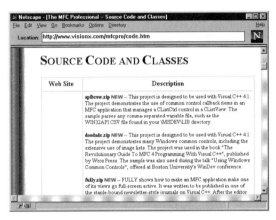

Figure 81 Free downloads.

MFC/VISUAL C++ INTERNET CORNUCOPIA

http://www.webcom.com/~sleslie/resources.html

This site is your "intersection" for hundreds of great links related to beta tests, conferences, demo-creation programs, mailing lists, retailers, books, configuration-management and version-control tools, text editors, installation programs, and more. You will find links to Usenet newsgroups, shareware, code libraries, consulting services, frequently asked MFC and Visual C++ questions, object-oriented development, training, compiler vendors, database products, FTP sites, magazines/newsletters, utilities, object-oriented software engineering tools, and custom utilities. The FTP sites include the Microsoft FTP server, the Oak Software Repository, and the Simtel NT Archive. This site's list of resources keeps "going and going . . . " In short, this site is a great place to start.

Figure 82 A host of options.

83

MICROSOFT'S VISUAL C++ FREQUENTLY ASKED QUESTIONS

http://www.microsoft.com/kb/faq/devtools/vc/vcmisc/

How can I optimize my help file access for Visual C++ under Windows 95 and Windows NT? Where can I get the patch for setting breakpoints on applications that are hosted on a Novell server? What Mx compiler options should I use to avoid an *LNK2005* error on *LIBC, LIBCMT*, and *MSVCRT* libraries? Why, in Windows NT 3.51, is the font size set in the Resource Editor not the same as in the application window? My DLL that calls *sin()* and *cos()* fails with incorrect results or produces general protection (GP) faults when used on a machine with no math coprocessor—help!—oh yeah, I'm using a 16-bit version of Visual C++. What's going on? If you have questions, this site has answers. If you have answers, share them here.

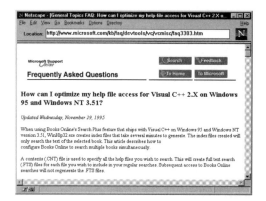

Figure 83.1 A sample question.

Figure 83.2 And another.

84

MICROSOFT'S VISUAL C++ INFORMATION (FREE SOFTWARE)

http://www.microsoft.com/VISUALC/

Come to this site for information on Visual C++ Enterprise Edition, Visual C++ Version 4.2 (which ships with enhanced support for ActiveX technologies), Visual C++ for the Macintosh, the RISC edition of Visual C++ Version 4.0, and other goodies. The goodies include white papers for all versions of Visual C++, along with hints and tips you will find nowhere else in cyber-space. You'll also find free software such as a great screen resolution switching application and an excellent search engine. The site's graphics are attractive, but not so intense that your compiler's version number may change during the long download. The Web Master has executed this site quite, quite well. Perhaps those folks at Microsoft know a thing or two about programming. What do you think?

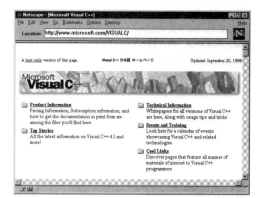

Figure 84.1 Official support from Microsoft.

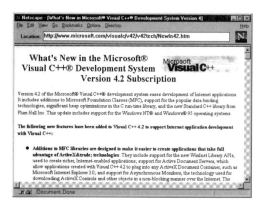

Figure 84.2 What's new.

OLDCORN'S C++ RESOURCES

http://www.bconnex.net/~coldcorn/c.htm

Maintained by Chris Oldcorn, C++ Resources comprises an excellent set of links to resources that relate to all aspects of C++ programming and application development. You'll find links related to enterprise client/server components, user-interface tools, OCX (OLE) controls, and C++ libraries for various applications. The site also discusses the *JOEY MFC* extension, which instantly makes Windows 3-D—it is cool. Also, you will encounter TCP/IP class libraries, C++ communications components, an MFC class library for an embeddable dialog/view editor, tools for creating cross-platform distributed objects, C++ object database tools, and the *MetaKit C++ Library* for persistent data. These aren't your run of the mill programming resources. Stop by this site—you'll learn a lot.

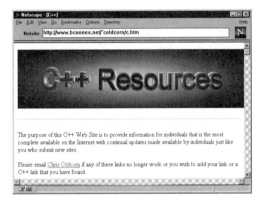

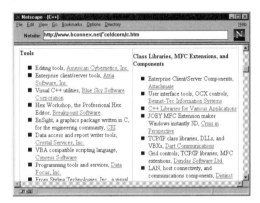

Figure 85.1 Oldcorn's C++ Resources.   *Figure 85.2 A few of your options.*

PORTING MFC 2.5 TO BORLAND 4.5 OR BETTER

http://www.htw.uni-sb.de/documents/mfc25-bc45.html

OK, real programmers have multiple compilers. Unfortunately, they will then need to move (port) the code they've written from one compiler to another. If, like many programmers, your compilers of choice are Borland's and Microsoft's, you'll want to check out this site. So, how do you port code between these compilers? For starters, you only do it with Borland 4.5 (or better), not 4.0 and not anything lower than that. You can't use anything lower than MFC 2.5, either. You need a specific Windows-Write File and a specific header-file (both of which are available at this site). Then, you need to modify some files, as detailed in the tutorial, make a new project in Borland IDE, and configure IDE settings as dictated by the author. All in all, the process this site outlines works just fine.

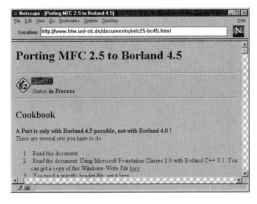

Figure 86.1 Porting details.   *Figure 86.2 Files to modify.*

AI CAFÉ C/C++ CGI HTML HTTP JAVA J++ PERL VBSCRIPT VRML WIN32 WINSOCK

STANDARD TEMPLATE LIBRARY (STL) FOR C++

http://www.cs.rpi.edu/~musser/stl.html

The Standard Template Library (STL) is a new C++ library that provides a set of easily composable C++ container classes and generic algorithms (template functions). The container classes include vectors, lists, sets, multisets, maps, multimaps, stacks, queues, and priority queues. The generic algorithms include a broad range of fundamental algorithms for the most common kinds of data manipulations, such as searching, sorting, merging, copying, and transforming. Come to this page, maintained by D.R. Musser of the Rennsselaer Polytechnic Institute, for much more information and for the library itself.

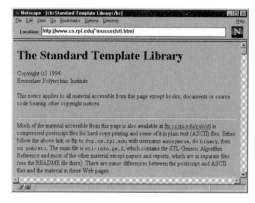

Figure 87.1 STL home page.

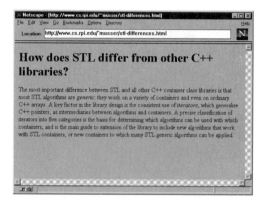

Figure 87.2 Facts about STL.

AI CAFÉ C/C++ CGI HTML HTTP JAVA J++ PERL VBSCRIPT VRML WIN32 WINSOCK

STL: A MODEST TUTORIAL

http://www.cs.brown.edu/people/jak/programming/stl-tutorial/home.html

Brown University's Jak Kirman believes you can learn a great deal about how generalization can simplify programming by understanding why the standard template library (STL) is constructed the way it is. With this in mind, he's put together a splendid on-line tutorial. The tutorial comprises a brief but elegant and insightful introduction to STL's five components (containers, iterators, algorithms, function objects, and allocators). The tutorial includes compact, to the point programming examples and really splendid illustrations that go a long way toward making STL-style object-orientation completely understandable. If you want to make your code more reusable, visit this site and try out the STL tutorial.

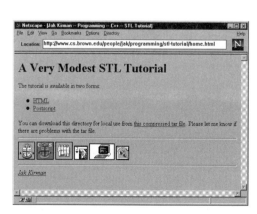

Figure 88.1 Oh, so modest.

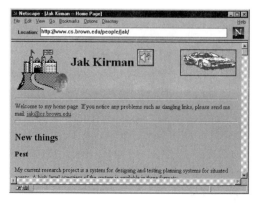

Figure 88.2 The author.

STL and Borland C++

http://www.cs.rpi.edu/~wiseb/stl-borland.html

The propaganda says that all versions of Borland C++ from 4.5 on are compatible with the standard template library (STL). But the propaganda lies—or at least does not tell the complete truth. Problems do exist. Data conversions, for example, may lose significant digits. Functions containing the <?> symbol may not be included. And, global STL comparison operators clash when a class provides the operators. These sort of things can screw up your day, year, life, and schedule big-time. These sort of things are just the sort of things that can leave you scratching your head in front of your boss and mumbling something brilliant like, "Gee, I thought it would run." Protect yourself before you start by accessing this tutorial.

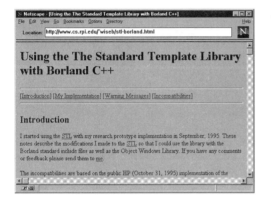

Figure 89.1 The introduction.

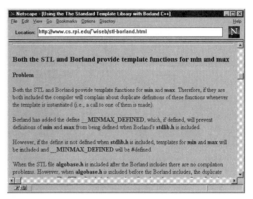

Figure 89.2 Some details.

STL Information from ByteWave

http://weber.u.washington.edu/~bytewave/bytewave_stl.html

If you are using or thinking about using the Standard Template Library (STL), put down what you are doing and visit this Web site. Compiled by Joseph Y. Laurino, this site includes great notes for STL newbies. ByteWave also includes great e-text editions of such STL "Bibles" as Sepanov's and Lee's *The Standard Template Library*, David Harvey's *The Tiny STL Primer*, and more. Add to this, links to newsgroups, mailing lists, lists of frequently asked questions, FTP software archives, on-line tutorials, and even Windows help-based versions of STL and ANSI C++ documentation. This excellent site goes a long way toward supporting the implementation of the STL programming model. Who said revolutions happen in the dark? They don't happen in the dark. They happen on the Web.

Figure 90.1 The STL Web site.

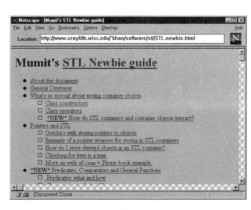

Figure 90.2 Some newbie notes.

STINGRAY: DOWNLOAD FREE DEMOS & WHITE PAPERS

http://www.stingsoft.com/

Come to Stingray for all the best in Microsoft Foundation Class libraries and other products for C++ object-oriented programming. You will find products which include *Objective Grid, Objective Toolkit, Objective Plug-In*, and more. Like their customers, the folks at Stingray are MFC developers. Also like you, they are sick and tired of fighting DLL/OCX battles. That's why they decided it would be much easier and quicker if C++ libraries were 100% MFC compatible (what a concept!). Thus, they devised their products to provide cleaner, "more" object-oriented solutions than the "controls" that programmers develop for the VisualBasic market that aren't object-oriented at all (ever tried deriving behavior from an OCX?). Check out these libraries.

Figure 91 Stingray home page.

THE TEN COMMANDMENTS FOR C PROGRAMMERS (ANNOTATED)

http://www.lysator.liu.se/c/ten-commandments.html

Thou shalt run lint frequently and study its pronouncements with care, for verily its perception and judgment oft exceed thine. Thou shalt not follow the NULL pointer, for chaos and madness await thee at its end. Thou shalt cast all function arguments to the expected type if they are not of that type already, even when thou art convinced that this is unnecessary, lest they take cruel vengeance upon thee when thou least expect it. If thy header files fail to declare the return types of thy library functions, thou shalt declare them thyself with the most meticulous care, lest grievous harm befall thy program. Thou shalt . . . Got the picture? Check out this site.

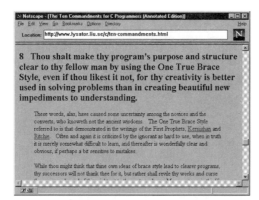

Figure 92.1 Commandment 8.

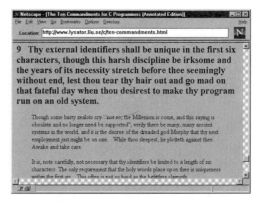

Figure 92.2 Commandment 9.

TTT: AN EXPERIMENTAL GUIDE TO C++

http://www.csu.edu.au/faculty/sciagr/inftech/comp/ttt/ttthome.htm

Devised by Erroll Chopping of Charles Sturt University, Australia, the Topic, Task and Test (TTT) System is an experimental suite of files and programs aimed at providing an interactive, Web-based on-line course on the fundamentals of C++ programming. After covering basic concepts such as variables and control structures, the tutorial moves on to address modularization with functions, batch processing, arrays, and structures (and, of course, arrays of structures). I am impressed with the tutorial's clearness of explanation, the elegance of the code samples, and the ease with which it makes sometimes complex topics understandable. I recommend this tutorial highly. It's a great way to get started.

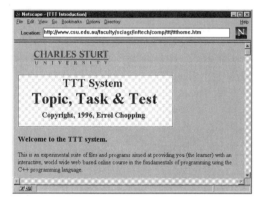

Figure 93.1 TTT Web site.

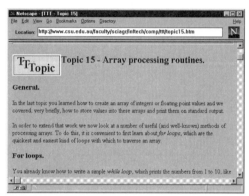

Figure 93.2 Array processing.

UNDERSTANDING C++: AN ACCELERATED INTRODUCTION

http://www.iftech.com/classes/cpp/cpp0.htm

This great hypertext tutorial addresses all aspects of C++, including C++ enhancements to C, vocabulary, classes, inheritance, operator overloading, handling pointers, and virtual functions. You'll also find a hyperlink to a great HTML introduction to C++ class hierarchies by the same authors. Note, a warning from the authors: They say the sections on operator overloading and handling pointers "get a little deep" into pointer details, perhaps needlessly so. If you are uncomfortable with pointers, you may safely move on to virtual functions and worry about pointers later. Like virtual functions and polymorphism are supposed to be a walk in the park?

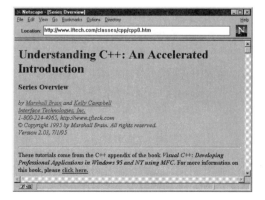

Figure 94.1 A free tutorial.

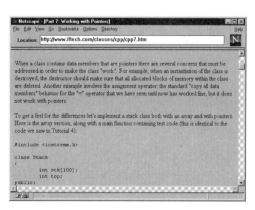

Figure 94.2 All about pointers.

AI Café C/C++ CGI HTML HTTP JAVA J++ PERL VBSCRIPT VRML WIN32 WINSOCK

THE VIRTUAL WINDOWS CLASS LIBRARY PROJECT

http://users.aol.com/vwcl/index.htm

The *Virtual Windows Class Library* (VWCL) is a non-commercial collection of powerful C++ tools that encapsulates the complexities of Windows development. All of the classes are designed to use the C++ language effectively and efficiently with minimal overhead added to the application. Code size and execution speed for applications built using VWCL are consistent with programs built using the standard SDK style C code. No multi-megabyte DLL's exist that you must distribute with applications using VWCL, as the code is normally (but not required to be) statically linked with the applications. Come to this informative Web page for more details.

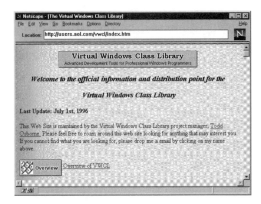
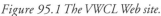

Figure 95.1 The VWCL Web site.

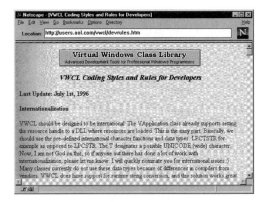

Figure 95.2 Coding styles and rules.

AI CAFÉ C/C++ CGI HTML HTTP JAVA J++ PERL VBSCRIPT VRML WIN32 WINSOCK

VISUAL C++ DEVELOPER: GET A FREE ISSUE

http://www.pinpub.com/level3/l3nvcd.htm

Each edition of Pinnacle Publishing's *Visual C++ Developer* covers a range of topics that include 16-bit and 32-bit delivery systems, static and dynamic MFC libraries, working with Windows 95 custom controls, building OLE data-sharing controls and automation servers, reducing the size of executable files, reducing an application's memory allocation needs, and managing large development teams effectively. With each monthly issue, you also receive a Developer's Disk packed with source code, objects, libraries, sample databases—even complete programs and utilities. Visit the Web site to order your free sample copy, complete with the valuable Developer's Disk. Good information.

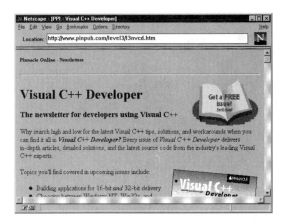

Figure 96 The Visual C++ Developer Web site.

VISUAL C++ DEVELOPERS JOURNAL

http://www.vcdj.com/

Launched in October 1996, *Visual C++ Developers Journal* is positioning itself to be the most comprehensive source of information available for Visual C++ developers. After all, it is not just a bi-monthly printed magazine, it integrates a great Web site along with hosting numerous technical conferences on both coasts. Come to the Web site to learn more about the *Visual C++ Developers Journal* in all of its various guises and to preview great upcoming articles such as "Is Java Ready to Replace C++ As Your Primary Development Language?" and "Combining Technologies to Build Your Visual C++ Applications." Also, check out the great developer resources they've assembled for you on-line.

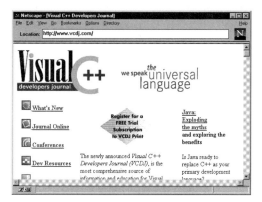
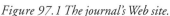

Figure 97.1 The journal's Web site.

Figure 97.2 Preview of beta issue.

VISUAL C++ AND MFC INTERNET RESOURCES

http://www.r2m.com/windev/MFC.html

At this site, you will find an outstanding set of links to pages packed with great "cut-and-paste" Visual C++ coding examples, as well as electronic magazines (zines) and on-line references for Visual C++ programmers. You will also find Visual C++ mailing lists and discussion groups, as well as vital information for cross-platform programming. The topics addressed include Windows 95 programming, integrating assembly-language programs with Visual C++ code, developing and using customized Visual C++ tool boxes, and more. And, of course, you get direct point-and-click to a wealth of powerful Visual C++ MFC libraries developed to make your programs more efficient, more robust, and (best yet) easier to write.

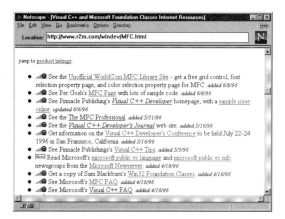

Figure 98 An array of options.

AI CAFÉ C/C++ CGI HTML HTTP JAVA J++ PERL VBSCRIPT VRML WIN32 WINSOCK

VISUAL C++ SERVICE PACK # 2 (SP2): FREE DOWNLOAD

http://www.microsoft.com/visual/hot/vc4sp2.htm

Are you experiencing problems and bugs in Visual C++ 4.0/4.2 with regard to sub-projects and debugging functions? You bet! Luckily, Bill Gates has come down from the mansion on the mountain to fix them. Or at least he's sent a few carpenters. All the patches and bug-fixes you need are in this packet, which you may download for free. The file is a 430K self-extracting .EXE and it downloads fairly quickly. And, after you plug in the patch, you'll be able to work with sub-projects to your heart's delight, and debug the dickens out of every line of code without ever once seeing your entire project suddenly crash down into the trash-heap (like it just might do without the patch).

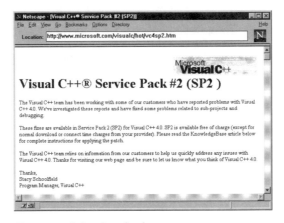

Figure 99 A free download.

AI CAFÉ C/C++ CGI HTML HTTP JAVA J++ PERL VBSCRIPT VRML WIN32 WINSOCK

V: A PORTABLE C++ GUI FRAMEWORK

http://www.cs.unm.edu/~wampler/v.html

Created by Dr. Bruce E. Wampler, *V* is, according to this site, "a C++ graphical user interface framework designed to provide an easy-to-use program system for building GUI applications." The *V* framework is small and provides the tools you will need to build all but the most special-ized applications. The V framework designers also focused on portability. You can currently run versions of *V* for X-Windows (Athena) that use customized 3-D widgets, as well as a version for Windows 3.1. In addition, versions for Win32/Windows 95 and OS/2 are underway. Best of all, the *V* system is available for free to all. Download it. Use it. Enjoy it.

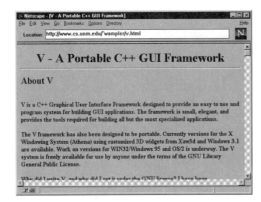

Figure 100.1 All about V.

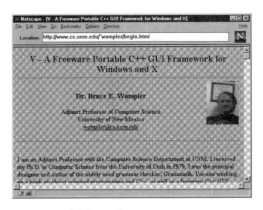

Figure 100.2 The author.

BEA: THE LEADER IN ENTERPRISE MIDDLEWARE SOLUTIONS

http://tuxedo.novell.com/

Depending on the existing hardware and software you must integrate into your client/server solution, you may require "middleware" which is software that sits between systems, possibly only to convert data formats or implement specific protocols. In 1995, three high-technology veterans founded BEA (from BEAcon) Systems, which focuses exclusively on enabling distributed applications to work seamlessly with legacy, client/server, and Internet environments. BEA delivers this capability by building a distributed application framework based on enhanced transaction and message management technology and services. In early 1996, BEA and Novell formed a partnership in which BEA became the developer and master distributor of *Tuxedo*, the leading portable transaction management system on UNIX, NT, and all non-NetWare platforms. Visit this Web site for specifics on *Tuxedo* and middleware.

Figure 101.1 Welcome to BEA.

Figure 101.2 Jolt information.

Figure 101.3 BEA products.

BUILDING YOUR OWN CLIENT/SERVER FOUNDATION

http://www.interex.org/interact/aug95/pp30-39.html

This authoritative tutorial article covers every aspect of client/server development, including SQL, two-tier versus three-tier architectures, middleware requirements, middleware components (including client, server, operations, and basic components), and listener processes. The tutorial also discusses development and operations utilities, time-zone management, security and authentication management, version control, and software distribution. Programmers must possess a strong working knowledge of all aspects of client/server programming. This tutorial is a great place to start building that knowledge.

Figure 102.1 Build your own.

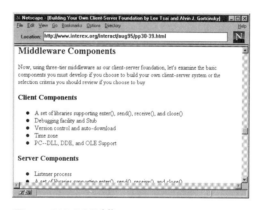

Figure 102.2 Middleware components.

CLIENT/SERVER ARCHITECTURE: A TUTORIAL

http://odo.elan.af.mil/pages/demos/web/cs_arc.html

At this site, you'll find complete details on fat-client models, fat-server models, the distribution-function model, the distributed-services model, the distributed-peer model, distributed-object computing, and more. Written by Wayne Eckerson, the tutorial explains how you distinguish each model by the way the model allocates components between clients and servers. As Eckerson writes, "Each has its strengths and weaknesses and is suitable for different types of business and processing requirements." Choosing the right model for your precise information system needs is precisely what this informative tutorial will help you do. Insightful discussion.

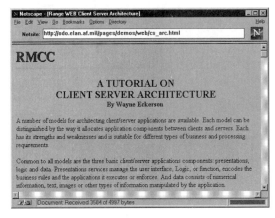

Figure 103 The tutorial.

CLIENT/SERVER COMPUTING: AN EXECUTIVE PRIMER

http://www.bitwise.net/iawwww/IAWWW-WP-CLNT-SRV-COM.HTML

Many companies use client/server computers throughout the organization. Many managers tout the development and productivity advantages the client/server model offers, even though they may know very little about the model itself. At this site, you will find a wonderful overview of all aspects of the client/server model. This document's purpose is to provide an executive overview of client/server computing from a technological, managerial, organizational, and leadership viewpoint. The primer's topics include metadata in the client/server environment, program design for client/server, administration of the client/server environment, corporate metadata, and common code administration, as well as client/server mainframe processing. A good read.

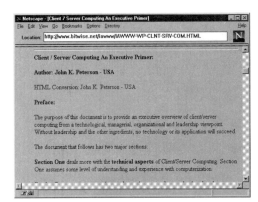

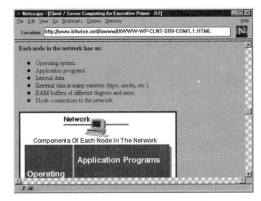

Figure 104.1 An executive primer.   *Figure 104.2 All about network nodes.*

MAIL PROTOCOLS (FREQUENTLY ASKED QUESTIONS)

http://www.umist.ac.uk/umist_info/popimapfaq.html

If you have ever struggled with setting up e-mail on a company-wide basis, you are well aware of the software complexities and questions that arise. Where can I get a POP server? Where can I get an IMAP server? What's the different between POP and IMAP? What are the relevant RFCs for POP and IMAP? Where can I get a POP client? Where can I get an IMAP client? At this site, you will find not only the answers to each of these questions (and many, many more), but also hyperlinks to appropriate downloads (for systems that include Mac System 7, Windows 3.1, Windows 95, NT, OS/2, and UNIX). Specifically, you will encounter *Eudora, Pegasus, pine, XLView, PopMail, mailx,* the *Cyrus IMAP* server, and many other products.

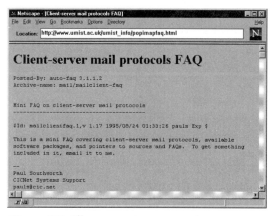

Figure 105 All your questions answered.

CLIENT/SERVER PROCESS CONTROL OVER A WAN

http://www.interex.org/hpuxusr/nov94/wong.html

Developing client/server applications for a local-area network is tough enough. What, then, do you have to watch out for when you deploy a client/server application over a wide-area network? This article, by Kevin Wong, explains in detail how one firm extended its HP 1000-based SCADA/process control system with the addition of a client/server based "CIM/21" software on HP 9000 Series 700 workstations. In reading how this firm implemented their system, you will learn how mechanisms such as *local buffering* are essential for client/server and distributed processing to minimize data loss when the wide-area network, workstations, software, or network equipment fail. A good read.

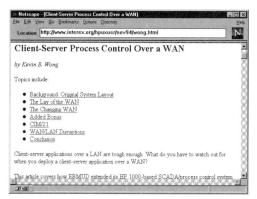

Figure 106.1 A great tutorial.

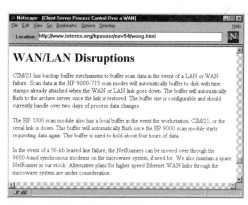

Figure 106.2 WAN/LAN disruptions.

1001 PROGRAMMING RESOURCES

1001100110001010101011001110110111110101110111110001101 AI CAFÉ C/C++ CGI HTML HTTP JAVA J++ PERL VBSCRIPT VRML WIN32 WINSOCK

107

CLIENT/SERVER AND RAPID APPLICATION DEVELOPMENT

http://www.agt.net/public/cipsweb/rad.html

The goal of the rapid application development special interest group (RAD SIG) of Calgary, Canada, is to share information about and to promote the use of client/server and distributed computing in relation to rapid application development (RAD) methods. Through the Web site (and via a mailing list), the group's members share information about how companies can move from mainframe development to client/server technologies. They also discuss tools and techniques that include GUI front-end software, and they examine object-oriented techniques for client/server implementations, and more. All told, this SIG is a marvelous source of client/server information "from the trenches" of the real-world system development.

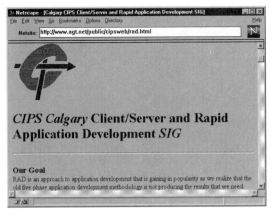

Figure 107 The SIG Web site.

108

CLIENT/SERVER: A SUCCESS STORY

http://www.interex.org/interact/jan95/client_server_success.html

Reprinted from *Interact Magazine*, Lisa Moose's "Client/Server: A Success Story" tells the tale of how the San Diego State University Foundation successfully implemented client/server technology, streaming valuable information from its core electronic systems into the hands of users. According to Ms. Moose, their success has stemmed from a fundamental focus on customer needs, a prosperous partnership with Hewlett-Packard, and a strong staff commitment. It also stemmed from "a dynamic vision to establish technological expertise as a tool to help the institution at large to excel. The net result is an elegant three-tiered client/server model that presides over robust HP systems and proficient end-users." Excellent real-world discussion.

Figure 108.1 A success story.

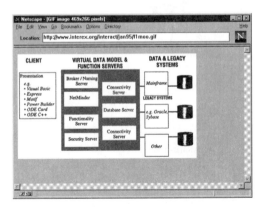

Figure 108.2 An illustration of success.

CLIENT/SERVER TECHNOLOGIES, INC., CONSULTING

http://www.com/cst/index.html

For many companies, choosing to outsource their client/server computing requirements will save money and development time. Client/Server Technologies, Inc. (CST), provides such servers, focusing primarily on Internet- and intranet-based solutions that require the design, implementation, and integration of Web servers, database servers, application servers, file servers, and legacy systems. CST specializes in security blueprints, security scanning and monitoring, and performance issues. CST also performs technology due-diligence (checks and validates the books) for major business ventures that have dependencies on client/server and Internet technologies. Find out more (actually, a great deal more) at the CST Web page.

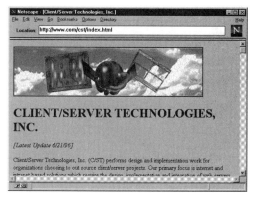

Figure 109.1 CST Web site.

Figure 109.2 A strategic relationship.

COGNOS CLIENT/SERVER PARTNER PROGRAM

http://cogweb.cognos.com/

Regardless of the client/server task at hand, you don't have to face (develop) your applications alone. From end-user data access to enterprise-wide mission-critical applications, the Cognos toolset (*Axiant, PowerHouse Client, PowerHouse, PowerPlay,* and *Impromptu*) is positioned to meet your needs. Whether you've embraced the client/server already, or need a path to get there, Cognos can provide you with the education, support, and tools you need to confidently attack client/server applications. Cognos partners can look for immediate results from client/server products that satisfy the entire enterprise: reporting and analysis, and application development. Visit the Cognos Web site for more information.

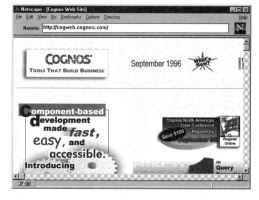

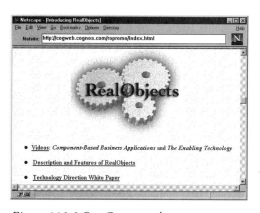

Figure 110.1 Cognos Web site.

Figure 110.2 One Cognos product.

Compuware Client/Server Development

http://www.compuware.com/

Would you like to sidestep the steep client/server learning curve, avoid the expense and delay of retraining your permanent staff, and develop easy-to-use applications that leverage your investment in information technology? In addition, wouldn't it be nice to extend the useful life of your existing systems, while satisfying demands for new user interfaces? Compuware can help you do all this and more. Compuware can step in and develop front ends and user interfaces that provide efficient client/server application, design cooperative and peer-to-peer communications (based on APPC, RPC, and named pipes), deliver distributed database technology (using DB2 SQL engines), and provide Windows-based, object-oriented development tools. Compuware may just be the solution you need.

Figure 111.1 Welcome to Compuware.

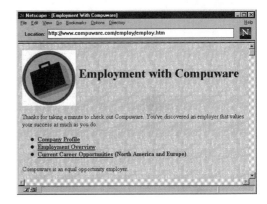
Figure 111.2 Employment with Compuware.

CoPath Client/Server Systems for Medicine

http://www.comedsys.com/cs.htm

Many client/server applications must satisfy the logical and physical flow of data. *CoPath Client/Server* solutions offer flexibility in managing the anatomic-pathology workflow, while also providing links to hospital-wide or enterprise-wide systems. The architecture of CoPath Client/Server applications enables a wide range of users within an organization to share information across functional boundaries, and thereby meet the organization's rapidly changing demands. *CoPath Client/Server* adds an array of features to both *Powersoft's PowerBuilder* tool set and the *Sybase* database that surpass any other combination of tools currently on the market. Visit the CoPath Web site for more information.

Figure 112.1 The CoPath App Manager window.

Figure 112.2 CoPath Web site.

DO-IT-YOURSELF CLIENT/SERVER (PICK)

http://www.picksys.com/links/pub/info/pickworld/0995clie.html

Bryan Buchanan explains a method for using Advanced Pick (AP) in the client/server environment. He emphasizes AP-on-UNIX implementations which provide C functions in UNIX, and systems where the UNIX environment provides Berkeley-style (BSD) sockets for accessing Pick. Buchanan has created a set of Windows-based routines that mirror the *_CP_xxx* routines in UNIX. When the client program calls one of these routines, the client passes the parameters to the server program on UNIX, which in turn calls the *_CP_xxx* routine. Buchanan's detailed tutorial explains the underlying process in detail. Take time to check out this information-rich Web page.

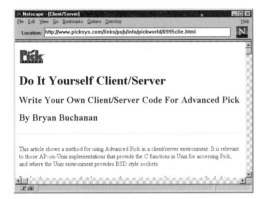
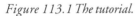

Figure 113.1 The tutorial.

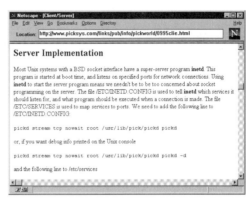

Figure 113.2 Server implementation information.

DOWNLOAD CLIENT APPS FOR PCS

http://oac3.hsc.uth.tmc.edu/staff/snewton/client-server.html

OK, so not everyone has the hardware to bring them into the twenty-first century, or even into Windows 95. If you are still using a DOS-based system (or Windows 3.x on top of DOS), use this site to download DOS-based gopher clients, WAIS clients, an Archie client for searching all the major public FTP archives, and a great news-reader client. This site offers the applications as self-extracting executable files. If you are using Windows, the archives include .PIF (Program Information File) files for running the clients. See, we didn't forget about you guys and gals.

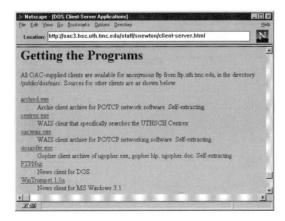

Figure 114 Help yourself.

THE ROAD TO CLIENT/SERVER PROCESSING: THE OPEN BLUEPRINT

http://www.software.ibm.com/openblue/PAPERS/EVERYONE.HTM

If you are struggling with, managing, or considering migrating to a client/server environment, do yourself a favor and read this great discussion by Diane Baron (originally written in 1994, but recently updated to reflect new technologies). Baron is the Program Manager for the Distributed Computing Environment (DCE) for IBM EMEA (IBM Europe, Middle East, Africa). She is one of the "heaviest hitters" and "saviest thinkers" around when it comes to client/server methodologies and technologies. Thus, she is the first to tell you that despite all the industry hype, client/server is not a cure-all and is no panacea. "So just what is it?" she asks rhetorically. "What are the key benefits? And how might you get there?" Her article provides the answers, and does so with panache!

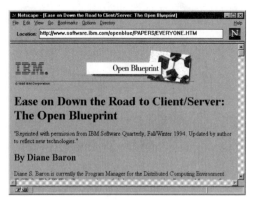
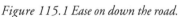

Figure 115.1 Ease on down the road.

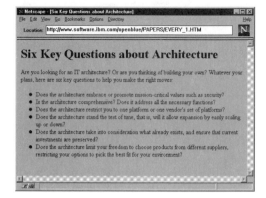

Figure 115.2 Six key questions.

EVALUATING CLIENT/SERVER FRONT-END TOOLS

http://www.cvm.com/cvm/provb.html

What does the latest client/server publicity flap say? Who rules the development-tool playoff this week? Last week the popular item was *VisualBasic*. This week *Gupta* is the star. Next week, *Powersoft's PowerBuilder* will be hot. Driven by publicity, and short on time, too many of us simply grab the software catalog, quickly review ratings on installation and ease-of-use and portability, and purchase hundreds, even thousands of dollars of software tools only to determine that the tool we purchased is easy to install but can't provide transaction control for the order-processing system we've been contracted to create. This article shows you how to choose your tools somewhat more astutely. A very good read.

Figure 116 Evaluating the tools.

FINANCIAL RULES-OF-THUMB FOR CLIENT/SERVER SYSTEMS

http://www.onr.com/oz/topic3.html

Client/server applications are really all about money. Aren't they? This site is packed with financial insights: 1) Every LAN server in your network will cost an average of $3,500 per month to maintain. 2) Automation of the help desk, configuration management, and software distribution are keys to LAN cost containment. 3) Regardless of what you initially spend on a LAN installation, you will spend twice that amount in six months to maintain it. 4) The education costs surrounding a client/server application will be twice as expensive as the programming it took to create the software. 5) Personnel costs will dominate your client/server project, potentially up to 70% of the total project costs. 6) . . . You get the idea.

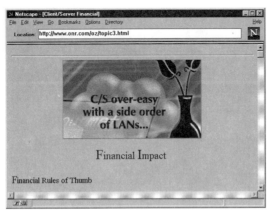

Figure 117 Rules of thumb.

THE FUTURE OF CLIENT/SERVER COMPUTING

http://www.tandem.com/new/letter/paranews2/csfuture.html

Yes, client/server computing is the future . . . but what is the future of client/server computing? Visit this site and benefit from Jack Karp's insightful analysis of what the client/server-computing future holds. Karp has spent over a decade analyzing the information industry. He has held senior research and consulting positions at Gartner Group, META Group, New Science Associates, and the Research Board. Karp regularly provides senior information-systems executives with comprehensive perspectives and analysis of the information industry and frequently speaks at major international conferences. By visiting this Web site, you can benefit from his vision without winging to some far-flung conference.

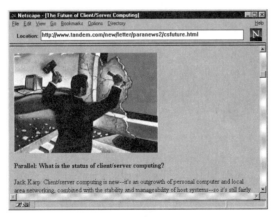

Figure 118 Looking at the future.

HEWLETT-PACKARD CLIENT/SERVER SOLUTIONS

http://www.dmo.hp.com/gsy/sp2.html

Hewlett-Packard, the established leader in providing UNIX solutions for open systems, recognized over a decade ago that the innovative user of client/server computing would reshape the business use of information technology (IT). As a leader in client/server computing, HP's offerings include high-performance scalable HP 9000 business servers, a broad range of client-side solutions that include PCs, workstations, and X-terminals, the HP-UX enterprise operating environment, distributed-computing middleware, high-speed networking technologies, and much more. Visit this informative Web site for more details.

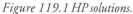

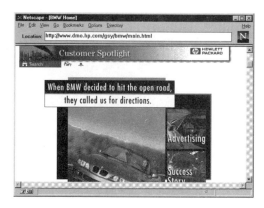

Figure 119.1 HP solutions.   *Figure 119.2 A satisfied HP customer.*

IBM'S ENTERPRISE 3GL CLIENT/SERVER APPLICATIONS

http://www.software.ibm.com/software/ad/ad3gl.html

A few years ago, "IBM client/server" tools would have been an oxymoron. But times change and so did "Big Blue." This site features a set of solutions for database and transaction-driven client/server applications. In addition, you will find workgroup development environment (with tight linkage to the host and LAN execution environments). The tools also introduce new technologies to the 3GL (third-generation language) programmer, such as support for object-oriented programming, multimedia, and visual construction. The tools allow programmers to introduce these new technologies into their application bases in an evolutionary manner. Visit this site for more details.

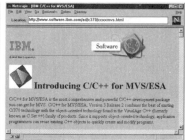

Figure 120.1 IBM's 3GL solution.   *Figure 120.2 COBOL solutions.*   *Figure 120.3 C language solutions.*

MEASURING CLIENT/SERVER PAYBACK: A REAL AUDIO INTERVIEW

http://www.mediapool.com/offtherecord/may.html

Is traditional return-on-investment (ROI) analysis a "dead science"? That's the view of Thornton May, vice president of research and education at Cambridge Technology Partners in Cambridge, Mass. May believes that companies must begin using multi-dimensional yardsticks to measure payback from technology. In this interview with Brian McWilliams, May explains how savvy information-systems executives succeed in this new environment, which he calls a "bid and ask negotiation marketplace." Stop and listen to the entire interview, which is available at this site as a Real Audio file. You may either listen to the interview right on-line, or download it and listen later. The interview runs for about eight minutes (8:22 minutes or 490Kb, to be exact). Good discussion in a cool (RealAudio) format.

Figure 121 Thornton May's firm.

MUSIC/SP CLIENT/SERVER SOFTWARE

http://musicm.mcgill.ca/~roy/http/mcs.html

MUSIC/SP Client/Server lets Windows-based users easily transfer files to and from a remote host running MUSIC/SP, without having to bother with FTP, 3270 protocols, host editors, or terminal emulators. It also lets users send and receive e-mail, as well as read and create e-mail off-line. Additionally, users may create and edit documents with the software's integrated WYSIWYG editor (including a built-in spell-checker), create and edit HTML documents, tailor menus to support a point-and-click interface for common tasks, and interface with dial-up terminal servers. A good solution for remote-host access.

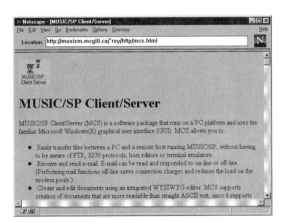

Figure 122 Information on MUSIC.

PROVIDING A CLIENT/SERVER INFRASTRUCTURE

http://www.interex.org/interact/feb95/net_mgmt.html

In this reprint of an extended-length *Interact Magazine* article, David Heck discusses such client/server topics as interpretability and integration, the impact of bandwidth, reliability and security, and resource management. These, explains Heck, are the critical areas of the network infrastructure that we must consider before client/server development can become a reality. Just one example: You must carefully consider the way in which the client initiates a link or connection to a database (such as sockets, NetIPC, NetBIOS) before you can choose, design, and evaluate a client-server solution. Heck's article will provide you with insight into all stages of the client/server development process.

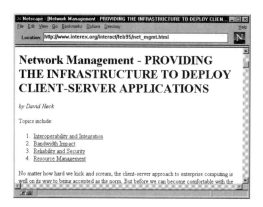
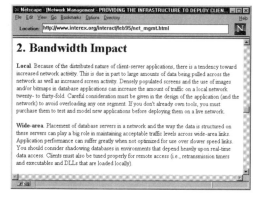

Figure 123.1 David Heck on network management.   *Figure 123.2 Bandwidth Impact.*

PERFORMANCE ENGINEERING IN CLIENT/SERVER ENVIRONMENTS

http://www.csc.com/about/perf_eng.html

This incisive tutorial explains how to use the methods and tools of performance engineering to design acceptable levels of performance into an installation's hardware configuration, network design, and data design. The discussion includes complete details on the importance of benchmarking and predictive modeling in this process. The tutorial emphasizes that you must engineer scalability into an application during the design phase. If you do not, the cost of scaling an application later may be prohibitive. Packed with hints and tips, the tutorial is well worth your read. It may save you much grief in the future.

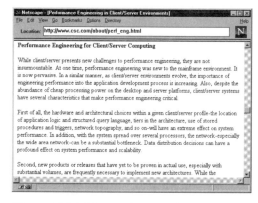

Figure 124.1 The tutorial.   *Figure 124.2 More on the tutorial.*

PITFALLS OF CLIENT/SERVER COMPUTING

http://www.onr.com/oz/topic4.html

According to this Web page, six basic pitfalls will "doom to failure" the well-intended client/server implementation: 1) Unrealistic expectations; 2) Selecting tools before you make decisions; 3) Lack of an adequate systems-management plan; 4) Incomplete or inaccurate data placement; 5) Organization power struggles; and 6) The use of client/server as an excuse. Any one of these, or any combination of them, is enough to send your project crashing down around you—often times more than just once. Visit this site and read the specifics. Then, post a list of the pitfalls within the offices of each of your client/server programmers.

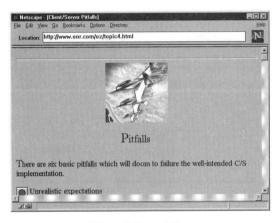

Figure 125 Pitfalls, pitfalls, pitfalls.

ROADMAPS TO OPEN CLIENT/SERVER & DISTRIBUTED COMPUTING

http://www.psgroup.com/

Many of Patricia Seybold's customers have asked her for pointers with respect to designing their client/server architectures. Her clients want to make sure they design robust, responsive systems and applications that take advantage of many of the technologies available on the market today. In response, the Seybold Group has created a set of step-by-step roadmaps to guide you through the many decision points involved in designing distributed applications. You will find roadmaps that help you select middleware, choose application-development tools, manage networks and systems, design enterprise electronic-mail solutions, select and implement groupware, select and implement workflow, and more. Come to Seybold's home page for more information. Thanks, Patricia.

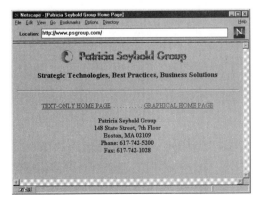

Figure 126.1 The group.

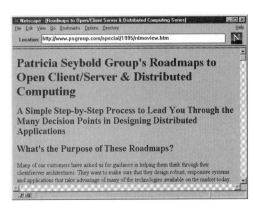

Figure 126.2 The roadmaps.

SoluTech Client/Server Solutions

http://205.242.177.130/

Don't struggle to get your client/server project off the ground. Instead, send it rocketing toward success with *SoluTech's PowerLaunch with PowerBuilder.* The software is a proven, cost-effective development methodology for client/server projects. Laying down a solid object-oriented framework, *SoluTech* will guide you through the sometimes overwhelming issues that always accompany a new project. To start, *SoluTech PowerLaunch* gives you development guidelines and standards (including GUI, *PowerScript*, and SQL guidelines). Next, *SoluTech* provides their design methodology which includes goal-setting, timelines, and project management. Finally, *SoluTech* offers ready-to-use, rigorously tested pluggable components.

Figure 127.1 SoluTech Web site.

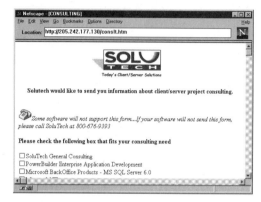

Figure 127.2 Consulting services.

Strategies for Client/Server Development in C: A Tutorial

http://www.pts.co.uk/pts/whtpaper/strat.cs.dev.wp.html

What are some of the issues you face when you move to C/C++ to develop client/server applications using a modern, three-tier architecture? This tutorial explains those issues and how to work through (or if necessary, around) them using CenterLine's *CodeCenter* and other proprietary tools. *CodeCenter* and other CenterLine tools are available for all leading UNIX platforms, integrate easily with other life-cycle development tools, offer interactive workspaces for prototyping and debugging, include comprehensive error detection, and provide an easy migration path from Cobol to C and then from C to C++. The products are good; and the tutorial is excellent. Visit the Web site for more details.

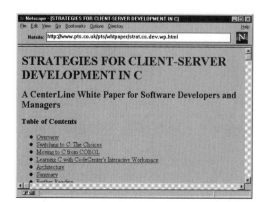

Figure 128.1 The white paper.

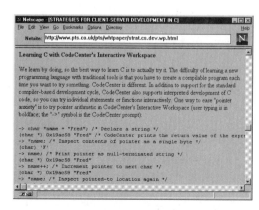

Figure 128.2 Learning with CodeCenter.

AI CAFÉ C/C++ CGI HTML HTTP JAVA J++ PERL VBSCRIPT VRML WIN32 WINSOCK 11001101001011100110111001101010001100110010010

TRANSTECH CLIENT/SERVER SEMINARS

http://www.interaccess.com/transtech/seminars.html

Are you still searching for an understanding of client/server processing? Transtech offers a number of seminars that introduce the client/server paradigm and give guidelines for migration to the client/server architecture. The seminar topics include application and data architecture, technical considerations, selecting candidates for client/server applications, organizational roles and issues, internetworking and network management, application framework, client/server application development lifecycle, development methodologies (including RAD methodologies), and much more. Visit the Transtech Web site for more information and, quite likely, many answers to your questions.

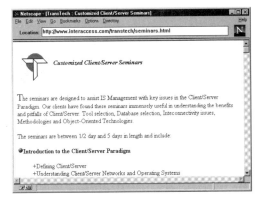
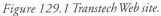

Figure 129.1 Transtech Web site.

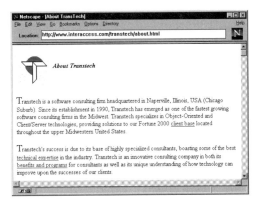

Figure 129.2 About Transtech.

AI CAFÉ C/C++ CGI HTML HTTP JAVA J++ PERL VBSCRIPT VRML WIN32 WINSOCK 11001101001011100110111001101010001100110010010

WHY CLIENT/SERVER?

http://www.pts.co.uk/pts/whtpaper/cli_serv.frame.html

Are you trying to convince your boss that your company needs to move to client/server computing? Are you trying to convince yourself? "At first glance," writes this site's author, "client/server computing has many appealing advantages. The first is that it complements downsizing. Moving to smaller machines inevitably leads to lower hardware cost and easier, less-expensive maintenance investments. Another advance is the modularity implied by client/server computing: the distribution of hardware resources leads to a more effective and equitable allocation of cost and responsibility." From this common-sense opening, the author goes on to discuss details of hardware and software considerations, data access alternatives, and more. A must-read paper.

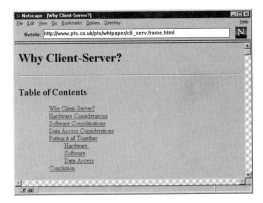

Figure 130.1 Why, why, why.

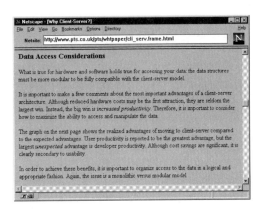

Figure 130.2 Data access considerations.

131

WHY IS CLIENT/SERVER COMPUTING LIKE TEENAGE SEX?

http://www-ems.enel.ucalgary.ca/people/vidya/teenage.html

Leave it to folks in Canada to bring client/server computing to a new dimension. Oh, well—their list seems to make sense: 1. It's on everyone's mind all the time; 2) Everyone talks about it all the time; 3) Everyone thinks everyone else is doing it; 4) Almost no one is really doing it; 5) The few who are doing it do it poorly or think it will be better the next time; 6) Everyone is bragging about their successes; 7) Very few actually have any successes; 8) The hope for success can lead to wasted time, effort, and money; and 9) Just as success in sex won't clear up your complexion, neither will success with client/server systems. Visit this site for additional insight.

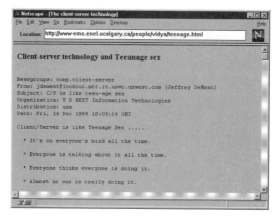

Figure 131 An unlikely comparison.

ADDITIONAL CLIENT/SERVER SYSTEM RESOURCES

- Migrating from Host-based Computing to Client/Server
  http://cause-www.colorado.edu/information-resources/ir-library/abstracts/cnc9448.html

- Client/Server Application Development Track
  http://www.techcalendar.com

- Managing Client/Server Environments: System Management Practices
  http://www.digital.com/.i/digest/htdocs/digest/course/ey-m901e-s0-w3.html

- CLC-RDBMS and Client-Server Concepts
  http://www.ini.net/shop/business/clc/outlines/rdbms.html

- Client/Server Software
  http://www.swan.ac.uk/mosaic/WM3_2.htm

- Faximum Software - Client/Server Questions & Answers
  http://www.faximum.com/products.d/qna.cs.html

- Yannis Manassis, Client/Server, Gupta Programmer
  http://www.corpus.nl/cornelius/freelanc/cv/cvmanass.htm

- DT2621 Client/Server Programming
  http://rokke.grm.hia.no/hia/fag/dt2621/dt2621-eng.html

ACCLAIM COMMUNICATIONS: DOWNLOAD AN EtherWAN DEMO

http://www.acclaiminc.com

Are you looking for information on state-of-the-art networking technology? Acclaim's products are perfect for those who wish to blend the benefits of LAN switching and WAN routing. These products include the *EtherWAN* access switch, as well as the well-known *Acclaim 3200FR/3000FR Frame Relay Routers*—arguably the most advanced integrated multi-protocol frame-relay access device and routers available today. Providing both scalability and performance, the *EtherWAN* access switch combines high-port count 10/100 Ethernet switching and integrated frame relay, ISDN and ATM (asynchronous transfer mode) technologies. All Acclaim products include *WindowsView* and *WebView*, Acclaim's integrated Wide Local Area Network (wLAN) management solution.

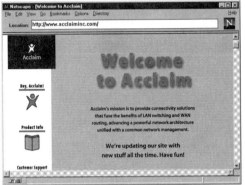

Figure 132.1 Acclaim Web site.

Figure 132.2 Late breaking news.

FREE

FREE SOFTWARE

COVERS DETAILS

OPEN TO ALL

THE ADSL FORUM

http://198.93.24.23/index.html

Telephone companies around the world are beginning to recognize the immense value they can still realize from their copper loop installations. Why? New transmission technologies give the phone companies the capability to construct broadband access networks with existing twisted-pair wiring. Asymmetrical Digital Subscriber Line (ADSL), an asymmetric modem capable of transmitting movies, television, and high-speed data over long copper links, has proved itself a viable technology for the future. This site's on-line forum concerns itself with technical and market issues related to ADSL access network system. The Web site includes tutorial information, as well as on-line dialogues, white papers, and more. Insightful.

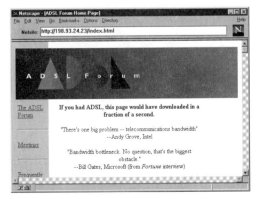

Figure 133.1 The Forum Web site.

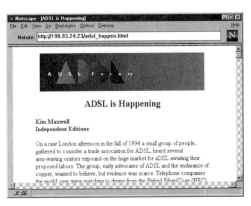

Figure 133.2 An article on ADSL.

FREE

FREE SOFTWARE

COVERS DETAILS

OPEN TO ALL

America's Network: Technology for the New Public Network

http://www.americasnetwork.com/

If you are into computers, you need to be into communications. Computers, after all, are becoming communication devices. Like the print version of this great publication, this site's electronic edition brings you a unique, well-organized package of original, independent reporting and business analysis of telecommunications technologies for today's public network. *America's Network* provides you with an independent benchmark of what technologies and strategies make the best business sense, which solutions work, and which remain to be proven. At this site, you'll find not only each bi-weekly issue of *America's Network,* but also selected back issues. You'll also find links to useful industry sites, a great itinerary of upcoming telecom events, and even an on-line job bank!

Figure 134.1 America's Network Web site.

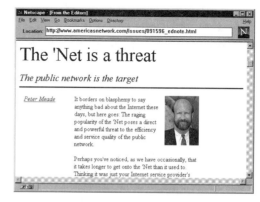

Figure 134.2 An editorial.

Banyan Systems

http://www.banyan.com

Founded in 1983, *Software Magazine* ranks Banyan as one of America's top thirty independent software companies. For more than a decade, Banyan has been the premier provider of enterprise networking products and services that enable organizations to integrate diverse computing resources into unified, global networks. Today, Banyan is using its network integration expertise to capitalize on the explosive trend towards extended enterprise networks. Banyan's core software technology is a suite of tightly-integrated services delivered consistently across multiple network environments throughout the enterprise. Visit Banyan's Web site for more information.

Figure 135.1 Banyan Web site.

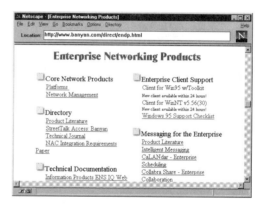

Figure 135.2 Some products.

COMMUNICATIONS/NETWORK TECHNOLOGIES

AI CAFÉ C/C++ CGI HTML HTTP JAVA J++ PERL VBSCRIPT VRML WIN32 WINSOCK 110011010010111100110111001101010100011001100100101

BAY NETWORKS

http://www.baynetworks.com

Internetworking is the process of connecting one or more networks. The Internet, for example, is a huge internetwork. Bay Networks is a worldwide leader in the internetworking market, providing innovative solutions that serve large enterprises, small businesses, and mobile workers. With revenues exceeding $1.7 billion, Bay Networks delivers the industry's most complete set of advanced internetworking products—from 10BASE-T to high-speed asynchronous transfer mode (ATM), from shared media hubs to high-performance multiprotocol routers, compact switches, and remote access servers. And with over 25 million nodes installed worldwide, Bay Networks products support more network connections than any other vendor. Visit this site and learn how to connect a wide variety of network architectures.

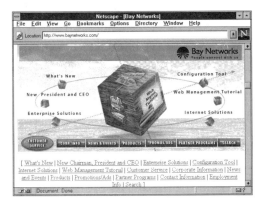

Figure 136.1 Bay Networks Web site.

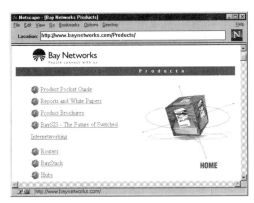

Figure 136.2 Bay products.

BUS-TECH: LAN TO MAINFRAME CONNECTIVITY

http://www.bustech.com/

Do you have a large mainframe hanging around whose processing power is disconnected from your company's large PC base? Bus-Tech provides simple, adaptable, economically-feasible connectivity solutions for linking legacy (older) IBM and Unisys mainframes to modern LANs. Bus-Tech's installed base of mainframe to LAN installations is now over 7,000 (many universities and research facilities) making Bus-Tech the undisputed market leader for mainframe interconnect controllers. Today, Bus-Tech has forged strategic partnerships with key industry giants (IBM, Microsoft, and Novell), resulting in Bus-Tech products that are more appealing to a broader range of users.

Figure 137.1 Bus-Tech Web site.

Figure 137.2 A few networking options.

1001100110001010101100111011011110101110111110001101 AI CAFE C/C++ CGI HTML HTTP JAVA J++ PERL VBSCRIPT VRML WIN32 WINSOCK

COASTCOM

http://www.coastcom.com/

In the future, users will send data, voice, and video over the same transmission media—which requires a high-speed channel. Coastcom is a leading supplier of equipment for connecting voice, data, and video communications to private and public networks. Founded in 1967, Coastcom supplies T1 and Frame Relay transmission equipment for a broad spectrum of commercial applications, including LAN connectivity, highway traffic control, and broadcast audio. Coastcom markets a full range of versatile intelligent multiplexers, digital program channels, and digital cross-connect systems. Visit this site for the latest information on state-of-the-art communication equipment.

Figure 138.1 Coastcom Web site.

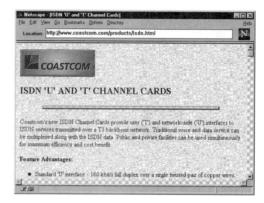

Figure 138.2 ISDN solutions from Coastcom.

1001100110001010101100111011011110101110111110001101 AI CAFE C/C++ CGI HTML HTTP JAVA J++ PERL VBSCRIPT VRML WIN32 WINSOCK

DOUGLAS COMER: NETWORKING GURU

http://www.cs.purdue.edu/people/comer

Comer is a noted authority on networks and internets (TCP/IP protocols), as well as the Xinu (yes, that's Unix spelled backward) operating system. His four-volume *Internetworking with TCP/IP* is a classic benchmark reference and tutorial. You can download the software that accompanies these books free from Comer's Web page. Comer's *Computer Networks and Internets* is an excellent, broad-based introduction to the topic. (Find more information about this book on the Web page.) You will also find several articles by Comer that you can read on-line, as well as information on seminars and tutorials Comer conducts, and how to go about obtaining his consulting services. Comer knows his stuff—check out this site.

Figure 139 The guru himself.

AI CAFÉ C/C++ CGI HTML HTTP JAVA J++ PERL VBSCRIPT VRML WIN32 WINSOCK 11001101001011110011011100110101010001100110010101

DISTINCT TCP/IP FOR WINDOWS

http://www.distinct.com/

Distinct Corporation has played a pioneering role in the advancement of interpretability (the ease with which one platform can interpret and run the software of another platform) among differing computer platforms. Initially founded as a network consulting and custom design firm in 1984, Distinct soon developed its own product line and, in 1988, shifted its resources to the development and marketing of its own connectivity products. Today, Distinct offers a full family of networking products designed to link disparate platforms over local- and wide-area networks. Utilizing Microsoft's Windows environment, Distinct's wide range of TCP/IP Developers Kits and TCP/IP applications offer state-of-the-art features which keep the company at the forefront of the networking industry.

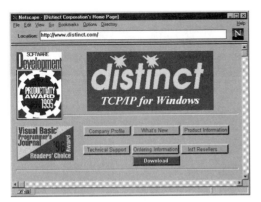

Figure 140.1 The Distinct home page.

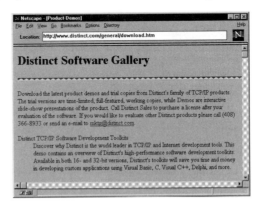

Figure 140.2 Download free software.

AI CAFÉ C/C++ CGI HTML HTTP JAVA J++ PERL VBSCRIPT VRML WIN32 WINSOCK 11001101001011110011011100110101010001100110010101

ENTERPRISE COMPUTER TELEPHONY FORUM (ECTF)

http://www.ectf.org

The Enterprise Computer Telephony Forum (ECTF) works toward industry agreement on implementation of the various standards for computer-telephony integration (CTI) technology to enable the entire communications market to grow. Telephony is the support of high-bandwidth multimedia services between computers via general switch telephone networks (GSTN), rather than ISDN lines. Their vision is standards-based, multi-vendor computer telephony services that meet all the needs of the enterprise. In other words, their goal is the creation of telephony standards that allow easy integration of a range of products that meet the company's requirements across multiple locations, and different hardware-and-software technologies. Visit this site and learn more about "open" telephony standards and the future direction of this key technology.

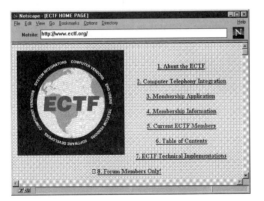

Figure 141.1 The ECTF home page.

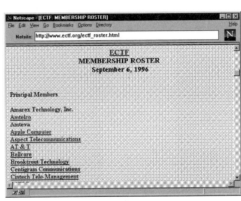

Figure 141.2 Directory of members.

FARALLON COMMUNICATIONS

http://www.farallon.com/

Today, everyone connects to the Internet. Tomorrow, they will also connect to intranets. Farallon Communications develops, markets, and supports complete, easy-to-use, plug-and-play Internet connectivity and networking solutions. With products that range from plug-and-play modems to real-time collaboration software, Farallon has emerged as a leader in the development of products that are easy to install and use. Specifically, Farallon's products include *Netopia* routers and modems (which provide high-speed Internet connectivity for individuals and workgroups), and its *Timbuktu Pro* collaboration software, which enables real-time, peer-to-peer collaboration on the Internet, Intranets, and LANs. If you are looking for Internet and intranet solutions, you will find them at Farallon today.

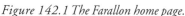

Figure 142.1 The Farallon home page.

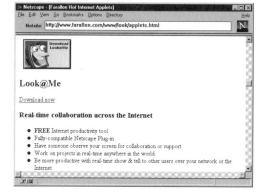

Figure 142.2 Download free Internet applets.

FLOWPOINT CORPORATION

http://www.flowpoint.com

FlowPoint provides ISDN bridge/router remote access network products for the small office and home (SOHO). The company strives to create superior-quality, full-featured products that allow efficient, seamless network integration between SOHOs and WANs. Since June of 1993, FlowPoint has been headquartered in Los Gatos, California. Flowpoint distributes its products worldwide through resellers, system integrators, distributors and private label partners. Come to this informative Web site for more information on FlowPoint and its products, including the FlowPoint 200 ISDN bridge/router and related items.

Figure 143.1 FlowPoint's home page.

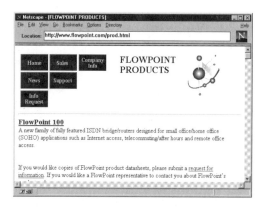

Figure 143.2 FlowPoint products.

AI CAFÉ C/C++ CGI HTML HTTP JAVA J++ PERL VBSCRIPT VRML WIN32 WINSOCK 110011010010111100110110011010100011001100100101

FORE SYSTEMS/ATM

http://www.fore.com

If you need to improve your company's network performance, consider FORE System's asynchronous transfer mode (ATM) products. FORE Systems offers one of the most comprehensive ATM product lines available, which includes: the *ForeRunner* series of switches and adapter cards, *PowerHub* LAN switches, *CellPath* WAN access products, *ForeView* network-management software, and *ForeThought* internetworking software. Their high-performance access devices provide network managers the flexibility to combine ATM with existing networks. FORE's combination of ATM-based intelligent switching hubs, LAN switches, and WAN-access devices enable customers to preserve their investment in existing network infrastructures while benefiting from the increase in network speed and capacity available via ATM technology.

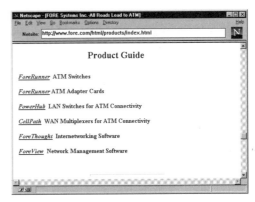

Figure 144.1 FORE Web site.   *Figure 144.2 FORE products.*

AI CAFÉ C/C++ CGI HTML HTTP JAVA J++ PERL VBSCRIPT VRML WIN32 WINSOCK 110011010010111100110110011010100011001100100101

FRAME RELAY FORUM

http://frame-relay.indiana.edu/

This site features everything you ever wanted to know about Frame Relay (a cost-effective, multiplexed communications interface for large host computers, ideal for applications that generate bursts of traffic). The Frame Relay Forum is comprised of vendors, carriers, users, and consultants committed to implementation of Frame Relay in accordance with national and international standards. Since 1991, they have maintained chapters in North America, Europe, Australia, New Zealand, and recently in Japan. This Web site is packed with information for the professional concerned with implementing and leveraging Frame Relay technology. It includes digital file implementation agreements, press releases, newsletters, and much more. This information is "stuff" you need to know!

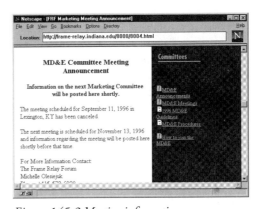

Figure 145.1 All the latest news.   *Figure 145.2 Meeting information.*

IMC NETWORKS

http://www.imcnetworks.com/

Come to IMC Networks for information on products that include the QuikCeiver 100 Mps Fast Ethernet TX or FX Transceiver, the MediaConverter/x 100 Mps Fast Ethernet Modular Media Converter, and the Fiber/Converter/5000 Single-Mode Fiber to Multi-Mode Fiber Converter. The QuikCeiver is IEEE 802.3 100Base-TX and 100Base-FX compliant, designed for direct connection to the MII port, and powered through the MII connection (which means, no external power supply is required). The key to IMC product designs is modularity. No other LAN connectivity supplier offers the modularity of IMC Networks. To find out more, access this useful collection of Web pages.

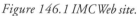

Figure 146.1 IMC Web site.

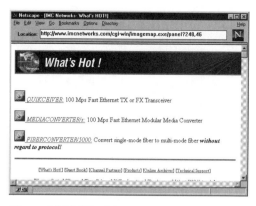

Figure 146.2 What's hot.

INTEROP ONLINE

http://www.interop.com

At Interop Online, you will find hundreds of great resources. During the twice-annual Interop conference and exhibition for TCP/IP based networking and communications professionals, this site features up-to-the-hour real-time show coverage. Throughout the year, you get the on-line access to InteropNet, a fantastic interpretability (the ease with which one platform can interpret and run the software of another platform) demo and network technology showcase; the Interop Buyer's Guide, your source for product and company information; live video Webcasting; a fantastic on-line magazine packed with articles and opinions; an astonishingly huge library of software demos called the "Software Room;" and tested networking shareware available for free downloading from the Ziff Davis software library! This site is a great resource!

Figure 147.1 Interop Online.

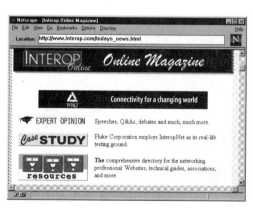

Figure 147.2 Interop Online Magazine.

AI CAFÉ C/C++ CGI HTML HTTP JAVA J++ PERL VBSCRIPT VRML WIN32 WINSOCK 1100110100101111001101110011010101000110011001001 01

RAJ JAIN: NETWORKING GURU

http://www.cis.ohio-state.edu/~jain/

Raj Jain is a Professor of Computer Information Sciences at Ohio State University, Columbus. Prior to this position, he was a Senior Consulting Engineer at Digital Equipment Corporation, where he was involved in the design and analysis of many computer systems and networks, including VAX clusters, Ethernet, DECnet, OSI, FDDI, and ATM networks. Jain has written extensively on all these subjects in several critically-praised books and in numerous journal articles, many of which you can download for free from this site. His papers include "Source Behavior for ATM ABR Traffic Management: An Explanation," and "The ERICA Switch Algorithm: A Complete Description." If you are looking for technical content about networks, visit this site.

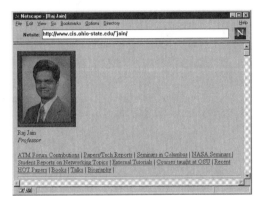

Figure 148.1 Raj Jain Web site.

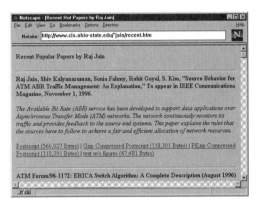

Figure 148.2 Download recent papers.

AI CAFÉ C/C++ CGI HTML HTTP JAVA J++ PERL VBSCRIPT VRML WIN32 WINSOCK 1100110100101111001101110011010101000110011001001 01

LANART

http://www.lanart.com/

Find networking Nirvana. LANart Corporation is the leader in optimizing virtual, switched, and shared LAN connectivity to the desktop. Their SegWay family of port switches, which received one of *Data Communications Magazine's* coveted "Hot Products Awards," as well as *LAN Times'* "Best of . . ." award, provides the ultimate way to empower Ethernet switches and virtual LANs. SegWay, says LANart, "meets the bandwidth, cost, security, flexibility, and management requirements of today's dynamic workplace environment and features a unique micro-segmentation capability that significantly reduces the cost of network moves, additions and changes." To find out more, access LANart's extensive Web site which is packed with details on all their products.

Figure 149.1 LANart Web site.

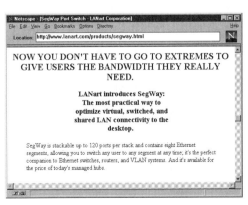

Figure 149.2 SegWay information.

LAN TIMES

http://www.wcmh/lantimes/

LAN Times is the premier LAN-related magazine. At this site, you will find the electronic version of this popular magazine. In short, this site provides it all: product reviews, special reports, trade shows and events, career development news and views, and late-breaking industry news. Perhaps most importantly, you get *LAN Times* Testing Center product reviews. The Testing Center conducts in-depth reviews on individual products, as well as comparisons of groups of products, including 100Base-TX switches, ATM analyzers, Java development tools, 10/100 NICs, firewalls, enterprise-wide webs, NetWare versus NT, SMP servers, routers for the branch office market, NT backup software, ISDN routers, and more. If you are looking for information on any LAN topic, this is a great place to start.

Figure 150.1 LAN Times Online.

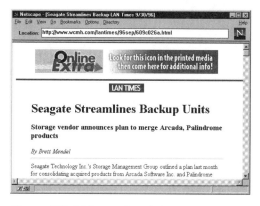

Figure 150.2 News and analysis.

MADGE NETWORKS

http://www.madge.com

Madge Networks is an enterprise networking (the networking of all computers, regardless of platforms, within an enterprise) company serving many of the world's largest users of information technology. Madge Networks is a company dedicated to helping customers become more competitive by maximizing their current LAN investment and preparing their network for the future. As an originator of ATM, Ethernet, ISDN, and Token Ring technology, Madge offers LAN and WAN switches, modular and stackable hubs, enterprise network management software, and adapters. Check out Madge's cost-effective solutions for your enterprise problems.

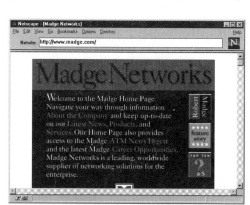

Figure 151.1 Madge home page.

Figure 151.2 News from Madge.

AI CAFÉ C/C++ CGI HTML HTTP JAVA J++ PERL VBSCRIPT VRML WIN32 WINSOCK 1100110100101111001101110011010101000110011001001

NICK MCKEOWN: SWITCHED ETHERNET GURU

http://www-ee.stanford.edu/~nickm/

Nick McKeown is a noted authority on switched Ethernets who harbors particular research interests in the areas of the "Tiny Tera" (a small, high-bandwidth switch—at the terabit level), scheduling algorithms for high-performance ATM switches, the "BayBridge" (a high-speed bridge/router between FDDI and SMDS—Switched Multimegabit Data Services), and (he has to rest sometime) kayaking. You will find McKeown's contact information at this site along with many papers rendered in Postscript, among them his 119-page thesis on scheduling algorithms for input-queued cell switches, and papers on designing multicast switch schedulers, and tetris models for multicast switches, to point out just a few. Take advantage of this network-switch Guru.

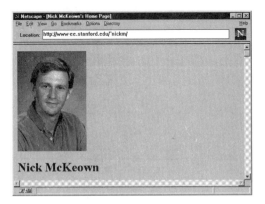

Figure 152.1 Nick McKeown home page.

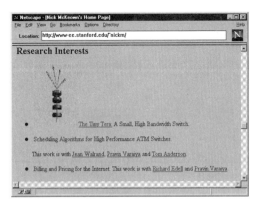

Figure 152.2 Research interests.

AI CAFÉ C/C++ CGI HTML HTTP JAVA J++ PERL VBSCRIPT VRML WIN32 WINSOCK 1100110100101111001101110011010101000110011001001

MOMA: MESSAGE ORIENTED MIDDLEWARE ASSOCIATION

http://198.93.24.24/home.html

MOMA is an international non-profit consortium of vendors, consultants, and customers concerned with the interpretability and functionality of distributed computing through message-oriented middleware. Their goal is to assist users, system integrators, and vendors in receiving maximum value through message-oriented middleware, and the education of the user and vendor communities. Another goal is to serve as an interchange for experiences and ideas related to the development and deployment of distributed applications based on message-passing technology. To that end, this Web site is something of an on-line "think-tank"—a meeting of messaging-oriented minds. Bring your questions, and answers, to MOMA.

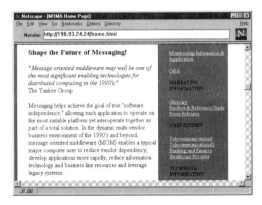

Figure 153.1 MOMA home page.

Figure 153.2 Letter from the President.

AI Café   C/C++   CGI   HTML   HTTP   Java   J++   Perl   VBScript   VRML   Win32   Winsock

154

Multi-Tech Systems: DSVD Products

http://www.multitech.com

Multi-Tech is a leading manufacturer of computer communications and networking products. Their name recognition has been realized through the long-standing quality of their modems and multiplexers. Multi-Tech is the inventor of the digital simultaneous voice-and-data (DSVD) technology for modems. To date, they have received six patents for DSVD technology, and they await several more. Their products include the *MiniArrayCWR*, *MiniArrayRNG*, and *MultiModem LAN* servers, the Internetworking products such as *LANTalker* and *RouteFinder100*, as well as the ATM/Frame Relay switching product *MultiFRAD*. Find out about the future today at Multi-Tech.

Figure 154.1 News from Multi-Tech.

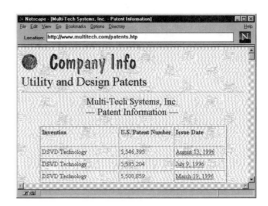

Figure 154.2 Multi-Tech patents.

AI Café   C/C++   CGI   HTML   HTTP   Java   J++   Perl   VBScript   VRML   Win32   Winsock

155

Netlink: Frame Relay Access

http://www.netlink.com/

Netlink is a networking company focused on transporting information over the fastest growing service in the history of data communications: *frame relay*. With Netlink, customers can reduce networking costs by migrating their mission-critical applications to the frame relay technology and by consolidating multiple traffic types over a common infrastructure. Users achieve these benefits with the assurance that the network will deliver their data with reliable and predictable response times. Netlink provides carriers with the security and speed of frame relay technology within economical cost structures, and with a firm guarantee of quality. Visit this sight for specifics on the frame relay technology.

Figure 155.1 Netlink Web site.

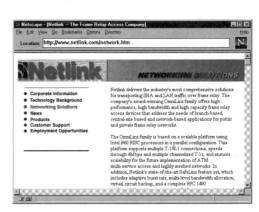

Figure 155.2 Netlink solutions.

NETWORK COMPUTING DEVICES

http://www.ncd.com/

The products of Network Computing Devices (NCD) give you and your users simultaneous, high-performance access to Windows NT, Java, UNIX, Mainframes, and AS/400s across easy-to-administer networks. One of their most popular products is *PC-Xware*. Find out how *PC-Xware* provides iron-clad X conformance. And discover how *WinCenter* delivers Microsoft Windows to multiplatform enterprise desktops in a fast, efficient, and inexpensive manner. Come to these Web pages to download a *PC-Xware* evaluation demo, a WinCenter evaluation demo, or demos of any one of NCD's other great software products. While you are at it, go for the demo of NCD's Marathon Intranet manager.

Figure 156.1 NCD Web site.

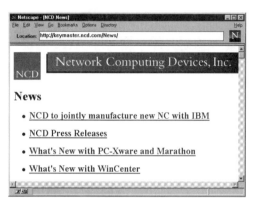

Figure 156.2 NCD news.

NETWORK HARDWARE RESALE

http://www.networkhardware.com

Do you need to implement a network on a budget? Think used equipment. Network Hardware Resale is one of the country's leading resellers of computer networking hardware. They buy, sell, and lease all types of new and used networking equipment, but they specialize in used Cisco Systems equipment. Other manufacturers they work with are: Livingston, Ascend, Adtran, US Robotics, 3com, Bay Networks, and Motorola/Codex/UDS. Network Hardware Resale offers significant discounts from the manufacturer's prices on their pre-owned and off-lease equipment. They fully refurbish and warrant their used equipment, providing a guarantee that the equipment meets the standards necessary to qualify for the manufacturer's maintenance agreement.

Figure 157.1 The Network Hardware Web site.

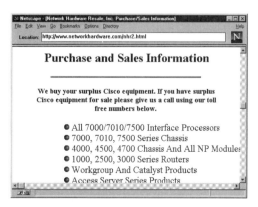

Figure 157.2 Turn used platforms into cash.

NOVELL

http://www.novell.com

Novell needs no introduction. As the network software leader, Novell connected PCs to create the LAN market, and then interconnected those LANs to build the WAN market. With the advent of global computing, Novell is integrating Internet technologies with business networks to create corporate intranets and business-class Internet services. Today, as the only major software company singularly focused on network software, Novell enables networks (LANs, Intranets, WANs, and the Internet) to combine into a single, managed Smart Global Network. To find out more about Novell, its products, its people, and its business strategy, come to this elegant and extensive Web site.

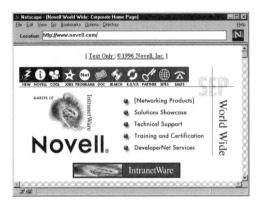

Figure 158.1 Novell home page.

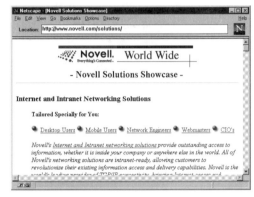

Figure 158.2 Novell solutions.

ONSTREAM NETWORKS

http://www.onstream.com

Where is the first place to turn for quality on-line information about T1, T3, SONET, and ATM? The home page of OnStream Networks, of course. Formerly known as T3plus Networking, OnStream Networks today is the only company focused exclusively on broadband wide-area networking. Broadband networks are high-bandwidth networks embacing ATM and SONET networks which support multimedia applications. The world's largest businesses and service providers (as well as the Internet itself) rely on OnStream's innovative nxT1/E1, T3/E3, SONET, and ATM products for business-critical data, and voice and multimedia communications. OnStream's clients include the top financial, healthcare, manufacturing, government, retail, and computer organizations in the world, along with leading service providers and Internet access providers.

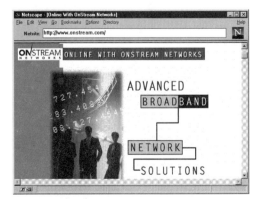

Figure 159.1 OnStream Web site.

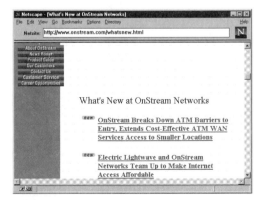

Figure 159.2 What's new.

AI CAFE C/C++ CGI HTML HTTP JAVA J++ PERL VBSCRIPT VRML WIN32 WINSOCK 1100110100101111001101110011010101000110011001001

PINE MOUNTAIN GROUP: NETWORK ANALYSIS

http://www.pmg.com

Face it, networks are complicated. In fact, keeping up with networking technologies can be a full-time job. The Pine Mountain Group regularly hosts or participates in various events designed to enhance and update the skills of professional network analysts. These events include skills seminars, public courses, trade shows, and conferences. To date, the Pine Mountain Group has trained thousands of technical and engineering professionals. They offer network analysis training courses, critical problem resolution services, re-architecture analysis services, the *On the Wire* network analysis newsletter, and products that include *TraceTool* librarian and translator, as well as a great network analysis protocol library.

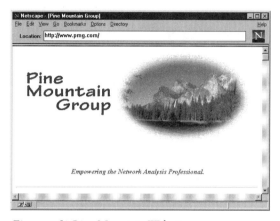

Figure 160 Pine Mountain Web site.

PIVOTAL NETWORKING

http://www.pivnet.com/

Pivotal Networking is dedicated to developing and marketing WAN and LAN router products. In various telecommunications scenarios, routers direct frames or data packets, as the case may be, to the correct segment of the network. Its R&D team consists of a group of seasoned software and hardware engineers with over 150 years of collective experience in the high-performance LAN and WAN networking industry. The firm's formal mission is to "apply innovative embedded system architecture and technology to forefront technological networking products with high reliability and impressive price-performance, and to address LAN and WAN needs in an integrated form." Pivotal offers frame relay access routers, port switching hubs, ISDN access routers, frame relay/ISDN access routers, and frame relay/ISDN/ATM access routers. See tomorrow's router technology today at Pivotal.

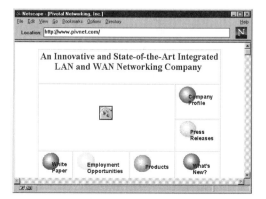

Figure 161.1 Pivotal Web site.

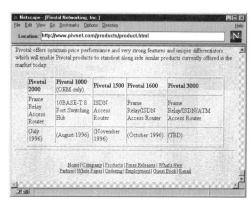

Figure 161.2 Pivotal products.

Questar Microsystems/NetQuest

http://www.questar.com/

Want to network like the big boys? Questar's *NetQuest* product line offers "a total solution for business connectivity, enabling small and medium-sized businesses to compete globally with the power of much larger companies, without the expense and duration of a company-wide systems integration project." Questar has high competence in digital-signal processing, computer telephony, data communication software design, and network management using TCP/IP, SMTP, and SNMP. Visit this Web site for information about Questar Microsystems, its products, and to access the free product demos that Questar invites you to download.

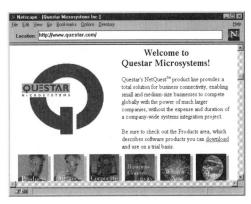

Figure 162.1 Questar's Web site.

Figure 162.2 Questar products.

Sahara Networks

http://www.saharanet.com

Sahara Networks' mission is to deliver leading edge access products (such as high-speed access systems) for broadband networks—applications which provide telecommunications service providers and corporate end-users with the flexibility to serve many applications over a single broadband wide area network (WAN) infrastructure. (Broadband networks are high-bandwidth networks embacing ATM and SONET networks which support multimedia applications.) Yes, we're talking about: Asynchronous transfer mode (ATM) devices. Sahara is a new outfit, and their first products are just hitting the streets in the autumn of 1996. But you keep your eye on them. Because like most other things associated with the Sahara, Sahara Networks is *hot*. Visit this site for information on Sahara's ATM implementation.

Figure 163.1 The Sahara home page.

Figure 163.2 Sahara products.

THE SMDS INTEREST GROUP

http://198.93.24.25/home.html

The Switched Multimegabit Data Services (SMDS) Interest Group defines itself as "an industry association of service providers, equipment manufacturers, users, and others working cooperatively to speed the proliferation and interpretability of SMDS services, products, and applications." The Interest Group develops technical specifications, promotes awareness of SMDS, stimulates new applications for SMDS, and ensures worldwide service interpretability, together with its international affiliates. In operation since 1990, the group maintains offices in Europe and the Pacific Rim. At their Web site, you'll find interesting articles and discussions concerning SMDS, as well as case studies.

Figure 164.1 SMDS Interest Group home page.

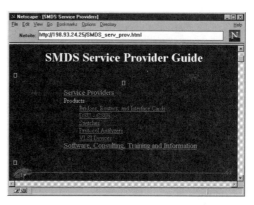

Figure 164.2 A great service provider guide.

TECHGUIDES TO COMMUNICATIONS

http://www.techguide.com

If you are like most of us, you have heard or seen many communications topics, but you are still a little fuzzy about the details. At this site, you will find free "textbooks" which you can view on-line or download. These textbooks address such subjects as frame relay, ISDN services, switching, scaling workgroup performance with switching and fast Ethernet, copper phone line technologies for multimedia, security solutions for enterprise networks, ATM services, SNA over frame relay, audio-video-document conferencing, intelligent network access, simultaneous voice and data technology, and mission-critical intranetworks. These great guides are sponsored by your friends at Sprint, ATG, AT&T, Premisys, MCI, Cascade, Network Systems, and Larscom. Go for it.

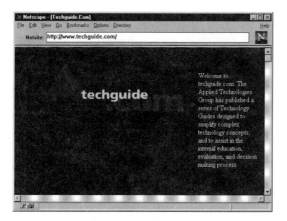

Figure 165 TechGuide Web site.

166

3COM CORPORATION

http://www.3com.com/

3Com derives its name from three words: *com*puter, *com*munications, and *com*patability. 3Com manufactures networking hardware that connects computers to one another across local and wide area networks (LANs and WANs). 3Com's systems—adapters, hubs, switches, routers, and remote access platforms—enable corporate, small office, home, and mobile users to link into computer networks anytime, anywhere. At the heart of 3Com's strategy is the desire to create a global data network. Visit this Web site for complete details on 3Com, its product data sheets, product white papers, performance tests and benchmarks, and more.

Figure 166.1 3Com Web site.

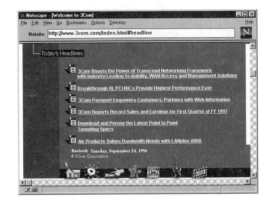

Figure 166.2 The latest product news.

167

TRITICOM: SOFTWARE TOOLS FOR LAN MANAGEMENT

http://www.triticom.com/

Triticom is the developer of many LAN management tools designed for network administrators and integrators. Their products include network monitors, protocol analyzers, bridges and routers, and Microsoft Windows network management software. Because Triticom's products are software-based, they provide reasonable performance at a lower price than many hardware-based products. Visit the Triticom Web site to sample great demonstration software, view technical support notes, review the latest lists of frequently asked questions concerning Triticom products, and to get the latest news about new product releases and updates.

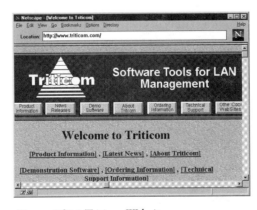

Figure 167.1 Triticom Web site.

Figure 167.2 Download demo software.

AI CAFE C/C++ CGI HTML HTTP JAVA J++ PERL VBSCRIPT VRML WIN32 WINSOCK 110011010010111100110111001101010100011001100100101

VISUAL NETWORKS: GREAT ON-LINE DEMOS

http://www.visualnetworks.com/

The Visual Networks home page states that the company "designs, manufactures, and markets an innovative family of management access products for organizations building networks based on public wide area data services, such as Frame Relay, ATM, and the Internet." Their lead product for frame relay management is called *Visual UpTime*. Their product for Internet access management is called *Visual OnRamp*. In March of 1996, Hewlett-Packard licensed Visual Networks' WAN monitoring technology and endorsed the Visual WAN Management Information Base (MIB) software architecture foundation on which standards-based WAN monitoring and management is deployed. Come to these pages for great on-line demos of *Visual OnRamp* and *Visual UpTime*.

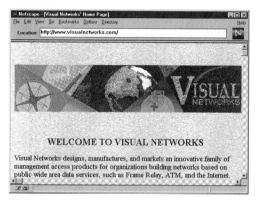

Figure 168.1 Visual Networks home page.

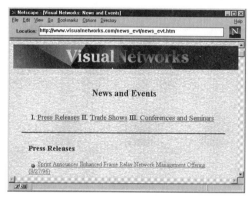

Figure 168.2 News and events.

AI CAFE C/C++ CGI HTML HTTP JAVA J++ PERL VBSCRIPT VRML WIN32 WINSOCK 110011010010111100110111001101010100011001100100101

WANDERLINK REMOTE ACCESS FOR NOVELL LANS

http://www.netutils.com/wlink.htm

Do you need remote access to your network? Don't forget security! WanderLink is a high-performance, secure, remote-access solution that lets remote PC users dial into a Novell NetWare network using standard phone lines. After you connect, your computer becomes a node on the network, gaining access to network resources such as file servers, e-mail, and printers. Plus, you can use the powerful remote control capability included with WanderLink to take over and operate any PC on the network. If you travel for business, or work in a branch office or at home, WanderLink lets you access all the network resources you'll need to get your job done.

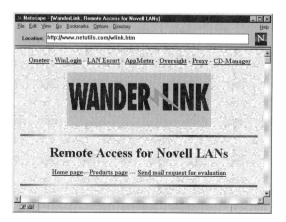

Figure 169 WanderLink Web site.

170

WHITTAKER XYPLEX

http://www.xyplex.com/

Whittaker Xyplex designs, develops, and markets high-performance LAN and WAN products that provide flexible network access, switching, and ATM solutions. According to the International Data Corporation (IDC), Whittaker Xyplex is the third largest provider of remote-access solutions in the world. Through its unique WANScape Internetworking architecture and its broad range of products, the company provides cost-effective platforms for multi-service wide-area network connectivity. As a bonus, at their Web site, Whittaker Xyplex provides a great on-line data communications glossary with extensive discussions of common (and not so common) terms and protocols.

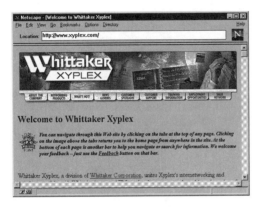

Figure 170.1 Whittaker Xyplex Web site.

Figure 170.2 Networking products.

171

WIRELESS LOCAL AREA NETWORKS: AN ON-LINE TUTORIAL

http://www.netplan.dk/netplan/wireless.htm

Wires and plugs. Wires and plugs. I hate all these wires and plugs. As it turns out, wireless LANs have been around for a number of years. However, the wireless LAN market is expected to really take off starting in 1997. The most obvious reason for this is the rapid evolution of mobile computing. In fact, a number of applications for wireless LANs are in use today. For example, hospitals use wireless networks to provide personnel with access to patient records from anywhere on the hospital floor. Likewise, other companies use wireless LANs to provide a bridge between cabled LANs that reside in different buildings. For more information on wireless LANs, access this great, free on-line tutorial.

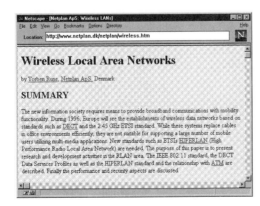

Figure 171.1 The tutorial.

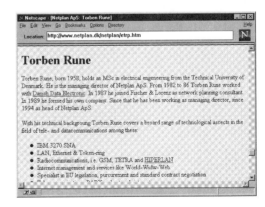

Figure 171.2 The author.

AI CAFÉ C/C++ CGI HTML HTTP JAVA J++ PERL VBSCRIPT VRML WIN32 WINSOCK 1100110100101110011011100110101010001100110010010l

ADOBE

http://www.adobe.com

If you want information on state-of-the-art graphics or type, Adobe is the place to start. Visit this site and get the scoop on the latest versions of *Photoshop*, plus details on PostScript Level 3. Check out great images in the Adobe Gallery and goof around with ATM Deluxe (Adobe Type Manager Deluxe). Then, download *PageMill* and the *Adobe Acrobat Reader*, along with Adobe Acrobat files packed with information on a range of products that include *Adobe Type Manager, Dimensions, Persuasion, Photoshop, Fetch, Premier, Illustrator*, and print drivers and utilities, as well as font utilities. As a bonus, you can even get information on job opportunities at Adobe, developer updates, and other cool stuff. Where would we all be without Adobe? Nowhere man. Nowhere.

Figure 172.1 Adobe Web site.   *Figure 172.2 Postscript information.*

AI CAFÉ C/C++ CGI HTML HTTP JAVA J++ PERL VBSCRIPT VRML WIN32 WINSOCK 1100110100101110011011100110101010001100110010010l

APPLE COMPUTER

http://www.apple.com

OK, so Apple's stock dropped faster than Newton's Apple. But many folks believe that Apple will bounce back. Visit the Apple Web site for product information, customer support, developer support, and all the latest product news and views. You will learn about Apple's strategic alliance with Sun and other players, the latest 200 MHz PowerMacs, 200 MHz servers, and more. Developers will be especially interested in Apple's "Developer World," where they will find information on developer programs, detailed specifications for porting Windows applications to the Mac platform, and loads of sample code, software developer's kits (SDKs), and utilities you can download for free. All told, the Apple Computer Web site is a vital resource for anyone developing software for Apple platforms.

Figure 173.1 Apple Web site.   *Figure 173.2 Mac OS information.*

AT&T Labs

http://www.att.com/attlabs/

AT&T does more than long distance. In the past, their labs have brought us operating systems and programming languages. Visit the AT&T site to access great articles from the *AT&T Technical Journal*—absolutely free. The journal's topics include Information Technology: Reuse Technologies and Applications, Information Technology Design and Development, AT&T Technology and the Environment, Multimedia Technology, The Evolution of the AT&T Network, and Undersea Communications Technology. You will also get the latest news on Research and Development projects at the AT&T Labs, including the work of their advanced speech products group on a funky speech synthesizer, the latest AT&T wrist-telephone (ala Dick Tracy!), and more.

Figure 174.1 AT&T Labs.

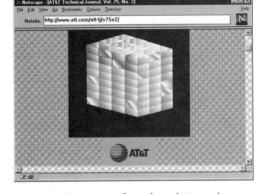

Figure 174.2 A page from the tech journal.

Autodesk

http://www.autodesk.com

Autodesk is the fourth largest PC software company in the world, the number one provider of PC multimedia tools, and the world's largest provider of technical content. Come to this site for information on *MapGuide* (the first available technology to support live, accurate, vector-based maps over the Internet), *Autodesk View* (fast, easy drawing and document access), *AutoCAD*, *PlantSpec* (industry-standard parts for plant design), *WorkCenter* (document and workflow management for the design team), and *WorkCenter for the Web* (Web-based access to documents organized in the WorkCenter). Also, visit this site for information on Kinetix, Autodesk's multimedia division.

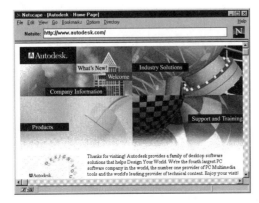

Figure 175.1 The Autodesk home page.

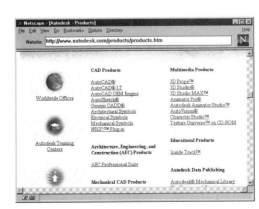

Figure 175.2 Autodesk products.

AI CAFÉ C/C++ CGI HTML HTTP JAVA J++ PERL VBSCRIPT VRML WIN32 WINSOCK 1100110100101110011011100110101010001100100100101

CISCO SYSTEMS

http://www.cisco.com

Cisco Systems is the leading global supplier of internetworking solutions, including routers, LAN and ATM switches, dial-up access servers, and network management software. These products, integrated by Cisco *IOS* (*Internetwork Operating System*) software, link geographically-dispersed LANs, WANs, and IBM networks. Cisco Systems news, products, and service information are available at this site on the Web, as well as details on new products in development, jobs openings, and more. Products include Cisco's outstanding *CiscoPro* internetworking solutions for small- to medium-sized businesses, which is available through value-added resellers around the world.

Figure 176.1 The Cisco Web site.

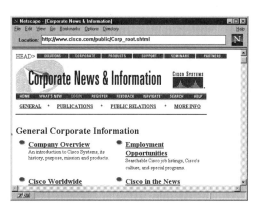

Figure 176.2 Cisco news and information.

AI CAFÉ C/C++ CGI HTML HTTP JAVA J++ PERL VBSCRIPT VRML WIN32 WINSOCK 1100110100101110011011100110101010001100100100101

DIGITAL EQUIPMENT CORPORATION

http://www.digital.com/

Digital is the leading worldwide supplier of networked computer systems, software, and services. Digital pioneered and leads the industry in interactive, distributed, and multi-vendor computing. An international company, Digital does more than half its business outside the United States, developing and manufacturing products and providing customer services in the Americas, Europe, Asia, and the Pacific Rim. Visit this Web page for Digital product information, Digital financial news and investor information, updates on Digital's new technology research and, of course, direct access to Digital's absolutely fabulous *Altavista* Internet search engine.

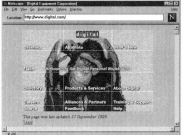

Figure 177.1 Digital's Web site.

Figure 177.2 A word from the CEO.

Figure 177.3 What's new.

THE OFFICIAL BILL GATES HOME PAGE

http://www.microsoft.com/corpinfo/bill-g.htm

What's Bill up to? Where is he speaking and what is he saying? Where will he be next week, next month, next year? And just how is the fabled house coming along? Get all these details and more at the Bill pages on Microsoft's corporate Web site. In addition to press releases and photographs, you can also access Bill's bi-monthly column, a series of essays he has written, and "Ask Bill" question-and-answer sessions. You can also access a brief biography of Bill—after developing BASIC for the first microcomputer, the MITS Altair, he dropped out of Harvard to found Microsoft with Paul Allen. The rest, of course, is history.

Figure 178.1 All about Big Bill.

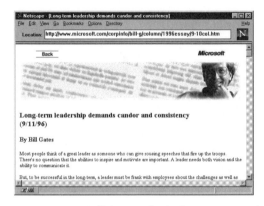

Figure 178.2 Bill Gates on leadership.

INTEL

http://www.intel.com

Check it out. Browse demos of "connected applications." Download *Intel Internet Phone* and other applets that include *Storm EasyPhoto*Net, Intel Intercast,* and the *Streaming Media* Viewer for PC multimedia. Browse details on all of Intel's various chips and boards. Submit your profile to "Custom News for You" and get regular content updates geared to meet your specific information needs. You can also read chapter excerpts from Intel CEO Andy Grove's fantastic book entitled *Only the Paranoid Survive.* Plus, of course, you'll also find great developer information and software, including Intel's great performance library suites and more. To stay current with technology, visit this site on a regular basis.

Figure 179.1 The Intel Web site.

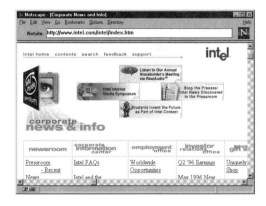

Figure 179.2 Corporate news and information.

AI CAFE C/C++ CGI HTML HTTP JAVA J++ PERL VBSCRIPT VRML WIN32 WINSOCK 1100110100101110011011100110101010001100110010010

JAMSA PRESS: BOOKS AND CDS FOR PROGRAMMERS

http://www.jamsa.com

In addition to *1001 Programming Resources*, Jamsa Press publishes many other books and multimedia CDs of interest to programmers and developers. These include the books *Internet Programming, Java Now!, Rescued by C++, Rescued by UNIX*, and *Success with C++*. Additional titles include *1001 Java Programming Tips, The Intranet Bible, Web Programming, Jamsa's C/C++ Programmer's Bible*, and the *Web Site Construction Kit*. Find out more about all these great products at the Jamsa Press Web site. The site also features Java demos, VRML virtual worlds, and ActiveX samples with source code.

Figure 180.1 Jamsa Press Web site.

Figure 180.2 A popular title.

Figure 180.3 And another.

AI CAFE C/C++ CGI HTML HTTP JAVA J++ PERL VBSCRIPT VRML WIN32 WINSOCK 1100110100101110011011100110101010001100110010010

LOTUS

http://www.lotus.com

Visit this site for information on a range of Lotus products and services. You will find complete details on *Notes* and *SmartSuite*, along with products related to messaging, the Internet, calendaring and scheduling, and business multimedia. You will also find great downloads and other support for developers, which include vital information about Lotus's collaboration on the new Internet Calendar Access Protocol (ICAP), and *Notes* developer tools that include the *Notes C++ API*, an easy-to-use object-oriented interface to Lotus *Notes*. In fact, Lotus invites you to download a free copy of the *Notes C++ API*. Check it out.

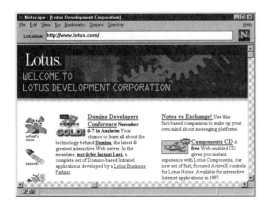

Figure 181.1 The Lotus Web site.

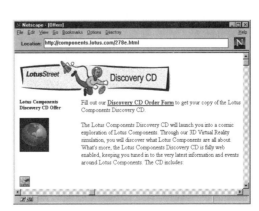

Figure 181.2 Get this free CD.

MICROSOFT

http://www.microsoft.com

Who has the absolutely coolest and most content-rich site on the entire Web? Why, Microsoft, of course! "Where do you want to go today?" Feel like downloading *Internet Explorer* and getting a bunch of great freebies along with it? This is the place to do it. Feel like receiving tour-de-force support for all Microsoft products, as well as information on upcoming releases and free downloads of bug-fixes and patches? This is the place to do it. Feel like joining Microsoft professionals in on-line chat sessions concerning products in development, as well as little-known turbo-geek secrets about the innards of Microsoft systems? Well, guess what! This is the place to do that too!

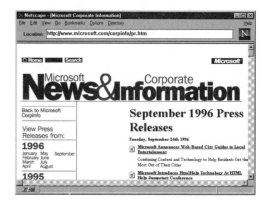

Figure 182.1 The Microsoft vision. *Figure 182.2 Microsoft press releases.*

NETSCAPE

http://www.netscape.com

Download great, free Netscape *Internet Foundation Classes* (IFC) designed to give Java developers a jump-start for creating Netscape ONE-compliant applications. Or, get the scoop on Netscape *AppFoundry*—a great collection of reusable business applications, powerful new enterprise development tools, and an innovative new on-line community dedicated to Information Systems professionals building corporate solutions on their intranets. Of course, you can also get the latest news about the ever-popular Netscape *Navigator* Web browser, including an invitation to download (or purchase) the browser's latest version. As a bonus, stop by the One Stop Software directory for a great collection of Java applets you can download.

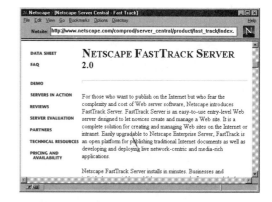

Figure 183.1 The Netscape Web site. *Figure 183.2 One of several free downloads.*

AI CAFÉ C/C++ CGI HTML HTTP JAVA J++ PERL VBSCRIPT VRML WIN32 WINSOCK 11001101001011110011011100110101010001100110010010 1

POWERSOFT

http://www.powersoft.com

Powersoft brings you the *PowerBuilder* family of products, which provide a comprehensive development environment for building fast, object-oriented applications that can go anywhere. Widely recognized as the de facto standard for client/server development, *PowerBuilder* delivers true object-orientation, enterprise database support, powerful team development tools, and cross-platform deployment capabilities. Visit this Web site for more information on Powersoft, technical-support, news and notes about products that include not only *PowerBuilder*, but also *Powersoft Portfolio, Optima++, S-Designor, Sybase SQL, NetImpact Studio*, and more!

Figure 184.1 The Powersoft home page.

Figure 184.2 A new Web development tool.

AI CAFÉ C/C++ CGI HTML HTTP JAVA J++ PERL VBSCRIPT VRML WIN32 WINSOCK 11001101001011110011011100110101010001100110010010 1

SANTA CRUZ OPERATION

http://www.sco.com

The Santa Cruz Operation (SCO) is the world's largest supplier of UNIX server and host systems, and a leading provider of software that integrates Windows PCs and other clients with UNIX servers from all major vendors. SCO envisions a future in which people and organizations can reach out to anywhere in the world, from anywhere in the world, to access, manage, and share the applications and information they need. The SCO corporate mission is "to be the leading supplier of UNIX system software for business critical environments." Come to this site for information on reseller partnerships, developer support, and more.

Figure 185.1 The SCO Web site.

Figure 185.2 Developer information.

186 SILICON GRAPHICS

http://www.sgi.com/

For more than ten years, companies have relied on Silicon Graphics systems for industrial design, database analysis, visual simulation, energy exploration, and entertainment—businesses in which creativity leads to competitive advantage, and where computer power and interactive visualization accelerate the creative process. Silicon Graphics brings you technology grounded in visualization, 3-D, color, sound, and multimedia. Silicon Graphics offers these technologies as a compatible family of systems ranging from inexpensive desktop clients to multiprocessor database or computer servers. Silicon Graphics systems push the leading industry standards. Visit the Silicon Graphics Web site for more details.

Figure 186.1 The Silicon Graphics home page.

Figure 186.2 Product information.

187 SUN MICROSYSTEMS

http://www.sun.com

Sun is king of the mountain with its Java technology these days. Visit this information-rich Web site to learn about all of Sun's products and programs, which include their workstation and server products, the *Netra* server family, SPARC and Java board, chip and technology products, and SPARC-storage products. You'll also get the scoop on Java products and technologies, *Solaris* operating system products, *Solstice* intranet-management products (including *Solstice WorkShop*), *WorkShop* developer products (including *Java WorkShop*), *NEO/Joe* object products, and x86 solutions. You will find no better place on the Web for product demos, white papers, live on-line support, and exciting new product news.

Figure 187.1 Sun's Web site.

Figure 187.2 An excellent on-line white paper.

Al Cafe C/C++ CGI HTML HTTP Java J++ Perl VBScript VRML Win32 Winsock 1100110100101110011011100110101010001100110010101

SYMANTEC

http://www.symantec.com

Symantec markets products for businesses in key areas which include utilities, development tools, and productivity applications. The company recently acquired Delrina Corporation and now offers a great collection of powerful communications software and electronic forms solutions. The company's products help customers build, manage, and use software on desktop PCs, as well as across heterogeneous networks of computers. In development tools, Symantec provides both 3GL and 4GL (third and fourth generation language) tools for building software applications. With respect to utilities, the company makes the products to manage a distributed computing environment while protecting against data loss. Visit this Web site for more details.

Figure 188 Symantec's Web site.

ADDITIONAL CORPORATE RESOURCES

Continental Resources: Computer Division
http://www.conres.com/ccj496.htm

High Tech Computers, Inc.
http://high-tech.com/

TETRANET / COMPUTERS - VRML
http://www.tetranet.net/vrml.html

Technopia and Farther Reaches
http://web2.airmail.net/pwa471/

Sutherland Communications Links
http://www.inforamp.net/~suth/links1.html

3Com Corporation
http://www.3com.com/index.html

Adobe Systems Incorporated Home Page
http://www.adobe.com/

Technology Online
http://www.tol.mmb.com/

189 AMULET FOR CROSS-PLATFORM DEVELOPMENT (FREE SOFTWARE)

http://www.cs.cmu.edu/Groups/amulet/amulet-home.html

Developed by Brad A. Myers of the Human Computer Interaction Institute at Carnegie-Mellon, *Amulet* is a user interface development environment for C++. The environment is portable across X11, Windows 95, Windows NT, and the Mac. *Amulet* includes many features specifically designed to make the creation of highly-interactive, graphical, direct manipulation user interfaces significantly easier. The environment's features include a prototype-instance object model, high-level input handling which includes an automatic undo feature, as well as a full set of widgets. Visit this site and download the compiler, the documentation, sample programs created with *Amulet*, and more.

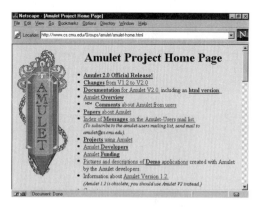

Figure 189.1 Amulet home page.

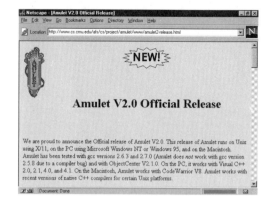

Figure 189.2 The latest release.

190 CROSS-PLATFORM PORTABILITY BETWEEN WINDOWS & X-WINDOWS

http://www.bristol.com/Bibliography/xj9602.html

This in-depth article by Chane Cullens is reprinted from *The X Journal* and forms an excellent tutorial on cross-platform portability. As Cullens points out, the gap between Windows 95 logo-compliant applications and applications created on UNIX using X/Motif tool kits is wide. "While the GUI look and feel between Motif and Windows 95 is similar," writes Cullens, " . . . the richness of the GUI in Windows 95 MFC applications tends to exceed standard Motif applications. Also, you need to have separate source-code streams when you use Win32/MFC on Windows and X/Motif on UNIX." To learn how to confront these and other problems, access Chane's excellent article on the Web.

Figure 190.1 The tutorial's first page.

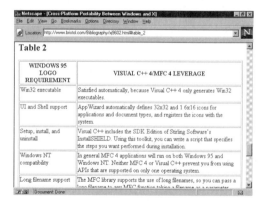

Figure 190.2 One of the many useful charts.

AI CAFÉ C/C++ CGI HTML HTTP JAVA J++ PERL VBSCRIPT VRML WIN32 WINSOCK 1100110100101111001101110011010101000110011000100101

CROSS-PLATFORM QUICKTIME: FREE DOWNLOADS

http://www.astro.nwu.edu/lentz/mac/qt/home-qt.html

QuickTime is an operating system extension that enables a machine to work with dynamic, time-based data such as animation, video clips and sound. (Still images are static data.) At this site, you can download everything and anything related to *QuickTime* and tools for porting *QuickTime* files across platforms. For starters, you get free access to *QuickTime, MoviePlayer*, and *Sound Manager* for the Macintosh, as well as *QuickTime for Windows*. You also get an extensive on-line tutorial concerning *QuickTime* programming for free, and additional free downloads of *SmartVid* (which converts AVI and *QuickTime* file formats under Windows), *Xanim* (an X-Windows animation viewer that includes support for *QuickTime* movies), *Flattmoov* (a small Mac program to "flatten" *QuickTime* movies so they are playable on non-Macintosh platforms), and more.

Figure 191 Choose your downloads at this site.

AI CAFÉ C/C++ CGI HTML HTTP JAVA J++ PERL VBSCRIPT VRML WIN32 WINSOCK 1100110100101111001101110011010101000110011000100101

CROSS-PLATFORM RESOURCES PAGE

http://www.bristol.com/Bibliography/bibliography.html

At this site, you will find an extensive list of resources that relate to cross-platform programming and application development. Specifically, you will find journal articles, books, third-party tools, conference presentations, product reviews, Visual C++ resources, and *The Portability Times* (featured in site 208). You will also find links to archives of downloadable programs, patches and applications of use to those involved in cross-platform development, extensive on-line documentation, and white papers. Finally, you will encounter numerous links to publishers of cross-platform tool kits. The page comes to you courtesy of the good folks at Bristol Technology, Inc.

Figure 192.1 Many available resources.

Figure 192.2 Learn about third-party tools.

193

CrossWind Technologies: Synchronize

http:///www.xwind.com

CrossWind Technologies brings you *Synchronize*, a cross-platform scheduling, task, and resource management software program. *Synchronize* runs on over 18 commercial UNIX servers as well as clients for Microsoft Windows, X.11/Motif, and ASCII-based desktops. It has a robust client/server architecture and supports distributed databases. Because *Synchronize* communicates directly across TCP/IP, developer access to critical information is instant, with none of the delays associated with file-based access methods, e-mail based scheduling, or slower transports. Plus, *Synchronize* is scaleable, offering enterprise collaboration for five to fifty-thousand users and beyond. If you are creating applications with a large team of developers, you should check out *Synchronize*.

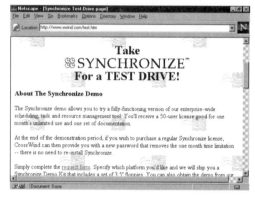

Figure 193.1 The CrossWind home page. *Figure 193.2 How about a test drive?*

194

Cross-Platform Portable Relational Database Toolkit

http://www.synervision.com/dvtool.htm

DataVision is a portable relational-database toolkit for client/server, distributed and embedded applications. *DataVision* combines the benefits of an embedded database (extremely fast response times, efficient memory utilization, flexible schemas, and low-level access) with the requirements for client/server applications (modular design and scalability). *DataVision* reads and writes data for heterogeneous platforms independent of the processor architecture and compiler and operating systems. Thus, developers who utilize *DataVision* need not need worry about which platform the database resides on. If your applications require such a hybrid database, take a close look at *DataVision*.

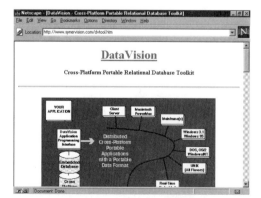

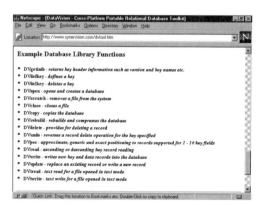

Figure 194.1 All about DataVision. *Figure 194.2 Example database library functions.*

AI CAFÉ C/C++ CGI HTML HTTP JAVA J++ PERL VBSCRIPT VRML WIN32 WINSOCK 11001101001011110011011100110101010001100100100101

ENCORE CROSS-PLATFORM SOLUTIONS

http://bbs.encore.com/

Providing scalable real-time universal storage, data retrieval, data sharing, and real-time system solutions for mixed-platform processing environments, Encore specializes in empowering corporations to enjoy the benefits of cross-platform data sharing. The company's product line features the Encore patented *Memory Channel* technology and the *Infinity* series of massively parallel scaleable systems that provide breakthrough performance and flexibility. The Encore *Infinity SP* storage products offer high-speed, massively scaleable I/O storage and throughput. The firm holds an ISO certification for quality assurance in production, installation, final inspection, and testing of computer systems. For a first look at the future of data storage and retrieval, check out this Web site.

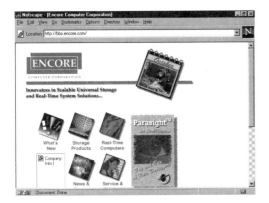

Figure 195.1 The Encore Web site.

Figure 195.2 What's new.

AI CAFÉ C/C++ CGI HTML HTTP JAVA J++ PERL VBSCRIPT VRML WIN32 WINSOCK 11001101001011110011011100110101010001100100100101

HUMMINGBIRD COMMUNICATIONS

http://www.hummingbird.com

Hummingbird Communications is committed to developing world-class cross-platform internetworking software solutions designed for seamless integration within corporate networks. They provide personal computers, including those running DOS, Windows 3.x., Windows NT, Windows 95, OS/2, and Mac System 7, with easy access to corporate information systems and graphical applications residing on mini and mainframe host computers. Hummingbird designs products based upon open systems and accepted industry standards. Visit this site for more information and potential intranet solutions. While you are there, download demo versions of Hummingbird's *MiniViewer* and *SOCKS* applications.

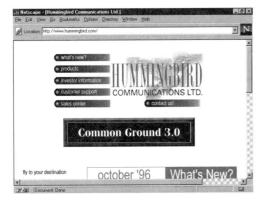

Figure 196.1 The Hummingbird Web site.

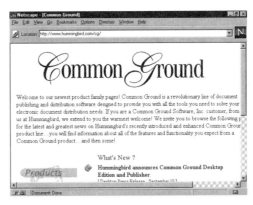

Figure 196.2 Hummingbird's Common Ground.

197

INSIGNIA SOLUTIONS

http://www.insignia.com

Insignia Solutions provides quality software solutions that let you run Windows applications on a range of platforms throughout your enterprise and over the Internet. Visit this site and check out *SoftWindows95* and *SoftWindows 3.0* for Power Macintosh, *Ntrique* (software that delivers Windows applications to UNIX workstations, X-terminals, PCs, and Macs), and more. Also, you will learn about the Insignia Solutions Partners Program, recently expanded to include Independent Software Vendors (ISVs), to access exhaustive on-line technical support, to review the Insignia products catalog, and to learn of job-opportunities at Insignia—the folks who are bringing Windows to the "rest of the world."

Figure 197.1 The Insignia Web site.

Figure 197.2 On-line demo.

198

ISA DIALOG MANAGER FOR CROSS-PLATFORM

http://www.isa.de/en/idm

The *ISA Dialog Manager* is a power user interface management system for the creation of portable graphical user interfaces for cross-platform computing. Dialog boxes created with the *ISA Dialog Manager* can be run on OSF/Motif (with Solaris, SCO, Linux, AIX, HP-UX, Ultrix, and OpenVMS), UNIX-based alphanumeric terminals, OS/2, Windows NT, and Windows. With the *ISA Dialog Manager*, a WYSIWYG editor supports you in the interactive design of a dialog-box layout that incorporates windows, menus, buttons, static texts, editable texts, lists, tables, and more. The package features object-oriented inheritance and powerful dialog-box dynamics described with an event-oriented rule language. Visit the Web page for more details.

Figure 198.1 Very good documentation.

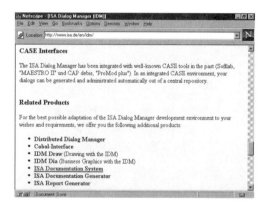

Figure 198.2 CASE interfaces and related products.

CROSS-PLATFORM COMPATIBILITY FOR BIOLOGICAL ANALYSIS

http://www.dnastar.com/

Lasergene is a well-established, internationally-renowned, bioinformatics computing suite for Windows and Macintosh. *Lasergene* is modular, supporting single as well as network users, and offers in-depth coverage of sequencing, primer design, sequence alignment, databases and database searching, protein analysis, and restriction map analysis. The Windows and Mac versions of *Lasergene* easily share sequence and project files, and feature the exact same menu, dialog, and screen systems. The *Biotechnology Software Review* named *Lasergene* "Product of the Year" in 1995. Now, this award-winning computing suite is brought to you, as is this informative Web site, by DNASTAR, Inc., the world's leading developer of biocomputing software products.

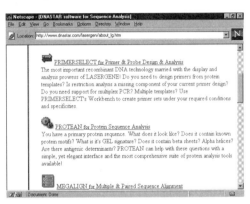

Figure 199.1 The Lasergene Web site.

Figure 199.2 More details on DNASTAR products.

THE LATITUDE CROSS-PLATFORM DEVELOPMENT KIT

http://www.quorum.com/latitude.html

Latitude is a "virtual" porting system produced by the Latitude Group specifically for Macintosh software developers wishing to port their Mac applications to the UNIX environment. Latitude presents applications on UNIX platforms with libraries that mirror the rich Macintosh toolbox. Developers rebuild their Macintosh application source code using Latitude on a UNIX workstation to produce a native UNIX executable. In addition to linkable libraries, Latitude includes utilities that facilitate the preparation of Macintosh source code for use on UNIX systems. If your two cross-platforms are UNIX and the Mac, you can use Latitude to bridge the platforms and save time writing new code. Visit this Web site for more information.

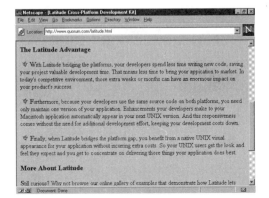

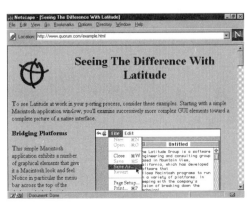

Figure 200.1 Details on Latitude.

Figure 200.2 And some samples.

THE MAC OS TO WINDOWS CROSS-PLATFORM PAGES

http://www.users.interport.net/~rrubin/xplat/xplat.html

In the spring of 1996, Apple Fellow Guy Kawasaki posted on his EvangeList mailing list that there was a need for a Web page that focused on cross-platform issues between Macs and PCs. Not long after Guy's request, Ross Scott Rubin jumped in to fill the gap. Ross is the author of many cross-platform articles in *MacWeek* and *Mac Home Journal*, and is also the author of the cross-platform chapter in the famous *Macintosh Bible*. "These pages," he writes, "contain information that we could not fit into the book. I hope you find them a useful resource." At this site, you'll find information on sharing data between systems, running DOS or Windows on a Mac (and vice versa), cross-platform peripherals, and much more. Thanks again Guy, for asking.

Figure 201.1 The Mac OS to Windows Web site.

Figure 201.2 Your menu of options.

METROWERKS

http://www.metrowerks.com

Founded in 1985, Metrowerks develops, markets, and supports a complete line of Mac-hosted computer-language products for building MacTMOS, Windows95, Windows NT, Magic Cap, BeOS, and Palm OS applications. Providing full support for C/C++, Object Pascal, and Java under one integrated development environment (IDE), Metrowerks' *CodeWarrior* products have become the industry standard for professional Mac-hosted software development—with more than 45,000 registered users in 70 countries. Come to this Web site for product information, on-line technical support, product information, job openings, and more.

Figure 202.1 The Metrowerks Web site.

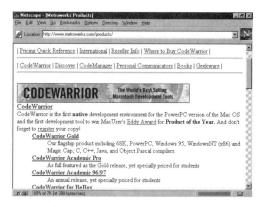

Figure 202.2 Product information.

AI CAFÉ C/C++ CGI HTML HTTP JAVA J++ PERL VBSCRIPT VRML WIN32 WINSOCK 1100110100101111001101110011010101000110011000100101

MRED CROSS-PLATFORM GUI DEVELOPMENT: FREE DOWNLOAD

http://www.cs.rice.edu/CS/PLT/packages/mred/

One of the most difficult pieces of an application to port between systems is the graphical user interface. *MrEd* is a graphical user interface development environment. *MrEd's* underlying language is *MzScheme*, extended with an object system and a thread package. The system's primitives include text-editing tools that can be employed with an application for editing a mixture of text and graphics. *MrEd* runs under the three major windowing systems: X-Windows, Windows, and Macintosh. Applications written using *MrEd* run on all three platforms. Visit this site and download *MrEd* as a compiled executable for any one of these platforms. While you are there, make sure you download the extensive on-line documentation.

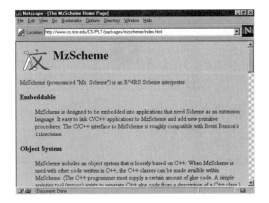

Figure 203.1 MrEd's MzScheme.

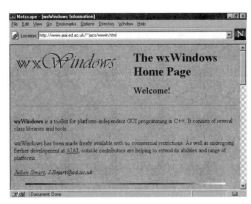

Figure 203.2 MrEd's graphical primitives.

AI CAFÉ C/C++ CGI HTML HTTP JAVA J++ PERL VBSCRIPT VRML WIN32 WINSOCK 1100110100101111001101110011010101000110011000100101

NAVIGATING AROUND THE CLIENT/SERVER ICEBERG

http://www.progress.com/WhitePapers/iceberg/progmain1.html

The first generation of cross-platform client/server application development tools marketed over the past five years offers rapid application development (RAD) for PCs and other platforms. Developers and business professionals using these tools focus on what they see on the screen rather than on the underlying complexity. And, because the GUIs these tools provide are quite sophisticated, developers assume that the tools are also sophisticated enough to handle other aspects of the application, such as complex business logic and data management. Unfortunately, this assumption is false. The sophistication of a first-generation tool's GUI represents only the tip of the iceberg. For more on this, see the great on-line tutorial.

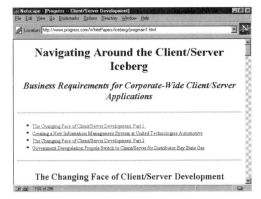

Figure 204.1 The tutorial's title page.

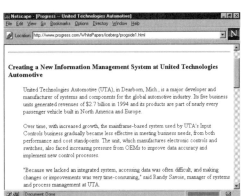

Figure 204.2 A case study.

205

NOMBAS: SCRIPTEASE CROSS-PLATFORM SCRIPTING

http://www.nombas.com

One of the recent trends in cross-platform processing is the use of scripts and scripting languages, such as Perl, JavaScript, and VBScript. Adding to this list, Nombas brings you ScriptEase, a safe portable scripting language for cross-platform applications. It used to be called *Cmm*, which stands for C-minus-minus. That means it is C "minus the hard stuff." That's right, ScriptEase is a streamlined version of C that packs the same functionality and power of C but lacks C's complex, time-consuming, and hazardous data manipulations. Programmers will find ScriptEase immediately familiar and immediately useful. New programmers will find ScriptEase easy to use. Visit this Web page for more information.

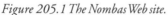

Figure 205.1 The Nombas Web site.

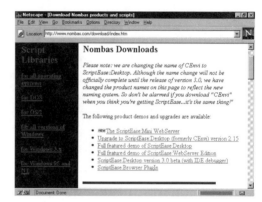

Figure 205.2 Download ScriptEase.

206

THE OPEN GROUP (X/OPEN & THE OPEN SOFTWARE FOUNDATION)

http://www.osf.org

The Open Group is an international consortium of vendors, ISVs (independent software vendors), and end-user customers from industry, government, and academia dedicated to the advancement of multi-vendor information systems. A consolidation of the two leading open systems consortia, X/Open and the Open Software Foundation (OSF) formed The Open Group in February 1996. Under the Open Group umbrella, OSF and X/Open work together to deliver technological innovations and wide-scale adoption of open systems specifications.

Figure 206.1 The Open Group Web site.

Figure 206.2 Open Group events.

CROSS-PLATFORM PROGRAMMING

AI CAFÉ C/C++ CGI HTML HTTP JAVA J++ PERL VBSCRIPT VRML WIN32 WINSOCK 11001101001011110011011100110101010001100110010101

207

OPEN SOFTWARE ASSOCIATES

http://www.osa.com

Open Software Associates is a leading supplier of cross-platform development tools for Internet and intranet applications, and the first company to offer a product solution for enterprise-scale, distributed applications. Open Software Associates is committed to helping you protect your existing investments in systems, tools, and staff, even while you move to new technologies and application paradigms. Their products include *OpenWEB, OpenUI* (for seriously scalable corporate applications), *OpenWEB Packer* (for packing *any* application to run across the net!), and more. Come to this site for details, white papers, technical support, and much more. Oh yeah, the site offers some cool demos you should take time to download.

Figure 207.1 Open Software Associates.

Figure 207.2 OpenWEB information.

AI CAFÉ C/C++ CGI HTML HTTP JAVA J++ PERL VBSCRIPT VRML WIN32 WINSOCK 11001101001011110011011100110101010001100110010101

208

THE PORTABILITY TIMES

http://www.bristol.com/Ptimes/ptimes.html

Get the latest news on cross-platform computing through Bristol Technology's great quarterly newsletter. You will find feature articles that examine how to use C++ templates across UNIX platforms, how to use structured storage with Microsoft Foundation Classes (MFC), and how to use the standard C++ template library (STL) with the MFC. You will also find information on client/server application development using Win32/MFC/OLE and UNIX-to-Windows NT cross-platform application development. Then, you will learn how to write fast portable Win32 applications and how to implement the Windows API on UNIX. Visit this Web site and subscribe.

Figure 208.1 The Portability Times.

Figure 208.2 Subscription information.

EXTENDING MFC FOR CROSS-PLATFORM PORTABILITY

http://www.bristol.com/Bibliography/drdobbs0495.html

This site features another article from Chane Cullens, this one reprinted from *Dr. Dobb's Journal.* At this site, Cullens explains that the basic idea of *serialization* is that an object should be able to write its current state, usually indicated by the values of its member variables, to a persistent store (a file). The object can later recreate its previous state by reading (or 'deserializing') the data from the store. The serialization process handles all the details of object pointers and circular references to objects. Since the object itself is responsible for reading and writing its own state, the object is responsible for implementing most of the cross-platform portability. Visit this site for more specifics.

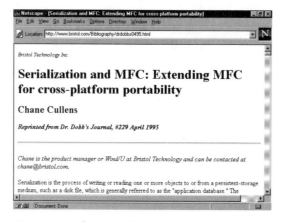

Figure 209 The tutorial's title page.

SUNRISE SOLUTIONS

http://www.sunrise-solutions.com/

Sunrise Solutions specializes in the evaluation of deployed technologies and their business effectiveness, development of information technology architectures, and implementation of Microsoft Windows NT and BackOffice products. In addition, they are specialists in the design of local- and wide-area networks, network installations, and software conversion to Windows 95 and Windows NT. Cross-platform computing, of course, brings with it some new and different uses that are not part of a traditional host-based network model. Sunrise Solutions has the expertise to deal with these issues and can help you create a network-centric client/server architecture that is right for your business. If you are looking for answers on cross-platform computing, start here.

Figure 210.1 The Sunrise Solutions home page.

Figure 210.2 What's new.

UNIFY CORPORATION

http://www.unify.com/

Looking for information on cross-platform database operations? Unify Corporation develops, markets, and supports advanced application development environments for the development, deployment, and management of high-end, business-critical, cross-platform applications. The company's flagship product, *Unify Vision*, combines a powerful and scaleable client/server architecture with a flexible and easy to use rapid application development technology. Other Unify products include the *Unify 2000* and *DataServer ELS* data servers, as well as the *Accell SQL* and *Accell IDS* 4GLs (fourth-generation languages). Visit Unify's impressive Web pages for complete technical support, product information, contact information, and sales and support details.

Figure 211 The Unify Corporation Web site.

USING OLE STRUCTURED STORAGE: PERSISTENCE OF DATA

http://crescent.progress.com/crescent/wp_oless.html

This tutorial discusses the OLE structured storage library and its new and powerful features which are available even to non-OLE applications. The discussion examines structured storage, how it differs from traditional serialization (an application's ability to write its current state to a persistent store—a file), and the advantages and disadvantages of each. You will also learn how to use structured storage in non-OLE applications, and the impacts of structured storage across Windows NT, Windows 95, UNIX, OpenVMS, and Mac platforms. To get started, download the site's Microsoft Powerpoint presentation or simply click to view the presentation right on-line.

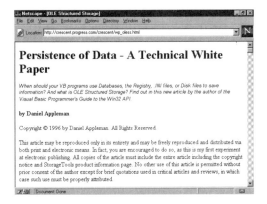

Figure 212.1 The tutorial's title page.

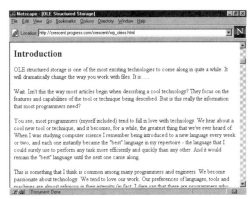

Figure 212.2 The introduction.

WILLOWS SOFTWARE

http://www.willows.com

Willows Software provides software tools and services for porting your 16- and 32-bit Windows applications to UNIX, the Mac, Java, real-time, and other systems. The Willows toolkits include Microsoft Foundation Classes (MFC) and Borland ObjectWindows Library (OWL) support. Willow Software invites you to download some exciting free software that includes demo versions of their various toolkits. You can also benefit from extensive on-line documentation. If you need to port Windows-based software and your schedule does not allow you much time, do yourself a favor and start with Willow Software tools.

Figure 213.1 The Willows Web site.

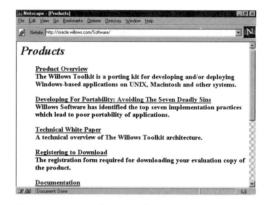

Figure 213.2 Willows Products.

WINDOWS CONTROLS VS. MOTIF WIDGETS

http://www.bristol.com/Bibliography/winhap7.html

Ah, yes. Windows controls and Motif widgets. "In each windowing environment," we are told, "these terms are used for the graphical user interface components that the end-user manipulates to achieve some goal." Of course, since Windows and Motif were both originally based on the Common User Access (CUA) user-interface specification, they share many similar components. But, they have dissimilarities as well. What, exactly, are the similarities and the dissimilarities? And how does one best work around the latter in order to create applications with inherent Windows-to-UNIX and UNIX-to-Windows portability? This article addresses these questions in detail.

Figure 214.1 The tutorial's title page.

Figure 214.2 More of the tutorial.

WINDOWS WITHOUT WALLS

http://www.byte.com/art/9602/sec11/art3.htm

The subtitle of the *BYTE* article, "Windows Without Walls," reads, "Portable applications for UNIX and Windows are a fact of life. Development problems don't have to be." In this informative piece, Denis Haskin points out that though UNIX is still the only platform for many mission-critical applications and database servers, the fact is that these systems simply must interact frequently and closely with the Windows world. And thus, the applications that companies deploy on both platforms are more critical than ever. Haskin goes on to delineate and solve many of the problems inherently involved in building and maintaining this important interface between platforms and systems. A must-read article.

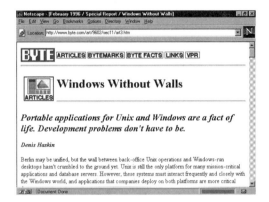

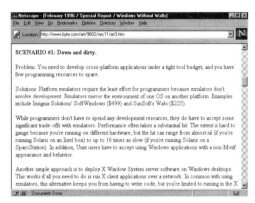

Figure 215.1 Windows Without Walls.   Figure 215.2 Part of the article.

WRITING PORTABLE C++ CODE

http://www.bristol.com/Bibliography/xplat2.html

You will encounter many different types of portability problems that are not language-specific, such as byte-swapping problems, 16/32/64-bit issues, operating-system differences, and so on. However, this article focuses on just C++ language-specific differences. In other words, it focuses on the portability issues that differences in various C++ compilers cause, such as those you would encounter when you move code from Microsoft's Visual C++ to a C++ compiler on a UNIX-based system. The tricks this article describes are neat, elegant, and efficient. A good read!

Figure 216 The start of the tutorial.

217

WRITING PORTABLE WIN32 APPLICATIONS

http://www.bristol.com/Bibliography/nt_developer.html

I hear you scoffing. Writing portable Win32 apps is no big deal, you say. After all, Win32 is a defacto cross-platform API for Windows NT on the Intel x86, Alpha, and MIPS, as well as Windows 95 and Windows 3.1. Yes, that's true, but this article goes far deeper than that, explaining how to write Win32 applications that you can easily port to the Mac and UNIX. That's right. You'll learn all the Zen of the Windows Portability Layer (WPL) found in Visual C++ 2.0 for NT, which lets you recompile your application with the Mac as a target and debug remotely using the Visual C++ debugger. And, you will also find information on Bristol Technology's great tool for moving Win32 apps onto UNIX platforms. Check it out.

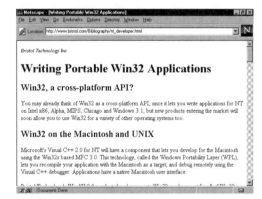

Figure 217.1 The title page.

Figure 217.2 More of the tutorial.

218

PUBLIC-DOMAIN CROSS-PLATFORM DEVELOPMENT TOOL KIT

http://www.awu.id.ethz.ch/~didi/wxwin/wx/wx_contents.html

Written by Julian Smart of the AI Applications Institute at the University of Edinburgh, *wxWindows 1.65* is a portable, public-domain C++ tool kit for creating graphical user interfaces. This site offers the software for free to all comers. The *wxWindows* tool kit currently maps to four native APIs: XView (Open Look), Motif, Microsoft Windows, and Windows NT. In addition to serving your GUI needs, *wxWindows* also supports a subset of Dynamic Data Exchange (DDE) for both PCs and UNIX machines. The model uses object-oriented clients, servers, and connections, all of which make it easy for you to write programs that communicate synchronously. And, it's free! You can't beat that.

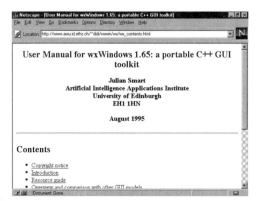

Figure 218.1 The user manual.

Figure 218.2 More of the manual.

zApp Developer's Suite

http://www.roguewave.com/products/zapp/

The *zApp Developer's Suite* provides four packages you can use to build cross-platform applications. To start, the *zApp Factory* is a visual programming environment. Next, the *zApp Interface Pack* provides a set of high-level visual objects and custom controls. And, *zHelp* provides tools that make it easy to build efficient, cross-platform help systems. These, combined with the *zApp Application Framework*, yield the suite that won an InfoWorld product comparison for cross-platform GUI application frameworks in February 1996. Visit this Web site for product information, example code, third-party extensions for *zApp*, the *zApp* object hierarchy, and free demos for you to download.

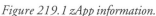

Figure 219.1 zApp information.

Figure 219.2 More zApp information.

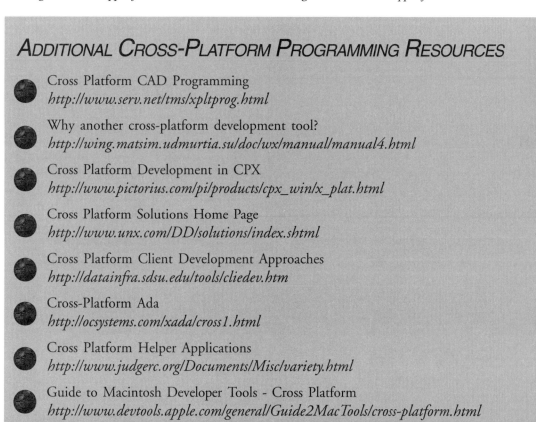

ADDITIONAL CROSS-PLATFORM PROGRAMMING RESOURCES

- Cross Platform CAD Programming
  http://www.serv.net/tms/xpltprog.html

- Why another cross-platform development tool?
  http://wing.matsim.udmurtia.su/doc/wx/manual/manual4.html

- Cross Platform Development in CPX
  http://www.pictorius.com/pi/products/cpx_win/x_plat.html

- Cross Platform Solutions Home Page
  http://www.unx.com/DD/solutions/index.shtml

- Cross Platform Client Development Approaches
  http://datainfra.sdsu.edu/tools/cliedev.htm

- Cross-Platform Ada
  http://ocsystems.com/xada/cross1.html

- Cross Platform Helper Applications
  http://www.judgerc.org/Documents/Misc/variety.html

- Guide to Macintosh Developer Tools - Cross Platform
  http://www.devtools.apple.com/general/Guide2MacTools/cross-platform.html

AN ENGLISH LANGUAGE FRONT-END FOR MICROSOFT ACCESS

http://users.aol.com/elfsoft/elfsoft.htm

Check out *Access ELF*, an English-language front-end (get it, ELF?) for Microsoft Access. *Access ELF* understands your plain-English questions and translates them, within seconds, into SQL, the native Access language. Just type your query, press a button, and see the answer flash instantly on your screen. You select whether to show the result as a data sheet, form, or graph. The setup is a snap. *Access ELF* customizes itself to your database with the push of one button. You won't have to deal with long "word-definition" dialogs—*Access ELF* includes its own 16,000 word dictionary. And, of course, the system is completely customizable. Perhaps that's why the software was a 1996 *PC Magazine* Shareware Awards Finalist.

Figure 220 Access ELF information.

1001100110001010101100111011011110101101110001101   AI CAFE C/C++ CGI HTML HTTP JAVA J++ PERL VBSCRIPT VRML WIN32 WINSOCK

ARBOR SOFTWARE CORPORATION: ESSBASE

http://www.arborsoft.com

Arbor Software "develops high performance, multidimensional database software for business planning, analysis, and management report applications." Their lead product, *Essbase*, pretty much owns the on-line analytical processing (OLAP) market. *Essbase* uniquely blends an innovative technical design with an open, client/server architecture. The result is a system which you can deploy for a broad range of strategic OLAP applications, including: product-flexibility analysis, customer-profitability analysis, sales analysis, budgeting, forecasting, financial consolidations, and manufacturing-mix analysis. Visit Arbor's Web site for more details.

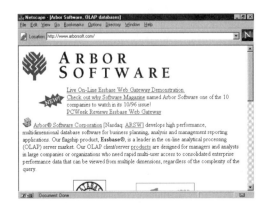

Figure 221.1 Arbor Software's Web site.

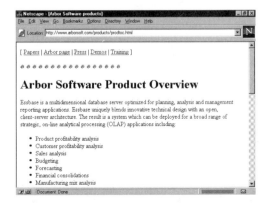

Figure 221.2 Arbor products.

AMULET CONSULTING DATABASE LINKS

http://www.amuletc.com/mirror/amuletc.htm

This site is packed with what the proprietor calls "Hot database links (including the Hot-Link of the Month) for the database software development industry." The proprietor is none other than Dan Gutierrez, contributing editor for *Internet Advisor* and *Data Base Advisor* magazines. Dan is also the author of the highly respected "Net Sightings" column in *Internet Advisor*. At this site, you will find links related to *Microsoft Access, Visual dBASE, Delphi, Paradox, Powerbuilder,* and a host of other products. All told, Amulet is a wonderful clearinghouse of information—one that I recommend highly. Do you have a link in mind that Dan has not discovered yet? If so, he'd be delighted to hear from you.

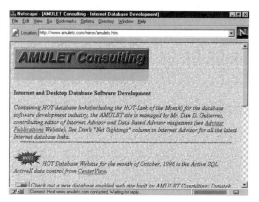

Figure 222.1 Amulet's Web site.

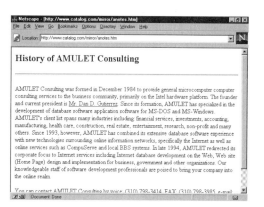

Figure 222.2 History of Amulet.

CHAD'S FOXPRO PAGE

http://www.dwave.net/~clemmer/foxpro.htm

Addressing all versions of *FoxPro,* Chad Lemmer provides great links to *FoxPro* pages across the Web, *FoxPro* FTP sites, *FoxPro* mailing lists, and *FoxPro* programs and utilities. Check out the *COB Editor* and *Extensions* which will save you thousands of keystrokes a day, *GPLIB 3.0* which contains invaluable Netware functions and procedures, an easy to use calendar class, *MessageBox()Function Builder* (an intuitive way to build the command!), and *DocBuild* for *Visual FoxPro* (which comments your code instantly!). And you'll find more at this site. Much more. So when you (or your code) are about to run out of gas, stop at this filling station along the Information Super Highway. Thanks, Chad.

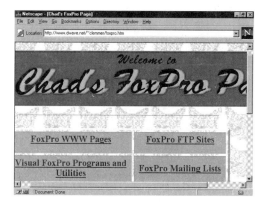

Figure 223.1 Chad's FoxPro page.

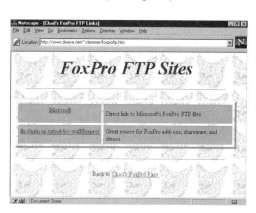

Figure 223.2 FoxPro FTP sites.

224

CHEE CHONG HWA'S MALAYSIAN CLIPPER SITE

http://www.jaring.my/cch/clipper

Dedicated to "Clipperheads" around the world, Chee Chong regularly updates and packs his site with great information, code, and more. You'll find information on dealing with bugs, how to avoid memory-low situations, the differences between various versions of *Clipper, Clipper* and Windows development, *Clipper* programming tips and tricks, and much more. The site also offers plenty of *Clipper* programs, files, and patches you can download. Also, the site features hot links to valuable technical references, articles, and white papers. Not only is this the richest *Clipper* oriented site on the Web, it is probably also the most up to date. Many thanks to the proprietor, Chee Chong Hwa.

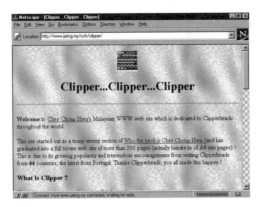
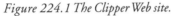

Figure 224.1 The Clipper Web site.

Figure 224.2 Who the heck is Chee Chong Hwa?

225

CINCOM: *TOTAL FRAMEWORK*

http://www.cincom.com/

TOTAL FrameWork is a breakthrough, component-based database application-assembly environment that lets customer-focused organizations build and execute customized (and cross-functional) business applications. Using the best of today's technology, including object-oriented and workflow technologies, *TOTAL FrameWork* is the first software environment to combine workflow automation with component-based application assembly and data integration. These three integrated components let you build strategic, cross-functional business databases that break down barriers between people, departments, and systems. Come to these pages for specifics on *TOTAL FrameWork* and other Cincom products.

Figure 225.1 Cincom home page.

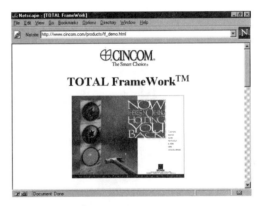

Figure 225.2 TOTAL FrameWork.

HTML HTTP Java J++ Perl VBScript VRML WIN32 Winsock

DATABASE PROGRAMMING

AI CAFÉ C/C++ CGI HTML HTTP JAVA J++ PERL VBSCRIPT VRML WIN32 WINSOCK 110011010010111100110111001101010100011001100100101

CLARIS: FILEMAKER PRO

http://www.claris.com

Claris Corporation, a wholly-owned subsidiary of Apple Computer, has grown during the past three years to become one of the world's eight largest PC software vendors. The DBMS *FileMaker Pro* for Windows 3.1, Windows 95, NT, the Mac, and PowerMac provides an easy to use, point-and-click application that brings the power of a fully relational DBMS to the smallest of platforms. This site is packed with specifics about *FileMaker Pro* (including technical discussions and samples). Check it out.

Figure 226.1 Claris home page.

Figure 226.2 FileMaker information.

CLIPPER RESOURCE PAGE FROM IRELAND

http://www.iol.ie/~pobeirne/cugi.html

Patrick O'Beirne of the Republic of Ireland provides a splendid collection of *Clipper* resources that includes links to *Clippings* Magazine, Cibertec (a cool Clipper site for Spanish-speaking users and developers), Allen Te's *Clipper Developer's Library*, Mark Schumann's great *Clipper* FTP site, and more. The site also provides you with an introduction to *Clipper*, several excellent *Clipper* course outlines, training materials for *Clipper*, a tutorial on using object-oriented technologies with *Clipper*, and an excellent tutorial on *Clipper* memory management. Many thanks to Mr. O'Beirne for a very worthwhile contribution.

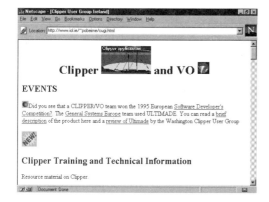

Figure 227.1 The Clipper Web site.

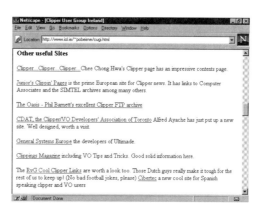

Figure 227.2 A few options.

228

CLIPPER SHAREWARE UTILITY

http://www.inforamp.net/~rpb/

Randall Banning is, as his page tells us, "a Clipper developer working in a Systems Integration Department for a large electronic manufacturing company. I design, develop, and implement various in-house applications." And, Randall uses *Clipper* a great deal. In that connection, he wrote *DBQ*, a shareware *Clipper* program designed to aid in the development and maintenance of *Clipper 5.3* databases. The utility customizes printer settings, and saves the existing environment. Visit this site and download *DBQ*. Give the software a test drive. I think you will like it—it's an efficient, time-saving utility.

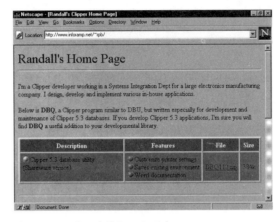

Figure 228 Randall Banning's home page.

229

CLIP-4-WIN

http://www.brainlink.com/clip-4-win/

Clip-4-Win provides *Clipper* programmers with immediate access to the complete Windows API and all the available resources such as buttons, dialogs, bitmaps, icons, menus, pens, and so on. With *CA-Clipper* and *Clip-4-Win*, the *Clipper* programmer develops programs for Windows using his or her familiar environment (using his or her favorite editor, linker, and libraries). *Clip-4-Win* supports VBX controls, ODBC2, SQL, and MAPI. It also supports more than 70 classes and comes complete with source code. You will also find an excellent browser that incorporates support for bitmaps and TrueType fonts, and also provides drag-and-drop, DDE server, and client support. Visit this Web site for more information on *Clip-4-Win*.

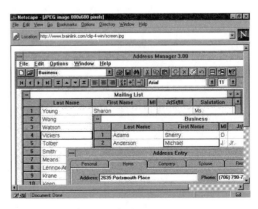

Figure 229.1 Clip-4-Win home page.   *Figure 229.2 A sample screen.*

COLIN'S FOXPRO PAGE

http://www.state.sd.us/people/colink/fox_page.htm

This Web site, maintained by Colin Keeler and hosted by the State of South Dakota's Web server, provides handy links to *FoxPro* resources on the Internet, facilitates the sharing of *FoxPro* information among developers, develops contacts between *FoxPro* developers and users around the world, and experiments with using *FoxPro* (and other database engines) for Web publishing. Visit this site for great *FoxPro* hints and tips, on-line chats, demo software you can download, example development projects, white papers, and previously undocumented *FoxPro* tricks.

Figure 230.1 Colin's FoxPro page.

Figure 230.2 More from Colin.

COMPUTER ASSOCIATES: INGRES ANSWERS

http://www.cai.com

The Computer Associates Web site is packed with great questions and answers related to their *Ingres* database product. For example: When using *Microsoft TCP/IP for Windows for Workgroups 3.11* with *CA-Ingres/Net*, how should I configure *WFW 3.11* and the *Microsoft TCP/IP stack*, and then, how I should I implement *CA-Ingres/Net 6.4/04 (net.win/00)*, *W4GL 2.0/01 (dev.win/02)*, and third-party telnet and FTP tools? Is that precise enough for you? You will find a detailed answer at this Web site, along with hundreds of other pertinent questions and answers. In short, the site is a gold mine of information for *Ingres* developers. So, save yourself some time and pay this site a visit.

Figure 231.1 The Computer Associates Web site.

Figure 231.2 Product information.

COOL CLIPPER LINKS

http://www.rad.net.id/users/personal/a/andijahj/clipper.html

This site features the Web's best clearinghouse of information about the *Clipper* DBMS. Andi Jahja maintains the site which contains dozens of links to *Clipper* usergroups, discussion groups, code archives, and other resources. You will also find access to *Clipper* newsgroups, technical support, and links to *Clipper* consultants and developers from around the world. Andi invites you to include your name on that list if you fit the bill. This is the spot on the Web where you can best make contact with other *Clipper* gurus, share hints and tips, and in the process save yourself a great deal of time, coding, and energy.

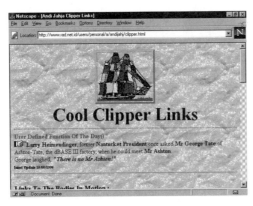

Figure 232.1 Cool Clipper Links Web site.

Figure 232.2 Some of the links.

dCLIP 4.0 FOR WINDOWS DOWNLOAD

http://www.dclip.com/

dCLIP for Windows is a true Windows version of *dCLIP* designed from *Clipper 5.2e* and *FiveWin 1.901*. The libraries that make up *dCLIP for Windows* are based on *dCLIP 4.0 for DOS*. The software's objective is to provide a powerful Windows client engine that integrates the dot-prompt, database-browsing, editing features, and the same compatibility with all *Clipper* RDD's (Requirement Driven Development) currently supported by *dCLIP 4.0 for DOS*. Additionally, all the data-driven sub-systems are fully compatible with the same data dictionaries used in the DOS version of *dCLIP*. Care for a test drive? Visit the Web site for a free demo download.

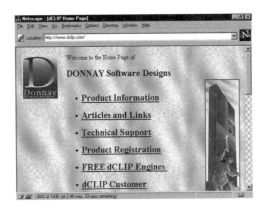

Figure 233.1 Donnay Software Designs.

Figure 233.2 Free dCLIP engines.

A TUTORIAL USING MACHIAVELLI

http://www_is.cs.utwente.nl:8080/keulen/me/docs/bunemanohori-tods94.html

This tutorial emphasizes the Machiavelli, a polymorphic language with static type checking. In Machiavelli, heterogeneous sets can be used, and a filter-operation is defined that can filter-out the elements of a particular type. In fact, the database in Machiavelli is a heterogeneous set of objects. Furthermore, Machiavelli inheritance is not based on subtyping (there is no subtyping in Machiavelli!), but on polymorphism. In addition to the extended tutorial on *Polymorphism and Type Inference in Database Programming*, this tutorial also includes links to places on the Internet where you can download Machiavelli and try it on for size.

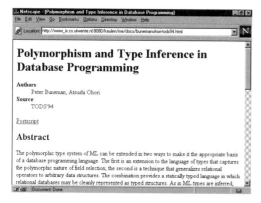

Figure 234.1 The tutorial home page.

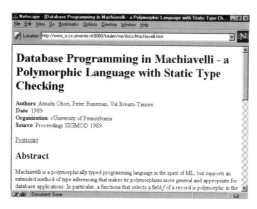

Figure 234.2 A related paper.

DATABASES & LOGIC PROGRAMMING: A BIBLIOGRAPHY SERVER

http://www.informatik.uni-trier.de/~ley/db/index.html

This outstanding site provides a dazzling hypertext bibliography of virtually all the vital literature on databases and logical programming. The site's bibliography includes not only books, but also magazine articles, journal articles, conference proceedings, symposia, and even on-line digital "literature." You may search the site's content by topic, author, keyword, year of publication, or any combination of these. If a link is available to an on-line text file, the site supplies it. All in all, it is hard to overstate how wonderful and vital a resource this bibliography server actually is. Check it out.

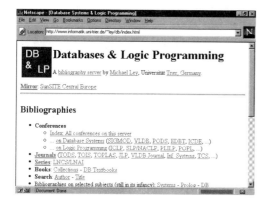

Figure 235.1 The Web site.

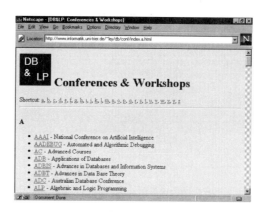

Figure 235.2 Conferences and workshops.

DATABASE PROGRAMMING USING VISUAL BASIC: A TUTORIAL

http://www.anglo.co.uk/vdb.html

This excellent tutorial explains the fundamentals of data access using Visual Basic. You will learn how to open and modify existing databases, how to use Visual Basic to access external database engines (such as *FoxPro, Oracle, Microsoft Access, dBase*, SQL servers, and so on), and how to write SQL queries to access and update existing databases. In addition, the tutorial discusses how to use Open Database Connectivity (ODBC), how to use the Windows APIs for Visual Basic database programming, and how Visual Basic provides data access capabilities based on the Microsft *Jet* database engine. You will also learn how to build databases using data access objects (DAO), and much more. The site leaves no question unanswered.

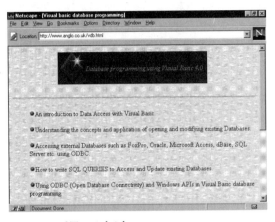

Figure 236 Tutorial title page.

DATABASE RESEARCH GROUP, UNIVERSITY OF CALIFORNIA, BERKELEY

http://s2k-ftp.CS.Berkeley.EDU:8000/postgres/

If you want to understand the theory behind database operations, you found the right site. Visit this excellent Web site for source code from the Berekely DBMS research projects, including *POSTGRES95*, *University POSTGRES*, and *University INGRES*. The site also provides a great archive of research papers on such topics as performance analysis of distributed database systems, implementation of rules in relational database systems, extending a database system with procedures, inclusion of new types in relational database systems, performance evaluation of operating system transaction managers, optimization of parallel query execution plans, file system performance as it relates to transaction support, and much more.

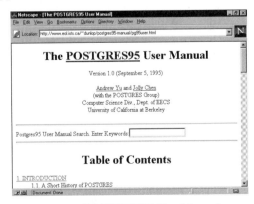

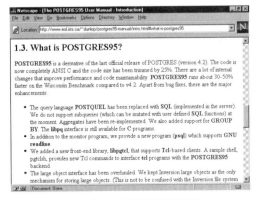

Figure 237.1 POSTGRES95 User Manual.   *Figure 237.2 What is POSTGRES95?*

DATABASE RESOURCES FROM "THE SQL PRO"

http://www.inquiry.com/techtips/thesqlpro/

This site provides hundreds of links to database companies, products, consultants, code libraries, white papers, technical support, and much more. You will also find resources that describe database publishing on the Web, as well as insightful articles and papers on database development. Some of the goodies you will find at this site include a hypertext catalog of free database systems you can download across the Web, a great history of SQL (the structured query language), an excellent on-line tutorial entitled "Understanding Relational Design," and a list of frequently asked questions regarding Open Database Connectivity. You will also find the on-line edition of *Database Programming and Design Magazine*, and more than a dozen newsgroups. In short, this site provides "one-stop shopping" for the professional database programmer searching for information on the Web.

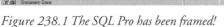

Figure 238.1 The SQL Pro has been framed!

Figure 238.2 Search for what you need.

DATABASE SYSTEMS LABORATORY: UMASS, AMHERST

http://www-ccs.cs.umass.edu/db.html

The current database research at the Database Systems Lab of the University of Massachusetts, Amherst, involves enhancing performance and availability of applications which require transaction support through the use of semantic information about objects, operations, transaction models, and the application. Individual projects focus on semantics-based concurrency control, specifying and reasoning about extended-transaction models, and the formal characteristics and performance aspects of epsilon serializability. Students in the lab are also working on language support for extended transaction models, support for recovery in shared-memory database systems, and more. This site is filled with state-of-the-art database research.

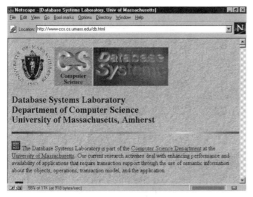

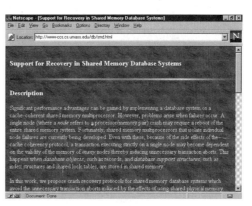

Figure 239.1 The Database Systems Web site.

Figure 239.2 A current project.

240

DATAFLIGHT SOFTWARE: TEXT DATABASE MANAGEMENT

http://www.dataflight.com

Dataflight Software's most popular database product is *Concordance for Windows*, which delivers a rich set of features that help you manage full-text databases. The features go beyond fast and accurate retrieval to include enhanced editing, record tagging, links to image retrieval systems, network-wide multi-user edits and updates, and more. The product includes edit validations supported with automatic case conversion, pop-up data entry lists, read-only fields, and data stamping. And, the report writer is easy and powerful. For more information, and for very cool and absolutely free Windows wallpaper, stop by the Dataflight Web site.

Figure 240.1 The Dataflight Web site.

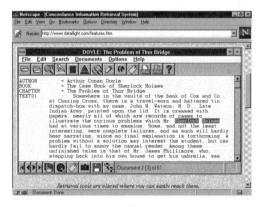

Figure 240.2 A Concordance screen.

241

DBINTELLECT TECHNOLOGIES

http://www.dbintellect.com/

dbINTELLECT tools enable you to leverage customer transaction data to establish long-term relationships. Through the application of advanced marketing models, data warehousing, data mining techniques, and more, dbINTELLECT can help you arm yourself with an optimally efficient business database. The dbINTELLECT tools fulfill your business vision through a blended product suite uniquely suited to your business. The tools marry the potential of a fully customized development effort to the speedy implementation of an off-the-shelf product—all, of course, based on the open-systems model. Visit this Web site for more information.

Figure 241.1 dbINTELLECT's Web site.

Figure 241.2 dbINTELLECT architecture.

DONOVAN LOUCKS' FOXPRO PAGE

http://www.primenet.com/~dloucks/foxpage.html

Donovan Loucks' Web page provides an excellent set of links to *FoxPro* sites across the Web, including Microsoft's own on-line *FoxPro* Knowlege Base and the Cobb Group's *Inside Visual FoxPro* newsletter. The site also features user-interface design resources that include the range of human-computer interaction (HCI) sites on the Web, user interface design tips from Janus Intermedia, and data normalization resources. Donovan Loucks, the proprietor of this site, works as a database consultant for several government agencies and private corporations in Phoenix, Arizona. He has put together a nice, useful set of resources at this site, for which we say, "Thanks."

Figure 242 Donovan's page.

DUNN SYSTEMS SOFTWARE: DOWNLOAD SECURE SQLBASE DEMO

http://www.dunnsys.com/

Dunn Systems is a computer consulting firm that focuses primarily on microcomputer systems. The folks at Dunn assist their clients in all aspects of development and decision making, including hardware and software specifications, custom programming, and multi-user installations. In this spirit, they have delivered *Secure SQLBase*, a product that gives you a secure wide-area network backbone capable of using powerful client/server tools to tap the unused power of the Internet. *Secure SQLBase* automatically provides encryption for all SQL database traffic. The software integrates RSA public key encryption into the SQLBase database engine. Visit this site and download a demo.

Figure 243.1 Dunn home page.

Figure 243.2 Dunn product information.

ELECTRIC FOXPRO: AN ALTERNATIVE TO FOXPRO PROGRAMMING

http://discover-net.net/~dhenton/ghtml/efox.html

This site is packed with an irreverent collection of undocumented *FoxPro* tips. The site's goal is to provide a forum for discussion about PC-database programming in *FoxPro*. The site will help you find resources, information, and even a place to complain. The site offers excellent discussions, solutions to hard-to-solve problems, and more. Take time to check out the site's many resources. And, while you are there, be sure to download the excellent data-environment extractor.

Figure 244.1 Electric FoxPro's Web site.

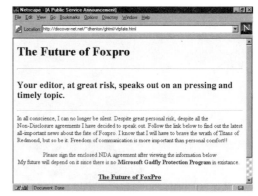

Figure 244.2 The future of FoxPro.

EMPRESS SOFTWARE

http://www.empress.com

Empress Software provides tools for data management, application prototyping, and for developing high-performance production applications. The sophisticated design of their integrated database package has made it the DBMS of choice for the most challenging database applications. *Empress DBMS* offers power, ease-of-use, integrity, and portability. With *Empress*, you can accept a wide variety of numeric, textual, and binary data types. You can also incorporate unlimited user definable functions and operators. And, you can store and manipulate large amounts of data, including binary data (such as image and sound in a variety of formats), as well as variable length text. Visit the Empress Web site for more details, as well as for some cool (free) downloads.

Figure 245.1 The Empress Web site.

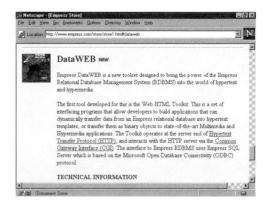

Figure 245.2 Empress DataWEB information.

EVERYWARE DATABASE DEVELOPMENT

http://www.everyware.com

EveryWare Development Corporation provides rapid, comprehensive, and visual Web-based database development tools. Their software provides solutions across all platforms and is ideal for database developers, Webmasters, and experienced programmers. EveryWare, an expert in rapid Web-based database integration, also develops Web-based, server-side analysis-and-reporting tools, shrink-wrapped business applications, and implementation consulting services. Their products include *Tango*, *Bolero*, *Butler SQL*, and *Connected*. Visit this Web site to learn specifics about these products and to download some neat, free demo packages that you will find quite useful.

Figure 246.1 EveryWare's Web site.

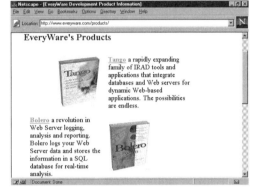

Figure 246.2 Products and demos.

FOURTH DIMENSION SOFTWARE

http://www.4ds.com/

OLTP (On-line Transaction Processing) is here to stay. Fourth Dimension Software is the premier provider of OLTP database solutions. Since 1982, Fourth Dimension Software has specialized in the design and development of software applications for use on Tandem computers. They have built their reputation on the ability to produce large-scale systems (based on complex databases) faster and more successfully than their competitors. Working on Tandem computers, they have always built systems that separate the presentation of data from its retrieval and processing. Client/server architecture fits perfectly with their design methodology, and client/server development is one of their greatest strengths. Drop in to learn more about Fourth Dimension and their great solutions.

Figure 247 The Fourth Dimension Web site.

248 · THE FOXPRO I/O ADDRESS: FOXPRO RESOURCES ON THE INTERNET

http://www.hop.man.ac.uk/staff/mpitcher/foxpro.html

This site provides the Web's most comprehensive set of links and resources available for all versions of *FoxPro* through *Visual FoxPro 5.0*. You will find links to related Web sites, FTP archives, mailing lists, USENET newsgroups, an electronic *FoxPro* newsletter, Microsoft's *FoxPro* pages, and even to a connection to *FoxPro* information on CompuServe. Other Web links you will encounter include the *FoxPro* Yellow Pages, and the *FoxPro* Tip-of-the-Month. If you are a serious *FoxPro* user, make this Web site your first stop on the Information Super Highway. You'll be glad you stopped by.

Figure 248.1 The FoxPro I/O Address.

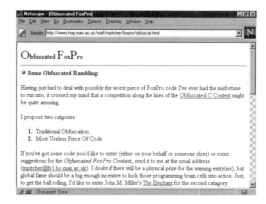

Figure 248.2 Obfuscated FoxPro.

249 · FOXPRO UTILITIES AND TUTORIALS FROM JASON LANDRY

http://206.10.225.118/genscrnx/

Visit this site and check out the great tools and tips from *FoxPro* programmer extraordinaire, Jason Landry. First, take time to read his outstanding tutorial on using *GENSCRNX* with *Visual FoxPro* to create great screens. Jason also explains how you can write your own *GENSCRNX* driver, and dives deep into *CDX2PRG*, a program that automatically creates a program that regenerates the index files in your database! Jason invites you to download various programs and drivers which include a driver that integrates a browser into a screen, and *SAYDIS* (a robust *GENSCRNX* driver that shades the text prompt to the left of an input whenever the input field is disabled). Very cool.

Figure 249.1 Jason's home page.

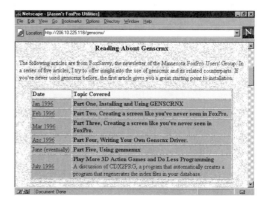

Figure 249.2 GENSCRNX stuff.

FOXPRO WWW DISCUSSION BOARD

http://dataperipherals.com/html/wwwboard/wwwboard.html

How do you design and implement efficient login screens? How do you preview a print-out without using the *Visual FoxPro* wizard? How can you clear a form within a *Visual FoxPro* program? How can you append records in grids? How can you print pictures in reports? Ask a question at this site, and you will get a flood of answers from other workers in the field who have already encountered your problem. If you see a question posted that you can answer, contribute your expertise. In short, this site demonstrates the philosophy of one hand washing the other, and a wonderful experiment in self-help cooperation on the electronic frontier.

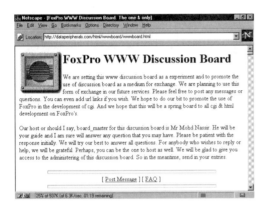
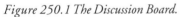

Figure 250.1 The Discussion Board. *Figure 250.2 Some posts.*

FREE DATABASE DOWNLOAD LIST

http://cuiwww.unige.ch/~scg/FreeDB/FreeDB.list.html

That's right. The database programs are free and they are at this site: *DiamondBase, PQL, Qddb, Typhoon, MetalBase, mSQL (miniSQL), REQUIEM, shql, Arjuna Distributed Programming System, EXODUS Project software, LINKCKS, OBST, pfl*, the *Triton Object-Oriented Database System, William's Object Oriented Database, YOODA (Yet another Object Oriented Database), Aditi Deductive Database System, ConceptBase, CORAL, AddressManager, EDB (the Emacs database), groc (Graphical REsource Organizer Kit), jinx, rdb*, the *Btree Library, B+tree Library, cbase*, and much more. Visit this site and download these databases for a test drive.

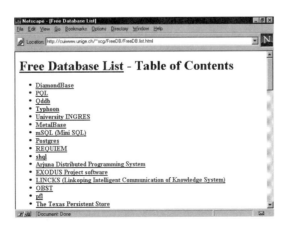

Figure 251 The Database list.

COMPARING LOTUS NOTES & RELATIONAL DBMSS

http://daniel.drew.edu/~tbeerley/notes.htm

Lotus Notes is a client/server application in that it allows groups of users to communicate and share data. This excellent paper, authored by Thomas J. Beerley of Drew University, compares *Lotus Notes* to other relational databases. As you will learn, you can think of *Lotus Notes* as a DBMS, by virtue of its information storage and retrieval capabilities. This is despite the fact that *Lotus Notes* was not founded on the relational model. This paper's purpose is to examine the similarities and differences between *Notes* and relational DBMS systems, and to explain the rationale behind any deviations *Notes* makes from the relational model. A recurring theme within the paper is that the relational model would prove inadequate handling the types of information and processes for which *Notes* is designed. This paper is a very good read.

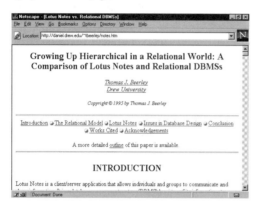

Figure 252.1 The title page.

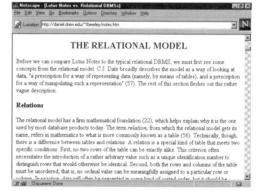

Figure 252.2 Part of the discussion.

ILLUSTRA INFORMATION TECHNOLOGIES, A DIVISION OF INFORMIX

http://www.illustra.com

Illustra, a division of Informix, is the leading supplier of object-relational database management systems (ORDBMS) and the first to bring a product to market in a growing category of information management systems: dynamic content management. The Illustra content management system generates, stores, and manages everything you will see at the Illustra Information Technologies (a division of Informix Software) Web site. Informix bases their Illustra product set on database server "snap-in" software called *DataBlade* modules. A *DataBlade* module is a collection of data structures, functions that manipulate them, and new (optimal) access methods. To find out more, access Illustra's informative and efficient Web site.

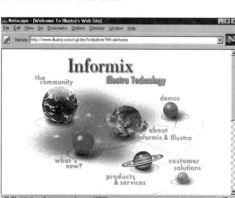

Figure 253.1 Informix Illustra's Web site.

Figure 253.2 Informix Illustra details.

INFORMIX

http://www.informix.com/

You need fast throughput, robust information integrity, speedy report generation, and a weekend off once in a while. You need reliable data backup, reliable security, and an interface so simple your help desk phone might stop ringing once in a while. Turn to Informix, a company which provides innovative database products and application and development tools to help you manage your corporate information efficiently, economically, and productively. For the past 15 years, Informix has proven its ability to deliver innovative database technologies to help its customers manage and grow their businesses. Informix thinks you and every other database system administrator on the planet need some time off. Find out how they can help you get it.

Figure 254.1 Informix in frames.

Figure 254.2 What's the latest?

JOSE'S VISUAL BASIC WORLD DATABASE PROGRAMMING CORNER

http://www.citilink.com/~jgarrick/vbasic/database/

This tutorial emphasizes the use of the *Jet* Data Access Objects (DAO), Structured Query Language (SQL), and a style of database programming that uses unbound controls. Jose Garrick delivers great discussions that include an introduction to the relational database model, techniques for optimizing database applications, database-design fundamentals, *Jet* and Access tools, and more. You will find no better resource on the Web for those who wish to master the Zen of creating fast, robust, efficient database applications using VisualBasic. And the price? Why, absolutely free, of course. Absolutely free!

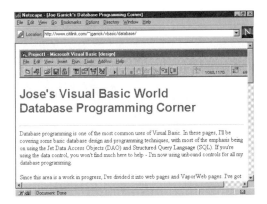

Figure 255.1 Jose's corner.

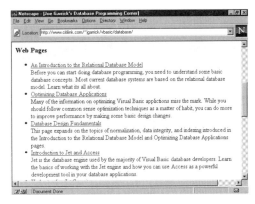

Figure 255.2 Some options.

JUST LOGIC SQL RELATIONAL DATABASE MANAGEMENT SYSTEM

http://www.justlogic.com/

Discover the *Just Logic SQL Database Management System*, a relational-database engine for use from within your C/C++ programs and for use as a database engine in your Web site. This product is ideal for professionals who write simple to very complex applications and need a database that delivers flexibility and performance. The product comes with three programming interfaces to suit your style. You get a complete set of C++ class definitions for easy access to all SQL features in true C++ programming style. You also get a C application program interface for complete access to SQL with pure C syntax, without precompilation. And, you get a standard C precompiler for application portability to or from other relational databases. If you are using C/C++ and SQL, don't miss this site.

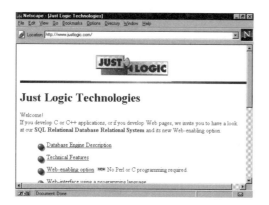

Figure 256.1 Just Logic's Web site.

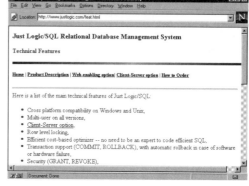

Figure 256.2 Technical features.

MATISSE DATABASE SERVER & CLIENT

http://www.adb.com

Matisse, from ADB, is the first in a new generation of OLTP (On-Line Transmission Processing), mission-critical, multimedia DBMS systems for efficient management of complex objects such as videos, documents, images, and audio. Leading DBMS experts, analysts such as Gartner Group and IDC, and many multinational firms who use *Matisse* daily in both corporate and industrial environments, recognize the reliability, performance, and technological advantages of *Matisse*. Visit this Web site for detailed information and technical support regarding *Matisse*. You will also encounter an outstanding *Matisse* demo. Use *Matisse* to query a database that manages thousands of photographs and videos on a virtual Web "gallery." Cool stuff.

Figure 257.1 Matisse home page.

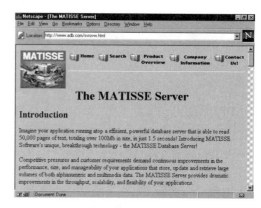

Figure 257.2 The Matisse server.

MICROSOFT ACCESS: OFFICIAL SITE

http://www.microsoft.com/msaccess/

Visit this site and find out all about *Microsft Access for Windows 95,* which quickly delivers relational database power to everyone from the novice to the expert user. The extensive documentation you'll find at this site explains how *Microsoft Access for Windows 95* uses second-generation learning tools to bring novice users up to speed quickly. It also explains how the *Microsoft Access Database Wizard* automatically builds tables, queries, forms, and reports, and how to use the new *Table Analyzer Wizard* to transform flat-file lists or spreadsheet data into a powerful relational database with little muss or fuss. Whether you're a first-time user or a database expert, you'll be interested in learning how *Microsoft Access* can help drive your business forward.

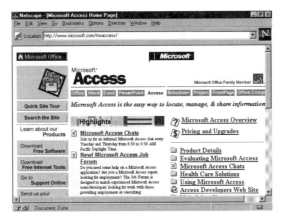

Figure 258 Official Access information.

MICROSOFT SQL SERVER: A FREE TRIAL

http://www.microsoft.com/sql/

Microsoft SQL Server 6.5 is the first DBMS designed specifically for the new world of distributed client/server computing. The software provides, in one box at one price, a complete and integrated system of database-management software to meet the challenges facing today's global businesses. The software also includes a built-in distributed transaction coordinator, heterogeneous-data replication, dynamic locking, Internet integration, increased performance, and scalability. In addition, the software benefits from better parallelization through the use of native Windows NT threads, improved asynchronous I/O, and a streamlined checkpoint process. Visit this site and download the 120-day evaluation-offer version which includes the *Programmer's Toolkit*!

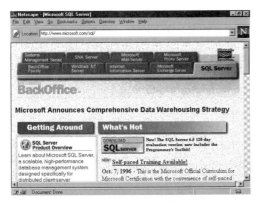

Figure 259.1 Microsoft SQL information.

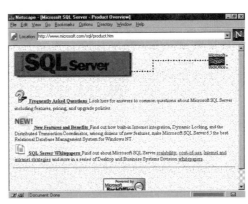

Figure 259.2 An overview.

1001 Programming Resources

001100110001010101100111011011110101011011110001101 AI CAFÉ C/C++ CGI HTML HTTP JAVA J++ PERL VBSCRIPT VRML WIN32 WINSOCK

260

FREE
FREE SOFTWARE

COVERS DETAILS

OPEN TO ALL

STRONG CONTENT

EXCELLENT REFERENCES

MiniSQL: Free Download

http://Hughes.com.au/product/msql/

MiniSQL (or *mSQL*) is a lightweight database engine created by Hughes that offers a subset of the ANSI SQL specification as its query language. *mSQL* performs simple operations very quickly, and it operates with very little memory. The package includes the *mSQL* server, a C programming interface for client software, and several tools. The site invites you to download a copy of this shareware (*not* freeware) for a 14-day trial. You can also get copies of some great user-contributed software available for *mSQL* that include interfaces to *mSQL* from *Perl, Tcl, REXX, Java*, and *Python*, Web interfaces, a Windows port of the client library, and much more. Visit this site and try out this software. The software may help you solve several small (mini) database requirements.

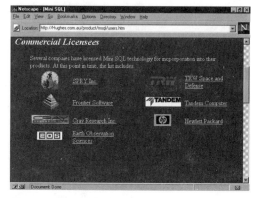

Figure 260.1 MiniSQL home pages.   *Figure 260.2 Who is using MiniSQL?*

261

FREE
FREE SOFTWARE

COVERS DETAILS

OPEN TO ALL

STRONG CONTENT

EXCELLENT REFERENCES

Neil's FoxPro Resources

http://adams.patriot.net/~johnson/neil/fox.html

This site features another great gateway to *FoxPro* resources on the Web! You will find job listings, special events, and announcements of interest to the *FoxPro* community. You'll also find *FoxPro* training and documentation (including publications and a great list of frequently asked questions), and details on *BarCodes* and related information (including TrueType Fonts for *FoxPro* bar-coding). The site also features a great collection of software archives and snippets, *GENSCRNX* drivers, mailing lists, newsgroups, *FoxPro* usergroups, the *Laguna* (software for interfacing *FoxPro* with CGI Web servers), and more. By providing you with a rich cornucopia of information options, Neil's *FoxPro* Resources can make your programming life a lot easier. I suggest a visit.

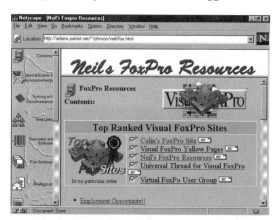

Figure 261 Neil's page.

AI CAFÉ C/C++ CGI HTML HTTP JAVA J++ PERL VBSCRIPT VRML WIN32 WINSOCK 1100110100101110011011100110101010001100110010101

O2 TECHNOLOGY: DATABASE SOLUTIONS FOR OBJECT DEVELOPERS

http://www.o2tech.com/

02 Technology is a leader in the fast-growing object-database market. The firm has been one of the main players in the definition of the object-database standard: *ODMG-93.* In fact, 02 shipped *the very first* object database compliant with this standard. Besides the standard ODMG (Object Database Management Group) interface to the 02 object database engine, 02 provides you with programming languages (02C and C), object-presentation builders (*02Look, 02Graph, 02Web,* and *02Report*) and a development environment (*02Tools* and *02Kit*). Via these tools, 02 gives you easier modeling, faster development, and simpler application modification and maintenance. Visit the 02 Web site for more information.

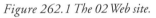

Figure 262.1 The 02 Web site.

Figure 262.2 Products.

AI CAFÉ C/C++ CGI HTML HTTP JAVA J++ PERL VBSCRIPT VRML WIN32 WINSOCK 1100110100101110011011100110101010001100110010101

THE OASIS: CA-CLIPPER FILE ARCHIVE

http://www.iag.net/~philb/

The Oasis file archive (which now includes the Reef file archive) is quite simply the Web's largest and best-maintained file archive for *CA-Clipper.* The Oasis archive allows *Clipper* programmers to satisfy their need for demos, utilities, source code, patches, and libraries. The site also provides direct access to the *comp.language.clipper* newsgroup. You can download any of the site's files, or you may donate your own submissions. "If you have any Clipper related material," writes the Webmaster, "please feel free to send it in for everyone to use." *Clipper* programmer extraordinaire, Phil Barnett, maintains this site. A worthwhile visit.

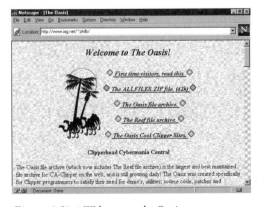

Figure 263.1 Welcome to the Oasis.

Figure 263.2 The Oasis Main Menu.

AI CAFÉ C/C++ CGI HTML HTTP JAVA J++ PERL VBSCRIPT VRML WIN32 WINSOCK

OBJECT DATABASE MANAGEMENT GROUP

http://www.odmg.org/

Portability in data. That is where your bread is buttered. That is where success lays. The aim of the Object Database Management Group (ODMG) is to develop a standard set of specifications that developers may incorporate into database programs to permit applications to access information stored in object-database management systems (ODBMSs) in a uniform way. The group also seeks to make their definitions available to others for general industry use, and to work with other standards-setting organizations such as the International Standards Organization (ISO). Make sure your data conforms to the standards of tomorrow. Stay in touch with ODMG.

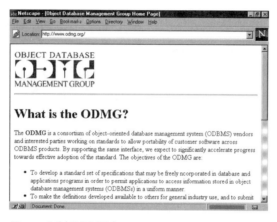

Figure 264 ODMG home page.

AI CAFÉ C/C++ CGI HTML HTTP JAVA J++ PERL VBSCRIPT VRML WIN32 WINSOCK

OBJECT ORIENTATION IN FOXPRO: A TUTORIAL

http://www.hop.man.ac.uk/staff/mpitcher/foxpro/foxoop.html

Can you create object-oriented programs in *FoxPro*? That's just one of the questions this tutorial answers. As you will learn, object-oriented programming techniques are not an alternate form of programming. Rather, they are an extension of structured programming—much the same way that structured programming inherits features from unstructured languages such as BASIC and assembly language. The tutorial's general notion is to enhance programming style and still maintain backward compatibility via object-oriented techniques. And, the technique the tutorial describes for *FoxPro* programming is simple and requires no external modules. Try it out!

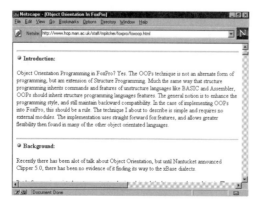
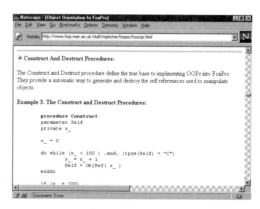

Figure 265.1 The start of the tutorial.   *Figure 265.2 More of it.*

AI CAFÉ C/C++ CGI HTML HTTP JAVA J++ PERL VBSCRIPT VRML WIN32 WINSOCK 110011010010111100110111001101010100011001100100101

MENU PROGRAMMING UTILITY FOR VISUAL FOXPRO

http://www.users.dircon.co.uk/~markh/fox.htm

Visit Mark's FoxPro Page and download *MnuClass*, which enables object-oriented menu programming with Visual *FoxPro*. Your host, Mark, is really annoyed that Microsoft has failed to update the menu builder in *Visual FoxPro*. "We have all the wonders of object-oriented programming," he writes, "but are doomed to using DEFINE MENU/PAD/POPUP and BAR for creating menus." Mark provides the best solution: a couple of class definitions that allow you to program your menus in a totally object-oriented manner. Previously awkward features (check marks, dynamically adding/removing options, changing the caption or message) are now "stupendously easy." Go for it.

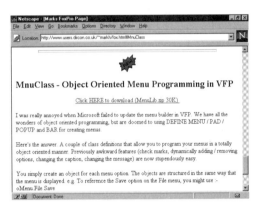

Figure 266.1 Mark's FoxPro Page.　　　　　　Figure 266.2 MnuClass details.

AI CAFÉ C/C++ CGI HTML HTTP JAVA J++ PERL VBSCRIPT VRML WIN32 WINSOCK 110011010010111100110111001101010100011001100100101

OMNISCIENCE ORDBMS

http://www.omniscience.com/broch.htm

Step into database luxury. The *Omniscience Object-Relational Database Management System (ORDBMS)* combines the power and flexibility of the object-data model with the robust features and reliability of the relational-data model. *Omniscience ORDBMS* is ideal for developers and users who require a powerful, object-relational database. You can easily run Omniscience ORDBMS on the same machine as your Windows tools and applications. It is part of a suite of integrated database products based on the advanced capabilities of object-oriented technology for today's client/server applications. Visit this site for much more information about the product, its development, its applications, its pricing, and technical support.

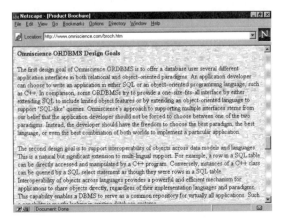

Figure 267 About ORDBMS.

1001 PROGRAMMING RESOURCES

1001100110001010101100111011011110101101111000110 | AI CAFÉ C/C++ CGI HTML HTTP JAVA J++ PERL VBSCRIPT VRML WIN32 WINSOCK

ONTOS

http://www.ontos.com

In cars, the name to remember is Rolls Royce. When it comes to database technology, the name to remember is Ontos. Ontos is the premier provider of object-oriented products and services for database management across the enterprise. Ontos provides object-based products and services that enable users to access, integrate, distribute, and manage information. The firm's products fall within a framework called the Ontos Virtual Information Architecture (Ontos VIA). Using Ontos VIA, users can access and integrate the enterprise's disparate data stores—stored in a variety of sources and formats. Visit the Web site for more information.

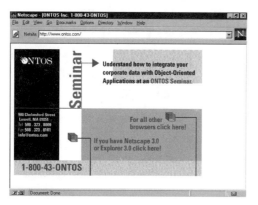

Figure 268.1 The Ontos Web site.

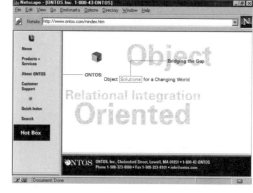

Figure 268.2 Ontos framed!

ORACLE CORPORATION

http://www.oracle.com/

Check out Oracle's new Workgroups Server demo! Download Oracle's WebServer 2.1 beta! Check on-line for Oracle OpenWorld details. As you probably know, Oracle is the world's largest independent provider of software and services for managing information. Current products include the noted *Oracle7* database engine and other products designed to help organizations of all kinds access and manipulate their business-critical information. Founded in 1977, with a vision of finding faster, less expensive ways of managing information, Oracle was the first to distribute products employing SQL, now the industry standard. Visit this Web site and test drive some software.

Figure 269 Oracle home page.

PICK SYSTEMS: DBMS FOR A MULTIDIMENSIONAL WORLD

http://www.picksys.com/

Saddam calls it the mother of all database systems. Pick Systems delivers multidimensional database technology enabling the development of practical, scalable, portable solutions. Pick's products include the *Multidimensional DBMS*, a multi-user and multitasking database-management system that fits real world data. A distinguishing characteristic of the *Multi-dimensional DBMS* is its ability to handle variable-length data, including multiple values and sub-values. When changes to the database occur, the DBMS lets you quickly and easily add fields to Pick files. Current versions of the software run on *AIX*, HP-UX, DG-UX, SCO UNIX, and *Microsoft MS-DOS*, as well as an *Advanced Pick/Protected Mode* for Intel hardware that requires no host operating system.

Figure 270.1 The Pick Web site.

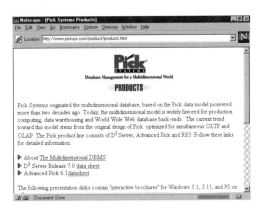

Figure 270.2 Pick products.

POET SOFTWARE: OBJECT DATABASES

http://www.poet.com/

Poet Software provides object-database solutions for desktop, groupware, and Internet applications. Their main product, *Poet*, is ideal for C++, Java, and OLE automation objects. *Poet* complies with the ODMG-93 object database standard, and runs on many platforms: Windows, Win95, Windows NT, NetWare, IntranetWare, OS/2, Macintosh, and UNIX. The *Poet Personal Edition SDK* is an entry-level system that allows affordable evaluation and prototyping. *Poet Professional Edition SDK* is a full client/server toolset for professional application development. Meanwhile, the *Poet Server* supports deployment of *Poet* applications.

Figure 271.1 The Poet Software Web site.

Figure 271.2 Poet products and services.

PROGRESS APPLICATION DEVELOPMENT ENVIRONMENT & RDBMS

http://www.progress.com/

The *Progress Application Development Environment* (ADE) is a complete, integrated set of object-oriented tools that give you the ability to build and deploy complete high-performance applications into a wide range of database environments. The *Progress RDBMS*, a component of *Progress ADE*, is a fully relational SQL-compliant database management system that runs on most UNIX, PC, and PC LAN operating systems, and delivers high performance for complex applications and large transaction volumes. Along with all this power, it is significantly easier to install, tune, and manage than its more expensive competitors. Visit the Progress Web pages for more information.

Figure 272.1 Progress home page.

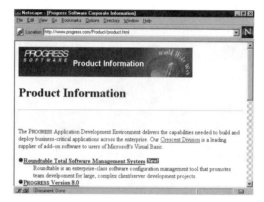

Figure 272.2 Progress products.

COMPARING PARADOX AND ACCESS

http://www.tietovayla.fi/borland/paradox/whitepap/pwvsacc.htm

So how do *Paradox* and *Access* compare? This site's author believes *Paradox* is much better. In fact, he believes it is more flexible, is closer to state-of-the-art productivity tools, is better for client/server installations, and generally surpasses the competition (most especially *Microsoft Access*). Perhaps he is right. Perhaps that is why *Paradox* is the fastest-growing corporate database standard for the Windows environment. Perhaps that is why corporations such as Bank of America, Chevron, and American Express are making *Paradox* the standard, claiming they love it for its stability and its ability to serve the needs of all corporate users. But, you'll find much more information at this site. Check it out.

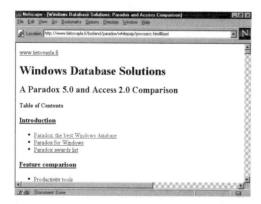

Figure 273.1 The white paper.

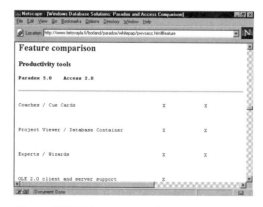

Figure 273.2 Feature comparison.

QUADBASE SQL SERVER

http:/www.quadbase.com/

What? You do database development without Quadbase SQL? Do you also ski blindfolded? Quadbase, founded in 1988, specializes in the area of open client/server SQL database-management systems and tools, and was one of the first firms to provide full-fledged SQL DBMS technology to PC users. Quadbase's main product, *Quadbase-SQL*, is a high-performance, full-featured, industrial strength SQL relational DBMS designed for mission-critical applications. The DBMS provides advanced features and query optimization techniques, and fully utilizes the symmetric multi-threading capability offered by Windows. The Netware and Windows NT versions also take advantage of asynchronous I/O to achieve optimum performance. Visit this site for technical support, product information, and free demo downloads.

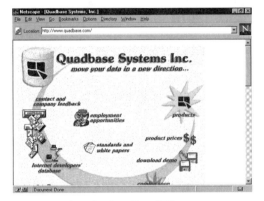

Figure 274.1 The Quadbase Web site.

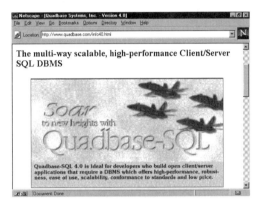

Figure 274.2 Quadbase products.

RAIMA: VELOCIS DATABASE SERVER

http://www.raima.com

Raima Corporation is an international developer of high-performance database tools. During the past ten years, more than 9,500 software companies have used Raima database engines in their commercial application software products and internal projects. Raima offers a suite of products and services designed to provide complete database developer flexibility and performance optimization. Professional C and C++ application developers worldwide use Raima database products in a wide range of commercial and line-of-business database applications. Raima's new generation ANSI SQL database engine, *Velocis Database Server*, is enjoying great popularity worldwide. Come to the site for more information, and for a free download of a *Velocis* demo.

Figure 275.1 The Raima Web site.

Figure 275.2 Raima products.

RVG CLIPPER COLLECTION—COOL CA-CLIPPER LINKS

http://asterix.urc.tue.nl/~rcrolf/cclinks.shtml

OK, *Clipper* developers, what is it you want? Shareware libraries? Newsgroups? Telnet sites? Web pages? Well, regardless of what you are looking for, it's a good bet that you will find it at this site. In addition, you will encounter newsletters, lists of frequently asked questions, *Clipper* patches, and usergroup Web sites. So far as shareware goes, how about "mousable" user-interface engines for *CA-Clipper*? How about a hot-link to the *SimTel Clipper* software repository? How about complete details on the *Blinker* linker, or a downloadable, shareware *Clipper Graphic Printing Library*? Or, how about a free demo of the *CodeColorizer* source code analyzer for *Clipper*? What are you waiting for? Click on the link and launch yourself into some cool stuff.

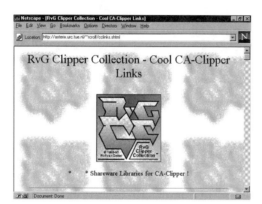

Figure 276.1 The RvG Clipper Web site.   *Figure 276.2 And what it offers.*

SOFTWARE AG

http://www.sagus.com/

Software AG's mission is to help you develop enterprise-wide, mission-critical applications that transform your information into a valuable, accessible, decision-making resource. Software AG will protect your considerable investment in information technology by allowing development and deployment across multiple platforms and by creating a solid foundation for current use and future-readiness. Visit the Software AG Web site for information on their *ADABAS* database-management product: a family of servers and add-on technologies that combine functionality with advanced, multi-platform data management. Learn how *ADABAS* can turn you into a database star within your organization.

Figure 277 Software AG.

SOLID INFORMATION TECHNOLOGY: FREE EVALUATION SOFTWARE

http://www.solid.fi/

Visit this site and get information on *Solid*, which is billed as "the industry's most powerful plug-and-play database server, offering cost-effective deployment and care-free maintenance." If you wish, you can download a free evaluation copy. Or, if you are already sold, you can order right on-line and receive a full license. The *Solid Server* is a care-free component DBMS for high-volume database applications, which is easy to embed and easy to administer, easy to distribute and easy to install. What is more, *Solid* is the first relational DBMS that is fully scalable from a standalone Windows notebook to symmetric multiprocessing and RISC UNIX environments. How is that for adaptability? Check it out.

Figure 278.1 The Solid Web site.

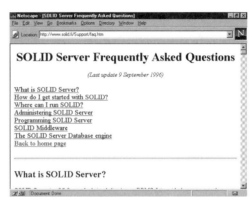

Figure 278.2 Solid FAQ.

SQL STANDARDS HOME PAGE

http://www.jcc.com/sql.stnd.html

This page provides a central clearinghouse for information about SQL (the structured query language). As such, this site is probably the best collection of SQL-related links to be found on the Web. You will find information on the current status of efforts to enhance SQL into a computationally complete language for the definition and management of persistent, complex objects. You will also find links to the key SQL standards committees around the world, details on NIST (National Institute of Standards and Testing) validation, and standard SQL publications and articles. Keith W. Hare maintains these useful pages, for which we owe him many thanks.

Figure 279.1 The SQL Standards home page.

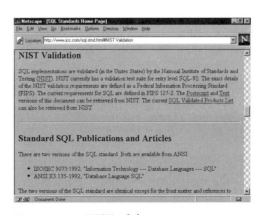

Figure 279.2 NIST validation.

280

SQL REFERENCE PAGE

http://www.contrib.andrew.cmu.edu/~shadow/sql.html

Assembled by Derrick Brashear, this remarkable set of SQL links include syntax information, programming resources, SQL software and tools, DBMS information, and more. You will find links to a catalog of free database software, a free download of Leroy Cain's *SQL parser*, remote database access protocols, RDA/SQL specialization protocols, and much more. Derrick warns, however, that he has not surveyed these resources for quality and variety. He has simply captured every link he could possibly find related to SQL. Some are bound to be more useful than others. And so it goes. The man can't do *all* our work for us, can he?

Figure 280.1 The SQL reference page.

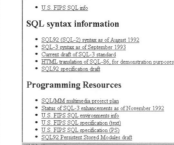

Figure 280.2 A few options.

281

SYBASE

http://www.sybase.com

Sybase is a worldwide leader in client/server software and services covering market requirements for on-line transaction processing (OLTP), data warehousing, mass deployment, and on-line electronic commerce. Sybase-branded products cover high-performance databases and middleware solutions, while their tools products are marked under the world-leading *Powersoft* brand. Visit this site for information (and demo downloads!) related to *Sybase System 11, Sybase SQL Server 11*, and more. Also, come to this site for *Sybase Magazine On-Line*, where you'll find the latest news, interviews, standards, discussions, tools, and customer profiles, along with late-breaking developments in enterprise computing in general.

Figure 281.1 The Sybase Web site.

Figure 281.2 What's new.

DATABASE PROGRAMMING

AI CAFÉ C/C++ CGI HTML HTTP JAVA J++ PERL VBSCRIPT VRML WIN32 WINSOCK 11001101001011110011011100110101010001100100100101

SYSDECO MIMER

http://www.mimer.se/

In Norse mythology, the giant Mimer stood guarding the well of wisdom, and the Gods came to him for information. This made Mimer the first information processing manager. Today, *Mimer* is an SQL-based relational database management system (RDBMS) developed by Sysdeco Mimer in Uppsala, Sweden. The *Mimer* database engine is a fast, robust, low price database handler providing high performance targeted at mission-critical client/server environments. And best of all, a new version compatible with Windows 95 has just been released! For complete details on *Mimer*, its attributes and tools, its installation and ease-of-use, visit the Sysdeco Mimer Web site.

Figure 282 Sysdeco Mimer.

THUNDERSTONE TEXT RETRIEVAL

http://www.thunderstone.com/

Thunderstone's flagship products, *Metamorph* and *Texis,* provide the most comprehensive set of text retrieval tools available. To date, Thunderstone has issued more than 400,000 licenses for database applications such as those supporting litigation support, competitive intelligence, help desk functions, document management, Internet databases, and real-time message handling. You will find Thunderstone tools in *WordPerfect,* the *Dow-Jones News Retrieval* search engine, and the Web database of *The Japan Times.* Come to Thunderstone's Web site for great demos that include Web content and category searches that are lightning fast.

Figure 283.1 Thunderstone home page.

Figure 283.2 Thunderstone products.

TM1 SOFTWARE

http://tm1.com/

TM1 develops on-line analytical processing (OLAP) database software products which progressive companies use world-wide to enhance insight and competitive advantage during planning and analysis. TM1 software enables users to share information and collaborate throughout a project. As users input numbers, results are available to everyone in real-time. No waiting for an answer. Everyone stays focused, moving toward the goal of making the right decision. Firms using TM1 products include AT&T, Hewlett Packard, BMW, Bristol Myers, Exxon, Pepsi Cola, Blockbuster, and Mercedes Benz. Strategic partners include Hyperion Software, IQ Software, and Platinum Software. Visit this site for more information.

Figure 284.1 The TM1 Web site.

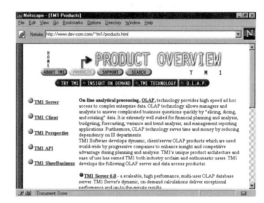

Figure 284.2 Products.

UNIDATA: DATA MANAGEMENT THAT WORKS

http://www.unidata.com/

Unidata enables businesses worldwide to develop sophisticated new applications and to effectively leverage legacy applications within open systems environments. How? Through easy integration of existing applications through Unidata's next-generation nested RDBMS. Only Unidata delivers the "total business solution" that moves existing application business logic intact to virtually any environment you use today or may use tomorrow. Unidata products include numerous system builder application tools in an integrated toolset. Visit this site for more information, product details, white papers, technical support, and lots more.

Figure 285.1 The Unidata Web site.

Figure 285.2 Software products.

UNISQL

http://www.unisql.com/

UniSQL is a leading provider of object-relational data-management technology for today's most complex client/server applications. Used by major engineering, telecommunications, healthcare, manufacturing, and defense organizations, the *UniSQL server* manages complex data far better, faster, and cheaper than relational systems. Products include the ODMG-compliant *UniSQL C++ Interface* and the ODMG-based *UniSQL Smalltalk Interface*. Visit the Web page for extensive information on all products, as well as white papers, tech support, partner-relationship information, demos, and much more of interest to people involved with the object-relational model.

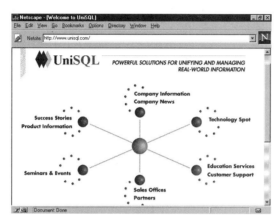

Figure 286 UniSQL's Web site.

VIRTUAL FOXPRO USER GROUP

http://205.205.57.1/vfug

The *Virtual FoxPro* User Group (VFUG) is an international multi-lingual *FoxPro* usergroup on-line around-the-clock seven days a week, 24-hours a day. VFUG is a non-profit organization for *FoxPro* and *Visual FoxPro* enthusiasts. At this site, you can exchange views, information, and tips, as well as find answers to your questions from *FoxPro* experts and developers from all over the world. If your country or city does not have a *FoxPro* usergroup, VFUG is your chance to become a part of one anyway. Membership includes regularly scheduled virtual meetings, a great electronic newsletter, and all the other benefits of belonging to the typical user group. Check it out.

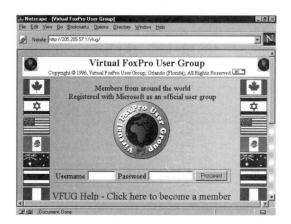

Figure 287 Virtual FoxPro User Group.

VISUAL FOXPRO YELLOW PAGES

http://205.205.57.1/foxpro/

Visit this site for a full, searchable library of downloadable *FoxPro* developer tools, free electronic newsletters for *FoxPro* users and developers, job listings in *FoxPro* for developers, useful code snippets, listings of independent *FoxPro* developers and consultants, and much more. If you are a developer, you may also, by the way, list your services at this site and add a link to your home page. The *Developer Tools Library* includes *DataExport* (for adding an export feature to a *FoxPro* database) and *DataImport* (for importing *FoxPro* database information to spreadsheets), *DBFtrieve* (for *Btrieve* access from *FoxPro*), and much more.

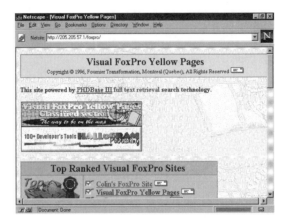

Figure 288 The Yellow Pages.

VMARK

http://www.vmark.com/

Founded in 1984, VMark is a leading provider of client/server database software and services. One of the top 100 software companies in the world, Vmark's products include the *UniVerse RDBMS* server, *HyperSTar* object-messaging middleware, and *ObjectStudio*, an object-oriented application development tool. The *UniVerse RBMS* server features operating system-friendly architecture, aggressive SQL support, a range of durability features, distributed processing optimization, nested transactions, and support for "document-centric" application development. Visit the VMark site for more information.

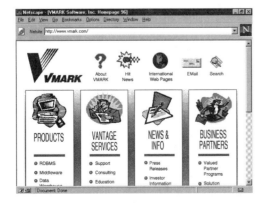

Figure 289.1 VMark's Web site.

Figure 289.2 VMark products.

AI CAFÉ C/C++ CGI HTML HTTP JAVA J++ PERL VBSCRIPT VRML WIN32 WINSOCK 110011010010111100110111001101010100011001100100101

AEROSOFT: DELPHI TAUTOBUTTON COMPONENT

http://www.aerosoft.com.au/delphi/

TAutoButton allows Delphi programmers to easily create a button using two bitmaps. *TAutoButton* is comprised of two distinct components, each of which is available in both 16- and 32-bit versions. One is a component with a masking capability, and the other is one which has the ability to make the button flash. But wait! That's not all! Another component lives on this server. It is called *TProgman* and it lets you add program groups and items to the program manager. All three components are very easy to use and require minimal programming. Visit the Web page for more information and a download of these three great freeware components.

Figure 290.1 The Aerosoft Web site.

Figure 290.2 Product details.

AI CAFÉ C/C++ CGI HTML HTTP JAVA J++ PERL VBSCRIPT VRML WIN32 WINSOCK 110011010010111100110111001101010100011001100100101

APIARY: OCX EXPERT

http://www.apiary.com/

Apiary is a leading provider of component software and development tools for the Windows desktop and client/server environments. Apiary's customers are independent programmers, software development companies, system integrators, and corporate information shops. Their most popular product is *OCX Expert*, which converts Borland Delphi 2.0 Visual Component Libraries (VCLs) into portable OLE controls quickly and painlessly. In fact, *OCX Expert* is probably the fastest and easiest way available to create high-performance 32-bit OLE controls using Delphi. Before *OCX Expert* you had to use C++ and the MFC. And, guess what? Not everyone wants to work with C++ and MFC. Some of us like to go *home* every once in a while.

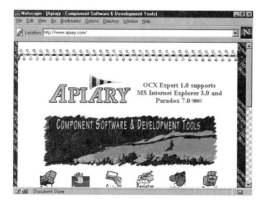

Figure 291.1 Apiary's Web site.

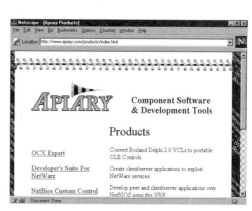

Figure 291.2 Product information.

ArGo Software Design

http://www.interlog.com/~argosoft

ArGo prides itself on creating outstanding Internet components for Delphi. ArGo's most popular item is *The Internet Mail Suite*, a native Delphi package. The folks at ArGo are also quite proud of *TValidator*, which lets you dial phone numbers from within Delphi applications. ArGo invites you to download a copy of the *Suite,* along with other programs. These products are so popular for many reasons, including low price, high reliability and stability, good technical support, frequent updates, full computability with Internet standards and, what is most important, all registered versions include full source code. Most components are available for both 16- and 32-bit platforms. Need I say more? Check it out.

Figure 292.1 The ArGo home page.

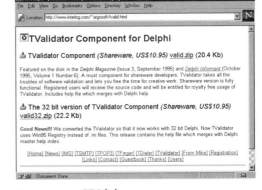

Figure 292.2 TValidator.

Big Wave Dave's Delphi Destination

http://www.lava.net/~drmcderm/

Big Wave Dave McDermitt hails from Hawaii and has assembled an excellent repository of information about Delphi programming. At this site, you will find links to on-line Delphi publications, Delphi newsgroups, Delphi component archives, and much more. One great component you'll find at this site is *TSmiley*, by Nick Hodges. If you're interested in getting into component writing, *TSmiley* is a great place to start. You'll also find another great download, *King Calendar*, which is a set of 15 calendar-oriented components that make adding calendar functionality to your applications a snap! Check out Big Wave Dave's pages for more information. Way cool, Big Wave Dave!

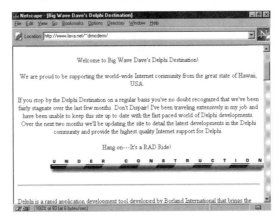

Figure 293 Big Wave Dave's page.

AI CAFÉ C/C++ CGI HTML HTTP JAVA J++ PERL VBSCRIPT VRML WIN32 WINSOCK 11001101001011110011011100110101010001100110010101

CALITZ BROTHERS DELPHI PAGE

http://ourworld.compuserve.com/homepages/calitz/

The Calitz Brothers provide files, components, answers to frequently asked questions, links to other Delphi and shareware sites, their own carefully-culled directory of "must have" shareware, Windows 95 programming tricks, and tips, and more. The Calitz Brothers custom components help you generate and print (or preview) professional looking reports, files, forms, and windows in minutes. You'll find components that can help you reduce your development time dramatically. In most cases, less than 10 lines of code are all you need! Using these components, creating complex reports is as easy as setting the properties of existing forms or grids and printing. Visit this site and check out demo versions. Best of all, you will also find that the demos come complete with source code!

Figure 294.1 Calitz Brothers home page.

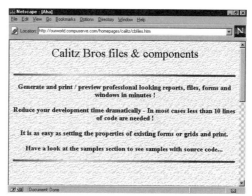

Figure 294.2 Files and components.

AI CAFÉ C/C++ CGI HTML HTTP JAVA J++ PERL VBSCRIPT VRML WIN32 WINSOCK 11001101001011110011011100110101010001100110010101

COMPONENT CREATE DEMO DOWNLOAD

http://www.compcreate.com/

Component Create, from Potomac Software, is one of the best tools you can use to create reusable code within Delphi applications. In fact, *Component Create* is probably the easiest way on the planet to create Delphi components. Programmers at American Express, Amtrak, AT&T, BASF, and PPG Industries rely on *Component Create* within their applications. The software multiplies programmer productivity by handling the drudge work, and freeing programmers to concentrate on the functionality of their new components. In short, to use *Component Create*, you point and click your mouse to set up the component. In return, you get quality, commented Pascal code. You can think of this process as the definition of "cyber-luxury." Visit this site and download a demo.

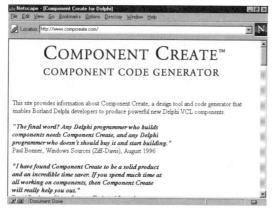

Figure 295 The Component Create Web site.

DASTECH: DOWNLOAD FREE EVALUATION SOFTWARE

http://www.dastech.com/

DASTech specializes in providing world class native Delphi components and products for the Windows 3.1, Windows NT, and Windows 95 environments. For example, DASTech provides Delphi TCP/IP networking components which simplify building distributed applications. Using DASTech components, programmers using Delphi 1.0 or 2.0 can quickly create outstanding client/server applications. To get a better feel for these components, visit this site and download an evaluation copy of *DelSock 2.0*, the 32-bit Delphi component for Windows NT and Windows 95. Visit this site for more information.

Figure 296.1 DASTech home page.

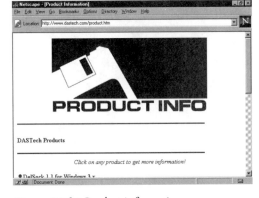

Figure 296.2 Product information.

DEATHSTROKE'S ALL-NEW HOME PAGE

http://www.infose.com/jerome/delphi.html

Relax. Take it easy. Be cool. That's what Jerome, your host at these pages, is doing. "OK," he writes, "this page might be small, but it's a CONTENT page." This Web site focuses on information, not links. Jerome features his own source code and articles, as well as code others have written for him. In addition, Jerome uncovers interesting things he has encountered in newsgroups. According to Jerome, the site's purpose is to provide a location where he can look when he forgets how to do something. Later on he adds, "Yes, I wrote components. Yes, sources are available. Yes, you can download 'em." Plus, he explains how to hide an application so that it doesn't appear in the Taskbar, and other neat tricks. Thanks, Jerome.

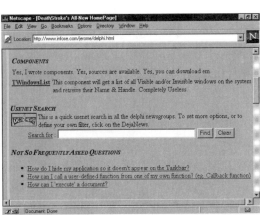

Figure 297 Components? I'll show you components!

AI CAFÉ C/C++ CGI HTML HTTP JAVA J++ PERL VBSCRIPT VRML WIN32 WINSOCK 110011010010111100110111001101010100011001100100101

THE DELPHI COMPANION

http://www.xs4all.nl/~dgb/delphi.html

The Delphi Companion is a fabulous Web clearinghouse for information and links related to Delphi books, articles, components, databases, frequently asked questions, FTP sites, patches, jobs, and usergroups. This site includes book review pages hosted by the Delphi Northbay Special Interest Group (SIG), as well as independent reviews of books from publishers such as Que, Borland/Sams, M&T, Addison-Wesley, Coriolis Group, Waite Group Press, Ventana Press, Osborne/McGraw Hill, IDG Books and, oh yes, Jamsa Press, which not only publishes some cool books on programming, but also my best-selling book *Net Worth: a Guide to Maximizing Wealth with the Internet*. The Delphi Companion's "articles file" is also especially valuable and includes, for example, links to on-line re-prints of every Delphi-related article ever to appear in *PC Week*.

Figure 298.1 The Delphi Companion Web site.

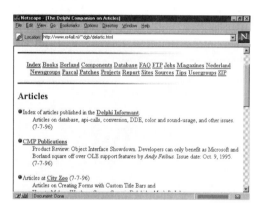

Figure 298.2 Delphi Companion articles.

AI CAFÉ C/C++ CGI HTML HTTP JAVA J++ PERL VBSCRIPT VRML WIN32 WINSOCK 110011010010111100110111001101010100011001100100101

DELPHI DEVELOPER'S JOURNAL

http://www.cobb.com/ddj/

Visit this site for great sample articles from the Cobb Group's *Delphi Developer's Journal*. For example, you will learn how to use the *dbiRegisterCallback* routine, a relatively unknown and under-used function in the Borland Database Engine (BDE). Or, master the Zen of how multiple threads can help you, where you might use them, and the basics of how to use them from within Delphi. Or . . . well, you get the picture. You may also subscribe to the *Journal* right on-line, which will immediately give you complete, unrestricted access to the entire rich information base that is the electronic edition of the *Delphi Developer's Journal*. This useful site comes to you from the Cobb Group, leaders in the field of literature for and by programmers.

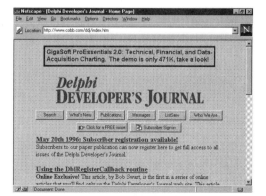

Figure 299.1 The Journal home page.

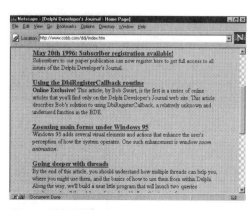

Figure 299.2 What's new.

300

THE DELPHI DELI

http://www.intermid.com/delphi/

Welcome to the Delphi Deli, where you can enjoy a meal of Delphi components, links, hints, tips, book reviews, and more. Learn, for example, how to write a *Poor Man's Internet Graphics Viewer (PIGViewer)*. Download (or upload!) components and "Delphi-Done-It" applications. Check out a cool collection of frequently asked questions. Check out a great article and demo program on using Colin Wilson's *keyboard.dcu* component. You will also find some cool screen resolution components as well. While you are there, master the Zen of looping .MID and .WAV files with *TMediaplayer* using John Pullen's *Roller* component. And, get the scoop on boxes, dialogs, resolution fixers, instance checkers, and enhancers. And that, my friends, is just the first course.

Figure 300.1 The Delphi Deli.

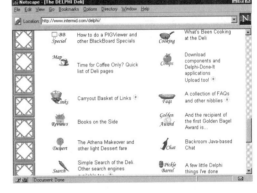

Figure 300.2 Some menu options.

301

THE DELPHI EXCHANGE

http://www.cswnet.com/~choate/dex/

The Delphi Exchange provides a splendid collection of resources. Visit this site for more than 420 Delphi-related Web links, as well as connections to development toolboxes, component file archives, lists of frequently asked questions, newsgroups, and more. You will also get a virtual Delphi classroom, a Delphi "newbie" page, an on-line Help center, on-line catalogs of Delphi-related materials, and even a Delphi job bank. The site also features regularly updated Delphi developer news. By the way, the chat page requires that you have a Java browser and that you turn the Java support on. The site has established a schedule for chat times and encourages your attendance during those times, but the facility is always available.

Figure 301.1 The Delphi Exchange.

Figure 301.2 On-line chat.

AI CAFÉ C/C++ CGI HTML HTTP JAVA J++ PERL VBSCRIPT VRML WIN32 WINSOCK 1100110100101111001101110011010101000110011001001 01

THE DELPHI HACKERS' CORNER

http://www.it.kth.se/~ao/DHC/

Anders Ohlsson maintains The Delphi Hackers' Corner. In addition to providing a fantastic set of Delphi-related links, he also invites you to download some great software. He's got a screensaver called *DoubleVision*, an application launcher (including Delphi source code) called *AppLaunch*, and a calendar program named *YACPU*. You will also find links to Delphi newsgroups, important Delphi client/server patches, desktop patches, *Visual Component Library* (VCL) source patches, and more. You will also get some neat demos including some that show you how to make a floating toolbar, use multiple status bars in different forms, move and resize a panel in run-time using your mouse, change cursors, and use a timer. Take time to check out the Delphi Hackers' Corner.

Figure 302 Delphi Hackers' Corner.

AI CAFÉ C/C++ CGI HTML HTTP JAVA J++ PERL VBSCRIPT VRML WIN32 WINSOCK 110011010010111100110111001101010100011001100100101

DELPHI INFORMANT MAGAZINE

http://www.informant.com/delphi/di_index.HTM

Delphi Informant Magazine received the 1995 Computer Press Rookie of the Year Runner-Up Award, so you know it's good. Visit this site for Delphi news and announcements, sample articles, file libraries, and a great set of links to all the best Delphi sites on the Web. You can read about and download *Delphi Finger*, an Internet Finger utility that just happens to let you add Winsock capability to Delphi applications. Examine and download *ReportSmith*, a robust reporting tool that lets you build powerful, complex reports featuring graphs, drill-downs, live data pivoting, and more. Then, learn how to implement Windows 95 and Windows NT multithreading capabilities within your Delphi 2 programs. All this and more awaits you at *Delphi Informant Magazine*. Very good stuff.

Figure 303.1 The Delphi Informant Web site.   *Figure 303.2 Sample articles.*

DELPHI INFORMATION CONNECTION

http://www.delphi32.com

What will you find at the Delphi Information Connection? The better question is: What won't you find? This site is packed with Delphi resources, links, component files you can download, and more. You will also encounter a Delphi beginners corner, Delphi publications, Delphi tips and tricks, the *Unofficial Delphi On-Line Newsletter*, Delphi newsgroups, and much more. The Component Files alone incorporate hundreds of files related to Winsock/Internet, clock/calendar displays, networks/ communication, editing, data and reports, tables and grids, buttons and panels, graphics and multi-media, game programming, installation, and registration. This site is your one-stop shop for every component and every bit of Delphi information you will ever need.

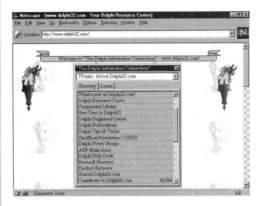

Figure 304.1 The Connection.

Figure 304.2 What's new.

DELPHI MAGAZINE

http://members.aol.com/delphimag/

Each issue of *Delphi Magazine* is packed with Delphi components, articles, technical reviews, and source code examples designed to help you get the most out of Delphi. The magazine's goal is to cater to the professional Delphi developer with solid, in-depth articles to which they will keep referring for months to come. *Delphi Magazine's* team of authors includes some of the most experienced and knowledgeable Delphi developers in the world. Subscribers from more than 40 countries are already enjoying *Delphi Magazine*. At this Web site, you will find great sample columns from the magazine along with back-issue contents, the table of contents for the current issue, subscription information, and more.

Figure 305.1 The Delphi Magazine Web site.

Figure 305.2 The Book Review Database.

AI CAFÉ C/C++ CGI HTML HTTP JAVA J++ PERL VBSCRIPT VRML WIN32 WINSOCK 1100110100101111001101110011010101000110011001001011

DELPHI POWER PAGE (FREE SOFTWARE)

http://www.jt.w1.com/

This site offers you hundreds of shareware tools and components developed by and for Delphi. All of the files are in zip format and contain a help file. An example of the valuable stuff you'll find in the Delphi Power Page is *Component Builder*, available in both 16- and 32-bit versions. *Component Builder* eliminates a lot of the drudgery of typing the code needed to define a new component. Using *Component Builder*, you describe the properties, methods, and event and message handlers you need. Then, you set the appropriate attributes for scope and dispatch, and *Component Builder* generates the source code complete with underlying variable declarations and procedure and function skeletons. If you're new to component writing, this utility can help you through the learning curve. Don't miss this site.

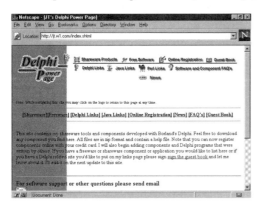

Figure 306.1 The Power Page.

Figure 306.2 Delphi resources.

AI CAFÉ C/C++ CGI HTML HTTP JAVA J++ PERL VBSCRIPT VRML WIN32 WINSOCK 1100110100101111001101110011010100011001100100101

DELPHI SUPER PAGE: SHAREWARE/FREEWARE COMPONENTS

http://sunsite.icm.edu.pl/delphi/index.html

Proudly created and maintained in Poland, the Delphi Super Page is an excellent, extensive collection of links which the Webmasters update with new files almost every day! The pages are filled with shareware and freeware you can download, which include such items as components that export data in a format you can easily import into SQL server databases, components that encapsulate the *SHBrowseForFolder* interface (thus allowing Win32 users to select a directory using the standard Explorer-like directory-tree dialog-box view), components that create Winhelp files, components that display 3-dimensional labels, and much more. You will find literally hundreds of shareware/freeware components to choose from. A great resource.

Figure 307 The Delphi Super Page.

308

DesignSystems: Home of User Interface Gizmos for Delphi

http://www.oz.net/dsig/

The goal of DesignSystems is to create components that help the Delphi community create better applications. "We want to make developing in Delphi more productive and more fun," they write. "Underlying our philosophy is the simple idea that we can delight the people that use our products by focusing on making their tasks easier. We hope that you will be delighted by our products and that your application design efforts become more delightful to those that use them." Be sure to check out *DSAppLock*, DesignSystems' component-based application protection for Delphi, which is one of the best new Delphi tools you'll find anywhere. The software achieves the DesignSystems' goal.

Figure 308.1 The DesignSystems Web site.

Figure 308.2 What's new.

309

Dr. Bob's Delphi Clinic

http://home.pi.net/~drbob/

Dr. Bob's clinic includes the latest Delphi news, updates and announcements, articles, and reviews (updated about once a week), and more. Dr. Bob's particular interest, however, is in Common Gateway Interface (CGI) applications written in Delphi 2.01. Dr. Bob invites you to download gobs of shareware and freeware including Version 2.01 of Dr. Bob's *Collection of Delphi Experts* (available in both 16- and 32-bit versions). This shareware collection consists of 12 different IDE experts, in more than 18 different types and forms. New software at the site includes the *ProgMan Expert*, with which you can turn the current project target into an icon in a Windows 3.x Program Manager group (or Windows 95 desktop folder). Thank you, Doctor Bob!

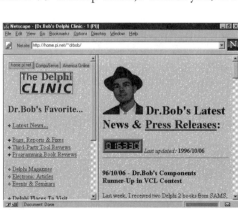

Figure 309.1 The Delphi Clinic.

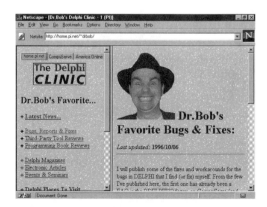

Figure 309.2 Bug reports and fixes.

GUERNSEY SOFTWARE COMPANY

http://www.scruz.net/~daley/

Guernsey Software, founded in 1995, is dedicated to distributing quality client/server and database software. "Until there is motivation to do otherwise," they write, "we are focusing our development efforts on writing components for Delphi." Their current product line includes a set of components, including *DirectODBC*, which is a set of ten components that provides direct access to Open Database Connectivity Interface (ODBC) sources. Using these components, you will no longer need to configure both BDE and ODBC. Likewise, you won't have to worry about re-distributing BDE. In addition, you have a choice of which vendor's ODBC driver you want to use. What a concept!

Figure 310.1 The Guernsey Web site.   *Figure 310.2 DirectODBC.*

HIGH GEAR NATIVE VCL COMPONENTS FOR DELPHI

http://www.high-gear.com/

Released in the autumn of 1996, *High Gear 2.0* is "awesome" (as the Woz would say). *High Gear 2.0* is a set of 30+ native VCL components for Delphi which include a database grid with state-of-the-art features that include: 3-D appearance and in-cell graphics, memo combo box, lookup combo box, and check box. Another component provides image support for the GIF file format. While other components offer MAPI (message application program interface) support that lets you enable e-mail within your applications, these components use MAPI to establish, use, and later terminate an e-mail session. Visit this Web site for more information on *High Gear 2.0.*

Figure 311 High Gear's Web site.

312

KINETIC SOFTWARE'S DELPHI COMPONENTS (DOWNLOAD DEMOS)

http://www.esper.com/kinetic/delphi.html

Kinetic Software offers a very cool collection of native Delphi components. The company offers each of its packages as native 16-bit or 32-bit components. Find out about *KSCalendar Date Kits, KSTransForm, KSPicButton, KSDirectPlay,* and the *Kinetic Card Game Development Kit.* The *KSTransForm* application is a Pascal Delphi component that you will want to use in every Delphi project you build in the future! From its amazing toolbars and awesome *About* boxes to beautiful custom windows, the *KSTransFrom* component gives you amazing control over your forms. Just drop a *KSTransForm* component on a Delphi form and you are set. Visit this Web site and download a demo of this and other packages.

Figure 312.1 The Kinetic Web site.

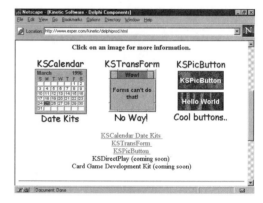

Figure 312.2 The components.

313

ANN LYNNWORTH'S DELPHI COMPONENTS AND UTILITIES

http://super.sonic.net/ann/delphi/cgicomp/

Ann Lynnworth has developed some great shareware Delphi components and utilities. If you want a quick glimpse of her software, visit this site and check out the on-line demos. Or, download the software itself which includes a component that helps you write to *stdout* and read HTML form data. You will also encounter other components that enable electronic mail under CGI control, create charts from live data, let you use the First Virtual Internet payment system for credit card charges from your Web site, create Delphi statistics for Web traffic analysis, and convert graphics. The site also includes ample applications (with source code), and lots of hints and tips on CGI programming using Delphi 2.0 and *stdin/stdout* (not *cgi-win*). Thanks, Ann, for the great software.

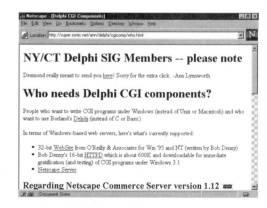

Figure 313.1 Lynnworth's Web site.

Figure 313.2 Who needs 'em?

MICROGOLD SOFTWARE: WITH CLASS DEMO DOWNLOAD

http://www.microgold.com/

Microgold's *With Class* is one of the easiest object-oriented analysis and design tools on the market, and it is fully compatible with Delphi. Visit the Microgold site and download a demo of either the 16- or 32-bit versions. You'll get 30 classes for 30 days. *With Class 3.1 Enterprise Edition* features reverse engineering, diagramming, and more. You can create a text specification for a system, class, attributes, operations, states, and transitions. You can also create a textual data dictionary and generate custom reports. And, you can import/export source code for C++ and Delphi. But, you won't know the full benefits of *With Class* until you've tried it. Remember, the demo is free, so you have nothing to lose. Check it out.

Figure 314 *The Microgold Web site.*

MIKE MARS'S DELPHI LINKS

http://www.webcom.com/mikemars/mikedelf.html

This site features dozens of Delphi-related links including those to *Chami CodeColorizer, Graphical Magick Productions, Digital Metaphor's Piparti Report Designer, DFL Software, Peter DeRanter's Delphi Page*, and more. You will also get links to newsgroups, on-line magazines and journals, component archives, third-party developers, sources for otherwise "undocumented" hints and tips, and even Michel Brazeu's *Spider Containers for Object Pascal*. You will also encounter international sites from Finland, Germany, Japan, and more. Thank you, Mike Mars, for a very useful resource.

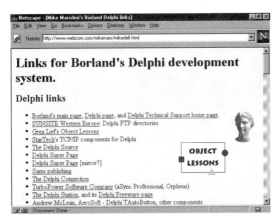

Figure 315 *The links.*

RAIZE COMPONENTS FOR DELPHI FREE TRIAL EDITION

http://www.raize.com/

Raize Software Solutions is pleased to offer you a free trial edition of *Raize Components for Delphi*. As is customary in most trial versions of Delphi components, the components in this trial edition are identical to those you will find in the released versions except that they are only available while Delphi is running. But hey, it is worth it for the free test drive, right? Specifically, we are talking about over 40 Delphi components, all of which have been designed for both 16- and 32-bit development. So, whether you are developing for Windows 3.1, Windows 95, or Windows NT, Raize will give you the edge you've been looking for. Check it out.

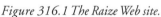

Figure 316.1 The Raize Web site.   *Figure 316.2 Raize products.*

SCIENTIFIC GRAPH COMPONENT (DOWNLOAD IT NOW!)

http://www.ee.princeton.edu/~phmertz/scigraph/scigraph.html

The *Scientific Graph Component for Delphi* plots arrays of numbers. Because the plots display coordinates, can easily zoom and pan, and allow users to measure the distances between points quickly, the plots are very user friendly. For developers, the component is easy to manipulate. In fact, the component comes with a help file which you can integrate into the Delphi environment with just one instruction. The component supports multiple plots, incremental plotting, chart recording, AutoScale toggling, and font and color properties. The site invites you to download the shareware, but you have to register before you'll get the source code. A powerful tool.

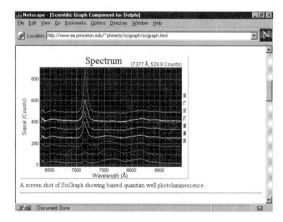

Figure 317 A sample.

AI CAFÉ C/C++ CGI HTML HTTP JAVA J++ PERL VBSCRIPT VRML WIN32 WINSOCK 110011010010111100110110011010100011001100100101

SILICON COMMANDER GAMES & DELPHI RESOURCES

http://www.silicmdr.com/delph.htm

Silicon Commander offers *TurboSprite 32* for Delphi 2.0. This set of components provides the easiest and most flexible way for Delphi developers to get started with *WinG* (a small freeware library provided by Microsoft that lets Windows programs achieve the graphic performance required by arcade-style games). The primary drawing surface of *TurboSprite 32* uses the *WING32* library to render Device Independent Bitmaps (DIBs). The package includes sprite management, collision detection, and full color-palette control. Silicon Commander invites you to download an evaluation copy of *TurboSprite 32*, along with a small *TurboSprite* demo program. They also invite you to view source code for some *TurboSprite*-derived classes.

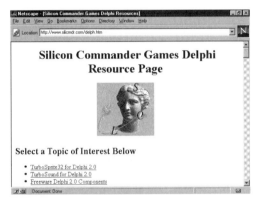

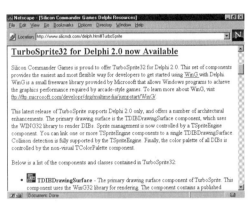

Figure 318.1 Silicon Commander.   *Figure 318.2 TurboSprite 32.*

AI CAFÉ C/C++ CGI HTML HTTP JAVA J++ PERL VBSCRIPT VRML WIN32 WINSOCK 110011010010111100110110011010101000110011001001011

TADDA! — TORONTO AREA DELPHI DEVELOPERS ASSOCIATION

http://www.tadda.com/

TaDDA is one of the largest Delphi user groups in the world. In addition, these folks have put together a very nice set of Web pages. You will find news about the organization, meeting schedules, and membership details. You will also get a great set of links to vendors, magazines, popular Delphi sites, consultants, and more. You'll also find links to component libraries, sample Delphi applications, 16- and 32-bit tutorials, white papers, technical support, Delphi authors, publishers of books about Delphi programming, and direct links to Borland's own on-line support facility. In short, TaDDA provides the very best and most authoritative Delphi documentation to be found anywhere. Thanks, Toronto!

Figure 319 TaDDa home page.

320

TCOMPRESS COMPONENT SET V2.5: FREE DOWNLOAD

http://www.spis.co.nz/compress.htm

TCompress Component Set V2.5 provides native Delphi components for the creation of multi-file compressed archives, as well as database, file, and in-memory compression using Delphi streams. The component has two compression methods (RLE and LZH) built in, with hooks for the easy addition of custom compression formats. In addition, the component supports compressed file protection using keys. Also, *TCompress* includes drop-n-plan components for automatic database, image and memory compression, based on Delphi's *TBDMemo* and *TBDImage* components. You will find that many images compress up to 98%, which provides massive savings in disk space, as well as reducing the file's download time across networks. Valuable software!

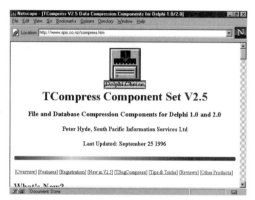

Figure 320.1 The TCompress Web site.

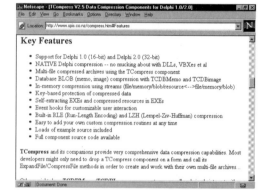

Figure 320.2 Key features.

321

THE TEMPLE OF DELPHI

http://www.coast.net/~jkeller/

Visit the Temple of Delphi, the site which invites you to praise and give homage to Borland's Delphi. The Temple has many chambers, all maintained by the Temple Monks who serve as Webmasters. The Main Chamber houses hundreds of components you can download. The Prophecy Chamber holds scrolls on which you'll find recorded what's been added to the Temple lately, and what will be added soon. The Monk's Chamber holds scrolls that introduce you to the Temple Monks. You will also find Delphi-related job listings, component reviews, technical information, lists of frequently asked questions, and links to other temples. Check it out.

Figure 321 The Temple.

AI CAFÉ C/C++ CGI HTML HTTP JAVA J++ PERL VBSCRIPT VRML WIN32 WINSOCK 110011010010111100110111001101010100011001100100101

WOLL2WOLL SOFTWARE FOR DELPHI (DOWNLOAD A DEMO)

http://www.woll2woll.com/

Delphi Informant Magazine recently named Woll2Woll Software's *InfoPower 2.0* for Delphi the 1996 Reader's Choice Product of the Year. Available in 16- and 32-bit versions (with and without source code), *InfoPower* gives Delphi programmers the power to define a data entry template with masks for the values users can enter into a form's fields. The software also lets programmers give end-users the ability to visually filter a table or query, or modify the *where* clause of an existing SQL statement. *InfoPower* also lets programmers give end-users the ability to easily and quickly increment or decrement numeric and date values by clicking the mouse button or by pressing the *up*-and-*down* cursor arrow keys. Best yet, you will discover much more.

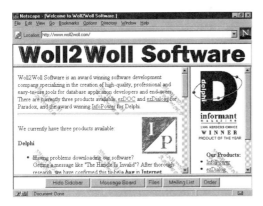

Figure 322.1 The Woll2Woll Web site.

Figure 322.2 InfoPower information.

ADDITIONAL DELPHI PROGRAMMING RESOURCES

Brant's Delphi Programming Page
URL: *http://bbs.roxboro.net/burnett/INDEX.HTM*

Eric's Delphi Links
URL: *http://www.inconnect.com/~ehuber/lks_dlph.htm*

Instant Delphi Programming
URL: *http://www.bsb.de/20/6/7/250084e.html*

DCU Store for Delphi Programmers. Delphi Tips &
URL: *http://www.wi.euv-frankfurt-o.de/~anke/Delphi.html*

DELPHI-L: Delphi Programming List
URL: *http://tile.net/LISTSERV/delphildelphi.html*

Mount Parnassus - Programming Tips
URL: *http://www.users.dircon.co.uk/~smithjt/tips.html*

The Unofficial Newsletter of Delphi User
URL: *http://www.doit.com/delphi/undu/dn0501g.htm*

Ask the Delphi Pro Book Review Capsules
URL: *http://www.inquiry.com/techtips/delphi_pro/books.html*

323

3-D SITE

http://www.3-Dsite.com/

This site features everything and anything about 3-D graphics for games and other things that go bump in the night. You will encounter *Talent Hunter* (the world's first truly interactive job board!), a series of weekly real-time panels on the topics of computer gaming and computer animation in 3-D, *Model Market* (a 3-D model store based on voluntary contributions), and a great bulletin board where game programmers and 3-D graphics programmers can chew the virtual fat. If you are looking to hire a 3-D game programmer or want to be hired as one, this is the spot. Likewise, if you want to connect with the folks at Sega and show them your great new creation, *3-D Site* is probably the place to do it. Good luck.

Figure 323 The 3-D Site Web site.

324

ACTIVISION

http://www.activision.com/

As one of the industry's first independent, third-party software developers (for Atari, Nintendo, and SEGA), ActiVision survived the interactive-video industry's initial rise and fall to become a leader in the field of interactive multimedia entertainment. The company not only survived, but resurfaced with an enviable line-up of titles and tremendous brand equity, including the Infocom list of 31 text adventures and the *Pitfall, Kaboom,* and *River Raid* series of action games. Today ActiVision is a diversified international developer and publisher of interactive multimedia entertainment software dedicated to delivering the highest levels of entertainment, production value, and technical sophistication. Visit their Web pages for more information, including job opportunities.

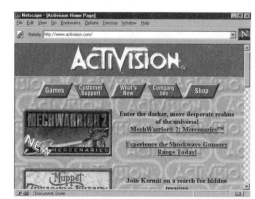

Figure 324.1 ActiVision home page.

Figure 324.2 A few of the games.

THE ADRENALINE VAULT: SHAREWARE GAMES ARCHIVE

http://www.avault.com/

OK, so you are tired of polymorphism, 3-D transformations, and light projections. Take a break and find new motivation by checking out the graphics in this site's unending list of video games. You can choose from among hundreds of games available for download: *Abuse, Admiral Sea Battles, Afterlife, Air Warrior, American Civil War, Amok, Anvil of Dawn, Apache, Archimedean Dynasty, Azrael's Tear, Ballblazer Champions, Battlecruiser 3000 A.D., Battle Island 2220, Bedlam, Big Red Racing, Birthright: The Gorgon's Alliance, Blood & Magic, Blast Chamber, Caesar 2, Capitalism, Chasm, Chaos Overlords, CyberJudas,* and *CyberMage: Darklight Awakening*. And that is just *A* through *C*, if you catch my drift.

Figure 325.1 The Adrenaline Vault Web site.

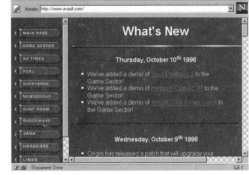

Figure 325.2 What's new.

COMPUTER GAMING MAGAZINE FROM ZIFF-DAVIS

http://www.zdnet.com/gaming/

At this site, you will find the Web edition of Ziff-Davis' fantastic *Computer Gaming* magazine. This Web edition features reviews and demos, as well as industry news you simply will not find anywhere else. You get detailed reviews of such games as *Paintball, Fire Fight, Virtual Fighter PC, Baseball Pro,* and more. You will also get great tutorial articles on topics such as how to set up TCP/IP with Windows 95 for on-line gaming. While you are there, take time to download such goodies as the *Eradicator* demo, and inflict maximum damage with *Computer Gaming's* exclusive *Quake level maps*. And the list goes on: demo archives, shareware games and freeware archives, patches, back issues, and more. Check it out.

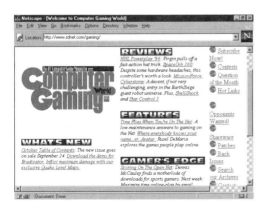

Figure 326.1 The Ziff-Davis gaming site.

Figure 326.2 An article.

327

CONSOLE PROGRAMMING WEB PAGE

http://www.aloha.net/~cdoty/console.htm

Master the black magic of *SNES* (Nintendo-style) programming, SEGA programming, Gameboy Programming, and more. The site's links include the *GameBoy Technical Page*, the *Jaguar Server Home Page*, *Gau's SNES Programming Page*, and more. The *Gameboy* resources include *GameBoy* programming information by "Dr. Pan," and a great *GameBoy* programming frequently asked questions. The *SNES* resources include information on color values, tile data formats, graphic modes, and more, including the Object Adapter Module (OAM) table data, a basic memory map, and sprite and screen format information. No serious programmer of console games can afford to be without the information this page presents.

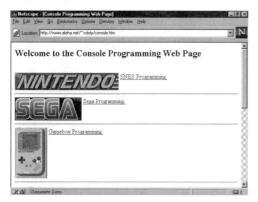

Figure 327.1 Console Programming Web page.

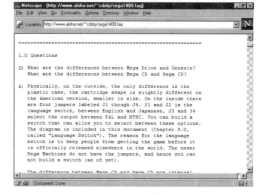

Figure 327.2 SEGA programming FAQ.

328

ELECTRONIC ARTS

http://www.ea.com/

All programmers seem to have a video game deep inside them that they are dying to write. Before you start cranking out the code, you might want to check out the software being produced by one of the industry's best. Electronic Arts is a leading global interactive entertainment software company that develops, publishes, and distributes software for IBM-compatible PCs and Macintosh computers. In addition, the company publishes software for "next generation" entertainment systems such as the *PlayStation*, *Sega Saturn*, and other major dedicated game systems. Since its founding in 1982, Electronic Arts has won more than 650 awards for outstanding software in the U.S. and Europe. Come to this site for product and corporate information and job openings.

Figure 328.1 Electronic Arts home page.

Figure 328.2 Origin information.

EPIC GAMES

http://www.epicgames.com/

Epic Games brings you *UNREAL*, *7th Legion*, *Fire Fight*, *Curly's Adventure*, and other great games. *Fire Fight*, of course, is the best "360 degree shooter" for the PC—featuring isometric view, rendered graphics, parallaxing backgrounds, digitized speech, and heart-pounding action for one to four players. *EXTREME PINBALL* is a must see, featuring ultra-realistic table dimensions, an animated arcade style scoreboard, multi-ball play, and a new music and sound system that changes with the music and game events. Visit this site for a lesson in state-of-the-art game programming and, while you are there, check out free demos and downloads.

Figure 329 Epic Games home page.

GAME DEVELOPER MAGAZINE

http://ww.gdmag.com/

Want to learn how to wrap *DirectX* common object model (COM) objects using Borland's Delphi, and how to access the objects as DLLs? Would you like a utility (created by AI expert Brian Stout) which illustrates the efficiency of various path-finding algorithms? What are the key differences between developing for the PC and the arcade? What is the hidden Zen behind the raw power of Bulk Synchronous Parallel (BSP) trees? And, how can Microsoft's *DirectInput* help you with your game programming? Every month, *Game Developer* addresses issues such as these, and much more. Visit this site for details.

Figure 330.1 Game Developer Web site.

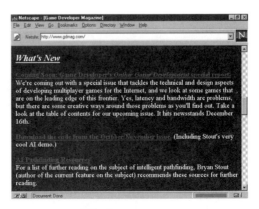

Figure 330.2 What's new.

GAMES DEVELOPMENT KIT FOR WINDOWS 95

http://www.mcs.com/~poschs/GDK/gdk.htm

This site is home to the Games Development Kit for Windows 95 (GDK95) which contains a set of routines written to simplify the creation of games for Windows 95. The routines implement common functions hiding many of the mundane programming tasks required for all games. The GDK95 is a static library (consisting of *DirectDraw* routines, a sprite library and routines, a process list and dispatcher, and an object list and manager) that you link in with your game source code. The site invites you to download the GDK95 shareware. You may also download a great demo of GDK95 in action called *GALAX* (a Galaxian clone). All in all, the GDK95 is a very remarkable tool that will prove essential for any Windows 95 game developer.

Figure 331 Download GDK95.

GAMES DEVELOPMENT RESOURCES

http://www.hull.ac.uk/php/cs8kpp/gameprog.html

The Games Development Resources site contains a fantastic set of links for the serious game programmer. You will find resources for creating demos, working with Space Network (SN) Systems developers tools, interactive fiction programming, Windows game programming, audio C/C++ library routines, HP game development, and much, much more. You will even have access to a digital *Games Programming Encyclopedia*. And, you get links to shareware and freeware archives, on-line tutorials, great on-line excerpts from the best game programming books around, and rules-of-the-road for efficient, modular, effective (and profitable!) game development for PC/Windows, Macintosh, and other platforms. Fantastic stuff.

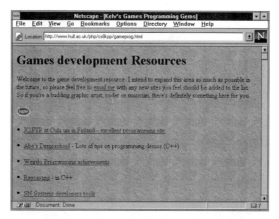

Figure 332 Games Development Resources.

GAMES DOMAIN CODING NEXUS

http://homepages.together.net/~adamd//game.html

OK. Get ready—You will find no better collection of game programming links anywhere else on the Web. Period. At this site, you will find links to newsgroups, code factories, and sites from which you can download games. For the "techies," this site has pages dedicated to game programming using C/C++, Delphi, assembly language, and even Pascal. You will learn how to master the Zen of graphics programming within games. You can participate in discussions which show you how to create dramatic graphics that run fast and efficiently, while at the same time dazzling the eye of the beholder. Get all the resources you need at Games Domain.

Figure 333.1 The Games Domain Web site.

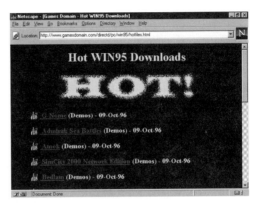

Figure 333.2 Windows 95 downloads.

GAME PROGRAMMING HOME PAGE

http://www.ocf.berkeley.edu/~emrek/gp/gameprog.html

Emre Kiciman is doing the world a favor by building and maintaining this outstanding game programming information and links page. You'll find theory, practice, documents, file formats, hardware information, links to other sites, and more. Check out the discussion on 3-D graphics which includes: 3-D math, projection, and textures. You will often find information on graphics operations such as: VGA and Mode-X palettes, bitmap operations, animation, scrolling, and fonts. Finally, you will find discussion on sound and sound cards, and miscellaneous items such as AI and compression and, of course, links—gobs and gobs of games-related links.

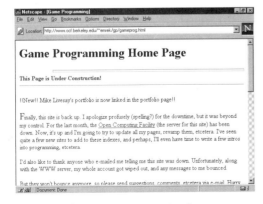

Figure 334.1 Game Programming home page.

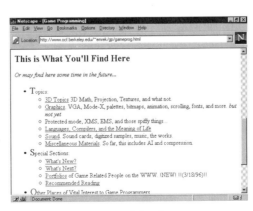

Figure 334.2 What you'll find here.

335

FREE
FREE SOFTWARE

OPEN TO ALL

STRONG CONTENT

EXCELLENT
REFERENCES

GAMES PROGRAMMING HOME PAGE FROM THE U.K.

http://www.ee.ucl.ac.uk/~phart/game

From the U.K. comes a site filled with tons of source code (tons of C/C++ and assembly language). You will find excellent, home-grown tutorials on different levels of graphics hardware, EMS, and XMS (the complete specifications and why and how to use them). You will also learn how to make good use of input technology, how to make your game "sound good," how to perform fixed-point arithmetic, and how to program in enemies (as well as how to make those enemies smart). You will also get links to the official *rec.games.programmer* frequently asked questions, and more. In short, the site is filled with very useful resources.

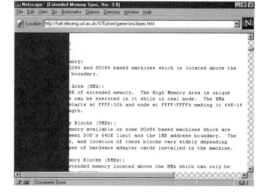

Figure 335.1 U.K. Games Programming home page. *Figure 335.2 The XMS Specification.*

336

FREE
FREE SOFTWARE

COVERS DETAILS

OPEN TO ALL

STRONG CONTENT

EXCELLENT
REFERENCES

GAMING ON OS/2 WARP

http://www.austin.ibm.com/os2games/

OS/2 Warp? Are they really serious? Yup. And there may be one or two serious visitors to this page as well. Who knows? Hey, it's *possible!* "Welcome to the IBM-sponsored OS/2 Games Home Page," they write. "Our goal is to provide OS/2 related information to both game developers and game enthusiasts wishing to combine the power of OS/2 Warp with PC-based games." At this site, for all you game programmers who are rushing to supply content for OS/2 platforms, you will find OS/2 entertainment tools, game development tools, and more. The support level and quality, I must say, are both excellent. But who do they think they are supporting?

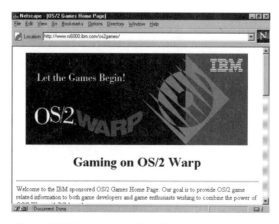

Figure 336 Let the games begin!

NATE GOUDIE'S GAMES PROGRAMMING PAGE

http://www.lehigh.edu/nsg2/public/www-data/prog.html

Nate Goudie has been programming since he got a Commodore 64 for Christmas way back in the sixth grade. Most of his time is devoted to games. You'll get a hot link to Nate's article "Designing Isometric Game Environments" from *Dr. Dobb's Games, Graphics,* and *Multimedia Sourcebook.* You will also find downloadable files of most of the games Nate has written, including *Kapture 2.0, Gunboat Duckhunt 1.0, Pinball Extravaganza, Maze Runner 3-D,* and educational software that includes *Statistical Nightmares 1.0,* and more. Nate also gives you links to several of his favorite game programming sites on the Web, all of which are worth checking out.

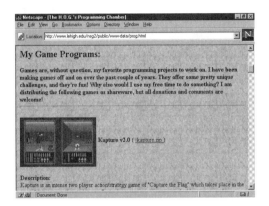

Figure 337.1 One of Nate's games.

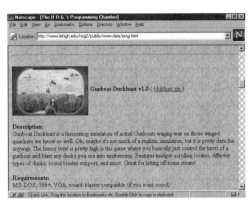

Figure 337.2 And another.

HAPPY PUPPY GAMES PAGE

http://www.happypuppy.com/

Do you program games and want to see what the competition is up to? Or, do you want a place from which to distribute your games shareware or freeware? Or, do you administer a network and want to find some "safe" games to store on the network, so that your users won't go downloading rogue software off the Internet, thereby infecting your systems with God only knows what? If you fit any of these three descriptions, then check out the Happy Puppy Games Page. Here you will find hundreds of great PC games, as well as reviews. Download *Interpose* (side-scroll space shooter), *Bug* (3D arcade adventure), *Guimo* (side-scrolling arcade), *Star General* (turn-based space combat), *Triple Play '97* (3D baseball), *Gazillionaire Deluxe* (galactic empire builder), and more. Or upload your own masterpieces. The choice is yours.

Figure 338.1 The Happy Puppy site.

Figure 338.2 Cool demos.

339

DJGPP DEVELOPMENT SYSTEM FREEWARE

http://www.delorie.com/

DJGPP is a 32-bit DOS development system based on the popular gnu tools. Using DJGPP and your PC, you can port many existing Unix programs to DOS, or rebuild your existing DOS program to be able to use more memory and run faster. These attributes are of special use to games developers. In fact, DJGPP is the development system that was used to create the classic *Quake* shareware game. The acronym that serves as the name for this freeware derives from DJ Delorie and the initials of several of his programming friends, who collaborated on building the system. You may download DJGPP here, along with full documentation and a useful list of frequently asked questions.

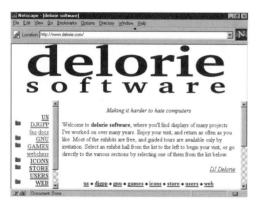

Figure 339.1 Get it from Delorie Software.　　　*Figure 339.2 Downloading details.*

340

IEIL: INTERACTIVE ENTERTAINMENT INDUSTRY LINKS

http://www.algonet.se/~hegge-t/ieil.htm

Interactive Entertainment Industry Links is run by Henrik Torstensson. This site provides a useful and extensive set of links related to all aspects of the computer game development/publishing industry. Here you'll find a great place to connect with other developers in the industry, swapping tools and techniques and tips along the way. One very nice feature of ieil is its set of dozens of links to job listings for many of the major companies in computer gaming, including AM Productions, 21st Century, 3D Realms, 5D Games, 7th Level, Ambrosia, Anarchy Entertainment, Black Dragon Productions, and other likely suspects.

Figure 340.1 ieil.　　　*Figure 340.2 Jobs in game programming.*

GAMES PROGRAMMING MEGASITE

http://members.aol.com/mreiferson/index.htm

From this site, you can download a great collection of icons, backgrounds and animated GIFs ... free! Games Programming MegaSite is probably the top game programming site on the Web. You will find downloadable 3-D engines (some with source code!) along with lots of other downloadable source code, demos, and shareware tools for serious game developers working with a range of operating systems including Windows 95, Windows 3.1 and MacOS. Also be sure to check out the "Useful Files" section which includes such goodies as a list of frequently asked questions on computer graphics algorithms, a text file on Doom programming techniques, and more. Cool stuff!

Figure 341.1 Games Programming MegaSite.

Figure 341.2 A game programming walkthrough.

LUCASARTS HOME PAGE

http://www.lucasarts.com/

Trying to debug that last error? "May the force be with you." Better yet, may George Lucas be with you. George Lucas and friends provide some of the coolest games and graphics going. Of course as you may know, LucasArts is a leading developer and publisher of entertainment and educational software. They publish an extensive line of interactive titles across multiple platforms. Each title combines compelling stories, painstaking character development, vivid setting, and sophisticated technology. Visit this site and download game demos and screen shots, read about soon-to-be-released products, and much more.

Figure 342 LucasArts Web site.

MIDI HOME PAGE

http://www.eeb.ele.tue.nl/midi/index.html

What would our games be without sound and music? And, what better tool for sounds and music than MIDI? This site contains stuff for the novice and expert alike. If you need elaborate MIDI specifications, you will find them at this site. If you need a simple overview of all the MIDI commands, you will find it, along with information about the MIDI standard formats and sample dumps. Likewise, if you only need an explanation of the differences between GM and GS, you will find it at this site. Finally, if you just want to listen to some cool GS MIDI sequences, and then get details on the setups used to create them, you can also do that at the MIDI Home Page. A wonderful source of MIDI content.

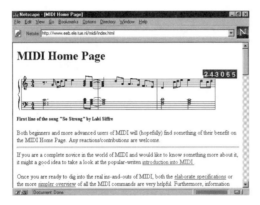

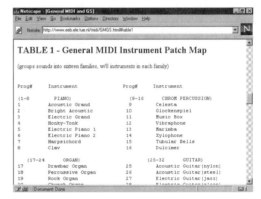

Figure 343.1 The MIDI home page.

Figure 343.2 Detailed documentation.

MIDI WEB

http://www.midiweb.com/

This site is another very cool stop on the Web for MIDI programmers. MIDI Web contains a huge collection of information resources on a range of MIDI subjects. Visit this site for the latest MIDI news, great downloadable MIDI files, technical guides and hardware information, tips and tricks for MIDI programming, utilities, demo programs, and more. Of course, you also get links—a very long list of links—to a classical MIDI library and other cool stuff. Note that MIDI Web has been ranked in the top 5% of all Web sites by Point Survey. All of this comes to you due to lots of hard work and dedication from Raymond Zwarts. Thanks, Ray, keep up the good work!

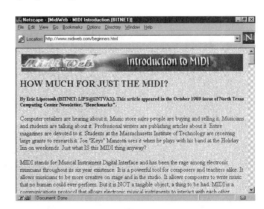

Figure 344.1 MidiWeb home page.

Figure 344.2 A great intro to MIDI.

AI CAFÉ C/C++ CGI HTML HTTP JAVA J++ PERL VBSCRIPT VRML WIN32 WINSOCK 110011010010111100110111001101010100011001100100101

PC DEMOS EXPLAINED

http://www.cdrom.com/pub/demos/hornet/html/demos.html

This is the first Web site dedicated to people who want to learn about creating great PC demos. The site includes definitions of terms, sound clips of demo music, links to other demo-related sites, and even pictures of cool demo effects. How can you build your own demo? What tools are the best to use? Where on the Web can you find the best demos to use as examples of what you should shoot for? This site answers all these questions and more. You can even access several demos from the site directly, including *Unreal, Panic, Second Reality*, and *Crystal Dream*. You'll also find a *Verses* demo featuring a great warping face of Bill Gates. Cool!

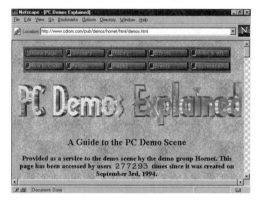

Figure 345.1 PC Demos Explained.

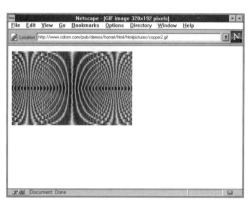

Figure 345.2 Pictures of cool demo effects.

AI CAFÉ C/C++ CGI HTML HTTP JAVA J++ PERL VBSCRIPT VRML WIN32 WINSOCK 110011010010111100110111001101010100011001100100101

PCROBOTS WWW PAGE

http://www.uni-frankfurt.de/~hbecker/pcrob.html

Would you like a challenge? *PCRobots* is a PC/DOS-based game (that you can download from this site). The principle behind *PCRobots* is to write a program which competes with other programs within a special environment provided by the *simulator*—the controlling program. In *PCRobots*, a "tank like" robot in a field symbolizes your program. Your program must control this robot and the robot's aim is to kill the other robots. Your program communicates with your robot using a special interrupt provided by *PCRobots*. The simulator executes the robots using its own custom multitasking. The download includes the appropriate libraries you need to create your program. Check out this site for more details.

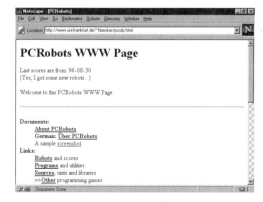

Figure 346.1 PCRobots home page.

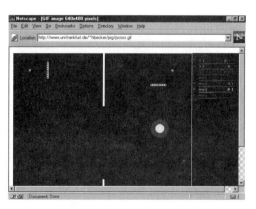

Figure 346.2 A sample screen shot.

PSY-Q TOOLS FOR CONSOLE GAME DEVELOPMENT

http://www.snsys.com/

Psy-Q development tools are a range of PC-based hardware and software tools specifically designed to speed up software development. Psy-Q development systems offer software authors (aka programmers) superior software tools and uncomplicated, super fast hardware adapters. Psy-Q tools have become so highly regarded the world over that SONY now uses them as the cornerstone for software development on their PlayStation. The Psy-Q development tools are the brainchild of one of the world's finest development teams: S.N. Systems. Visit their plush Web site for more information on how you can reduce your programming time.

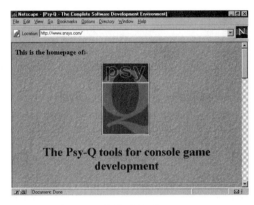

Figure 347.1 Psy-Q Tools Web site.

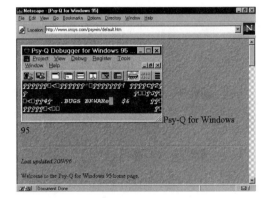

Figure 347.2 The debugger for Windows 95.

RINGZERO GDK FOR DELPHI

http://www.sage-inc.com/RingZero.htm

Sage Software's *RingZero* Game Developers Kit (GDK) is a Delphi 2.0 component suite that gives your programs direct access to *DirectDraw*, *DirectSound*, *DirectPlay*, and *DirectInput*. The *draw* facility, for example, uses the Microsoft Common Object Model (COM) programming interface, which provides a wrapper for *DirectDraw* to facilitate access from Delphi. In a similar way, the *sound* facility provides a wrapper for *DirectSound*. The folks at Sage Software invite you to download the *RingZero* beta. They also invite you to sample some great *RingZero* third-party demos. If you are developing games in Delphi, or if you simply want to enhance your Delphi applications, check out this GDK.

Figure 348 The RingZero Web site.

SEGA ONLINE

http://www.sega.com

Who owns computer gaming? Why, SEGA of course. Visit this Web site for news on *SEGA Saturn Net Link, NIGHTS* (the most revolutionary next-generation game), *World Series Baseball II for Sega Saturn,* and more. You can also download demos of many SEGA games, including *BUG* (the animated 3-D action game). What else? Well, let's see. Any good game programmer is bound to be interested in jobs at SEGA and, at this site, you'll find a great listing of openings. Also, be sure to check out the information on *SEGASoft,* the SEGA Music Group, SEGA Gameworks, the SEGA Channel, and the SEGA Foundation. You'll find it all at this site. The one downside: the pages take forever to load at 28.8.

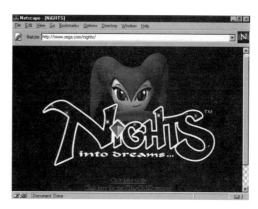

Figure 349.1 The SEGA Web site.　　　Figure 349.2 SEGA Nights.

WINDOWS GAMES, EDUCATIONAL SOFTWARE, ETC.

http://www.nova.edu/Inter-Links/cica/games.html

Do you need to take a break, but still want to look busy? Is it Friday night and you have no life? This site is jam packed with all sorts of shareware and freeware. You will find Windows-based games available for download that include: *Aces-Up Solitaire, Accordion Solitaire, Clock Solitaire, a "Kitty in the Corner" game, Monte Carlo Solitaire, Pyramid Solitaire, King Albert Solitaire, Klondike Solitaire, Maze Solitaire, Shamrock Solitaire, Sly Fox Solitaire, St. Helena Solitaire, Triplet Solitaire, Yukon Solitaire, Cyberspace Crossword Puzzle, Connect 4, Hi/Low Betting Card Game, Magic Eight Ball, NFL Statistical Analysis and Prediction software,* and more.

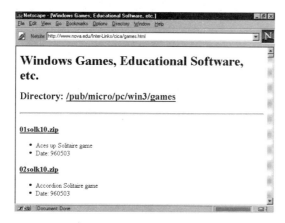

Figure 350 Take your pick.

ACM SIGGRAPH

http://www.siggraph.org/

Everyone in computing knows what SIGGRAPH is, right? OK, well, just in case: SIGGRAPH is the Association of Computing Machinery's (ACM's) Special Interest Group (SIG) on computer graphics (GRAPH, get it?). SIGGRAPH is committed to providing educational resources and guidance to the computer graphics community, and they do a darn fine job of it. Visit this site for organizational, membership, conference, and workshop information. You will also find educational resources, professional chapter information, art and design resources, SIGGRAPH publications, the SIGGRAPH calendar, and more. In particular, be sure to check out the site's listing of Educational Resources files. If you are interested in computer graphics, SIGGRAPH is a great place to start.

Figure 351.1 The SIGGRAPH Web site.

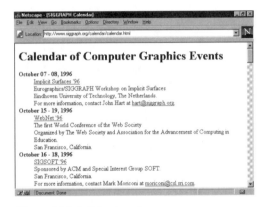

Figure 351.2 Calendar of events.

ADVANCED VISUAL SYSTEMS

http://www.avs.com/

If a picture is really worth a thousand words, you will want to add visualization tools to your programming repertoire. Advanced Visual Systems provides quality software tools and solutions which transform data into visual information. AVS/*Express* is a multi-platform, component-based software environment for visualizing complex data and for building applications with interactive visualization and graphics functions. Their products include *AVS/Express*, *AVS5*, *Gsharp,* and *Toolmaster. AVS/ Express* provides object kits that contain numerous reusable objects for building visualization components applications. *AVS/Express* employs an innovative object-oriented visual programming interface to create, modify, and connect these objects. Visit AVS's Web pages for more information.

Figure 352.1 The AVS Web site.

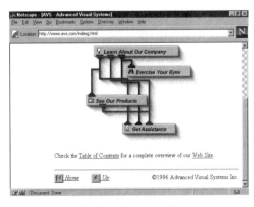

Figure 352.2 Click on the topic of interest.

RT EDITOR FOR WINDOWS (SHAREWARE)

http://www.geocities.com/SiliconValley/3526/

RT Editor is a fantastic shareware ray-tracing engine (ray-tracing is the process of creating photo-realistic images on the computer by simulating the effects of lighting and shadows) and editor for Windows 3.x with Win 32, Windows NT, and Windows 95. The shareware supports depth bitmaps for stereogram, VRML, antialiasing, texture and bump mapping, Phong illumination, and more. The shareware also supports boxes, spheres, cylinders, and boundary representation (with Phong interpolation). The built-in editor supports polyline, bezier and NURBS curve editing, texture map editing, and layers. As a bonus, the program can read and write file DSF from programs such as 3D Studio! The Web page includes a direct link for download along with an extensive gallery of great RT-generated images.

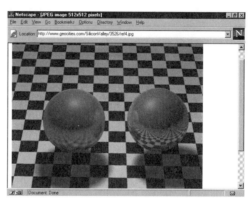

Figure 353.1 RT Editor home page. *Figure 353.2 A typical image.*

APPLE QUICKTIME VR WEB SITE

http://qtvr.quicktime.apple.com/

Two words describe Apple's *QuickTime VR*: Really Cool! Award-winning *QuickTime VR* software for the Mac and Windows brings Virtual Reality to your desktop—without requiring you to install any special equipment. Use *QuickTime VR* to experience a 3-D photograph or rendered representation of any person, place, or thing. Use your mouse and keyboard to rotate objects, zoom in and out of a scene, look around 360 degrees, and navigate from one scene to another. Via these Web pages, you can "virtually" hold priceless art objects in your hands. And you can link to an estimated 5,000 Web sites around the world that offer *QuickTime VR* experiences.

Figure 354.1 The QuickTime home page. *Figure 354.2 Free authoring tools!*

Applied Chaos Laboratory, Georgia Tech

http://acl1.physics.gatech.edu/aclhome.html

A ton of cool stuff based on chaos and fractals is going on at Georgia Tech. The main mission of the Applied Chaos Laboratory is to investigate basic nonlinear phenomena with an emphasis on future applications. The research ranges from fundamental computational studies of nonlinear dynamics to advanced 3-D fractal graphics programming. The laboratory's founding principal is that interdisciplinary research into basic nonlinear phenomena and dynamics will result in a variety of novel applications. Come to this site for great fractal graphics generation engines, awesome source-code examples, and stunning fractal graphic images.

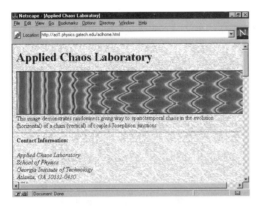

Figure 355.1 The Applied Chaos Web site.

Figure 355.2 Edna St. Vincent Millay on chaos.

Avalon: 3-D Object Repository

http://avalon1.viewpoint.com/

Avalon is a 3-D object repository for the Internet. Since July 1985, Viewpoint, a commercial 3-D model vendor, has run "Avalon." At this site, you will find 3-D objects (stored in multiple formats), utilities, file-format documents, and more. You will also get textures, demos, lists of frequently asked questions, and compression utilities. The sampling of 3-D objects includes aircraft, anatomical items, animals, architecture, dinosaurs, military items, characters, plants, vehicles, watercraft, and more. Although Viewpoint is a commercial vendor, they insist that the Avalon models will remain free to all. Many thanks to Viewpoint for maintaining this enormous resource.

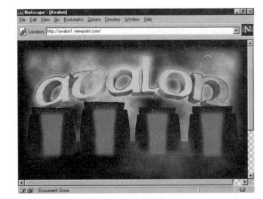

Figure 356.1 The Avalon Web site.

Figure 356.2 Your choices.

THE BEAUTY OF CHAOS

http://i30www.ira.uka.de/~ukrueger/fractals

Would you care to make a journey into the hidden (or not so hidden) depths of the Mandelbrot set? At this site, you will find a database of more than 500 images which becomes your guide to discovering the beauty of chaos, as represented in fractal graphics. The images you will encounter on your screen are already precalculated (stored in a rendered format). Just point and click to explore deeper and deeper, finding new layers of beauty and symmetry the deeper you dive. All these wonders are courtesy of Uwe Kruger of Germany, a leading researcher in chaos theory, and a clever and masterful creater of multidimensional fractal graphics of the very first order.

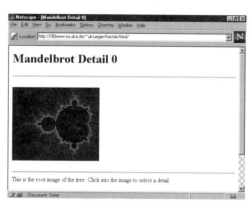

Figure 357.1 The Beauty of Chaos Web site.   Figure 357.2 Click on the image to select a detail.

BSP TREE FREQUENTLY ASKED QUESTIONS

http://www.qualia.com/bspfaq/

A Binary Space Partitioning (BSP) tree is a data structure that represents a recursive, hierarchical subdivision of n-dimensional space into convex subspaces. Great. What's that you say? At this site, you will find answers to all of your questions regarding BSP trees. How do you build a BSP tree? How do you partition a polygon with a plane? How do you remove hidden surfaces or compute analytic visibility with a BSP tree? How do you accelerate ray-tracing with a BSP tree? How do you perform collision detection with a BSP tree? How do you handle dynamic scenes with a BSP tree? And so on. Visit this site for the answers to these questions and to learn how you can use BSP trees within real applications today.

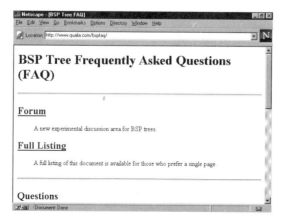

Figure 358 BSP specifics.

CHAOS GROUP, COLLEGE PARK, MARYLAND

http://www-chaos.umd.edu/

The Chaos Group at the University of Maryland, College Park, focuses on various areas of chaotic dynamics that range from the theory of dimensions to fractal basin boundaries, chaotic scattering, and controlling chaos. What, you ask, are fractal basin boundaries? These little goodies arise in dissipative dynamical systems when two or more attractors (objects that limit the trajectory of a fractal set) are present. In such situations, each attractor has a basin of initial conditions which lead asymptotically to that attractor. The basin boundaries are the sets which separate different basins. Confusing? Would some pictures help? You know, some graphics. Find them at this site, along with detailed discussions of how and why Chaos generates them.

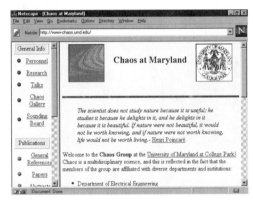

Figure 359.1 The Chaos Group Web site.

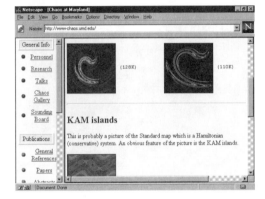

Figure 359.2 Some great images.

CLEMSON UNIVERSITY VR PROJECT

http://chip.eng.clemson.edu/vr

The immersion of human participants in virtual environments is a technological reality achieved through the use of head-mounted display (HMD) devices and high-speed image transfer. Clemson University's VR Project examines how virtual reality can aid instruction in architecture, bioengineering, computer science, electron microscopy, mechanical engineering, performing arts, and even psychology. In short, the project's goal is to immerse students in the use of virtual reality with instruction. The project is a cross-college effort whose results will be felt within all fields of academia. Visit this site for more information.

Figure 360.1 The VR Project home page.

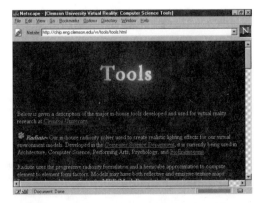

Figure 360.2 In-house tools developed at Clemson.

AI CAFÉ C/C++ CGI HTML HTTP JAVA J++ PERL VBSCRIPT VRML WIN32 WINSOCK 11001101001011110011011100110101010001001100100101

dFORM: VRML DESIGN FOR SCIENCE & EDUCATION

http://www.dform.com/

dFORM envisions and creates educational and research-oriented interactive 3-D environments for the Internet. dFORM's innovative production method combines 3-D models with animation, text, and audio to develop interactive navigable multimedia environments that enhance and facilitate the presentation of information. Leveraging cutting-edge technologies, dFORM is dedicated to pushing and expanding these technologies into new areas, as well as developing and adopting new technologies. From simple classroom presentations to detailed database visualizations, dFORM empowers people to learn effectively through the Internet. Visit this site for futuristic learning techniques.

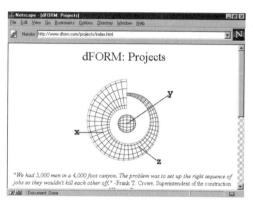

Figure 361.1 The dFORM Web site.

Figure 361.2 dFORM projects info.

AI CAFÉ C/C++ CGI HTML HTTP JAVA J++ PERL VBSCRIPT VRML WIN32 WINSOCK 11001101001011110011011100110101010001001100100101

DIVISION

http://www.division.com/

As the world leader in virtual prototyping software, systems, and services, Division provides you with ways to improve your product development, enhance productivity, and reduce costly prototypes. With direct experience in a wide range of application areas, including collaborative design and engineering, architectural design, training, simulation, and other mission-critical applications, Division can provide you with optimal integrated solutions. Division's products include *dVISE Virtual Prototyping Software*, which won *Computer Graphics World's* First Place Editor's Choice Award not long ago. This is an interactive digital prototyping solution for collaborative design and engineering. Visit the Web pages for more information.

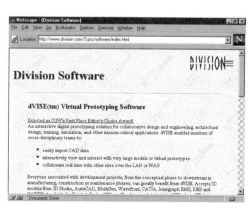

Figure 362.1 The Division Web site.

Figure 362.2 Division software solutions.

363

Electric Labs

http://www.electriclabs.com/

Electric Labs is a testing ground for ideas and experimental projects using VRML. Visit the lab to get a taste of projects that use the latest technologies to create dazzling effects with *Quicktime VR*, VRML, and 3-D computer animation. You can also venture down into the "Basement" to check out some "super secret stuff" the boys and girls at the lab have been working on. While you are there, feel free to add to the "graffiti galleries" scattered across the walls. And before you split, please leave your name and e-mail address at the lab's registry, so that these wacky scientists can e-mail you when next they put a new project on display. Awesome stuff.

Figure 363.1 Choose Java or non-Java Web pages.

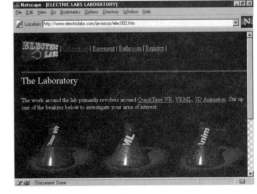

Figure 363.2 Cool stuff in the laboratory.

364

Forte Technologies: Download Some Great (Free) Stuff

http://www.fortevr.com/

What great stuff? Man, give me the details. OK, this is the list. Forte invites you to download the VFX1 Software Developers Kit (VDK) v.2.03, the newest versions of Forte's many DOS and Windows 95 drivers, and an even newer version of their driver for *Duke Nukem 3-D*. Got a problem with *Quake*? Download Forte's beta driver for that baby. And you'll find more at this site as well. Forte, the folks who bring you the great VFX1 headgear, is leader in the field of virtual reality. In addition to downloads and product news, this site delivers great software libraries, the latest in virtual reality news and information, terrific on-line tech support, great developer information, and more. Cool!

Figure 364.1 The Forte Web site.

Figure 364.2 Product information.

AI CAFÉ C/C++ CGI HTML HTTP JAVA J++ PERL VBSCRIPT VRML WIN32 WINSOCK 110011010010111100110111001101010100011001100100101

FRACTAL DESIGN ON-LINE

http://www.fractal.com/

Fractal Design is at the forefront of the digital-imaging revolution. The firm is the producer of super graphics products that they say they design to "empower your creativity." These products include *Painter*, the world's most popular paint program, and *Ray Dream Studio* for the Mac and Windows, a powerful and affordable 3-D modeling and animation suite. Come to this Web site for demo downloads, great galleries, cool links, and extensive product information. You will also find top-drawer technical support. Fractal Design invites you to download their Web page's background, which changes daily, and take it with you along with other goodies. Great fun.

Figure 365.1 The Web site.

Figure 365.2 Cool images.

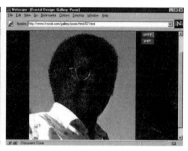
Figure 365.3 More cool images.

AI CAFÉ C/C++ CGI HTML HTTP JAVA J++ PERL VBSCRIPT VRML WIN32 WINSOCK 110011010010111100110111001101010100011001100100101

FRACTAL GALLERIES

http://www.glyphs.com/art/fractals

To begin with, you get some great, illustrated tutorials addressing such issues as *What is a Fractal?*, *Fractals as Art, Fractals as a Programmer's Art*, and *The Computer as Brush*. Next, you get links to some of the most beautiful fractal images you can find on the Internet. The programming emphasis at this site is on *WinFract*, a wonderful tool for creating fractal images under Windows 3.1, Windows NT, and Windows 95. The images that you'll find at Fractal Galleries are mostly 70-80Kb JPEGs. If you want to learn how to create fantastic fractal images in the Windows environment, Fractal Galleries is a good place to start your journey.

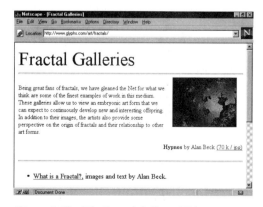
Figure 366.1 The Fractal Galleries Web site.

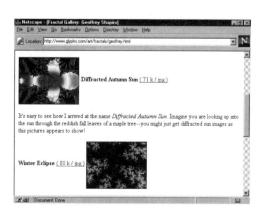
Figure 366.2 Images by Geof Shapiro.

FRACTAL IMAGE COMPRESSION PROJECT, UNIVERSITY OF WATERLOO

http://links.uwaterloo.ca/

The Fractal Image Compression Project at the University of Waterloo is part of a general research program dedicated to the study of fractal analysis, iterative function systems, and fractal transforms from both theoretical and practical perspectives. The research is funded primarily by grants from the Natural Science and Engineering Research Council of Canada (NSERC)—and they are getting their money's worth. This site's pages are fantastic. Check out "A Hitchhiker's Guide to Fractal Compression for Beginners." Also be sure to check out the valuable summaries of ongoing fractal compression research at Waterloo, where the trail to the future in this field is being blazed.

Figure 367 The Fractal Compression Web site.

FRACTAL IMAGE ENCODING

http://inls3.ucsd.edu/y/Fractals/

This cool site is maintained by Uval Fisher, the author of *Fractal Image Compression: Theory and Application to Digital Images* and *Fractal Image Encoding and Analysis*. As you might guess, you will find some great images stored at this site which you can download or view on-line. You will also find much information and many links related to fractal image encoding and corresponding topics. The site also includes bibliographies and other references, conferences and announcements, links to Internet resources, papers, software, and much more. Fisher also invites you to download some fantastic fractal image generation software. Bravo!

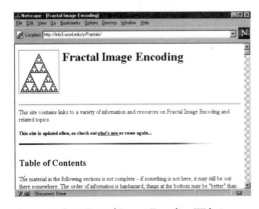

Figure 368.1 Fractal Image Encoding Web site.

Figure 368.2 Available software.

THE FRACTAL MICROSCOPE

http://www.ncsa.uiuc.edu/Edu/fractal/

"The Fractal Microscope," writes the Webmaster, "is an interactive tool . . . for exploring the Mandelbrot set and other fractal patterns." The on-line module combines supercomputing and networks with simple Macintosh and X-Window interfaces to reveal much about computer graphics, scientific notation, coordinate systems, graphing, number systems, convergence, divergence, and self-similarity. The images are astonishingly beautiful and include a Mandelbrot set visualized and shaded in blue, along with a large gallery of additional fractal images. The on-line presentation is designed to be run in conjunction with NCSA imaging tools such as *DataScope* and *Collage.* Check it out.

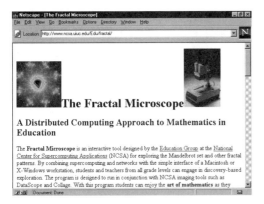

Figure 369.1 Fractal Microscope Web site.

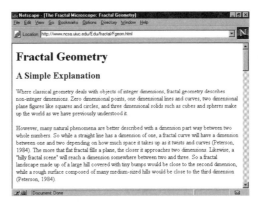

Figure 369.2 All about fractal geometry.

FRACTINT: FREE DOWNLOAD

http://spanky.triumf.ca/www/fractint/fractint.html

Fractint is a freeware fractal generator for IBM PCs and compatibles. It is by far the most versatile and extensive fractal program available for any price, and the authors work very hard to keep it that way. The latest release of *Fractint* (version 19.5) has fantastic deep-zooming capabilities. Additionally, the authors have made several ports of this software, which you can download for different environments, including Windows and the X-Window system for UNIX. These are also available for download. While you are visiting, be sure to check out the *Fractint* user's gallery, as well as the great collections of parameter files, formula files, and color-map files, along with some very useful *Fractint* add-ons. Great stuff.

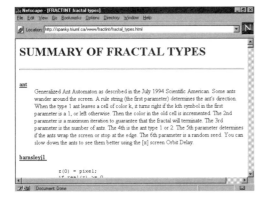

Figure 370.1 Summary of Fractint fractal types.

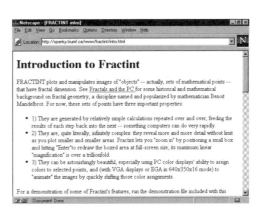

Figure 370.2 Introduction to Fractint.

GRAFICA OBSCURA

http://www.sgi.com/grafica/

Visit this site and check out *Grafica Obscura*, Paul Haeberli's "evolving computer graphics notebook." One of the site's highlights is *The Impressionist*, which, if you have a Java-enabled browser, will serve as a paint program that lets you create a painted representation of a photograph. Another highlight is Paul's portfolio of digital pictures which includes both photographic and synthetic (entirely generated on computer) images. Just try to tell the difference! You will also find good information on synthetic lighting for photography, details for a multi-focus method for controlling depth of field, and specifics about image merging, interpolation, and extrapolation. Finally, don't miss *Dynadraw*, a paint program that uses dynamics (computer graphic rendering technique) to filter mouse positions. If you are "into" image manipulation, *Grafica* is a must-see site.

Figure 371.1 The Grafica Obscura Web site.

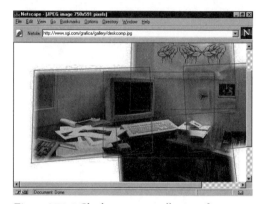

Figure 371.2 Check out a great collection of images.

THE HUMAN INTERFACE TECHNOLOGY LAB

http://www.hitl.washington.edu/

This site probably contains the Web's greatest collection of information on virtual reality (VR). The University's Human Interface Technology Lab (HITLAB) is a research and development lab charged with transforming virtual reality concepts and early research into practical, market-driven products. The lab's research strengths include interface hardware and virtual environments software. These researchers hope to develop a new generation of human-machine interfaces. Visit the lab's pages to learn how these virtual architects are leading the way in the design of previously unimagined virtual spaces.

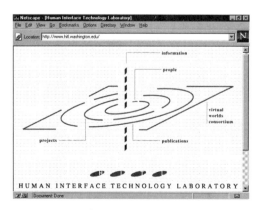

Figure 372.1 The HITLAB Web site.

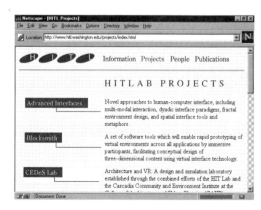

Figure 372.2 Projects.

AI CAFÉ C/C++ CGI HTML HTTP JAVA J++ PERL VBSCRIPT VRML WIN32 WINSOCK 11001101001011110011011100110101010001100110001010

IAN'S VR BUYING GUIDE

http://www.cs.jhu.edu/~feldberg/vr/vrbg.html

Are you looking for a great list of virtual reality products? Well, you've found it at this site. "I got one too many paper cuts flipping through company brochures announcing their landmark, break-through, cross-over VR products," writes Ian. What we are talking about is a great list with full product information and clickable links to suppliers of head-mounted displays (HMDs), other types of displays, 3-D sound convolvers (uses changing mathematical parameters to revise or filter the contents of an image or sound file), data gloves, 3-D mice and wands, haptic (based on the sense of touch) feedback devices, position/orientation trackers, software, and more. Thanks, Ian!

Figure 373.1 Software information.

Figure 373.2 Displays.

AI CAFÉ C/C++ CGI HTML HTTP JAVA J++ PERL VBSCRIPT VRML WIN32 WINSOCK 11001101001011110011011100110101010001100110001010

ICE: INTEGRATED COMPUTING ENGINES

http://www.iced.com/

Integrated Computing Engines (ICE) provides high-performance computing products for rendering complex graphics, which include 2-D special effects and 3-D photorealistic animations. ICE computing engines work with Windows and Mac systems to create rendering "superstations." Their products are open and interface with leading graphics applications to provide breakthrough rendering speeds for a broad base of performance-starved end-users. ICE's customers include post-production artists, animators, and CAD engineers. These users create print, video, film, CD-ROM, and Internet content in the communications, entertainment, and manufacturing industries. For solutions to your high-speed graphics needs, visit the ICE Web site.

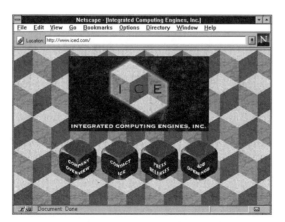

Figure 374 The ICE Web site.

ITERATED SYSTEMS

http://www.iterated.com/

Founded by two mathematics professors from Georgia Tech, Iterated Systems *invented* fractal transform technology and, in doing so, demonstrated that fractals are the answer for sharp, fast images and video for the Web and other multimedia technologies. Iterated Systems envisions and develops new and more efficient ways to represent still images and full-motion video as data. Using these fractal-based technologies, applications can transmit such images with speed and quality far beyond that which is obtainable using other formats. Iterated's products let applications use fractal images in hundreds of ways, from e-mailing family photos to friends, to quickly downloading complex images from a Web site. Cool.

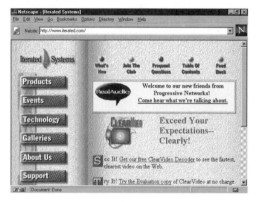

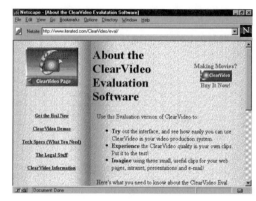

Figure 375.1 The Iterated Systems Web site.

Figure 375.2 Free evaluation software.

LIGHTSCAPE VISUALIZATION SYSTEM: GET A FREE DEMO CD

http://www.lightscape.com

The Lightscape Visualization System is an advanced lighting and visualization application for creating accurate images of how a 3-D object would appear if it were physically built. The system uses radiosity technology to produce accurate photometric (the measure of a light's brightness or luminosity) simulations of diffuse lighting, soft shadows, and color bleeding surfaces—images with a natural realism that applications cannot attain with other rendering techniques. Because it supports industry-standard photometric formats and natural daylighting, Lightscape is a powerful tool for design and visualization analysis. Come to this Web page for more details. In addition, you can request a great, free demo CD.

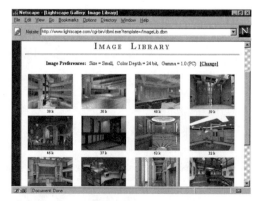

Figure 376.1 The Lightscape Web site.

Figure 376.2 A cool gallery.

MESH MART

http://cedar.cic.net/~rtilmann/mm/

Mesh Mart provides a source of 3-D mesh object files for the growing number of 3-D modeling artists and developers. Although "art purists" may wish to design all their own mesh objects, the rapidly increasing demand for 3-D renderings and virtual reality environments is creating a demand for reusable objects. A small number of object meshes are available from several FTP sites. And, some are available from various commercial sources. Mesh Mart offers a place for both user-buyers and developer-sellers of mesh objects to get together (to mesh, so to speak) and exchange their wares. What a wonderful idea. Cool art.

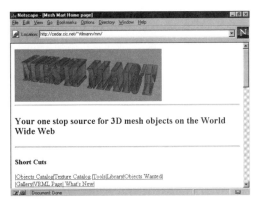

Figure 377.1 Mesh Mart home page.

Figure 377.2 3-D picture of the week.

METATOOLS: THE VISUAL COMPUTING SOFTWARE COMPANY

http://www.metatools.com/

MetaTools is a dynamic, creative developer and publisher of state-of-the-art graphic imaging, special effects, and multimedia software applications for Mac, Windows, and Silicon Graphics systems. MetaTools publishes the award-winning *Kai's Power Tools* and *KPT Convolver*—both powerful plug-in filters for imaging software such as *Adobe Photoshop* and *Fractal Design Painter*. MetaTools also publishes *KPT Bryce*, an innovative Mac-based 3-D landscape generator, and *KPT Vector Effects*, which are plug-in extensions for *Adobe Illustrator* and *Macromedia Freehand*. If you've benefited from these tools in the past, you will want to visit this site to check out the newly developed *KPT VideoWare* line of tools.

Figure 378.1 The MetaTools Web site.

Figure 378.2 Bryce 2 information.

UNIVERSITY OF MICHIGAN VR LAB

http://www-VRL.umich.edu/

Created in 1993, the Virtual Reality Lab at the University of Michigan focuses its attention on industrial applications of virtual environments. The lab's research includes immersive virtual reality, augmented reality, and other variations of virtual reality. Their research emphasizes virtual prototypes of automotive and marine designs, simulations of manufacturing processes, architectural walk-through models, free-form shape designs, accident simulations, and more. Visit this site for complete information on all ongoing projects, including summaries, images, animations, videos, and VRML models. The site also includes a very good, short introduction to VRML. Exciting stuff!

Figure 379 The Lab's introduction to Virtual Reality.

MR TOOLKIT FROM THE UNIVERSITY OF ALBERTA

http://web.cs.ualberta.ca/~graphics/MRToolkit.html

The *Minimal Reality (MR) Toolkit* is a set of software tools for the production of virtual reality systems and other forms of three-dimensional user interfaces (for HP, SGI, DEC, and IBM RS6000 workstations). The software consists of a set of subroutine libraries, device drivers, support programs, and a language for describing geometry and behavior. MR provides a device-independent, portable platform for the development of virtual reality applications. In fact, with the tools at this site, you can easily port the applications you develop at one site to other sites with minimal or no change to the source code. The tool kit includes an object-modeling language, 3-D modeling software, and an environment manager for running multi-user applications.

Figure 380.1 The MR Toolkit Web site.   *Figure 380.2 Check out the graphics.*

MULTI-DIMENSIONAL ARRAYS IN C/C++

http://www.graphics.cornell.edu/faqs/array.html

Programs that manipulate graphics images often store the images using multi-dimensional arrays. Unfortunately, dealing with multi-dimensional arrays in C and C++ is not always easy, especially when the program must allocate the array dynamically. At this site, you will find a collection of techniques for working with multi-dimensional arrays. One method, for example, involves allocating many separate slices for the array. "There is an advantage to this approach," writes the author, "in that it will be reasonably fast, since the only work in indexing into the array will be a sequence of dereferences. The disadvantages are that it will allocate lots of small chunks of memory, and won't work with any pre-existing arrays." The site's discussion is insightful.

Figure 381.1 And another solution.

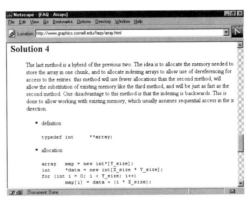

Figure 381.2 And another.

NAN'S COMPUTER GRAPHICS PAGE

http://www.cs.rit.edu/~ncs/graphics.html

Nan Schaller provides an exhaustive set of Web links which reference all phases of graphics programming—in various programming languages and for various platforms. At this site, you will find extensive links that discuss animation, art, color, on-line computer graphics courses, visualization and design, desktop publishing, file formats, fractals, multimedia, 3-D images, computer-graphics societies, software, standards, stereoscopy, and virtual reality. The sites include archives that contain computer-graphics literature which you can download, software and image libraries, and much, much more. This is the best central clearing house for computer-graphics information anywhere on the Web.

Figure 382.1 Nan's home page.

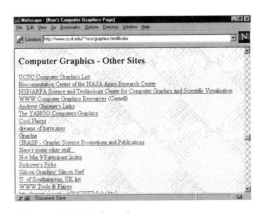

Figure 382.2 A few other options.

383

OPENGL: A TUTORIAL BY HARRY SHAMANSKY

http://hertz.eng.ohio-state.edu/~hts/opengl/article.html

OpenGL is a device- and software-independent software interface with which applications can generate interactive 2-D and 3-D computer graphics. Harry Shamansky delivers a great on-line tutorial addressing *OpenGL* as a professional tool for programmers. Harry cuts right to the chase—informing us quite bluntly that *OpenGL* is NOT: a tool kit or high-level API, a windowing system, a descriptive graphics system, or an object-oriented environment. And, he also states quite plainly what *OpenGL* IS: an immediate-mode system and a procedural system that is at once application-format flexible and display-list functional. Shamansky explains quite clearly how *OpenGL* solves the interface dilemma. If you need to get up to speed on *OpenGL* quickly, turn to Harry Shamansky's Web-based *OpenGL* tutorial.

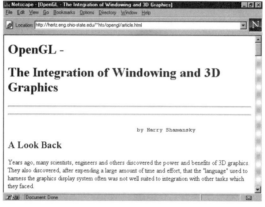

Figure 383 The title page.

384

OPENGL AT IBM

http://www.austin.ibm.com/software/OpenGL/

Come to this site for detailed on-line documentation, standards, patches, and bug reports related to IBM's OpenGL3-D programming API for IBM AIX, the Common Desktop Environment (CDE), Windows NT for the RS/6000, and other environments. This site also provides an automated "application finder." Type in the details of your network's computers and configuration, the graphics tasks you want to accomplish, and the software you already have installed. Then press ENTER and the "wizard" will display a list of robust, versatile, and compatible graphics solutions from a range of vendors, complete with hyperlinks. This can save you a lot of time coming up with the proper software solution for your installation.

Figure 384.1 IBM's OpenGL home page.

Figure 384.2 RS6000 information.

OPENGL WWW CENTER

http://www.sgi.com/Technology/openGL/opengl.html

What is *OpenGL*? As this site tells us: "*OpenGL* is a software interface for applications to generate interactive 2-D and 3-D computer graphics. *OpenGL* is designed to be independent of operating system, window system, and hardware operations, and it is supported by many vendors." This site delivers complete information and resources related to *OpenGL*. You will find the details on the *OpenGL* architecture review board, *OpenGL* licensing information, and the *OpenGL* Performance Characterization Project Proposal. In addition, the site provides *OpenGL* performance benchmarks, everything you would ever want to know about *OpenGL* extensions, and more. If you are a graphics programmer, you need to understand *OpenGL*. And if you want to understand *OpenGL*, visit this site.

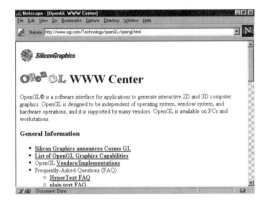

Figure 385.1 OpenGL WWW pages.

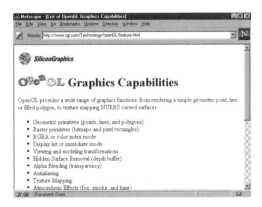

Figure 385.2 OpenGL graphics capabilities.

OPEN VIRTUAL REALITY TESTBED HOME PAGE

http://www.nist.gov/itl/div894/ovrt/OVRThome.html

The mission of the Open Virtual Reality Testbed is to facilitate the development of standard interfaces and testing methodologies to the many novel types of human interface devices programmers are now integrating into Virtual Reality environments. Visit this site and check out VRML manipulation tools that allow users to view VRML files by toggling between wire-frame and solid displays, and between wire-frame and link-following displays. Also, come to this site for information on research into manufacturing applications, image-based virtual reality, navigational information, immersion studies, virtual environments for health care, and much more. State-of-the-art stuff!

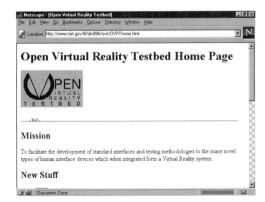

Figure 386.1 The Open VR home page.

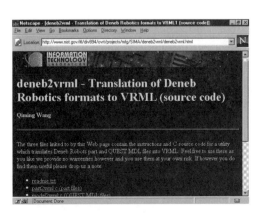

Figure 386.2 Free tools.

AI CAFE C/C++ CGI HTML HTTP JAVA J++ PERL VBSCRIPT VRML WIN32 WINSOCK

387 PERSISTENCE-OF-VISION (POV) RAY-TRACING TOOL DOWNLOAD

http://www.povray.org/

POV-Ray is based on David Buck's original ray-tracer, *DKB-Trace*, and has been (and still is) developed and supported by a crowd of people on the CompuServe Graphics Developers' Forum. Two things make the Persistence-of-Vision Ray-Tracer (*POV-Ray*) stand above the rest. First, the software is freeware. Second, the freeware distributes the source code which lets you compile the software for use on virtually any platform. This software is without a doubt the most used ray-tracing package going. Now, after more than two years, a new release of *POV-Ray* (3.0) is officially available. Download it at this site, and start having fun.

Figure 387.1 The POV-Ray Web site.

Figure 387.2 Super cool images.

AI CAFE C/C++ CGI HTML HTTP JAVA J++ PERL VBSCRIPT VRML WIN32 WINSOCK

388 CLIFF PICKOVER: COMPUTER GRAPHICS GURU

http://sprott.physics.wisc.edu/pickover/home.html

The *Los Angeles Times* recently proclaimed, "Cliff Pickover published nearly a book a year in which he stretches the limits of computers, art, and thought." Cliff's computer graphics have been featured on the covers of many popular magazines. And, his research has recently received considerable attention by the press, including CNN's "Science & Technology Week," *The Discovery Channel, Science News, The Washington Post, Wired,* and even *The Christian Science Monitor. Scientific American* has featured his graphic work several times, calling it "strange and beautiful, stunningly realistic." Treat yourself to a visit with the guru at his Web pages, which are no less interesting than the man himself. A must-see site.

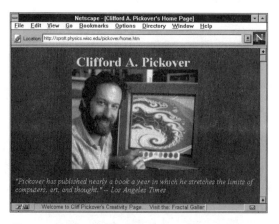

Figure 388 The Cliff Pickover home page.

AI CAFÉ C/C++ CGI HTML HTTP JAVA J++ PERL VBSCRIPT VRML WIN32 WINSOCK 110011010010111001101110011010101000110011001001 01

PIXAR ANIMATION STUDIOS

http://www.pixar.com/

Steve Jobs' (you remember Steve—he co-founded Apple Computer) Pixar is an Academy Award-winning animation studio with the technical, creative, and production capabilities to create a new generation of animated feature films, CD-ROMs, and related products. Pixar's objective is to combine proprietary technology and world-class creative talent to develop computer-animated feature films. Pixar films presents characters using a state-of-the-art three-dimensional appearance. The films feature memorable characters and heartwarming stories. What parent has not sat through *Toy Story* at least once with his or her kids? Pixar is responsible for many important technological breakthroughs in the application of computer graphics to filmmaking, and you can learn all about those breakthroughs at the Pixar Web site.

Figure 389.1 Pixar home page.

Figure 389.2 Toy Story images.

AI CAFÉ C/C++ CGI HTML HTTP JAVA J++ PERL VBSCRIPT VRML WIN32 WINSOCK 110011010010111001101110011010101000110011001001 01

PIXEL-PLANES HOME PAGE

http://www.cs.unc.edu/~pxpl/home.html

The Pixel-Planes Project is a research group dedicated to building graphics engines with an emphasis on scalability and real-time rendering. Their goal is also to provide hardware and software platforms upon which new graphics and computer-interaction techniques can be explored. The project's name reflects one of the principle techniques used for fast rendering: the basic building block is a plane of processors, each with a few bytes of its own memory, operating in unison. A pixel plane associates each picture element (pixel) on the screen with a unique processor. This elegant solution can produce some stunning, rapid results. Visit the home page of the Pixel-Planes Project for more details.

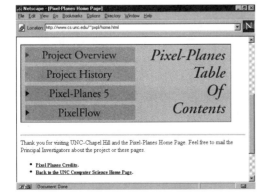

Figure 390.1 Pixel-Planes home page.

Figure 390.2 Pixel-Planes 5.

1001 PROGRAMMING RESOURCES

1001100110001010101100111011011110101110111110001101   AI CAFÉ C/C++ CGI HTML HTTP JAVA J++ PERL VBSCRIPT VRML WIN32 WINSOCK

391

POLYRAY IMAGES & SOFTWARE

http://skynet.ul.ie/~stephen/graphics.html

Polyray is a shareware rendering program for producing scenes that consist of 3-D shapes and surfaces. To create a scene, designers use a range of primitives such as *box, sphere,* and so forth to three-variable polynomial expressions and (and slowest of all) surfaces containing transcendental functions like *sin, cos,* and *log. Polyray* supports rendering in a number of different modes: ray-tracing, Zbuffered polygon, wire-frame and hidden line, and raw triangles. *Polyray's* texturing is not limited to a few predefined styles—you can use mathematical expressions to modify any part of the shading. Binaries are available for HP-UX, Linux, FreeBSD, Sun OS 4 & 5, SGI/IRIX 4 & 5, and DOS.

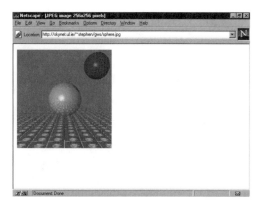

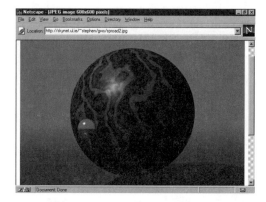

Figure 391.1 A great image.   *Figure 391.2 And another.*

392

RADIANCE: FREE DOWNLOAD

http://radsite.lbl.gov/radiance/HOME.html

Visit this site and check out the freeware *Radiance*—a "synthetic imaging system." This UNIX freeware (with a DOS port) comprises a suite of programs for the analysis and visualization of lighting in design. Input files for *Radiance* specify the scene geometry, materials, luminaries, time, date, and sky conditions (for daylight calculations). In addition, the files include calculated values such as spectral radiance (luminance + color), irradiance (illuminance + color), and glare indices. You can display the simulation results as color images, numerical values, or contour plots. To obtain the DOS port, you must go to the ADELINE Web site (*http://radsite.lbl.gov/Adeline/HOME.html*).

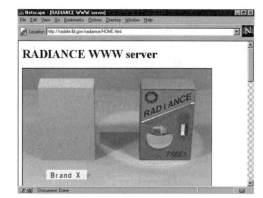

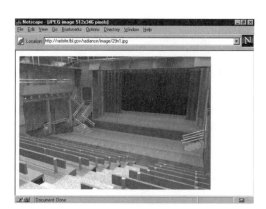

Figure 392.1 The Radiance web server.   *Figure 392.2 A Radiance image.*

AI CAFÉ C/C++ CGI HTML HTTP JAVA J++ PERL VBSCRIPT VRML WIN32 WINSOCK 1100110100101111001101110011010101000110011000100101

RAYSHADE: FREE DOWNLOAD

http://www-graphics.stanford.edu/~cek/rayshade/rayshade.html

Rayshade is a free ray-tracing package originally developed in 1988 for UNIX, but it has been rewritten and improved several times since then and now includes ports for DOS, Amiga, Mac, and OS/2. Many universities use this program to teach ray-tracing and, consequently, for research on rendering and object generation. Because of its extensibility, you will find a large number of user-contributed additions and modifications to the base renderer. Thus, many incredible images and ideas have first seen "light" under *Rayshade*, which you can download free from this site. Also, you can download many of the user-contributed additions and modifications. And don't forget to tour the great *RayShade* gallery.

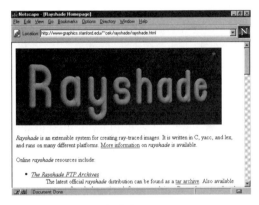
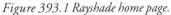

Figure 393.1 Rayshade home page.

Figure 393.2 A fantastic Rayshade image.

AI CAFÉ C/C++ CGI HTML HTTP JAVA J++ PERL VBSCRIPT VRML WIN32 WINSOCK 1100110100101111001101110011010101000110011000100101

REALIMATION: VIRTUAL REALITY DEVELOPMENT TOOL

http://www.realimation.com/

RealiMation is a set of software tools designed to assist in the development of Virtual Reality and Simulation systems. Acting as an interface between a host and an application, *RealiMation* allows developers to create small to very large systems for any application environment. And, the simulation system's hardware independence assures its portability and upgradeability. You can use *RealiMation* to create and manipulate virtual worlds, to control the development of object behavior within the virtual world, and to manage the development of a terrain that will adapt as objects move through a scene. Visit this site for specifics on *RealiMation* and to check out the free downloads.

Figure 394.1 RealiMation home page.

Figure 394.2 A free download.

395

RUTGERS VIRTUAL REALITY LAB

http://www.caip.rutgers.edu/vrlab/

The emphasis at the Rutgers Virtual Reality Lab is on forced-feedback in virtual environments and in particular on RM-II, a human-machine interface for haptic (based on the sense of touch) display in virtual reality and telerobotics. RM-II reads hand gestures (hand-master) and displays forces (haptic displays) up to four fingers in real-time. Developers have integrated the system into a number of virtual-reality simulations that are available on-line. The recently developed RM-II is a standalone system—a configuration that allows developers to connect a multitude of hardware platforms to it using Ethernet or RS232. This new system, called the RM-II Smart Interface System (RM-II-SIS), is a working example of cutting-edge virtual reality. Visit this Web site for more information and cool VR demos.

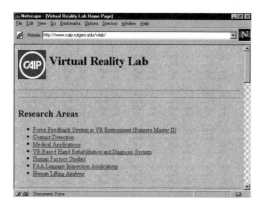

Figure 395.1 The lab's home page.

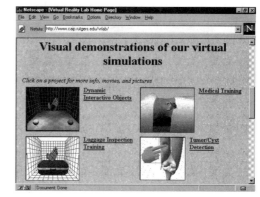

Figure 395.2 Check out great demo software.

396

THE SPANKY FRACTAL DATABASE

http://spanky.triumf.ca/

The Spanky Fractal Database is an outstanding collection of fractals and fractal-related material, which the site freely distributes across the net. Most of the software "Spanky" gathered at this site is from various FTP sites and is generally freeware or shareware. The site contains links to an enormous number of images and shareware. Check out interactive fractal explorers and other software; read on-line journal articles (and even some complete books) about fractals; access digital bibliographies and resource lists; and hot-link to the personal home pages of leading fractal gurus such as Michael Barnsley and others. This is probably the best collection of fractal resources anywhere on the Internet. Thanks, Spanky. And please, thank Alfalfa as well.

Figure 396.1 Spanky Web site.

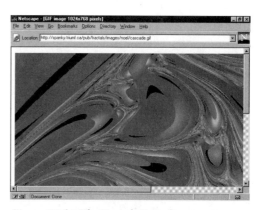

Figure 396.2 The Cascade Fractal.

THEMEKIT: SOFTWARE FOR VIRTUAL REALITY

http://www.themekit.co.uk/

Themekit provides software for Virtual Reality graphics engines, software, and tools. Their lead product, *MindRender*, is a high-performance programmer's API. And, *MindFormer* is a WYSIWYG image-designer package for use with *MindRender*. The combination of these packages enables the production of stunning real-time visuals for 3-D applications. The engine's interactive capabilities enable the rapid development of games and other programs. Apart from extremely fast true-perspective texture-mapping, *MindRender* excels at interactive feedback through the API. *MindRender* can report on any pixel location giving details such as polygon, surface, instance, and architecture labels.

Figure 397 The Themekit Web site.

VIEWPOINT: 3-D DIGITAL CONTENT PROVIDER

http://www.viewpoint.com

The folks at Viewpoint Datalabs International are the same folks who maintain the fantastic Avalon repository, discussed in site 356. Viewpoint offers the world's largest and most comprehensive selection of quality 3-D models. Their huge selection of 3-D models (datasets) is available in varying resolutions and in more than 75 file formats. The images are compatible with all major 3-D software. Passion, talent, and a commitment to accuracy, quality, and integrity has made Viewpoint the world's leader in 3-D modeling and 3-D data distribution. Viewpoint's custom and catalog products and services are used by many of the world's best modelers, animators, producers, and developers of 3-D animations and special effects. If you model or program 3-D images, this is a must-see site.

Figure 398.1 The Viewpoint Web site.

Figure 398.2 A sample Viewpoint file.

VIRTUAL REALITY ALLIANCE OF STUDENTS & PROFESSIONALS

http://www.vrasp.org/vrasp/

The mission of the Virtual Reality Alliance of Students and Professionals (VRASP) is simply to *exist* as a virtual entity where artists, scholars, and professionals can interact and share their understanding of virtual reality. The group discusses all forms of enabled, interactive 3-D experiences. Further, their mission is to examine what VR is, is not, and ought to be. Toward this end, VRASP is now committed to becoming the coolest virtual entity in cyberspace: an online community revolving around you, the virtual reality enthusiast. VRASP encourages everyone to become involved. Indeed, VRASP has designed their Web site with "audience" participation in mind. Jump in and join the scene.

Figure 399.1 The VRASP Web site.

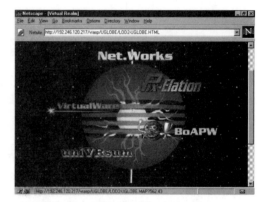

Figure 399.2 VRASP projects and products.

THE VIRTUAL REALITY STORE

http://www.thevrstore.com/

If you are looking for a place to shop on-line for Virtual Reality headgear, Virtual Reality chairs and joysticks, gaming computers, shutter glasses, 3-D video systems, books and CD-ROMs that discuss the art and science of Virtual Reality, software and shareware for Virtual Reality applications, Virtual Reality globes, and more—this is the spot! You will be amazed at the number of cool things you can buy. Also, make sure you always check the "Product of the Month," which the site offers at a special discount. When I visited, the Product of the Month was Forte VFX1 headgear (available at astonishingly great prices—as if it had all fallen "off the back of the truck." But it hadn't.) The Virtual Reality Store is wholly owned and operated by Watkins Comnet, Inc., of Aurora, Colorado. Check it out!

Figure 400 The Virtual Reality Store Web site.

AI CAFÉ C/C++ CGI HTML HTTP JAVA J++ PERL VBSCRIPT VRML WIN32 WINSOCK 11001101001011110011011100110101010001100100101

THE VISUALIZATION TOOLKIT

http://www.cs.rpi.edu/~martink/

The *Visualization Toolkit (VTK)* is a software system for 3-D computer graphics and visualization. In sum, it is a C++ class library and a Tcl implementation based on the class library. The VTK supports nearly every UNIX-based platform, as well as PCs running Windows NT and Windows 95. Object-oriented principles strongly influence the library's design and implementation. The graphics model in the *VTK* is at a higher level of abstraction than rendering libraries like *OpenGL* or *PEX*, which means creating useful graphics and visualization applications is much easier. Visit the Web page for more information and direct links to FTP sites for downloading.

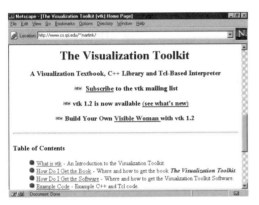

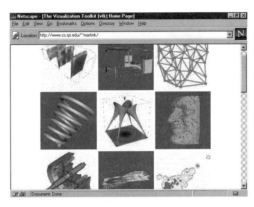

Figure 401.1 The Toolkit home page.

Figure 401.2 Some sample images.

AI CAFÉ C/C++ CGI HTML HTTP JAVA J++ PERL VBSCRIPT VRML WIN32 WINSOCK 11001101001011110011011100110101010001100100101

VIRTUS CORPORATION

http://www.virtus.com/

Virtus Corporation is a pioneer in Virtual Reality and real-time 3-D visualization software. With its emphasis on low-cost, high-quality 3-D design and presentation graphics, Virtus brought powerful, affordable virtual-reality software to the desktop computer. Virtus now enables users to build complete 3-D worlds. Their products include the *Virtus 3-D Website Builder, Virtus WalkThrough Pro, Virtus VR, Alien Skin,* and *Textureshop,* as well as the freeware VRML browsers, *Virtus Voyager* and *Virtus Player,* which Virtus invites you to download. Both browsers support Macs, PowerMacs, and Windows 95, with Voyager being the newer and more powerful of the two. Visit this site and learn more about these outstanding products.

Figure 402.1 The Virtus home page.

Figure 402.2 Free demo download!

VREAM

http://www.vream.com/

VREAM makes *WIRL*, a state-of-the-art VRML browser (the most recent ActiveX version is available now for a free download), along with other cool stuff. According to *VRML Review*, "WIRL has gotta be the hottest thing out . . . Fantastic!" Likewise, according to *Stroud's Consummate Apps List* "[WIRL is] a phenomenal new interactive 3-D VRML browser . . . If ever there was an app that showed sure signs of being the next 'big thing' or the next 'killer app,' WIRL is that app." In fact, *WIRL* was the very first Virtual Reality browser to extend VRML functionality to include object behaviors, cause-and-effect relationships, and logic. How is that for a claim to fame? You may download if you'd care to. So, would you care to?

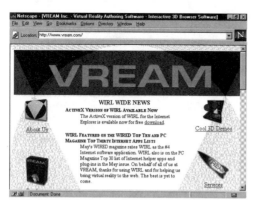

Figure 403.1 The VREAM Web site.

Figure 403.2 Free downloads!

VRML: VIRTUAL WORLDS

http://www.telecide.com/vrmlpub.htm

This site features pages that exist for demonstration and experiments with VRML. To start, visit the site, download, and install one of several available VRML viewers. Then, explore a 3-D model of the Webmaster's multimedia production suite. Make yourself at home. Look around. Poke under the desks and through open doors. Look out the windows. Check out the computers. Boy, there's a lot of computers. These guys must really like computers. And they look so real—almost as if this were a parallel world, a virtual world, a digital reality. Hey, that's what we can call it: Virtual Reality! What's that you say? Someone already came up with that? Darn. I've missed yet another chance to coin a phrase. Anyway, if you are looking for a good place to start your VRML exploration, this site is it.

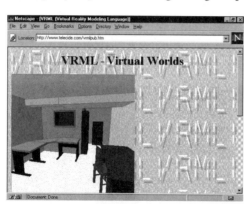

Figure 404.1 VRML - Virtual Worlds.

Figure 404.2 Stroll around.

WEBDOG'S GUIDE TO VIRTUAL REALITY: DOWNLOADS A'PLENTY

http://www.webdog.com/vr.html

This site features lots of cool links, including many downloadable VRML browsers and other goodies. Check out *Liquid Reality* (dynamic 3-D worlds based on Java), *Live3-D* for Macintosh (a slick VRML plug-in), and *ExpressVR* (another plug-in for Mac Netscape). For those of you who like to chat, you will find Microsoft *V-Chat* (a mutlimedia, multiuser chat environment), *OnLive* (real-time multipoint voice chat within 3-D virtual environments for Windows 95), and *The Palace* (excellent chat, with graphics, for PC and Mac). Last, but not least, you will encounter *QuickTime VR* (3-D QuickTime movies you can navigate through with a Mac), *VRWeb*, *DIVE* (Distributed Interactive Virtual Environment), *Virtual Society*, and more. Wow! All this good stuff in one place.

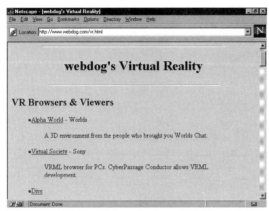

Figure 405 Webdog's Virtual Reality.

XFORMS HOME PAGE: FREE DOWNLOAD

http://bragg.phys.uwm.edu/xforms

Xforms is a GUI tool kit based on *Xlib* for X-Window systems. The tool kit features a rich set of objects, such as buttons, sliders, and menus. *Xforms* integrates these objects into an easy and efficient object and event callback execution model that allows fast and easy construction of X-applications. The library is extensible and you can easily create and add new objects. Visit these pages for coding examples and more, including tools for PERL-, Ada95-, Python-, and Fortran-binding for *XForms*. And of course, download the *XForms* library itself for a variety of platforms along with the source code, 50+ demo programs, and a GUI builder that you can use to design what you see is what you get (WYSIWYG) user interfaces, and which will automatically write the corresponding C code for you.

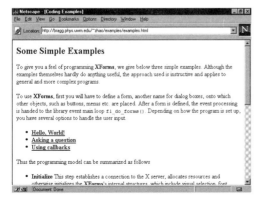

Figure 406.1 Xform's coding examples.

Figure 406.2 How to get Xforms.

407

FREE
FREE SOFTWARE

COPYRIGHT DETAILS

OPEN TO ALL

STRONG CONTENT

EXCELLENT
REFERENCES

ZIFF-DAVIS INTERACTIVE VRML INFORMATION

http://www.zdnet.com/zdi/vrml/

Get authoritative VRML discussion and analysis from Marc Pesce, the "grand poobah" of VRML and native of my home town, North Kingstown, RI! Download fantastic 3-D and VRML files from Ziff-Davis' extensive software library, including an excellent VRML browser. And, check out *ZD3-D*, designed to serve as an all-encompassing interactive source for 3-D technology, and dedicated to providing a rich virtual experience, direct access to hundreds of emerging 3-D Web sites, and a wealth of news, events, articles, and columns focusing on virtual reality. Count on Ziff-Davis Interactive and *ZD3-D* to keep you updated on the latest development on the 3-D and VRML fronts.

Figure 407.1 The ZD3-D Web site.

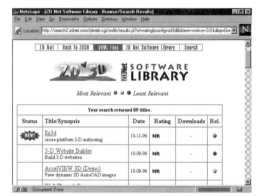

Figure 407.2 Download fantastic files.

ADDITIONAL GRAPHICS, CHAOS, AND VIRTUAL REALITY RESOURCES

Fractal Spectrum
http://www.fractal.cornell.edu/spectrum/spectrum.html

RGB fractal compression tools
http://www.jyu.fi/~kuru/fractalCompression/index.html

Complexity
http://www.cs.buffalo.edu/~goetz/al.html

CTC Math/Science Gateway: Mathematics
http://www.tc.cornell.edu/Edu/MathSciGateway/math.html

Physics Around the World: Software
http://www.physics.mcgill.ca:8081/physics-services/physics_software2.html

Complex (Adaptive) Systems Information
http://www.seas.upenn.edu/~ale/cplxsys.html

Lines, Triangles, and Fractals, Oh my!
http://www.mnsinc.com/garfield/chaos/fractal.htm

Fractals - Computer Generated
http://unite2.tisl.ukans.edu/UNITEResource/820994437-81ED7D4C.rsrc

3-D ACTIVEX CONTROLS

http://www.activex3d.com

So, you probably realize that the type of applications you can design with the 3-D Virtual Reality OCX control are limitless. At the TegoSoft Web site, you will find just a few examples of applications that you can design using the 3-D Virtual Reality OCX control. These include games programs (*Doom*-like games), fancy user interfaces, virtual showrooms, and more. Use these applications as springboards for your own ideas. Use them as models of what is possible, as ideals of something to be aspired to, or as benchmarks to be beaten! Perhaps you may be the one to take ActiveX3D to its next level. Perhaps you are the Picasso we've been waiting for. Cool stuff.

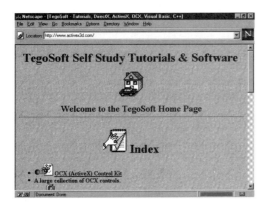

Figure 408.1 *TegoSoft home page.*

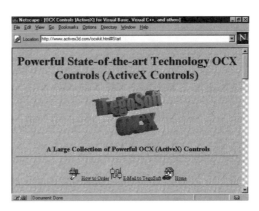

Figure 408.2 *The tools.*

ACTIVEX CONTROLS AND CONTROL SAMPLES

http://www.microsoft.com/icp/

ActiveX. You've got to love it. After all, it implements an exciting open technology that brings the power of the personal computer to the connectivity of the Internet. As all the pros know, ActiveX controls are what were formerly called *OLE controls*. But now, according to the Microsoft propaganda, ActiveX controls "combine the versatility of controls with the power of the most up-to-date Internet protocols." And, they let programmers build custom browsers, file viewing applications, newsgroup readers, mail clients, and other awesome applications. Visit this site and download the ActiveX controls, and cool samples from Bill Gates and all the fun dudes at Microsoft.

Figure 409.1 *Support from Microsoft.*

Figure 409.2 *All about ActiveX.*

1001100110001010101100111011011110101110111110001101　AI　CAFÉ　C/C++　CGI　HTML　HTTP　JAVA　J++　PERL　VBSCRIPT　VRML　WIN32　WINSOCK

FREE
FREE SOFTWARE

COVERS DETAILS

OPEN TO ALL

STRONG CONTENT

EXCELLENT REFERENCES

AOLPRESS: FREE WEB AUTHORING SOFTWARE!

http://www.aolpress.com/press/index.html

In its continuing effort to support and promote publishing on the Web, America OnLine (AOL) now offers, at no charge, *AOLpress* and *AOLserver* software. This is the same software used by AOL and GNN for its personal and professional Web publishing services. *AOLpress* is software for client-side authoring and *AOLserver* is software for server-side operations. This free distribution is AOL's gift to the Web community. And, the software couldn't be nicer. AOL designed *AOLpress* both to make Web authoring more accessible to beginners and to save valuable time and effort for professional Web publishers. Best of all, *AOLpress* Web sites can be published on any server—not just AOL's. Download it!

Figure 410.1 The AOLpress Web site.

Figure 410.2 AOLpress features.

1001100110001010101100111011011110101110111110001101　AI　CAFÉ　C/C++　CGI　HTML　HTTP　JAVA　J++　PERL　VBSCRIPT　VRML　WIN32　WINSOCK

FREE
FREE SOFTWARE

COVERS DETAILS

OPEN TO ALL

STRONG CONTENT

EXCELLENT REFERENCES

BLACK DIAMOND SURROUND VIDEO SDK

http://www.bdiamond.com/surround/surround.htm

Black Diamond's *Surround Audio Software Development Kit* (SDK) provides you with the tools you need to create awe-inspiring Internet surround sound. Visit this Web site to find out all about the SDK and to check out the *Surround Video*, which the folks at Black Diamond tell us is a "great way to view panoramic images on the Web." You'll find a demo; so if you are using *Microsoft Internet Explorer 3.0*, the download will automatically include the components you need to view the demo. If you are using Netscape, you will need to download a Netscape plug-in from the Black Diamond support page, and then copy it to your plug-ins directory before you can view the demo. Cool stuff.

Figure 411.1 The Surround Video Web site.

Figure 411.2 Support information.

AI CAFÉ C/C++ CGI HTML HTTP JAVA J++ PERL VBSCRIPT VRML WIN32 WINSOCK 110011010010111100110111001101010100011001100101

CGI-LIB.PL HOME PAGE

http://www.bio.cam.ac.uk/cgi-lib/

The *cgi-lib.pl* library makes CGI scripting in Perl easy enough for anyone to process forms and create dynamic Web content. The library is very simple to learn and easy to use. Designed for operation under Perl5 and Perl4, *cgi-lib.pl* is very efficient. It offers compatibility with all CGI interactions, including *File Upload*. The library also features convenient utility functions, supports Perl5 security features, and includes debugging facilities. The site invites you to download version 2.12 or the simpler, though less robust, version 1.14. You will also find extensive documentation. If you plan to add CGI to your Web site, using the *cgi-lib.pl* library is a great way to start.

Figure 412.1 *The cgi-lib.pl home page.*

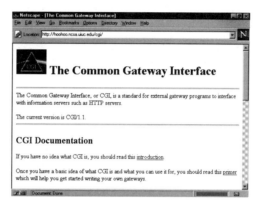

Figure 412.2 *CGI explained.*

AI CAFÉ C/C++ CGI HTML HTTP JAVA J++ PERL VBSCRIPT VRML WIN32 WINSOCK 110011010010111100110111001101010100011001100101

CMX VIEWER FOR NETSCAPE: FREE DOWNLOAD

http://www.corel.com/corelcmx/

View Corel CMX files (vector format) right on-line! Simply download the *CMX Viewer* plug-in for Netscape for Windows and place it in the Netscape/Programs/Plug-ins directory of your computer. The good folks at Corel offer you a viewer plug-in which is available to you free of charge. That's because they'd love to see more people creating CMX files for the Internet. And the viewer is absolutely free: so why not stop by for a download today and start enjoying some outstanding Corel graphics via the Internet.

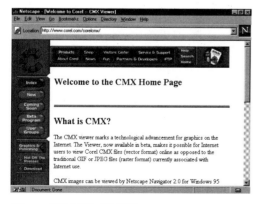

Figure 413.1 *The CMX home page.*

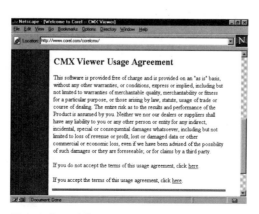

Figure 413.2 *The usage agreement.*

DUMMY

http://www.sausage.com/dummy.htm

Creating a personal Web page that's both interesting and visually appealing is still something of an art form. Considering that very few people have bothered to apply even the most basic design principles to their Web sites, a heavily-assisted HTML document composer, such as *Dummy*, is long overdue. *Dummy* is designed to take first-time Web-site authors by the hand, providing them with a step-by-step guide to Web-site creation using pre-generated style templates and a range of options. *Dummy* makes it very, very easy to create compact, elegant, ergonomically-correct Web documents. It is a veritable, automated, "Strunk & White" of digital style.

Figure 414.1 Sample Dummy screen.

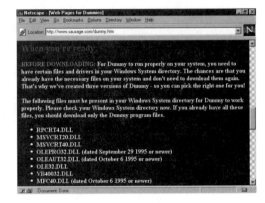

Figure 414.2 Download instructions.

EGOR: JAVA ANIMATION!—TRIAL COPY DOWNLOAD

http://www.sausage.com/egor.htm

Egor is the world's first commercial Java animator application. Use *Egor's* simple frame-by-frame assembler to create your own Java animations. You can add sounds, associate URLs with each frame or with the whole animation, and more. *Egor* is a simple and effective way to get your Web site moving and shaking with Java! The Web site invites you to download and try *Egor* on for size. The software is yours to play with for as long as you'd like to play. Check out *Egor's* awesome powers in your own time, off-line. Then, when you are ready to publish *Egor's* animations on your Web pages, simply register *Egor* for a modest fee (under $100). And, that's certainly fair, isn't it?

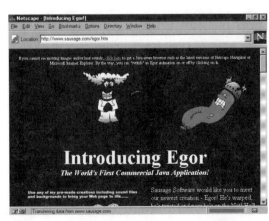

Figure 415 The Egor Web site.

EMISSARY INTERNET SOFTWARE: FREE BETA DOWNLOAD

http://www.attachmate.com/emissary/11.htm

Emissary Internet Software from Wollongong is a revolutionary new way to bring the power of the Internet to your PC with one Windows application. With *Emissary*, you can send mail, copy and retrieve files, manage interactive Telnet sessions, keep up on news, and browse the Web. At last, you don't have to juggle multiple programs, protocols, and data formats to access the information and services you need. *Emissary* is built on Wollongong's Client Object Linking Technology (or COLT) architecture. This innovative, extensible architecture enables Wollongong to build in capabilities not available in any other Internet software product. Visit this Web site, download the beta, and then go for a test drive.

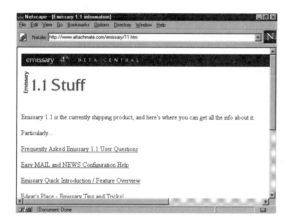

Figure 416 *Emissary's Web site.*

ENVOY FROM TUMBLEWEED SOFTWARE

http://www.twcorp.com/

Learn about *Envoy* portable document technology, and how it compares with HTML and *Adobe Acrobat*. Take advantage of the site's invitation to download *Envoy* viewers and plug-ins for free, along with demos of Tumbleweed's other products. While you are at this site, be sure to read about the new *Envoy ActiveX for MS Internet Explorer*! Of course, it also has a Netscape plug-in. *Bitstream's TrueDoc* font-embedding technology ensures that all the fonts used in authoring the document are available for display on any system. Come to the Tumbleweed Web site for more information.

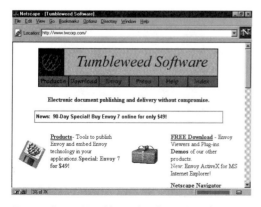

Figure 417.1 *Tumbleweed Software's Web site.*

Figure 417.2 *Product information.*

FIGLEAF INLINE PLUG-IN FOR NETSCAPE: DOWNLOAD A DEMO

http://www.ct.ebt.com/figinline/

FIGleaf Inline is a *Netscape Navigator* plug-in that lets you view, rotate, and scroll around a variety of raster and vector graphic formats within a *Netscape Navigator* window. *FIGleaf Inline* adds rotation of all images to 0, 90, 180, or 270 degrees, and enables you to view multipage files. The plug-in displays scrollbars when the user zooms in on an image, or when the image is too large for display in the default window. Versions are available for Windows 95 and Windows NT, UNIX Sun OS 4.1.3, UNIX Solaris 2.4, and UNIX IRIX 5.3. If you like the demo version, you can purchase the full version of the product for just $19.95.

Figure 418.1 The FIGleaf Web site.

Figure 418.2 Product details.

FLASH: FREE DOWNLOAD

http://www.sausage.com/flash.htm

Flash is a small user-friendly tool that lets you, the Webmaster, display scrolling text within a browser's status line—sort of like ticker-tape. *Flash* is a great way to pass subtle bits of information to your viewers. The site invites you to download a fully functional copy of *Flash* which entitles you to a free 14-day evaluation period, after which the authors hope you will purchase the software for the modest sum of $25. Important note: because of a bug (confirmed by Microsoft) that makes the *Internet Explorer 3.0* incompatible with many FTP servers, you cannot download this software using *Internet Explorer 3.0*. Instead, use the *Netscape Navigator* or an FTP client to download the software.

Figure 419.1 What Flash looks like.

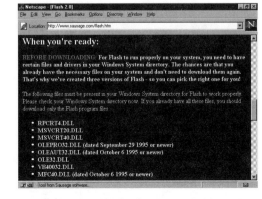

Figure 419.2 Downloading instructions.

AI CAFÉ C/C++ CGI HTML HTTP JAVA J++ PERL VBSCRIPT VRML WIN32 WINSOCK 1100110100101111001101110011010101000110011001001011

SPREADSHEET PLUG-IN FOR NETSCAPE—DOWNLOAD A DEMO

http://www.visualcomp.com/f1net/download.htm

Published by Visual Components, *Formula One/NET* is the first Internet spreadsheet component that lets you embed live spreadsheets and charts directly into a *Netscape Navigator* window. You may also want to check into *Formula One/NET Pro*, which adds a pop-up Workbook Designer for Netscape. *Formula One/NET Pro* comes with a fully functional, 32-bit, standalone spreadsheet application which can read and write Excel workbooks. Both programs come with 16- and 32-bit OLE controls which you can use in leading development environments, including Visual Basic, Visual C++, and PowerBuilder. Visit the Web pages for more information and for the downloads.

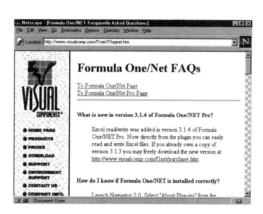

Figure 420.1 *The Formula One/NET Web site.*

Figure 420.2 *Formula One FAQ.*

AI CAFÉ C/C++ CGI HTML HTTP JAVA J++ PERL VBSCRIPT VRML WIN32 WINSOCK 1100110100101111001101110011010101000110011001001011

FRONTPAGE 97 FOR WINDOWS 95: FREE DOWNLOAD

http://www.microsoft.com/frontpage/

FrontPage 97 is Microsoft's entry into the HTML-editor and Web-site-management market. The *FrontPage 97* software keeps track of your site's links and makes it easy for you to change your Web site design. Visit this site and check out *FrontPage 97*. You will find that *FrontPage 97* includes major enhancements and new functionality over the previous version and includes a great Bonus Pack of extra goodies. The added features of *FrontPage 97* with Bonus Pack include support for the newest Internet technologies (such as ActiveX and Java), and Microsoft Image Composer, a sophisticated application for composing WEB-ready images. Great stuff.

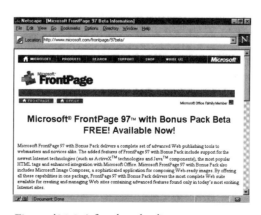

Figure 421.1 *FrontPage 97 information.*

Figure 421.2 *A free download!*

HOMESITE FOR WINDOWS 95: DOWNLOADABLE SHAREWARE

http://www.dexnet.com/homesite.html

HomeSite is a versatile editor for creating Web pages. Its long list of features include automatic, customizable color-coding of HTML tags, a built-in HTML 2.0 browser, explorer-style pane for drag-and-drop access to documents and images, support for multiple undo operations, a frame wizard, support for style sheets and ActiveX controls, search and replace tools for text in single files or entire directories, auto-detection of image sizes, full-screen view for maximum viewable space, rulers marked with standard screen sizes, drag-and-drop tools for handling HTML documents, images and multimedia files from Windows 95 Explorer, and much more. Wow! Awesome software.

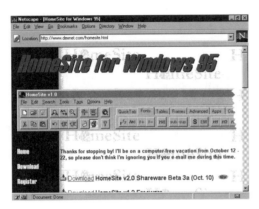

Figure 422.1 Download HomeSite 2.0 today!

Figure 422.2 HomeSite's built-in browser.

iHTML

http://www.ihtml.com/

iHTML (Inline HyperText Markup Language) is a toolkit that uses database technology to create customized content and integrated Web-site-management functions. *iHTML* supports the easy creation of sites that are dynamic (can change on the fly), have commercial appeal, and provide more features to the user. *iHTML* gives you the tools to build dynamic Web sites that allow real-time interaction between the user and the data your site presents. The *iHTML* site invites you to download and test-drive *iHTML*. See for yourself if it does not make your Web-authoring life simpler, faster, and better while doing the very same thing for the pages you create. Go for it.

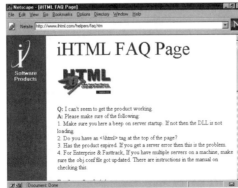

Figure 423.1 An iHTML FAQ.

Figure 423.2 Test drive the software.

AI Café C/C++ CGI HTML HTTP Java J++ Perl VBScript VRML Win32 Winsock 110011010010111100110111001101010100011001100100101

INTERNET OUTFITTERS

http://www.netoutfit.com/

If you need a professional quality Web site, or if you want to rework an existing site, you need to visit the Internet Outfitters Web site. Internet Outfitters provides content design and other services to the Web authoring/publishing community. The company (formed in 1994) provides design services and technical expertise for the Web. The company specializes in collaborative projects with corporate customers and employs a partnership philosophy in dealing with both clients and vendors. Their creative team specializes in everything from concept to delivery and from graphics to on-line marketing. Their in-house technical team delivers the best in hardware and software tools primed for the Internet. Their clients include CompuServe and Toshiba America. Visit their Web pages for more information.

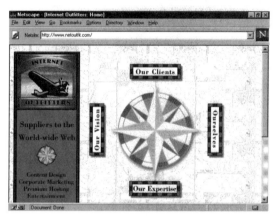

Figure 424 *The Internet Outfitters home page.*

AI Café C/C++ CGI HTML HTTP Java J++ Perl VBScript VRML Win32 Winsock 110011010010111100110111001101010100011001100100101

JAVA WEB SITE

http://java.sun.com

At this site, which is the Internet home of *JavaSoft*, you will find an enormous array of topics that relate to Java, including technical support, documentation, developer's information, and much more. Visit this site for the Java Developers Kit (JDK), general information and white papers, a great on-line Java tutorial, information on Java language and API, and more, including the official Java Language Specification and the official Java Virtual Machine Specification. What else? Lots. Check out the job opportunities in Sun's Java Group. Or buy a Java mug, T-shirt, or cap. Or get the latest news on what the techies at Sun are dreaming up for Java's next revision.

Figure 425.1 *The Java Web site.*

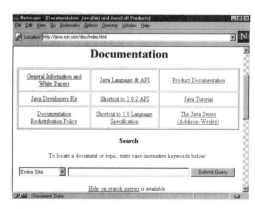

Figure 425.2 *Java documentation.*

LONE WOLF WEB DESIGN

http://www.primenet.com/~shauna/

If you don't have time to create your own Web site, or if you simply don't have the skills, check out Lone Wolf, a premier provider of Web design and Internet consulting services based in Phoenix, Arizona. Lone Wolf provides all the services your organization needs to establish a successful and enticing Internet presence, including market research, graphic design, Internet consulting, and more. If your organization is considering establishing or enlarging its on-line presence, the folks at Lone Wolf are well worth talking to as they offer research, consulting, training, graphics, and Web design expertise. They are also available as a sub-contractor to those Web shops who wish to subcontract. Check their (elegant) Web pages for more information.

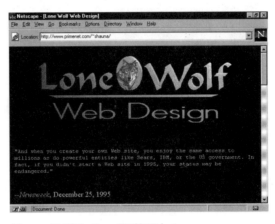

Figure 426 The Lone Wolf Web site.

MAKE IMAGE MAPS WITH WEBMAP FOR MAC

http://www.home.city.net/cnx/software/webmap.html

This site provides one of the best tools available for creating image maps on your Web site. This robust software supports both client-side and server-side image maps. It is easy to use and very powerful. Note that the freeware has been honored by *MacWorld* Magazine and several other publications as a "must have" application for editing Web image maps. By combining a clean, intuitive, easy-to-use interface, the freeware has won the hearts of millions of users worldwide. Of course, it helps that this stellar tool is also extremely inexpensive at just $25. This is one of the best deals on the Web.

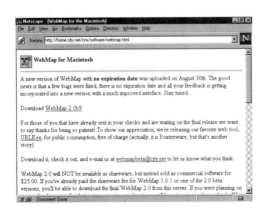

Figure 427.1 The WebMap Web site.

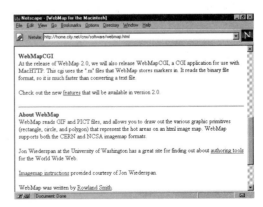

Figure 427.2 WebMap details.

AI CAFÉ C/C++ CGI HTML HTTP JAVA J++ PERL VBSCRIPT VRML WIN32 WINSOCK 11001101001011110011011100110101010001100110010010101

MATT'S WEB PAGE EDITOR FREEWARE

http://www.goshen.edu/~mattdm/edithtml/

Visit this site and check out and then download *Matt's Web Page Editor*. This software, says the author, is a "handful of Perl CGI scripts and HTML files. You can use it for free, as long as you give me credit." The scripts and HTML files combine to let users edit their Web pages from their forms-capable browsers, rather than from a UNIX shell account. Obviously, this approach is much easier for both users and administrators. The scripts seem quite elegant and efficient, and the editor runs quite nicely, enabling an easy and effortless approach to editing Web pages that even a novice will be quick to master. This all comes to you courtesy of Matt Miller of Goshen College. Thank you, Matt!

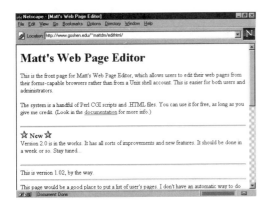
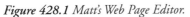

Figure 428.1 Matt's Web Page Editor.

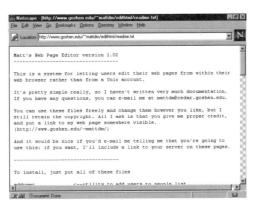

Figure 428.2 Complete on-line documentation.

AI CAFÉ C/C++ CGI HTML HTTP JAVA J++ PERL VBSCRIPT VRML WIN32 WINSOCK 11001101001011110011011100110101010001100110010010101

PERL WEB CLIENTS & OTHER PERL GOODIES

http://pubweb.nexor.co.uk/public/perl/perl.html

This site provides a great basic reference and tutorial page on Perl. The pages include a list of frequently asked questions, as well as HTML versions of the manual that comes with Perl4 and Perl5. If you find these useful, the site recommends that you download a local copy for yourself. You also get the complete texts of *Programming Perl: The Complete Perl4 Reference* and the book, *Software Engineering with Perl*. And, you get links to other sites including one that contains some general-purpose Perl5 modules for the Web. You can also connect to Plexus (an http server implemented in Perl), a great Web client library distribution for Perl4, an object-oriented URL module for Perl5, and an object-oriented Web module for Perl5. If you use Perl, you must visit this site.

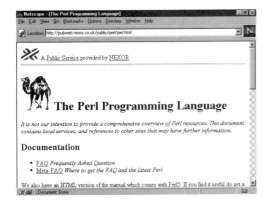

Figure 429.1 The Perl Web site.

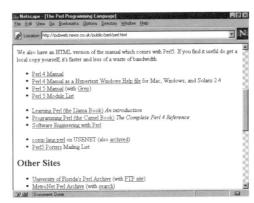

Figure 429.2 A few of your options.

PERL FOR WIN32 FAQ

http://www.perl.hip.com/PerlFaq.htm

How does one go about installing Perl for Win32? What are some of the problems, and solutions, involved in porting your working UNIX script to Perl for Win32? How can you get HTML files through the HTTP protocol with NT-based Perl scripts? How do I run my Perl script as a CGI-script? And so forth. The questions go on and on. You will also get information on debugging, GUI-creation, incorporating sounds and 3-D images, and other arcane aspects of the mysterious voodoo associated with using Perl for Win32 to create dazzling Web installations. Great stuff.

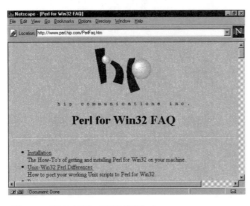

Figure 430.1 The FAQ Web site.

Figure 430.2 Installation questions.

REALAUDIO PLAYER 3.0: FREE DOWNLOAD

http://www.realaudio.com/products/player/index.html

RealAudio represents the standard for playing streaming audio on the Net. *RealAudio* enabled Web sites can even provide live audio, such as concerts, radio programs, and more. The *RealAudio Player* is available on a free download basis for individual use. For under $30 you can step up to *RealAudio Player Plus*, which provides all the standard *RealAudio* features plus near-CD quality over standard modems with *PerfectPlay* and lets you scan and preset hundreds of live *RealAudio* sites, plus record your own *RealAudio* content. For most folks, however, *RealAudio Player 3.0*, which is the one available free, will fit the bill nicely.

Figure 431 RealAudio Web site.

SHOCKWAVE DOWNLOAD FROM MACROMEDIA

http://www.macromedia.com/shockwave/

Shockwave, Macromedia's collection of Windows and Mac audio and video tools for multimedia authoring, is taking the planet by storm, especially in its new release with streaming audio. Visit this site and download a copy of *Shockwave*. In addition, you can access a hyperlink gallery that takes you to the "best of the best" shocked sites across the Internet. Also, take time to dip into extensive Macromedia Technotes, lists of frequently asked questions, and more. In addition, you will get at all the tools and information you need to create Internet multimedia and high-impact graphics with *Shockwave*.

(**Note:** *Before doing anything at this site, Windows95/NT Netscape 3.0 users should download the free Shockwave updater first thing, in order to avoid problems with streaming audio.*)

Figure 432.1 Download Shockwave today.

Figure 432.2 Shockwave Gallery.

SPOTTED COW MEDIA WEB TOOLBOX

http://www.spottedcow.com/tools.htm

At this site, you will find an exhaustive set of links that relate to Active-X, HTML editors, Web utilities, and other neat stuff. You will get all the tools you need to create your own Web pages and more. Visit this site often to see what new code the gurus have brewed up. You'll also find tons of stuff that relates to Java, JavaScript, and VBScript. We are talking games, applets, and much more—all the information and tools you need to make your Web pages come to life. More? OK. How about Netscape compatible plug-ins, Perl and CGI tools, and free downloadable Web browsers. Who do you have to thank for all this? The spotted cow, of course. *Mooooooo!*

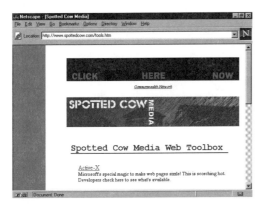

Figure 433.1 The Spotted Cow Web site.

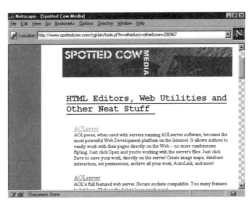

Figure 433.2 Lots of cool options.

434

TOOLVOX FROM VOXWARE: FREE DEMO DOWNLOAD

http://www.voxware.com/

ToolVox is a high-quality, low-cost way to add speech audio content to Web pages. Based on Voxware's revolutionary *MetaVoice* compression technology, *ToolVox* delivers better quality speech with 53:1 compression. That's better than three times smaller than its closest competitors! The software delivers speech quickly and reliably, even over 9.6Kbs modems, international connections, or busy servers. And, users have the option to slow down playback to improve comprehension, or speed-up playback to shorten listening times, without changing voice pitch. The site invites you to download and try a free demo of the outstanding *ToolVox*. Do so and give it a try.

Figure 434.1 The Voxware Web site.

Figure 434.2 ToolVox information.

435

TRUESPEECH PLAYER/FREE PLUG-IN FOR WINDOWS 95/NT

http://www.dspg.com/plugin.htm

TrueSpeech is a plug-in that lets you embed *TrueSpeech Player* control functions in your Web pages. The software is easy to use and elegant in function. The Start, Stop, and Rewind buttons are small and unobtrusive. (Note that *TrueSpeech* has been integrated into the final release of *Internet Explorer 3.0*, and plugs in easily to the *Netscape Navigator*.) This page, in addition to inviting you to download the *TrueSpeech Player*, also provides detailed technical support and answers a host of pertinent questions, such as: "How can I set up my Web site to support a *TrueSpeech* plug-in?" Access this Web site for more information, and download the software.

Figure 435 The TrueSpeech Web site.

AI CAFÉ C/C++ CGI HTML HTTP JAVA J++ PERL VBSCRIPT VRML WIN32 WINSOCK 1100110100101111001101110011010101000110011001001011

VIVOACTIVE PLAYER FREE DOWNLOAD FOR ACTIVEX

http://www.vivo.com/

The *VivoActive Player* for ActiveX lets you view videos on demand from any Web site. You don't need any special server software, and you can view the videos over a modem connection and from behind corporate firewalls. In other words, this is the world's first serverless streaming video product. Users report (in great numbers) that they get excellent video quality even at very low data rates. Because *VivoActive Player* has no server component, the software eliminates the high cost and hassle usually attendant to supplying streaming video. Now, even over 28.8 modems, Web surfers can watch and listen to uninterrupted streaming video and audio. The site invites you to download *VivoActive*. Do it! Do it now!

Figure 436.1 *The VivoActive Web site.*   **Figure 436.2** *VivoActive information.*

AI CAFÉ C/C++ CGI HTML HTTP JAVA J++ PERL VBSCRIPT VRML WIN32 WINSOCK 1100110100101111001101110011010101000110011001001011

VRML FOR INTERNET EXPLORER (DOWNLOAD IT NOW!)

http://www.microsoft.com/ie/ie3/

Go virtually (get it?) anywhere on the Web. "Why surf a two-dimensional Web when you can explore on-line worlds in 3-D?" ask the gurus at Microsoft. "VRML Support for Internet Explorer is a fully integrated add-on module that lets you explore virtual worlds with your mouse, keyboard, or joystick. VRML Support provides fast and easy access to virtual worlds created with VRML. So, stop just surfing the Web, and start exploring with *Microsoft Internet Explorer* with VRML Support." Microsoft invites you to download the package. Microsoft also invites you to explore some very cool 3-D worlds using *Microsoft Internet Explorer*. My advice? Go for both options.

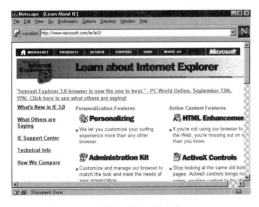

Figure 437.1 *Tools for all kinds of support.*   **Figure 437.2** *Including VRML support.*

VR SCOUT DEMO FOR WINDOWS 95 & NT

http://www.chaco.com/vrscout/

VR Scout is Chaco's VRML viewer, which displays 3-D graphics from the Web. Using *VR Scout*, you can fly through a 3-D scene, rotate a 3-D object to view it from any side, or walk through it. *VR Scout* has a headlight to illuminate scenes that don't contain their own lights. *VR Scout*, using the *Microsoft Reality Lab 3-D* graphics engine, is hardware-accelerated on a variety of 3-D graphics boards. The *VR Scout* has been rated by several independent sources as the best implementation of the VRML standard. Are you using Windows 3.1? You can download the *VR Scout* "External Viewer," which also does the job nicely.

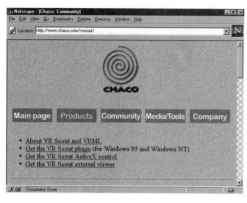

Figure 438.1 Chaco's Web site.

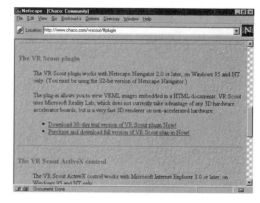

Figure 438.2 Download VR Scout today!

WEBDBC: DOWNLOAD A FREE DEMO

http://perdix.ndev.com/ndc2/response/

This site features a powerful, easy-to-use Web database development environment which provides the widest support for platforms, standards, and databases. *WebDBC* lets Webmasters create forms that insert data into their choice of database, create queries that retrieve data, and create template files to display the results. By supporting Windows 95, Windows NT, MacOS, and UNIX, *WebDBC* thrives in multi-platform, multi-vendor corporate environments. By adhering to open standards, *WebDBC* gives Web-site developers total flexibility in choosing the components for their site. So, visit this site, download a free demo, and try *WebDBC* on for size.

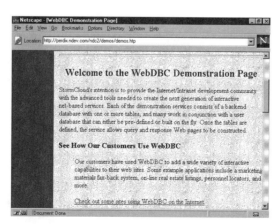

Figure 439 See WebDBC in action.

AI Café C/C++ CGI HTML HTTP Java J++ Perl VBScript VRML Win32 Winsock 11001101001011110011011100110101010001100110010101

THE WEB DEVELOPER'S VIRTUAL LIBRARY

http://www.stars.com/

This site features hundreds of links related to all aspects of Web development, including HTML, VRML, CGI, plug-ins, Perl, and much more. One particularly useful aspect of this site is a bulletin board for postings by Webmasters seeking mirror sites (very cool!). Also, you get libraries of images, icons, HTML editors and browsers, META tagging information, style guides, GIF animations, Shockwave information, and highly useful forums on all aspects of Web development from page design to attracting "hits." You will find few more useful Web resources for developers than this one. Check it out. You'll be glad you did. The library is good stuff.

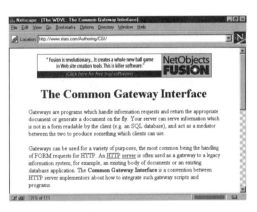

Figure 440.1 *Your many options.*

Figure 440.2 *CGI information.*

AI Café C/C++ CGI HTML HTTP Java J++ Perl VBScript VRML Win32 Winsock 11001101001011110011011100110101010001100110010101

WEB MEDIA PUBLISHER: SHAREWARE DOWNLOAD

http://www.wbmedia.com/publisher/

This site provides another strong 32-bit HTML editor which is loaded with a host of powerful features. The editor supports long file names (great for those *html* and *shtml* extensions). It provides full support for all browsers, incorporating HTML 3.2, Netscape 3.0, and MSIE features. The editor spellchecks your document with a dictionary consisting of over 100,000 words while, at the same time, automatically skipping all HTML tags. The editor also provides automated FTP-upload features that enable you to upload your files to any Web server, without having to leave the *Web Media Publisher* environment. Finally, the editor lets you view images while you add or link them to documents (no more surprises!) Check out *Web Media Publisher*.

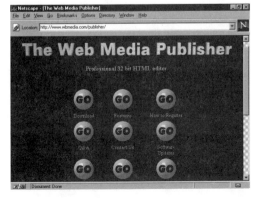

Figure 441.1 *The Web Media Publisher Web site.*

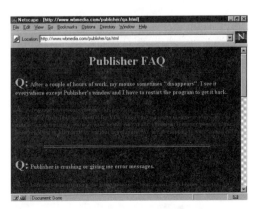

Figure 441.2 *Web Media Publisher FAQ.*

WINFRAME WEB CLIENT TECHNOLOGY FROM CITRIX

http://www.citrix.com/ms081396.htm

WinFrame is software that enables Windows application launching and embedding (ALE) across the Web. And now the technology is a part of *Microsoft Internet Explorer 3.0*. With *WinFrame*, you can run full-blown 16-bit and 32-bit Windows applications embedded in or linked to HTML Web pages. The *WinFrame* client is an ActiveX control and is based on the Citrix ICA distributed Windows Protocol. Thanks to *WinFrame*, organizations can create resources using standard Windows development tools and deploy them over the Internet to customers in an easy-to-use, intuitive Windows format. Cool.

Figure 442.1 WinFrame information from Citrix.

Figure 442.2 WinFrame Demo Room.

ADDITIONAL INTERNET AND WEB TOOL RESOURCES

- Macintosh TCP/IP Programming Libraries
  http://www.metrowerks.com/tcpip/lib/lib-index.html

- Macintosh TCP/IP Programming Libraries (Pascal)
  http://www.metrowerks.com/tcpip/lib/pascal-libs.html

- DECUS F94: NE005: Socket Programming for TCP/IP
  http://www.decus.com/F94sess-abs/ne005.html

- TCP/IP Programming Libraries (C++)
  http://www.metrowerks.com/tcpip/lib/cpp-libs.html

- TCP/IP Networks and Network Programming
  http://ruby.ils.unc.edu/210inls/syllabus.html

- TCP/IP Version 3 Release 1 for MVS
  http://www.raleigh.ibm.com/tcm/tcmover.html

- TCP/IP - Running a successful network" seminar TCP/IP - TCP/IP in the Computing
  http://www.integralis.com/training/tcpsem.html

- An Introduction to TCP/IP Programming
  http://www.tgv.com/products_and_services/education_services/old/internet/5programming.html

ACME JAVA SOFTWARE: FREE WEB TOOLS

http://www.acme.com/java/software/

If you are looking for tools to make your Web site development more productive, this is the site. "All of this is completely free for any use, educational, commercial or whatever," writes the Webmaster. "I do have to earn my grocery money, though. I'm available for consulting, and would be very interested in work that builds on these Java utilities." The utilities are certainly neat and needed. You will find various stripped-down animation applets, colorful moving splines, a simple status display for your Java virtual machine, an applet that will always show the current phase of the moon, and an applet that displays information on available fonts. They are all yours to download for free. So go for it.

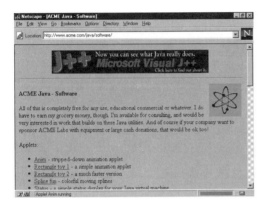

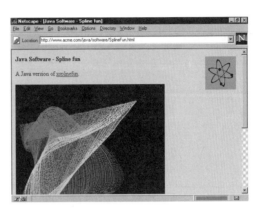

Figure 443.1 The Acme Web site.

Figure 443.2 Spline fun.

BLACK COFFEE: THE WORLD'S BEST-KNOWN JAVA APPLETS

http://www.km-cd.com/black_coffee/

Wow! Browse through this extensive database for complete Java applications and Java resources such as code libraries, tools, and tutorials. You'll find 10 business applications, 71 games, 62 graphics applications, 23 JDK (Java Developer's Kit) demos, 11 network applications, 8 science applications, 18 Web applications, and no less than 22 utilities from which to choose. Also, be sure to check out the 9 JavaScript code libraries you will find along with the 16 GUI toolkits. Take time to follow some of the links to Web sites that make cool use of Java. All of this is brought to you courtesy of Knowledge Media, Inc., as a service to the Java programming community on the World Wide Web.

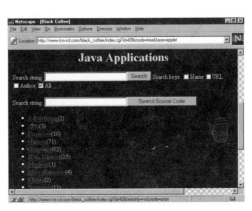

Figure 444.1 Pour me a cup.

Figure 444.2 Search the available applications.

Blue Skies for Java

http://cirrus.sprl.umich.edu/javaweather/

The weather underground was something very different way back when the Vietnam War was raging, and I was a campus radical. Today, it is more refined. More tame. It has devolved, in fact, into a group of turbo-geeks at the University of Michigan who create Java applets for weather maps and other weather-related graphics. One of their coolest creations is an applet called *Blue Skies for Java*. This applet creates interactive weather maps that contain a weather image which supports embedded textual information on current conditions and forecasts. In addition to downloading *Blue Skies for Java*, the site also invites you to view some excellent weather maps.

Figure 445.1 Blue Skies for Java.

Figure 445.2 Cool weather maps.

Jim Buzbee's Hershey Font Page

http://www.nyx.net/~jbuzbee/font.html

Jim Buzbee has implemented what he calls the "Hershey Font Set for Java." The *Hershey Font* class has methods for loading a specified *Hershey* font, setting the rotation, horizontal alignment, vertical alignment, character width, character height, font line width, italics, and "slant" specification. "I now have everything you need to use this class in an on-line zip file," writes Jim. "Note that I retain the copyright for my code and classes, but you may feel free to use it for non-commercial purposes." The fonts look great and load easily. Help yourself. Also, send Jim a thank you note if you get a chance.

Figure 446 The Hershey Font in various guises.

CafeBabe from Open Solutions: Free Download

http://members.aol.com/opensolinc/opensolution.html

CafeBabe is a Java class file viewer. The applet provides you with a user-friendly interface for viewing revisions, super-class names, and methods within a class file. You will find *CafeBabe* a valuable tool for understanding how Java classes work at the virtual machine level. This site invites you to download either the 16-bit or 32-bit version of *CafeBabe*. You are also invited to learn more about Open Solutions, a firm which provides answers to information processing problems based upon open standards including, but not limited to, Java. Download and test-drive the software. You are bound to like it.

Figure 447 The Open Solutions Web site.

Club Java from Virtual Rendezvous

http://www.magpage.com/~ashert/javaindex.htm

Virtual Rendezvous, its proprietors tell us, is "a small, virtual corporation of like-minded individuals, companies and organizations dedicated to the designing, building, and fostering of a more socially-focused version of cyberspace." In this spirit, they have put together a virtual gathering place for all those interested in Java development, thus facilitating a community of Java programmers and developers brought together to give, take, and share information, comment, opinion, and tools. At this rendezvous, you'll find jobs, consultants, links to other Java sites, links to remote Java compilers, a great Java bibliography, links to Java user groups, mailing lists, and much more. Check it out.

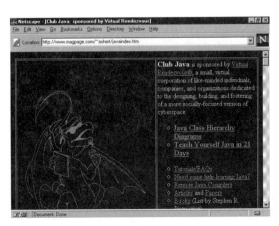

Figure 448 Club Java's Web site.

AI CAFÉ C/C++ CGI HTML HTTP JAVA J++ PERL VBSCRIPT VRML WIN32 WINSOCK

COOL JAVA APPLETS & GAMES BY MARK BOYNS

http://www.sdsu.edu/~boyns/java/

This site is loaded with very cool and absolutely free Java-based applets and games that include *Missile Commando II* (based on the arcade game *Missile Command*), *Miata* animation for *Miata.net*, *Centipedo*, *Crazy Counter!*, *Netscape Animation Fun*, *StarBase* (shoot objects before they destroy the Star Base!), *Missile Command* (the first effort modeled on *Missile Command*), and the ever-popular *Slot Machine*. Now, I'm sure there are lots of important reasons why you need to play these games. I mean, without checking out stuff like this, how will you be sure you are up with the state-of-the-art in Java programming? I mean, you owe it to your employer and to your clients to check out how *StarBase* is rendered, don't you?

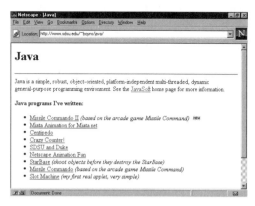

Figure 449.1 Your options.

Figure 449.2 Check out Missile Commando II.

AI CAFÉ C/C++ CGI HTML HTTP JAVA J++ PERL VBSCRIPT VRML WIN32 WINSOCK

CUP O'JOE JAVA SHOP

http://www.cupojoe.com/

The Cup O'Joe Java Shop is dedicated to providing high-quality Java resources for the serious developer. The folks at Cup O'Joe strive to present only those items which can actually assist developers in achieving their Java-related project and career goals. Cup O'Joe provides you not only with the hottest new applets and classes, but also any other information you may find relevant and useful. Visit this site for applets, applications, classes, white papers, technical support, utilities, digital reprints of important journal and magazine articles, and much, much more. You know, there is nothing quite like a nice "Cup O' Joe."

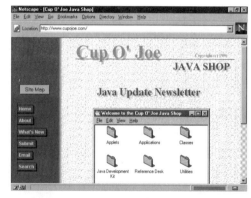

Figure 450.1 The Cup O'Joe Web site.

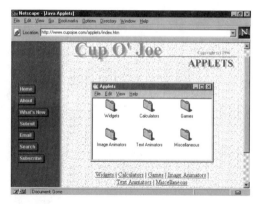

Figure 450.2 Choose from among many applets.

DIGITAL ESPRESSO: JAVA NEWS

http://www-elec.enst.fr/java/DigitalEspresso/DigitalEspresso.html

"Are you tried of wading through hundreds of messages on the Java-related mailing lists to get to the real nuggets of information? Don't you wish there was some place where you could just read the high-points?" asks the Webmaster. "Well, search no longer!" That's what Digital Espresso is all about. Digital Espresso is a weekly summary of the traffic appearing in the Java mailing lists and newsgroups. The summaries are unbiased, providing a clear reflection of what the various authors intended. At this site, you will find product announcements, press releases, happenings, course offerings, bug and warning notices, class exchange information, and much, much more. Check it out.

Figure 451.1 The Digital Espresso Web site.

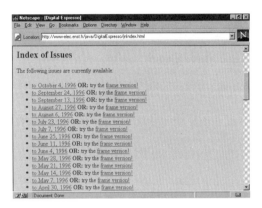

Figure 451.2 Index of issues.

DIPPY BIRD'S JAVA PAGE

http://www.dippybird.com/

The Dippy Bird Web site is loaded with gobs of great information on Java. Would you care for Java documentation in Windows Help format? Dippy Bird's got it! Do you currently use Microsoft Visual C++ for Java development? Really? Want to learn how to integrate it with the Java documentation in Windows Help format? Dippy Bird will be happy to teach you. Dippy Bird also has documentation on JavaScript and Netscape plug-ins in Windows Help format. Finally, the site invites you to read about our hero, Dippy Bird, in the hypertext treatise entitled "What is Dippy Bird and How Is it Used?" by Blair P. Houghton. By the way, Dippy Bird is fed and cleaned up after by Bill Bercik. Check out this site and the bird, but more importantly, the Java content.

Figure 452.1 Dippy Bird's Web site.

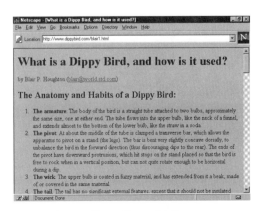

Figure 452.2 What is Dippy Bird?

THE E PROGRAMMING LANGUAGE

http://www.communities.com/e/epl.html

E is a programming language designed for developers who write distributed applications. It builds on the strength of Sun's Java language, an open standard that already provides some flexibility for developers writing Web applets. However, developers are finding that Java is not well-suited to more ambitious distributed applications because Java's incomplete security model requires unacceptable trade-offs between expressive power and safety. The E language improves on Java's security model and provides other powerful communications-oriented features. Come to these informative Web pages for many more details on E and how it can change your programming life.

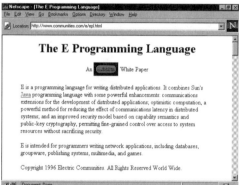

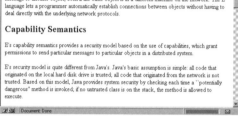

Figure 453.1 E Programming Language Web site.   *Figure 453.2 More on E.*

EARTHWEB'S GAMELAN: THE JAVA DIRECTORY

http://www.gamelan.com/index.shtml

Yes, this site features everything you ever wanted to know about Java, and more. We are talking downloadable applets, all the latest VRML and Java news, product announcements, white papers, user chat boards, newsgroups, and more. You also get expert product reviews, links to downloadable applets, browsers, and authoring tools, as well as links to the home pages of such "fathers of invention" as Mark Pesce: the big Daddy of VRML. While you are browsing the site, feel free to click on a music clip for some great background sounds: mostly Indian sitar stuff. Very soothing. "Agh! I feel so peaceful. Now if this code would only compile!"

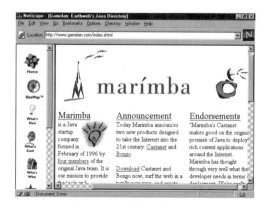

Figure 454.1 Gamelan's Web site.   *Figure 454.2 Marimba information.*

ESPRESSOGRINDER: DOWNLOAD THE QUICKEST JAVA AROUND

http://wwwipd.ira.uka.de/~espresso/

Are you interested in a Java compiler that takes up less space but works faster than any other compiler you are likely to find anywhere? If so, check out *EspressoGrinder*. The "grinder" translates beta-level Java programs into Java bytecode. Of course, it requires the beta-level Java Developers' Kit (JDK), which is available free from Sun Microsystems. After you are armed with the JDK, you can use *EspressoGrinder* as a drop-in replacement for Sun's *javac* compiler. *EspressoGrinder* works about twice as fast as *javac* and is more compact. Also, the software works on both UNIX and Windows 95 systems. *EspressoGrinder* is well worth a test drive by any serious Java programmer.

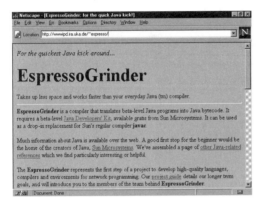

Figure 455.1 The EspressoGrinder Web site. *Figure 455.2 Software details.*

DANNY GOODMAN'S JAVASCRIPT PAGES

http://www.dannyg.com/javascript/

Danny Goodman has written many successful books on AppleScript, as well as JavaScript. His Web pages are packed with application excerpts from his book, selected, as he writes, "to demonstrate JavaScript concepts of concern to scripters." The pages also feature a challenge: Java versus JavaScript— do you know the difference? Java, of course, is a full-fledged object-oriented programming language that you use to create standalone applications and mini-applications called *applets*. JavaScript is a small language that, as Danny reminds us, "does not create applets or standalone applications." Rather, you embed JavaScript right within an HTML file. Take time to visit Danny's site. You'll be glad you did.

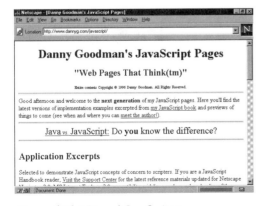

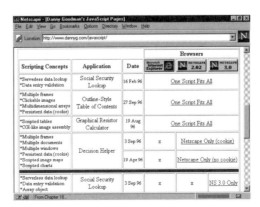

Figure 456.1 Danny's JavaScript pages. *Figure 456.2 Some cool software.*

GUIDE TO JAVA!!!

http://www.surinam.net/java/java.html

At this site, you will find links to the JARS (Java applet rating service); freeware, shareware, and commercial Java products; utilities programs; zines (electronic magazines) and books; Java news; Java training and seminars; and super cool Web pages using Java. You will also find information on Java user groups, a fantastic Java business listing, a Java Who's Who, answers to frequently asked questions, and much more. You also get links to Java tutorials, class hierarchy information, and essential Java developer links. This is one of several excellent clearinghouses for Internet-based Java information. Who is in the Who's Who links? Stop by and see!

Figure 457 A large array of options.

IBM CENTRE FOR JAVA TECHNOLOGY DEVELOPMENT

http://ncc.hursley.ibm.com/javainfo/

The IBM Centre for Java Technology Development is a one-stop Web site for news, information, and access to various IBM code ports for *AIX 4.1.3* or later, *OS/2 Warp Version 3 Java Developer's Kit*, and Windows. Visit this site and download the Windows applet development kit and other new Java technology from IBM's *alphaWorks* library. Then, read about the Java support built into *OS/2 Warp 4*. You might take time to download the beta for *Netscape Navigator* for *OS/2 Warp*. David Mounce, of IBM's staff in the United Kingdom, maintains this whole set of pages. David also provides cool links, developers information, links to discussion groups, and more.

Figure 458.1 Java at IBM.

Figure 458.2 The alphaWorks library.

JAMBA FROM AIMTECH: FREE TRIAL DOWNLOAD

http://www.aimtech.com/prodjahome.html

Jamba is a Java authoring software tool that enables Internet developers to create interactive, media-rich applets without programming or scripting. Built on industry standard object-oriented software technology and Sun's new Java technology, *Jamba* meets the growing demand for easy-to-use tools that enhance the interactivity of a company's Internet efforts. What is more, *Jamba* supports ActiveX in several ways. And, *Jamba* includes an ActiveX player which is both an ActiveX server and an ActiveX *Document* object. For more details on *Jamba*, and for a free download of a trial version, visit the Aimtech Web pages.

Figure 459 Jamba home page.

jaNet: DOWNLOAD A FREE JAVA NEURAL NETWORK TOOLKIT

http://www.isbiel.ch/Projects/janet/index.html

jaNet is a Java-based neural network toolkit. With *jaNet* you can design and optimize an ideal neural network for your private application. And, when the network is ready and cooked, you can save it in a file. You can then include the network in your application using *jaNet.backprop*, which is also available at this site for you to download. Not only may you download *jaNet* and *jaNet.backprop*, but you can also access the source under the GNU General Public License (GPL). There is one drawback—for now, the documentation is only available in French; however, it'll probably be translated into English some time soon. *Parlez-vous Français?*

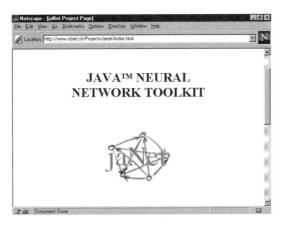

Figure 460 The jaNet Web site.

461 JPAD JAVA EDITOR: SHAREWARE DOWNLOAD

http://www.sni.net/express/

JPad is a basic Java editor published by ModelWorks and integrated with Sun's Java tools. *JPad* makes it easy to write, compile, and run Java programs in a single environment. New features in *JPad 2.0* include syntax coloring and access to on-line Java documentation. *JPad* also includes a project manager with class, package, and file views, as well as template insertion, and syntax coloring for Java, JavaScript, and HTML. *JPad* also supports the Java development environment and Sun's Java Development Kit (JDK). Its powerful syntax checking is ideal for finding errors in JavaScript-enabled HTML pages. Visit this site and download the shareware today. You'll be glad you did.

Figure 461.1 The ModelWorks Web site.

Figure 461.2 JPad Pro details.

462 JAVACHART APPLETS AND CLASSES

http://www.ve.com:80/javachart/

Check into *JavaChart*, a great new class library for creating charts in Java. Whatever types of charts you need, *JavaChart* can handle it, including bar, pie, line, and area charts, as well as combinations of various types of data representations (mixed bar and area charts, for example). Note that *JavaChart's* extensible architecture also permits Java programmers to add new kinds of charting elements that combine with existing chart elements. *JavaChart* is loosely modeled after Visual Engineering's C language charting library, *Visual C-Chart*, a product that has been in production for many years and is a part of many commercial software products. If you create charts, this is a must-see site.

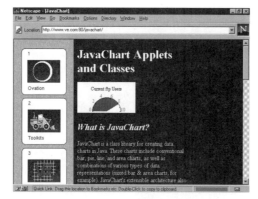

Figure 462.1 JavaChart Applets and Classes.

Figure 462.2 Check out some cool applets.

JAVA APPLETS AT GEORGIA TECH

http://www.cc.gatech.edu/grads/k/Colleen.Kehoe/java/local.html

Visit this Georgia Tech site for some great Java applets with source code. The goodies include a simple Java version of *MindSweeper*, an illustrated tutorial on 2-D transformations, a simple scientific calculator, and *JavaCup* (a Java-based constructor of useful parsers or, in other words, a system for generating look ahead left to right parsers from simple specifications). Of course, you also get many more applets, as well as links to a multitude of additional Java sites on the Web. All of this comes to you courtesy of Webmistress Colleen Kehoe, who is also the author of yet another applet available at this site: an adaptive Java-based survey that is generated "on-the-fly." Thanks, Colleen.

Figure 463.1 Java at Georgia Tech.

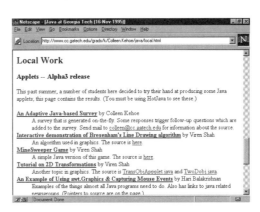

Figure 463.2 Download these applets.

THE JAVA BOUTIQUE

http://www.j-g.com/java/

"The Java Boutique," writes the Webmaster, "is a resource for Internet users that would like to add Java Applets to their own Web sites. The boutique currently houses more than 100 working Applets, along with instructions for downloading and including the applets within other Web pages." You will find audio applets, educational applets, games applets, text applets, utilities applets, and visual applets. Be sure to check out *billsClock* (an attractive analog clock with a moving second hand) and *GuestbookIII* (which lets guests add comments to a browser-based guest log on the Web). You will find much more here—go for it.

Figure 464 The Java Boutique.

465

JAVA CLASS VIEWER (FREE DOWNLOAD)

http://www.intac.com/~robraud/classinfo.html

The *Java ClassViewer* is an application with which you can view the methods and variables defined in the Java class file. The program also lets you browse into any other class that is referred to within the class file. The *Java ClassViewer* is most useful when the source code is not available for your review and as a verification and troubleshooting tool. The viewer is written in Java; therefore, it works on any Java-supported platform. However, you can't run the application as a downloaded applet because downloaded applets don't have access to the local hard drive. To use the *ClassViewer*, you have to have Java Virtual Machine available, which you can download from Sun Microsystem's Java site. A very good applet.

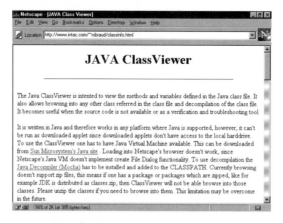

Figure 465 The ClassViewer.

466

THE JAVA COMPANION

http://www.xs4all.nl/~dgb/java.html

Visit this site for Java white papers, overviews, applet and API packages, the complete Java language specification, along with downloadable Java tools from Sun, IBM, Netscape, and Symantec, as well as Borland's *Java Debugger*. You will also find links to great Java sites which include *Blackdown*, the Java-Linus porting project, Dimension X Java, the Coriolis Group's Java pages, MindQ Publishing, Marimba Corporation, and more. The Java Companion is an excellent clearinghouse of links, tools, and information by and for Java developers operating at all levels of expertise. This site is well worth your visit. You are sure to find some gem at this site of which you were not previously aware.

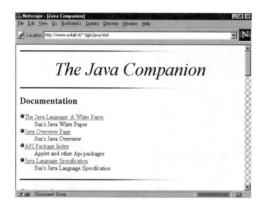

Figure 466.1 The Java Companion.

Figure 466.2 Corporate links.

JAVA DEMO SITE

http://193.92.55.33/java/

Visit the Java Demo Site and check out dozens of cool examples of Java applets which include *Clock* (an animated clock showing Greek time), *Animator* (a sequence of animations), *Arc Test* (an Arc test demonstration), *Barchart* (a charting example), *Blink* (colorful blinking text), *bouncing heads* (heads bouncing on a box), *Card Test* (an example of playing cards), *Dither Test* (shows the ins and outs of dithering), *Draw Test* (demonstrates Java drawing capabilities), *Fractal* (Java-generated fractal graphics), and much more. You will also get image-map applets, jumping-box applets, a great example of scrolling images, the famous tic-tac-toe game, and lots of other great stuff. A cool visit!

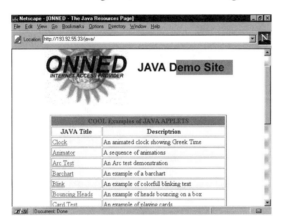

Figure 467 The Java demo site.

JAVA LAUNCHING PAD

http://ng.netgate.net/~aronoff/JavaLinks.html

This site is a one-stop shop for Web-based Java information! You will find white papers, executive summaries, bibliographies, the latest scoop on add-ons to the Java APIs, documentation, tutorials, presentations, lists of frequently asked questions, magazine articles on Java, and applet libraries. In addition, the site provides you with access to all the Java materials from *GeekWeek@Pikes.Peak*, JavaScript information, and more. Be sure to check out "Java: The Inside Story," an interesting article on the history of Java and its genesis out of C++. Also, treat yourself to the information on *Java Beans*, which provides support for persistent data, inter-component GUI management, messaging, layout control, and more.

Figure 468.1 The Launching Pad.

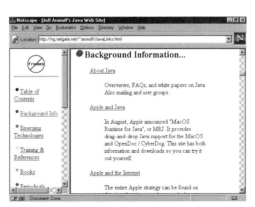

Figure 468.2 Background information.

1001 PROGRAMMING RESOURCES

1001100110001010101011001110110111110101110111110001101   AI CAFE C/C++ CGI HTML HTTP JAVA J++ PERL VBSCRIPT VRML WIN32 WINSOCK

JAVALINKS FROM TEAMJAVA

http://www.teamjava.com:80/links/

This site is packed with hundreds of great links to Java sites from the around the globe. Included are links to excerpts from Java documentation and books, Java forums, Java-based on-line games, applet collections, Java "advocate" links, non-English Java sites, Java products, JavaScript links, and much more. You also get links to Macintosh Java resources, VRML resources, software archives, universities doing cutting-edge graphics research involving Java, technical notes, and white papers. Furthermore, you will find links to Sequter Software, Object Design, Future Tense, WebLogic, QuickStream, Cedar Ridge Software, Rogue Wave, and other leaders in the field of Java tools and programming.

Figure 469 The TeamJava Web site.

JAVA AND THE NEXT OBJECT MODEL: A NATURAL CONVERGENCE

http://www.next.com/WebObjects/Java.html

At this site, you will find a great white paper from NeXT that discusses how their Object Model and Java can overcome HTML limitations by improving client performance, enabling the creation of dynamic, real-time Web applications, and by providing the ability to create a wide variety of user-interface components. As the paper explains, NeXT's Object Model enhances Java's capabilities and addresses current server-side limitations by giving developers the ability to distribute applications over multiple server machines, increasing platform independence, and integrating Web applications with the organization's existing client/server computing environment. A good read from a technology leader.

Figure 470.1 The discussion.

Figure 470.2 The NeXT Web site.

JAVA OASIS: FREE JAVA SOFTWARE REPOSITORY

http://www.oasis.leo.org/java/

"Java Oasis," writes its Webmaster, is "a repository for free Java related software and documentation. We, the Java Oasis Team, tried to restrict ourselves to software and documentation which is of interest, especially for developers. But for all others who are interested in Java, there should be something in our archive for you, too." And, indeed there is. Visit Java Oasis for Java-enabled Web browsers, applets and applications written in Java, and more. Everything you find at this site is either freeware, public domain, or covered under the GNU General Public License (GPL). Best yet, all the software includes source code. So, go for it!

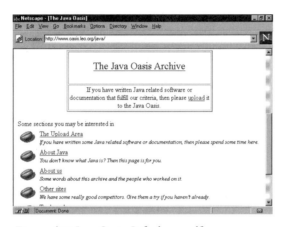

Figure 471 Java Oasis. Refresh yourself.

JAVA ON-LINE TUTORIAL FROM SUN

http://java.sun.com:80/books/Series/Tutorial/TOC.html

Sun's great tutorial starts off with a review of object-oriented programming concepts and then gets in to the nuts and bolts of the Java language. You will learn the ins-and-outs of applets, methods for drawing images and event handling, what applets can and can't do, the art of adding an applet to an HTML page, and how to send messages to other applets on the same page. You will also learn how to use Java to create a graphical-user interface, how to create and manipulate images, how to implement secure networking, and much more, including how to incorporate C/C++ routines in native method implementations. All in all, you will find no better Java introduction on the Web.

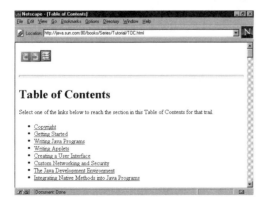

Figure 472.1 The Table of Contents.

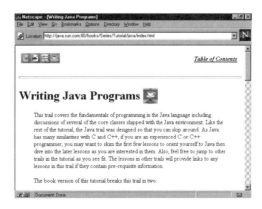

Figure 472.2 Writing Java Programs.

AI CAFE C/C++ CGI HTML HTTP JAVA J++ PERL VBSCRIPT VRML WIN32 WINSOCK

JAVA SECURITY: FROM HOTJAVA TO NETSCAPE AND BEYOND

http://www.cs.princeton.edu/sip/pub/secure96.html

As Java emerges as a standard for embedding programs into Web pages, a number of people are making serious studies of Java's security. Though Java's security is better than that of most other Internet-programming tools, the potential scope of Java's deployment requires rigorous study and the maintenance of a high security standard. Most analysts, including the authors of this timely on-line paper, believe that developers must improve Java's security in several ways. Some of these improvements will fix small, localized bugs, while other fixes require significant changes in Java's structure. Tune into this site for more details.

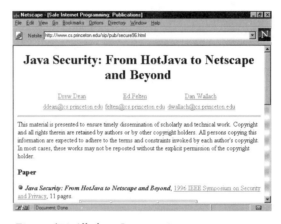

Figure 473 All about Java security.

AI CAFE C/C++ CGI HTML HTTP JAVA J++ PERL VBSCRIPT VRML WIN32 WINSOCK

JAVA SPECIAL INTEREST GROUP

http://www.sug.org/java-sig.html

The Java Special Interest Group (Java SIG) recognizes the simple fact that if you use the World Wide Web, Java is your future. Java SIG is quickly becoming *the* national user group for anyone interested in developing, publishing, or even just playing with Java and *HotJava*. First and foremost, Java SIG is a channel of communication, connecting Java users and developers all over the world. In addition, Java SIG is a source of hot news and information about all the latest Java developments. Check out Java SIG and its cool library of applets, its great book reviews, and its list of links to local Java groups in your area.

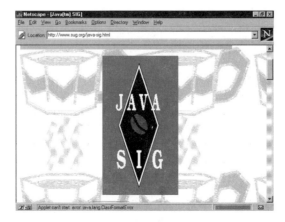

Figure 474 The Java SIG Web site.

AI CAFÉ C/C++ CGI HTML HTTP JAVA J++ PERL VBSCRIPT VRML WIN32 WINSOCK 11001101001011110011011100110101010001100100100101

JAVA USER RESOURCE NETWORK (JAVA URN)

http://www.nebulex.com/URN/

This site features the premier information base for Java related programming, applets, products, and services. Whether you just want to try a taste of Java, or if you are pulling an "all nighter" of programming, and you have a critical question whose answer you must know NOW, the Java User Resource Network (Java URN) is the place to come. In fact, the URN can provide you with all you need to know about the latest and greatest Java blends (such as J++). That's right. Now all the resources you need are organized at one site. You will find applets, consultants, developers, links to related Java sites, Java news, and much more. This site is one for you to bookmark.

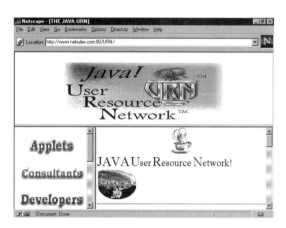

Figure 475 The URN Web site.

AI CAFÉ C/C++ CGI HTML HTTP JAVA J++ PERL VBSCRIPT VRML WIN32 WINSOCK 11001101001011110011011100110101010001100100100101

JAVOLOGY ON-LINE E-ZINE OF JAVA NEWS & OPINIONS

http://www.magnastar.com/javology/

This constantly updated, on-line e-zine (electronic magazine) covers *Java Beans*, Java for *Netscape ONE* and ActiveX, and Java security, as well as new Java products. You will find specifics on all the best Java books, interactive Java tutorials, interactive Java atlases, and other similar topics. You'll find dozens of articles at this site, not a few of which explain how you can seamlessly integrate Java programs with other applications like *Netscape Navigator*, *Internet Explorer*, *VisualBasic*, *Word*, and *Excel*. No serious Java developer or user should skip a single "issue" of *Javaology*, the on-line e-zine of Java news and opinions.

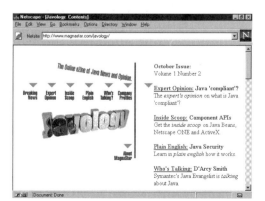

Figure 476.1 Javology.

Figure 476.2 Expert opinion.

THE JAVASCRIPT INDEX

http://www.c2.org/~andreww/javascript/

This very useful site is packed with JavaScript source-code listings, demo applets, documentation, links to people, and other resources related to the world of JavaScript. You will find programmer pages, widgets, source code, magazine and journal article reprints, calculators, games, newsgroups, tutorials, mailing lists, chat rooms, and more. Note: the site requires JavaScript capability. Also, the site's blinking red dots mean that a section of the index has been recently updated. Andrew Wooldridge built and maintains the whole site with *BBEdit*. The JavaScript Index has won several awards and ranks as a Crest Top 25 site.

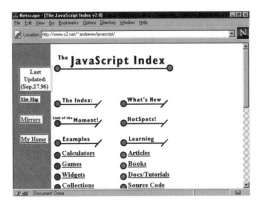

Figure 477.1 The JavaScript Index.

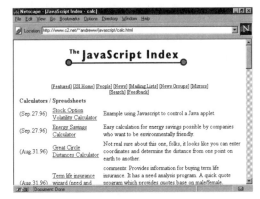

Figure 477.2 Calculators.

JAVAWORLD MAGAZINE

http://www.javaworld.com

What doesn't the on-line home of IDG's *JavaWorld* have? What does it leave out? Nothing. Visit this site to find expert tutorials, tips, tricks, applet reviews, tools, newsgroup summaries, and more. Any time you visit, you will find 50 or more new stories and news briefs, as well as details on such pertinent topics as how to build commercial-quality Web applets with Java, how to work with *Lucent's Inferno* development kit, the Zen of floating-point math, Netscape's JavaScript "privacy" bug, and more. And, every day you'll find a reading assignment. On the day I visited, the reading assignment was a fundamental chapter on Java class loader basics with an "extra-credit" sidebar addressing the observer interface and the observable class. Great content!

Figure 478 The JavaWorld Web site.

JPP—A PREPROCESSOR FOR THE JAVA LANGUAGE

http://www.digiserve.com/nshaylor/jpp.html

JPP (Java preprocessor) is a preprocessor that adds closures and operator overloading to Java. This new version of the preprocessor has fixed a bug that had previously prevented its use on UNIX platforms. The precise features that *JPP* adds to Java are block closures, local variable renaming, operator overloading, assert and trace macros, conditional compilation, and nested comments. The preprocessor accomplishes this by converting an input *JPP* file into a standard *java* file that you then compile using any standard Java compiler. The *JPP* file contains normal Java statements with syntactic extensions for the new features. This all comes to you courtesy of the author, Nick Shaylor.

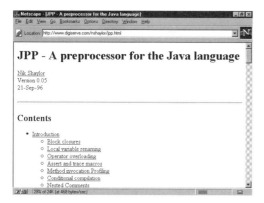

Figure 479.1 The JPP Web site.

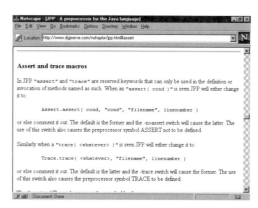

Figure 479.2 Assert and trace macros.

A JAVA PROGRAMMING ENVIRONMENT (FREE DOWNLOAD!)

http://www.dstc.edu.au/projects/kalimantan/

This package was formerly known, in another life, as *Espresso*. *Kalimantan* is a collection of basic tools designed to simplify the task of constructing serviceable applications and applets using Sun's Java programming language. *Kalimantan* builds on the Sun-supplied Java API with a graphically oriented interface to useful facilities. *Kalimantan* works with Sun's Java Developers Kit (JDK) and has been tested under Solaris 2.4 and Windows 95. The *Kalimantan* environment currently consists of an inspector to examine the internal variables of objects and a debugger to monitor the execution of Java applications. This a great tool and it's free!

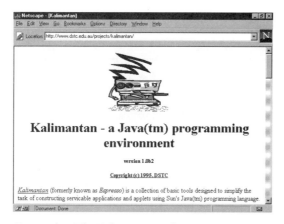

Figure 480 The Kalimantan Web site.

Kawa Java IDE: Download for 30-Day Free Trial

http://www.fni.net/kawa/

Kawa is a Java Integrated Development Environment (IDE) that helps programmers build Java applications and applets directly on 32-bit machines. Kawa supports the Windows 95, NT 3.51, and NT 4.0 platforms. *Kawa* is powerful and very intuitive. It uses the project-development metaphor that you find in all modern development tools. *Kawa* includes a project editor, project manager, GUI debugger, class browser, and on-line help for the Java API, as well as the Java Language Reference, a class editor, and much more. Note that, while professionals are asked to register their copy of the IDE after 30-days for a moderate fee, the IDE is free to students and faculty members using the IDE for instructional purposes.

Figure 481.1 The Kawa Web site.

Figure 481.2 The latest Kawa news.

Liquid Reality & Liquid Motion: Demo Download

http://www.dimensionx.com/products/index.html

Check out *Liquid Reality* and *Liquid Motion*, two state-of-the-art Java development tools from DimensionX. *Liquid Reality* provides a robust set of Java class libraries designed for the creation of tools and viewers for interactive VRML 2.0 worlds. *Liquid Motion* is an authoring tool for creating animations in Java. In general, *Liquid Motion* is a drag-and-drop tool that lets you create animated scenes with backgrounds and soundtracks, sprites with different behaviors, drawn paths, and so on. When you save your animation, *Liquid Motion* outputs a set of class files that make up a new Java applet. You don't have to write a line of code (unless you want to)! Visit this site and download a demo copy of one or both items.

Figure 482 Liquid Reality's Web site.

AI CAFE C/C++ CGI HTML HTTP JAVA J++ PERL VBSCRIPT VRML WIN32 WINSOCK 1100110100101111001101110011010101000110011001001 01

MAC OS RUNTIME FOR JAVA: FREE DOWNLOAD

http://www.devtools.apple.com/mrj/

If you are doing serious Web development for the Mac platform, you need to check out Apple's Java execution environment—*Mac OS Runtime for Java* (*MRJ*), which you can download. To run *MRJ*, you need Power Macintosh or a 68030 or 68040 Macintosh, System 7.5 or later, 8MB RAM (16MB or more recommended), 5MB of free disk space, and *OpenDoc 1.0.4*, or later. So climb aboard a train headed toward the future of Mac programming: *Mac OS Runtime for Java*.

Figure 483.1 Mac OS Runtime for Java.

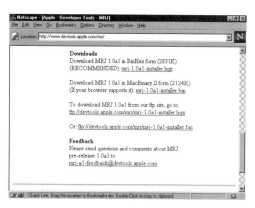

Figure 483.2 Download information.

AI CAFE C/C++ CGI HTML HTTP JAVA J++ PERL VBSCRIPT VRML WIN32 WINSOCK 1100110100101111001101110011010101000110011001001 01

MINDQ PUBLISHING

http://www.mindq.com/

MindQ has developed the first true multimedia Java CD-ROM entitled "An Introduction to Programming Java Applets." This is not a book with a CD-ROM, but rather a CD-ROM that does not require a book. The CD-ROM uses excellent graphics, animation, narration, and video to optimize your learning. It also provides a rich glossary and extensive visualizations and animations to show sample Java programs in execution. This CD-ROM is ideal for first-time programmers with its graphical introduction to object-oriented programming. Visit the MindQ Publishing Web site for more information. Also, note that this CD-ROM requires Windows 95 or NT.

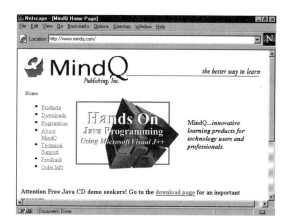

Figure 484 MindQ home page.

MOCHA: JAVA DECOMPILER —A FREE DOWNLOAD

http://web.inter.nl.net/users/H.P.van.Vliet/mocha.htm

What does a decompiler do? Well, you know how a Java compiler takes source code and produces bytecodes? Well, *Mocha*, and other decompilers like it, do exactly the opposite. *Mocha* reads bytecodes and converts them back to Java source code. Although the source code produced by *Mocha* seldom matches the original source code exactly (comments, for example, are lost), it is surprisingly close. Its output is certainly good enough to enable you to understand or modify the Java program. This Web site invites you to download *Mocha* for a test-drive, which can come in very handy on those days when you inadvertently delete a Java source file.

Figure 485.1 Mocha information.   *Figure 485.2 A Mocha example.*

MOVING FROM C++ TO JAVA

http://www.ddj.com/ddj/1996/1996.03/aitken.htm

Gary Aitken, this site's Webmaster, does a great job of highlighting the differences between C++ and Java, and how to surmount them. What are these differences? Briefly: Java executes on a virtual machine. Java is totally object-oriented. Separate header files don't exist in Java. Packages partition the name-space in Java. Exceptions are first-class characteristics in Java. Strings are different from character arrays in Java. Java has limited support for constant objects and methods. Java has no pointers. Java has no parameterized types. Java is a "garbage collected" language. Java does not implement multiple inheritance. Java *does* support multithreading. And, Java comes with a diverse set of predefined classes. Whew! Visit this site for details. Thanks, Gary.

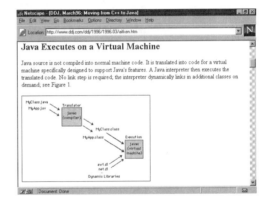

Figure 486.1 A great tutorial.   *Figure 486.2 More of the tutorial.*

JAN NEWMARCH'S JAVA TUTORIALS

http://pandonia.canberra.edu.au/java/

Jan Newmarch provides a host of vital facts regarding all aspects of Java Web programming. This site's contents include a detailed tutorial on GUI programming using Java, various articles Jan has written on Java for *X Advisor*, a discussion of the *awtCommand* Class, a discussion of Java *Emacs* support, and much more. Visit this site for in-depth considerations and explanations of the *Event* class, geometry layout, *GridBag* layout, the New Event model, and more. All told, Jan's site provides a very useful resource and performs a very vital service to the Java programming community.

Figure 487 Jan's great resource.

OBJECT ENGINEERING WORKBENCH FOR JAVA

http://www.isg.de/OEW/Java/info.html

Object Engineering Workbench (OEW) for Java is a graphical design and documentation tool for all applications written in Sun Microsystem's Java programming language. The tools feature a relational database schema design and reverse engineering. *OEW for Java* provides object-oriented analysis, design, implementation and documentation of Java-based applications in a standalone, integrated development environment. *OEW for Java* is now available for Microsoft Windows 95, Windows NT, OS/2, Sun Solaris, and HP-UNIX. Visit this site to learn about *OEW for Java's* built-in code generator and other benefits. You can also download some cool tools, if you insist.

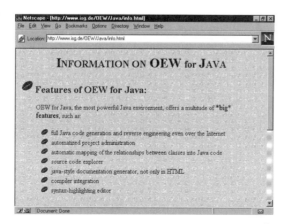

Figure 488 Details on the product.

489

ON-LINE JAVA TUTORIAL

http://www.thedswgroup.com/java/tutorial/

This site features a great on-line tutorial of such fundamentals as: GUI development, creating and using objects, using the Borland debugger, programming for the Internet, *HotJava*, security, and upcoming advances in Java technology. The *HotJava* chapter covers every aspect of using *HotJava*, Sun's Web browser written entirely in Java. The chapter explains how to open a URL with *HotJava*, how to customize *HotJava's* display settings, how *HotJava* stores its configuration and help screens, how to allow applets to access files on your hard drive, and how to modify the security restrictions on network connections and system access in *HotJava*. For all this and more, visit the On-Line Java Tutorial.

Figure 489.1 Java Tutorial Table of Contents.

Figure 489.2 Perspectives on Java.

490

PENUMBRA SOFTWARE: UNLEASH THE POWER OF JAVA

http://www.penumbrasoftware.com/

Penumbra means "a space of partial illumination (as in an eclipse) between the perfect shadow on all sides and the full light," according to *Webster's Dictionary*. To software developers, the word denotes a developer and publisher of excellent Java tools, with the leader of the pack being *Mojo*—a comprehensive Java development environment consisting of a GUI *Designer* and *Coder*. The drag-and-drop *Designer* lets anyone create simple applications without first having to master the Java language or coding principles. The *Coder* organizes objects into a visible hierarchy and keeps all objects easily accessible for direct coding. Visit the Penumbra pages for more information.

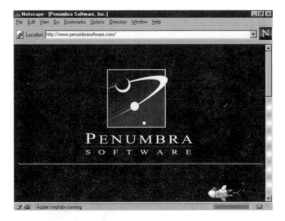

Figure 490 Penumbra's Web site.

PRO-C INCORPORATED JAVA TOOLS: WINGEN FOR JAVA DOWNLOAD

http://www.pro-c.com/

The coolest thing in Pro-C's arsenal is *WinGEN for Java*—the world's first true Java source-code generator for building platform independent Internet, intranet (client/server), and database applications. The product offers developers the ability to interactively design and automatically generate applications for any Java enabled platform. The folks at Pro-C invite you to download and try out a free demo of *WinGEN for Java*. Visit the Pro-C Web site for more information.

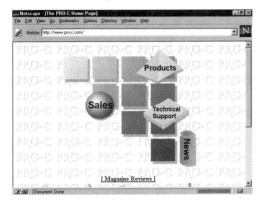

Figure 491.1 *Pro-C home page.*

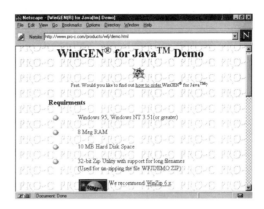

Figure 491.2 *WinGEN demo.*

QUINTESSENTIAL DIVA FOR JAVA: BETA DOWNLOAD

http://www.qoi.com/javaside.html

Diva for Java, formerly known as *Javaside,* provides an integrated-development environment for editing, compiling, and testing Java, Perl, and HTML files. *Diva* requires Windows 95 or Window NT 3.51+, and the Java SDK. The site invites you to download the beta and try the product on for size. Eventually, the software will be released as *Quintessential Diva.* But a word of warning: the beta is inordinately buggy. In fact, developers have made many major changes to the underlying code in between the software's alpha and beta versions, so be prepared.

Figure 492.1 *Diva home page.*

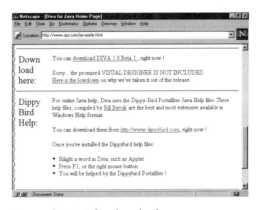

Figure 492.2 *A free download.*

Rapid Application Development for Java (Demo Version)

http://www.radja.com/

Rapid Application Development for Java (*RadJa*) is a visual programming environment that enables you to create Java applets and applications without the need for programming in Java code. The *RadJa* environment consists of two main windows which serve as workspaces. The left window provides an actual view of the running *RadJa* program. The right window is a logical view, or related source of the program. The user may build and change *RadJa* programs in either window. The site invites you to download an evaluation version for Windows 95, NT, and UNIX free of charge. You will also find complete documentation, white papers, and on-line support at the *RadJa* Web site.

Figure 493 The Radja Web site.

Roaster from Natural Intelligence

http://www.natural.com/

Roaster is an outstanding Mac development environment for Java. *Roaster* requires a PowerMac with 30MB of free disk space and at least 8MB of available RAM. *Roaster's* integrated-development environment is similar to programs such as Symantec's *ThinkC*, in which you store a collection of related source and HTML files within a project space. *Roaster* includes a project window, editor, debugger, and two Java compilers (Sun's *javac* compiler and a new native PowerMac compiler developed by Natural Intelligence). Visit this Web site for more information on *Roaster*, including complete white papers and technical support.

Figure 494 The Natural Intelligence Web site.

AI CAFÉ C/C++ CGI HTML HTTP JAVA J++ PERL VBSCRIPT VRML WIN32 WINSOCK 1100110100101111001101110011010101000110011001001001

SHLURRRPP . . . JAVA: THE FIRST USER-FRIENDLY JAVA TUTORIAL

http://www.neca.com/~vmis/java.html

What a fun tutorial! Have a sample: "Undoubtedly, Java has flung open a whole slew of possibilities to spruce up a page on the Internet. Every little Johnny in the world, who has anything close to a GK, knows that Java can change lives. *How*, is the question . . . As regards the concepts of Java, there are quite a few potatoes in the sack. We promise to bring you all of them in elaborate detail . . ." This tutorial is, in fact, in addition to a lot of fun, just plain elegant and enlightening. You will learn a lot. And, you will not realize you are learning a lot because you will be having so much fun. Treat yourself to this wonderful introduction to Java programming

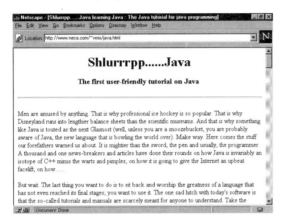

Figure 495 The tutorial's title page.

AI CAFÉ C/C++ CGI HTML HTTP JAVA J++ PERL VBSCRIPT VRML WIN32 WINSOCK 1100110100101111001101110011010101000110011001001001

SQUIRREL SOFTWARE: JAVA APPLETS

http://www.squirrel.com.au/

Visit this site and download the *Squirrel Selector*, a Java applet that makes drop-down list-boxes and push-buttons available on Web pages. As well as being fun (and easy) to use, the selector's controls provide a better use of screen space. Also, check out the *Squirrel Shopping Cart*—an applet that makes it easier for you to browse through a Web catalog by organizing articles into departments. You just add items to your shopping cart and a tally shows you how much you've spent. At the end, take your basket to the check-out stand and make your payment. You'll find lots of other cool stuff at this site, much of it available for free downloading. Visit *Squirrel Software* for many useful Java Web tools.

Figure 496 Java applets from Squirrel.

497

SubArctic: Java-Based User Interface Toolkit Freeware

http://www.cc.gatech.edu/gvu/ui/sub_arctic/

Designed by Scott Hudson and Ian Smith at the Graphics, Visualization, and Usability Center of the Georgia Institute of Technology, *SubArctic* is not just another *awt* widget set. No, *SubArctic* is much more than that—*SubArctic* is a complete, fully-functional, industrial-strength toolkit you can use for all your user-interface needs. *SubArctic* is highly extensible and supports a number of sophisticated effects not available in other toolkits. And, it provides the basic infrastructure to build much more. The product includes animation support based on a high-level path model with controlled timing and support for effects such as anticipation and follow-through. Visit this site and download *SubArctic* complete with source code!

Figure 497 SubArctic freeware.

498

Symantec Café for Java Development

http://cafe.symantec.com/

Available in versions for both Windows 95 and the Mac, *Symantec Café* makes it easy to develop dynamic Java applications and applets. For programmers who are new to Java, the program's visual tools, Wizards, on-line help, and sample applications get you started quickly. For more experienced programmers, *Café* offers sophisticated, time-saving tools for development and debugging which yield unmatched productivity. With *Café*, you get the easy-to-use Java language, as well as a highly productive development environment that includes project management tools and a full collection of flexible editing and browsing tools. Visit this Web site for more information.

Figure 498 Symantec Café options.

AI Café C/C++ CGI HTML HTTP JAVA J++ PERL VBSCRIPT VRML WIN32 WINSOCK 110011010010111100110111001101010100011001100100101

THINGTONE'S JAVA WORKSHOP

http://users.aol.com/thingtone/workshop/index.htm

Thingtone's *Java Workshop* is a collection of instructive Java programs and annotated source-code examples written especially to help the experienced programmer become productive with the Java programming language. The folks at Thingtone released the programs, applets, classes, and tutorials you will find at this site with two goals in mind. The first is simply to explore the possibilities of Java. The second is to distill Thingtone's lab experiments into a simple form that will help others who wish to learn and explore Java, too. You will find a growing archive of cool programs, demonstrating animation, concurrency, and much more. Check it out.

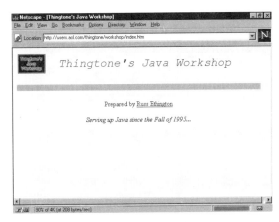

Figure 499 Thingtone's Java Workshop.

AI Café C/C++ CGI HTML HTTP JAVA J++ PERL VBSCRIPT VRML WIN32 WINSOCK 110011010010111100110111001101010100011001100100101

THE UTK JAVA SITE

http://sunsite.utk.edu/java/

This site, from the University of Tennessee at Knoxville, is one of the best-designed Web sites I've seen. You'll find lots of great information, including links, tutorials, and applets. The site includes a monthly survey of the latest developments in the Java universe, discussion and support groups, on-line magazines and newsletters, results of the Java Cut, and other international and national contests. You will also find hundreds of developer tools from free and commercial sources, Java tutorials (including extensive documentation on the Java programming language), details on Java bugs and fixes, discussions on security, and information on experimental innovative applications of Java. Before you leave, also be sure to pick out some goodies from the applet orchard.

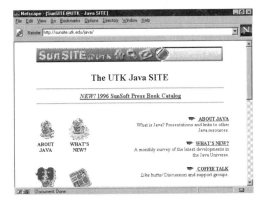

Figure 500.1 The UTK Web site.

Figure 500.2 What's new.

VERIFYING FORM INPUT WITH JAVASCRIPT: A WHITE PAPER

http://gmccomb.com/javascript/valid.htm

This informative white paper explains, in detail, exactly how, using JavaScript, you can check user input before the browser sends the data to the CGI program. In this way, you can keep the CGI program to a bare minimum. And, because the browser only sends the data after it has been validated, the server need not be bothered (to process the form) until the form entry is known to be good. Reducing the server and CGI program's workload in this way saves valuable system resources. After explaining these fundamentals, the white paper goes on to provide a rudimentary example of how to use *JavaScript* for form input validation. Check the pages, authored by Gordon McComb, for more information.

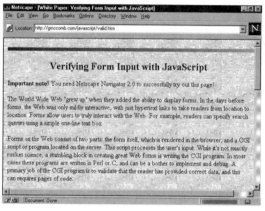

Figure 501 The tutorial.

VISUALJAVA

http://www.eas.asu.edu/~lu/visualJava.html

visualJava is a Java applet that allows users to experiment with and create Java applets without having to write a single line of Java code or understand anything about objects or types. But *visualJava* is not just for non-programmers. The *visualJava* package is an extensible, open system that enables programmers to write complex and useful *visualJava* components for use by those who do not have the time to learn Java. Such components can be as simple as a text-field or as complex as a visual SQL component. You will find lots of cool details about *visualJava* at this site, along with a complete interactive *visualJava* tutorial. Check it out.

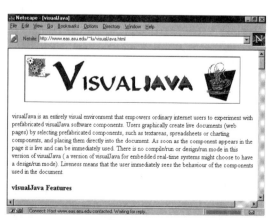

Figure 502 The visualJava Web site.

AI CAFÉ C/C++ CGI HTML HTTP JAVA J++ PERL VBSCRIPT VRML WIN32 WINSOCK 1100110100101111001101100110101010001100110010101

AN APPLE A DAY

http://www.AmbrosiaSW.com/AppleDays/

At this site, Heng-Cheong Leong does an incredible job updating this daily showcase of Apple and Macintosh technologies. Heng-Cheong also adds a bit of daily news to go along with his Apple A Day. Get the latest news. Know the minute Netscape releases a new update to its popular Mac Web browser. Find out what will, and will not, be included in the next release of *Cyberdog*. Discover what is quite possibly the best Mac-based Web-site creation-kit ever produced. And receive live Webcasts from important Apple and Macintosh conferences and seminars. Many thanks to Heng-Cheong Leong for this great resource.

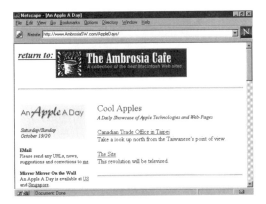
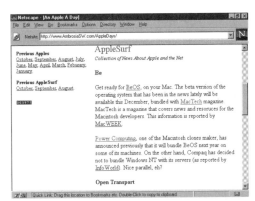

Figure 503.1 An Apple A Day.   *Figure 503.2 More of the site.*

AI CAFÉ C/C++ CGI HTML HTTP JAVA J++ PERL VBSCRIPT VRML WIN32 WINSOCK 1100110100101111001101100110101010001100110010101

ANDREW'S MACTCP DRIVE-THRU!

http://www.echonyc.com/~andrewj/drive-thru.html

"Tired of having to dig through endless directories at different sites to find the latest and greatest versions of the Macintosh Internet clients you need?" asks Andrew. At Andrew's MacTCP Drive-Thru, you will find just about every Mac-based Internet client program you"ll ever need. From browsers, to FTP clients, to Telnet and more, Mac users will find links to the software at this "Drive-Thru." The software is waiting for you to swing by. Go for it.

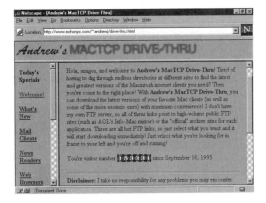
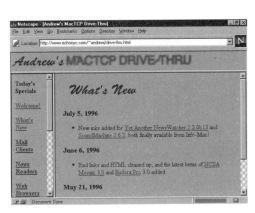

Figure 504.1 The Drive-Thru.   *Figure 504.2 What's new.*

505

APPLE COMPUTER: A HISTORY

http://www.apple-history.pair.com/history.html

This site provides a broad history of Apple Computer, from the invention of the Apple I in 1976 to its present troubled times. Apple's history has been a rocky one, and the company that started in Steve Wozniak's garage has had many ups and downs. You'll find, however, an underlying theme in the history of Apple: *innovation.* Apple Computer has had more industry firsts than any other personal-computer company in the world. This innovation has always set Apple apart from the others. Visit this site and travel from the fabled garage to the legendary "Sculley versus Jobs battles" of the mid-80s, through the Spindler years, and into the Anelio ascendancy.

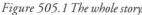

Figure 505.1 The whole story.

Figure 505.2 Spotlight on Jobs.

506

APPLE DIRECTIONS

http://dev.info.apple.com/appledirections.html

Apple Directions, an on-line business report, is meant to communicate Apple's strategic, business, and technical directions every month to help you maximize your development dollars. Whether you are an executive, a marketing or technical manager, a value added reseller (VAR), an in-house developer, or a consultant, Apple Directions tells you where Apple is going, so that you can plan your next business moves accordingly. Apple Directions is the only publication that provides the official Apple viewpoint about the latest Apple technologies, strategic plans, and innovations. This is really an invaluable information source. Don't miss it.

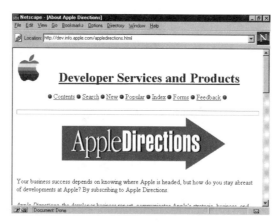

Figure 506 The Apple Directions Web site.

AI CAFÉ C/C++ CGI HTML HTTP JAVA J++ PERL VBSCRIPT VRML WIN32 WINSOCK 110011010010111100110111001101010100011001100100101

APPLE FLAVORED JAVA

http://www.mbmdesigns.com/macjava/

As you might guess, Apple Flavored Java focuses on the creation and implementation of Java-based applications on the Apple Macintosh and PowerMacintosh platforms. Come to this site for great applets, cool source code, tutorials, information, links, and a lively, interactive discussion area. When you visit, be sure to investigate the "What's Hot" area. Updated daily, you'll find the latest news and announcements about all aspects of Java-based programming on the Mac platform in this section. For example, you might come to this site for details on Symantec's great new *Visual Cafe* suite for building applets using visual tools with drag-and-drop operations.

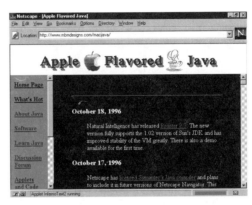

Figure 507.1 Apple Flavored Java.   Figure 507.2 What's hot.

AI CAFÉ C/C++ CGI HTML HTTP JAVA J++ PERL VBSCRIPT VRML WIN32 WINSOCK 110011010010111100110111001101010100011001100100101

APPLEHOLICS ANONYMOUS

http://www.appleholics-anonymous.com/

The Appleholics Anonymous award goes to deserving Mac sites. And in the process of doling out the award, the Webmaster creates a wonderful collection of Mac-oriented links. All of the sites feature the same statement on their primary pages: "No Microsoft products were used in the creation of this site." All the sites are so well designed, so intuitive, so clickable, so easy to navigate that you'll be mesmerized. And all of the sites are so graphically rich. Unlike some sites on the Web, each is easy on the eye and ergonomically-correct. Ah, that says something about the Mac, doesn't it? You bet. Check out the winners of the Appleholics Anonymous award.

Figure 508.1 Appleholics Anonymous.   Figure 508.2 Hot Apple News.

THE APPLE MEDIA PROGRAM

http://www.amp.apple.com/

Visit this site for complete information on a range of Apple multimedia programs and tools, including *Cyberdog*, the *Apple Interactive Music Toolkit*, *Hot Sauce*, *QuickTime*, and more. The Apple Media Program (AMP) gives you access to some of the best minds and most successful members of the multimedia community. Designed for content developers and the creative community, AMP offers a breadth of resources and information to help keep new media developers up-to-date on Apple's offerings for authoring and playback. AMP provides technical information, white papers, and software. The site also offers great co-marketing opportunities, special-discount hardware-purchase privileges, third-party discounts, and more. Check it out.

Figure 509.1 Apple Media Program.   *Figure 509.2 Map of the AMP site.*

THE COMPLETE CONFLICT COMPENDIUM

http://www.quillserv.com/www/c3/c3.html

This excellent site comprises a detailed listing of all the software conflicts on the Macintosh, and how to fix them. You can search by symptom, product name, Mac model, or System Software. The site assigns each conflict a confidence rating from one to five, where one is dubious and five is completely certain. The site goes on to provide contact information and links to related software vendors. Also, check out the "Hmmm Zone," which is an area where you can post questions or reply to the questions that others have posted. You'll also find a useful discussion of how the folks at Complete Conflict Compendium maintain this site. If you are troubleshooting Mac hardware or software, this site is a great place to start.

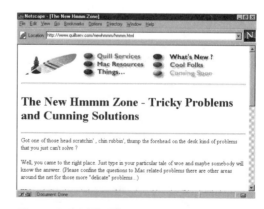

Figure 510.1 The Compendium.   *Figure 510.2 The Hmmm Zone.*

AI Café C/C++ CGI HTML HTTP Java J++ Perl VBScript VRML Win32 Winsock 1100110100101110011011100110101010001100110010101

Corey's MacOS Page

http://corey.imc.sfu.ca/mac/

This site comes highly recommended by both *MacWorld* Magazine and by yours truly. Visit the site for engaging facts and trivia, along with some startling "educated guesses" about the future of Mac hardware and software. Also, visit the site for system updates, reviews of commercial-software releases, shareware and freeware archives, demo downloads, benchmarks, technical notes, and other documentation. The site also features Web links, Mac-based games, Mac-oriented mailing lists, and even an engaging list of MacOS suggestions from you, the users. What a concept! Now, if we could only be sure that the designers at Apple actually sometimes visit this page and read the suggestions. Wouldn't that be wonderful?

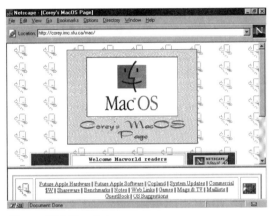

Figure 511 Corey's site.

AI Café C/C++ CGI HTML HTTP Java J++ Perl VBScript VRML Win32 Winsock 1100110100101110011011100110101010001100110010101

CU-SeeMe

http://cu-seeme.cornell.edu/

CU-SeeMe is a free video-conferencing program available to anyone with a Macintosh or a Windows-PC and a connection to the Internet. With *CU-SeeMe*, you can video conference with another site located anywhere in the world. By using a reflector (software at a designated Web site that "controls" the exchange and flow of the video packets), multiple parties at different locations can participate in a *CU-SeeMe* conference, each from his or her own desktop computer. This is the only software available *free* for personal computers that allows desktop video conferencing with more than one other site. (In fact, the software supports up to 8 parties in any one video conference.) Macintosh and Windows-PC users alike should be sure to check out *CU-SeeMe*, brought to you courtesy of Cornell. Ultra cool stuff.

Figure 512 The CU-SeeMe Welcome page.

CULT OF MACINTOSH

http://www.gulf.net/~stone/mac/

The Cult of Macintosh is a tribute to the men and women who made Mac what it is today, and what it will be tomorrow and beyond. The Cult of Macintosh provides hundreds of links to Apple support, cool Mac games, Mac newsgroups, lists of frequently asked Mac questions, MUGs (that's Macintosh User Groups). You will also find periodicals, PowerBook trivia, vendors of Mac software and hardware, software archives, and even Mac people such as Mark Anbinder, Aaron Anderson (publisher of *the Mac Net Journal*), Don Crabb (columnist for *MacWEEK* and *MacUSER*), Bill Dickson, Adam Engst, Aaron Giles, Elliotte Rusty Harold, Peter Lewis, Tony Lindsey (publisher of *Mac*Chat*), Matthias Neerarcher (converter of UNIX software to Macintosh), and many others. A great resource.

Figure 513 Join the cult.

THE CYBERDOG POUND

http://www.microserve.net/~dhughes/index.html

"We all have our vision of where to take the future of *Cyberdog* and its third party parts," writes the Webmaster. "And . . . it's obvious Apple hasn't committed to providing a section on their *Cyberdog* home page for users to send in their most wanted features. Now, here's your chance. Let Apple and the *Cyberdog* developers know what you want to see in the future." This site not only lets you spout off, but you can also get great information on where *Cyberdog* is at and where it is going. You will also find fantastic links to other exceptional *Cyberdog* pages, and more. The page includes information about *Cyberdog*-related items such as *MacOS Runtime for Java*, the *Open Document Helper*, *Rapid-I Button*, and assorted other additions and add-ons, some of which you can download at this site.

Figure 514.1 The Cyberdog Pound.

Figure 514.2 Give developers your opinion!

digital**A**pple Central

http://www.digitalapple.com/

The digitalApple site is another fantastic clearinghouse of Macintosh-oriented information on the Internet. Visit this site for cool tools to help customize your desktop, a great Mac "Who's Who" complete with hyperlinks, software archives, and much more. While you are there, be sure to check out the digitalApple "Snap Gallery." You see, words can tell you quite a bit, but pictures can tell you more. The digitalApple "Snap Gallery" provides screen snaps of the latest and greatest *MacOS* system software, utilities, games, and more. This site also features detailed information on customizing your Mac environment with every tool from *ResEdit* to *Aaron*.

Figure 515.1 digitalApple Central.

Figure 515.2 Cool Stuff Archive.

Download Internet Software for the Mac

http://community.net/~csamir/macapp.html

This site offers you one-stop shopping for the Mac-based tools you can use to browse the Web or utilize the net. You will find links to *Netscape Navigator, Internet Explorer, NewsWatcher, Eudora, Fetch, Homer* (an IRC client), *Talk* (allows you to do just that, talk), *Telnet, Turbo-Gopher, Anarchie, Finger, Blue Skies* (a fun weather application), *Mac Wais, Disinfectant,* and *STuffit Expander.* You can click directly on a link to perform an FTP download of these popular Macintosh applications. Catherine Samir, who maintains this site, has created an eminently useful set of links.

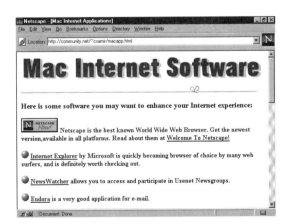

Figure 516 Download it here!

517

DylanWorks

http://www.harlequin.com/full/dylan.html

What is *Dylan*? A new object-oriented programming language developed at Apple Computer. Apple carefully designed *Dylan* to allow the development of libraries, components, and applications comparable in size and performance with those developed in static languages like C++. What makes *Dylan* so attractive is that it achieves these results from a dynamic base, retaining the advantages in improved productivity, flexibility, and robustness attainable through the use of existing dynamic languages like Smalltalk and Lisp. The language features a clean, uniformly object-oriented model. It also features automatic memory management. Visit these pages for more information on *Dylan*.

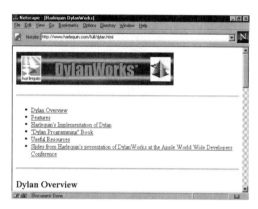

Figure 517.1 DylanWorks information.

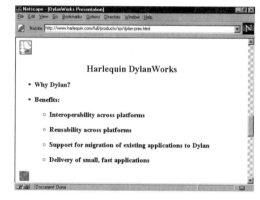

Figure 517.2 Dylan benefits.

518

THE ENTERTAINING MACINTOSH: MAC GAMES

http://www.princeton.edu/~pjcreath/macgames/

OK, all work and no play . . . I know. This wonderful site contains information on more than 200 games—who released them, when they were released, what the current versions are, and any special requirements (like CD-ROM or PowerPC-only). The site also contains lists of all known URLs related to each game, including direct links to files you can download. The site's total URL count is over 800! In addition, you will get information on over ninety game companies, including their Web URL, their e-mail address, their snail-mail address (you know, using the postal service), as well as their phone/fax/BBS numbers. All this comes from Peter Creath. Thanks, Peter.

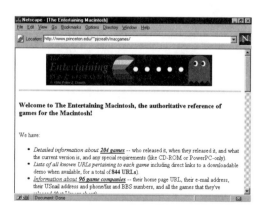

Figure 518.1 The Entertaining Macintosh Web site.

Figure 518.2 Some of the listings.

AI CAFÉ C/C++ CGI HTML HTTP JAVA J++ PERL VBSCRIPT VRML WIN32 WINSOCK 11001101001011110011011100110101010001100110010101

EVANGELIST

http://www.evangelist.macaddict.com/

"The purpose of this Web site," writes the Webmaster, "is to help people evangelize Apple, Macintosh, and Newton—and to make the world a better place!" The site actually contains archived messages from EvangeList, Guy Kawasaki's mailing list of "good news about Apple, Macintosh, and third-party developers—plus links to other useful Web sites." The list is quite popular and has exploded in size and influence. As of the summer of 1996, the list had some 30,000 direct subscribers. This is a big number when you consider Adam Engst's rule of thumb that seven users read the message on a list-serve mailing list for every user that has directly subscribed.

Figure 519.1 The EvangeList Web site.

Figure 519.2 Recent messages.

AI CAFÉ C/C++ CGI HTML HTTP JAVA J++ PERL VBSCRIPT VRML WIN32 WINSOCK 11001101001011110011011100110101010001100110010101

EVERYTHING MACINTOSH

http://www.cs.brandeis.edu/~xray/mac.html

This site is the best in its coverage of *corporate* sites that relate to Mac computing. You'll find hundreds of links that include About Software, Aeon Technology, AG Group, Aladdin Systems, Alisa Systems, Allegiant, Andyne, Attain, Bare Bones Software, Bentley Systems, Berkeley Systems, Blue Ridge Technologies, Bungie Software, Cambridge Soft, Carnation Software, Casady & Greene, Civilized Software, Compatible Systems, Connectix Corporation, Daystar Digital, Delorme Mapping, Dubl-Click Software, Fairgate Technologies, Farallon, Folio, Forefront, Global Village, Gryphon Software, Helix Technologies, and many others. If you are looking for Mac hardware and software, this site is a great place to start.

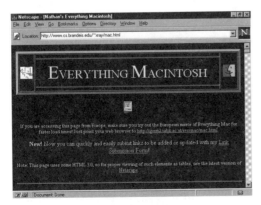

Figure 520.1 Everything Macintosh.

Figure 520.2 Corporate sites.

521

FREE
FREE SOFTWARE

OPEN TO ALL

STRONG CONTENT

EXCELLENT REFERENCES

EXTREME MAC

http://www.extreme-mac.com/

John Mueller runs Extreme Mac, one of the most useful Mac Web sites on the Internet. Many sites only have links that lead you from one site to another, and keep you jumping from site to site in search of a page where all resources are at your fingertips. On the other hand, you will find all your references here at Extreme Mac. And, what is more, the links just don't hang out there in cyber-space buck-naked (as simply a hot link). No sir. Mueller himself regularly reviews the sites and comments on their contents. Mueller guides you to the best of the best in Mac Web resources. His instincts are invariably correct. His standards are painstakingly high. And his lightning wit is a pleasure.

Figure 521.1 Extreme Mac.

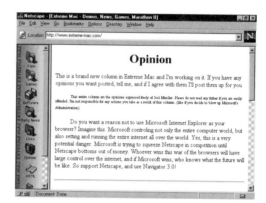

Figure 521.2 Great editorials.

522

FREE
FREE SOFTWARE

COVERS DETAILS

OPEN TO ALL

FETCH 3.0.1 — FREE DOWNLOAD

http://www.dartmouth.edu/pages/softdev/fetch.html

Fetch is a user-friendly Macintosh FTP client that supports point-and-click, drag-and-drop file transfers to and from any machine with an FTP server over a TCP/IP network. *Fetch* is free to users affiliated with an educational institution or a charitable non-profit organization. All other users may purchase a license for a modest fee. The latest release features support for multiple connections, bookmark lists, *AppleScript*, *Internet Config*, and *Open Transport*. *Fetch* is an excellent, robust application, which is probably why it won MacUser's 1996 Shareware Award. In any event, the site invites you to try *Fetch* on for size. I am quite sure you will like it.

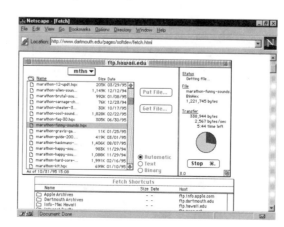

Figure 522 A Fetch screen.

AI Café C/C++ CGI HTML HTTP JAVA J++ PERL VBSCRIPT VRML WIN32 WINSOCK 110011010010111100110111001101010100011001100100101

FONT FAIRY'S FREE FONT SITE

http://home.earthlink.net/~ewhall/fontfairy/freefonts.html

Font Fairy, writes the site's proprietor, is the home of "guilt-free typographic treasures." These fonts, she writes, "are not just any fonts, but high-quality commercial ones. In the real world, they would set you back over a thousand dollars if you were to buy them all, but here in Font Fairyland they are free and legal." At this site, you can nab free and legal fonts developed by Acute Type, Bitstream, Castle, Matt Chisholm, ClickArt, Digital Ink, Emboss, Emigre, Exploding Font Company, FontHead Design, Fountain, Handcrafted Fonts, Letraset, Patricia Lillie, Linotype, Microsoft, Mountain Lake, nonDairy Fonts, Phil's Fonts, Quadrat, and other vendors. Check it out!

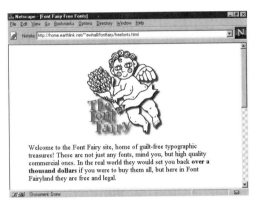
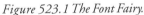

Figure 523.1 The Font Fairy.

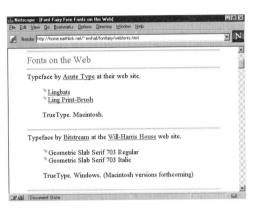

Figure 523.2 Some fonts on the Web.

AI Café C/C++ CGI HTML HTTP JAVA J++ PERL VBSCRIPT VRML WIN32 WINSOCK 110011010010111100110111001101010100011001100100101

FREEPPP 2.5 & INTERNET SETUP MONKEY

http://www.rockstar.com/

Rockstar Studios maintains this site and is a founding member of the *FreePPP* Group, as well as a primary developer of the *Internet Setup Monkey* configuration utility and *FreePPP*. Both of these items are for folks who want to connect their Mac computers to the Internet quickly, easily, and cheaply. Whether you are configuring Mac clients for local intranets or for dial-up Internet connections, these products will make your job very easy. Each program creates foolproof setup packages that install and configure system software and popular Net applications with the click of a button. Check out *FreePPP* and *Internet Setup Monkey*.

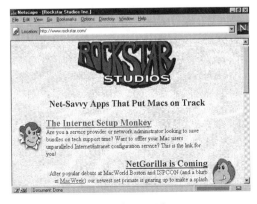

Figure 524.1 The Rockstar Web site.

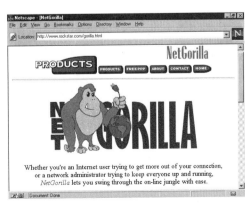

Figure 524.2 NetGorilla, a new product.

AI Café C/C++ CGI HTML HTTP Java J++ Perl VBScript VRML WIN32 Winsock

GIFCONVERTER: A MAC VIEWING AND MANIPULATION TOOL

http://www.kamit.com/gifconverter.html

GIFConverter can display the following graphic types and convert between them: GIF, JPEG (and progressive JPEG), PICT, MacPaint, CompuServe RLE, TIFF, RIFF, EPS, and PNG. *GIFConverter 2.4* also introduces many new features, including scriptability, recordability, and integration with *Frontier* and *Menu Sharing*. The site invites you to download this shareware along with complete documentation. You may try out *GIFConverter* free for 15 days. After that, if you continue to use the program, the authors request that you pay a modest registration fee. The software is excellent, and well worth trying on for size.

Figure 525.1 The GIF Converter Web site.

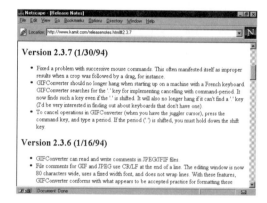

Figure 525.2 Release notes.

AI Café C/C++ CGI HTML HTTP Java J++ Perl VBScript VRML WIN32 Winsock

THE HAPPY MAC

http://atlantic.net/~jlf/macresources.html

This site offers you links to general Macintosh sites: Mac publications and news, Mac Usenet groups, Mac hardware sites, PowerMac sites, Mac software, Mac-based Internet and Web software, Mac vendors, Mac programmer and hacker pages, and Mac shopping sites. Among the cool hacking sites you'll find linked at The Happy Mac are Hecklers on Macs, Hacks and Cracks, Mac Hacks, and the inimitable Whacked Mac Archives. You will also find links to the Land O' Mac Geeks and the fabulous *Developer's Workbench*. Mac vendors include Global Village, DayStar Digital, Intuit, and Iomega. This is a great site if your are intent on keeping your Mac a "Happy Mac."

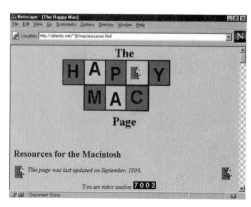

Figure 526.1 The Happy Mac.

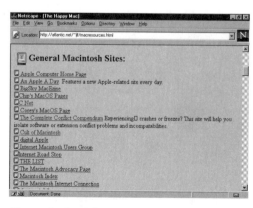

Figure 526.2 A few options.

AI CAFÉ C/C++ CGI HTML HTTP JAVA J++ PERL VBSCRIPT VRML WIN32 WINSOCK 11001101001011110011011100110101010001100110010101

THE HYPERCARD HOME PAGE

http://www.glasscat.com/hypercard.cgi

The HyperCard home page is quite simply the largest on-line resource available for HyperCard programmers, instructors, and enthusiasts. Visit this site for more than 140 links to discussion groups, resources for learning HyperCard, books about HyperCard, and the Web sites of authors who write those books. You will also find HyperCard links for educators, developer home pages, and Apple servers and newslinks, as well as "weird and wonderful" unclassifiable goodies. The HyperCard developer tools you will encounter include a neural-network browser, *CodeCacher*, *Myst* (the most commercially successful HyperCard stack ever), speech recognition plug-ins for HyperCard, and much more.

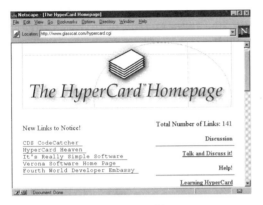
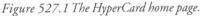

Figure 527.1 The HyperCard home page.

Figure 527.2 Great technical support.

AI CAFÉ C/C++ CGI HTML HTTP JAVA J++ PERL VBSCRIPT VRML WIN32 WINSOCK 11001101001011110011011100110101010001100110010101

THE IBM POWERPC PAGE

http://www.chips.ibm.com/products/ppc/index.html

The IBM PowerPC Page is the place to learn all about the PowerPC microprocessor and the PowerPC platform. You can look up performance data or check out current products and services. While you are there, be sure to look in the Developer's Corner, where you'll find everything you need to know about the PowerPC microprocessor. The Developer's Corner includes technical specifications, software and hardware providers, firmware sources and requirements, PowerPC microprocessor-compatible boards and add-ins, design tools, and much more. You'll also find a complete technical library of white papers, references, and other technical support documents. Great content.

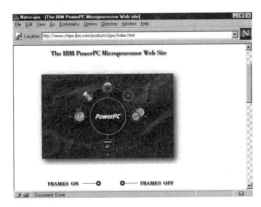

Figure 528.1 The IBM PowerPC Web site.

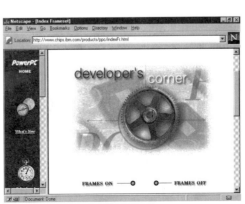

Figure 528.2 Developer's corner.

529

ICONFACTORY: MACINTOSH ICONS THAT DON'T SUCK

http://members.aol.com/icnfactory/index.html

So I thought to myself: *Gee, I really wanna do something for those cool guys over there at the Iconfactory but they won't take my money. After all, their icons come as freeware. What can I do for them to show my support for their non-sucky icons? Hey, wait a minute. I know! I'll list 'em in the Mac section of my new book. That way, thousands of people around the world will find out about the Iconfactory and all their great non-sucky icons. And that's how I'll thank them for the Great Pumpkin Icon Collection of icons featuring Charlie Brown and friends that I just downloaded today, and the Star Trek icons I downloaded last week, and the Looney Tunes icons I got last month.*

Figure 529.1 The Iconfactory Web site.

Figure 529.2 A few options.

530

INTERNET ONLY MACINTOSH USER'S GROUP

http://www.iomug.org/

Internet Only Macintosh User's Group (I/O MUG) exists only on the Internet, in virtual space, and is an officially recognized MUG. The group is dedicated to enhancing the use of Macintosh computer systems by sharing information, support, and insights with Macintosh computer users throughout the global community. Unlike "traditional" MUGs that serve particular locations and interest groups, I/O MUG reaches out to the entire world, offering user group advantages, privileges, and camaraderie to all that do not have the advantage of a MUG in their area, or that cannot attend regular meetings or find them inconvenient. Go for it. Membership is free. This site is a great place to find answers to your questions.

Figure 530.1 The I/O MUG Web page.

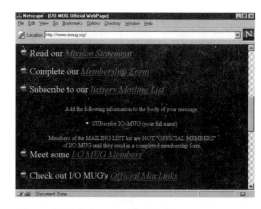

Figure 530.2 A menu of options.

THE INTERNET ROADSTOP

http://www.digiserve.com/roadstop/

The Internet Roadstop is a Macintosh resource with daily news, the hottest Mac links, reviews of the current Mac systems, and a free e-zine with topics concerning the Mac and Internet world. Each article provides an in-depth report on a topic that deals with the Mac. In addition to feature articles, the e-zine includes reviews of the newest Mac products, mini-previews which let users take a look at new Mac products not yet in release, and monthly columns authored by experts on Mac systems and software. While you will encounter many daily Mac news sites on the Web, this one is unique in the depth of its coverage. Drop by.

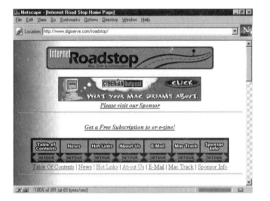
Figure 531.1 The Internet Roadstop.

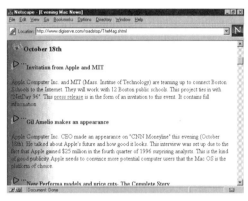
Figure 531.2 The latest news.

THE INTERNET STARTER KIT FOR MACINTOSH, 3RD EDITION

http://www.mcp.com/hayden/iskm/iskm3/index.html

This is the complete book from Adam Engst in an on-line edition—the whole thing! In fact, it's even a little more than the complete book, since at least one chapter at his site didn't make it into print. Now, to be honest, this large collection of Web pages demonstrates exactly why digital publishing is not going to render paper books obsolete any time soon, if at all. It gets a little tiring, reading 300+ pages of text on screen. On the other hand, the Web edition of the book does not, like the paper edition, cost $35. It will not, unlike the paper edition, clutter up your bookshelves after you are done with it. And, unlike the paper edition, it is environmentally correct in that no trees were destroyed in connection with its publication. It's a good read, check it out.

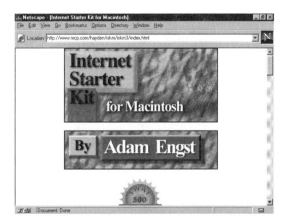
Figure 532 The entire book right on-line!

533

ISDN FOR MACINTOSH FREQUENTLY ASKED QUESTIONS

http://www.public.usit.net/marty104/pubs/Mac-ISDN-FAQ.html

John Martellaro created and maintains this Web site at which he addresses every possible question about Macintosh ISDN. Why do I want ISDN? Do I need to rewire my house? What is the simplest way to get a Macintosh connected? What will the phone company need to know to start installation? What information do I need from the phone company? What is Motorola's BitSURFR, and how do I connect and configure it for the Macintosh? Can I keep using my analog phone and modem? What is the difference between an ISDN terminal adapter and an ISDN router? What is the serial port speed of the Macintosh? And so on.

Figure 533.1 Macintosh ISDN FAQ.   *Figure 533.2 A question and an answer.*

534

JR'S PAGE OF MAC PAGES

http://members.aol.com/jrspacer/macp.html

What hidden advantages make this Mac page better than many others? After all, it lacks the snazzy graphics and animations, the fancy formatting, hourly or daily updates, the big corporate sponsorships, and so on. So, what's so special about it? Only the following. First, enhanced speed and reliability. This page has minimal graphics and animations in order to speed its download to users and minimize crashes. Second, the site incorporates more speed enhancements. In fact, the developers have hand-optimized each page's HTML for speed loading. Third, the proprietor does not list empty, irrelevant, misleading, risky, or frustrating sites. He has done away with the trivial and the shallow. He gives you the best of the best of Mac Internet resources. Thanks, JR.

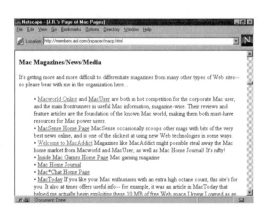

Figure 534.1 A few options.   *Figure 534.2 And a few more.*

AI Café C/C++ CGI HTML HTTP Java J++ Perl VBScript VRML WIN32 Winsock 11001101001011110011011100110101010001100110010010T

THE MAC MONITOR DATABASE

http://www.nashville.net/~griffin/monitor.html

The Mac Monitor Database, writes its Webmaster, "has specifications and compatibility information on thousands of monitors." You may search manufacturers and models alphabetically to get details on Apple displays, Rasterops displays, Sony displays, Hitachi displays, SuperMac displays, E-Machines displays, Radius displays, Ikegami displays, NEC displays, and more. You can also visit this site for similar information on video adapters and accelerators, as well as detailed technical support on a number of hardware compatibility issues. All of this comes to you courtesy of Griffin Technology Corporation of Nashville.

Figure 535.1 The Mac Monitor Database.

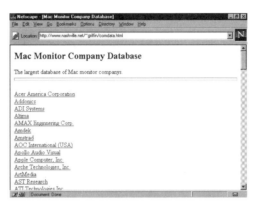

Figure 535.2 The manufacturer database.

AI Café C/C++ CGI HTML HTTP Java J++ Perl VBScript VRML WIN32 Winsock 11001101001011110011011100110101010001100110010010T

MAC NET JOURNAL

http://www.dgr.com/web_mnj

This is the Web site for the *Mac Net Journal*—a fast growing monthly digital publication for Mac users that is making quite a splash. You can read the Web version of *Mac Net Journal* in either a full-graphics (beautiful) or text-only (efficient) mode. You can also download the *Mac Net Journal* in a *DOCMaker* version and view it on almost any Macintosh computer. Or, you can subscribe to the journal's e-mail distribution by sending e-mail to *mchuff@wolfenet.com*. The subscription is free. The Web site is free. The download is free. Everything is free. The whole enchilada. And, if you'd care to submit an article or review, you are free to do that as well. You'll find the Web site contains guidelines for writers.

Figure 536.1 The Mac Net Journal Web site.

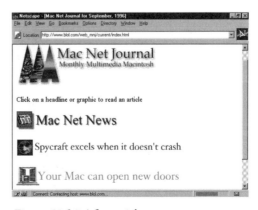

Figure 536.2 A few articles.

537

MAC ON THE NET: DOWNLOAD MAC INTERNET SOFTWARE

http://www.moxienet.com/macnet/

This site contains links to software that you can use with your Mac to access the Internet. Rather than maintaining an enormous list of all software available anywhere, the site's Webmaster tries to make Mac On the Net a compilation of quality software, organized in appropriate categories. "Having a product listed in Mac On the Net is free," he writes, "but I insist that all entries must be reviewed by myself before being entered into the catalog. I feel that this is my responsibility to visitors to this site, in order to provide as accurate information as possible." The result is an excellent archive driven by high standards, which result in the highest quality content. Check it out.

Figure 537 Mac on the Net.

538

THE MAC ORCHARD

http://www.spectra.net/~dsaur/orchard.html

Nothing is more vital to your Internet experience than the most powerful, up-to-date Internet applications, which is why the Mac Orchard provides an extensive list of the most popular and important Mac shareware and freeware applications available today. Each application has a brief description and evaluation, along with a link to make it easy to download. Where appropriate, the Webmaster has indicated links to current beta versions of applications. You will find chat and talk applications, VRML applications, e-mail applications, MUSH/MUD software, and much more. All told, the Mac Orchard is a very valuable resource—Newton would have loved it.

Figure 538.1 The Mac Orchard Web site.

Figure 538.2 What's new.

AI CAFÉ C/C++ CGI HTML HTTP JAVA J++ PERL VBSCRIPT VRML WIN32 WINSOCK 1100110100101111001101110011010101000110011001001011

MACPLAY HOME PAGE

http://www.macplay.com/

What a fantastic assortment of games: *Alone in the Dark, Blackthorne, Battle Chess, Beat the House, Castles: Siege & Conquest, Descent, Dungeon Master, Frankenstein: Through the Eyes of the Monster, Kingdom, Mummy: Tomb of the Pharoh, Mario's Game Gallery, Power Pete, Prisoner of the Ice, Sim City, Star Trek, Tommy, Adventure, Voyeur, Virtual Pool,* and many others. Visit this site for complete details on the games, the company that makes them, upcoming new releases, and more. Of course, you will also find demos—lots of very cool demos—along with full technical support and excellent sneak peeks of games in development.

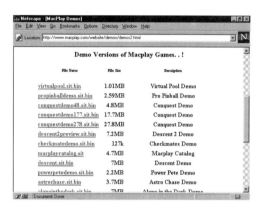

Figure 539.1 MacPlay.   Figure 539.2 Cool demos.

AI CAFÉ C/C++ CGI HTML HTTP JAVA J++ PERL VBSCRIPT VRML WIN32 WINSOCK 1100110100101111001101110011010101000110011001001011

THE MAC PRUNING PAGES

http://www.AmbrosiaSW.com/DEF/

This site features an indispensable guide to exactly what is dispensable on your Mac. The information on this page will completely satisfy your curiosity as to exactly what each and every control panel/ extension on your Mac is and does. This site comprises every trivial fact any Mac user will need to prune his or her system folders of unnecessary extensions, control panels, and other goodies in the interest of both conserving RAM and ensuring maximum compatibility. Visit this site for RAM usage figures, incompatibility notes, and a few "secret gems" of information that may surprise you. All of these details come from the bowels of Apple Tech Notes and other arcane Bibles of the Mac.

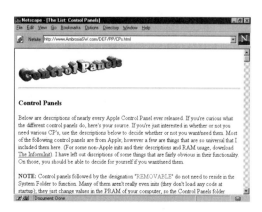

Figure 540.1 The Mac Pruning pages.   Figure 540.2 Control panel information.

541

THE MAC RESOURCE PAGE

http://www.macresource.pair.com/

The Mac Resource Page provides timely news summaries relating to the Mac and *MacOS*. The site also offers feature stories that provide extended coverage of important events, software reviews, and how-to primers. And, it provides links to essential Mac software and information sites. One of the best aspects of this very good site is the weekly RAMWatch Update, which tracks RAM prices. Also, be sure to check out the very good on-line "Primer of MIME Types." Eric David Belsey, who maintains this site, is an Assistant Professor of Mathematics at the University of Miami, Florida. This is an excellent site, which deserves tenure.

Figure 541 The Mac Resource Page.

542

THE MAC TRADING POST

http://www.en.com/users/william/mac/mactrade.html

At the Mac Trading Post, you can buy, sell, or swap used Mac machines, Mac-related software, and third-party add-ons. Advertise at this site free! You must, of course, follow the license instructions for the product you wish to buy, sell or, trade. And, of course, the Webmaster is not responsible for any transactions that occur due to the listings on this page. You must make the arrangements for delivery of all products with the persons with whom you cut deals. The Mac Trading Post has no part in any transaction other than to be a free space where people who want to buy, sell, or swap can connect with each other. So tune in, turn on, and connect.

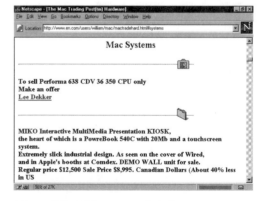

Figure 542.1 The Mac Trading Post.   *Figure 542.2 Mac systems for sale.*

MACADDICT MAGAZINE: FREE TRIAL ISSUE & CD

http://www.macaddict.com

MacAddict is a monthly magazine for the Macintosh computer enthusiast. If you are a Mac owner and you use your computer for music, games, graphics, education, personal finance, and Internet access, you're going to love *MacAddict*. Every month you'll find tons of how-to's, reviews and ratings on new products, coverage of the latest Mac technologies and what they'll mean for you, and an all-new interactive CD-ROM disc packed with shareware, demos, and other cool goodies. Visit the Web pages to find out more about *MacAddict*, including the risk-free subscription offer which entitles you to one free issue of the magazine (CD included) with no obligation. Check it out.

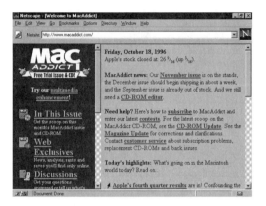

Figure 543.1 The MacAddict Web site.

Figure 543.2 The "deal."

MACFIXIT: FREE DOWNLOADS

http://www.macfixit.pair.com/

Formerly known as the SadMacs Update Site, MacFixIt contains an extensive download library comprising a large archive of trouble-shooting related freeware and shareware utilities. The site also includes links to many trouble-shooting files on Apple's Web site. As a bonus, you also get *MacFixIt Reports*, which are extended reports on specific troubleshooting topics (such as "Troubleshooting System 7.5.5"). The indomitable Ted Landau maintains the MacFixIt site. He is the author of the books *Sad Macs* and *Bombs and Other Disasters*. He is also an editor of the current edition of *The Macintosh Bible*, and a professor of psychology at Oakland University, in Michigan. Don't miss this site.

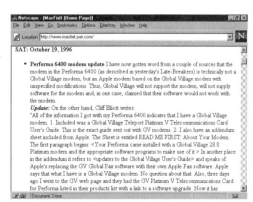

Figure 544.1 The MacFixIt home page.

Figure 544.2 Hardware updates.

MACINTOSHOS.COM

http://www.MacintoshOS.com/

Brent Crandall maintains MacintoshOS.com, which he designed with the novice and expert user in mind. MacintoshOS.com is a complete Internet destination that includes a great shareware library incorporating the Internet's finest applications. Visit this site and get the latest information from the Mac industry in the *Industry Insider* report. And find solutions to the most pesky technical problems amid the *Troubleshooting* files. In declaring this an official "Hot Site," USA TODAY said of these pages, "Mac computer users have a cool new destination on the Web. MacintoshOS.com offers troubleshooting tips, a shareware library, and a Macintosh museum in a quick, clean format." Well said.

Figure 545.1 MacintoshOS.com.

Figure 545.2 Troubleshooting tips.

MACINTOSH CLONE COMPARISON PAGE

http://ng.netgate.net/~engstrom/cc.html

The graphs on this page represent a performance comparison between popular Mac models and Mac clones. The testing that produced the graphs was done using *MacBench 3.0* with results, other than 6300 results, supplied by the Ziff-Davis labs. *MacBench* profiles popular software programs such as *Adobe Photoshop*, *Word 6.0*, and *QuarkXpress* among a variety of others and applies these profiles to the various subsystems being tested. The models they tested were, for the most part, base models shipped from the manufacturer. The site will display additional performance results for new models as the results become available. Note: This site contains a lot of graphics, so expect this page to take about 30 seconds to load even if you have a good connection at 28.8 kpbs.

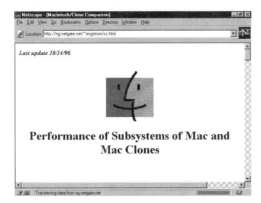

Figure 546.1 The Mac Clones Web site.

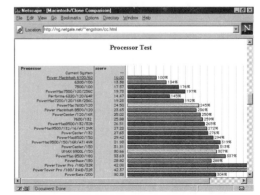

Figure 546.2 A sample graph.

AI CAFÉ C/C++ CGI HTML HTTP JAVA J++ PERL VBSCRIPT VRML WIN32 WINSOCK 11001101001011110011011100110101010001100110010010

MACINTOSH COMMON LISP (MCL) FROM DIGITOOL

http://www.digitool.com/

Originally developed by Apple, *Macintosh Common Lisp (MCL)* is now published by Digitool. *MCL* lets you complete programming projects in one-third to one-half the time as projects developed with C/C++. What's more, you will find *MCL*-based programs easier to modify, update, and expand than their C counterparts. *MCL* is a uniquely fast, LISP-based environment. Additionally, the software takes less than 2Mb of disk space and runs in a 4Mb memory partition, instead of the usual 12Mb. Some of the most exciting new software products are developed in *MCL*, including the new programming languages *Dylan* and *SK8* (HyperCard done right!). Check it out.

Figure 547.1 The Digitool home page.

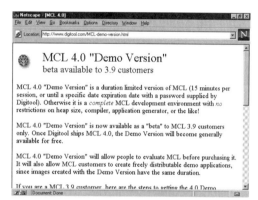

Figure 547.2 MCL 4.0 announcement.

AI CAFÉ C/C++ CGI HTML HTTP JAVA J++ PERL VBSCRIPT VRML WIN32 WINSOCK 11001101001011110011011100110101010001100110010010

MACINTOSH EVOLUTION

http://www.primenet.com/~ericy/MacEvolution.html

This site features excellent performance comparisons between different types and models of Mac computers. Eric Yang, the site's Webmaster, has created some fantastic performance comparison charts that track the performance differences of various PowerPC processors. In one chart, he plots the performance of each PowerPC processor against its clock speed. Yang gathers his figures from various sources. Some of the data points on the graphs represent actual ratings, while others are estimates published by Motorola, IBM, and other suppliers. Because system performance can vary greatly depending on bus-speed, cache size, and other variables, you should view all of these charts as estimates, and only use them as tools for general comparison.

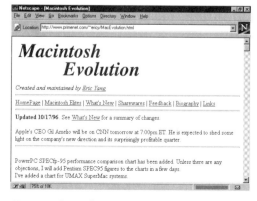

Figure 548.1 The Macintosh Evolution.

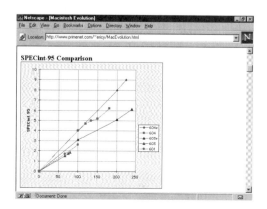

Figure 548.2 A sample chart.

549

FREE
FREE SOFTWARE

COVERS DETAILS

OPEN TO ALL

STRONG CONTENT

EXCELLENT
REFERENCES

MACINTOSH GRAPHICS RESOURCES

http://www.users.interport.net/~jashear/mac_graphics.html

This site offers an amazing collection of hundreds of carefully selected Mac resources that relate to graphics. You will find information on software and hardware vendors, periodicals, and more. The site also features information on 3-D modeling, EPS (encapsulated PostScript) rendering, desktop publishing, EPS rasterization, video editing, image editing, palette reduction, and multimedia authoring. You will also find links to hardware vendors which include Adaptive Solutions, Afga, APS, ART, Color Savvy Systems, Connectix, DayStar Digital, Eastman Kodak, GCC, Iomega, Lasergraphics, Matrox, Power Computing (Mac clones), SuperMac (Mac clones), Videomedia, ViewSonic, and Xerox. If you are into graphics, either for fun or for a living, this site is one you must visit.

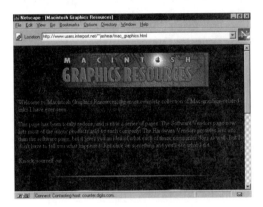

Figure 549.1 Macintosh Graphics Resources.

Figure 549.2 Software vendors.

550

FREE
FREE SOFTWARE

COVERS DETAILS

OPEN TO ALL

STRONG CONTENT

EXCELLENT
REFERENCES

MACINTOSH INTERNET CONNECTION

http://www.themic.com/

Who you gonna call when news happens? Who do you turn to for details when new Mac prices are announced, when the new *Quicken* hits the streets, or when the *QuickMail Pro* ship date is set? Why, you will turn to the Macintosh Internet Connection, of course. These guys have all the latest information. Plus, they have an enormous collection of links to Mac products and resources. In fact, their motto is "Come for the news, stay for the links." We are talking about links to on-line magazines, software archives, software and hardware companies, Internet tools, Mac support, and even Mac mail-order companies. Do yourself a favor and visit the Macintosh Internet Connection.

Figure 550.1 The Macintosh Internet Connection.

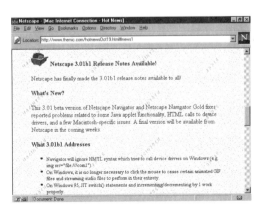

Figure 550.2 Late-breaking news.

THE MACINTOSH MIDI USER'S INTERNET GUIDE

http://www.aitech.ac.jp/~ckelly/mmuig.html

Visit this site for explanations on how to use MIDI with a Macintosh. You will find complete MIDI documentation, details on MIDI players, along with MIDI plug-ins for Netscape, and more. You'll also find digital resources related to MIDI sequencers, MIDI utilities, and tools for unzipping and zipping software. Additionally, the site provides links to Mac-based MIDI software archives around the world, as well as information on software synthesizers, *QuickTime MIDI*, and more. You will find more than a hundred links from which you can choose. Charles Kelly created and maintains this site. Bravo!

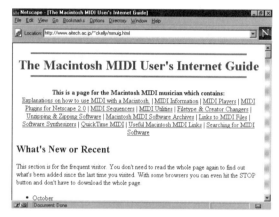

Figure 551 The MIDI Guide.

MACINTOSH MOTHERBOARD BATTERY PAGE

http://www.academ.com/info/macintosh

First, a warning: This page has *lots* of graphics. So, if you have a slow connection (like a modem line), you will want to turn off your browser's *AutoLoad Images* settings. That being said, this page is also very useful. The site intends to answer the eternal question: "How do I replace my desktop's motherboard battery?" This question, of course, often follows right behind the question "Why is it that when I boot my Macintosh, the monitor is set to black and white and the date is wrong?" In short, this site provides you information that can quite literally save the life of your machine and, along with it, your own personal sanity. We can't put a price tag on your sanity. But in any event, this Web site is free.

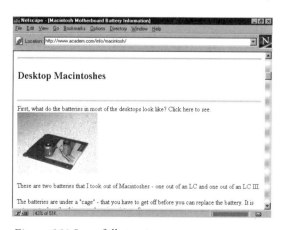

Figure 552 Lots of illustrations.

553

MACINTOSH MULTIPLE DOMAIN (MULTINODING/MULTIHOMING) FAQS

http://home.waidsoft.com/macfaq/

This list of frequently asked questions discusses how to set up one Mac server to handle the Web sites for two different domains. Although it is easy for a single mail server to process mail for several domains, maintaining *www.thiscompany.com* and *www.thatcompany.com* as separate Web sites is more complex. In addition, many users are confused by the terminology. *Multihoming* is most commonly used by Mac people but conflicts with a general networking term: *multinoding*. Better yet, stick with *multiple Web domains*, and you will be fine. The list of frequently asked questions provides current solutions, useful links, and a mailing list that can keep you up to date with the latest trends.

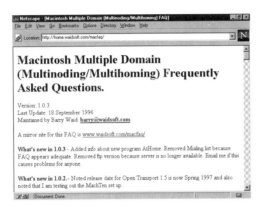

Figure 553.1 Mac Multiple Domain FAQs.

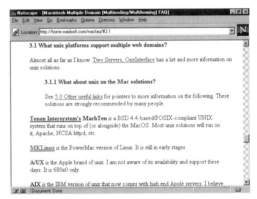

Figure 553.2 A question and an answer.

554

MACINTOSH NETWORKING

http://www.louisville.edu/~lmlars01/indulge/

Compiled by Lee Larson of the Mathematics Department at the University of Louisville, this document is a compendium of Larson's well-tested methods for getting connected to the Internet. This site is also a collection of his self-professed "ornery opinions about what software to use after the connection is accomplished and from where you can get it." Lee's opinions change with the complexion of cyberspace. "The Internet is a moving target," he writes, "and my opinions change right along with it. New tools and capabilities show up every day, and the tool I recommend today might not be the same one I enthusiastically recommended yesterday." And that is why we love him. Thanks, Lee.

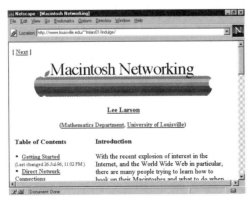

Figure 554.1 Macintosh Networking.

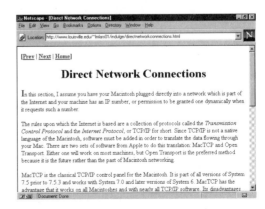

Figure 554.2 Direct network connections.

AI CAFÉ C/C++ CGI HTML HTTP JAVA J++ PERL VBSCRIPT VRML WIN32 WINSOCK 11001101001011110011011100110101010001100110010101

MACINTOSH PROGRAMMING RESOURCES

http://www.astro.nwu.edu/lentz/mac/programming

Cool. A set that provides a wealth of information specifically for programmers! You will find links to frequently asked programming questions, assembly-language and C/C++ resources, information on *OpenDoc*, and more. You will also find details on *QuickTime* programming, porting applications to the PowerPC, working with third-party network services, working with *Macintosh Common Lisp* (MCL), working with *MacPerl*, working with Mops (the Fourth-based object-oriented programming language), understanding *MacScripting*, and dealing with the *Thin C* development environment. Also, while you are there, check out the Apple DTS sample code, details on the *WorldScript-Aware Styled Text Engine* (WASTE), and an extensive introduction to *QuickDraw GX* programming. This all comes courtesy of Robert Lentz.

Figure 555.1 Macintosh Programming Resources.

Figure 555.2 Some selections.

AI CAFÉ C/C++ CGI HTML HTTP JAVA J++ PERL VBSCRIPT VRML WIN32 WINSOCK 11001101001011110011011100110101010001100110010101

MACINTOSH TCP/IP PROGRAMMER'S GUIDE

http://www.metrowerks.com/tcpip/index.html

This site provides a great collection of resources for programmers who are creating TCP/IP client or server software for Macintosh computers. Visit this site for links to Eric Behre's fantastic *MacTCP* and Related Macintosh Software page along with lists of frequently asked (difficult) questions about programming with *MacTCP* and *Open Transport*. You will also find TCP/IP networking guidelines and references (including standards and communications protocols), Apple documentation for *MacTCP* and *OpenTransport*, programming libraries (including freeware and shareware source-code libraries for programmers developing TCP applications on the Macintosh), and much more.

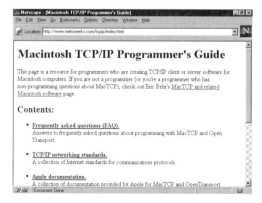

Figure 556.1 The Programmer's Guide.

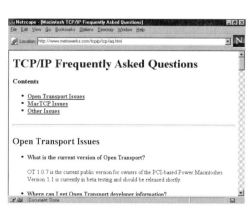

Figure 556.2 Frequently asked questions.

MACINTOSH *UNIX* SOLUTIONS PAGE

http://w3.one.net/~beef/Unix.html

Visit this site for detailed support and technical information about a range of Mac and UNIX solutions. You will find specifics on *Apple A/UX, Mach-Ten, Linux, MacBSD, MacMiNT,* and *MacMinix. Mach-Ten* is, by the way, a Mac port of BSD UNIX, produced by Tenon Intersystems. Likewise, *MacBSD* is a freeware port of *NetBSD (4.4BSD-Lite)* for the Mac. Currently, *MacBSD* runs only on the 680x0 Macs and, like *A/UX*, is an entire operating system unto itself. Visit this Web site for complete details on these products and other flavors of Mac UNIX.

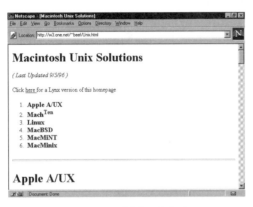

Figure 557.1 Macintosh Unix Solutions.

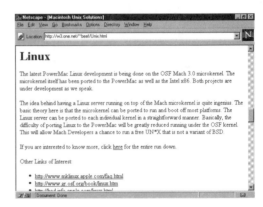

Figure 557.2 Linux information.

MACINTOSH *WORLD WIDE WEB* FREQUENTLY ASKED QUESTIONS

http://arpp.carleton.ca/mac/

How can I set up a Web server on my Mac? How can I extend what my server does? How can I write a CGI application in *Applescript*? How can I configure *MacTCP* to let me run applications locally without a network? How can I switch between networked and non-networked configurations? How can I use domain names when I don't have a name server available? How can I have multiple names for a single machine? How can I announce my new server on the net? How can I implement client-pull in an HTML document? How can I serve *QuickTime* movies. How can I link a *FileMaker Pro* database to my server? You will find answers to all these questions, and more, at this great site.

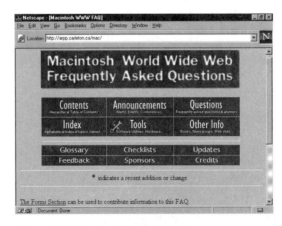

Figure 558 Macintosh WWW FAQ.

MACINTOUCH HOME PAGE

http://www.macintouch.com/

MacInTouch provides all the very latest Mac news, bug-chat, and other timely information. The site is a clearinghouse for current information—all the most current information. For example, when I visited the page, the big talk was about a glitch with 1.2GB disk drives in some PowerMac 7200/120 and WGS 7250 models manufactured between mid-August and early September. The problem? You can't power off the computer when an external hard drive is attached and powered on. Apple was keeping mum about it—you know, not telling anyone. MacInTouch got the word out, just as it did about the fact that every official release of *Open Transport* has been "incomplete and faulty." Visit this site for a little taste of the truth.

Figure 559.1 MacInTouch home page.

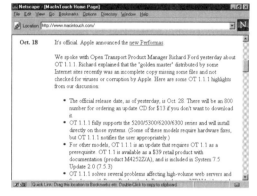

Figure 559.2 All the latest news.

MACMOM

http://home.earthlink.net/~sq_peg/macmom/

MacMom offers basic tips, links, and witicisms designed to entertain and inspire adult women to actually use the Mac computers they've already bought for the kids or inherited from their friends or relatives. The site was created and is administered by an actual Mac Mom who has pulled together an inspired, witty collection of "tips and motivational nudges" specifically targeted to "grown-up (chronologically, your emotional condition is irrelevant) women." The site is packed with examples of things you can do with "a few simple programs, a little ingenuity, and the courage that comes from having confidence in yourself and your ability to use your Macintosh." (Pssst. You guys may want to check this stuff out too!)

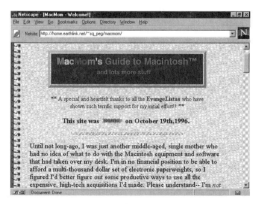

Figure 560.1 MacMom's Guide to Macintosh.

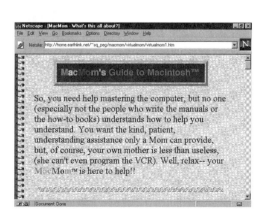

Figure 560.2 This is one user-friendly Mom.

561

MacNuggets

http://darkwing.uoregon.edu/~dd1i/MacNuggets

Sure, a ton of Mac sites are available on the Web. Luckily, you can visit this site to learn which Mac sites are the true gems. MacNuggets gives you over 500 thorough (and I mean *thorough*) reviews of Mac sites across the Web, and features weekly updates. This guy is extremely critical, sometimes even brutal. Nevertheless, his reviews are completely independent, and they can save you a great deal of time messing with sites that are inadequate, slow, or just plain stupid. MacNuggets uses a site rating system. Five nuggets = a gold mine. Four nuggets = hi ho silver. Three nuggets = a diamond in the rough. Two nuggets = scrap iron. And one nugget = fool's gold. The critic, Daniel de Grandpre, is doing a great service to the Mac community with MacNuggets.

Figure 561.1 MacNuggets.

Figure 561.2 What's new?

562

MacOS Hardware Rumor Page

http://home.earthlink.net/~jasonbear/index.html

Want some good Mac gossip? Look no further. The Webmaster, Jason Baringer, started this site because he had to visit five different sites a day to find out all the different *MacOS* hardware rumors. "There had to be a better way," he writes. "But there wasn't. So I created one." What batteries are going to be in the next generation PowerBooks, and why will they be an improvement? What RAM configuration will come standard with the next generation PowerMac, and how will those babies be priced? How will the oncoming clone wars impact Mac prices and configurations in general? For all this gossip and more, visit the MacOS Hardware Rumor Page. Thanks, Jason.

Figure 562 The Rumor Page.

MACSENSE: THE MACINTOSH E-ZINE

http://tkb.colorado.edu/OLM/MacSense/MS.html

MacSense provides a monthly electronic magazine (e-zine) which focuses on the mainstream Mac market. Each issue details the most significant news stories in the world of Mac computing and explores how the news will impact Mac users. The e-zine is filled with vibrant color graphics and in-depth product reviews. Also, because *MacSense* is created and distributed electronically, it exploits the most environmentally friendly method of publishing! Cool. Visit the Web page for details on *MacSense*.

Figure 563 The MacSense Web site.

MACSHARENEWS

http://netmar.com/macsn/

MacShareNews is a well-established, electronic publication that reports on new and interesting Mac-based shareware, as well as all kinds of freeware and demo programs (even the strange and uncommon!) available on the Net. *MacShareNews* is free and comes to you via e-mail as a self-reading *eDOC* document of about 60k. The publication releases new issues every seven to twenty days. To subscribe, just fill out the form on this Web page and you are "in." Then, you can rely on the latest edition of *MacShareNews* to direct you to all the hottest, latest, greatest Mac shareware files newly archived on the Internet. It's a very convenient service. Give it a try.

Figure 564.1 MacShareNews.

Figure 564.2 The on-line subscription form.

565

MacTCP Monitor—Free Download

http://gargravarr.cc.utexas.edu/mactcp-mon/main.html

MacTCP Monitor is a utility that gives users a better idea of how their Macs are interacting with a network. Specifically, the program graphs the amount of data read and written via the TCP network protocol which forms the basis of most Internet operations, including the ever popular FTP, HTTP, Gopher, POP, IMAP, SMTP, and NNTP protocols. In addition to graphing all of the TCP data read and written, *MacTCP Monitor* provides a visual indication of the state of up to 64 TCP connections. *MacTCP Monitor* is handy for users who want to see how fast their system is moving data to or from the network, and for programmers writing TCP based code.

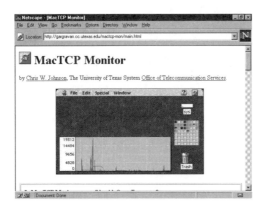

Figure 565.1 The MacTCP Monitor Web site.   *Figure 565.2 On-line documentation.*

566

MacToday Magazine

http://www.MacToday.com/

MacToday Magazine bills itself as an "irreverent, off the wall, PC-slamming, totally-biased look at the Macintosh." This "alternative" Macintosh magazine offers witty, yet in-depth considerations of all aspects of Mac programming, systems development, hardware, desktop publishing, and more. A sample: "Apple finally has a big name making Macintosh clones: Motorola. So now you can choose to buy your Mac from companies that make cellular phones, scanners, and accelerator cards, or from a startup that's never made anything. Reportedly, Apple is meeting with other possible clone makers, including companies that sell hamburgers, farm equipment, and detergent." Give *MacToday* a try.

Figure 566 The MacToday Web site.

AI Café C/C++ CGI HTML HTTP Java J++ Perl VBScript VRML WIN32 Winsock 11001101001011110011011100110101010001100110010010

#MACWAREZ

http://www.eskimo.com/~adrenal/macwarez.html

Internet Relay Chat (IRC) is the Internet's closest thing to CB radio. Using IRC, users select specific channels and then "chat" using their keyboards. *#macwarez* is an IRC channel located on Efnet (a series of channels) created for Mac users to discuss the most recent commercial software. On *#macwarez*, users can chat about the latest versions of the most popular (and arcane!) Mac software, and hear user reviews and comments designed to help users decide on whether a given piece of software is worth buying. This site also features discussion about downloadable software that includes *Ircle* and several other excellent IRC clients. You'll need one of these, of course, to access *#macwarez*. And, then you'll need to access an Efnet server such as *irc.ais.net*. Visit this Web site for instructions on how to get started.

Figure 567 #macwarez.

AI Café C/C++ CGI HTML HTTP Java J++ Perl VBScript VRML WIN32 Winsock 11001101001011110011011100110101010001100110010010

MacWEEK Online

http://www.macweek.com/

You have got to investigate *MacWEEK's* site on the World Wide Web. At this site, you will find selected top stories from the latest edition of *MacWEEK*, reviews from past issues, contact information, and more. Each weekday, *MacWEEK* posts new stories, features, and opinion pieces. And, you will find the majority of stories from each week's printed issue are available by the Monday of publication. The site's updates usually take place between 6:00 and 8:00 pm, PST. Visit this site to get the latest word on all aspects of the Mac and related products. Be the first to know when Linotype cuts scanner costs, or when the new version of *After Dark* hits the Internet. Don't be left behind. Check out *MacWEEK Online*.

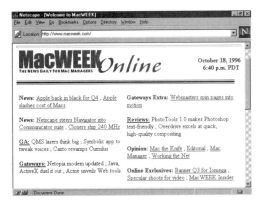

Figure 568.1 MacWEEK Online.

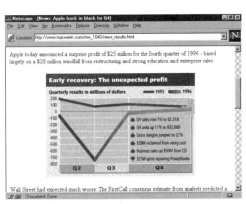

Figure 568.2 Apple turns a profit!

Macworld OnLine

http://www.macworld.com/

Macworld OnLine not only includes late-breaking Mac-oriented news and views, but also digital reprints of important interviews and editorials from the pages of *Macworld*. Visit this site and browse articles and essays from past issues of *Macworld* (searching by topic, date, or author). Then, stroll through *Macworld's* great archive of robust, elegant Mac shareware and freeware. You can then dive even deeper into *Macworld's* custom, proprietary library of tools and utilities. And, while you are there, join the *Macworld* editors and writers in considering important issues that involve all of us who spend time living in cyberspace, such as privacy, censorship, and free access to information. Find all this and more at *Macworld OnLine*.

Figure 569.1 The MacWorld Web site.

Figure 569.2 Hot Mac news.

Marathon Central

http://www.marathon.org/

Visit Marathon Central, hosted by Mark McWilliams, for an interactive demo of *Marathon Infinity* as well as for links to such cool related pages as Travis Vils's Map of the Month, FrigidMan's Maps, the Group Map Project (hosted by Ben Matasar), the Mad Hackerz Maps Page, the Pfhactory Page, the Bungie Home Page (official Web site for the creators of the Marathon series), and more. You will also get links to great utilities, including a Physics model editor, an object placement editor, a WAD (you know, from the game *Doom*) converter, and other invaluable, robust tools. You will find no better set of information related to Marathon series of games anywhere on the Internet.

Figure 570 Marathon Central.

AI CAFÉ C/C++ CGI HTML HTTP JAVA J++ PERL VBSCRIPT VRML WIN32 WINSOCK 110011010010111100110111001101010100011001100100101

MCL CODE LIBRARY

http://hamp.hampshire.edu/~adaF92/MCL/

Visit this site for gobs of freeware and shareware for Macintosh Common LISP (MCL), including GUI code for generating 3-D interfaces. You can also access the *Defsystem Project Manager*, a visual browser for systems created with Mark Kantrowitz's portable *DEFSYSTEM* utility, which presents a "twist-down" view, like the *Metrowerks CodeWarrior* or *Symantec's C* project windows. You may also want to check-out *Drop & Drag Color Panel*, which implements a simple color picker as a floating palette, with the usual red, green, and blue sliders. Or perhaps you are interested in some simple but elegant extensions of the *MCL* interface designer. You'll find it all there for the taking. Check it out.

Figure 571.1 The MCL code library.

Figure 571.2 What's new.

AI CAFÉ C/C++ CGI HTML HTTP JAVA J++ PERL VBSCRIPT VRML WIN32 WINSOCK 110011010010111100110111001101010100011001100100101

UNIVERSITY OF MICHIGAN PUBLIC DOMAIN AND SHAREWARE ARCHIVE

http://www.umich.edu/~archive/

This site features one of the largest Mac-based software archives on the Internet. The archive contains over 5,000 files and is updated regularly. One of the archive's additional strengths is that the Webmasters review all the files before they add them. This means that the quality of the files is usually high, and that descriptions of all files are available. By the way, this site has become so popular that it is often difficult to access. Thus, several corporations and universities have formed their own mirrors of the software at the University of Michigan to ease the load. At this site, you'll find detailed information on mirrors and how to connect to them. In other words, if you *can connect* to this site, you will find other addresses you can use to access the software if you *couldn't connect* to this site. I get it!

Figure 572.1 The archive.

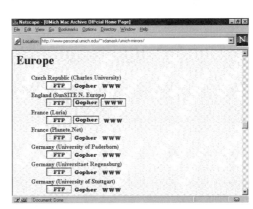

Figure 572.2 Mirror sites for Europe.

Microsnot: A Microsoft Parody

http://www.microsnot.com/

Visit this site fast, before Bill Gates finds out about it and sends his company goons around to smash the server. Check out cool press releases on this parody of the Microsoft Web pages. "Microsnot Becomes a Nuclear Power" reads one headline, "Competitors, customers, and beta testers quake in fear of Microsnot Bomb 1.0." And, don't miss the announcement that "Microsnot acquires England." You can point and click your way to information on how to license the English language, the works of William Shakespeare, British countryside screensavers, and other proprietary items. And, don't miss the release announcing that Bill Gates will run for President. "Buying the election will be cheaper than buying the country."

Figure 573.1 The Microsnot Web site.

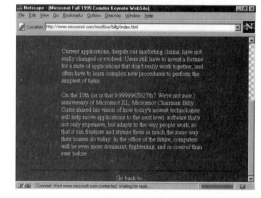

Figure 573.2 A true confession.

MkLinux for Power Macintosh: Free Download

http://www.mklinux.apple.com/

Apple Computer is supporting a project with the Open Software Foundation Research Institute (OSF-RI) to port Linux, a freely distributed version of UNIX, to a variety of Power Macintosh platforms. *MkLinux* operates on the OSF RI Mach (Mk) microkernel, running natively on the PowerPC microprocessor. Do you need some details in order to know if the freeware is for you? The software requires 250Mb of free disk space, with 400Mb recommended. It also requires a minimum 8Mb of RAM, with 16Mb recommended. The software supports virtually all PowerMachines, as well as *Mach 3.0* and *Linux version 1.2.13.* And yes, *X-Windows* is included. So why don't you just relax and go for a download?

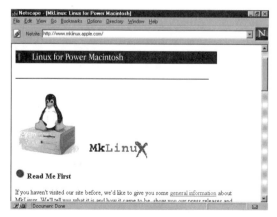

Figure 574 The MkLinux Web site.

AI CAFÉ C/C++ CGI HTML HTTP JAVA J++ PERL VBSCRIPT VRML WIN32 WINSOCK 11001101001011110011011100110101010001100110010101

MOTOROLA POWERPC WEB SERVER

http://www.mot.com/SPS/PowerPC/

Visit this site for complete information on Motorola chips and PowerPC software products. Motorola, after all, is leading the way in PowerPC development tools. They offer a strong lineup of RISC-based software products created specifically to help speed the development of PowerPC microprocessor applications, hardware, and operating systems. Motorola software development tools are produced in parallel with chip development, to help developers get the full performance potential from PowerPC microprocessors. While you are at this site, be sure to look into information about their new *C/C++ SDK, PowerPC edition for MacOS*. Also, check-out *Power PC Architecture HAL for Windows NT*.

Figure 575.1 The PowerPC home page.

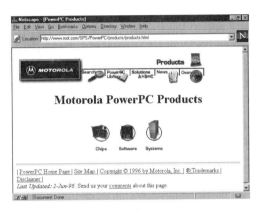

Figure 575.2 Product information.

AI CAFÉ C/C++ CGI HTML HTTP JAVA J++ PERL VBSCRIPT VRML WIN32 WINSOCK 11001101001011110011011100110101010001100110010101

NCSA MAC MOSAIC HOME PAGE

http://www.ncsa.uiuc.edu/SDG/Software/MacMosaic/

The National Center for Supercomputing Applications (NCSA) Mosaic software is the "classic" distributed-hypermedia system designed for information discovery and retrieval on the Internet. NCSA Mosaic is the grandpa on which all the other browsers are based. But grandpa, revised and improved, is still available at this site for free. And it ain't bad. NCSA Mosaic provides a single elegant interface to a variety of protocols, data formats, and information servers. The latest version provides forms support, tables support, support for in-line JPEGs, and more. It also supports strikethrough text, superscript and subscript, as well as a user-configurable color background, custom menus, and other goodies. So, what are you waiting for? Go grab a copy.

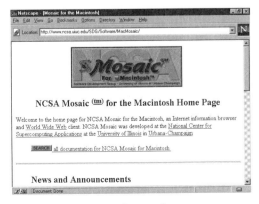

Figure 576.1 Mosaic for Mac home page.

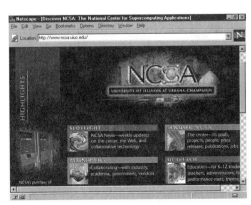

Figure 576.2 Brought to you by the NCSA.

577

NETSCAPE PLUG-INS FOR THE MAC

http://wso.williams.edu/~jsolomon/plugins.html

This site features direct connections to downloads for a number of great plug-ins for *Netscape for the Macintosh*. The plug-ins you will find include: *Plug Master* (a nifty application that lets you control which plug-ins load when you run Netscape), *ViewMovie XT* (displays *Quicktime* movies, as well as AU and AIFF formatted data within Netscape), *KM's Multimedia Plug* (supports *Quicktime*, MPEG, MIDI, AIFF, WAV, and more), *MovieStar* (allows for viewing of *Quicktime* movies *while they are still loading*), *InterVU MPEG Player* (allows viewing of MPEG *while they are still loading*), *Future Splash* (an animation plug-in with inline streaming and smaller file sizes than equivalent plugs, which you can also view while loading), and much more.

Figure 577.1 A few options.

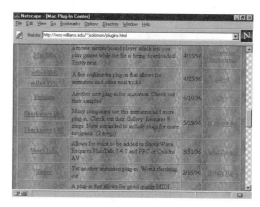

Figure 577.2 And a few more.

578

NEXUS MAC RESOURCES

http://www.go-nexus-go.com/macresources

Programmers, check this out! The Nexus Mac Resources site offers a fantastic clearinghouse for all things Macintosh on the World Wide Web. You will find hundreds of links to Apple sites, publishers of Mac software, archives of Macintosh freeware/shareware, manufacturers of Mac hardware, on-line technical support, lists of frequently asked questions, games, graphics, music and multimedia resources, publications, programming resources, and much more. Your host, Nexus, is, of course, one of the premier purveyors of Macintosh parts and accessories. If there is any one site on the Web that Macintosh programmers and users should be sure to bookmark, this is it.

Figure 578.1 Mac Resources.

Figure 578.2 A few newsgroup options.

MAC, POWERMAC, AND POWERPC COMPUTING

AI CAFÉ C/C++ CGI HTML HTTP JAVA J++ PERL VBSCRIPT VRML WIN32 WINSOCK 11001101001011110011011100110101010001100110010010

JOHN NORSTAD WEB SITE

http://charlotte.acns.nwu.edu/jln/

John Norstad is the author of some of the very best Macintosh freeware around. And, he is offering all of it to you for downloading at this site. First, John is the author of *Disinfectant*, the great anti-viral program for the Mac. He is also the author of *NewsWatcher* (a Usenet newsreader for the Mac), *Ph* (a Macintosh Ph directory services client), *MacTCP Switcher* (a utility program to make it easier to switch between *MacTCP* configurations), *Mail Tools* (a Web gateway to make it easier for people to turn vacation and mail forwarding on and off), *popassed* (a *UNIX* server for the *popassed* protocol used by the *Eudora* "Change Password" command), and *Kill Idle* (a utility program to kill idle *AppleShare* guests after one hour). All of these programs are good stuff. Thanks, John.

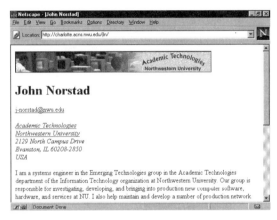

Figure 579 Norstad's Web site.

OBJECT PLANT SHAREWARE

http://www.softsys.se/ObjectPlant/

Object Plant is a Mac shareware program for object-oriented analysis and design. The notation used by *Object Plant* is based on the object modeling technique (OMT). The program features class diagrams (object models), state diagrams, event trace diagrams (message trace diagrams), diagram support for PICT and EPS formats, as well as primitive code generation. The latest release of *Object Plant* includes an interface model item which lets you add static information to class attributes and operations, and incorporates an extended code generation template language. Download the shareware and give it a try. It comes from Mikael Arctaedius in Stockholm.

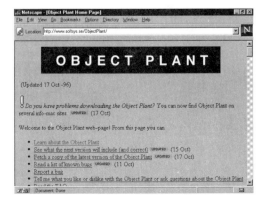

Figure 580.1 Object Plant home page.

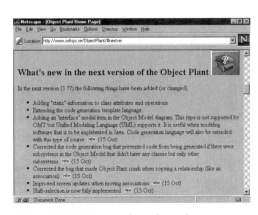

Figure 580.2 Latest info on the package.

1001 Programming Resources

`10011001100010101011001110110111101011101110001101  AI CAFÉ  C/C++  CGI  HTML  HTTP  JAVA  J++  PERL  VBSCRIPT  VRML  WIN32  WINSOCK`

581

OPEN TRANSPORT PAGE

http://msproul.rutgers.edu/macintosh/OpenTpt.html

At this site, you will find links and information related to each and every aspect of Apple's *Open Transport*. Of course, you will find links to locations where you can download *Open Transport*. But beyond that, you also get *Open Transport* development information, version histories, on-line documentation, lists of frequently asked questions, and details on using *Open Transport* with TCP/IP, SLIP, and PPP. In addition, you will find links to Mentat (the firm which wrote the STREAMS and TCP/IP protocol stack that Apple uses as the core of *Open Transport*), to a free *OTTool PING* utility for *Open Transport*, and to great on-line guides like the *Macintosh TCP/IP Programmer's Guide*.

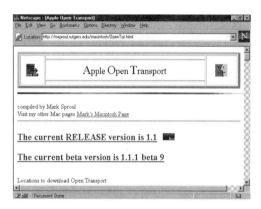

Figure 581.1 Download Open Transport.

Figure 581.2 Open Transport information.

582

THE PERFORMA PROBLEM PAGE

http://www.ganson.com/jganson/performa.html

A number of Performas—especially those with 603 or 603e chips—have been plagued with problems. Those who have bought them still love them, but they desperately want things to work properly. This site is dedicated to identifying and dealing with frequent freezes and monitor color changes, *Open Transport* problems, serial ports refusing to perform basic hardware handshaking tasks, Global Village modem connection problems, and more. The site also addresses such mysterious happenings as the ever-popular volume button crash, video system remote control crashes, mangled sound from streaming audio, and other things that go bump in the night. So, if you are having problems with your Performa, visit this site and take the first step toward finding a solution.

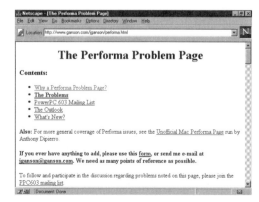

Figure 582.1 The Performa Problem Page.

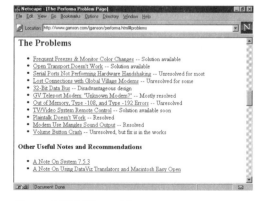

Figure 582.2 The problems.

AI CAFÉ C/C++ CGI HTML HTTP JAVA J++ PERL VBSCRIPT VRML WIN32 WINSOCK 1100110100101111001101110011010101000110011001001010

PHOTOSHOP PROFESSIONAL TIPS & TRICKS

http://www.tema.ru/p/h/o/t/o/s/h/o/p/

Cool site—difficult URL. Most of the things this site describes are undocumented features or things hardly interesting for beginners. In other words, these pages explore power-user techniques: the real hidden voodoo of Mac-Photoshop excellence. The site is packed with great scanning tips, explanations of how to create drop shadows, color-separation tips, and dozens of special effects. You will learn to use RAM effectively, create 3-D objects, create irregular multicolor gradients, and more. The site's author is Art Lebedev who is one of the great and most-revered gurus of Photoshop excellence. He is also a devout Mac-head.

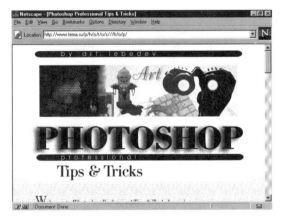

Figure 583 Photoshop Tips and Tricks.

AI CAFÉ C/C++ CGI HTML HTTP JAVA J++ PERL VBSCRIPT VRML WIN32 WINSOCK 1100110100101111001101110011010101000110011001001010

POWERCOMPUTING: MAC CLONES

http://www.powercc.com/

PowerComputing is the second licensed manufacturer of Mac clones, and the first one that really competes with Apple. They have some neat machines at prices that really are better than similar machines from Apple. Most notably, they have a form on their Web site that lets you custom configure your "dream machine" and get a price quote instantly. If you've ever spent time trying to get pricing information from an Apple-authorized dealer, this form is a dream come true. The down-side, of course, is that supply has not yet caught up with demand. So, if you actually order a machine, you may have to wait several weeks for delivery. We live in an imperfect world.

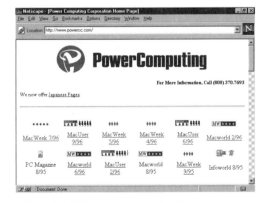

Figure 584.1 Power Computing home page.

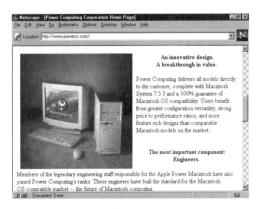

Figure 584.2 Beautiful machines.

POWERMAC INFO FROM APPLE

http://support.info.apple.com/ppc/index.html

Visit this site for information on a range of PowerMac and PowerPC native applications, sorted alphabetically by company and with direct links to company Web sites. In addition, the site provides complete details on Power Macintosh configurations, optimization resources, and more. You will find configurations for the Power Macintosh Advantage, the Mac Performa 5200, 5400, 6100, 5200, and 6300 series, and all PowerMacs from the 5200 up to the latest 9500 machines. The site also includes Mac upgrade information and patches, details on PowerMac logic-board and processor-card upgrades, and PC compatibility cards for PowerMac machines. Check it out.

Figure 585.1 The Power Macintosh home page.   *Figure 585.2 The week's new native applications.*

THE POWERMACINTOSH RESOURCE PAGE

http://rampages.onramp.net/~stevent/powermac.html

Visit this site and join its Webmaster, Steve Tannehill, as he waxes philosophical views on various aspects of life with the PowerMac. Also, check out his meticulously maintained news archive, as well as the extremely valuable PowerMac 7500 Problem Page. "Now that warranties are about to expire on the early PCI Macs," Steve writes, "it seems that some serious problems are coming to light. Although the problems are not entirely new, they appear to be news to many people." Take, for example, the Level 2 cache problem. Did you know that some 7500s are unable to run with *any* Level 2 cache (even Apple's)? Hmmm. Steve Tannehill can be quite enlightening. I'm sure Apple just loves little revelations like this.

Figure 586.1 PowerMac Resource Page.   *Figure 586.2 Link to After Dark Online.*

PRISTINE'S MAC LINKS

http://www.eskimo.com/~pristine/maclinks.html

Wow. This site provides an awesome collection of Mac-based links. You will find information on hardware drivers, Java, text editors and tools, compression and encoding, Mac tutors, document viewers, games, Internet phones and video-conferencing, servers, VRML and 3-D, and Mac graphics, as well as IRC (talk and chat). You will also find information on desktop publishing, Mac assembly-language programming, Mac Internet connections, and much more. Priscilla Showalter, to whom we say "Thanks," maintains this site. To speed up your access to these links, Priscilla has set up mirror sites for North America and Europe.

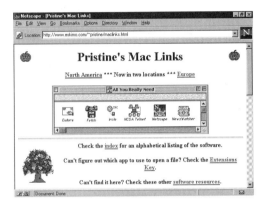

Figure 587.1 Pristine's Web site.

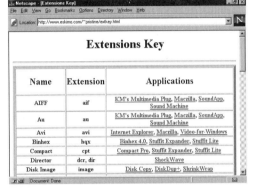

Figure 587.2 A valuable extensions key.

15 QUESTIONS TO ASK MICROSOFT ABOUT WINDOWS 95

http://www.austin.ibm.com/pspinfo/15qs.html

Want to see the best questions on Windows 95? Guess what? None of the answers are what you want them to be. Perhaps the questions aren't either: Does Windows 95 protect the contents of its system cache against intrusion by Win32 programs? How is Microsoft dealing with the issue of Virtual Device Driver (VxD) instability? Is it true that Windows 95 doesn't fully protect its own operating system code against Win32 application failures? When running DOS applications, does Windows 95 fully virtualize the PC's hardware to protect against buggy applications? Does Windows 95 track objects dynamically? Does Windows 95 make consistent use of drag and drop? Is the Windows 95 interface consistent and object-oriented? Well?

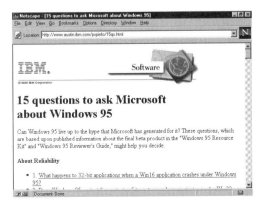

Figure 588.1 15 Questions.

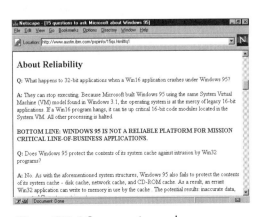

Figure 588.2 Some questions and answers.

589

PROVIDING INTERNET SERVICES VIA THE MAC OS

http://www.freedonia.com/pism/

You can buy the book, by Carl Steadman and Jason Snell, from Addison-Wesley for gobs of money, or you can access this interactive on-line edition for free. The chapters start with the basics of Internet services and making your initial connection and then move to sending and receiving electronic mail, mail-based services, serving files via FTP, Gopher fundamentals, Web publishing, domain-name services, remote administration and maintenance, and character entities. The on-line edition is even better than the paper edition because the authors update it regularly and the links on pages are clickable. This is an exhaustive, lucid resource for anyone using the Mac as a basis for any and all Internet services.

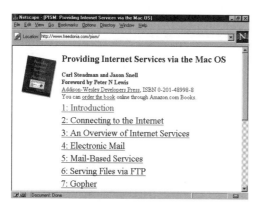

Figure 589.1 The entire book right on-line.

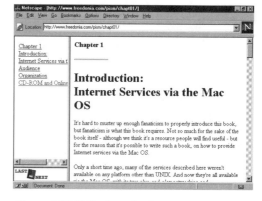

Figure 589.2 The Introduction.

590

QUADRA 630 PAGE

http://www.halcyon.com/honky/q630

This site provides the ultimate directory of Quadra information anywhere. "This page contains all the information I have gathered from various sources over the first year of owning my Quadra 630," writes the Webmaster. "There is quite a bit of information." The Quadra 630 is a nice machine with many capabilities for a low-end model. In fact, the Quadra 630 is something special, as one of the last Macs based on the original Mac chip architecture, the Motorola 6800X0. This site includes technical information, the *MacBench* benchmarks, hardware specifications, technical notes, reviews, upgrade information, and details on video options.

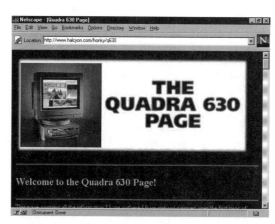

Figure 590 The Quadra 630 Page.

QuickDraw GX Fan Club

http://www.ixmedia.com/quickgx/default.html

QuickDraw GX, Apple's imaging technology for the Mac, changes the way you print, use type, and work with graphics on the Mac. The *QuickDraw GX* Fan Club you will find at this site shares information about *QuickDraw GX* and encourages its use and development. You will find pages devoted to each of the three elements of the *GX* technology: printing, typography, and graphics. Other related pages provide information on *GX-Smart* applications, printer and fax drivers, *GX*-savvy fonts, and utilities, including printing extensions. If you are interested in learning as much as possible about *GX*, the *QuickDraw GX* Fan Club is the place to come.

Figure 591.1 The Fan Club.

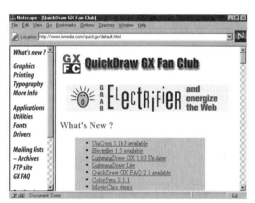

Figure 591.2 What's new?

Frequently Asked Scanning Questions

http://www.infomedia.net/scan/

Are you having trouble getting your scans "just right?" This site may have your answer. "By popular demand from the gang at the PageMaker Listserv," writes Jeff Bone, "this scanning FAQ is being made available as an HTML document." And, what an excellent document it is. As respected Web-Mac maven Elliotte Rusty Harold has written, "this detailed, well-organized, and well-written document is easily the best introduction to scanning I've seen anywhere, not just the best one on the Web. Furthermore, as well as serving its stated purposes of teaching readers about scanning, it's an excellent example of clear Web design that stands in marked contrast to the graphics-rich, content-poor sites we've learned to expect." Can't say much more than that.

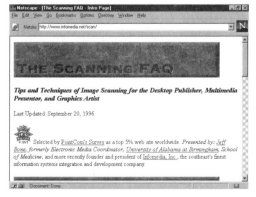

Figure 592.1 The Scanning FAQ.

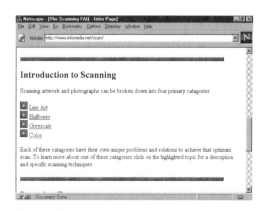

Figure 592.2 Intro to scanning.

1001 Programming Resources

10011001100010101011001110110111101011101111000110 AI CAFÉ C/C++ CGI HTML HTTP JAVA J++ PERL VBSCRIPT VRML WIN32 WINSOCK

SITELINK

http://www.tiac.net/users/jbrochu/SiteLink.shtml

SiteLink's philosophy is excellence, and nothing short of excellence. To be listed on SiteLink, a Mac Web resource must be something special. "Mac users are accustomed to applications that have a high standard of excellence in user interface design and aesthetics," writes the Webmaster. "We deserve the same level of quality in our Web browsing." Therefore, SiteLink tries to present only the best of the Mac on-line Web experience in both content and presentation. "Although there are several sites that attempt to exhaustively list every Mac-related site on the Web, SiteLink is not, and will never be, such a site." Come to SiteLink for quality.

Figure 593 SiteLink.

SLIRP FREQUENTLY ASKED QUESTIONS & RELATED LINKS

http://www.webcom.com/~llarrow/tiafaqs.html

SLiRP is a free TCP/IP emulator for SLIPP/PPP link-level protocols which let users with a shell account on a UNIX system act as if they are using a real SLIP/PPP account. This means you can use programs like *Netscape Navigator, Mosaic, FTP,* and so on from your home machine using only a shell account. *SLiRP* is absolutely free and comes with source code! The TCP/IP code is based on 4.4BSD which is widely regarded as very stable and complete. This means it does all the things expected of TCP implementations and includes congestion avoidance, exponential backoff, round-trip time calculations, delayed ACKs, Nagle algorithms, and more. Visit this site for more information, as well as to download SLiRP.

Figure 594.1 SLiRP resources.

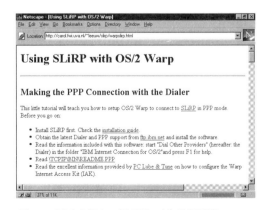

Figure 594.2 Using SLiRP with OS/2 Warp.

Stairways Shareware/Peter Lewis

http://www.share.com/peterlewis/

Peter Lewis is the Picasso of Macintosh shareware. At this site, you will find all his creations on display within his gallery of shareware. Visit this site to download *Anarchie* (an FTP client), *NetPresenz* (an HTTP, FTP, and Gopher server), *Assimilator* (for Mac-lab maintenance), *Mac TCP Watcher 2.0* (a useful TCP/IP test suite in one program), *ObiWan* (a general Help system considered essential by most Mac programmers who have their heads "screwed on straight"), *Talk* (for live person-to-person text conversation), *Finger* (an implementation of UNIX finger), *SOCKS* (a Mac implementation of the SOCKS firewall), and *Balloon Help Compiler* (a plug-in for *CodeWarrior*, which helps you create balloon help in your applications). Wow. Great stuff.

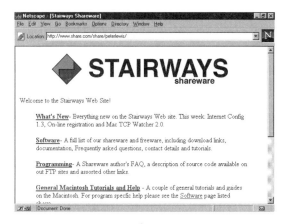

Figure 595 Stairways Web site.

utexas Mac Archive

http://wwwhost.ots.utexas.edu/mac/main.html

This site is a beautifully designed, graphically driven software archive for the Mac provided by the University of Texas. You won't find quite as many files at this site as you will in other Mac archives (at least by Texas standards), but the files have been well-selected. And, every file has a description and an icon. Visit this site for anti-virus software, AppleTalk network software, compression/translation software, games software, graphics software, sound playing and manipulation software, and system folder additions that include extensions, control panels, desk accessories, and more.

Figure 596.1 The archive.

Figure 596.2 Index by Date.

597

TIDBITS

http://www.tidbits.com/

Available in English, Chinese, Dutch, French, Japanese, and Spanish, *TidBITS* is a great, free weekly electronic publication edited and produced by Adam and Tonya Engst. *TidBITS* emphasizes Macintosh/Internet connectivity and programming. Every other issue of *TidBITS* includes *DealBITS*, a collection of exclusive hardware, software, and book deals for Mac users. To subscribe to *TidBITS*, simply enter your e-mail address into the on-line form you'll find at this Web site. While you are there, take time to read the past issues—they are quite informative.

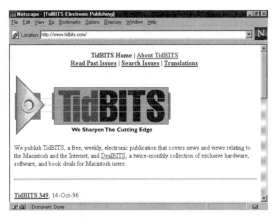

Figure 597 TidBITS.

598

TODD'S INTERNETWARE DOWNLOAD SITE

http://www.cjnetworks.com/~tfrazier/internet.html

Download all your favorite Internet connectivity software at this site: *Eudora, Fetch, FreePPP, HTML Markup, Ircle, Netscape Navigator, Newswatcher, NCSA Telnet, SiteMarker, Sound Machine, tn3270, TurboGopher,* and more. What? You don't know what *tn3270* is? It's a terminal emulation program that lets you Telnet to IBM mainframes from your Mac. In addition, you will find links to an on-line edition of the *Internet Starter Kit for the Macintosh,* as well as other key "net" software. Check it out. Thanks, Todd.

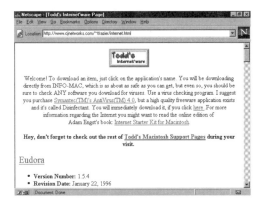

Figure 598.1 Todd's download site.

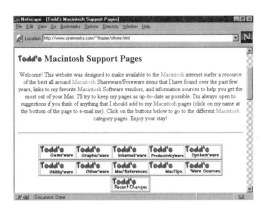

Figure 598.2 Todd's other pages.

AI CAFE C/C++ CGI HTML HTTP JAVA J++ PERL VBSCRIPT VRML WIN32 WINSOCK 1100110100101111001101110011010101000110011001001

TOP TWENTY TIPS FOR MACINTOSH WEBMASTERS

http://www.clearway.com/team/clearway/mac-web-tips/home.html

What kind of Mac Webmaster are you? If you're the kind who creates Web pages, images and text, you're a Content Consultant and you probably want to read the section of this document entitled "Cool Content" *(without programming—even animations!).* If you're the kind of Mac Webmaster who needs to keep a Mac Web server up and running smoothly, you're a Site Administrator, and you probably will want to read the section entitled "Creating Solid Infrastructure." And, of course, everyone should check out the section on how to connect with the Macintosh Webmaster community. All told, this is a very useful resource, no matter what it is you do in cyberspace.

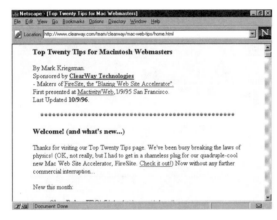

Figure 599 Top twenty tips.

AI CAFE C/C++ CGI HTML HTTP JAVA J++ PERL VBSCRIPT VRML WIN32 WINSOCK 1100110100101111001101110011010101000110011001001

THE ULTIMATE MACINTOSH

http://www.freepress.com/myee/ultimate_mac.html

This extensive collection of links includes connections to software archives, as well as great information and tools related to Mac graphics and sound, hardware, programming, publications, games, vendors, and newsgroups. You will also find the latest details on *System 7.5.5, CyberDog, Netscape for Mac, QuickTime, Photoshop for the Mac,* as well as late-breaking Mac news from *MacInTouch, MacSOURCE, MacSense,* and *MacCentral.* Additionally, you get connections to Mac software archives at the University of Texas, and other sites, including the Link Everything Online Macintosh Archive (Germany). Check it out.

Figure 600.1 The Ultimate Macintosh.

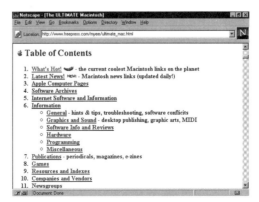

Figure 600.2 Table of Contents.

THE WELL CONNECTED MAC

http://www.macfaq.com/

This site provides yet another great compendium of Mac-based links. In addition, this site includes lists of frequently asked Mac questions, vendor information (more than 1,400 vendors of Mac hardware, software, and peripherals), Mac software archives, a Mac trade-show calendar, periodicals and on-line journals, mailing lists, and, of course, links to other Web sites (more than 400 of them). This site is the brainchild of Elliotte Rusty Harold, author of the *Java Developer's Resource*. The Well Connected Mac is sponsored by C/NET: The Computer Network (*http://www.cnet.com*). So, after you enjoy the site, send a thank you note to Elliotte, then click the icon to visit C/NET, and thank them as well.

Figure 601 The Well Connected Mac.

WHY MACINTOSH?

http://www2.apple.com/whymac/

Why Macintosh? Because the Mac is simply the greatest. But my writing it doesn't make it so. You need studies, reports, and independent product comparisons to convince you. And that is what you'll find archived at this site. If you are already a die-hard "Macker," or a recent convert, you'll be interested in the *free* evangelizing goodies you can get. How about some great Macintosh logo stickers for your car, house, computer, office, or forehead? Get them at Why Macintosh? How about benchmark reports and studies that clearly show how the PowerPC beats the living daylights out of Pentium and Pentium Pro when it comes to performance? How about a free video which compares the Macintosh and a PC running Windows 95 with predictable results? Go for it.

Figure 602 Why Macintosh?

AI CAFÉ C/C++ CGI HTML HTTP JAVA J++ PERL VBSCRIPT VRML WIN32 WINSOCK 110011010010111100110111001101010100011001100100101

4SITE: ASSOCIATION OF INTERNET PROVIDERS

http://www.algohio.com/4site/

As the only formal association of independent Internet providers, the goal of 4site is to provide members with high-quality business and marketing tools that will give them a competitive edge over other local and national on-line services. Membership to the association includes the 4site electronic newsletter, *Insight*, which will keep you up to date on association and industry news. Membership also includes use of the member newsgroup for getting and giving advice alongside your fellow industry professionals. Note: this is an exclusive newsgroup, just for members. You also get, of course, unrestricted access to the vast resources of the 4site Web pages which are packed with useful professional tools.

Figure 603 4Site home page.

AI CAFÉ C/C++ CGI HTML HTTP JAVA J++ PERL VBSCRIPT VRML WIN32 WINSOCK 110011010010111100110111001101010100011001100100101

ACCREDITED STANDARDS COMMITTEE X3

http://www.x3.org/

Standards—hah! Who needs 'em? I don't want others to use my stuff and I'm not interested in theirs. For the rest of you, however, these are the standards. Accredited Standards Committee X3, more commonly known simply as X3, is a committee accredited by the American National Standards Institute (ANSI) to develop voluntary standards for information technology. X3 standardization efforts encompass the storage, processing, transfer, display, management, and retrieval of information. X3's mission is to provide an efficient and effective process for the development of national standards and for participation in the development of national standards. A higher, yet related, goal is to strengthen and maintain U.S. leadership in the global standards arena by providing a visible, focused and effective national consensus body.

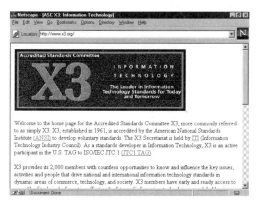

Figure 604.1 X3 home page.

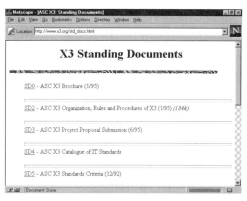

Figure 604.2 Standing documents.

ACM SIGMOD

http://bunny.cs.uiuc.edu/

ACM SIGMOD is the Association of Computing Machinery's Special Interest Group on Management of Data. Visit the ACM SIGMOD for membership information, as well as for information on great database conferences around the nation and around the world. You will also find free, public domain database software, database research groups and projects, database publications, database job openings, database research funding, and more. While you are there, check out abstracts from selected conferences, great on-line journals and magazines (e-zines), news of events that may impact database research funding, and, of course, links to other servers of potential interest. A strong resource.

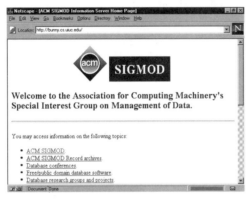

Figure 605.1 The home page.

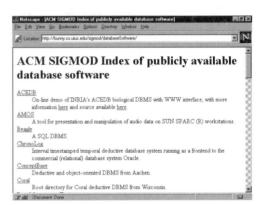

Figure 605.2 Free software.

ALLIANCE FOR INTERNATIONAL SOFTWARE DEVELOPMENT

http://www.aisd.com/

The Alliance for International Software Development (AISD) is a group of software development, consulting, and marketing companies from around the world. AISD members set high standards for software quality, provide continuing educational opportunities for employees, and develop long-term relationships with customers and the community. Many AISD member organizations are based in India. It is worth noting that the National Association of Computer Software and Services estimates that by the end of 1996 there will be 75 software firms in India that are certified under the ISO 9000 standard set by the European Union—a number greater than the number of firms so certified in the U.S.

Figure 606 The AISD Web site.

AI Café C/C++ CGI HTML HTTP Java J++ Perl VBScript VRML Win32 Winsock 11001101001011110011011100110101010001100110010101

ASSOCIATION FOR APPLIED INTERACTIVE MULTIMEDIA (AAIM)

http://www.aaim.org/

Are you just starting with multimedia or do you want to know how others use multimedia technology? The Association for Applied Interactive Multimedia (AAIM) supports professionals using and development multimedia. From a modest beginning five years ago, the organization has grown to include professionals from business and industry, higher education, K-12 education, the military, medicine, hardware and software producers and manufacturers, suppliers, and state, local, and federal government. AAIM conducts at least one major conference per year for the purpose of bringing together practicing multimedia professionals, and those considering using multimedia and related technologies. While the focus is on multimedia, AAIM presents papers and seminars on a wide variety of technologies.

Figure 607.1 The AAIM home page.

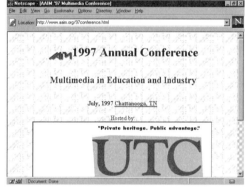

Figure 607.2 Conference information.

AI Café C/C++ CGI HTML HTTP Java J++ Perl VBScript VRML Win32 Winsock 11001101001011110011011100110101010001100110010101

ASSOCIATION FOR MULTIMEDIA INTERNATIONAL

http://www.ami.org/

Association for Multimedia International (AMI) is a non-profit, international association serving professionals who promote, produce and use the World Wide Web, video, computer multimedia, slide multi-image, mixed media, and integrated media projects to communicate, educate, entertain, and persuade. Founded in 1974, AMI attracts worldwide membership. The AMI International Festival occurs annually every summer, and brings together the world's best multimedia talent for a week of professional networking, forums, and seminars, along with the world's largest and most prestigious festival competition for all forms of multimedia. Check it out.

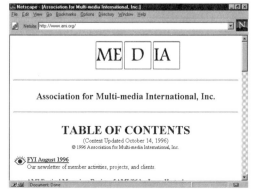

Figure 608.1 The AMI home page.

Figure 608.2 Press releases.

ASSOCIATION FOR MULTIMEDIA COMMUNICATIONS

http://www.amcomm.org/

Association for Multimedia Communications (AMC) is dedicated to promoting and expanding the use of interactive multimedia as a communication tool by gathering, researching, and distributing information through lectures, demonstrations, and published materials. Visit the AMC Web site for association information, industry news, membership and meetings information, special-events information, and more. Ed Rynearson and Todd Germann constructed and still maintain this extensive, well-designed, and highly informative Web site. If you design or are considering interactive multimedia products, don't miss this site.

Figure 609 The AMC home page.

ASSOCIATION OF SHAREWARE PROFESSIONALS (ASP)

http://www.asp-shareware.org/

The Association of Shareware Professionals (ASP) began, in April, 1987, as a small group of software authors and vendors marketing innovative programs through the concept of shareware. The ASP founders intended to strengthen the future of shareware as an alternative to commercial software by encouraging broader distribution. To this end, ASP works to inform the user community about shareware programs, assist members with the distribution (and therefore, the marketing) of their products, provide a forum for ASP members to share ideas and experiences, and foster a high degree of professionalism among the membership by setting appropriate standards and promulgating a code of ethics. Visit this Web site for more information.

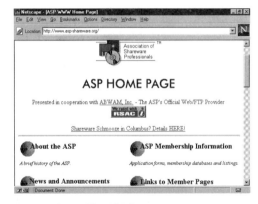

Figure 610.1 The ASP home page.   *Figure 610.2 News and announcements.*

AI CAFÉ C/C++ CGI HTML HTTP JAVA J++ PERL VBSCRIPT VRML WIN32 WINSOCK 11001101001011110011011100110101010001100110010010 1

BROAD ALLIANCE FOR MULTIMEDIA TECHNOLOGY & APPLICATIONS

http://www.bamta.org/

The Broad Alliance for Multimedia Technology and Applications (BAMTA) is an alliance whose purpose is to advance networked multimedia through open-systems solutions. BAMTA's mission is to accelerate the development of networked multimedia technologies and applications. Networked multimedia encompasses both the technology and the applications that allow the distribution of multiple data types over networks. To achieve this result, several industries must collaborate to create, manage, transport, and use digital content. BAMTA addresses the technological issues and offers a working structure for cooperative effort between different types of organizations. Visit this site for more information.

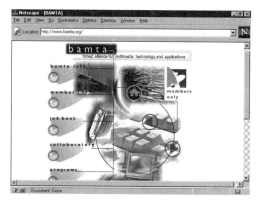

Figure 611.1 BAMTA home page.

Figure 611.2 Job bank.

AI CAFÉ C/C++ CGI HTML HTTP JAVA J++ PERL VBSCRIPT VRML WIN32 WINSOCK 11001101001011110011011100110101010001100110010010 1

BIMA: BRITISH INTERACTIVE MULTIMEDIA ASSOCIATION

http://www.bima.co.uk/

The British Interactive Multimedia Association (BIMA) is the United Kingdom trade association for the multimedia industry. Founded in 1985, BIMA members include end-users, application developers, hardware manufacturers, distributors, lawyers, publishers, consultants, and disc pressers. BIMA provides a forum for the exchange of information and views amongst its members. In this way, it promotes a wider understanding of multimedia and its benefits. BIMA also establishes relationships at national and international levels with professional bodies, governmental departments, other European training and educational bodies, and other trade associations around the world.

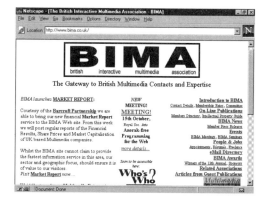

Figure 612.1 BIMA home page.

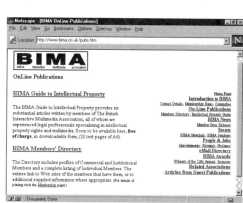

Figure 612.2 Online publications.

CENTER FOR DEMOCRACY AND TECHNOLOGY (CDT)

http://www.cdt.org/

The Center for Democracy and Technology (CDT) is a non-profit, public-interest organization based in Washington, DC. CDT's mission is to develop and advocate public policies that advance constitutional liberties and democratic values in new computer and communications technologies. Visit this site for complete information on this important fight, links to companion organizations such as the Electronic Frontier Foundation, informative publications, details about which "politicos" are for freedom of expression on the Internet and which against, and other engaging tidbits. While you are there, be sure to read the document entitled "First Annual Report and 1996 Work in Progress."

Figure 613 Support free speech!

COMPUTER HISTORY ASSOCIATION OF CALIFORNIA (CHAC)

http://www.chac.org/chac/

The Computer History Association of California is a charitable, nonprofit corporation established in 1993 to study, preserve, protect, and popularize the history of electronic computing. The Association publishes a great quarterly journal called the *Analytical Engine*. It also collects and archives hardware, software, and documents significant to the history. In addition, it cooperates in an informal network of other institutions specializing in computer history while overseeing the newsgroup, alt.folklore.computers. By the turn of the century, the organization plans to establish a major, comprehensive, public museum of computing, probably in the Silicon Valley itself. Visit this Web site for more details.

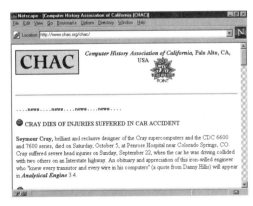

Figure 614.1 Obit for Seymour Cray.

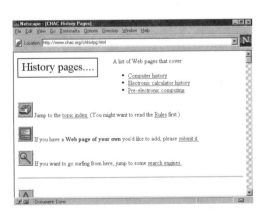

Figure 614.2 Computer history resources.

AI CAFE C/C++ CGI HTML HTTP JAVA J++ PERL VBSCRIPT VRML WIN32 WINSOCK 11001101001011110011011100110101010001100100100101

COMPUTER PROFESSIONALS FOR SOCIAL RESPONSIBILITY

http://snyside.sunnyside.com/home/

Computer Professionals for Social Responsibility (CPSR) is a public-interest alliance of computer scientists and others interested in the impact of computer technology on society. As technical experts, CPSR members provide the public and policy-makers with realistic assessments of the power, promise, and limitations of computer technology. As concerned citizens, CPSR members direct public attention to critical choices concerning the applications of computing, and how those choices affect society. The organization's current priorities include the Global Internet Liberty Campaign and other campaigns focusing on the issue of privacy, free-speech, and commerce. This site is an excellent stop along the Information Super Highway.

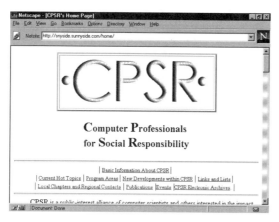

Figure 615 The CPSR home page.

AI CAFE C/C++ CGI HTML HTTP JAVA J++ PERL VBSCRIPT VRML WIN32 WINSOCK 11001101001011110011011100110101010001100100100101

DSDM CONSORTIUM

http://www.dsdm.org

DSDM Consortium is a non-profit organization dedicated to defining, promoting and continuously evolving a world-wide standard for Rapid Application Development (RAD). Of course, DSDM stands for Dynamic Systems Development Method, which is a public domain RAD method developed through capturing the experience of a large consortium of vendor and user organizations. Programmer's in many countries, including the U.K., now consider DSDM the defacto RAD. Visit this elegantly designed, ergonomically correct Web site for complete information on DSDM, RAD in general, and the DSDM Consortium in particular.

Figure 616.1 DSDM's home page.

Figure 616.2 News.

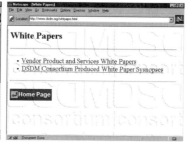

Figure 616.3 White papers.

ELECTRONIC FRONTIER FOUNDATION

http://www.eff.org/

The Electronic Frontier Foundation (EFF), in the words of its masthead, is a "non-profit civil liberties organization working in the public interest to protect privacy, free expression, and access to public resources and information on-line, as well as to promote responsibility in new media." The Electronic Frontier Foundation is well worth joining. Every day, lawmakers make decisions that will affect your life on-line—decisions about what sorts of technology you can use to protect the privacy of your communications, and what services you will be able to get over the emerging national-information infrastructure. The EEF works to insure that the civil liberties guaranteed in the Constitution and the Bill of Rights are applied to new communications technologies. Visit and join. Your rights and interest are at stake.

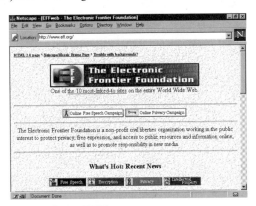

Figure 617.1 EFF home page.

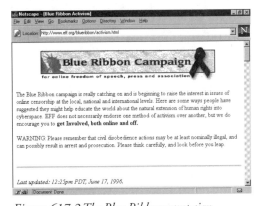

Figure 617.2 The Blue Ribbon campaign.

eTRUST

http://www.etrust.org/

eTRUST's mission is to establish user trust and confidence in electronic transactions. The organization seeks to promote the mass adoption of electronic commerce by creating an infrastructure to establish and evolve guidelines on issues such as privacy, security, and authentication. eTRUST's first project addresses on-line privacy. The organization has developed and will license recognizable and credible symbols ("trustmarks") of privacy and security to on-line merchants. The ultimate beneficiaries of the eTRUST program are on-line users who use these trustmarks to make informed choices. eTRUST is a non-profit, membership association. Visit this site for information on an important organization.

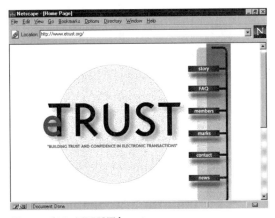

Figure 618 eTRUST home page.

AI CAFE C/C++ CGI HTML HTTP JAVA J++ PERL VBSCRIPT VRML WIN32 WINSOCK 11001101001011110011011100110101010001100110010101

THE EUROPEAN ASSOCIATION FOR COMPUTER GRAPHICS

http://www.cwi.nl/Eurographics/

Eurographics is a European-based non-profit organization which organizes many different activities, publications, and conferences for its members, which include researchers, developers, educators, and those who work in the computer-graphics industry as users or providers of computer graphics hardware, software, and applications. The organization's regular events and services include the Eurographics Annual Conference (which is the premier annual computer-graphics conference on the continent), and publications which include a great quarterly journal, *The Computer Graphics Forum*. This journal is a highly respected and authoritative source on all aspects of computer graphics programming and development. Even if you aren't in Europe, you can benefit from this site via the Web.

Figure 619.1 Eurographics home page.

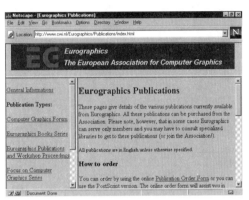

Figure 619.2 Publications information.

AI CAFE C/C++ CGI HTML HTTP JAVA J++ PERL VBSCRIPT VRML WIN32 WINSOCK 11001101001011110011011100110101010001100110010101

FIBRE CHANNEL ASSOCIATION

http://www.amdahl.com/ext/CARP/FCA/FCA.html

One key to faster data communication is the wide-spread use of fiber optics. The primary purpose of the Fibre Channel Association (FCA) is to provide a support structure for system integrators, peripheral manufacturers, software developers, component manufacturers, communications companies, and computer-service providers who wish to utilize Fibre Channel technology. Visit this site for frequently asked questions regarding the Fibre Channel, their standards, products, and technical notes, as well as complete membership information on why and how you would join the Fibre Channel Association. You will also find the latest news, notes, and magazine articles related to Fibre Channel technology, conference announcements and proceedings, and details on fiber optic tests and methods.

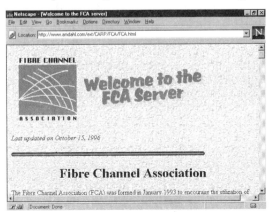

Figure 620 Fibre Channel home page.

INFORMATION SYSTEMS SECURITY ASSOCIATION

http://www.uhsa.uh.edu/issa/

Is it secure? Maybe? Don't know? The folks at this site may know. The Information Systems Security Association (ISSA) is, according to its masthead, "an international organization of information security professionals and practitioners. ISSA provides education forums, publications and peer interaction opportunities that enhance the knowledge, skill and professional growth of its members." Visit this site for information on membership in ISSA, along with a wealth of resources that include on-line security papers and publications, virus information and tools, disaster recovery information and tools, system patches, and much more. What you learn at this site may well prove vital. Check it out.

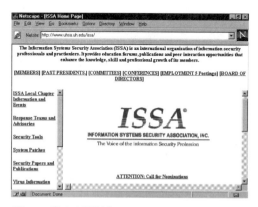

Figure 621.1 ISSA home page.

Figure 621.2 Security tools.

INDEPENDENT COMPUTER CONSULTANTS ASSOCIATION (ICCA)

http://www.icca.org/

Man, I wish I had someone to bounce ideas off of. Hey, based in St. Louis, Missouri, the Independent Computer Consultants Association is, as its Web site tell us, "a national not-for-profit organization providing professional development opportunities and business support programs for independent computer consultants." As you might guess, the membership is comprised of computer and software professionals who are journeying through the cyber-landscape as journeymen freelancers. These are the folks who use, recommend, and install the latest products, and help corporations and individuals leverage (to the hilt) the potential of the technology they already own. Does this sound like you? Then, consider joining ICCA.

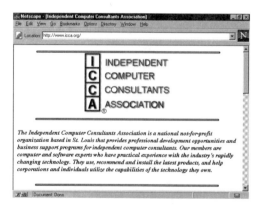

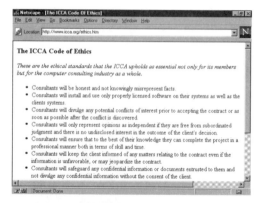

Figure 622.1 The ICCA home page.

Figure 622.2 Code of ethics.

AI CAFÉ C/C++ CGI HTML HTTP JAVA J++ PERL VBSCRIPT VRML WIN32 WINSOCK 110011010010111100110111001101010100011001100100101

INTERMEDIA PROFESSIONALS ASSOCIATION

http://www.his.com/~kara/ipa.html

According to its Web site, Intermedia Professionals Association (IPA) is "an informal organization dedicated to enabling production of innovative, content-driven interactive experiences. A key part of their Web pages is the "Intermedia Professionals Association Report," which casts a critical eye on the present state of Intermedia art and technology, while at the same time looking toward the future, "what can be, where we want to be and the steps necessary to achieve these goals." Visit this site for industry gossip, insider chat, recent success stories, reviews and comments on commercial interactive and multimedia projects, and much more.

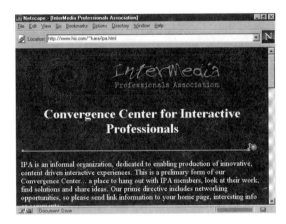

Figure 623 Intermedia home page.

INTERNATIONAL COMPUTER MUSIC ASSOCIATION (ICMA)

http://music.dartmouth.edu/~icma/

The International Computer Music Association (ICMA) is a worldwide organization of individuals and institutions involved in the technical, creative, and performance aspects of computer music. The organization serves composers, computer software and hardware developers, researchers, and musicians who are interested in the integration of music and technology. ICMA also presents the annual International Computer Music Conference, fosters professional networking, creates specialized publications and recordings, sponsors research, and supports competitions and awards for excellence in computer-generated music. If your in to music and PCs, don't miss this site.

Figure 624.1 The ICMA home page.

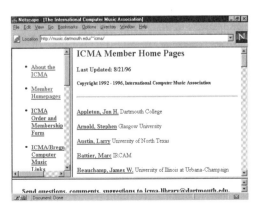

Figure 624.2 Member home pages.

INTERNATIONAL INTERACTIVE COMMUNICATIONS SOCIETY

http://www.intac.com/~virtual/

International Interactive Communications Society (IICS) is the premier world-wide, non-profit organization for interactive media professionals. Dedicated to the advancement of interactive arts and technologies since 1983, members of IICS include professionals involved in the rapidly integrating digital "convergence" industries: multimedia, computing, telecommunications, education, mass media, consumer electronics, publishing, and entertainment. IICS is unique in the broad spectrum of media issues it addresses, and for the talent, information, networking and educational resources it provides to its international membership. Visit this Web site for the "Virtual Chapter" of IICS for more information. It's a worthwhile stop.

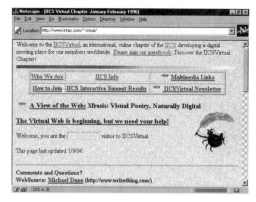

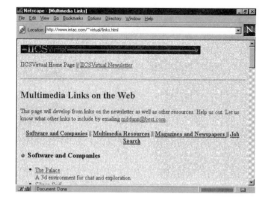

Figure 625.1 The IICS virtual chapter home page.   *Figure 625.2 Multimedia links.*

INTERNATIONAL TELECOMMUNICATIONS UNION

http://www.itu.ch/

The International Telecommunications Union (ITU) is headquartered in Geneva, Switzerland. The organization, the Web site tells us, "is an international organization within which governments and the private sector coordinate global telecommunications networks and services. ITU activities include the coordination, development, regulation and standardization of telecommunications and organization of regional and world Telecom events." Visit this Web site for more information on all these things, as well as a broad collection of ITU publications, a great World Telecommunication Policy Forum, information on international mobile telecommunications, and more.

Figure 626 The ITU home page.

AI CAFÉ C/C++ CGI HTML HTTP JAVA J++ PERL VBSCRIPT VRML WIN32 WINSOCK 11001101001011110011011001101010100011001100100101

INTERNET ENGINEERING TASK FORCE (IETF)

http://www.ietf.cnri.reston.va.us/home.html

Stop! This group is one you need to know. The Internet Engineering Task Force (IETF) is the protocol engineering and development arm of the Internet. The IETF is a large, open, international community of network designers, operators, vendors, and researchers concerned with the evolution of the Internet architecture and the smooth operation of the Internet. The group is open to any interested individual. The actual technical work of the IETF is done in its working groups, which are organized by topic into several key areas (for example, routing, network management, security, and so on.) To get acquainted with the IETF, I recommend going to their Web home page and accessing the document entitled *The Tao of IETF.*

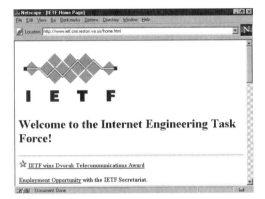

Figure 627.1 The IETF home page.

Figure 627.2 *A recent honor.*

AI CAFÉ C/C++ CGI HTML HTTP JAVA J++ PERL VBSCRIPT VRML WIN32 WINSOCK 11001101001011110011011001101010100011001100100101

INTERNET PRIVACY COALITION: GOLDEN KEY PROGRAM

http://www.privacy.org/ipc/

Washington says don't do it. You are not supposed to have secure data. Does that make sense? The mission of the Internet Privacy Coalition (IPC) is to promote privacy and security on the Internet through widespread public availability of strong encryption. If you've spent any time at all on the Web, you've noticed the IPC's "Golden Key" on many sites. The Golden Key campaign has been launched to raise awareness and support for the preservation of the right to communicate privately and the legalization of techniques which make that possible. Visit the IPC site, grab a Golden Key logo, and display it on your Web pages to show your support for the right to privacy and the freedom to use good tools of privacy *without governmental restraints.* Shame on you Washington. The McCarthy era is over.

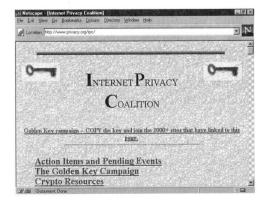

Figure 628.1 IPC homepage.

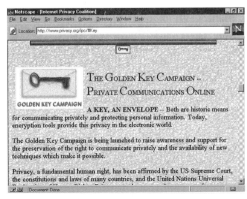

Figure 628.2 The Golden Key campaign.

ISO ON-LINE: INTERNATIONAL ORGANIZATION FOR STANDARDIZATION

http://www.iso.ch/

Stop. Read. This is another organization you must know. The International Organization for Standardization (ISO) is a worldwide federation of national standards bodies from some 100 countries. ISO is a non-governmental organization established in 1947. The ISO's mission is to promote the development of standardization and related activities in the world with a view to facilitating the international exchange of goods and services, and to developing cooperation in the spheres of intellectual, scientific, technological, and economic activity. ISO's work results in international agreements which are published as International Standards. Visit the ISO's Web site for more information on the organization and its efforts.

Figure 629.1 ISO home page.

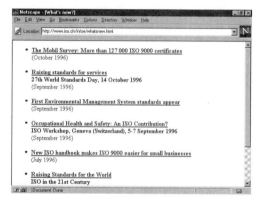

Figure 629.2 What's new.

METADATA COALITION

http://www.metadata.org/

The Metadata Coalition is comprised of vendors and users "allied with a common purpose of driving forward the definition, implementation and ongoing evolution of a metadata interchange format and its support mechanisms." Towards this end, they have formed the Metadata Interchange Initiative. This program brings industry vendors and users together to address a variety of difficult problems and issues with regard to exchanging, sharing, and managing metadata. The Metadata Coalition is a gathering of interested parties with a common focus and shared goals, rather than a traditional standards body or regulatory group.

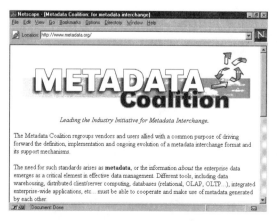

Figure 630 The Metadata Coalition home page.

AI CAFE C/C++ CGI HTML HTTP JAVA J++ PERL VBSCRIPT VRML WIN32 WINSOCK 11001101001011110011011100110101010001100110010010

MMCF: MULTIMEDIA COMMUNICATIONS FORUM

http://www.mmcf.org/

The Multimedia Communications Forum (MMCF) is, as its Web site tells us, "an international non-profit research and development organization of telecommunications service providers, multimedia application and equipment developers, and end-users who realize the revolutionary potential of multimedia communications." The group's members are dedicated to accelerating the market acceptance of multi-vendor, multimedia solutions which can users can use across different types of networks. One particularly nice aspect of this site is the hyperlink to the MMCF software roundtable which is hosted by IBM, Hursley, United Kingdom. These folks are discussing some good stuff. Check it out.

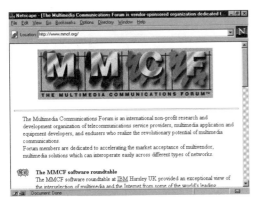

Figure 631.1 MMCF home page.

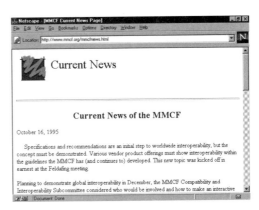

Figure 631.2 MMCF forum news.

AI CAFE C/C++ CGI HTML HTTP JAVA J++ PERL VBSCRIPT VRML WIN32 WINSOCK 11001101001011110011011100110101010001100110010010

NATIONAL ASSOCIATION OF PROGRAMMERS

http://www.naponnet.org/

The National Association of Programmers is an association dedicated to programmers, developers, consultants, and students in the computer industry. The association's goal is to provide information and resources that give members a competitive edge in today's fast-paced, ever-changing computer industry. Whether you are a corporate professional or an independent entrepreneur, membership in the National Association of Programmers will let you share with others your commitment to excellence, knowledge, and professionalism. Membership offers many benefits including a quarterly newsletter and other good stuff.

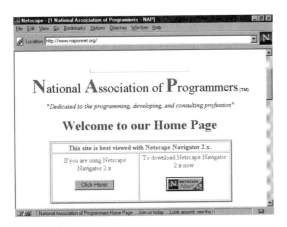

Figure 632 NAP home page.

AI Café C/C++ CGI HTML HTTP Java J++ Perl VBScript VRML Win32 Winsock

National Association for Women in Computing

http://www.halcyon.com/monih/awc.html

The Association for Women in Computing (AWC) is a national, nonprofit, professional organization dedicated to the advancement of women in the computing field. AWC's purpose is to provide opportunities for professional growth through networking and through programs on technical and career-oriented topics. AWC encourages high standards of competence and promotes a professional attitude among its members. One of the organization's major goal is, of course, to promote awareness of the issues affecting women in the computing industry. Visit this site for more information on AWC, including details on chapters in California, New York, Massachusetts, New Jersey, Washington state, the District of Columbia, and other areas.

Figure 633.1 The AWC home page.

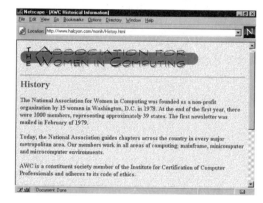

Figure 633.2 A history.

AI Café C/C++ CGI HTML HTTP Java J++ Perl VBScript VRML Win32 Winsock

National Computer Security Association (NCSA)

http://www.ncsa.com/

The National Computer Security Association (NCSA) is an independent organization offering objective views and opinions on computer-security issues. NCSA strives to improve computer security through the sharing of knowledge, dissemination of information, and certification of security products. In fact, NCSA has become the premier provider of security and reliability information, as well as information on the ethics related to these issues. NCSA also provides fundamental resources related to security training, testing, research, and more. Among other things, you will want to check out information on the Web surfer regarding the many NCSA conferences and seminars scheduled throughout the year.

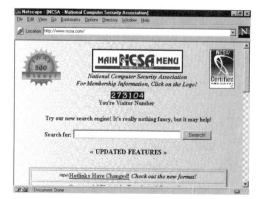

Figure 634.1 NCSA home page.

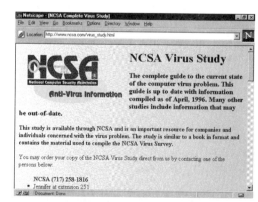

Figure 634.2 NCSA virus study.

NATIONAL MULTIMEDIA ASSOCIATION OF AMERICA

http://www.nmaa.org/

The industry refers to the Web site of NMAA (National Multimedia Association of America) as a "multimedia proving ground" because this is the place to come to test new theories, ideas, and concepts. In fact, that is what the organization is all about. Consider: the multimedia vehicle of today is *virtually guaranteed* to be outdated and completely different five years from how. Because the industry is changing at such a rapid pace, NMAA was formed to involve all who wish to be involved in exchanging ideas about changing technologies. Previously, no national exchange for such discussions existed. Now NMAA provides the vital forum. Check it out.

Figure 635.1 The NMAA Web site.

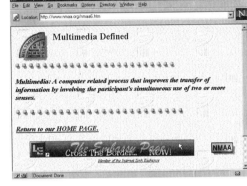

Figure 635.2 Multimedia defined.

OLAP COUNCIL

http://www.olapcouncil.org/

On-line Analytical Processing (OLAP) is an information technology that lets analysts and executives gain insight into raw data quickly by looking at the data using a variety of views (data manipulations). The OLAP Council's mission is to educate the market about OLAP technology, provide common definitions, sponsor industry research, and help position OLAP technology within a broader IT architecture. In addition, the Council works toward establishing guidelines for interpretability between multiple OLAP vendors' client and server tools. The value of OLAP is that it performs multidimensional analysis of enterprise data, including complex calculation, trends analysis, and modeling. Derived from end-user requirements, OLAP enables end-users to perform ad hoc analysis of data in multiple dimensions, thereby giving them the insight and understanding they need for better decision making.

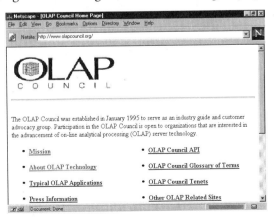

Figure 636 OLAP home page.

PORTABLE APPLICATION STANDARDS COMMITTEE (PASC)

http://www.pasc.org/

No you can't move the standards as you would like. That's not the point. The Portable Application Standards Committee (PASC) is chartered by the Institute of Electrical and Electronics Engineers (IEEE) to define standard application service interfaces—most notably those in the POSIX family. PASC includes an executive sub-committee (chaired by Lowell Johnson of Unisys Corporation), a logistics committee (chaired by Barry Needham of Amdahl Corporation), and several interpretations committees (chaired by Andrew Josey of X/Open). Visit this Web site for full information on all aspects of each and every PASC sub-committee, as well as membership and publication information.

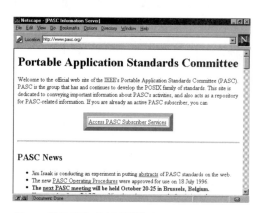

Figure 637.1 The PASC Web site.

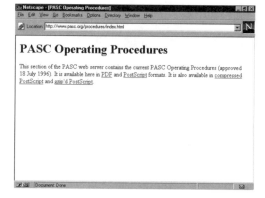

Figure 637.2 PASC operating procedures.

PROFESSIONAL INTERNET PROVIDER ASSOCIATION

http://www.pipassoc.com/

Are you looking for Internet insights from the experts? The members of the Professional Internet Provider Association are comprised of Internet access providers, Web presence providers, manufacturers of hardware for the Internet industry, and Internet software developers who strive toward superior customer service, quality Web viability, and access to the greatest community in the universe: the Internet! The association's purpose is to exchange ideas, solve problems, and help others with similar experiences. By working together, members can accomplish exceptional results. By sharing ideas, they avoid struggling over the same hurdles others have already learned to successfully navigate. Join the party.

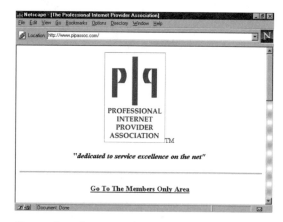

Figure 638 The PIPA Web site.

SOFTWARE PUBLISHERS MARKETPLACE

http://spmarket.com

Since the dawn of the PC industry, independent software developers have produced an estimated 10,000 CD-ROM titles and tens of thousands of software titles. The average retail outlet (including catalog companies and superstores) carries less than 500 titles. These 500 titles are, for the most part, developed by companies who can spend as much as $100,000 per title just to launch it in the marketplace. This leaves thousands of titles that have little, if any, retail space. The Software Publishers Marketplace provides, for its member publishers, an easy-to-browse site for the inexpensive promotion of titles that would otherwise have trouble reaching their market. Small software publishers are well-advised to look into joining Software Publishers Marketplace.

Figure 639.1 Sotware Publishers Marketplace.

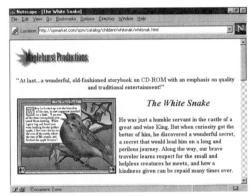

Figure 639.2 One offering.

SOFTWARE SUPPORT PROFESSIONALS ASSOCIATION

http://www.sspa-online.com/

Since 1989, the Software Support Professionals Association (SSPA) has provided a value-added forum where service and support professionals in the software industry can share ideas, discuss developing trends, and network with their peers. Today, SSPA enjoys worldwide recognition with nearly 600 member companies, and is comprised of technical and support professionals from the world's leading firms. SSPA is dedicated to enhancing the roles of software support professionals, both those who manage internal help desks and those who serve retail software buyers. To this end, SSPA endeavors to serve as a vehicle for growth for the profession of software support management.

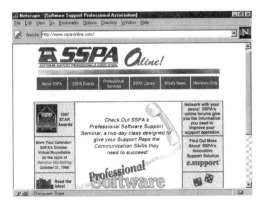

Figure 640.1 SSPA online.

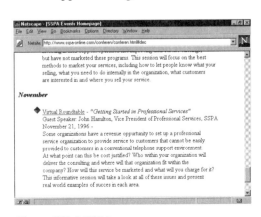

Figure 640.2 SSPA events.

TRANSACTION PROCESSING PERFORMANCE COUNCIL (TPC)

http://www.tpc.org/

The Transaction Processing Performance Council (TPC) is a non-profit corporation founded to define transaction processing and database benchmarks. Any company can run TPC benchmarks based on published standards. TPC then audits and reviews the benchmarks. *TPC-C* and *TPC-D* are the two current benchmarks:. The former is a popular on-line transaction processing (OLAP) benchmark. The latter relates to a broad range of decision support (DS) applications that require complex, long-running queries against large complex data structures. Visit this Web site for information on these and newly proposed benchmarks.

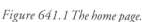

Figure 641.1 The home page.

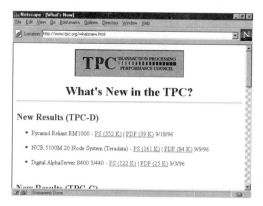

Figure 641.2 What's new.

USENIX & SAGE

http://www.usenix.org/

USENIX is the UNIX and advanced computer systems professional and technical association, while SAGE stands for the System Administrators Guild. Since 1975, USENIX has brought together the community of engineers, systems administrators, scientists, and technicians working on the cutting edge of the computing world. SAGE is a special technical group of the USENIX. SAGE co-sponsors conferences on system and network administration, publishes a bi-monthly newsletter, conducts an annual system administration salary survey, and fosters relationships with international affiliates. Visit this Web site for detailed information on both organizations.

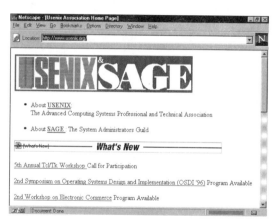

Figure 642 USENIX & SAGE home page.

AI CAFÉ C/C++ CGI HTML HTTP JAVA J++ PERL VBSCRIPT VRML WIN32 WINSOCK 110011010010111100110111001101010001100110010101

APPLIED KNOWLEDGE

http://www.aki.com/

Applied Knowledge is a firm dedicated to the advancement of client/server systems and *PowerBuilder* development through the use of object-oriented technologies and design methodologies. It is organized around research and development that results in tools and techniques that continually meet the challenge of client/server system development. Applied Knowledge is a *Powersoft* CODE partner, committed to continued improvement and advancing technologies through open architectures and integrated products. Their products include *Progency*, a professional designed library for *PowerBuilder* developers. Visit this site for more information. Find out how *Progency* can save you a lot of headaches.

Figure 643.1 Applied Knowledge.

Figure 643.2 Products.

Figure 643.3 Links.

AI CAFÉ C/C++ CGI HTML HTTP JAVA J++ PERL VBSCRIPT VRML WIN32 WINSOCK 110011010010111100110111001101010001100110010101

AUSTIN SOFTWARE FOUNDRY

http://www.foundry.com/

The Austin Software Foundry is a premier software development company based in Austin, Texas. They are recognized leaders in object-oriented solutions, and they are noted for building powerful object-oriented tools for *PowerBuilder* developers, including tools for object-oriented analysis, design, and development, along with tools for object declaration and management. They also sell a splendid component-software library for *PowerBuilder*. Through it all, the Austin Software Foundry keeps up a strong dedication to efficiency and quality. Visit their incisive, informative Web site for much more information. Find out how Foundry tools can improve your applications while saving you time in the process.

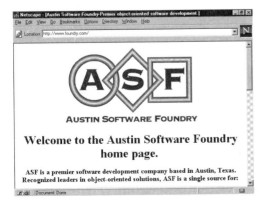

Figure 644.1 Austin Software Foundry Web site.

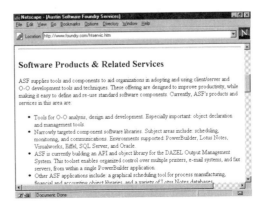

Figure 644.2 Some product information.

645

BEARD TECHNOLOGY: PROFRAME CLASS LIBRARY

http://www.beardtech.com/

PowerBuilder developers: how much project time and money do you waste coding the same functionality over and over? Imagine code that is reusable across all applications. Imagine a situation where every completed project contributes to the next development effort! Imagine placing a *datawindow* on a window and having it function *immediately*! Imagine never coding a *Retrieve*, *InsertRow*, *Update*, or *DeleteRow* operation *ever again*! If this sounds a little bit like heaven, then you can find heaven at the Beard Technology Web site in the form of Beard's *ProFrame Class Library*. The time you save may be your own.

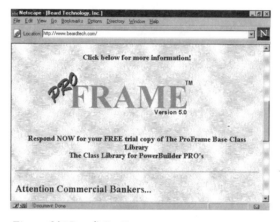

Figure 645 Beard's ProFrame.

646

BUILDING CLIENT/SERVER APPLICATIONS USING POWERBUILDER

http://hsb.baylor.edu/~vaughnr/cover.htm

Visit this site for a fantastic on-line tutorial from Baylor University that addresses every aspect of *PowerBuilder* application development from the ground up. The tutorial's chapters discuss creating windows (including copied windows and inherited windows), event scripting, string-control interactions, scripting calculators, instance variables and scripts, user functions, debugging, creating a database, adding data to a database, simple data windows, master detail data windows, reports and printing, dropdown *datawindows*, the library painter, and more. If you want to get up to speed with *PowerBuilder* in a hurry, this site is a great place to start.

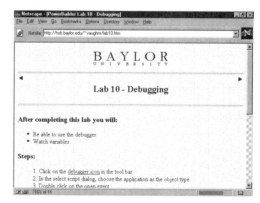

Figure 646.1 The tutorial.

Figure 646.2 The start of a chapter.

CORE GROUP INNOVATIONS

http://www.pics.com/byte/

Core Group Innovations markets two products, *Visual Security* and *Visual Libraries*, for *PowerBuilder* applications. *Visual Security* provides row- and column-level security. *Visual Libraries* goes beyond being a library to also being an application framework for *PowerBuilder*. The mission of Core Group Innovations is to provide *PowerBuilder* programmers with tools that enable them to write programs that are every bit as robust and technologically advanced as any being written in other programming languages. In short, the *PowerBuilder* programmer can achieve remarkable, professional results without having to have advanced object-oriented programming skills.

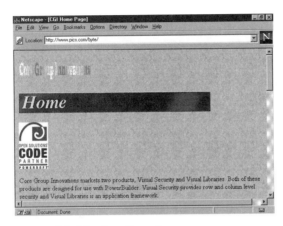

Figure 647 The Core Group home page.

GREENBRIER & RUSSEL: FREE POWERBUILDER TOOLS

http://www.gr.com/

The folks at Greenbrier & Russel have a gift for you. They are giving away *PowerBuilder Foundation Class* extensions software for free! The *PowerBuilder Foundation Class (PFC) Library* included with *PowerBuilder 5.0* is indeed a robust, object-oriented class library. However, to further enhance the capabilities of the PFC, Greenbrier & Russell have developed *PFCPlus*—free, downloadable software for use with *PowerBuidler 5.0*. The *PFCPlus* software contains a variety of useful objects not currently found in *PowerBuilder's PFC*, along with source code, full documentation, and a sample application! *PFCPlus* includes application services, window services, *datawindow* services, and much more. Check it out!

Figure 648.1 Greenbrier & Russel Web site.

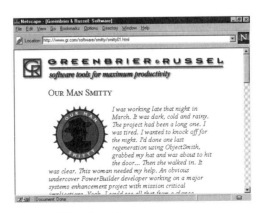

Figure 648.2 An odd story.

Janiff Software: PowerBuilder Tools

http://www.janiff.com/

Janiff Software publishes a number of great *PowerBuilder* resources, including *APOL* (a fully object-oriented class library that helps you build highly functional business applications), *BatchMan* (the first enterprise reporting and report delivery system for *PowerBuilder*), *QuickLook* (the fastest, most intuitive on-demand *PowerBuilder* browser available), *Secure It* (which lets a user secure an application without being a *PowerBuilder* expert and without having to write code), the *Workbook* object (which allows users to run *datawindow* reports and then store them for a later review), and the *Outliner* object (which lets users view relationships among nodes in a tree). Visit this site and check out these tools.

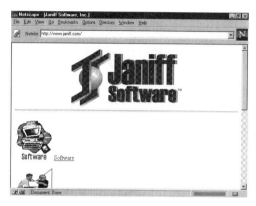

Figure 649.1 Janiff Software Web site.

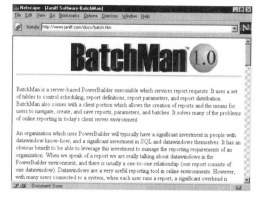

Figure 649.2 Product information.

Millennium Software: PowerBuilder Tools

http://www.pbase.com

Millennium Software brings you a host of tools including *Millennium Dispatch*, a *PowerBuilder* application which automates the execution of Windows-based executables and *PowerBuilder* reports. This application addresses the needs of large, mission-critical applications with batch requirements. *Millennium Dispatch* provides distribution reports to diverse locations based on pre-defined distribution lists, catalog management of all reports defined for an application, asynchronous launching of reports and executables based on pre-defined schedules, enforcement of application security for viewing, creating and launching reports, automatic load leveling, and much more. Wow!

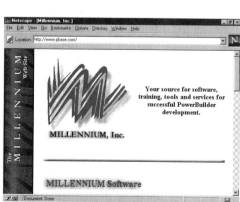

Figure 650.1 Millennium Web site.

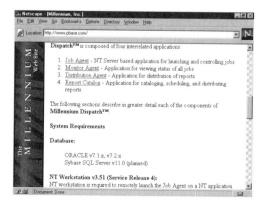

Figure 650.2 Dispatch information.

PARADIGM COMPUTER SOLUTIONS

http://www.pdcs.com/

Paradigm Computer Solutions specializes in client/server application development using *PowerBuilder*, and they have been providing application development and support to a host of satisfied clients since 1991. Their products include several *PowerBuilder* application startup libraries and a *PowerBuilder*-based application development template called *PowerPlate*, which provides a set of development tools and guidelines targeted at new *PowerBuilder* developers. PowerPlate also provides a consistent and straightforward approach to building *PowerBuilder* applications. Most of a typical application's functionality has been built into *PowerPlate*. Visit this Web site for more information.

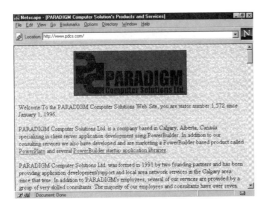

Figure 651.1 The Paradigm Web site.

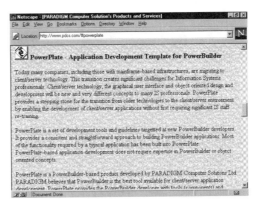

Figure 651.2 PowerPlate information.

.PBL—POWERBUILDER LINKS PAGE

http://www.opcenter.net/~david_levine/

Maintained by David Levine, the *PowerBuilder* Links Page is perhaps the best clearinghouse of information and links related to *PowerBuilder* you will find on the Web. This site features extensive resources related to *PowerSoft*, analysis and data modeling, class libraries and frameworks, VBX and OCX controls, add-ons, testing tools, databases, books and magazines, usergroups, and more. You will also find a great list of *PowerBuilder* frequently asked questions. Finally, the site's links to class libraries and frameworks, *PowerArchitect*, *Progency*, *Pro Frame*, *ObjectSolutions*, *Super!*, *ObjectStart*, *Enterprise Builder*, and other products alone are worth your visit.

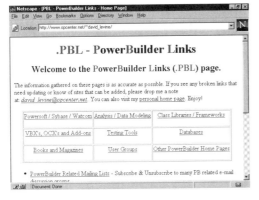

Figure 652.1 .PBL - PowerBuilder Links.

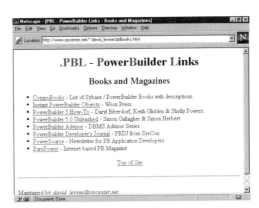

Figure 652.2 Book and Magazine links.

653

PB NEWBIE

http://www.ashok.pair.com/

Hosted by Ashok Ramachandran, this site is the first (and, so far as I can tell, the only) site on the Web devoted to *PowerBuilder* beginners. You will find gobs of great tips, tricks, and fundamentals, along with first-rate tutorial essays and articles. Connect to the "PB Newbie forum," the only threaded discussion group for *PowerBuilder* "virgins." Access a great list of frequently asked questions that take nothing for granted and leave nothing to the imagination. Scroll through excellent *PowerBuilder* primers and tutorials, including Baylor University's outstanding on-line tutorial. And, check out a host of other tools and references. If you are going to get started with *PowerBuilder*, this is the place to do it.

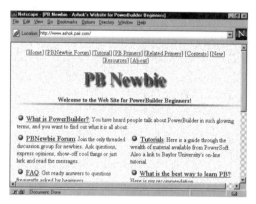

Figure 653.1 PB Newbie.

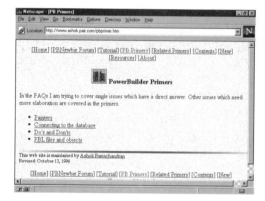

Figure 653.2 PowerBuilder Primers.

654

POWERARCHITECT FROM AJACOM

http://www.ajacom.com/

PowerArchitect is a "*PowerBuilder* architecture" that provides developers with a fresh alternative to existing class libraries and frameworks. Specifically designed for use with all new client/server development projects, not only does *PowerArchitect* have a full set of class libraries, it also provides an easy step-by-step methodology for coding *PowerBuilder* applications. *PowerArchitect's* three levels of inheritance provide programmers with a consistent coding standard while minimizing development time and increasing productivity. Novice as well as experienced developers will find *PowerArchitect* an easy tool to learn and use. Visit this Web site for more details.

Figure 654.1 AJACOM Web site.

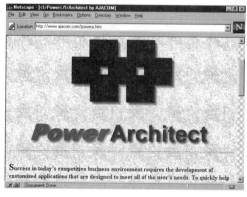

Figure 654.2 PowerArchitect information.

AI CAFÉ C/C++ CGI HTML HTTP JAVA J++ PERL VBSCRIPT VRML WIN32 WINSOCK 1100110100101110011011100110101010001100110010010

POWERBUILDER HOME PAGE (UNOFFICIAL)

http://www.servtech.com/public/bigelow/pb/pb.htm

This site is a wonderful resource for *PowerBuilder* developers. You will find, among many other things, a fantastic list of frequently asked *PowerBuilder* questions, as well as downloadable objects, detailed white papers, *PowerBuilder* news and views, expert hints and tips, and more. You will also find book reviews, industry forecasts, on-line chat sessions that constitute a "virtual" *PowerBuilder* usergroup, and links to such important resources as the *PowerBuilder Developer's Journal* and exclusive *PowerBuilder* articles provided by the experts at Tenax Engineering. All told, this site is a valuable stop on the Information Super Highway for any serious *PowerBuilder* developer.

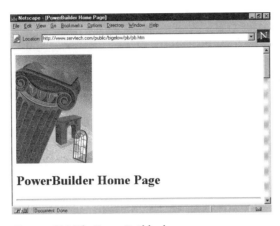

Figure 655 The PowerBuilder home page.

AI CAFÉ C/C++ CGI HTML HTTP JAVA J++ PERL VBSCRIPT VRML WIN32 WINSOCK 1100110100101110011011100110101010001100110010010

POWERBUILDER INTERACTIVE

http://pk.com/PowerBuilder/

This site features a tremendous collection of information and links related to *PowerBuilder Winsock* programming, using *PowerBuilder* with ActiveX controls, and much more. The page includes a large and useful *PowerSocket Library* of demo programs which include a POP3 client application, a routine that shows HTTP requests made by a Web browser, a *PowerSocket* domain name registration utility, and more. You'll also get the latest *PowerBuilder* announcements and news, reviews of great (and not so great) new *PowerBuilder* books, connections to *PowerBuilder* usergroups around the country and around the world, and even an excellent chat area. Check it out!

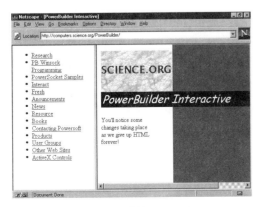

Figure 656.1 PowerBuilder Interactive.

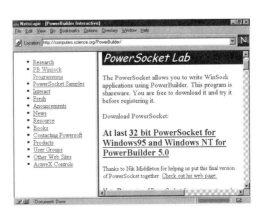

Figure 656.2 PowerSocket shareware.

657

POWERBUILDER JOBS LISTING

http://www.pbjobs.com/

Need a programmer? This site lets you list your employment needs for free. And you can search for a job here for free as well. Hey, the price is right either way! The site lists the job's country, state, and region. Let's see. What is in demand today? A company in Phoenix requires a Senior PowerBuilder Developer. The pay is up to $70,000 with a full-benefits package. The needed RDBMS expertise includes Sybase, Oracle, or Informix (take your pick). You'll get your own office (no cubicles here!). Out of town? No problem. The company will pay for both your interview and your moving expenses. And, you'll be working for a fast-class shop with many Fortune 1000 clients. Come to think of it, I think *I'll* apply!

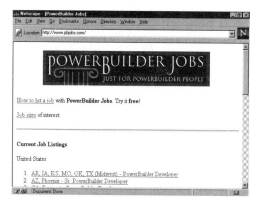

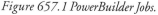

Figure 657.1 PowerBuilder Jobs.

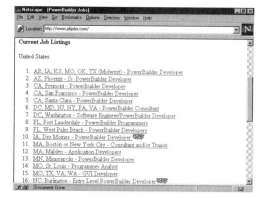

Figure 657.2 Some listings.

658

POWERBUILDER PITSTOP

http://ourworld.compuserve.com/homepages/stanner/

Check out the latest tricks and tools, including screen shots, sample code, and applications to download. And be sure to treat yourself to the host of great *PowerBuilder* tips you'll find at this site which include approaches related to dropdown calendars, non-visuals for parameter passing, *datawindow* service objects, multi-table updates from *datawindow*, *dropdown* calculators, drag-and-drop row sequencing, "the world's smallest leap year calculation," instance-level menu references, controlling menu-close events, dropdown searches, getting faster graphics without bitmaps, single click column sorting, and much more. This site is a great pit stop!

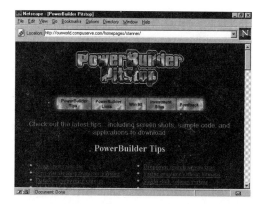

Figure 658.1 PowerBuilder Pitstop.

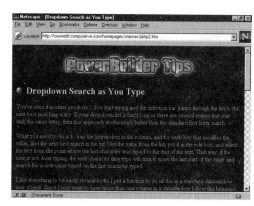

Figure 658.2 One of the tips.

AI CAFÉ C/C++ CGI HTML HTTP JAVA J++ PERL VBSCRIPT VRML WIN32 WINSOCK 110011010010111100110111001101010100011001100100101

POWERBUILDER TIPS

http://ourworld.compuserve.com/homepages/Howe/

As its name implies, this site is dedicated to providing useful tips of value and interest to *PowerBuilder* developers. Visit this site and benefit from the experience and wisdom of your *PowerBuilder* peers. Or, if you have a tip or technique to share, come to this site and share it. The host of this site, Ken Howe, also has a number of objects which he invites you to download, including public-domain objects, shareware programs, and more. The tips are very useful and include how to add a *Groupbox* control, find the Windows directory, make Windows stay on top, get the user's LAN ID, and display text at any angle. Great tips!

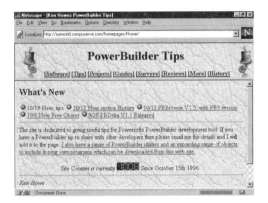

Figure 659.1 PowerBuilder Tips.

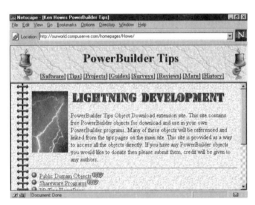

Figure 659.2 Free PowerBuilder Objects.

AI CAFÉ C/C++ CGI HTML HTTP JAVA J++ PERL VBSCRIPT VRML WIN32 WINSOCK 110011010010111100110111001101010100011001100100101

POWERTOOL 5.0 FROM POWERCERV

http://www.powercerv.com/

The tools with which you develop can have a dramatic impact on how well and how quickly you meet your goals. *PowerTOOL* is the leading *PowerBuilder* object class library and inheritance methodology embodied in a collection of pretested *PowerBuilder* templates, windows, functions, and component objects that you can easily integrate (using inheritance) into your application. *PowerTOOL* lets you complete your applications much faster and with fewer bugs, than would otherwise be possible. The result is a more efficient, error-free application with significantly lower ongoing maintenance costs. Visit this Web site and download a free demo!

Figure 660.1 PowerCerv home page.

Figure 660.2 PowerTOOL information.

PURE POWER: YOUR SOURCE FOR POWERBUILDER INFO

http://www.magicnet.net/purepower/

This site features a great set of *PowerBuilder* links and resources, and also a *PowerBuilder* tip of the week. This was the tip when I visited: "Isn't it unfortunate that grid-style *DataWindows* have lines going into the header band? When I want the look of a grid *DataWindow* without creating a grid-style *DataWindow*, I add horizontal and vertical lines to create a grid. But, to save myself from a lot of sizing work, I set up a couple of attributes on these lines. On vertical lines, I select Properties (right-click on the line object), click the Expressions tab, and enter 0 (zero) for *y1* and *rowheight()-1* for *y2*. That way, *PowerBuilder* sizes the vertical lines automatically." Visit this Web site for more great tips. You will be glad you stopped by.

Figure 661 Pure Power.

RATIONAL SOFTWARE CORPORATION

http://www.rational.com/

Rational Software brings you *Rational Rose for PowerBuilder*. As you will learn, *Rational Rose* supports the revised Booch '93 notation that unifies object-oriented analysis and design notation, captures your analysis model, supports model transformation from analysis to design, represents your design model, and automatically generates *PowerBuilder PowerScript* for your application. In addition, the software can reverse engineer your application's *PowerBuilder PowerScript*, automatically generate SQL/DDL for relational databases, map persistent objects to relational databases, and provide version control and multiuser development support. Visit the Rational Software Web site for more information.

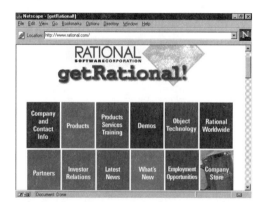

Figure 662.1 The Rational Web site.

Figure 662.2 Downloads and demos.

RIK'S POWERBUILDER DOJO

http://www.pics.com/byte/dojo.htm

Rik's *PowerBuilder* Dojo provides a vast cornucopia of resources, tools, and answers. Your host, Rik Brooks, maintains the site in order to provide open communications between *PowerBuilder* professionals around the world. Ideally, as a group, these developers can discern industry trends and better position themselves for future innovations. The site features especially good resources for distributed computing from both the client and server sides. And, you'll find a great tutorial on the Zen of the *connection* object, which contains information that lets the objects address themselves to the right place. Visit Rik's Web site for more information.

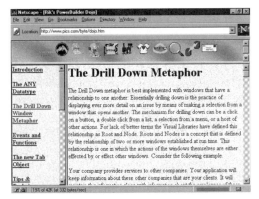

Figure 663.1 *The Drill Down Metaphor.*

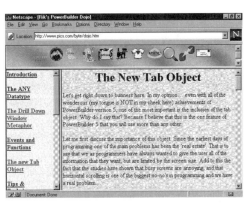

Figure 663.2 *The New Tab Object.*

SERVERLOGIC

http://www.serverlogic.com/

Server Logic tools streamline and enhance PowerBuilder development, letting you go home sooner while at the same time leaving better software projects behind you. Headquartered in Bellevue, Washington, ServerLogic Corporation was founded in 1992 to deliver advanced client/server application development tools and services. ServerLogic is one of *Powersoft's premier* CODE and consulting partners, and the firm is known worldwide for providing one of the most comprehensive lines of class libraries available for *PowerBuilder* application development. Their products include the *PowerClass Application Framework*, the *PowerLock Security Library and Administration Program*, and the *PowerObjects Modular Object Library*. Visit the Web pages for more information on the many great tools and services available from ServerLogic.

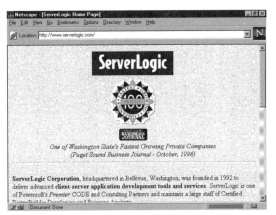

Figure 664 *ServerLogic Web site.*

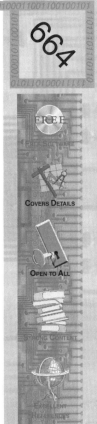

FREE
FREE SOFTWARE

COVERS DETAILS

OPEN TO ALL

665

SHERBORN CONSULTING ASSOCIATES POWERBUILDER KIT

http://www.ultranet.com/~sca/scapbsk.html

Just starting to write applications with *PowerBuilder*? Then, consider doing yourself a favor. Check out the SCA *PowerBuilder Starter Kit*. Start yourself off with a great foundation class library that you can easily enhance and modify to suit your particular needs. You've got nothing to lose. The kit is shareware. If you don't like it, just stop using it and don't pay the registration fee. But, I think you'll like it not only because it provides a robust class library, but also because it is full of useful examples that can speed you along the learning curve. Visit this Web site for more information.

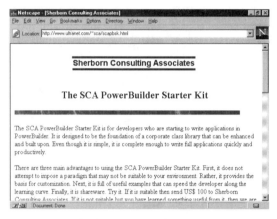

Figure 665 The SCA PowerBuilder Starter Kit.

ADDITIONAL POWERBUILDER PROGRAMMING RESOURCES

Using Powerbuilder 5: Special Edition
http://www.davison.net/cgi-bin/vlink/0789707543

Languages/Programming - Powerbuilder Computer Books from Open Group
http://www.opengroup.com/open/books/langpwr.html

Software Development using Powerbuilder, Training, Internet consultancy
http://www.prime-digest.w1.com/prime/

Building Object-Oriented Applications with Powerbuilder
http://www.anatec.com/pb_ooapp.htm

Powerbuilder vs Delphi
http://cism.bus.utexas.edu/issues/issue233/issue233.html

Powerbuilder info
http://win-www.uia.ac.be/u/wsmet/powerbuilder.html

Detail Report for CSCE (Powerbuilder) LTD
http://www.powersoft.com/partners/code/catalog/2422.htm

Powerbuilder: The Basics
http://www.cp-consulting.com/pb_bas_o.htm

AI CAFÉ C/C++ CGI HTML HTTP JAVA J++ PERL VBSCRIPT VRML WIN32 WINSOCK 1100110100101111001101110011010101000110011001001

AMERICAN PROGRAMMER

http://world.std.com/~cic/amprog/amprog.htm

Hailed as "the Harvard Business Review of the software field," and as "a literate and highly useful newsletter from one of the best thinkers in managing computer technology today," *American Programmer's* mission is to provide software engineers and data-processing (DP) organizations with no-nonsense information and a critical perspective that will help them gain a competitive edge in the global marketplace. Launched by industry expert Ed Yourdon in 1988, the monthly journal, *American Programmer*, has become an essential survival tool for systems analysts, IS/DP managers, and software industry executives around the world. Visit this Web site for details.

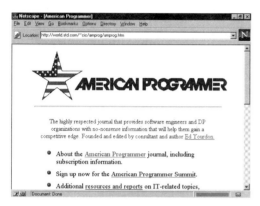

Figure 666.1 American Programmer.

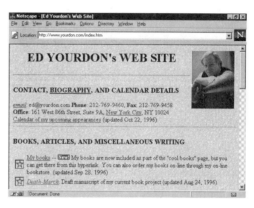

Figure 666.2 Founder, Ed Yourdon.

AI CAFÉ C/C++ CGI HTML HTTP JAVA J++ PERL VBSCRIPT VRML WIN32 WINSOCK 1100110100101111001101110011010101000110011001001

APPLICATION DEVELOPMENT STRATEGIES NEWSLETTER

http://world.std.com/~cic/ads/ads.htm

Design and development automation should be an essential element in your effort to integrate hardware, software, operational techniques, and management strategies. Such automation can help you cut waste, increase efficiency, streamline operations, safeguard quality, and boost profits. The benefits of automation include reusability, fast and easy detection of errors and inconsistencies, interactive prototyping, timetable budget control, and more. How can you get the information you need to get the maximum benefits from the new design and development automation tools and techniques? By reading *Application Development Strategies*. That's how. Visit this Web site for more information.

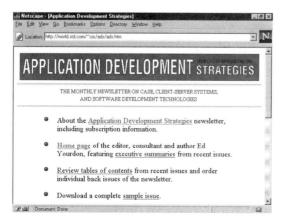

Figure 667.1 Application Development Strategies.

BackOffice Magazine

http://www.backoffice.com

Microsoft *BackOffice* is a family of server-based products from Microsft. *BackOffice Magazine* focuses on NT computing and Microsoft BackOffice. At this site, in the Internet edition of *BackOffice*, you will find a great "ComUnity" white paper, along with essays and articles on creating a Microsoft enterprise, the Windows NT server, the SQL, and exchange and system-management servers. You will also find great trade-show information, server-hardware surveys, and considerations of *Diskeeper*, object modeling, OLE bugs, the Service Management System (SMS), using Visual C++ with NT, scalability, memory-mapped files, and ISDN as it relates to NT. The articles are detailed while at the same time easy to understand. If you work in an NT environment, add a browser bookmark to this site.

Figure 668.1 The BackOffice Web site.

Figure 668.2 Free subscription.

BoardWatch Magazine

http://www.boardwatch.com/

Each issue of *BoardWatch Magazine* features 128 pages of great articles, features, profiles, interviews and reviews concerning the Internet, the World Wide Web, BBSs (bulletin board systems), and the communications industry. Published monthly, *BoardWatch Magazine* is read by the "movers and shakers" in the on-line community, including 2,200 Internet service providers, thousands of software developers and consultants and, essentially, anyone involved in developing and providing on-line services. The magazine includes great Windows 95 networking coverage, as well as detailed editorials related to HTML, Java, and all the rest. Check out the *BoardWatch Magazine* Web site for more information.

Figure 669 The BoardWatch Web site.

AI CAFÉ C/C++ CGI HTML HTTP JAVA J++ PERL VBSCRIPT VRML WIN32 WINSOCK 1100110100101110011011100110101010001100110010010

BYTE MAGAZINE

http://www.byte.com/

Visit this Web site for the on-line edition of *BYTE Magazine.* The site is packed with great editorials, product reviews, downloads, links, and more. You will find articles on Windows programming, Internet telephony, private branch exchanges (PBX), Java programming, Web publishing, and much more. You will also find great columns by John Udells and others. Udells' monthly commentary relates directly to the *BYTE Magazine* pages, where Udells espouses his theories on Web publishing each month. In this case, however, his theories are put into practice right alongside his prose. The result is an informative, ergonomically correct, uniquely intuitive, and useful set of Web pages. Check it out.

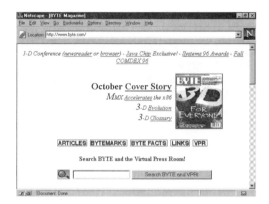

Figure 670.1 The BYTE Web site.

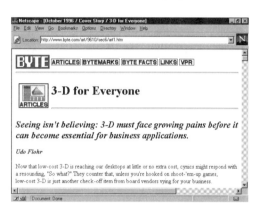

Figure 670.2 October '96 cover story.

AI CAFÉ C/C++ CGI HTML HTTP JAVA J++ PERL VBSCRIPT VRML WIN32 WINSOCK 1100110100101110011011100110101010001100110010010

CED MAGAZINE

http://www.cedmagazine.com/

CED stands for Communications Engineering and Design. If you are responsible for planning, building, and maintaining a state-of-the-art broadband network, then *CED Magazine* is quite simply "required reading." Recent articles from this Web site include "Does broadband data need eye candy?", "Digital TV equals big electric bills," "How to look through your customer's walls," and "Software has to be useful, not perfect." You can find issues dating back through 1994 archived on the Web site, and a robust search engine lets you search articles by topic, author, and date. You may also subscribe to the print edition right on-line. So take time to try out *CED Magazine.*

Figure 671.1 The CED Web site.

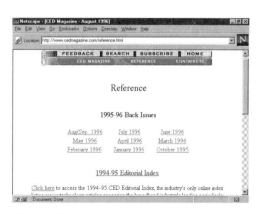

Figure 671.2 Access back issues.

CD-ROM Advisor: 1001 Ratings & Reviews

http://www.cd-rom-advisor.com/

CD-ROM Advisor is a magazine committed to reviewing the latest CD-ROM titles. Their reviews and ratings are based on the opinions of independent consumers like you—the actual users of CD-ROMs. You'll find no hype, no jargon, and no fluff at this site. In addition, each issue presents cutting-edge feature stories of interest to CD-ROM users from leading journalists in the field like Steven Kent, John Quain, Warren Buckleitner, and others. *CD-ROM Advisor* is the only publication that delivers this user-based information both in print and on a CD-ROM bound into each issue. Check out the Web pages for many more details, including subscription information.

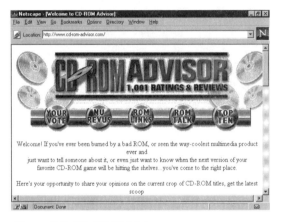

Figure 672 CD-ROM Advisor.

CIO Magazine

http://www.cio.com/CIO/

CIO Magazine is the leading source of information "for those interested in the strategic application of information technology." CIO, of course, stands for "Chief Information Officer." Visit this site and learn, for example, how among the IT (information technology) professionals on today's more innovative development teams are people you wouldn't normally expect to find: psychologists, social scientists and, of all things, users. You will also get articles on such useful topics as how to stay ahead of the technological curve, how to create compensation packages that will attract and keep quality personnel without bankrupting your bottom line, and how to choose from among the various server software suites.

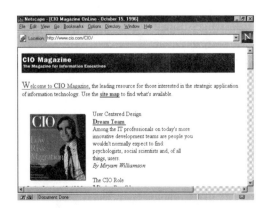

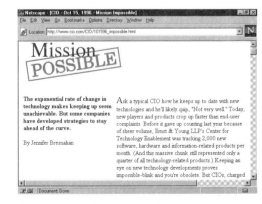

Figure 673.1 CIO Magazine.

Figure 673.2 A sample article.

AI CAFE C/C++ CGI HTML HTTP JAVA J++ PERL VBSCRIPT VRML WIN32 WINSOCK 110011010010111100110111001101010100011001100100101

CLICK INTERACTIVE MAGAZINE

http://click.com.au/

This site features the interactive on-line magazine by and for interactive on-line programmers, packagers, artists, and publishers. A typical issue includes, well, let's see. Is there really a typical issue? I think not. One current issue includes a discussion of the art of computer animated story telling by the experts at Pixar (you know, the folks that brought you *Toy Story*), an interview with interactive on-line storyteller Andrew Denton, a peek inside the MIT labs which are pioneering the future of human-computer interaction, and a clickable playground that is, in fact, a "Musical Toys Web Safari." This is a publication in which the unorthodox is common, and the unexpected is actually what you should plan to encounter. Don't miss it.

Figure 674 Click Interactive Magazine.

AI CAFE C/C++ CGI HTML HTTP JAVA J++ PERL VBSCRIPT VRML WIN32 WINSOCK 110011010010111100110111001101010100011001100100101

COMMUNICATION SYSTEMS DESIGN

http://www.csdmag.com/

The Web site for *Communication Systems Design* includes a monthly feature article from the magazine, subscription information, the editorial calendar for the next 12 months, editorial and sales staff contact information, author's guidelines, and information on how to submit articles. In the site's TechTalk section, you'll find existing and emerging communications technologies. In the site's Guts and Glory section, you'll find discussions of uniquely innovative designs for communications systems. In the Open Channel section, you'll find guest columnists commenting on all aspects of communications engineering design. The site is filled with good information. Go for it.

Figure 675.1 Communication Systems Design.   *Figure 675.2 TechTalk - a monthly feature.*

COMPUNOTES

http://users.aol.com/CompNote/

CompuNotes is a weekly publication available through e-mail and on the Web. *CompuNotes* covers the IBM computing world with software and hardware reviews, late-breaking news, cool Web links, and even more cool FTP archives, and interviews. *CompuNotes* also has a monthly contest, which it invites all readers to enter free of charge, with the prize always being a software package of some value. Never dull, *CompuNotes* is an engaging, invigorating, and sometimes irreverent window into the constantly changing world of PC computing and programming. As such, and as a free publication, it is well worth looking into.

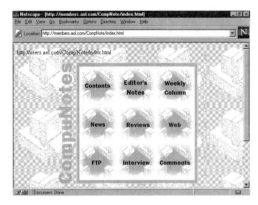

Figure 676.1 The CompuNotes Web site.

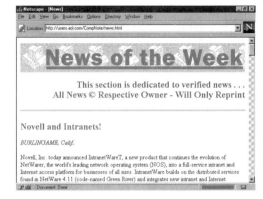

Figure 676.2 News of the week.

COMPUTER GRAPHICS WORLD

http://www.cgw.com/

Computer Graphics World magazine bills itself as "the ultimate resource for 3-D graphics information." The magazine covers computer-aided design (CAD), animation, visualization, virtual reality, and multimedia. Every month, the on-line edition of *Computer Graphics World* includes a great new gallery of digital images, as well as details on current news and products, cool links, and a design studio "lab" exercise. You will also find a directory of shows and events, a great bookstore of graphics-related books, a useful job directory, and a link to an "image of the month" that lurks somewhere in cyberspace. Note that to enjoy this graphics-intensive and Java-enhanced site, Netscape 3.0 is a *very* good idea.

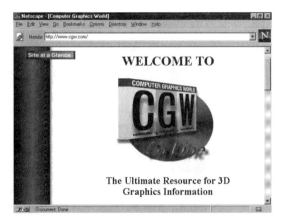

Figure 677 Computer Graphics World.

COMPUTERLIFE—UK

http://www.zdnet.com/clifeuk/

ComputerLife is probably the leading British magazine covering all aspects of PC computing. Visit this site for great digital reprints from the magazine, the latest computing news from Europe and around the world, a choice selection of the "top 20 downloads" on the Internet, subscription information, and much more. If you'd like, add your own Web site to the large file of reader Web sites. Also, fill out a form and sign yourself up for "Personal View," a customized newsfeed available absolutely free. All told, *ComputerLife UK* is a fantastic resource for computer professionals whether they live in the UK or not! Do yourself a favor and check it out.

Figure 678.1 Computer Life - UK.   Figure 678.2 Top 20 downloads.

COMPUTERLIFE—US

http://www.zdnet.com/complife/home/home.html

The digital edition of *ComputerLife Magazine* is packed with great stuff. Visit this Web site for the tip of the day, the download of the day, the contest of the week, and details on the latest print issue of the magazine. You will also find great feature articles on such topics as how to buy a personal digital assistant, video-phones, the Cyrix's 6.86-P200, and more. In addition, you will encounter Dr. Livingston's Online Shopping Safari Guidebook, and a tour of *ComputerLife's* digital house (the "CyberHome"). Finally, the site offers you hardware and software reviews, cool files you can download, and a great archive of the print magazine's past issues. All very useful. All very interesting.

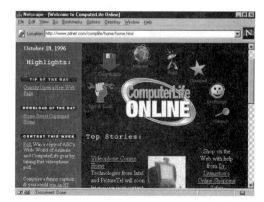

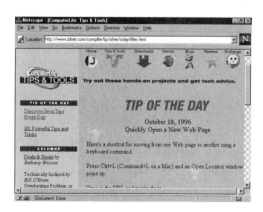

Figure 679.1 ComputerLife Online.   Figure 679.2 Tip of the day.

680

COMPUTER-MEDIATED COMMUNICATION MAGAZINE

http://www.december.com/cmc/mag

Computer-Mediated Communication Magazine reports on people, events, applications, and studies related to the arts of computer networking and telecommunications. Sample articles deal with mentoring and the Internet, enhancing professional development in special education through the Web, extra-verbal communication in cyberspace, and a great meditation on Web literacy. The site also features book and software reviews, profiles of industry leaders, and much more. The editor and publisher is John December, who has contributed a great dissertation on how to teach students to write for the Web. Take time to visit this site.

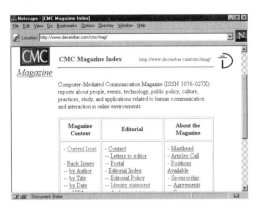

Figure 680.1 The CMC Web site.   *Figure 680.2 Editorial policy.*

681

COMPUTER RESELLER NEWS

http://techweb.cmp.com/crn/issues/706/

If you buy or sell any product related to computers or communications, you need to read *Computer Reseller News*. This great weekly publication addresses the information needs of those folks involved in the computer reseller industry. This site is the place to turn to for all the latest industry gossip: when Motorola surprises everybody with a new chip, when revised microprocessor predictions are published, when Digital posts a $66 million loss, and so on. The publication is absolutely fabulous in both its print and Web editions. Perhaps that is why *Computer Reseller News* has received top honors from the Computer Press Association for best newspaper for the last three years running! That right. Three years in a row. Check it out.

Figure 681 Computer Reseller News.

PUBLICATIONS

AI CAFÉ C/C++ CGI HTML HTTP JAVA J++ PERL VBSCRIPT VRML WIN32 WINSOCK 1100110100101111001101110011010101000110011001001010

COMPUTER SHOPPER

http://www.zdnet.com/cshopper/

Computer Shopper, whether in its print or the Web edition, is more than just a fat book of advertisements. Yes, it is packed with buying advice and shopping tools, but *Computer Shopper* also houses respected pundits commenting on technology trends and forecasts, as well as timely talk and analysis on all aspects of systems, peripherals, motherboards, and software. And, it is an outstanding guide to great downloads, links, BBSs, and events (both in real and virtual space). Plus, of course, you get all those great ads that offer the best equipment and software at the best prices—direct from warehouses and manufacturers. Visit the digital edition of an old friend, the *Computer Shopper*.

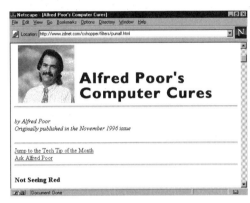

Figure 682.1 Computer Shopper.   Figure 682.2 Alfred Poor, pundit.

COMPUTER TELEPHONY MAGAZINE

http://www.computertelephony.com/ct_home.html

Computer Telephony covers all aspects of computer telephony (CT), including text-to-speech applications, open call-centers, voice-data-fax on one call, heavy-duty application generators, specialized switching applications and resources, CT standards, low-density voice cards, CT applications, TAPI, power protection, video-conferencing, and collaborative computing. You will also find discussions on PC-based call centers, high-density fax cards, single-slot board level components, PC telephony applications, Webphony (supercharging the Net with CT), pulse-to-tone converters, Windows telephony middleware, and more. This high-tech discussion defines the future of computing. Don't miss it.

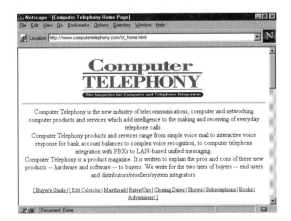

Figure 683 The CT home page.

684

COMPUTERWORLD

http://www.computerworld.com/

This Web-based edition of *ComputerWorld* is a wonder to behold. Updated more than once a day, the site is packed with the latest news and views. Keep an eye on the Microsofts, Netscapes, Digitals, and IBMs. Don't let technology sneak up on you. Keep abreast of the latest development in software, hardware, networks, and security. Get the word on what's in alpha, and what's in beta, and how folks are reacting to the new software. You will find it all there, at one convenient, literate, information-rich location—at the Web site of your old friend, *ComputerWorld*. You'll find no better place to get the good word.

Figure 684.1 ComputerWorld Web site.

Figure 684.2 Up-to-date news.

685

DATA COMMUNICATIONS MAGAZINE

http://www.data.com/

At the Web site for *Data Communications* you will find fantastic articles, editorials, and reviews concerning ATM (asynchronous transfer mode), frame relay and other vital data communications topics. The information at this site includes great case studies, user surveys, lab tests, technical tutorials, and even a networking directory within which you may register yourself as an available freelance consultant or programmer. On the ATM front, you get a great ATM glossary, as well as news and reviews related to ATM switch tests, juggling ATM traffic, voice communication over ATM, and a bit of essential reading entitled "ATM Bandwidth: Waste Not, Want Not." On the frame-relay front, be sure to read the piece on encryption suitable for frame-relay.

Figure 685 Data Communications Magazine.

DATA MANAGEMENT REVIEW

http://dmreview.com/

Data Management Review focuses on data warehouse and client/server solutions for enterprise systems. Visit this site for informative articles on such topics as data visualization, IT (information technology) strategies, business process re-engineering (BPR), data warehousing, client/server connections, enterprise systems, and management skills that relate to all these things. As a fringe benefit, for those high-tech stock investors amongst us, *Data Management Review* features a financial column written by Steve Uyhely, who, though a relative unknown, has quite a track record. His model portfolio has been yielding returns in excess of 40% for some time now, and he utilizes both fundamental and technical analysis in his stock selection process. His column is *very* interesting.

Figure 686.1 DMR's Web site.   *Figure 686.2 Get a free subscription!* *Figure 686.3 The contents of an issue.*

DATAMATION MAGAZINE

http://www.datamation.com/

Datamation Magazine is essential reading for all computer professionals. Visit the *Datamation* Web site for great articles, tutorials, and reviews related to Java, Internet telephony, enterprise and distributed applications, data warehousing, linking the Web to your legacy data and applications, deciding between UNIX and NT, and hot new database technologies. You will also find articles that discuss the future of UNIX, how to fix the year 2000 problem *now*, betting your job on *BackOffice*, guarding the till at the CyberMall, the future of the Web and the Internet, and other timely issues. I like the article which asks the question: Is the World Wide Web just a boomtown on the electronic frontier? Is it a bubble waiting to burst? Hmmm. Now *that* is something to think about.

Figure 687.1 The Datamation Web site.   *Figure 687.2 The October '96 issue.*

THE NEWSLETTER OF WORLD-WIDE INFORMATION SYSTEMS

http://www.netline.com/dsr/

Data Storage Report explores the market and technology forces driving business through its myriad twists and turns. Recent issues have examined how the contracting PC industry is affecting disk drive suppliers and analyzed the forces driving the growth of the World Wide Web, such as interactive gaming, cyber-shopping, PC TV, and Java. *Data Storage Report* is a 16-page monthly publication continuously published since 1984. The Web pages provide general information on *Data Storage Report* and fundamental information on the data storage market using information from the *Report.* For lots of insightful analysis and opinion, visit this Web site.

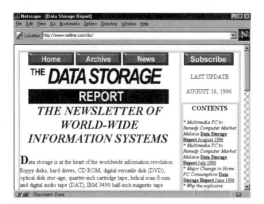

Figure 688.1 Data Storage Report.

Figure 688.2 The August '96 issue.

DATABASE MAGAZINE

http://www.onlineinc.com/database/

Database Magazine is, as its Web site tells us, "written for the 'hands-on' searcher, managers of information facilities and others who use information technology. It provides practical, how-to advice on effective use of databases and systems, plus innovative tips and techniques, reviews, and product comparisons. It covers databases in online, CD-ROM, disk, and tape formats, and resources on the Internet." The Web site contains selected full-text articles and news from each issue of the magazine, as well as recent editorials, author guidelines, and a completely searchable database of the contents of back issues. If you design, implement, or manage a database, add the *Database* Web site to your list of must-visit sites.

Figure 689.1 The Database Web site.

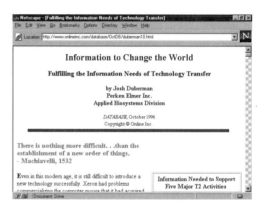

Figure 689.2 Selected articles published on the Web.

AI CAFÉ C/C++ CGI HTML HTTP JAVA J++ PERL VBSCRIPT VRML WIN32 WINSOCK 1100110100101111001101110011010101000110011001010

DATABASE PROGRAMMING AND DESIGN MAGAZINE

http://www.dbpd.com/

Visit the Web site of *Database Programming and Design Magazine* for hot product news and articles by industry leaders on such topics as VLDB (Very Large Databases), data mining, data integrity and concurrency, accelerated index searching, decision support techniques, database monitors, how and why to be a "procedural" database administrator, and much more. You will also find articles on such topics as the seven habits of highly effective data modelers, and business rules as they relate to object-role modeling. You will also get great columns like "Data Architect" (written by Barbara von Halle) and "According to Date" (by C.J. Date). This site is a great stop along the Information Super Highway.

Figure 690 The Database Programming home page.

AI CAFÉ C/C++ CGI HTML HTTP JAVA J++ PERL VBSCRIPT VRML WIN32 WINSOCK 1100110100101111001101110011010101000110011001010

DATABASED ADVISOR

http://www.advisor.com/db.htm

Written by database professionals for database professionals, *Databased Advisor* strives to give more than generalities and "food for thought," providing the in-depth guidance, specific details, and real-world wisdom that empowers you to take immediate, well-informed action. Rely on *Databased Advisor* each month for extensive reviews, test drives, beta previews, and new product news. Covering leading Windows client and database server software and hardware, *Databased Advisor* is hard to beat when it comes to extensiveness, clarity, and reliability. Recent issues include discussions of ActiveX and thin-client computing, Java, and other related topics.

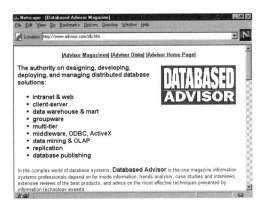

Figure 691.1 Databased Advisor.

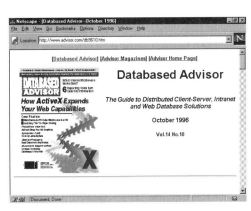

Figure 691.2 The October '96 issue.

DBMS MAGAZINE

http://www.dbmsmag.com/

DBMS Magazine is a magazine for all database programming professionals. You will find great articles on such topics as understanding and managing text bases, along with expert opinion by such authorities as Grady Booch, Ivar Jacobson, and Jim Rumbaugh. You will also find great monthly on-line columns, including "Enterprise C/S" (written by Judith Hurwitz), "Data Warehouse Architect" (written by Ralph Kimball), "SQL for Smarties" (written by Joe Celko), "C/S Developer" (written by David Linthicum), "Server Side" (written by Martin Rennhackkamp), and "Desktop DBMS" (written by Tom Spitzer). Add to that some fabulous product reviews and you've got one useful publication. Check it out.

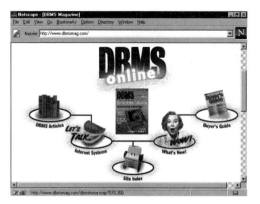

Figure 692.1 The DBMS Web site.

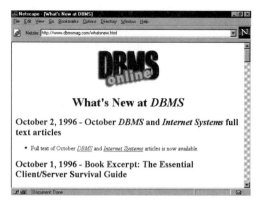

Figure 692.2 What's new.

DIGITAL VIDEO MAGAZINE

http://dvlive.com/Home.html

What a cool site. Visit *Digital Video Magazine's* Web Site, called DVlive, for astonishing on-line digital video demos, along with its service directory, product reviews, digital-video downloads, technical information, tutorials, feature articles, and case studies. You will also find a fantastic media gallery, daily digital-video news, industry news, surveys, on-line chats, and great editorials and commentary. Get the scoop on how virtual-set technology puts people and objects anywhere. Learn why models "are in the eye of the beholder." And, learn how to, quite literally, "master the blues" without spending a million dollars to do it. This is one great magazine and one great on-line review of a great magazine.

Figure 693.1 The DVlive magazine Web site.

Figure 693.2 Articles from the magazine.

DR. DOBB'S WEB SITE

http://www.ddj.com/

For years, programmers have benefitted from *Dr. Dobb's* magazine. Now, you can benefit from *Dr. Dobb's* on-line. Come this site for digital reprints, tables of contents, subscription information, and source code related to both *Dr. Dobb's Journal* and *Dr. Dobb's Sourcebook*. While you are there, be sure to check out the extensive on-line source code library. You see, in addition to the source code published in the magazines, many of *Dr. Dobb's* articles have additional source code that simply cannot fit in the magazines. Much of that code is available at this site, on-line for you to peruse and enjoy. Visit this site for the source code and also for issue themes, contents, and selected articles from issues of the *Sourcebook*, going back to 1994, and issues of the *Journal*, going back to 1993. There's no point in not stopping by, because the Doctor is *in*.

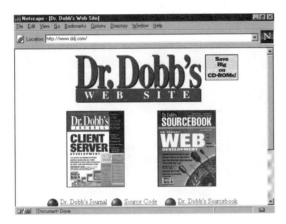

Figure 694 Dr. Dobb's Web site.

EMBEDDED SYSTEMS PROGRAMMING

http://www.embedded.com/

Embedded Systems Programming is a publication for engineers, software designers, and project leaders whose daily work includes supervising, designing, writing, testing, and integrating programs used in microcontroller and embedded microprocessor-based systems. At this Web site, you'll find information on the monthly magazine, news which the site updates weekly, source code related to magazine articles, conference information, and many other valuable items. While you are visiting the Web pages for *Embedded Systems Programming*, be sure to access and participate in the Embedded Forum, where you'll find active discussion related to embedded systems development and design.

Figure 695.1 Embedded Systems home page.

Figure 695.2 Late-breaking news.

ENT MAGAZINE

http://www.entmag.com/

ent Magazine focuses on enterprise solutions for mangers of Windows NT. At this site, you will find digital reprints of articles, features, editorials, commentaries, and forecasts. In addition, the site features a great hypertext special report entitled "Windows NT and Manufacturing." You will also find an index to back issues, a buyer's guide, and subscription information. A handy resource guide provides carefully selected links to other sites on the Web that are bound to be of interest to Windows NT developers, programmers, and administrators. Interested in advertising in the printed version of the magazine? No problem. You'll also find a complete media kit right on-line. Go for it.

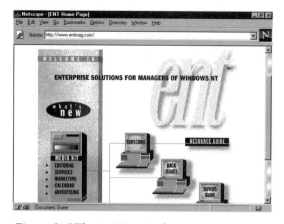

Figure 696 The ent Magazine home page.

FAMILY PC

http://www.zdnet.com/familypc/

Family PC is the magazine that focuses on computing in the home and for the home. In short, the magazine focuses on hardware and software for everyday living. At this Web site, you will find great reviews and product information not only related to hardware but also software for personal-financial planning, gaming, edutainment (you know, mixing learning and fun), and reference. The Web site also includes news, views, reviews, special features, projects and crafts, contests, and an index to back issues. Also, be sure to check out *Family PC's Guide to the World Wide Web*. Use the Guide to find out the whos, whats, wheres, and hows of the Web by pointing and clicking. The Guide includes 50 of the best family sites on the Web.

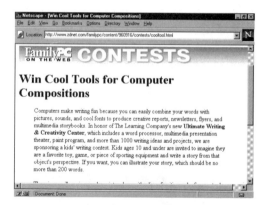

Figure 697.1 Family PC Web site.   *Figure 697.2 A sample article.*

IEEE COMPUTER SOCIETY PUBLICATIONS

http://www.computer.org/pubs/pubs.htm

The Institute of Electrical and Electronic's Engineers (IEEE) Computer Society's publications include applications-oriented magazines that foster active communication between practitioners and the research community, and research-oriented transactions that document the state of the art in computer science. Magazines include *IEEE Internet Computing, Computer, IEEE Software, IEEE MultiMedia, IEEE Computational Science and Engineering, IEEE Computer Graphics and Applications, IEEE Parallel & Distributed Technology, IEEE Micro, IEEE Expert, IEEE Design & Test Computers,* and *IEEE Annals of the History of Computing.* If it's from the IEEE, you know it's good.

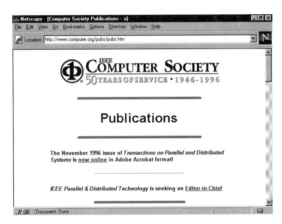

Figure 698 IEEE publications.

INSIDE OS/2: FREE ISSUE

http://www.cobb.com/ios/index.htm

Inside OS/2 is the Cobb Group's monthly journal of tips and techniques for using OS/2. At this site, the Cobb Group invites you to sign up to receive a free issue of the journal on a trial basis. While you are there, you can also check out many excellent digital reprints of key articles from recent editions of the journals, along with great free tips, such as how to change PATH setting without rebooting, using drag-and-drop to add program objects to a menu, and how to use the Program Manager for WIN-OS/2 sessions. Add to that some great downloadable shareware and writers who are leading authorities in the field, and you've got one fine publication.

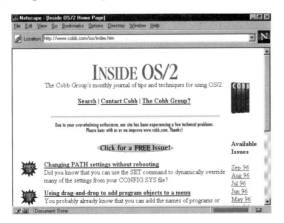

Figure 699 Inside OS/2.

700

INTERNETWORK MAGAZINE

http://www.internetworkweb.com/

The Internet, Web, and soon, intranets, are shaping every aspect of our lives. *InterNetwork Magazine* is the place to visit for all the latest internetworking news and views, as well as product information. You can get the scoop on late-breaking mergers and acquisitions or access interviews with industry insiders, such as Intel President and CEO, Andy Grove. Next, you can partake of "Random Musings" by such guest columnists as Yancy Lind. Then, you can get details on current developments within the "Big 4"—Cabletron, Cisco, 3Com, and Bay Networks. As a cool fringe benefit of visiting these pages, you may use *Excite* to search for digital reprints of articles in the *InterNetwork* archives. Check out the Web site for more details.

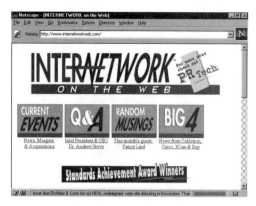

Figure 700.1 InterNetwork Magazine.

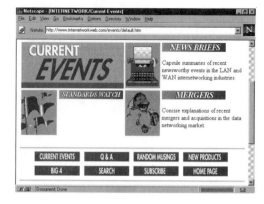

Figure 700.2 The latest news.

701

IMAGING WORLD MAGAZINE

http://www.iwmag.com/

Imaging World provides workflow news, information, and solutions for corporate information managers. This site's on-line edition features a great daily newswire that covers all aspects of the digital-imaging trade, such as the Kodak and Wang connection, Digital Systems' ViewStar technology, StorageTrek developments, the Computer Associates acquisition of Cheyenne Software, FileNet enhancements, and TMSSequoia's imaging plug-in for the Mac. You will also get editorials and commentaries, product reviews, buyer's guides, software libraries, and hot links to vendor sites including Artist Graphics, Canon, Cardiff, Cornerstone, and Fujitsu. If you are into imaging, don't miss this site.

Figure 701 Imaging World Web site.

AI CAFÉ C/C++ CGI HTML HTTP JAVA J++ PERL VBSCRIPT VRML WIN32 WINSOCK 1100110100101111001101110011010101000110011001001011

INTERNET & JAVA ADVISOR

http://www.advisor.com/ia.htm

The *Internet & Java Advisor* is a monthly, technical guide to building Internet, intranet, Web, and Java solutions. As this Web site informs us, the magazine is "the complete technical guide to achieving the business benefits of Internet and Java technology." The articles are written by experts who explain exactly how to design, build, deploy, and manage net-based applications. As you know, the business benefits of net-based technologies are unmatched. Learn to use them profitably by reading *Internet & Java Advisor*.

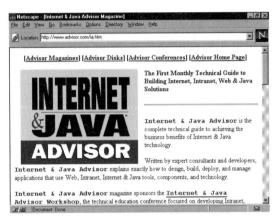

Figure 702 Internet & Java Advisor.

AI CAFÉ C/C++ CGI HTML HTTP JAVA J++ PERL VBSCRIPT VRML WIN32 WINSOCK 1100110100101111001101110011010101000110011001001011

HP PROFESSIONAL MAGAZINE

http://www.hppro.com/

HP Professional bills itself as "the independent magazine for Hewlett-Packard enterprise computing." The magazine's mission is to provide unbiased reporting and analysis on interoperability solutions using HP 9000 workstations and servers, as well as PCs, LANs, and HP 3000 systems. The magazine's audience includes the typical IS/IT (information systems/information technology) manager working in a multiplatform computing environment. Visit this Web site for HP news and views, new product announcements, and reviews. In addition, you will find excellent feature stories, case studies, editorials, commentaries, and monthly columns that are sure to enlighten and educate. Also, check out the special on-line report entitled "Client/Server on the HP 3000."

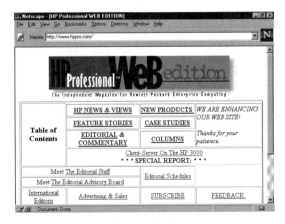

Figure 703 HP Professional Web site.

LAN MAGAZINE

http://www.lanmag.com/

The on-line edition of *LAN Magazine* is full of great reviews, articles, and interviews. You will find detailed discussions of fire walls that keep your company's Internet connection safe from hackers, tips and tricks for making your network secure enough for electronic commerce, wireless infrared devices that work with Windows 95 to produce network connections out of the air for laptops equipped with infrared "eyes." The site also features notes and opinions from the groupware battlefield, the subtle art of making the Internet your WAN, and more. You'll also find some great tutorials, such as one on how to integrate CGI with Web servers. All in all, the information presented at this site is extremely valuable.

Figure 704.1 The LAN Magazine Web site.   *Figure 704.2 A sample article.*

LAN TIMES

http://www.lantimes.com/

LAN Times is the premier magazine for those charged with building, supporting, maintaining, and administering local area networks (LANs). The magazine's Web site is packed with feature articles, product reviews, industry trends and forecasts, and editorials designed specifically for LAN professionals. Looking for comprehensive product and vendor information? Find it in the LAN Times as well. I am talking about getting the scoop on more than 6,000 products from more than 850 vendors and publishers with on-line presence. How is that for *comprehensive*? The site also features software and demos you can download. And, if you aren't yet getting the printed version of *LAN Times*, you get information for subscribing at this site.

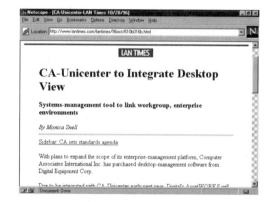

Figure 705.1 LAN Times Online.   *Figure 705.2 News updates.*

AI CAFÉ C/C++ CGI HTML HTTP JAVA J++ PERL VBSCRIPT VRML WIN32 WINSOCK 1100110100101111001101110011010101000110011001001011

LINUX JOURNAL

http://www.ssc.com/lj/

Linux is the most popular free UNIX available today. Each issue of *Linux Journal* offers articles that appeal to newcomers and serious technical articles for long-time UNIX users. Although *Linux Journal* is Linux-specific, many of the articles are of interest to UNIX users and other users of freely redistributable software. Also, for the many UNIX users, *Linux Journal* offers articles on commercial uses for Linux. Regular columns include interviews with prominent Linux personalities, book and product reviews, and great code snippets in the "Kernel corner." Recent article topics include customizing Emacs, learning C++ with Linux, using Ethernet with Linux, porting DOS applications to Linux, and so on. Stop by.

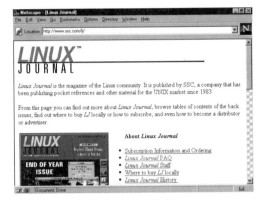

Figure 706.1 The Linux Journal Web site.

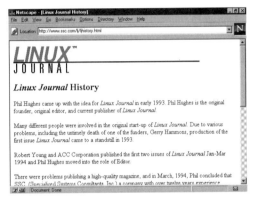

Figure 706.2 The history of Linux Journal.

AI CAFÉ C/C++ CGI HTML HTTP JAVA J++ PERL VBSCRIPT VRML WIN32 WINSOCK 1100110100101111001101110011010101000110011001001011

MICROSOFT SYSTEMS JOURNAL

http://www.msj.com/

Microsoft Systems Journal (MSJ) bills itself as "the developers' source for Windows," and that is just what it is. Visit this site for digital reprints from the journal along with MSJ's comprehensive source-code archive. Also, visit this site for Miller-Freeman's *Tools for Windows* database which contains product information for thousands of products of interest to Windows developers. While you are at the *MSJ* Web site, register in the on-line guestbook and receive advanced notice of special events for Windows programmers. Only *MSJ* gives you in-depth coverage directly from Microsoft about writing software for Microsoft's operating systems. Visit the Web pages for more information.

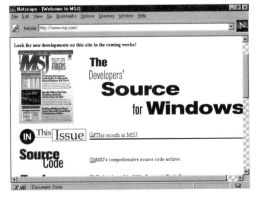

Figure 707.1 MSJ Web site.

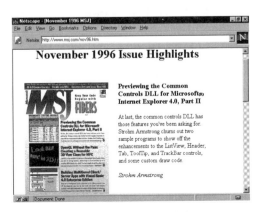

Figure 707.2 November '96 highlights.

M<small>IDRANGE</small> S<small>YSTEMS</small>

http://www.cardinal.com/midrange/

Midrange Systems is an independent newspaper addressing IBM AS/400 and RS/6000 server computing. You may apply for a free subscription right on-line. You may also access late-breaking industry news, and read the latest edition of the paper. The paper and the site are each packed with useful feature articles, editorials, commentaries, case-studies, and product reviews. You'll also find a useful buyer's guide, a forecast of the status of midrange systems in the year 2,000 (along with a consideration of the notorious calendar problem!), and more. Access *Midrange Systems* on-line for a rewarding time.

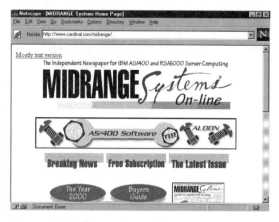

Figure 708 Midrange Systems home page.

T<small>HE</small> N<small>ET</small>

http://www.thenet-usa.com/

The Net is a magazine which bills itself as the ultimate Internet guide. It is very good at flagging hot new sites, telling you where to go in cyberspace, and why. The on-line edition is equally excellent. Month after month, you can visit this site for articles about current news affecting the on-line community, rated reviews of the hottest Web sites around, and practical information for the newbie and guru alike. Each issue of the print edition comes with *netPower*, a CD-ROM disc packed with games, demos, Windows, and Mac shareware, as well as quick links to some of the hardest-to-access sites. Visit this Web site and check out the magazine. It's very cool.

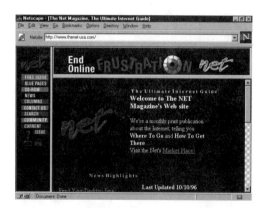

Figure 709.1 The Net.

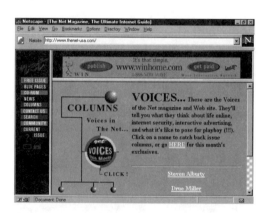

Figure 709.2 Columns online.

AI CAFÉ C/C++ CGI HTML HTTP JAVA J++ PERL VBSCRIPT VRML WIN32 WINSOCK 1100110100101111001101110011010101000110011001001101

NETWARE CONNECTION MAGAZINE

http://www.nwconnection.com/

At this site, you'll find great on-line articles concerning *NetWare 4.11* and *IntranetWare*, John Young's ongoing attempts to move Novell forward, CNE Net, how to synchronize your network servers, *NetWare 4.1* SET parameters, managing *NDS* with *NWADMIN*, and more. The site also includes the full text of monthly issues going back to July 1995. In addition, you will find a fantastic library of shareware and freeware, Netscape plug-ins, and utilities. The utilities include e-mail programs, graphical software, network-management tools, printing utilities, security programs, TCP/IP connectivity software, and virus scanning utilities. The great editorial is free. The program archive is free. And you are free to partake of it all.

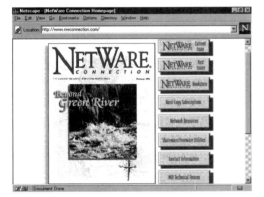

Figure 710.1 NetWare Connection.   *Figure 710.2 Software archive.*

AI CAFÉ C/C++ CGI HTML HTTP JAVA J++ PERL VBSCRIPT VRML WIN32 WINSOCK 1100110100101111001101110011010101000110011001001101

NETWORK BUYER'S GUIDE

http://www.sresearch.com/

The on-line edition of the *Network Buyer's Guide* includes some very, very cool stuff. How cool, you ask? Well, I'll let you be the judge. Something I like a lot is the on-line Java applet developed by Interpose which lets you calculate your network downtime costs. Just enter a few key bits of data, and the applet calculates and displays the costs. Want more? OK. Are you tired of the average, dry, dull white papers? Then, check out the newest wave in technical promotions, Custom Strategic Profiles, as presented on these Web pages. Awesome. Spectacular. Oh yeah, you'll also find buyer's guides for storage, networking, and other products. But then you guessed that already.

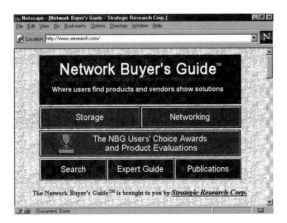

Figure 711 Network Buyer's Guide.

712

THE NETWORK OBSERVER

http://communication.ucsd.edu/pagre/tno.html

The Network Observer (TNO) is a free on-line newsletter about networks and democracy edited by Phil Agre who teaches in the Department of Communication at the University of California, San Diego. Every issue includes a few short articles plus some regular departments. You will usually find book reviews, commentaries, editorials, guest opinions, and even interviews with people prominent in the discussion of free speech and privacy in cyberspace. I think the publication is both excellent and important, and I encourage you to access this Web site to sign up for a free subscription.

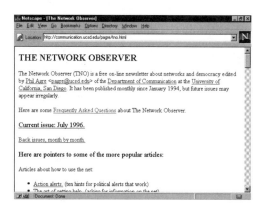

Figure 712.1 The Network Observer.

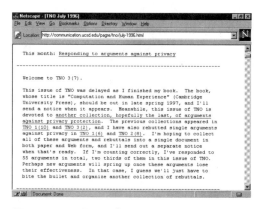

Figure 712.2 Responding to arguments.

713

NEWS/400 MAGAZINE

http://www.news400.com/

News/400 is a great magazine for AS/400 professionals. Published 16 times a year, *News/400* brings you information that will help you make strategic business decisions, solve business programming problems, broaden your knowledge of programming techniques, improve your AS/400's productivity, and access AS/400 hardware and software products. In each issue of *News/400*, you'll find load-an-go utilities, product reviews, new product announcements, technical articles, and much more. Finally, the Web contains digital reprints of many great articles, along with a timely MidWeek News Update. Check it out.

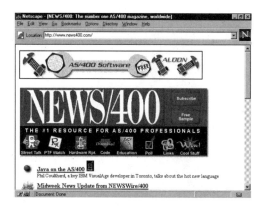

Figure 713.1 The News/400 Web site.

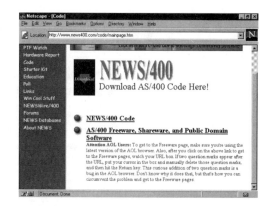

Figure 713.2 Download some excellent code.

AI CAFÉ C/C++ CGI HTML HTTP JAVA J++ PERL VBSCRIPT VRML WIN32 WINSOCK 1100110100101111001101110011010101000110011001001011

ORACLE MAGAZINE

http://www.oramag.com/

Published by Oracle corporation in both a print and Web-interactive edition, *Oracle Magazine* is authoritative and, at the same time, a lot of fun. Check out the comic strip entitled *The Adventures of the WebMaster*! In addition to comics, check out the great articles and columns by the likes of Ian Smith, Jill Donley Rege, Aliza Sherman, Glen Lipka, and others. In addition, the site contains great Oracle tips and tricks from the gurus deep within the Oracle labs—such as how to display "invisible" records in Oracle forms. What else? Well, let's see. You've got free access to archives of digital reprints from back-issues of the magazine. Great content.

Figure 714.1 Oracle Magazine.

Figure 714.2 The comic strip.

AI CAFÉ C/C++ CGI HTML HTTP JAVA J++ PERL VBSCRIPT VRML WIN32 WINSOCK 1100110100101111001101110011010101000110011001001011

OS/2 E-ZINE

http://www.haligonian.com/os2/

OS/2 e-Zine strives to be a high-quality publication bringing the best in news, reviews, and opinions to the OS/2 community. The e-zine promotes the use and discussion of OS/2 and its native software. Visit this site for all the latest on *OS/2 Warp 4, OS/2-CIM, Cosmos 4.0,* and much more. You will also find a great OS/2 help desk, as well as reviews and opinions by OS/2 experts. The e-zine is packed with "how to do its" and beta software and demos you can download. You will also find an outstanding list of frequently asked questions. If you are into OS/2, take a look at *OS/2 e-Zine.*

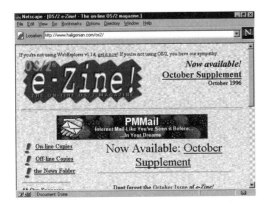

Figure 715.1 OS/2 e-Zine.

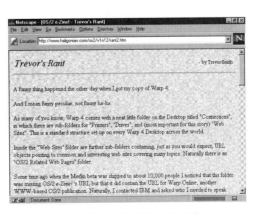

Figure 715.2 Editorial by Trevor Smith.

1001 PROGRAMMING RESOURCES

0011001100010101010110011101101111010111011110001101 AI CAFÉ C/C++ CGI HTML HTTP JAVA J++ PERL VBSCRIPT VRML WIN32 WINSOCK

PATHWORKS MANAGER NEWSLETTER

http://www.cardinal.com/pm/

Path Works is network software from Digital Equipment Corp. (DEC) systems. *Pathworks Manager* is an independent newsletter devoted to helping managers of PathWorks networks solve their networking problems. The newsletter achieves this goal by providing high-quality, in-depth technical information about PathWorks integration, performance, troubleshooting, and upgrades. *Pathworks Manager* is the only publication focused exclusively on providing highly technical information of this type. The newsletter tailors its coverage to the needs of a highly sophisticated readership through articles contributed by recognized PathWorks experts. *Pathworks Manager* is published monthly.

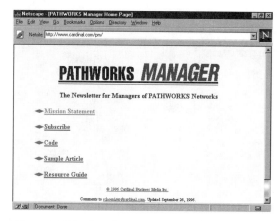

Figure 716 Pathworks Manager Newsletter.

PC COMPUTING

http://www.zdnet.com/pccomp/

PC Computing is the leading magazine for programmers and users of IBM PCs and compatible machines. Visit the *PC Computing* Web site for links to the 1001 best downloads on the Web, as well as *PC Computing's* top picks from the 1001 best sites on the Web. Also, check out the sneak peeks at new products and upcoming *PC Computing* articles, great digital reprints of key feature articles from recent issues of *PC Computing*, fantastic technical tips, and lists of frequently asked questions. You will also find CD-ROM reviews by "CD-Ron," the "Talk to Us" BBS, and fun sweepstakes. Of course, the pages also include complete subscription information for *PC Computing*. Check it all out right now.

Figure 717.1 PC Computing home page.

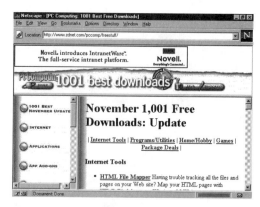

Figure 717.2 1001 Downloads.

AI CAFÉ C/C++ CGI HTML HTTP JAVA J++ PERL VBSCRIPT VRML WIN32 WINSOCK 1100110100101111001101100110101010001100110010010

PC GRAPHICS & VIDEO MAGAZINE

http://www.pcgv.com/

PC Graphics & Video Magazine is a publication of Advanstar Communications, a global producer of magazines, expositions, and other media. *PC Graphics & Video's* editorial focus is on creative applications running Microsoft Windows and Windows NT operating systems, as well as other PC-based operating systems. That's right, the bias is definitely pro-PC and anti-Mac, which is something new in desktop graphics. This bias is a sign of the evolution in technology. "In my toolbox," writes the editor, "I want the fastest, most versatile, most economical platform and the greatest array of software choices. As a PC user, I now can say that's what I've got."

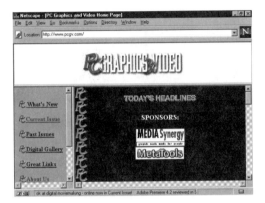

Figure 718.1 PC Graphics & Video Magazine.

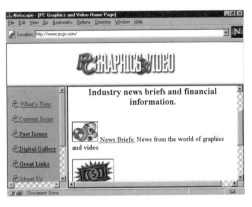

Figure 718.2 The latest news.

AI CAFÉ C/C++ CGI HTML HTTP JAVA J++ PERL VBSCRIPT VRML WIN32 WINSOCK 1100110100101111001101100110101010001100110010010

PC LAPTOP MAGAZINE

http://www2.pclaptop.com/pclaptop/

PC LapTop Magazine provides a wealth of information for laptop PC users. Visit this Web site for a host of very helpful articles on such topics as using Usenet newsgroups, how to get organized with your computer, keeping up with changing technologies, how to speed up your Web surfing by properly configuring your laptop browser, how to have "fun" with fatal errors (or, in other words, how to avoid aggravating error messages), the latest in (non-mouse) pointing devices, and more. You'll also find articles explaining how to keep your laptop running, without a plug-in, for 30 hours or more, how to foil computer kidnappers and data snatchers, and how wireless modems are entering the business mainstream. You will find a lot of valuable information at this site. Don't miss it.

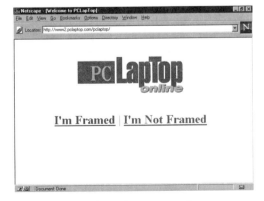

Figure 719.1 Choose frames or no-frames.

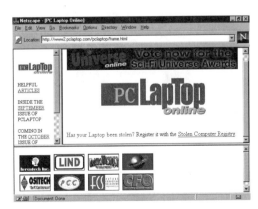

Figure 719.2 I like frames.

PC Magazine

http://www.pcmag.com/

PC Magazine is the world's best selling monthly magazine for users, administrators, and programmers. So what if these pages take *forever* to load the pages at 28.8, they are still worth waiting for because they are absolutely packed with great articles, reviews, features, commentary, and downloads. The site includes hundreds of reviews of the latest Internet tools, interactive reviews, PC Labs test results for hundreds of software products, and up-to-the-minute news, trends, and analysis. You'll also get columns by Dvorak, Willmott and Miller, and more. When I visited, a great ongoing Web discussion board was going full-blast on the topics of development platforms and mapping technology. You will always find something new and different at each visit to this site. Visit often.

Figure 720.1 PC Magazine.

Figure 720.2 A sample article.

PC Week

http://www.pcweek.com/

This great on-line edition of *PC Week* is a "must" resource for every serious PC developer and programmer. The site features product reviews, editorials, feature articles, industry trends analysis, and much, much more. You also get great downloads of software carefully selected by the *PC Week* staff (with a demanding eye for excellence). When I visited, a late-breaking news articles was on tap about how Marimba's *Castanet* is rocking the Java-world, about Microsoft's net income rising 22% (what else is new), the future of *dBASE* and *Paradox*, and IBM's move to scrap its InterPersonal Computer in order to avoid overlaps with designs by its AS/400 group. This site is packed with vital information you cannot do without. Stop by.

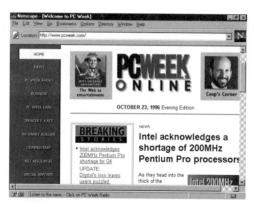

Figure 721.1 PC Week Online.

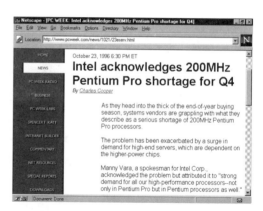

Figure 721.2 Breaking news.

PC WORLD ONLINE DAILY NEWS

http://www.pcworld.com/

The scope and content of the *PC World OnLine Daily News* are best summarized with a sampling of headlines: "On-line Companies to Focus on Content," "Uninstaller 4 Offers Some Improvement Over Predecessor," "Screen Phone Report: $300 Devices Catch On Slowly," "Compaq to Build Handheld PC with Microsoft Windows CE," and "Prodigy Targets World with New Internet Service." You will find audio reports—"Daily News Radio Summaries"—available in RealAudio 28.8 and 14.4 formats. You will also find detailed coverage of important topics that include computer viruses, newsgroup "cancel wars," clonemaker battles, Java development, and related subjects. All good stuff.

Figure 722.1 PC World Online.

Figure 722.2 A sample article.

POWERBUILDER ADVISOR

http://www.advisor.com/pa.htm

PowerBuilder Advisor bills itself, quite correctly, as a "comprehensive guide to successful *PowerBuilder* client/server development." *PowerBuilder Advisor* is written by and for professional *PowerBuilder* developers. It shows you how to take full advantage of Sybase-Powersoft's *PowerBuilder* and related products to design and deploy client/server database applications. Building on *Databased Advisor's* pioneer *PowerBuilder* coverage, the new *PowerBuilder Advisor* tackles the full range of development issues, such as Internet/intranet connectivity, project management, analysis, replication, distributed data strategies, N-tier techniques, and more. If you work with *Powerbase*, you owe it to yourself to visit this site.

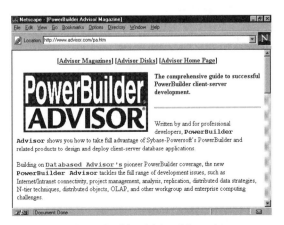

Figure 723 PowerBuilder Advisor Magazine.

AI CAFÉ C/C++ CGI HTML HTTP JAVA J++ PERL VBSCRIPT VRML WIN32 WINSOCK

RS/MAGAZINE

http://www.cpg.com/rs/

RS/Magazine focuses on the PowerPC workstation. Each month, the magazine delivers analyses of late-breaking news and spotlights products and services for the RS/600 and other open systems in what is fast becoming a PowerPC world. The magazine's monthly columns include "Systems Wrangler" (a sometimes irreverent, but always informative and useful look at RS/6000 systems administration), "AIXtensions" (covers the wide world of RS/6000 system interfaces, peripherals, and add-ons), "Q&Aix" (addresses often-asked questions about the most vexing AIX problems), "Datagrams" (a guide to the complexities of wide area networking), and "Work" (using UNIX tools for everyday office chores).

Figure 724.1 RS/Magazine Web site.

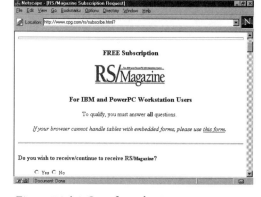

Figure 724.2 Get a free subscription!

AI CAFÉ C/C++ CGI HTML HTTP JAVA J++ PERL VBSCRIPT VRML WIN32 WINSOCK

SCO WORLD MAGAZINE

http://www.scoworld.com/

SCO World is an independent, international magazine dedicated to helping computing professionals turn SCO (Santa Cruz Operations) and third-party products into effective business computing solutions. Published monthly by Venture Publishing, *SCO World* is not affiliated with the Santa Cruz Operation. The editorial focus is on the SCO market, UNIX-Intel technology, comparable third-party hardware, and software and connectivity products. Recent articles consider Granite Digital's Grand Central SCSI switch, Commtouch's *ProntoMail*, Wyse's Color Terminal, and related topics. Visit this Web site for sample contents and for information on subscribing to the print edition.

Figure 725 SCO World Web site.

AI CAFÉ C/C++ CGI HTML HTTP JAVA J++ PERL VBSCRIPT VRML WIN32 WINSOCK 1100110100101111001101110011010101000110011001001010

SYS ADMIN HOME PAGE

http://www.samag.com/

Sys Admin Magazine targets UNIX system administrators who seek to improve their system's performance or extend its capabilities. Each month, *Sys Admin Magazine* gives you coverage of systems analysis and monitoring, security, backup, crash recovery, shell scripts, X-Windows, system automation, and integrating multiple hardware platforms. Unlike other UNIX magazines, *Sys Admin Magazine* focuses on system-level processes, rather than the latest database or spreadsheet. Not only does *Sys Admin Magazine's* coverage include multiple versions of UNIX, it spans a variety of platforms as well. Visit the Web pages for more information on this outstanding publication.

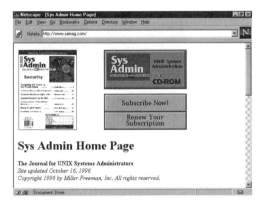

Figure 726.1 Sys Admin Magazine home page.

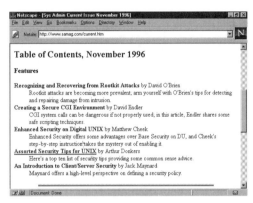

Figure 726.2 November '96 Contents.

AI CAFÉ C/C++ CGI HTML HTTP JAVA J++ PERL VBSCRIPT VRML WIN32 WINSOCK 1100110100101111001101110011010101000110011001001010

UNIX REVIEW

http://www.unixreview.com/

UNIX Review helps UNIX professionals develop and administer superior systems and solutions. Each month, *UNIX Review* offers concise, detailed analysis of the latest UNIX technologies, software development, products, standards, and UNIX-related business worldwide. The magazine covers all elements of UNIX-based operating systems: software, hardware, peripherals, and support services. The Web pages include subscription information, digital reprints of selected articles from current and back issues of *UNIX Review*, and a great on-line buyer's guide, complete with thousands of product listings and a full-text and fielded search engine. If you've worked with UNIX for some period of time, you've undoubtedly read *UNIX Review*. Now access the information on-line.

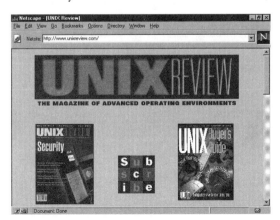

Figure 727 The UNIX Review Web site.

UNIXWORLD ONLINE

http://www.wcmh.com/uworld/

UnixWorld is a free, Web-based (no printed edition) magazine that provides practical, tutorial-oriented articles and columns for beginner to expert users, programmers, and system administrators of platforms running the UNIX operating system. The magazine's recent articles include "The vi/ex/ Editor: The Subtle Substitute Command" by Walter Zintz, "An Introduction to Tcl and Tk" by Brent Welch, and more. You'll also get some great tips and techniques for exchanging files between UNIX and DOS via FTP (courtesy of Becca Thomas), and an answer to the age-old question "Can a pipe have more than one exit?" supplied by Ray Swartz. Check out *UnixWorld*.

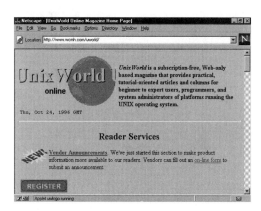

Figure 728.1 UnixWorld home page.

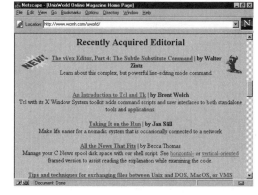

Figure 728.2 A sampling of content.

UPSIDE

http://www.upside.com/

Upside Magazine is meant to provide technology executives with provocative, insightful analyses of the individuals and companies leading the digital revolution. For example, a recent issue featured an article with Heidi Roizen (one of Apple's controversial but technically astute marketing gurus) in which she explained why she took her new job at Apple, how she plans to turn things around, and what it is like to be looking down the barrel of the Apple developers' shotgun. You also get useful entrepreneur forums, an *Upside* back issues archive, great guest columnists such as Richard Brandt and David Kline, and much more. While you are at this site, check the archives for Dave Kline's great piece entitled "NetProfit: The Internet Advertising Shell Game."

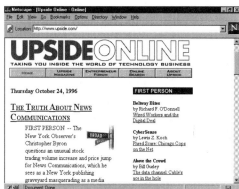

Figure 729.1 The Upside Web site.

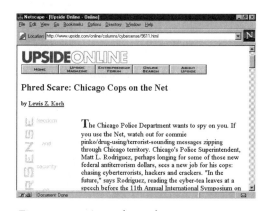

Figure 729.2 A sample article.

AI Café C/C++ CGI HTML HTTP Java J++ Perl VBScript VRML Win32 Winsock 110011010010111100110111001101010001100110010010 1

THE WEB MAGAZINE: WEB CENTRAL STATION

http://www.webmagazine.com/

Web Central Station is the on-line home of *The Web Magazine*. Visit this site for great editorials and also for those things you won't find in the print edition of the magazine. Check out their "Sites of the Day"—three particularly "browse worthy" sites the magazine selects each day. Then, check out Web Central's on-line exclusives. That's right. You get all-new, exclusive on-line content twice a week. The pieces are by some of the savviest writers and the most top-knotch columnists who report the latest trends in digital and pop culture. Then, check WebReviews, which contains all the site reviews from current and back issues of the magazine. This site is one to bookmark, kids.

Figure 730.1 Web Central Station.

Figure 730.2 An article about on-line race hate.

AI Café C/C++ CGI HTML HTTP Java J++ Perl VBScript VRML Win32 Winsock 110011010010111100110111001101010001100110010010 1

WEB DEVELOPER MAGAZINE

http://www.webdeveloper.com/

Web Developer is a monthly magazine for those who sponsor, build, maintain, and market Web sites. You will get the latest security suggestions for specific servers and learn how to make the introduction of Java to CGI a pleasant one. Next, you will learn to make your Intranet more manageable using cutting-edge tools. Also, the magazine shows you how implementing a few design fundamentals can make for fantastic looking frames. Pick up expert HTML tips and tricks you won't find anywhere else on the planet. You will also hear from Steve Bush on what it is like to be Microsoft's top Webmaster. Finally, you will benefit from detailed reviews of site-management tools and other valuable software.

Figure 731 Web Developer Magazine.

732

0011001100010101011001110110111101011101111000101   AI CAFÉ C/C++ CGI HTML HTTP JAVA J++ PERL VBSCRIPT VRML WIN32 WINSOCK

WEB INFORMANT MAGAZINE

http://www.informant.com/wi/

Published monthly, *Web Informant* is packed with technical "how-to" articles, product reviews, book reviews, news from the Internet community, Internet usergroup information, and much more. Each month *Web Informant* includes articles that demystify Web, Internet, and intranet development, and which make you immediately productive developing applications for the Web. You will find feature articles on Java and JavaScript, Perl, Web-page design, server-configuration issues, fire walls and security, HTML, VRML, and database application development. Don't miss the *Web Informant.*

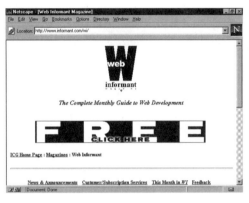

Figure 732.1 Web Informant.

Figure 732.2 A sampling of the contents.

733

0011001100010101011001110110111101011101111000101   AI CAFÉ C/C++ CGI HTML HTTP JAVA J++ PERL VBSCRIPT VRML WIN32 WINSOCK

WEBMASTER MAGAZINE

http://www.cio.com/WebMaster/

WebMaster Magazine is devoted to those professionals who are devoted to doing business on the Web. Recent issues contain goodies such as an interview with Tim Berners-Lee ("the man who gave away the Web"), considerations of various P&L business models for Web-based commerce, the possible benefits of giving intranet access to a few select outsiders, and more. Interspersed with all this are editorials, commentaries, expert-developer forums, and Web-tool reviews. One particularly great feature of the on-line edition is the Professional WebMaster Forum. Sign on to the forum and chime in about who you are, what you do, why you do it, and what your problems are (you might start with the problems you are having on your Web site and work from there).

Figure 733.1 WebMaster Web site.

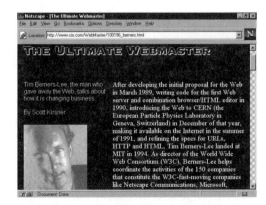

Figure 733.2 Article about Tim Berners-Lee.

AI CAFÉ C/C++ CGI HTML HTTP JAVA J++ PERL VBSCRIPT VRML WIN32 WINSOCK 11001101001011110011011100110101010001100110010101

WEBTECHNIQUES MAGAZINE

http://www.webtechniques.com/

WebTechniques is the hottest monthly magazine for professionals who develop, design, and maintain Web sites. Keep up with emerging Web technologies, tools, and techniques. *Web Techniques* give you in-depth feature articles that will help you grasp the intricacies of Java, mobile agents, Internet security, VRML, and more. The site includes fantastic "how-to" articles related to the latest tools and coolest techniques and strategies. It also provides expert columnists discoursing on HTML, Java, page design, Perl/CGI, legal issues, and Web administration hassles. And, it offers exceptional Web site case study "profiles" from which you can learn exactly how all the most innovative Web pages were built.

Figure 734.1 The WebTechniques Web site.

Figure 734.2 A sample article.

AI CAFÉ C/C++ CGI HTML HTTP JAVA J++ PERL VBSCRIPT VRML WIN32 WINSOCK 11001101001011110011011100110101010001100110010101

WEB WEEK

http://www.webweek.com/

Web Week is a great weekly publication for Web developers and other professionals—and you will find much of the magazine is available to you at this site, right on-line! You will learn why Netscape is betting on groupware as the third wave for the Net, why Lotus has unveiled an "Intranet for Rent" plan, how well Sun is doing (and why), how police have enlisted intranet technology in drug dragnets, why Oracle is diving into e-commerce software, why Netscape is (begrudgingly) incorporating ActiveX technology in its products, how the streaming audio market is heating up, and much more. The news is timely, insightful, informative and well-written. Check it out.

Figure 735.1 Web Week.

Figure 735.2 Ask Dr. Website.

WINDOWS 95 PROFESSIONAL

http://www.cobb.com/w9p/index.htm

Windows 95 Professional is a monthly print newsletter designed to help you and your users discover new ways of enhancing your productivity with Windows 95. Each issue of *Windows 95 Professional* is packed with information designed to help you migrate smoothly to Windows 95. The issues will help you understand the new features of Windows 95, install Windows 95 for individual workstations and networks of computers, exploit Windows 95's networking capabilities, and solve network problems without leaving your desk. Best yet, it will help you stay up-to-date with bug fixes, patches and workarounds. Check out the Web pages for *Windows 95 Professional*, for digital reprints of the newsletter and other goodies.

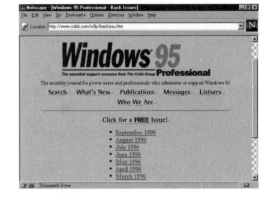

Figure 736.1 Windows 95 Professional.   *Figure 736.2 Search back issues.*

WINDOWS DEVELOPER'S JOURNAL

http://www.wdj.com/

Windows Developer's Journal is, as its Web pages inform us, "an independent monthly magazine that provides practical technical information for advanced Windows programmers. The editorial focus is on solutions to real-world Windows programming problems contributed by practicing Windows programmers." The articles typically include code examples and all published code. In addition, the site features code too extensive for publication. Visit this site for great information, articles, and product reviews related to development tools, utilities, and more. Care to contribute an article? Then, check out the Author's Guidelines that you will find available right on-line. Anyone who programs Windows should stop by and visit the *Windows Developer's Journal*—a magazine by and for programmers.

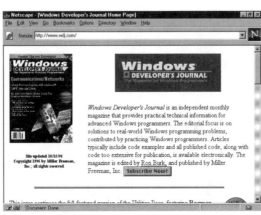

Figure 737 Windows Developer's Journal home page.

AI CAFÉ C/C++ CGI HTML HTTP JAVA J++ PERL VBSCRIPT VRML WIN32 WINSOCK 1100110100101111001101110011010101000110011001001010

WINDOWS MAGAZINE

http://www.winmag.com/

The Internet edition of *Windows Magazine* is updated daily and is absolutely packed with great information, articles, reviews, commentary, downloads, and demos related to Windows 3.1, Windows 95, NT, and more. You can keep your system in shape with *Windows Magazine's* new, constantly-updated databank of Windows add-ons, patches, and updates. Then, check out the new NT Enterprise supplement to *Windows Magazine*, targeted to IS (information systems) professionals. You can also download *Windows Magazine's* latest picks of some of the best Windows shareware, which include a cool compression utility, great search tools, and more. And, check out the great calendar of Windows events, the daily news, and the daily *Windows Magazine* "hot spot" on the Web.

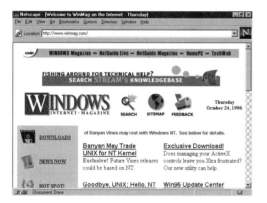

Figure 738.1 Windows Magazine.

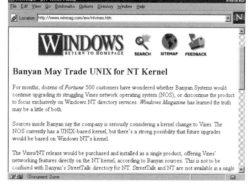

Figure 738.2 Breaking news.

AI CAFÉ C/C++ CGI HTML HTTP JAVA J++ PERL VBSCRIPT VRML WIN32 WINSOCK 1100110100101111001101110011010101000110011001001010

WINDOWS NT MAGAZINE

http://www.winntmag.com/

Windows NT Magazine is a monthly business publication written for technical decision makers using the Windows NT operating system and related applications. The magazine provides practical, hands-on information to help IS (information systems) teams deploy business-critical applications based on Windows NT and *BackOffice*. The magazine's editorial content is technical, striking a balance between tactical and strategic information. The magazine is full of information on how to implement various features of a Windows NT workstation and server, as well as information about related third-party products. Visit this Web site for more information.

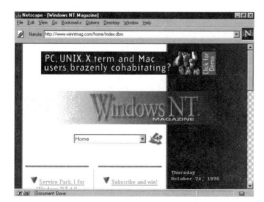

Figure 739.1 Windows NT Magazine.

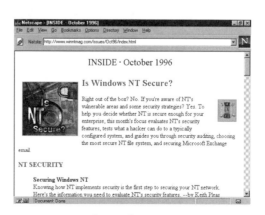

Figure 739.2 The October '96 issue.

WINDOWS SOURCES

http://www.zdnet.com/wsources/

Windows Sources is a magazine that covers all aspects of Windows programming, development, and use. The magazine's coverage extends to both Windows 95 and Windows NT, with the occasional, nostalgic look back at old man 3.1. Visit this site for great articles, reviews, editorial, and downloads. Also, you will find exclusive software "first looks" at upcoming reviews of products like *SufinBoard*, *GoldMine*, *DemoShield*, *Automate*, *Internet Fastfind*, *Character Studio*, *Asymetrix WebPublisher*, *EchoSearch*, and more. You'll also find cool links to other Windows pages, magazine subscription information, special offers, and much more. Stop by.

Figure 740.1 Windows Sources.

Figure 740.2 Tip of the day.

WINDOWS WATCHER NEWSLETTER

http://www.windowswatcher.com/

Windows Watcher is a newsletter that monitors the Windows industry to inform readers about key technologies and products. Starting with the October 1995 issue, *Windows Watcher* has moved many key columns and reviews from the hardcopy, print-edition of the newsletter to these Web pages, thus greatly expanding the number of products they can cover. To help you learn more about the products and their manufacturers, the articles include direct links to, as they put it, "some of the more progressive vendor's home pages." The listings are categorized and cross-linked by product type, date reviewed, company name, and product name. *Windows Watcher* is a great way to stay current.

Figure 741.1 Windows Watcher Newsletter.

Figure 741.2 Links to sample articles.

WIRED MAGAZINE: HOTWIRED

http://www.hotwired.com/wired/

HotWired is the on-line edition of *Wired* magazine. It does not contain the same amount of prose and images as the paper edition, but it is still notoriously cool. You'll find all the standard columns, including "Rants and Raves" (reader feedback), "Electric Word" (bulletins from the front line of the digital revolution), "Scans" (people, companies, and ideas that matter), "Fetish" (technolust), "Reality Check" (the future of nanotechnology), "Raw Data" (lots and lots of stats), and more. You'll also find the "Geek Page," considerations of cyber-rights, and profiles of personalities involved in creating, defining, and refining the new frontier of cyberspace. Too cool.

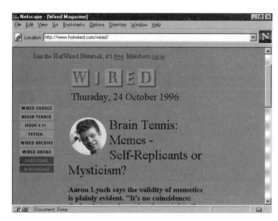

Figure 742 Care for a little brain tennis?

ADDITIONAL PUBLICATIONS AND RELATED RESOURCES

- CCG - Tech Links - Programming
  http://www.cconsulting.com/techlink/programming.html

- YPN: Tech: Programming
  http://www.ypn.com/tech/a386.

- Nerd World : SOFTWARE - DEVELOPERS
  http://www.nerdworld.com/nw1659.html

- Useful Links
  http://www.imagine-net.com/artbeatswebtools/lglink.html

- Distance Learning
  http://www.usit.net/hp/ttpm/DistLrning.html

- Alias Wavefront
  http://www.alias.com/

- Computers: Hi-Tech share index
  http://www.australian.aust.com/computer/stocks.htm

- Virginia Tech Research: VirtualReality
  http://ei.cs.vt.edu/~mm/s96/sspace/VirtualReality_918.html

JOHN PERRY BARLOW

http://www.eff.org/~barlow/barlow.html

A character whose life appears to come out of the writings of both Ken Kesey and William Gibson, John Perry Barlow is a noted lyricist (for the Grateful Dead), retired Wyoming cattle rancher and, in his own words, "the only former Republican County Chairman in America willing to call himself a hippie mystic without lowering his voice." Barlow is also a founder of the Electronic Frontier Foundation, a contributing writer for *Wired*, and a highly respected commentator on computer security, virtual reality, digitized intellectual property, and "the social and legal conditions arising in the global network of connected digital devices."

Figure 743.1 John Perry in the flesh.   Figure 743.2 Anti Reform Act.   Figure 743.3 The Times editorial.

GAVIN BELL: VRML ARCHITECT

http://www.mailbag.com/users/gavin

Gavin Bell is the chief architect of VRML 2.0, and he is the man who wrote the proposal that turned into the VRML 1.0 specification. He is also an accomplished juggler. Furthermore, the course notes for the tutorial on VRML 2.0 that he presented at Eurographics '96 are available at his personal Web site. He also provides historical notes on the development of VRML, and a couple of utility programs that you might find useful. For example, you can download source code for a program that calculates a single rotation given a series of rotations. (If you can't figure out how to set the orientation field of VRML cameras, then this program might be for you.) Check it out.

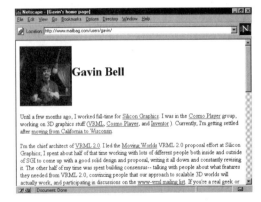
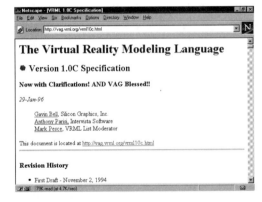

Figure 744.1 Gavin Bell home page.   *Figure 744.2 The original VRML 1.0 spec.*

AI CAFÉ C/C++ CGI HTML HTTP JAVA J++ PERL VBSCRIPT VRML WIN32 WINSOCK 11001101001011110011011100110101010001100110010 1

TIM BERNERS-LEE

http://www.w3.org/pub/WWW/People/Berners-Lee/

Meet the man who invented the World Wide Web. That's right. He works at MIT right now, but back then Tim was working at CERN, the European Particle Physics Laboratory. In 1989, Tim first proposed connecting the Web as a system for transferring ideas and research among scientists in the high-energy-physics community. Berners-Lee's original proposal defined a very simple implementation that used hypertext, but did not include multimedia capabilities. In 1990, there was an implementation for Steve Jobs NeXT computer. And in 1992 CERN began publicizing the Web and encouraging the development of servers. The rest is history. Thanks, Tim!

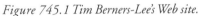

Figure 745.1 Tim Berners-Lee's Web site.

Figure 745.2 He directs the W3C.

AI CAFÉ C/C++ CGI HTML HTTP JAVA J++ PERL VBSCRIPT VRML WIN32 WINSOCK 11001101001011110011011100110101010001100110010 1

GRADY BOOCH: AN INTERVIEW WITH "GEEK CHIC"

http://www.geekchic.com/repliq8.htm

The intrepid interviewer from *Geekchic* gets to the heart of Grady Booch, the father of object-orientation. Which is his favorite programming language? C++, of course. What is his favorite operating system? The MacOS. His favorite newsgroup is comp.object. His favorite Web pages include those of Rational Software (his employer), IBM, Apple, and the Vatican. His sport is racquetball. His car, like OJ's, is a Bronco II. He reads upwards of 10 books a week, likes to travel, loves to sing and play music, and build model trains. His favorite book in the world is Douglas Hofstadter's *Godel, Escher, Bach*. His favorite movie is *Casablanca*. Visit this Web site for more information.

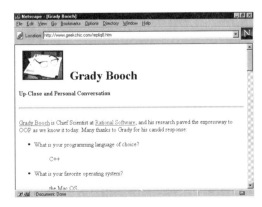

Figure 746.1 The interview.

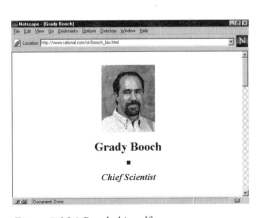

Figure 746.2 Booch, himself.

Brainstorms: Howard Rheingold's Experiment in Futurism

http://www.well.com/user/hlr/

Can many-to-many media help us think together about the future? Can everybody join Howard in turning Brainstorms into something that resembles a jam session more than it does an on-line magazine? Is it possible to make sense of what is happening and still have fun? Toward that end, Brainstorms is a forum for intelligent opinions and observations about technology-related prospects for the future. At this site, you'll find an on-line forum where both audience and authors can talk together about *what it all means.* Participants include *you,* along with Howard Rheingold, William Calvin, Joi Ito, and others.

Figure 747 Brainstorms.

Stewart Brand

http://www.well.com/user/sbb/

Do you want to visit with someone in the know? If so, Stewart Brand's Web site pretty much speaks for itself: "Since co-founding The WELL back in 1984 (see resume), I've been busy as a principal with Global Business Network, and have been on the boards of the Electronic Frontier Foundation and the Sante Fe Institute, and consulted for Ecotrust and MIT's Media Lab. A substantial item on the home page of Global Business Network is the list of all the books I've recommended for the GBN "Book Club" since 1988 and my reviews—a couple of hundred of them." Brand is also a founder of the *Whole Earth Catalog,* and author of the critically praised book, *How Buildings Learn.*

Figure 748.1 Stewart Brand home page.

Figure 748.2 One of his brainchildren.

AI CAFÉ C/C++ CGI HTML HTTP JAVA J++ PERL VBSCRIPT VRML WIN32 WINSOCK 11001101001011110011011100110101010001100110010010

CAL-STATE, SAN MARCOS, WINDOWS SHAREWARE ARCHIVE

http://ftp.csusm.edu/winworld.html

This archive gives Windows users access to a vast cornucopia of Windows-based shareware. Most of the applications you will find are in zip form, so you need to have an unzip program like PKUNZIP (which you can find at this site) or its Windows equivalent WINZIP (which you can also find at this site). Some of the programs may require the VisualBasic Run-time DLLs, which are also available. A particularly nice feature of this site is the shareware search engine, which helps you quickly find what you are looking for, allowing you to search either by shareware function, title, or author. Not bad. For added convenience, recent uploads are listed in their own section, so that you can browse what's new.

Figure 749.1 The archive.

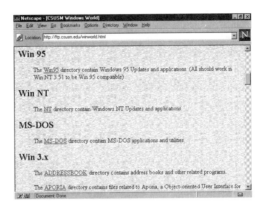

Figure 749.2 Some options.

AI CAFÉ C/C++ CGI HTML HTTP JAVA J++ PERL VBSCRIPT VRML WIN32 WINSOCK 11001101001011110011011100110101010001100110010010

CENTER FOR ON-LINE ADDICTION

http://www.pitt.edu/~ksy/

Do you find yourself spending more and more time on the net? The Center for On-Line Addiction has been dedicated to promoting awareness of the phenomena of Internet addiction. Since its inception in January 1995, the center has conducted extensive empirical research lead by Dr. Kimberly S. Young. Internet Addiction has now gained credibility among mental health professionals as a clinically significant disorder which negatively impacts social, occupational, family, and financial functioning. In addition, the center has identified problem areas that mental health professionals, educators, and human resource managers are experiencing due to individuals' becoming addicted to the Internet in the same manner one would become addicted to drugs, alcohol, or gambling.

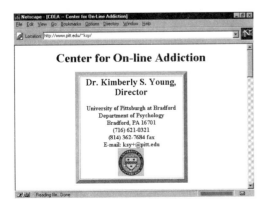

Figure 750.1 Center for On-line Addiction.

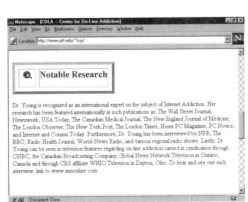

Figure 750.2 The proprietress.

AI CAFE C/C++ CGI HTML HTTP JAVA J++ PERL VBSCRIPT VRML WIN32 WINSOCK

751

COAST TO COAST TELECOMMUNICATIONS SOFTWARE REPOSITORY

http://www.coast.net/SimTel/

This archive has just launched a new games section that is bound to become the ultimate spot on the Web for shareware and freeware games. Watch this rapidly expanding section of the Repository for the hottest new releases. Another excellent sub-archive you will find at this site is the Windows 95 Collection, a fantastic array of applications and utilities. You will also find software for DOS, Windows 3.1, Windows NT, and OS/2. The Windows 95 collection includes fax software, edutainment (there's that word again), desktop publishing applications, file utilities, graphics software, Java and Internet applications, network software, programming tools, sound and other multimedia tools, and much more.

Figure 751.1 The Repository.

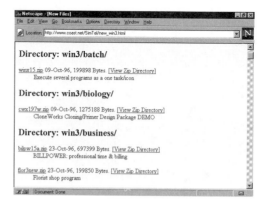

Figure 751.2 Some Windows options.

AI CAFE C/C++ CGI HTML HTTP JAVA J++ PERL VBSCRIPT VRML WIN32 WINSOCK

752

CYBERBABIES: A HYPERTEXT STUDY OF KIDS AND COMPUTERS

http://sunsite.unc.edu/ckind/Schaefer.html

How young can they start? Very young. The sooner the better. You can find software for kids at age fifteen months and up. But there are complications. The mouse—yes, that user friendly mouse—is not friendly at all to the very young. They just don't get how to manipulate it. The relation of the mouse on the pad to the cursor on the screen is an abstract concept for the very young to grasp, neuronally challenged as they are. Next question: What do the very young use the computer for? The same thing you do: entertainment, information, and the manipulation of data. Sure, it is simple manipulation of simple data, but the fundamentals are the same. Visit this site for more information.

Figure 752.1 Cyberbabies.

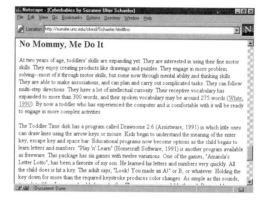

Figure 752.2 No Mommy, me do it.

AI CAFÉ C/C++ CGI HTML HTTP JAVA J++ PERL VBSCRIPT VRML WIN32 WINSOCK 11001101001011110011011100110101010001100110010101

CYBERIA: FIGHTING THE CHILL OF THE INFORMATION AGE

http://www.well.com/user/pb/cyb/

This site is the on-line home of the weekly column "Cyberia: Fighting the Chill of the Information Age," by Paul Bissex. The man is full of opinions: good opinions, useful opinions. And, Paul cleverly crafts his opinions, presenting them with wit and just the right amount of cynicism to make things spicy. Titles of recent articles include "Talking Heads," "Net Reading," "The Database Investment Act," "Everything's Mediated," "What the Hell is 'Content'?" "Rules of the Net," "Spam Hall of Shame," and "Are On-line Activists Stuck On-line?" Also check out "Where is Cyberspace?" "The V-Chip Hits the Fan," "The Millennium Problem," and "The Web: Desktop Publishing Redux?" Take time out to visit this site.

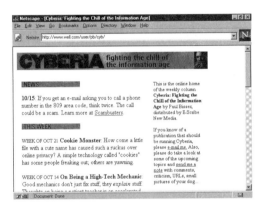

Figure 753.1 Cyberia.

Figure 753.2 A sample article.

AI CAFÉ C/C++ CGI HTML HTTP JAVA J++ PERL VBSCRIPT VRML WIN32 WINSOCK 11001101001011110011011100110101010001100110010101

CYBERLIT HOME PAGE

http://omni.cc.purdue.edu/~stein/stein.htm

Treat yourself to the Cyberlit (Cyberpunk Literature) Home Page, an exploration of the evolving cyborg body of fiction, animae, and cyberculture. While you are there, check out some current trends in contemporary culture and find some interesting links to related sites. On the literature side of things, you'll find complete information, starting with William Gibson's 1984 classic *Neuromancer*, which established a landscape in which a number of important theoretical postulations about the future of contemporary culture were free to operate. This landscape is where the cyberpunks have lived and moved and had their being, ever thereafter. Man, I thought C++ was confusing.

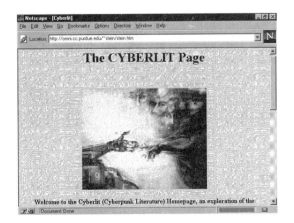

Figure 754 The Cyberlit home page.

755

ESTHER DYSON

http://www.eff.org/homes/dyson.html

Esther Dyson is President of EDventure Holdings, a small but diversified company focused on emerging information and technology worldwide and on the emerging computer markets of Central and Eastern Europe. Dyson is also active in industry affairs. She is chairperson of the Electronic Frontier Foundation and a member of the U.S. National Information Infrastructure Advisory Council. She co-chairs the NII AC's Information Privacy and Intellectual Property subcommittee. Dyson's EDventure publishes Release 1.0, a highly regarded monthly newsletter, and sponsors PC (Platforms for Communication) Forum and the East-West High-Tech Forum. For discussion on a wide range of topics, check out this Web site.

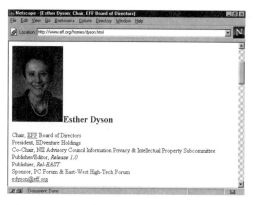

Figure 755.1 Esther Dyson.

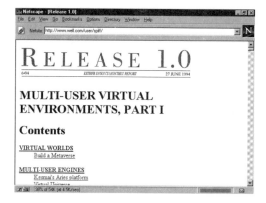

Figure 755.2 And her publication.

756

DAVID J. FARBER

http://www.eff.org/~farber

Are you looking for information with some research to back it up? David Farber is the Alfred Fitler Moore Professor of Telecommunications at the University of Pennsylvania and is on the Faculty Council of the SEI Center for Advanced Studies in Management of the Wharton School. At UPenn, Farber is Director of the Distributed Computing Laboratory where, with Professor John Smith, he manages leading edge research in high-speed networking. He is also a founder of Caine, Farber & Gordon (CFG), a leading supplier of software-design methodologies to industry. His Web site is chock full of essays, articles, and random thoughts on the present and future in cyberspace, as well as articles about Farber from such publications as the *Philadelphia Inquirer*.

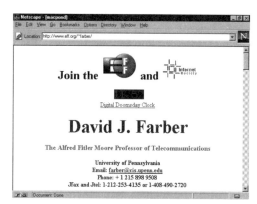

Figure 756.1 David J. Farber Web site.

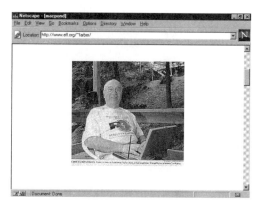

Figure 756.2 The man himself.

AI CAFÉ C/C++ CGI HTML HTTP JAVA J++ PERL VBSCRIPT VRML WIN32 WINSOCK 110011010010111100110110011010101000110011001001011

FEED MAGAZINE

http://www.feedmag.com/

At first glance, *FEED* magazine seems to play into the take-no-prisoners advance of contemporary techno-culture. *FEED*, after all, is a creature of the Web, born and bred in the binary soup of zeroes and ones. In other words, the proprietors of *FEED* are firm believers in the promise of new, interactive media. However, they are not inclined to see *FEED* as a paradigm shift or a radical break with tradition. Sure, you can't just drop a page-bound magazine into cyberspace and expect nothing to change. But neither can you throw away the centuries of development that produced modern journalism in its linear form. Thus, the editors of *FEED* seek a balance. And it is a good balance. Check it out.

Figure 757 FEED.

AI CAFÉ C/C++ CGI HTML HTTP JAVA J++ PERL VBSCRIPT VRML WIN32 WINSOCK 110011010010111100110110011010101000110011001001011

SCOTT FRAIZE, JAVA GURU

http://www.dimensionx.com/people/scott

Scott Fraize is the chief technical officer (CTO) of Dimension X. He grew up in Sudbury, Massachusetts and started hacking with C and UNIX at age 13. Fraize went to school at the University of Rochester, where he received a degree in Cognitive Science. While he was there, he also worked on and off for Networking Services at MIT, where he built most of the original software for their campus-wide information system, *TechInfo*. Years later, he got involved in writing Mosaic applications in Perl, which led him to an infatuation with VRML, which in turned led to an infatuation with Java. And as anyone might guess, that is the focus today at Dimension X.

Figure 758 Scott Fraize Web site.

GEEK CHIC

http://www.geekchic.com/geekchic.htm#replique

Geek Chic is pronounced "geek sheek" as in "tre's chic," which, the Webmaster reminds us, is French for "way cool." So, now it is chic to be a geek. And these pages document why and how. Visit this site for interviews with Ed Yourdon, Edger Dijkstra, Bjarne Stroustrup, and other geek celebrities who "are hounded constantly by the press, talk shows, and crowds of admirers . . . are rarely able to come out of their secluded homes without leading a trail of the curious." Survey the gallery of "Nude Nerds," or upload your own offering if you dare. Take the "Are You Geek Chic" quiz. Review an extensive chronicle of the history of geekdom in literature and the cinema. You'll find more. Check it out.

Figure 759.1 Geek Chic Web site.

Figure 759.2 A geek wannabe.

Figure 759.2 Geek mythology.

GIGGLEBYTES

http://www.currents.net/magazine/backiss/archciss.html?GIGG

"Gigglebytes" is Lincoln Spector's humor column in *Computer Currents*. At this site, you will find digital reprints of the column going back several months. "The first place to look for sex on the Internet is the World Wide Web," he writes. "Why? Because popular opinion states that the Web is the sexiest part of the Internet, and if I didn't care about popular opinion, I'd probably be writing about socks on the Internet. So I headed over to my favorite Web search tool, Alta States, and searched for the word 'sex.' Guess what? I found it. In fact, there are more sites with the word 'sex' than the phrase 'cheap airfare.' (There are so many of both, by the way, that there just has to be an overlap. That's frightening.)" And so on. Take a break and check out Gigglebytes.

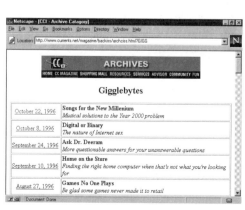

Figure 760.1 Gigglebytes.

Figure 760.2 A sample article.

SITES TOO COOL TO PASS UP

AI CAFÉ C/C++ CGI HTML HTTP JAVA J++ PERL VBSCRIPT VRML WIN32 WINSOCK 11001101001011110011011100110101010001100100100101

JOHN GILMORE

http://www.cygnus.com/~gnu/

John Gilmore's pet project for 1996 is to secure 5% of the Internet traffic against passive wiretapping. "If we get 5% this year, we can secure 20% next year, against both active and passive attacks, and 80% in 1998. The whole Internet will have been secured. Want to help?" Gilmore is a founder of Cygnus Support, the Electronic Frontier Foundation, The Little Garden (a small Internet provider in San Francisco), and the CyberPunks (an informal group dedicated to dissemination of cryptography information). Gilmore hosts a mailing list on the latter topic. Cygnus, of course, is a well-known firm which provides commercial support for free software. Don't worry—I am (pretty) sure you can visit his site without your lines being tapped.

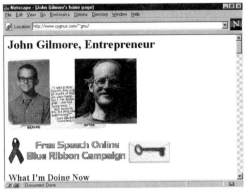

Figure 761.1 Before and after Woodstock.

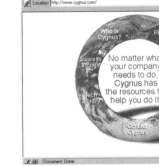

Figure 761.2 Cygnus home page.

MIKE GODWIN

http://www.eff.org/~mnemonic/godwin.html

Mike Godwin is staff counsel for the Electronic Frontier Foundation, where he informs users of electronic networks about their legal rights and responsibilities, instructs criminal lawyers and law-enforcement personnel about computer civil-liberties issues, and conducts seminars about civil liberties in electronic communication for a wide range of groups. Godwin has published articles for print and electronic publications on such topics as electronic searches and seizures, the First Amendment and electronic publications, and the application of international law to computer communications. Many of these engaging papers are warehoused at this site on-line for you to peruse.

Figure 762.1 Mike Godwin Web site.

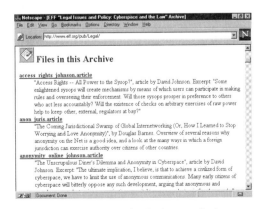

Figure 762.2 Writings by Godwin and others.

The Hacker Crackdown: Full Text On-line

http://www.cs.wesleyan.edu/HTML/The-Hacker-Crackdown/

At this site, you will find the full e-text of Bruce Sterling's classic *The Hacker Crackdown: Law and Disorder on the Electronic Frontier*. Sterling has added a special Preface and Afterword exclusive to this electronic edition, every chapter of which is available to you as freeware. Sterling has made the book available as freeware because, as he writes, ". . . information wants to be free. And the information inside this book longs for freedom with a peculiar intensity. I genuinely believe that the natural habitat of this book is inside an electronic network. That may not be the easiest direct method to generate revenue for the book's author, but that doesn't matter."

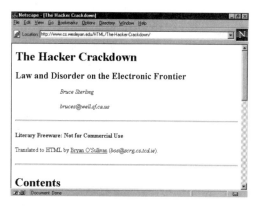

Figure 763.1 The "title page."

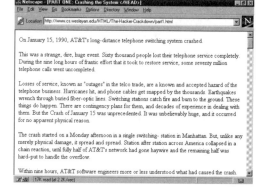

Figure 763.2 Some prose.

Hacking

http://www.ling.umu.se/~phred/hack.html

Access questions and comments about hacking, phreaking (illegally using phone lines for free, phone-break, get it?), and cracking. Learn what hacking is NOT about (hacking is not about destroying things. The media has misused the word "hacking" far too often while talking about criminals). Find out about the hacker ethic which says: 1) Access to computers should be unlimited and total. 2) All information should be free. 3) It is wise to distrust authority and promote decentralization in computing, as in all things. 4) Hackers should be judged by the nature, ends, and content of their hacking. 5) It is possible to create art and beauty on a computer. 6) Computers can change your life for the better. Stop hacking and check out Hacking.

Figure 764 Hacking.

AI CAFÉ C/C++ CGI HTML HTTP JAVA J++ PERL VBSCRIPT VRML WIN32 WINSOCK 11001101001011110011011100110101010001100110010101

HYPNO SUPER SHAREWARE

http://www.hypno.com/share.html

Visit this site and download some fantastic shareware from Hypnovista Software. As the Webmaster says: "Download em' . . . look at em' . . . distribute em' everywhere!" This is all fun stuff, such as *Box-O-Candy*, a free interactive digital valentine for your Mac or Windows computer. A slot-machine mechanism determines whether your sweetheart loves you or loathes you. Then, be sure to open the box to discover happy bouncing chocolates. Each chocolate contains a different creamy digital liquid center. You'll also find a great screen saver, available only for Windows. It is a portrait of Vincent Van Gigabyte, the famous beat poet turned art director. What do you have to lose? It's free.

Figure 765 Super free stuff.

AI CAFÉ C/C++ CGI HTML HTTP JAVA J++ PERL VBSCRIPT VRML WIN32 WINSOCK 11001101001011110011011100110101010001100110010101

JARGON FILE RESOURCES/THE NEW HACKER'S DICTIONARY

http://www.ccil.org/jargon/jargon.html

Jargon File is the on-line edition of *The New Hacker's Dictionary*, which is available in bookstores. You will find almost all the entries from the print edition at Jargon File on-line. The only stuff missing from the on-line edition is some nice front matter in the form of a Foreword and Introduction by Guy Steele and Eric Raymond, as well as Guy Steele's infamous *Crunchly* cartoons, which serve as interior illustrations. But, you can visit the Web edition for the standard entries. You will find explanations of all the slang, jargon, and techno-speak associated with computing, as well as essays on such topics as "Hacker Speech Style" and "Hacker Writing Style." Go for it.

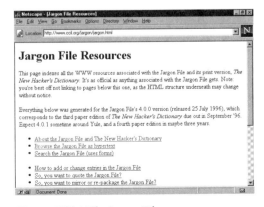

Figure 766.1 The Jargon File.

Figure 766.2 Add your own jargon.

767

JUMBO SHAREWARE & FREEWARE ARCHIVE

http://www.jumbo.com/

Jumbo bills itself as "the coolest shareware site on the Web." And, it may well be. You will find over 72,000 pieces of shareware addressing ActiveX (authoring tools, forms and layouts, multimedia, VRML), business applications (spreadsheets, financial and accounting applications, word processing), desktop-publishing applications (graphic design utilities, photographic tools, morphing tools), on-line tutorials (foreign languages, SAT tutors, vocabulary builders), games (action, 3-D, arcade, shoot-em-ups, puzzles, fantasy, adventure), Java (source code, applets, libraries, demos, examples), the Internet and Web (browsers, e-mail tools, FTP tools, news readers, terminal software), and much more. Wow!

Figure 767 Jumbo!

768

DONALD KNUTH

http://www-soe.stanford.edu/compsci/faculty/Knuth_Donald.html

Any programmer who hasn't read Donald Knuth's *The Art of Programming* from cover to cover (in every edition) should be taken out and shot. Well, perhaps that is a bit extreme. But it would be rather like an author who had never bothered to look at Strunk & White's classic *Elements of Style*. For *The Art of Programming* exists to help all programmers write clean, efficient code. In short, the book is an elegant and succinct style guide for programmers. Knuth is also responsible for developing the *TeX* document compiler and the *METAFRONT* character compiler, each of which have done much to make technical documents pleasant to behold. In 1979, Knuth received the National Medal of Science. Visit this site for more enlightenment.

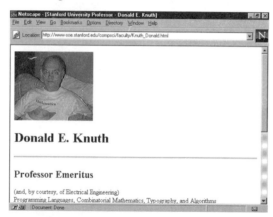

Figure 768 Donald E. Knuth.

JANE METCALFE

http://www.eff.org/homes/metcalfe.html

Jane Metcalfe serves on the board of the Electronic Frontier Foundation and, with her partner Louis Rosetto, is the founder of *Wired* Magazine. Prior to founding *Wired*, Metcalfe worked at *Electric Word* magazine, an Amsterdam-based cult magazine covering such leading edge technologies as machine translation, optical character recognition, and speech recognition. She is a cyber-entepreneur who lives on the technical edge and sponsors the creation of images and prose worthy of the 21st century, in which she and the people she hangs with already live. Join them.

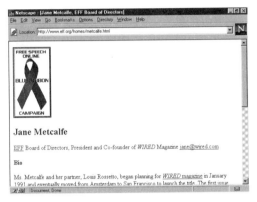

Figure 769.1 The Jane Metcalfe Web site.

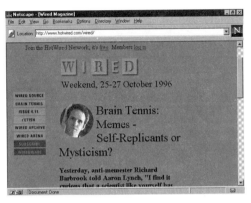

Figure 769.2 And her magazine.

THE NET.LEGENDS FREQUENTLY ASKED QUESTIONS

http://www.math.uiuc.edu/~tskirvin/home/legends.html

This site features a collection of legends of the Net—urban legends, if you will. Folklore. "Not all the following are completely factual entries," writes the author. "In some cases, the true facts are known only to one person, or are lost in the mists of time, while in others the facts pale in relation to the mythology." Learn of McElwaine, the legendary flamer who terrorized newsgroups for years and then disappeared totally and completely from the scene. Or how about Gary Strollman? He also disappeared, but first became famous in newsgroup circles for his postings about aliens who were hunting him down like a dog. The woods are full of characters. Are they real or imagined? A little of both, I guess.

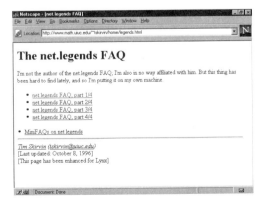

Figure 770.1 net.legends FAQ.

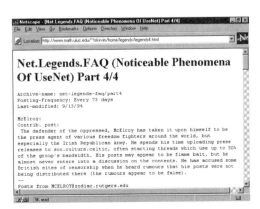

Figure 770.2 Some details.

771

NICHOLAS NEGROPONTE

http://nicholas.www.media.mit.edu/people/nicholas/

Nicholas Negroponte is author of the bestseller *Being Digital* and also the founder and director of MIT's Media Laboratory. Negroponte's is a multi-million dollar research center which focuses exclusively on the study of future forms of human communications from entertainment to education. Negroponte studies at MIT, where, as a graduate student, he specialized in the then-new field of computer-aided design. He has held visiting professorships at Yale, the University of Michigan, and the University of California at Berkeley. In 1968, he founded MIT's pioneering Architecture Machine Group. Visit his Web pages for more information. And don't miss his monthly column in *Wired*.

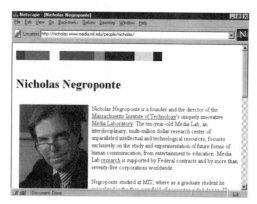

Figure 771.1 Negroponte himself.

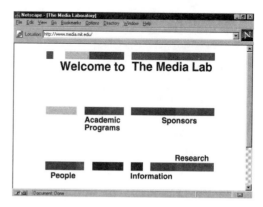

Figure 771.2 And his lab.

772

MARK PESCE: VRML GURU

http://www.hyperreal.com/~mpesce/

A native of my home town of North Kingstown, Rhode Island, Marc Pesce is the Big Daddy of VRML. Visit this site and check out some of his papers and lots of other cool stuff, including his speech given at the Fifth International World Wide Web Conference. You will also encounter papers with such titles as "Lessons Learned from VRML," "The Future of VRML," "The Web VRevolution," "Growing VRML," and more. You will also find information about his book, *VRML: Browsing and Building Cyberspace*, along with lots of cool graphics to play around with. This is one cool guy. But of course, he's from North Kingstown. Cheers.

Figure 772.1 Pesce.

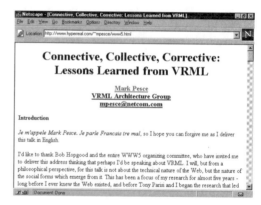

Figure 772.2 And one of his speeches.

AI CAFÉ C/C++ CGI HTML HTTP JAVA J++ PERL VBSCRIPT VRML WIN32 WINSOCK 11001101001011110011011100110101010001100110010010 1

KEVIN POULSEN: FAMOUS HACKER

http://catalog.com/kevin/

Does it follow, since he is a famous hacker, that Kevin Poulsen rejects all forms of authority. Not at all. "In the matter of boots," he writes, quoting Bakunin, "I refer to the authority of the bootmaker; concerning houses, canals or railroads, I consult that of the architect or engineer." Well, actually, Kevin does reject most authority. He has done some serious time for hacking. But he is funny. Just check out his list of frequently asked questions: "Who the hell are you and what are you doing here? You think this is funny? Do you really expect me to believe that? How did you get in here? Could I see your driver's license and proof of insurance?"

Figure 773.1 Kevin's Web site.

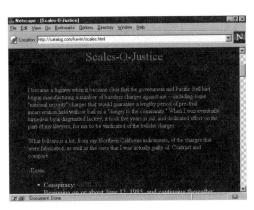

Figure 773.2 How Kevin got framed.

AI CAFÉ C/C++ CGI HTML HTTP JAVA J++ PERL VBSCRIPT VRML WIN32 WINSOCK 11001101001011110011011100110101010001100110010 1

HOWARD RHEINGOLD'S TOOLS FOR THOUGHT

http://www.well.com/user/hlr/texts/tftindex.html

Before today's first-graders graduate from high school, hundreds of millions of people around the world will join together to create new kinds of human communities, making use of a tool that a small number of thinkers and tinkerers dreamed into being over the past century. Howard Rheingold's classic 1985 book, *Tools for Thought: The People and Ideas of the Next Computer Revolution,* has already had many of its predictions fulfilled in the form of the Internet, the Web, and VRML and Java technologies. The book is available in its entirety, in hypertext, at this site on the Web, courtesy of Howard himself. Feel free.

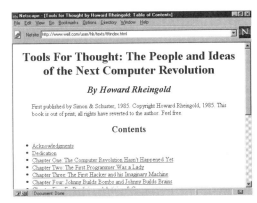

Figure 774.1 Tools for Thought.

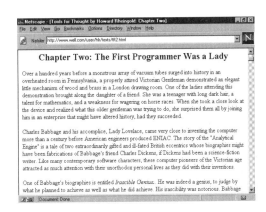

Figure 774.2 Some prose.

775

SHAREWARE.COM

http://www.shareware.com/

Shareware.com is a service from C/NET: The Computer Network that features the *Virtual Software Library* (VSL) search engine and much more. At this site, you can search for, browse, and download the best software including freeware, shareware, demos, fixes, patches, and upgrades—from top-managed software, archives and computer vendor sites on the Internet. You can also keep abreast of new arrivals and the most popular files by subscribing to Shareware Dispatch, Shareware.com's weekly e-mail newsletter. Also, archive managers can also register their FTP archives to make their files searchable from Shareware.com. So, whether you want to gather or distribute some shareware, this is a site to check out.

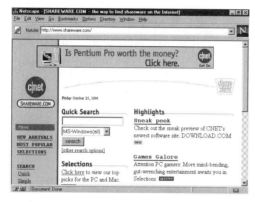

Figure 775.1 Shareware.com.

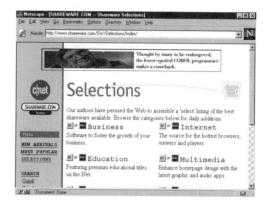

Figure 775.2 A few options.

776

DWIGHT SILVERMAN: COLUMNIST, THE HOUSTON CHRONICLE

http://www.neosoft.com/~dwights/dsframe.htm

Dwight Silverman's computing column appears every Sunday in the *Houston Chronicle*'s Business section, a four-page pull-out devoted to personal technology. The column also moves every week on the *New York Times* Wire Service, where it is picked up by at least a dozen papers weekly; and a lot more papers run it occasionally. The name of the column, "Computing," may not be very inventive, but it is quite descriptive. The column is, quite simply, about using personal computers. "Computing" includes hardware and software reviews, tips to make computing more enjoyable, and dispatches from cyberspace. Check out the great archive of recent columns that you'll find at this Web site .

Figure 776.1 Dwight Silverman's page.

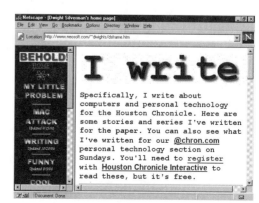

Figure 776.2 What he does.

AI CAFÉ C/C++ CGI HTML HTTP JAVA J++ PERL VBSCRIPT VRML WIN32 WINSOCK 1100110100101110011011100110101010001100110010101

SOCIETY, CYBERSPACE AND THE FUTURE

http://www.cco.caltech.edu/~rich/aspen.html

How can new interactive communication technologies enhance harmonious and functional communities at all scales worldwide? This question is what the folks at the Aspen Institute spent some time figuring out. Their result is this report. New communications technology can, and must, play an essential role in connecting individuals within diverse, dispersed communities. However, as with previous new technological development in communications, negative effects on the stability and functionality of communities are also latent. This report visualizes both potentially positive and negative effects on communities and identifies specific near-term actions and policies which can enhance broad, informed participation in content-rich networks. An excellent read.

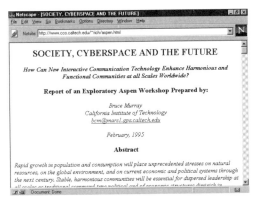

Figure 777.1 Well worth a read.

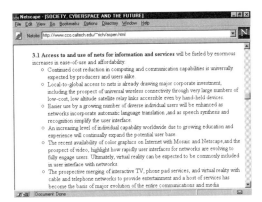

Figure 777.2 A piece of it.

AI CAFÉ C/C++ CGI HTML HTTP JAVA J++ PERL VBSCRIPT VRML WIN32 WINSOCK 1100110100101110011011100110101010001100110010101

THE SOFTWARE SITE

http://softsite.com/

This shareware, freeware, and demo archive focuses on games for Windows 95. Visit this site to get a taste of Ultimate Software's newest slot games for Windows, along with great word games such as *Bog 2* (an addictive word game similar to *Boggle*), *WORDS for Windows 95* (spell selected words by maneuvering falling letters), *Word Search Rampage* (comes complete with over 300 puzzles), and *Word Wrestle* (a new computer game for the whole family to enjoy). If you'd prefer a little more excitement, try *Primordial Life*, an action-arcade game that creates a world filled with artificially living "biots" which battle between themselves and against you!

Figure 778 The Software Site.

1001 PROGRAMMING RESOURCES

1001100110000101010110011101101111010110111100011101 AI CAFÉ C/C++ CGI HTML HTTP JAVA J++ PERL VBSCRIPT VRML WIN32 WINSOCK

779

SYNCHRONIZED, AN INTERNET NOVEL BY WILLIAM H. CALVIN

http://www.well.com/user/wcalvin/bkf1toc.html

William H. Calvin is a neurophysiologist whose popular non-fiction books include *How the Shaman Stole the Moon*, *The River That Flows Uphill*, *How Brains Think*, and *The Cerebral Code*, the last of which was published by MIT Press. He now has published his new "Internet novel," entitled *Synchronized*, on the World Wide Web. The storyline involves stock-market manipulations, detective work via the Internet, and tracking down a kidnap victim (via the Internet). No, *Synchronized* has not yet been published in what Calvin calls "dead tree media." It is only available at this site in a digital, cyberspace edition. While you peruse the table of contents, a back fugue entertains you via streaming audio. The sequel, *Unlisted*, is also available.

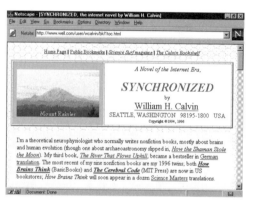

Figure 779.1 Synchronized, the novel.

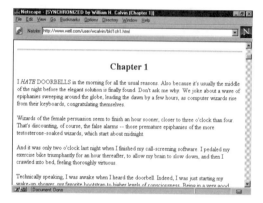

Figure 779.2 The start of the story.

780

JEFFREY ULLMAN

http://db.stanford.edu/~ullman/

Jeffrey Ullman is the co-author of some of the best reference books available, including *Elements of ML Programming*, *Foundations of Computer Science*, *Principles of Database and Knowledge-Base Systems*, *Compilers: Principles, Techniques and Tools*, *Introduction to Automata Theory, Languages and Computation*, and *The Deisgn and Analysis of Computer Algorithms*. Ullman is the Ascherman Professor of Computer Science at Stanford University. Visit this Web site for details on his latest publications, downloads of recent papers in Postscript format, and complete information on Ullman's recent research into database theory, database integration, data mining, and education using the information infrastructure.

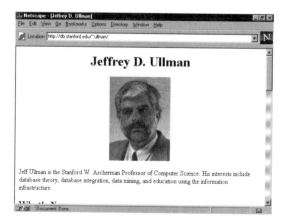

Figure 780 Sometimes mistaken for Robert E. Lee.

THE VIRTUAL COMMUNITY

http://www.well.com/user/hlr/vcbook/index.html

I will let Rheingold speak for himself. "I can see that thousands of people are reading or at least looking at each chapter of this book every month," writes Rheingold. "Excellent! I put these words out here for the Net without charge because I want to get as much good information distributed as possible right now about the nature of computer communications. But I am also competing with myself. Harper Collins' paperback edition pays me about a dollar a book. So, if you like what you read on-line, go out and buy a copy of the ink-and-dead-trees edition and give it to someone who needs to read this. Thanks! Your support will help me spend more time cooking up cool stuff to post here."

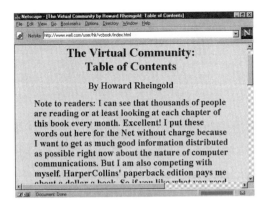

Figure 781.1 The Virtual Community.

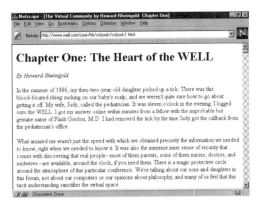

Figure 781.2 Some prose from Chapter 1.

THE WELL

http://www.well.com/

The Well is an on-line community started in 1985. Some have referred to the Well as the first civilization in cyberspace. It's a community with a strong sense of place and is populated by many of the most colorful people on the Net. The Well is best known for its hundreds of conferences and its knowledgeable customer support. When you visit the Web pages of The Well, you may take a tour to see exactly why The Well is the most celebrated on-line community around. Visit with some of the eccentric, brilliant, and beautiful Well members who publish some of their best stuff at the Well for the world to enjoy. And check out the Well Gopher, an acclaimed library of articles collected or authored by Well members.

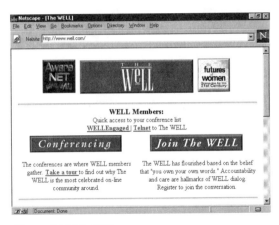

Figure 782 The Well.

783

WINSITE: THE PLANET'S LARGEST WINDOWS SOFTWARE ARCHIVE

http://www.winsite.com/

What's all the buzz about? Why has *www.hot100.com* placed WinSite in its list of the "Hot 100 Web sites" on the Internet? Why has PointCom (Point Survey) identified WinSite as being in the top 5% of all Web sites? Why, in October of 1996, did the Cool Staff at CoolCentral.Com designate WinSite as the "Cool Site of the Hour?" Well, perhaps the buzz is because WinSite is quite literally the world's largest software archive for Windows shareware anywhere on the Internet. WinSite emerged out of the former CICA Windows FTP archives, and is run by the three gentleman who founded that earlier, popular venture. Don't miss out on this site.

Figure 783.1 The WinSite Web site.

Figure 783.2 Hot software.

784

STEVE WOZNIAK

http://www.woz.org/Pages/staff/Steve/Steve.html

We all know the "Woz." He is nearly as famous as the "Fonz." Wozniak was, of course, the fellow who co-founded Apple Computer with Steve Jobs. He is now a happy and contented kabillionaire spending much of his copious free time teaching kids. You can see him do it via Wozcam, which you will find at Steve's Web site. Wozcam uses a video camera mounted in the classroom, *WebStar*, and a framesaver script that grabs images of what is going on in class and shoots those images into cyberspace. Other goodies you'll find at this site are details of Steve's role in founding Apple Computer, and information on other sordid enterprises he and Jobs had going before the Apple thing.

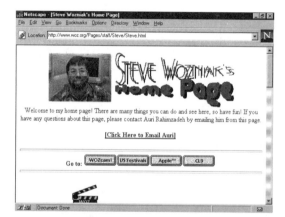

Figure 784 Steve Wozniak's home page.

AI CAFÉ C/C++ CGI HTML HTTP JAVA J++ PERL VBSCRIPT VRML WIN32 WINSOCK 11001101001011110011011100110101010001100110010101

3COM 3C590 ETHERNET DRIVER FOR FREEBSD

http://www.owlnet.rice.edu/~fgray/if_vx.html

Do you need to better understand 100Mps Ethernet cards? Fred Gray has written a driver for the 3Com 3c590 PCI-based Ethernet adapter. The driver is based heavily on the existing EtherLink III driver (*if_ep.c*) by Herb Peyerl, Andres Vega Garcia, Serge Babkin, and friends. Gray's driver is meant to be suitable as a basis for supporting the Fast EtherLink 100Mbps cards. Note that this should only be of interest to those using *FreeBSD 2.1* or earlier, as the driver is distributed with *FreeBSD-current and 2.2*. The driver interfaces are, of course, considerably different between these two versions of *FreeBSD*.

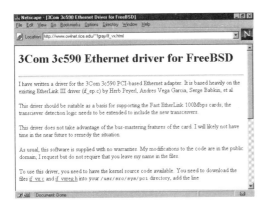

Figure 785.1 Driver information.

Figure 785.2 Author, author!

AI CAFÉ C/C++ CGI HTML HTTP JAVA J++ PERL VBSCRIPT VRML WIN32 WINSOCK 11001101001011110011011100110101010001100110010101

HOW TO AVOID 40 COMMON X-PROGRAMMING ERRORS

http://www.rahul.net/kenton/40errs.html

The *X-Window System* has come a long way since *Version 11* was first released in 1987. Now, thousands of *X*-programmers are developing thousands of *X*-applications. Together these *X*-programmers have probably made millions of programming errors, many of them the same programming errors, over and over again. In this valuable article, *X*-expert Kenton Lee reviews the 40 most common *X*-programming errors, and delineates methods for how to avoid them. The errors include design and style errors, syntax errors, usage errors, *X-Toolkit* usage errors, interoperability errors, and more. Save yourself some time, some grief and, perhaps, some embarrassment. Read Kenton Lee's article.

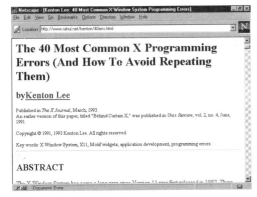

Figure 786.1 The title page.

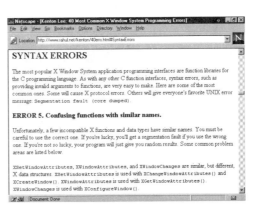

Figure 786.2 Syntax errors.

AIX FREQUENTLY ASKED QUESTIONS

http://euch6h.chem.emory.edu/services/aix-faq/

This great list of frequently asked *AIX* questions was pulled together by Frank Wortner. The questions cover general concepts, system administration, backups, memory, and process management, shells, commands, main pages, *InfoExplorer*, video, graphics, X11, networks and communications, *AIX 4.1*, and much more. You'll also find questions related to C/C++, FORTRAN and other compilers, GNU and public domain software for *AIX*, third party products for *AIX*, and much more. How do I make an informative prompt in the shell? How do I set up *ksh* for *emacs* mode command-line editing? How do I put my own text into *InfoExplorer*? Get the answers to these and other timely questions.

Figure 787.1 The questions.

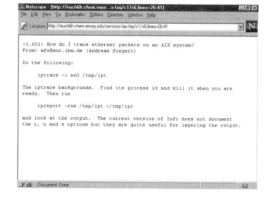

Figure 787.2 A question and an answer.

AIX PUBLIC DOMAIN SOFTWARE LIBRARY

http://aixpdslib.seas.ucla.edu/aixpdslib.html

This site is packed with public domain programs for *AIX 3.1.5*, *AIX 3.2*, and *AIX/ESA*. The programs include text formatters (including *TeX*), text editors (including *aXe*), desktops and X-Windows file managers (*fvwm, gwm, tvtwm, xdtm, xtdp, xfilemanager*, and *xfm*), spreadsheet programs (*oleo, ss, xspread*), mail programs (including *coolmail*), mail and news readers (including *elm, knews, mm, pine, rn, slrn, tin, trn*, and more), plotting tools (including *drawII, gnuplot, plotmtv, tgif, transfig, xfig, Xmgr*, and *xpaint*), FTP file browsers (including *archive, chimera, gopher, kermit, lynx, llnlxdir, llnlxftp, mftp, midaswww, ncftp, xarchie*), and more. If you use *AIX*, you can't afford to miss this site.

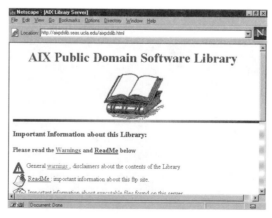

Figure 788 The AIX library.

AIXPORT

http://AIXPort.sut.ac.jp/

Visit this site for a great deal of technical information, documentation, and frequently asked questions from IBM and other sources, including the "AIX Guidebook," a great paper entitled "Performance Optimization with Enhanced RISC," and more. You will also find a fantastic collection of freeware and shareware for *AIX 4.1.x*, including some programs precompiled by the Information Processing Center at the University of Tokyo. These tools include *NCSA Mosaic for X-Windows*, a tool for querying Archie-anonymous FTP databases using *Prospero*, communications software for serial and network connections, DVI file utilities, and much more. The pages are available in English or Japanese.

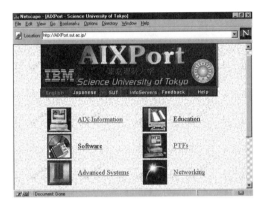

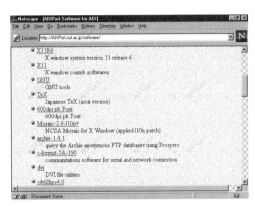

Figure 789.1 AIXPort.

Figure 789.2 Some software choices.

ANTICRACK: UNIX SECURITY

http://www.teu.ac.jp/siit/~tominaga/anticrack/

AntiCrack is a password checking program that checks raw (not encrypted) UNIX passwords, making it far faster than the *Crack* program. *AntiCrack* uses rules and dictionaries in the same manner as *Crack* does, so if you already use *Crack*, you can use your rules and dictionaries for *AntiCrack* as they are. *AntiCrack* is written in standard C. Visit this site for complete documentation on *AntiCrack*, a direct FTP link for downloading, and much more information. Note that the documentation is available in Japanese as well as English, since the software originates in Japan.

Figure 790 AntiCrack information.

APPLE NETWORK SERVERS FOR *AIX*

http://www.solutions.apple.com/products/NetServer

Designed from the ground up as high-performance servers for departmental networks, the Apple Network Servers 500 and 700 are the fastest, most powerful, reliable, and expandable servers Apple has ever developed. These servers run *AIX for Apple Network Servers*, a robust version of IBM's industry-standard *AIX* operating system. Apple has tuned *AIX* for these servers and has tightly integrated the servers running *AIX* with *MacOS* desktop computers. These Apple Network Servers are ideal for customers who currently use UNIX-based servers to support *MacOS* desktop systems, and those who are in mixed Mac, Windows, and UNIX environments. Visit this Web site for more information.

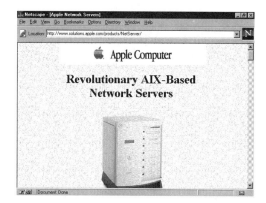

Figure 791.1 Server info from Apple.

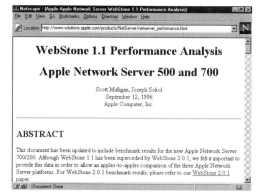

Figure 791.2 WebStone benchmarks.

THE ULTIMATE *HP-UX* TOOLBOX FOR WEB PUBLISHING

http://www.swcp.com/~fugelso/kelley/iworks95/

From a user's point-of-view, the Web is a wonderful place filled with information and entertainment. From the developer's point-of-view (from one who seeks to publish on the Web), it can be a scary place. The Web is filled with uncertainties, fraught with danger, and clogged with an overwhelming amount of informal (and often unreliable) documentation. The author of these Web pages has spent a lot of time learning which tools to use (and which not to use) to create Web documents in the HP-UX environment. At this site, she gathers links to those tools, along with her own very useful comments and documentation. Thank you, Kelley Fugelso.

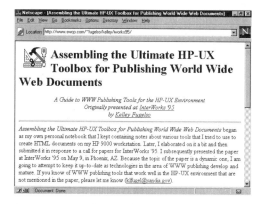

Figure 792.1 The initial page.

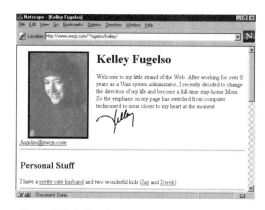

Figure 792.2 Your hostess.

ATM FOR LINUX

http://lrcwww.epfl.ch/linux-atm/

Come on. You like being on the cutting edge, don't you? You like noodling around with code and systems and applications with which no one else has as yet noodled. In that case, push the envelope and check out ATM for Linux. "ATM support for Linux is currently in the pre-alpha stage," writes the Webmaster. "There is an experimental release, which supports raw ATM connections (PVCs and SVCs), IP over ATM, LAN emulation, Arequipa, and some other goodies." At this site, you can download the distribution (including full source), along with complete documentation and other cool stuff. And you'll find a mailing list to which you can subscribe. The pre-alpha came out in September 1996. Check it out.

Figure 793.1 ATM for Linux.

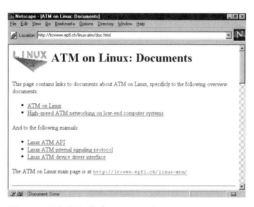

Figure 793.2 Full documentation.

MALCOLM BEATTIE'S PERL5 MASTERPIECES

http://users.ox.ac.uk/~mbeattie/perl.html

Malcolm Beattie is something of a Perl programming legend—a Leonardo of the language, a Michaelangelo. At this site, you can learn about and download some of his masterpieces, most of which you've probably heard of already. For example, you'll see such wonders as: the *Tk* extension, a native Perl object-oriented interface to John Oousterhout's *Tk GUI library*, and the *Safe* extension, which lets you create compartments within which you can evaluate your Perl in a restricted environment. Other extensions include *Tcl* (a small but complete interface into *libttcl* and other *Tcl*-based libraries), *Mmap* (lets you *mmap* in a file as a Perl variable on platforms that support *BSD* and *POSIX*), and many other items. If you are into Perl, don't miss this site.

Figure 794 Malcolm Beattie's stuff.

BERKELEY SOFTWARE DESIGN, INC.

http://www.bsdi.com/

Berkeley Software Design, Inc. (BSDI) designs, develops, markets, and supports high-performance Internet and network server software for Internet service providers, corporate users, and embedded system vendors. Their most popular product is the *BSD/386* operating system, a full-function, *POSIX*-compatible, UNIX-like system based on the BSD software from the University of California at Berkeley, combined with components engineered by BSDI. Based in Colorado, BSDI continues to develop and advance the *BDS/OS* as the underlying platform for advanced computing. Check it out.

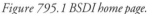

Figure 795.1 BSDI home page.

Figure 795.2 What's hot.

CALDERA: LINUX DEVELOPMENT SOLUTIONS

http://www.caldera.com/

Caldera is a Utah corporation founded in 1994. Caldera's goal is to create and integrate easy to use network-aware software, and to distribute, support, and sell that software via the Internet, as well as through more traditional channels. The core of all this is the *Caldera Network Desktop* system, which is an operating environment based on the *Linux* operating system combined with numerous value-added components such as a full-featured desktop metaphor and *NetWare* client. Their products also include the *Caldera Internet Office Suite*, and the *Caldera WordPerfect & Motif Bundle*. Visit this Web site for more information.

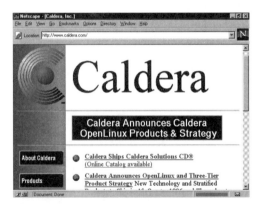

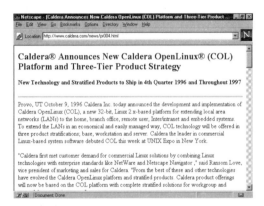

Figure 796.1 The Caldera Web site.

Figure 796.2 A news release.

CGI: COMMON GATEWAY INTERFACE

http://hoohoo.ncsa.uiuc.edu/cgi/overview.html

The Common Gateway Interface (CGI) is a standard for interfacing external applications with information servers, such as HTTP or Web servers. Normally, when you visit a Web site that displays and processes a form, that site is using CGI. In other words, when the user submits the form, the server runs a special program, a CGI-based program that processes the form. After the program examines the form's contents, the form can display another form. Visit this site for specifics on the CGI interface. Also, most programmers write their CGI scripts in Perl. If you are truly interested in CGI, examine this book's index for sites that discuss Perl.

Figure 797.1 The CGI Web site.

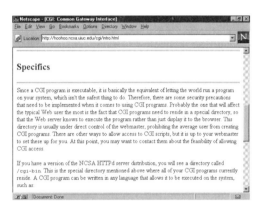

Figure 797.2 A CGI Primer.

CGI-LIB.PL HOME PAGE

http://www.bio.cam.ac.uk/cgi-lib/

The *cgi-lib.pl* library has become the defacto standard library for creating CGI (Common Gateway Interface) scripts using the Perl programming language. This site is the official Web site for *cgi-lib.pl*—the place where you can find the most up-to-date releases of the library. The *cgi-lib.pl* library makes CGI scripting in Perl easy enough for anyone to process forms and create dynamic Web content. The library is designed for operation under Perl5 and Perl4, is compatible with all CGI interactions, offers convenient utility functions, and is compatible with Perl5 security features (such as *taint*). The library also includes sophisticated debugging facilities, and is a good starting point for migration to more sophisticated libraries. If you are just getting started with CGI, make sure you have the *cgi-lib.pl* file at your disposal.

Figure 798.1 The home page.

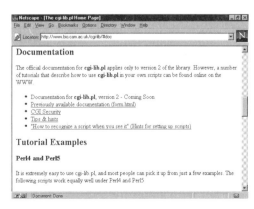

Figure 798.2 Documentation.

CMU SNMP FOR LINUX: USER'S GUIDE

http://www.cis.ufl.edu/~dadavis/cmu-snmp.html

SNMP (Simple Network Management Protocol) is an Internet standard for exchanging network management information. This site at CMU (Carnegie Mellon University) provides you with a free, downloadable implementation of SNMP which Juergen Schoenwaelder and Erik Schoenfelder have ported to *Linux*. The current version of CMU SNMP is 2.1.2. At this site, you will find the complete technical documentation for CMU SNMP, together with direct FTP links for downloading the application. The supporting documentation is easy-to-understand, in-depth, and to-the-point. All in all, this is a first-rate bit of software and a first-rate job of documenting software. Well done!

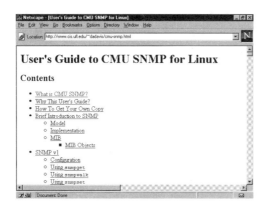

Figure 799.1 Table of Contents.

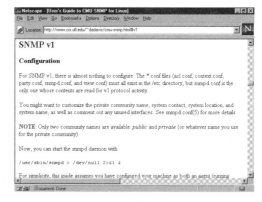

Figure 799.2 A section of the tutorial.

COMMON LISP HYPERMEDIA SERVER

http://www.ai.mit.edu/projects/iiip/doc/cl-http/home-page.html

OK kids, release 60.53 is now available, free! This is a Web server implemented in Common LISP in order to facilitate exploratory programming in the interactive hypermedia domain and to provide access to complex research programs, particularly AI systems. The server was initially used to provide interfaces for document retrieval and for e-mail servers. More advanced applications include interfaces to systems for inductive rule learning and natural-language question answering. Continuing research seeks to more fully generalize automatic form-processing techniques developed for e-mail servers to operate seamlessly on the Web. Visit this site for the software with source code, along with extensive documentation. If you have ever programmed in LISP, you know this site took considerable programming expertise.

Figure 800.1 The Common Lisp Server.

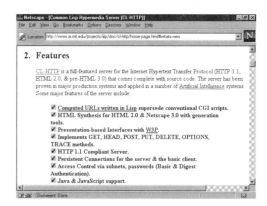

Figure 800.2 Details.

AI CAFÉ C/C++ CGI HTML HTTP JAVA J++ PERL VBSCRIPT VRML WIN32 WINSOCK 110011010010111100110111001101010100011001100100101

COMPETITIVE AUTOMATION: JOIN TECHNOLOGY

http://www.join.com/

Competitive Automation is the industry leader in DHCP (Dynamic Host Configuration Protocol) technology. With its *JOIN* product, Competitive Automation provides turnkey solutions to customers in need of simple, centralized IP (Internet Protocol) administration. By adopting the DHCP industry standard, *JOIN* delivers centralized IP administration in heterogeneous networks with machines running different operating systems and hardware platforms. Networks supported by *JOIN* range from a small LAN to enterprise-wide networks with thousands of nodes. *JOIN* is available for *Sun OS, Solaris, Digital UNIX,* and *HP-UX*. Visit this Web site for more information.

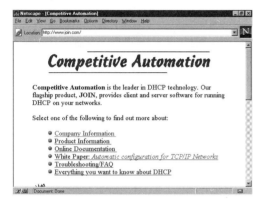

Figure 801.1 Competitive Automation.

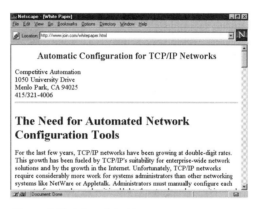

Figure 801.2 A useful white paper.

AI CAFÉ C/C++ CGI HTML HTTP JAVA J++ PERL VBSCRIPT VRML WIN32 WINSOCK 110011010010111100110111001101010100011001100100101

DEBIAN GNU/LINUX

http://www.debian.org/

Debian *GNU/Linux* is a complete UNIX-compatible operating system for IBM-PC and compatible machines with an 80386. Debian *GNU/Linux* uses the *Linux* kernel and includes hundreds of software packages, such as most GNU software, *TeX*, and the *X-Window System* (*XFree86* version). Debian *GNU/Linux* is best known for its upgradability. You can upgrade the software incrementally and "in place," which means you can upgrade individual packages or entire systems as software becomes available, without having to reformat and reinstall. Visit this Web site for more information on *GNU/Linux*.

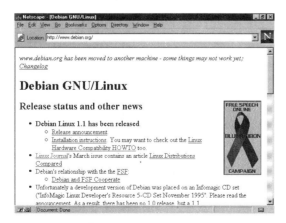

Figure 802 Debian GNU/Linux.

DEBUGGING X-WINDOW SYSTEM PROTOCOL ERRORS

http://www.rahul.net/kenton/perrors.html

X-protocol errors are common symptoms of *X-Window System* application programming bugs. This Web site discusses simple, but unusually efficient, techniques for understanding *X*-protocol errors and correcting the associated programming problems. Other topics you will find in this site's article address synchronization, stack trace, combining stack trace and error-message data, subroutine libraries, and error messages as they relate to subroutine libraries. The article discusses the data presented in the error message, techniques for identifying the particular line of code in your program that is associated with the error, and how to use the *X*-documentation to find the specific problem within that line of code. If you work in the *X-Window* environment, don't miss this article.

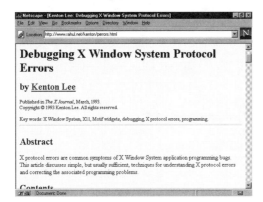

Figure 803.1 Title page.

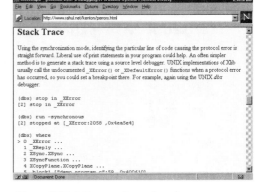

Figure 803.2 Prose and sample code.

DIGITAL UNIX INFORMATION CENTER

http://www.unix.digital.com/

Digital *UNIX 4.0* and the DEC (Digital Equipment Corporation) Alpha architecture deliver full, native 64-bit computing. While other UNIX vendors rush to catch up, Digital offers one easy step to a modern computing solution that will carry you into the next century. With its advanced operating system features, Digital UNIX is a modern operating system designed to handle both commercial and technical computing needs equally well. Furthermore, because Digital UNIX is a standard-compliant UNIX operating system, it protects your investment by providing an integrated environment that works with new and existing platforms. Visit this Web site for more information on a state-of-the-art operating system.

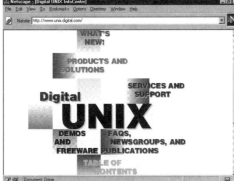

Figure 804.1 Digital UNIX.

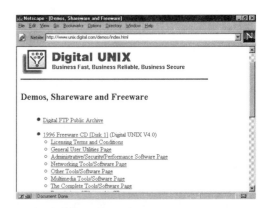

Figure 804.2 Demos and freeware.

AI CAFÉ C/C++ CGI HTML HTTP JAVA J++ PERL VBSCRIPT VRML WIN32 WINSOCK 11001101001011110011011100110101010001100110010010

DONOHUE'S RS/6000 PAGE

http://www.s6000.com/

Donohue's RS/6000 Page is dedicated to providing information about IBM RS/6000 third-party vendors and products. These products and vendors include hardware, software, and services, as well as job opportunities. The Web site also provides on-line catalogs and a wealth of information and links about RS/6000 systems. Of course, IBM RS/6000 is the acronym for the IBM RISC System/6000—a series of computers ranging from notebook to mainframe-sized systems with an architecture originally targeted for technical opportunities like numerically intensive applications. These RISC-based machines have an open architecture and utilize a UNIX-based operating system. Visit Donohue's pages for more information.

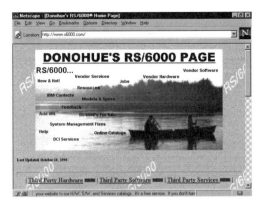

Figure 805.1 Donohue's RS/6000 Page.

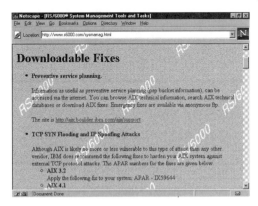

Figure 805.2 Downloadable fixes.

AI CAFÉ C/C++ CGI HTML HTTP JAVA J++ PERL VBSCRIPT VRML WIN32 WINSOCK 11001101001011110011011100110101010001100110010010

EST: ENHANCED SOFTWARE TECHNOLOGIES

http://www.estinc.com/

Enhanced Software Technologies (EST) is the maker of *BRU* (*Reliable Backup Utility* for the UNIX operating system). EST has been selling *BRU* for several years and offers versions of it for almost every version of UNIX and UNIX-like operating systems available today. *BRU* is a command-line utility that uses a syntax similar to *tar*. In fact, if you already have a legacy of *tar*-based backup scripts, you can simply replace all instances of *tar* in your script with *bru* and continue using the same scripts! Then, as you become more comfortable with the many optional features *BRU* provides over standard *tar*, you can updgrade your old scripts. Convenient.

Figure 806.1 EST's Bru page.

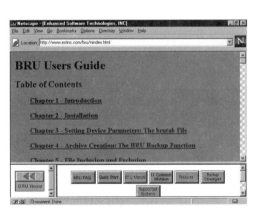

Figure 806.2 BRU Users Guide.

EXCLAIM!—X-WINDOWS SPREADSHEET

http://www.unipress.com/cat/exclaim.html

eXclaim is a fast, easy-to-use spreadsheet designed for *X-Windows*. This full-featured UNIX-based spreadsheet offers excellent performance and advanced *X*-features including mouse control, pull-down menus, scroll bars, dialog boxes, and *X*-graphics. The spreadsheet is fast too, recalculating in a fraction of the time required by other spreadsheets. The package accepts standard files from a range of other spreadsheet applications, including *Lotus* and *Excel. eXclaim* ports not only their files, but also their macros, allowing continued use of existing spreadsheet models. Furthermore, *eXclaim* includes a full complement of mathematical, statistical, and logical functions, as well as the ability to filter data through other applications.

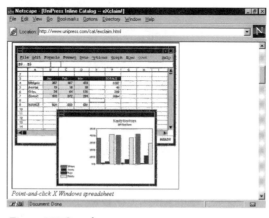

Figure 807 Sample screens.

FREEBSD CCD DRIVER

http://stampede.cs.berkeley.edu/ccd/

As its author tells us, the "concatenated disk (*ccd*) driver will let you concatenate multiple disk partitions into one 'virtual' disk. You can either concatenate them serially or stripe across them. The stripe unit ('interleave size' in *ccd* terminology) is configurable to optimize performance." The *ccd* driver for *FreeBSD* is robust but is still alpha quality, so beware. At this site, you will find versions for *FreeBSD-2.1, FreeBSD-2.1.5, FreeBSD-stable*, and *FreeBSD-current*. An earlier version of this same driver was included in the original *VSD* from the University of California. You will find a link at this site to Jason Thorpe's version of the driver for *NetBSD*, which includes added dynamic configuration and disk-label support.

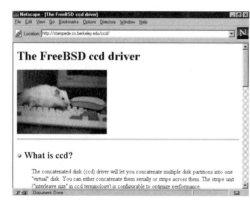

Figure 808.1 Mousing around.

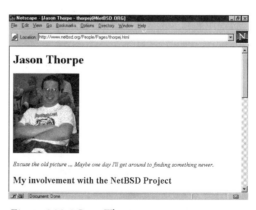

Figure 808.2 Jason Thorpe.

AI CAFÉ C/C++ CGI HTML HTTP JAVA J++ PERL VBSCRIPT VRML WIN32 WINSOCK 11001101001011110011011100110101010001100110010010

FreeBSD Home Page

http://www.freebsd.org/

FreeBSD is a non-*Linux* free *UNIX* alternative. It is an advanced *BSD UNIX* operating system for PC-compatible computers which offers an exceptional combination of features. *FreeBSD* provides excellent support for TCP/IP networking and makes an ideal Internet server or desktop system. In short, *FreeBSD* provides robust network services even under the heaviest loads. Throughout it all, *FreeBSD* uses memory efficiently to maintain good response times for hundreds, or even thousands, of simultaneous user processes. It also provides advanced features for performance, security, and even binary compatibility with other popular operating systems. Check out *FreeBSD*.

Figure 809.1 The FreeBSD Web site.

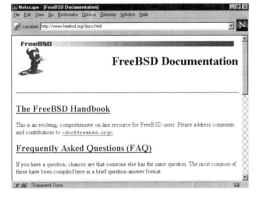

Figure 809.2 Documentation.

AI CAFÉ C/C++ CGI HTML HTTP JAVA J++ PERL VBSCRIPT VRML WIN32 WINSOCK 11001101001011110011011100110101010001100110010010

Free Software for Digital UNIX

http://www.digital.com/info/misc/pub-domain-osf1.txt.html

This site contains a dynamic list of pointers that have been sent in from users around the world who have made software for *Digital UNIX* available free to other users over the Internet. Browse these offerings and take whatever you'd like. Also, if you have any freeware that you'd care to register for listing at this site, you'll find details on how to do that right on-line. The offerings include a device-independent network-transparent audio server, a new tool for fast text searching allowing errors, an easy-to-install user-level NFS (network file system) server that provides transparent file-system access to FTP sites, and an *autonice daemon* which lowers the priorities of long-lived jobs. Visit this site for more information.

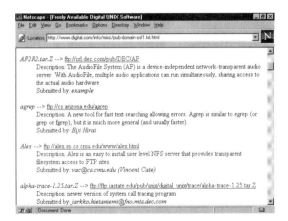

Figure 810 Free software.

811

Freeware Drivers

http://www.3am-software.com/

3am Software is actually Matt Thomas, who has graciously written and makes available several freeware PC network adapters for *FreeBSD, NetBSD, BSDI's VSD/OS,* and *Novell's UnixWare 2.0.* Of course, like all freeware, this stuff comes with a caveat: "This is purely a hobby and is completely unrelated to my real job," writes Matt. "That means that if my drivers don't work, corrupt your data, or cause 'the end of the world as we know it,' it's not my fault!" Still, while Matt doesn't guarantee to fix all reported problems, he does try to do so in a timely manner. "However, problems are often due to broken hardware or brain-dead BIOS; and those I can't fix." This is cool stuff. Thanks, Matt.

Figure 811.1 3am Software's home page.

Figure 811.2 Useless information.

812

GNU's Not Unix

http://www.cs.pdx.edu:80/~trent/gnu/

No, *GNU* is not UNIX. But it is pretty darn close. At this site, you will find links for getting *GNU* software, along with extensive documentation and technical support, as well as information on mailing lists, and so on. This site is the brainchild of Richard Stallman, who has long lived with the goal of creating a free operating system that people can use and improve on. In so doing, Stallman has established a worldwide community of people sharing software. Stallman chose to model his effort on AT&T's proprietary UNIX operating system. Hence, the project's tail-chasing name: *GNU's Not Unix.* In this connection, Stallman is the author of *Emacs,* the extensible text editor for UNIX. Visit this site for more information.

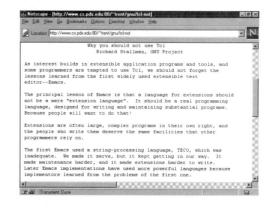

Figure 812.1 GNU's not Unix!

Figure 812.2 Why you should not use Tcl.

AI CAFÉ C/C++ CGI HTML HTTP JAVA J++ PERL VBSCRIPT VRML WIN32 WINSOCK 11001101001011110011011100110101010001100110010101

GOLDMEDAL UNIX SOFTWARE

http://www.goldmedal.com/gm/

Are you looking for off-the-shelf UNIX solutions for business computing? GoldMedal offers UNIX groupware, e-mail, and office solutions. In fact, they provide seven software configurations of easy to use and install applications for most major variants of UNIX. Their groupware suite features electronic mail, group scheduling and calendars, resource management, cooperative documentation, software integration, menu customization, a personal information manager, and a sophisticated text editor. Additional products include an excellent personal and departmental relational database, a superior word processing/editing tool for the construction of simple or complex documents, and a multi-dimensional (3-D) spreadsheet using *X-Window* graphics.

Figure 813 GoldMedal home page.

AI CAFÉ C/C++ CGI HTML HTTP JAVA J++ PERL VBSCRIPT VRML WIN32 WINSOCK 11001101001011110011011100110101010001100110010101

GRAPHICS EFFECTS BY MANIPULATING X COLORMAPS

http://www.rahul.net/kenton/colormap.html

Most *X-Window* system programs use some color graphics. Most of these programs generate their graphics using traditional raster-manipulation (bitmapped or pixel-based graphics) techniques. Raster manipulation is easily understood but, unfortunately, it doesn't always give satisfactory results. This tutorial presents some alternatives based on colormap manipulation. Colormap-manipulation techniques supplement, and sometimes replace, raster manipulation techniques. Depending on the application, colormap manipulation may significantly improve performance and prevent undesirable graphic artifacts. This great tutorial comes from *X*-maven Kenton Lee.

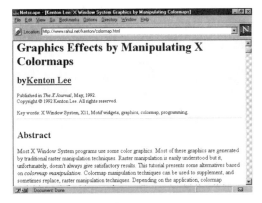

Figure 814.1 The title page.

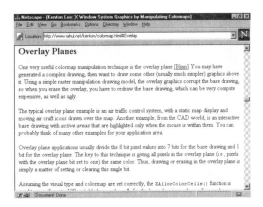

Figure 814.2 Overlay planes.

HP-UX Software Porting & Archive

http://hpux.cae.wisc.edu/

This great software archive is maintained by the Model Advanced Facility at the College of Engineering, University of Wisconsin, Madison. The archive includes nine distributed-computing software packages, thirty-five public domain text and binary editors, forty-nine games that involve arcade-style action, and forty-five pieces of GNU software (with ports to HP-UX, if necessary). You will also find fifty public domain compilers, interpreters and translators, fourteen mathematics packages in the subject of linear algebra, twenty-seven programs for network administration, twelve programs which deal specifically with FTP, and much more. Kind of sounds like the "Twelve Days of Christmas."

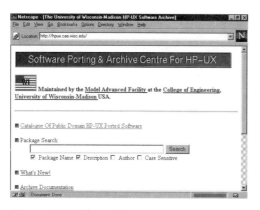

Figure 815.1 The archive.

Figure 815.2 The newest package in the archive.

Hypermail 1.02: Freeware

http://www.eit.com/software/hypermail/hypermail.html

Are you looking for an easier way to read, respond, and potentially browse your e-mail? *Hypermail* is a program that takes a file of mail messages in a UNIX mailbox format and generates a set of cross-referenced HTML documents. Each file the software creates represents a separate message in the mail archive and contains links to other articles, so the user can browse the entire archive in a number of ways by following links. In addition, *Hypermail* will convert references in each message to e-mail addresses (so you can quickly send a response) and convert URLs to hyperlinks (so you can browse the corresponding link). Furthermore, four index files are created which sort articles by date, thread, subject, and author.

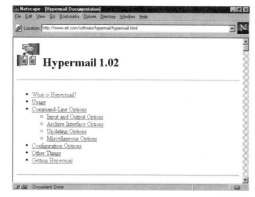

Figure 816.1 Hypermail.

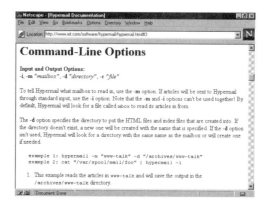

Figure 816.2 Command-line options.

AI CAFÉ C/C++ CGI HTML HTTP JAVA J++ PERL VBSCRIPT VRML WIN32 WINSOCK 11001101001011110011011100110101010001100110010010

"INDIRECT" MOTIF WIDGET RESOURCES

http://www.rahul.net/kenton/m_res.html

"Many Motif features are controlled by 'indirect' widget resources," writes Kenton Lee. Indirect widget resources allow one widget to control the behavior of another widget. "These resources are well documented," writes Lee, "though perhaps not where you might normally look." In this article, Lee discusses places in the Motif documentation where you should look for resources such as these. He also gives examples of some of the most confusing indirect resources. The article includes discussions of super class resources, parent class resources, and combination and convenience widgets. I know of no other discussion of this arcane aspect of Motif that is so incisive and so complete. Go for it.

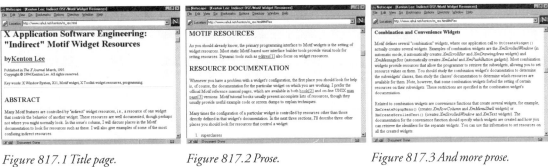

Figure 817.1 Title page.   Figure 817.2 Prose.   Figure 817.3 And more prose.

AI CAFÉ C/C++ CGI HTML HTTP JAVA J++ PERL VBSCRIPT VRML WIN32 WINSOCK 11001101001011110011011100110101010001100110010010

IRIX 5.3 FROM SILICON GRAPHICS

http://www.sgi.com/Products/software/5.3.announce.html

IRIX 5.3 is an operating system from Silicon Graphics that features paralleled TCP/IP, improved virtual memory performance, kernel tuning for databases, outstanding NFS performance, caching file system support, enhanced IO4 serial driver performance, and superior digital media tools. The system is upwardly compatible revision of *IRIX 5* (which incorporates substantial functionality from *UNIX System V, Release 4.1* and *4.2*). *IRIX 5.3* is available on all Silicon Graphics computers, and was designed to preserve customer software investments by providing binary compatibility with applications developed under earlier versions of IRIX 5. Visit this Web site for more information.

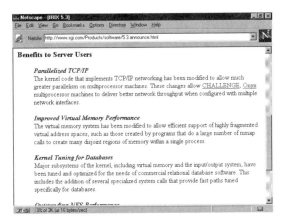

Figure 818 IRIX benefits to service users.

819

ISDN FOR LINUX

http://alumni.caltech.edu/dank/isdn/isdn_sw.html

Two sets of widely used ISDN solutions exist for *Linux*. The first set embraces external solutions, such as ISDN terminal adapters or ISDN/IP routers. These are not *Linux*-specific and, hence, are not addressed at this Web site. Instead, this site addresses *Linux*-specific solutions (the second set of solutions) such as *isdn4linux*, a *Linux* device driver for Teles-compatible cards and the ICN ISDN card which has been a standard part of the *Linux* kernel for a while now. Other tools addressed include Joel Kat's driver for the Combinet EVERYWARE 1000 series, the *Sonix Volante PC ISDN driver*, and the *SpellCaster DataCommute/BRI device drivers*. Many thanks to Harold Milz for this useful set of pages and links.

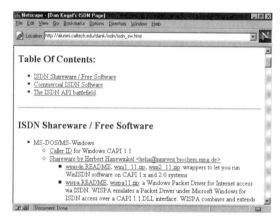

Figure 819 ISDN shareware and freeware.

820

JAGUBOX'S A/UX HOME PAGE

http://jagubox.gsfc.nasa.gov/aux/

This Web site is packed with *A/UX* explanations, solutions, and tools. At this site, you will find an extensive list of frequently asked questions, a host of Apple-supplied fixes for various 3.0 binaries, dozens of patched or new daemons for use under *A/UX*, various GNU-stuff (everything from patches to complete ports) that's been ported for *A/UX*, an extensive collection of patches for various packages that enable them to compile/run under *A/UX*, and more. You also get Apple technical-notes for *A/UX* in MS-Word format, a directory of important security-related tools, tutorials, and helpful utilities for use under *A/UX*. Many thanks to Jim Jaagielski for a very useful resource.

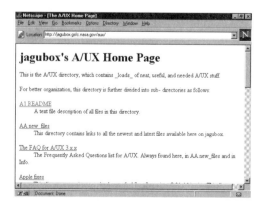

Figure 820.1 jagubox's home page.

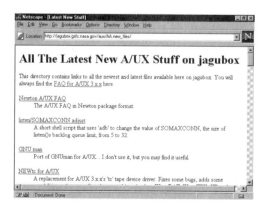

Figure 820.2 Newly added files.

JAVA-LINUX

http://www.blackdown.org/java-linux.html

Focusing on the *Java Development Kit 1.0.2* (*JDK 1.0.2*) for *Linux*, this Web site answers a host of questions such as: which libraries do I need? Where can I find more information on *ELF*? Where and how do I get *JDK* for Linux? What are the bugs, and how do I fix 'em? You will also find cool tools, including replacement scripts and a *Linux-ELF* version of the native libraries required for Marimba's *bongo* and *castanet* packages. All of these wonderful resources have been marshaled for you, with goodness of spirit and purity of heart, by Karl Asha, who clearly has a firm grasp of exactly where the future of *Linux* lays.

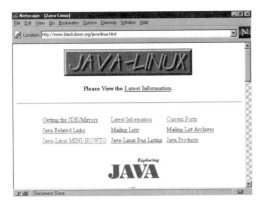

Figure 821.1 Java-Linux information.

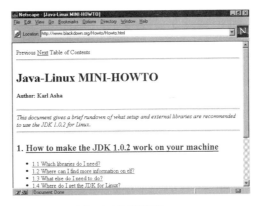

Figure 821.2 A mini HOWTO.

LIBWWW-PERL

http://www.ics.uci.edu/pub/websoft/libwww-perl/

"*libwww-perl,*" the author informs us, "is a library of Perl packages/modules which provide a simple and consistent programming interface to the World Wide Web. This library is being developed as a collaborative effort to assist the further development of useful WWW clients and tools." This library is freeware. The *libwww-perl* software architecture and standard distribution package are copyrighted by the University of California, but only for the sole purpose of retaining consistency and coherence in the distribution of the library. The library strongly encourages contributions, which it will include in the standard package with full citation to the developers. If you work with Perl, don't miss this Web site.

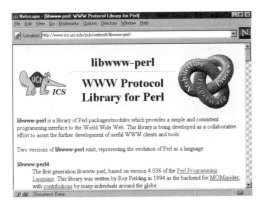

Figure 822.1 libwww-perl.

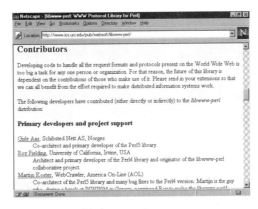

Figure 822.2 Tis better to give ...

LINUX HOME PAGE

http://www.linux.org/

Linux. We've all learned to love it—and not just for its price tag. As you may know, *Linux* is a free, distributable implementation of UNIX for the *x86*, Motorola 68K, Digital Alpha, and Motorola PowerPC machines. *Linux* supports a wide range of software, including *X-Windows*, *Emacs*, and TCP/IP networking (including SLIP/PPP/ISDN). *Linux* was originally written by Linus Torvalds of Helsinki, Finland. After just two years, *Linux* has become one of the most popular free UNIXs available, and is continually being developed and improved by *Linux* and teams of people all around the world. Come here for a download and extensive documentation.

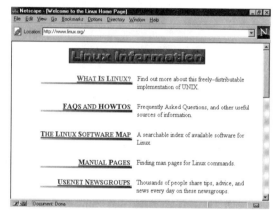

Figure 823 Linux information.

LINUX 2.x INFORMATION HEADQUARTERS

http://www.ecsnet.com/

This site is loaded with great links and information. Visit this site to learn what is new with *Linux 2.x*, how to upgrade from version *1.2* to *2.x*, other programs that need upgrading along with *Linux*, and much more. You will also get several major how-to documents and mini-how-tos, great mailing list archives, and *Linux* documentation files. Add to that *Linux 2.x* patches that include kernel patches and unofficial patches complete with source code. In addition, you also get links to exceptional sites related to *Linux* security, *Linux SMP*, the Kernel Configuration Database, the Kernel Hacker's Interactive Guide, *Linux's* Favorite Penguin logo, and much more.

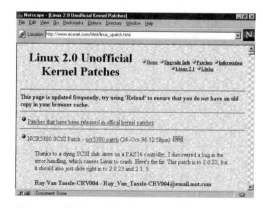

Figure 824.1 More Linux information.   *Figure 824.2 Unofficial patches.*

AI CAFÉ C/C++ CGI HTML HTTP JAVA J++ PERL VBSCRIPT VRML WIN32 WINSOCK 1100110100101111001101110011010101000110011001001101

THE LINUX CONFIGURATION PAGE

http://www.hal-pc.org/~david/linux/linux.config.html

Need help installing *Linux*? Like to get your hands on some custom configuration files to make your job shorter and your life easier? Turn to the *Linux* Configuration Page. At this site, you'll find both desktop and laptop configurations. You will also find configuration information for Pentium-based processors, Zeos 486 DX2/66 machines, 386-based machines, and much, much more. Others have spent hours, days, weeks, and months confronting the technical glitches that confront you. Others have already solved the configuration problems that threaten your sanity, if not your livelihood. Why labor needlessly? Why pit your wits against unforgiving systems when you've got a cheat-sheet waiting for you at the *Linux* Configuration Page?

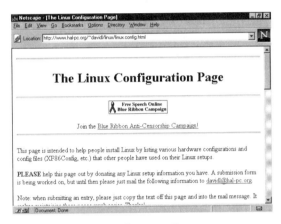

Figure 825 Linux Configuration Page.

AI CAFÉ C/C++ CGI HTML HTTP JAVA J++ PERL VBSCRIPT VRML WIN32 WINSOCK 1100110100101111001101110011010101000110011001001101

THE LINUX DOCUMENTATION PROJECT

http://sunsite.unc.edu/mdw/linux.html

This site features the Web's premier clearinghouse of links and information related to *Linux*. Visit this site for lists of frequently asked questions, information sheets, newsgroups, user groups, mailing lists, and related links. You will also encounter *Linux* documentation, as well as books that include *Installation and Getting Started, Kernel Hackers' Guide, Network Administrator's Guide, Programmer's Guide, System Administrator's Guide*, and the *Linux Users' Guide*. You will also get links to "how-to" pages, as well as links to more than a hundred *Linux*-related sites on the Web. This is a site that every serious *Linux* user will want to bookmark.

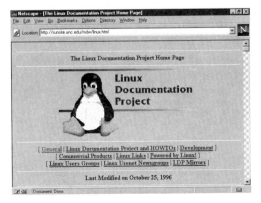

Figure 826.1 Linux Documentation Project.

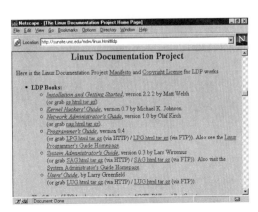

Figure 826.2 Books available on-line.

Linux ELF How To

http://www.sjc.ox.ac.uk/users/barlow/elf-howto.html

This site features documents that describe how to migrate your *Linux* system to compile and run programs in the *ELF* binary format. The tutorial considers what *ELF* is, whether you should upgrade, and why. It explains how to upgrade to *ELF*. And, it gives you a blow-by-blow description of exactly how to go about getting the job done, covering the installation, how to build programs using *ELF*, the Zen of patches and binaries, and more. The tutorial is packed with examples, source code, and case studies. It leaves nothing abstract. Everything is made concrete through the force of good, strong, robust examples. And this magnifies the value of the exercise tenfold.

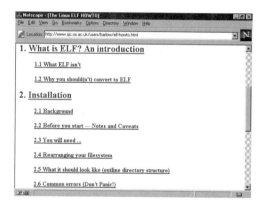

Figure 827.1 Table of Contents.

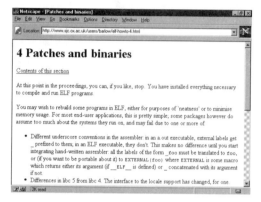

Figure 827.2 Some prose.

Linux FSSTND (aka, FHS)

http://www.pathname.com/fhs/

So, what goes where, and why? Inquiring minds want to know. *Linux FSSTND* (File System Standard)is available at this site in HTML, PostScript, DVI, and plain text formats. *FSSTND*, as this page tells us, "specifies a standard file-system structure for *Linux* systems, including the location of files and directories, and the contents of some system files. Just to make things good and confusing, *FSSTND* is also referred to as the File-system Hierarchy Standard (FHS). Daniel Quinlan, a fine Irishman, maintains these pages on *FSSTND* (or FHS, take your pick), not that there ever was an Irishman who wasn't quite fine.

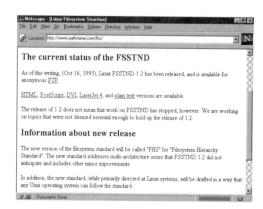

Figure 828.1 The current status.

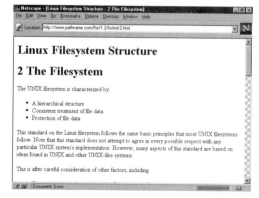

Figure 828.2 Filesystem details.

LINUX GAZETTE

http://www.redhat.com/linux-info/lg/gazette_toc.html

An official member of the *Linux* documentation project, the *Linux Gazette* says its mission is to make Linux "just a little more fun," while at the same time sharing ideas and discoveries. The basic idea behind these two concepts is that *Linux* is one cool operating system, whose price for admission is a willingness to read, learn, tinker (a.k.a, *hack*!), and then share your experiences. Designed to facilitate this process, the *Gazette* is a witty compilation of basic tips, tricks, suggestions, ideas, and short articles. The *Gazette* started out as a personal project of John M. Fisk, but has grown to include contributions provided free by a growing number of Linux authors. *Linux Gazette* is a non-commercial, free publication.

Figure 829.1 *Linux Gazette.*

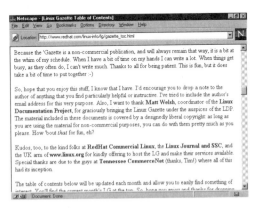

Figure 829.2 *Some prose.*

LINUX INTERNATIONAL

http://www.li.org/linux-int/

"Just as the *Linux* operating system fits in with most kinds of computers without costs," write the Webmasters, "so we at *Linux* International help *Linux* users and *Linux* itself without making a profit. The volunteers who created *Linux* are now joined by volunteers who specialize in promoting it. We know how good *Linux* is and want it to become an accepted competitor to products from the largest computer companies." But *Linux* International is much more than just an advertising organization. As well as promoting the existing advantages and compatibility of *Linux*, they also coordinate development projects and support the creation of top-drawer documentation. If you use or are thinking of using *Linux*, visit this site.

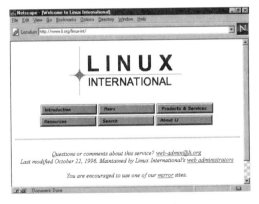

Figure 830.1 *Linux International.*

Figure 830.2 *Late breaking Linux news.*

831

THE LINUX LAPTOP HOME PAGE

http://www.cs.utexas.edu/users/kharker/linux-laptop/

This site features several how-to style documents that describe the *Linux* setup and configuration for specific brands of notebooks. You will find those how-tos listed in alphabetical order by vendor name. The laptops these how-tos cover include the AST 900N, AT&T Globalyst 200S, Compaq 430C, Compaq Concerto, Compaq Contura Aero, Dell Latitude, Digital, Epson Action Note 910C, EPS Technologies Apex XL-133, Gateway 2000 Solo, HP Omnibook, IBM Thinkpad, Micron Millennia Transport, NEC Versa, Olivetti Echos, ProStar NP5200, Samsung SENS810, Sharp PC 8600 and 8800 series, Tadpole P1000 Series, Texas Instruments Extensa, Toshiba Satellite, Toshiba 2100 series, and many other machines. If *Linux* is making its way to your laptop, check out this site.

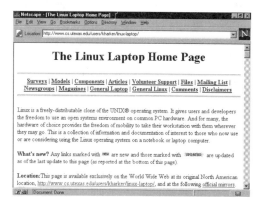

Figure 831.1 The Linux Laptop home page.   *Figure 831.2 Articles and presentations.*

832

LINUX LIBRARY

http://www.redhat.com/linux-info/lg/linux_library.html

The Web is crowded with *Linux* pages filled with links to frequently asked *Linux* questions and how-tos. The *Linux* Library is, according to its editor, an attempt to pull together the rest of the documents that have been written about *Linux* and that lay neglected in the furthest outposts of cyberspace. The *Linux* Library brings together software documentation for various problems which are not usually addressed by other *Linux* sites. The *Linux* Library also includes links to major archive sites for the larger software packages such as *XFree86*, the *Andrew User Interface System (AUIS)*, *TeX* and *LaTeX*, *InterViews*, and several others.

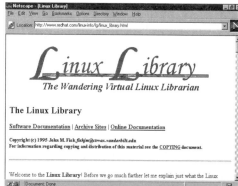
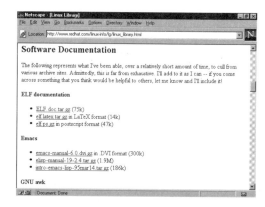

Figure 832.1 Linux Library.   *Figure 832.2 Software documentation.*

AI CAFÉ C/C++ CGI HTML HTTP JAVA J++ PERL VBSCRIPT VRML WIN32 WINSOCK 11001101001011110011011100110101010001100110010010

THE LINUX MACHINE

http://www.visi.com/~hjeand/Linux.html

This site offers another wonderful clearinghouse of news, information, and software for *Linux* users. Andrew Hjelle created and maintains the *Linux* Machine. At this site, you will find general information, news and newsgroups, books and documentation, on-line help desks, mailing lists, and links to software. I especially like the how-to files, which include a boot prompt how-to, a boot disk how-to, a bus mouse how-to, a *Linux ELF* how-to, a *Linux* Ethernet how-to, and also how-tos related to fire walls, hardware computability, and more. Note: this site is international and multilingual, incorporating English, Danish, German, Hebrew, and other languages.

Figure 833.1 The Machine.

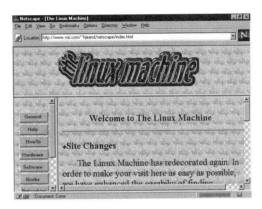

Figure 833.2 The Machine, framed.

AI CAFÉ C/C++ CGI HTML HTTP JAVA J++ PERL VBSCRIPT VRML WIN32 WINSOCK 11001101001011110011011100110101010001100110010010

LINUX MEMORY SAVERS

http://rsphy1.anu.edu.au/~gpg109/mem.html

Lots of people out there are running Linux on 386 boxes with 4Mb RAM and older hard disks. The patches available at this site implement options that will let such users trim some excess (unused) functionality from their kernels and reclaim some of that valuable memory for running applications. (Note that memory taken up by the kernel can't be swapped to disk; thus, it reduces the amount of real memory available to run user programs and the like.) Most of these patches are against the current *1.2.13* kernel, as that is quite a bit smaller than the *1.3.x* development kernels to begin with. These patches come from Paul Gortmaker. Thanks, Paul.

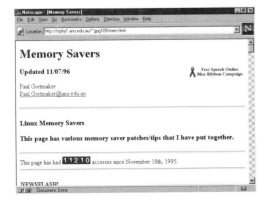

Figure 834.1 Linux memory savers.

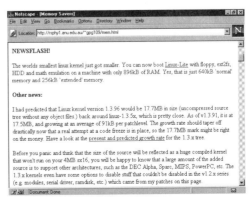

Figure 834.2 The latest news.

LINUX MIDI AND SOUND PAGES

http://www.digiserve.com/ar/linux-snd/

"The aim of these pages," writes the Webmaster, "is to contain links to all homepages and/or FTP-sites of MIDI + sound software available for *Linux* on the Net with a short, but comprehensive, description of what you will find at each link." At this site, you will find dozens of links related to system drivers, MIDI software, sound-card mixers, network-audio tools, digital-audio tools, module players and editors, CD-audio tools, sound-synthesis packages, documentation and information sources, and much more. Arne Di Russo constructed and maintains these pages.

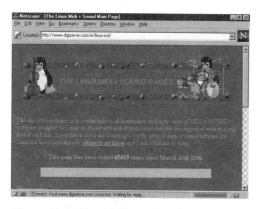

Figure 835.1 Linux MIDI + Sound Pages.

Figure 835.2 Main index.

LINUX NETATALK—A HOW-TO

http://thehamptons.com/anders/netatalk/

Netatalk, which runs with *Linux*, is a program which lets your UNIX-based computer look like an Appletalk file-server on a LAN. *Netatalk* exports a piece of the UNIX file system via the Appletalk protocol. Using *Netatalk*, Mac computers can mount UNIX volumes as if they were standard Appletalk network drives. This document is a guide to help the *Linux* system administrator set up *Netatalk*. You can download *Netatalk* from this site via a direct FTP link to its proprietors at the Research Systems UNIX Group, at the University of Michigan. The tutorial comes courtesy of Anders Brownworth.

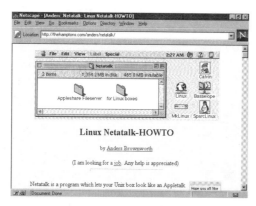

Figure 836.1 Linux Netatalk-HOWTO.

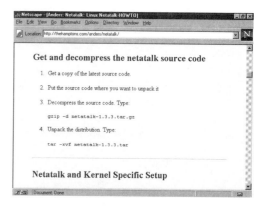

Figure 836.2 Steps in the process.

AI CAFÉ C/C++ CGI HTML HTTP JAVA J++ PERL VBSCRIPT VRML WIN32 WINSOCK 110011010010111100110111001101010000110011001001

LINUX POWERPC HOME PAGE

http://www.linuxppc.org/

Linux has found a new home! Volunteers around the world are banding together to port the *Linux* operating system to a number of PowerPC platforms. Their aim is to provide an alternative production-quality operating system for Bebox, FirePower, IBM, and Motorola users. Their goal is also to make available to the *Linux* community the price and performance advantages of PowerPC hardware. When will this all be ready? Right now! A *1.3* kernel is available, and the group is continuing their work. Unfortunately, PowerMac folks will be disappointed as the *Linux* PowerPC port does not support Apple hardware at this time. What you want is the *Mklinux*, which this book discussed in the Mac section (site 574).

Figure 837.1 Linux PowerPC information.

Figure 837.2 Project Documents.

AI CAFÉ C/C++ CGI HTML HTTP JAVA J++ PERL VBSCRIPT VRML WIN32 WINSOCK 110011010010111100110111001101010000110011001001

LINUX PROBLEM SOLVING PAGE

http://vortex.cc.missouri.edu/~rhys/linux.html

This Web site addresses a range of common problems encountered by *Linux* programmers, developers, and users. The problems discussed include difficulties with *ELF* upgrades, problems with *2.0.x* kernels, difficulties with kernel modules, other compiling quandaries, hardware problems, *X-Windows* problems, and more. The site also addresses common questions about upgrading your kernel, networking, security, *X-Windows*, and related topics. A sample problem? OK. "I compiled support for my NE2000 card as a module, but I get errors on bootup and 'inconfig' doesn't work." Know the answer? No? OK, find it on the *Linux* Problem Solving Page.

Figure 838.1 Linux Problem Solving Page.

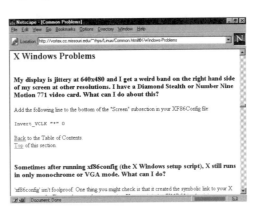

Figure 838.2 X-Windows Problems.

LINUX SERVICES FOR MACINTOSH & WINDOWS USERS

http://www.eats.com/linux_mac_win.html

Linux is an excellent operating system for providing services for many of the standard TCP/IP Internet resources. In addition, if you are running *Linux*, you can share files, printers, and desktop print-to-fax capability with your Mac and Windows users. This site shows you how. It covers Internet services (routing, electronic mail, USENET news, and the Web), file and print services (file and printer sharing for non-UNIX users), fax service (desktop fax for non-UNIX platforms), and more. Among the tools discussed is *MacFlex*, a Mac client for the UNIX-based fax server software *HylaFAX*, which you can also download from this site.

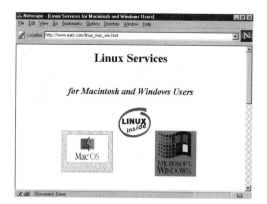

Figure 839.1 Linux Services for Mac and Windows.   Figure 839.2 File and print services.

LINUX-SUPPORTED HARDWARE LINKS

http://linux.crynwr.com/

At this site, you will find links to dozens of hardware manufacturers who support the *Linux* operating system. Included in this list are makers of multiport serial cards, *Linux* workstations, ISDN BRI terminal adapters, frame relay synchronous communication cards, Digital Alpha workstations, high-performance frame relay WAN adapters, and hard-disks. Manufacturers include Cyclades, VA Research, PromoX, SpellCaster, Sangoma, SW Technologies, Control, DCG Computers, EDV Consulting, SDLcomm, Baastrup & Bayard Software Design, and other companies. Russell Nelson maintains this site and asks that you let him know if he has left anyone off the list who should be on it.

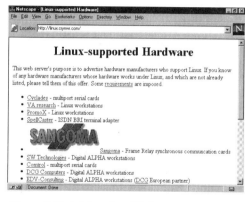

Figure 840.1 A long list of links.   Figure 840.2 One of the options.

AI CAFÉ C/C++ CGI HTML HTTP JAVA J++ PERL VBSCRIPT VRML WIN32 WINSOCK 1100110100101111001101110011010101000110011001001001

LINUX TOYS

http://www.redhat.com/linux-info/lg/linux_toys.html

"Welcome to the Linux ToyBox!" writes John Fisk. "This is a collection of software for the *Linux* that (1) compiles cleanly or is a binary distribution, (2) does what it claims to do (read: "*it works*"), (3) looks nice, (4) I like. Pretty subjective, eh? Well, that's what this is all about. After scrounging around various *Linux* archive sites, downloading *way* too much stuff, trying to set it up, and managing to get at least *some* of it running, I've arrived at a list of software that, quite frankly, I really like." Sounds good to me. You will find editors, the *Andrew User Interface System*, productivity tools and utilities, graphics packages, and much more. Go for it.

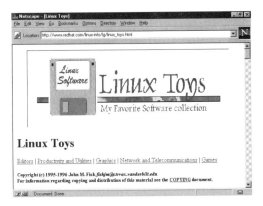

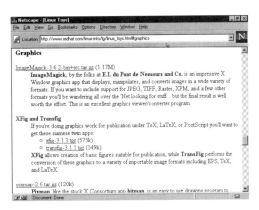

Figure 841.1 The toy box.

Figure 841.2 Graphics toys.

AI CAFÉ C/C++ CGI HTML HTTP JAVA J++ PERL VBSCRIPT VRML WIN32 WINSOCK 1100110100101111001101110011010101000110011001001001

BRIAN LITZINGER'S DRIVERS

http://www.mpress.com/

Visit this site to get Brian Litzinger's *FreeBSD CYB* driver for Cyclades multiport-serial cards, his *FreeBSD TM* driver for the OmniMedia Talisman MPEG card (and his programmer's guide), and *FreeBSD WC* driver for the DVI watchdog reset card. The first, *FreeBSD CYB*, is a production-quality driver that has been in use for a year or more by a number of people, including several ISPs. And the last, *FreeBSD WC*, is something entirely neat. Basically, if your system stops working, the board will push the hardware reset switch for you—without disabling your current reset switch. Also, it uses a relay to push the reset button so it works on most motherboards!

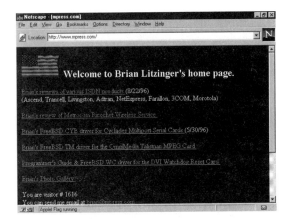

Figure 842 Litzinger's drivers.

1001100110001010101100111011011110101110111110001101 AI CAFÉ C/C++ CGI HTML HTTP JAVA J++ PERL VBSCRIPT VRML WIN32 WINSOCK

MATT'S CGI/PERL SCRIPT ARCHIVE

http://www.worldwidemart.com/scripts/

Matt's Script Archive contains many free Perl and CGI scripts to benefit the Internet and Web community. If you're looking for CGI scripts to spice up your pages, this site is where you want to come. Each script's link leads to a page where you can download the script, look at demonstrations and working examples of the script in action, and check out the script's frequently asked questions. All of this and you don't pay a penny! Who says you can't get something for nothing anymore? Visit this site for programs such as *Guestbook, Free for All Link Page, WWWBoard, Counter, TextCounter, Simple Search, FormMail, Random Image Displayer, Random Link Generator*, and more. Thanks, Matt.

Figure 843.1 The Archive.   *Figure 843.2 One of Matt's programs.*

1001100110001010101100111011011110101110111110001101 AI CAFÉ C/C++ CGI HTML HTTP JAVA J++ PERL VBSCRIPT VRML WIN32 WINSOCK

MATT'S UNIX SECURITY PAGE (YES, A DIFFERENT MATT)

http://www.deter.com/unix/

Matt makes it clear that this is by no means a complete listing of *all* the UNIX-security information and tools on the Internet. "What is hosted here," he writes, "is what I personally find useful and/or interesting." Let's see. What do we have at this site? I like the comprehensive checklist for securing your UNIX system. That's very useful. I also like the very interesting paper by Steven Bellovin describing the various attacks, probes, and miscellaneous packets floating past AT&T Bell Labs' net connection—fascinating stuff. So is the detailed paper on security problems in the TCP/IP protocol suite. And, I also found some papers by Matt Blaze himself, who is famous for cracking the *Clipper* chip while at Bell Labs. Very cool.

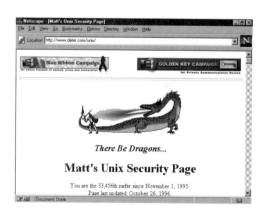

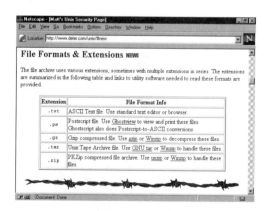

Figure 844.1 Matt's UNIX Security Page.   *Figure 844.2 File Formats and Extensions.*

AI CAFE C/C++ CGI HTML HTTP JAVA J++ PERL VBSCRIPT VRML WIN32 WINSOCK 1100110100101111001101110011010101000110011001001011

FREEBSD MBONE TOOLS

http://rah.star-gate.com/~hasty/mbone.html

MBONE is a virtual network layered on top of portions of the physical Internet. In short, MBONE exists to provide a multimedia backbone for the net, over which users can video conference and much more. MBONE supports the routing of IP multicast packets (since that function has not yet been integrated into many production routers). The MBONE network is composed of islands that directly support IP multicast, such as multicast LANs like Ethernet, linked by virtual point-to-point connections called "tunnels." At this site, you can download MBONE and, after you install it, join in the FreeBSD Lounge. This lounge gets really wild when people from all over the world join in. But be forewarned: If you have a slow data link (less than 56kb) to the Internet, then forget about MBONE. Even a 128kb ISDN line is barely enough to due heavy bandwidth demands.

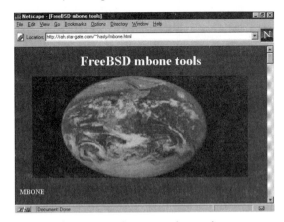

Figure 845 MBONE lives on mother earth.

AI CAFE C/C++ CGI HTML HTTP JAVA J++ PERL VBSCRIPT VRML WIN32 WINSOCK 1100110100101111001101110011010101000110011001001011

MEDIA WAREHOUSE

http://www.rahul.net/kenton/xconf96/mw.html

Media Warehouse is an application from Silicon Graphics' *X-Window* System desktop devised to help people manage their multimedia data (audio, movies, images, 3-D, text, and hypertext). Users often copy multimedia data from one *X*-based application to another. Media Warehouse helps users interchange multimedia data between applications, save multimedia data within a persistent database, and browse through the database. This incisive article by *X*-guru Kenton Lee examines all the major features of Media Warehouse and details some of the more interesting *X*-related components.

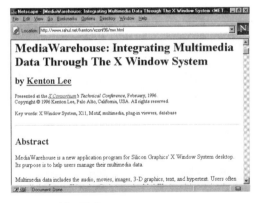

Figure 846.1 Title page.

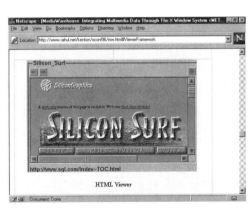

Figure 846.2 An illustration.

THE MINIX HOME PAGE

http://www.cs.vu.nl/~ast/minix.html

Minix is a free UNIX clone. Andrew S. Tannenbaum wrote the *Minix* system from scratch and, therefore, he did not include any AT&T code: not in the kernel, the compiler, the utilities, or the libraries. For this reason, the system is available with the complete source code. The current version of *Minix* runs on Intel-based PCs. Due to its small size, microkernel-based design, and ample documentation, *Minix* is well suited to people who want to run a UNIX-like system on their personal computer and learn about how such systems work. Indeed, this is one of the main reasons Tannenbaum created the system in the first place. Visit this site for free download.

Figure 847.1 Minix home page.

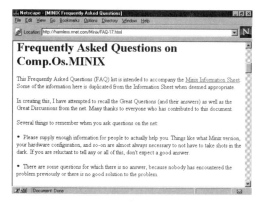

Figure 847.2 An FAQ.

THE NETBSD PROJECT

http://www.NetBSD.ORG/

The *NetBSD* Project is the collective effort to produce a free, available, and distributable UNIX-like operating system. *NetBSD* is based on a variety of free software, including *4.4BSD Lite* from the University of California, Berkeley. The software runs on a large number of hardware platforms and is highly portable. It comes with complete source code, and is user-supported. *NetBSD* is distributed in two forms: formal releases and *NetBSD*-current. Formal releases are done periodically and include well-tested binaries, source code, and install tools. *NetBSD*-current is a nightly distribution of the latest sources, meant for serious hackers who want to work with the absolutely latest software.

Figure 848.1 The NetBSD Web site.

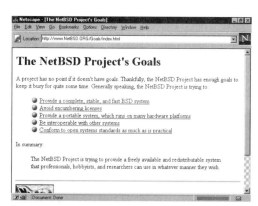

Figure 848.2 Project goals.

AI CAFÉ C/C++ CGI HTML HTTP JAVA J++ PERL VBSCRIPT VRML WIN32 WINSOCK 1100110100101111001101110011010101000110011001100101

NETWORK INFORMATION TECHNOLOGY

http:///www.nit.com/

Network Information Technology (NIT) offers products for customized security. The *NetBSD* Project is the collective effort to produce a free, available, and distributable UNIX-like operating system. *NetBSD* is based on a variety of free software, including applications for access control, password management, intrusion detection, monitoring and audit, and privilege delegation. NIT's most important product may be *Root Access Control*, which offers a unique and innovative approach to address the UNIX system's most common security risk, root access. *Root Access Control* lets you easily and effectively control root access across enterprise-wide networks by delegating privileges without giving away the root password. Visit this site for more information, a GUI demo, and a demo download.

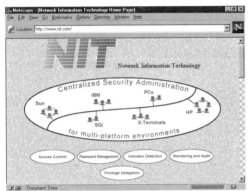

Figure 849.1 Network Information Technology.

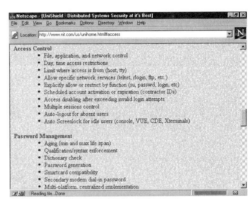

Figure 849.2 Access and password management.

AI CAFÉ C/C++ CGI HTML HTTP JAVA J++ PERL VBSCRIPT VRML WIN32 WINSOCK 1100110100101111001101110011010101000110011001100101

OLYMPUS TUNEUP: DEMO DOWNLOAD

http://www.olysoft.com/

Olympus TuneUp monitors 100% of SCO (Santa Cruz Operations) UNIX-system activity to provide a complete performance snapshot. *Olympus TuneUp* warns you, via fax or e-mail, before the system reaches critical threshold. The software diagnoses system problems so that you, the system administrator, know exactly what is wrong and how to fix it. The software also manages over 75 tunable parameters to maximize system performance. And, it fixes system performance by building a new kernel with resource allocations based on actual use, not theoretical estimates. Are you interested? Who wouldn't be. Visit this Web site for more information and a demo download.

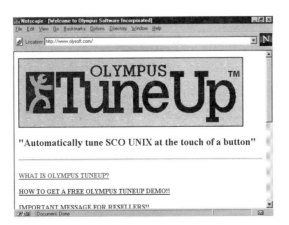

Figure 850 Olympus TuneUp.

851

OpenBSD

http://www.openbsd.org/

The *OpenBSD* Project involves continuing development of a free multi-platform *4.4BSD*-based UNIX-like operating system. *OpenBSD* looks a lot like *NetBSD* (which it is derived from, following the *4.4BSD* roots), but is now being developed separately. Generally, *OpenBSD* is *NetBSD* "plus more stuff." *OpenBSD* fixes many *NetBSD* problems and includes a new *curses* library, including *libform*, *libpanel*, and *libmenu*. The software also includes an *ipfilter* for filtering dangerous packets, better *ELF* support, integration of the GNU tools, numerous security-related fixes, and much more. And, it is free!

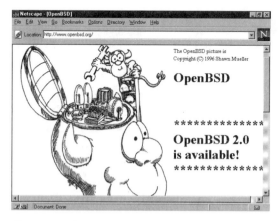

Figure 851 OpenBSD 2.0.

852

PERL ARCHIVE AT THE UNIVERSITY OF FLORIDA

http://www.cis.ufl.edu/perl/

Larry Wall wrote and currently maintains Perl (the Practical Extraction and Report Language). Perl is a language for processing text. Sounds pretty harmless, doesn't it? Perhaps at one time it was pretty harmless, but in its present state, with its sophisticated pattern matching capabilities, straightforward I/O, and flexible syntax, Perl is anything but harmless. In fact, by borrowing heavily from C, *sed, awk*, and the UNIX shells, Perl has become the language of choice for many I/O, file processing, process management, and system-administration tasks. Visit this site for great freeware Perl tools, extensive documentation, and more.

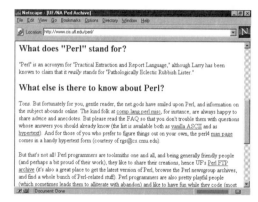

Figure 852.1 Loads of great Perl information.

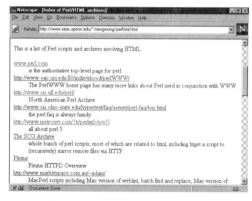

Figure 852.2 An index of Perl/HTML archives.

THE PERL PAGE (UNOFFICIAL)

http://www-cgi.cs.cmu.edu/cgi-bin/perl-man

This site features complete—and I mean *complete*—documentation for Perl. This extensive documentbegins with a Perl script and covers options, data types and objects, syntax, compound statements, simple statements, and more. The site also details the range of expressions (including pre-defined functions and "special" operations) with attention to flow-control operations, operators (including file-test operators), arithmetic functions, conversion functions, string functions, array and list functions, file operations, directory reading, I/O operations, search and modification operations, system interaction routines, IPC and networking operations, and other aspects. You will not find a more extensive documentation for Perl anywhere on the Web.

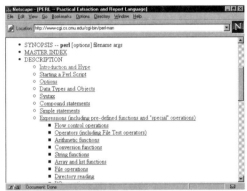

Figure 853.1 Table of Contents.

Figure 853.2 Expressions.

THE PERL DATA STRUCTURES COOKBOOK

http://www.perl.com/perl/pdsc/

The Perl Data Structures Cookbook provides recipes for building up complex data structures in Perl. Tom Christiansen, one of the leading gurus of Perl development and a real pioneer, extracted the recipes for the Cookbook from a much larger and more expository document to be published and included with the standard Perl distribution. Christiansen's goal is to provide cookbook-like, cut-and-paste examples of the most-often used data structures in Perl. Think of the recipes as a quick reference guide and the expanded versions (also available at this site) as tutorials.

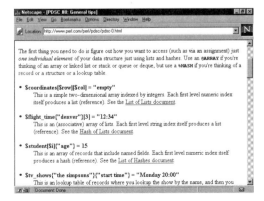

Figure 854.1 A few of the recipes.

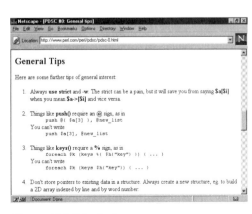

Figure 854.2 And a few more.

THE PERL LANGUAGE HOME PAGE (OFFICIAL)

http://www.perl.com/perl/

Visit this site for the latest Perl news, a short description of what this Perl thing is all about, a discussion of what's new in Perl5, and lots more. You will also get the scoop on where to download Perl5 source, documentation in various forms (including lists of frequently asked questions and book lists), how to get a corporate support contract for Perl, how to get professional training courses for Perl, and where to find/submit Perl bug reports. Plus, you get connections to newsgroups, mailing lists, and related sites. These pages come courtesy of the Perl Institute, a non-profit organization dedicated to making Perl more useful for everyone.

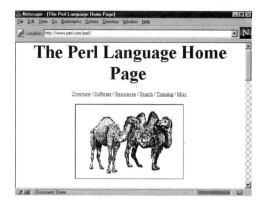

Figure 855.1 The Perl Home Page.

Figure 855.2 Perl software.

PLATFORM COMPUTING CORPORATION

http://www.platform.com/

Platform Computing Corporation is a world-leading systems software company specializing in UNIX-based workload-management solutions. Their focus is on products and solutions to increase productivity and maximize the use of computing resources through efficient computing in networked environments. Platform's primary product, *LSF* (Load Sharing Facility), is a fully-integrated suite of software designed to turn a heterogeneous network of machines into a single, integrated system. *LSF* distributes interactive batch and parallel jobs across the network to reduce job response time, increase throughput, and improve resource accessibility. Visit the company's Web site for more details.

Figure 856.1 Platform Computing.

Figure 856.2 Some news.

AI CAFÉ C/C++ CGI HTML HTTP JAVA J++ PERL VBSCRIPT VRML WIN32 WINSOCK 110011010010111100110111001101010100011001100100101

PREVENTING WIDGET RESOURCE SYNTAX ERRORS IN X-WINDOWS

http://www.rahul.net/kenton/rdebug.html

You may think that the programming interface to *X-Toolkit* resources is so simple that errors in this area are rare. One of the nice features of the *X-Toolkit* is that it does provide a simple interface to a powerful feature and this simple interface does cut down on programming errors. Still, mistakes are common. In this article, the author looks at the most common resource syntax errors, ways to avoid the errors, and ways to debug them. By reading this piece, you should learn how to identify resource syntax errors in your code, either when writing the code or later when debugging it. Either way, you are sure to save yourself a lot of time.

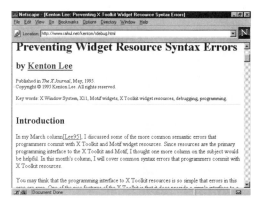

Figure 857.1 The title page.

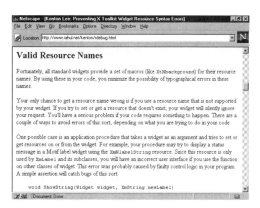

Figure 857.2 Part of the article.

AI CAFÉ C/C++ CGI HTML HTTP JAVA J++ PERL VBSCRIPT VRML WIN32 WINSOCK 110011010010111100110111001101010100011001100100101

PULSAR SYSTEMS

http://www.pulsarsystems.com/

Are you looking for turnkey communications for the UNIX environment? Pulsar Systems offers a complete line of products and services for UNIX-based systems: hardware, communications equipment, software, custom software design and implementation, feasibility studies, and consulting services. Their offerings include *FaxMan* (a fully automated faxing system optimized for outgoing messages), *FaxREAX* ("fax on demand" tool), *umagrst* (a unique *UNIX* utility to read Prime MAGSAV tapes), *PULSARLINK* (a *UNIX* replacement for PRIMELINK), *FormsXPRESS* (forms design and documentation), *WebKit* (Internet enable your *UniVerse* applications), and *WordMark* (a complete word processing system that integrates database, spreadsheet and graphics into a single character mode or graphical solution).

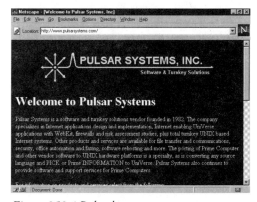

Figure 858.1 Pulsar home page.

Figure 858.2 Unix product information.

AI CAFE C/C++ CGI HTML HTTP JAVA J++ PERL VBSCRIPT VRML WIN32 WINSOCK

QUICKCAM THIRD-PARTY DRIVERS INFORMATION

http://www.crynwr.com/qcpc/

QuickCam is one of the most popular, affordable video cameras for PC-based video conferencing. This site exists primarily for developers who are developing for platforms other than Windows or the Mac, since Connectix directly supports these operating systems through the drivers and software they bundle with the QuickCam. At this site, you will find drivers for *Linux*, *FreeVSD*, and *Plan9*. You will also find links to other sites that have images (in some cases, live images) taken by the QuickCam running on operating systems other than Mac or Windows. Finally, you can even get source code for QuickCam drivers on other operating systems. This very useful set of pages comes courtesy of Russ Nelson.

Figure 859 Some cool related links.

AI CAFE C/C++ CGI HTML HTTP JAVA J++ PERL VBSCRIPT VRML WIN32 WINSOCK

SLIP FOR LINUX: A GUIDE

http://www-leland.stanford.edu/~wkn/Linux/slip/slip.html

This document describes how to initiate a SLIP connection using the *Linux*-based *Dip* program. Other topics you will find in this document include the remote net connection program *ringd*, and the *fetchmail* program which continuously retrieves your e-mail from a POP server (as long as your net connection is setup and running). You will also get all the details on how to set up *Dip*, how to use *Dip* to manually initiate a SLIP connection, using a *Dip* script to automatically initiate a SLIP connection, and using a *Dip* script to terminate a SLIP connection. This great tutorial comes to us from Ken Neighbors, to whom a big *thank you* is due.

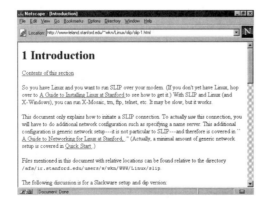

Figure 860.1 Introduction.

Figure 860.2 Using Dip.

AI CAFÉ C/C++ CGI HTML HTTP JAVA J++ PERL VBSCRIPT VRML WIN32 WINSOCK 110011010010111100110111001101010100011001100100101

SOFTWAY SYSTEMS: OPENNT DEMO DOWNLOAD

http://www.softway.com/OpenNT/

Softway Systems is a leading developer of UNIX products and technology for Microsoft Windows NT. Their most important product is *OpenNT*, which provides seamless integration between UNIX and the Windows NT environment in one single machine within a single operating system. The product allows simultaneous access to the multitude of powerful UNIX programs and utilities and the myriad of Windows NT applications, while at the same time maintaining strict conformance to open systems standards for Windows NT. Sound appealing? Of course it does. Download a free 30-day trial demo today, and take *OpenNT* for a test drive.

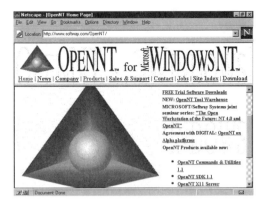

Figure 861.1 OpenNT home page.

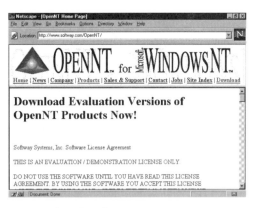

Figure 861.2 Free demos!

AI CAFÉ C/C++ CGI HTML HTTP JAVA J++ PERL VBSCRIPT VRML WIN32 WINSOCK 110011010010111100110111001101010100011001100100101

TAKEFIVE SOFTWARE: SNiFF+

http://www.takefive.com/

TakeFive Software's *SNiFF+* is an integrated development environment for UNIX programmers working with C, C++, Java, FORTRAN, CORBA IDL, and other languages. *SNiFF+* supports reverse engineering, configuration management, workspace management, and provides the most comprehensive set of browsers and parsers to be found anywhere. A Documentation Editor automates the documentation of source code and promotes its reuse. To aid software implementation, *SNiFF+* also includes a graphical editor, compiler, and debugger. Visit this Web site for much more information and an invitation from TakeFive to download demo copies of various *SNiFF+* tools.

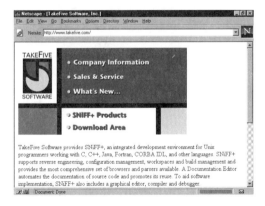

Figure 862.1 The TakeFive Web site.

Figure 862.2 Product information.

TWINCOM INTERNATIONAL

http://www.twincom.com/

Twincom International is a software house focusing on UNIX system software. Founded in 1991, Twincom releases products for volume shadowing and server mirroring on different UNIX platforms. With operations in Europe and the U.S.A., installations have taken place worldwide in mission-critical applications. The typical applications are: point of sale, telecommunications, on-line reservation databases, production plant databases, and health-care provider information systems. Visit this Web site for additional information about Twincom and its great collection of UNIX solutions.

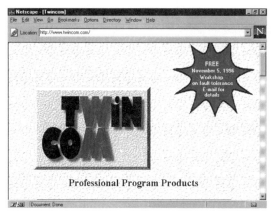

Figure 863 The Twincom Web site.

UNIFORUM

http://www.uniforum.org/

UniForum, the Webmaster tells us, "is the largest international, vendor-independent non-profit association that helps individuals and their organizations increase their Information Systems' effectiveness through the use of open systems, based on shared industry standards. Central to UniForum's message is the delivery of high quality educational programs, trade shows and conferences, publications, on-line services, and peer group interaction." Visit the UniForum Web site for up to the minute *UNIX* news and views, a calendar of events, job postings, an open systems products directory, press releases, and much more.

Figure 864.1 UniForum Home Page.

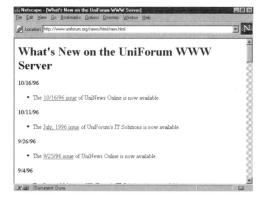

Figure 864.2 What's new.

AI CAFÉ C/C++ CGI HTML HTTP JAVA J++ PERL VBSCRIPT VRML WIN32 WINSOCK 11001101001011110011011100110101010001100110010101

THE UNIX REFERENCE DESK

http://www.geek-girl.com/unix.html

At this site, you will find extensive links and resources providing support and information with regard to UNIX applications and programming, *IBM AIX* systems, *HP-UX* systems, UNIX for PCs, UNIX for Sun systems, the *X-Window* system, UNIX networking and security, and even some UNIX humor. A particularly nice feature of this site is the UnixHelp for Users section which comprises a beginner-level introduction to the UNIX operating system that assumes no prior knowledge whatsoever. You also get a splendid, extensive directory of frequently asked UNIX questions, manuals for all versions of UNIX, and much more. Check it out.

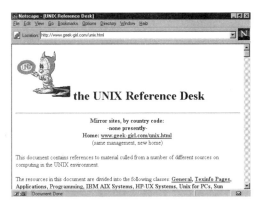

Figure 865.1 A devil of a reference.

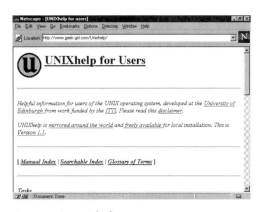

Figure 865.2 Help for users.

AI CAFÉ C/C++ CGI HTML HTTP JAVA J++ PERL VBSCRIPT VRML WIN32 WINSOCK 11001101001011110011011100110101010001100110010101

THE UNIX TEXT EDITOR: VI

http://albrecht.ecn.purdue.edu/~taylor/4ltrwrd/html/unixman.html

This document provides new users with an easy way to get acquainted with UNIX and *vi* (the UNIX-based text editor). "Although much of the material contained within has the same tantalizing appeal of arithmetic," writes the author, "please try to contain your excitement." Actually, the thing is written in a highly amusing manner and covers everything you need to know about *UNIX* and *vi*, from files and directories through basic commands, special characters, and *vi* text editing. The author is Chris Taylor, whose autobiography appears within these pages. Chris reports that he "hasn't been convicted of grand theft auto in the last five years and has never been convicted of a violent crime." Gotta love that!

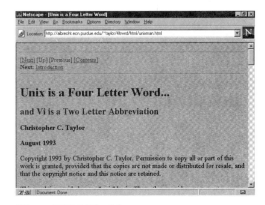

Figure 866.1 The title page.

Figure 866.2 The author.

UNIX Guru Universe

http://www.polaris.net/ugu/

This site advertises itself as the largest UNIX resource on the Internet. You will find system-administration resources that include articles and tutorials, consultants, FTP sites, GNU resources, mailing lists, magazines, organizations, patch archives, publications, software, usergroups, and Web tools. You will also find extensive resources related to UNIX networking, security, help, conferences and shows, vendors, jobs, and more. I counted several hundred links. However, this site has one downside: while it contains a ton of links—more than you'll find anywhere else on the Web—the links have no annotations. All you see are names. An abstract would be nice. But you can't have everything.

Figure 867.1 Unix Guru Universe.

Figure 867.2 A large collection of links.

A UNIX Tutorial: HP-UX

http://www.eel.ufl.edu/~scot/tutor/

This site features a tutorial which covers some of the features of *HP-UX*. Scott Miller composed the tutorial for use by the students and faculty at the University of Florida Department of Electrical Engineering. The tutorial starts with the fundamentals of *UNIX* and then runs through the concepts of creating files and directories, working with processes, file processing, using the network, managing files and directories, and more. The tutorial also includes a very useful hypertext command index. Scott invites comments and criticism via a handy form that you will find linked to the tutorial's main title page.

Figure 868.1 Tutorial table of contents.

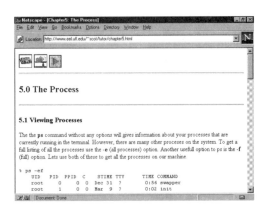

Figure 868.2 Processes information.

AI CAFÉ C/C++ CGI HTML HTTP JAVA J++ PERL VBSCRIPT VRML WIN32 WINSOCK 1100110100101111001101110011010101000110011001001001

EL WEASEL'S LINUX PAGE

http://www.ghg.net/crholmstrom/linux.html

"This page is seriously under construction," writes El Weasel. "This is a little project of mine to help out *Linux* newbies cut through the ambiguous world of the *UNIX* interface. I will attempt to make all information on this page as user friendly as possible." And, so it is. He has lots of resources and links at this site, including direct connects to *Linux* downloads. However, the nicest thing about these pages is El Weasel's straightforward, precise, and detailed answer to the question: "How do I set up *Linux*?" This excellent tutorial alone is worth the veritable "price of admission," which, in this case, happens to be absolutely free. If you are just starting out with *Linux*, this is the place to start.

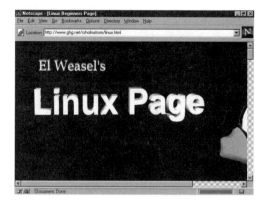

Figure 869.1 Linux Page.

Figure 869.2 Linux info desk.

AI CAFÉ C/C++ CGI HTML HTTP JAVA J++ PERL VBSCRIPT VRML WIN32 WINSOCK 1100110100101111001101110011010101000110011001001001

WINDSOR'S NETBSD HINTS AND TIPS

http://www.warped.com/~windsor/netbsd/

"I've helped many a new user through different parts of their *NetBSD* experience," writes Ron Windsor. Now he has decided to "HTML-ize" his expertise. And thank goodness for that! You will find files that tell you how to install *NetBSD* on Amigas, Ataris, HP300s, Macs, PCs, Sparc, and Sun workstations. Windsor also explains what size you should make your partitions, and how to partition your devices. And you'll find many more questions which Windsor answers. Do I need to compile a kernel? If so, how do I do that? How do I configure Ethernet for the first time? How can I get and install *X-Windows*? And, perhaps, most importantly: How do I get *Linux-Doom* running on my *NetBSD* machine?

Figure 870.1 NetBSD Hints and Tips.

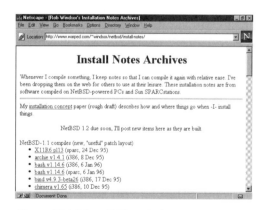

Figure 870.2 Install Notes Archives.

THE WINE PROJECT

http://www.linpro.no/wine/

No, we're not talking Chardonay. *Wine* is an emulator that lets Windows applications run on *ix86* UNIX-based systems (currently *NetBSD, FreeBSD, SCO OpenServer, Unixware,* and *Linux*) running *X11.* As a library, it allows the use of the Windows API for *Unix/X11.* The license is *BSD*-like. *Wine* is similar in goals to *Sunsoft's Wabi* product, and to *Willows Software's TWIN XPDK. Wine* is still alpha code, so it may or may not work to varying degrees on your system. At this site, you will find a direct link with which you can download *Wine,* complete with source, plus extensive documentation and a great list of frequently asked *Wine* questions. You'll also find an extensive list of programs that work under *Wine.*

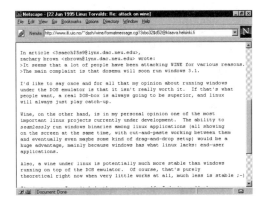

Figure 871.1 Linus Torvalds comments on Wine.

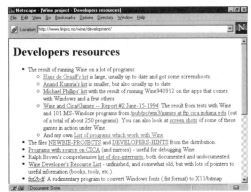

Figure 871.2 Wine Developers Resources.

X CONSORTIUM

http://www.x.org/

The X Consortium is a leader in developing standards and technology for Open Systems Computing. They're the authors of *X*—the recognized standard for computing interoperability. The X Consortium is committed to fostering the development, continued evolution, and widespread adoption of those standards. The X Consortium is supported through membership fees from over sixty member organizations. Currently, the X Consortium charges no license fees for the use of the *X-Window* system standards, or the sample implementations they have developed. These are made available to the computing community free of charge, in the interest of promoting open systems and interpretability. Visit this site.

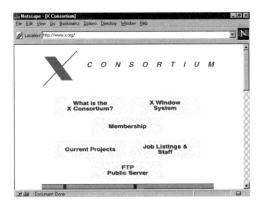

Figure 872.1 X-rated.

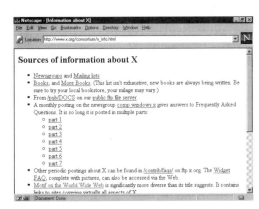

Figure 872.2 X-Window information.

AI CAFÉ C/C++ CGI HTML HTTP JAVA J++ PERL VBSCRIPT VRML WIN32 WINSOCK 11001101001011110011011100110101010001100100100101

X: END OF STORY

http://www.gaijin.com/X/

Visit this site for *X* tools tips, resources, and settings along with great configuration files and more. You will also find tools and information related to date-books, editors, games, graphics, mail, and managers that include *Tcl/Tk*. Among the tools you'll find at this site are *Marx* (an *X*-based scripting language), *PyXForms* (a development system using *python* and *XForms*), *V* (a freeware portable C++ GUI framework), the *Xi* interactive programming language, *Xaw95* (the widget set with a Windows95 look-and-feel), the *Hungry Viewkit* (a sophisticated C/C++ framework), *Lesstif* (a freeware clone of *Motif 1.2*), and much more.

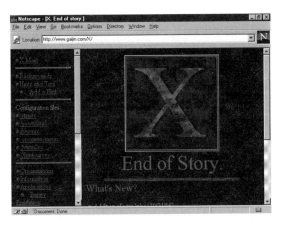

Figure 873 X: End of Story.

AI CAFÉ C/C++ CGI HTML HTTP JAVA J++ PERL VBSCRIPT VRML WIN32 WINSOCK 11001101001011110011011100110101010001100100100101

X-WINDOW SYSTEM PERFORMANCE TUNING

http://www.rahul.net/kenton/perf.html

When many *X-Window* system application programmers think of performance, they think of *drawing speed*—the time the application takes to draw or refresh its graphical displays. Experienced software engineers, however, know that application performance engineering can be somewhat more complex than solely optimizing drawing speed. "The performance of *X*-based application programs goes beyond simple drawing speed," writes the author. "This paper discusses several performance metrics as well as techniques you can use to improve the performance of your application." The techniques are concise, elegant, and proven. Avail yourself of them.

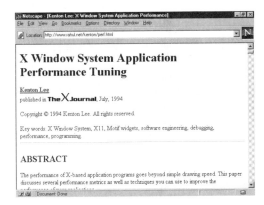

Figure 874.1 The title page.

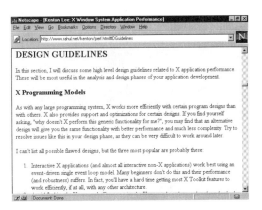

Figure 874.2 Design guidelines.

XFree86

http://www.xfree86.org

The *XFree86* Project is a non-profit effort to produce *XFree86*, the *X-Window* server for PC-based UNIX and UNIX-like systems. *XFree86-3.1.2.G* is now available as a download from this site. The site provides the program complete with source code, free of charge. (Note that there is an ongoing effort to port the servers, libraries, and some of the clients of *XFree86* to OS/2. The port runs parallel to the Presentation Manager desktop, similar to a *WinOS/2* fullscreen session. OS/2 binaries of the latest beta release are available.) No work is being done at the moment for an MS-DOS or Windows port. Joe Moss maintains the *XFree86* pages. Thanks, Joe.

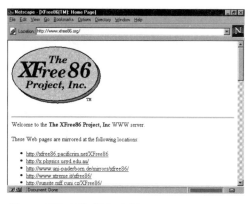

Figure 875.1 The XFree86 home page.   *Figure 875.2 The official FAQ.*

XPM Format and Library

http://www.inria.fr/koala/lehors/xpm.html

"*XPixMap (XPM)* consists of an ASCII image format and a C library," writes Arnaud Le Hors. "The format defines how to store color images (X Pixmap) in a portable and powerful way. The library provides a set of functions to store and retrieve images to and from *XPM* format data, being either files, buffers (files in memory), or data (include files)." While *XPM* is not an X Consortium standard, it is already a defacto standard. *XPM* is used in many applications, both commercial and non-commercial. Several vendors distribute the *XPM* library, as contributed software, on the platforms they sell. Visit these Web pages for much more information, as well as a download.

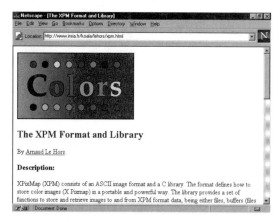

Figure 876 The XPM Format and Library.

AI CAFÉ C/C++ CGI HTML HTTP JAVA J++ PERL VBSCRIPT VRML WIN32 WINSOCK 11001101001011110011011100110101010001100110010100

ABRISOFT TOOLS FOR VISUAL BASIC

http://www.abrisoft.com/

If you are a Visual Basic programmer, this site features a set of tools you won't want to miss. Abrisoft is a maker of OCXs (OLE controls) and other tools for Visual Basic. Abrisoft publishes *User Options OCX*, a tool that lets users fully customize programs at run-time. Additional products include *Self-Translator OCX* (which lets you translate your program into foreign languages without changing source code), *DemoCop OCX* (which turns your Visual Basic application into a demo that runs for a certain number of days), and *FormAide OCX* (which lets you enhance your form *Resize* controls proportionally while at the same time "remembering" your previous position). Visit this Web site for information on these and other outstanding Abrisoft products.

Figure 877.1 The Abrisoft Web site.

Figure 877.2 User Options OCX.

Figure 877.3 Self-Translator OCX.

AI CAFÉ C/C++ CGI HTML HTTP JAVA J++ PERL VBSCRIPT VRML WIN32 WINSOCK 11001101001011110011011100110101010001100110010100

ADVANCED VISUAL BASIC

http://vb.duke-net.com/

The Advanced Visual Basic Web site contains information for the seasoned Visual Basic programmers who are already over the fundamental hurdles of learning the nuts and bolts of the programming environment and are ready to take on some real fancy tricks and tips. The page is maintained by Chris Duke who says it is "a page by a developer written for developers. It assumes you already know about OLE automation, object-orientation, and hopefully have a few years of VB programming under your belt." At this site, you will find information on VBScript, tuning Visual Basic, and other arcane aspects of graduate-level Visual Basic. In a world overflowing with newbie information, this site is a refreshing change.

Figure 878.1 Advanced Visual Basic.

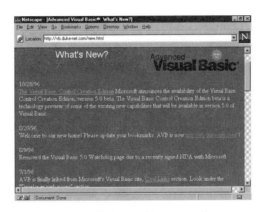

Figure 878.2 What's new? Version 5.0 beta.

APEX SOFTWARE CORPORATION

http://www.apexsc.com/

Apex's award-winning *TrueGrid Pro* data-bound grid control is widely recognized as one of the best VBX custom controls ever written for Microsoft Visual Basic 3.0. *TrueGrid Pro* creates grids for the display and editing of tabular data. After that success, Microsoft chose Apex to develop *DBGrid*, a data-bound ActiveX control (an OCX) that ships with both Visual Basic 4.0 and Visual C++ 4.2. Today, Apex's flagship product, *TrueDBGrid*, combines the rich feature set of *TrueGrid Pro* with the ActiveX functionality of *DBGrid*. Other Apex products include *VBA Companion* (an OLE/ActiveX object browser), and *MyData Control*, an event-driven control for Microsoft Visual Basic 4.0. Visit these Web pages for complete information on the good people at Apex and their products.

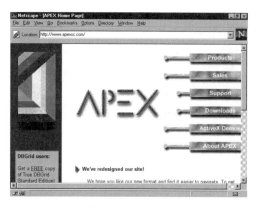

Figure 879.1 The Apex home page.

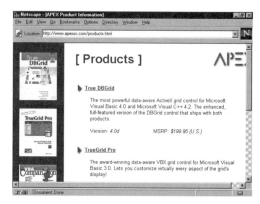

Figure 879.2 The products.

ASK THE VB GURU

http://itrc.uwaterloo.ca/~jauger/vbguru/vbguru.htm

Have you got a question about Microsoft's Visual Basic? Is there something that you would like to know how to do and just can't seem to be able to figure out? Have you tried *everything* and just can't get that application running? Have you resorted to lighting incense candles and muttering incantations over your PC, praying to the Gods of computing to tame the savage beast in your machine and make Visual Basic do everything Bill Gates says it can do? If you are at the end of your rope, if you think there is no place else to turn—be of good cheer. There is a solution. And the VB Guru knows what it is. He'll tell you, if you will only gather yourself to ask.

Figure 880 Go ahead and ask him.

ASK THE VB PRO

http://www.inquiry.com/thevbpro/

Got a question about Visual Basic? Is the VB Guru (featured in Site 880) on vacation? Ask the VB Pro, Eric Smith, who has been using Visual Basic since 1991 and is a veteran of Anderson Consulting. Or, leave your question on the bulletin board and the VB Guru will address it. Or, just survey previous questions and answers to see if the Guru has already solved your problem for another programmer. In addition to the great set of questions and answers, this site provides the latest Visual Basic news and views, monthly giveaways, component information, book and product reviews, an archive of in-depth Visual Basic-related tutorials and white papers, a fantastic VBScript archive and "Control Center," and more. Thanks, Eric.

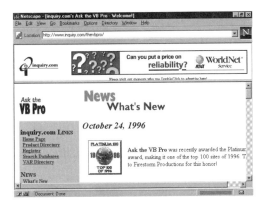

Figure 881.1 The VB Pro.

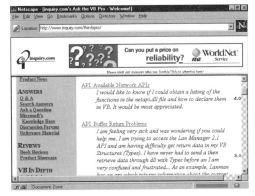

Figure 881.2 Q&A.

ATTAP: ALL THINGS TO ALL PEOPLE/VISUAL BASIC RESOURCES

http://w3.one.net/~dreitz/

I am not sure why this site is called All Things to All People. I just don't know. And, the name is never explained anywhere within the pages. Nevertheless, the site is an outstanding, extensive clearinghouse of links and resources related to all aspects of Visual Basic programming and development. You will find basic references and links, Visual Basic tools and libraries, Visual Basic programming tips, links to Visual Basic User Groups (VBUGs) around the world, Visual Basic education links (courses and tutorials), and much more. As a bonus, you get an excellent tutorial on how to use Visual Basic in the creation of a Web site. Good stuff.

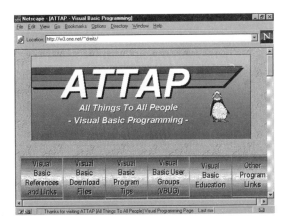

Figure 882 ATTAP.

GARY BEENE'S VISUAL BASIC WORLD/BEGINNER'S CORNER

http://web2.airmail.net/gbeene/begin.html

"I get the same questions over and over. 'How do I get started in VB?' This page provides a 'cookbook' set of instructions and tips which should provide the answer for this question!" At this site, you will find great step-by-step instructions, general guidelines, and an informative on-line tutorial. The tutorial covers all aspects of the Integrated Development Environment (IDE), coding, subroutines and functions, standard controls and properties, menus, graphics, displaying/printing, error handling, files, and more. The tutorial goes on to look at code libraries, custom controls and properties, databases, VB multimedia, and other advanced topics. If you are just getting started with Visual Basic, this is a great place to start.

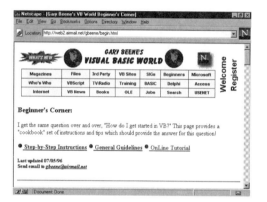

Figure 883.1 The Visual Basic Web site.　　　　Figure 883.2 General guidelines.

CARL & GARY'S VISUAL BASIC HOME PAGE

http://www.apexsc.com/vb

Hosted by Visual Basic experts Carl Franklin and Gary Wisniewski, this site features a definitive source of information about Visual Basic, add-on products, and the Visual Basic user community on the Internet. "Our ongoing mission," Carl and Gary write, "is to create a virtual gathering place for Visual Basic programmers throughout the world. . . . This page is dedicated to the free exchange of software, ideas, and information. We do not accept money for advertising. Instead, we allow any and all third party vendors to publish their pages on our server free of charge. . . . We believe this and other information is good for the (Visual Basic user) community." And so it is. Visit this site for some outstanding Visual Basic information.

Figure 884.1 Carl & Gary's.　　　　Figure 884.2 Late breaking news.

CHRIS & TIM'S RAD HOME PAGE

http://www.zetnet.co.uk/rad/

This outstanding Web site includes extensive information on writing VBXs (Visual Basic controls) and provides great archives for Visual Basic 3.0 and 4.0. You will also find resources for using JavaScript with Visual Basic, an excellent Borland Delphi archive, and more. While you are there, be sure to check out the tutorial on writing dynamic link libraries, the detailed list of frequently asked Visual Basic questions, and the superb Visual Basic tutorial. Of the tutorial, they say: "This isn't going to turn you into a programmer overnight, but it is a start. Hopefully we'll show you by example how to program a simple application and therefore explain the structure of a VB program and some of the design techniques." Trust me. Chris and Tim are being modest. They do far more than that.

Figure 885.1 Chris & Tim's.

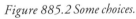

Figure 885.2 Some choices.

COMPONENT GRAPHICS: DOWNLOAD SOME FREEBIES

http://www.cginc.com/

Component Graphics provides portable and robust software technology in the form of highly reusable components. Component Graphics has successfully developed components for Microsoft Visual Basic. As Microsoft's OLE and other object models come to wider use, Component Graphics is the company to count on for rock-solid, easy to use component solutions. Visit this site to download *CGTabBar*, the latest in Windows 95 utilities. *CGTabBar* simplifies the Windows 95 desktop by organizing programs and files into easy to use tabs. The site also invites registered *ErgoPack 3.0* users to download the *ErgoPack 3.01* patch. Check it out.

Figure 886.1 Component Graphics.

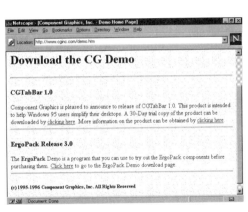

Figure 886.2 Downloads!

885

886

CRESCENT CUSTOM CONTROLS

http://crescent.progress.com/

He (or she) who writes the best custom controls will win. Win what? The best jobs, best assignments, the most respect, and so on. Crescent is dedicated to enhancing the success of Visual Basic developers by delivering tools and services that heighten their productivity and provide the foundation for creating reliable, scaleable, business-critical applications. By leveraging a 10-year track record of developing successful tools and components for the BASIC and Visual Basic environments, Crescent provides components and corporate and client/server solutions that are acclaimed throughout the industry. Crescent, a division of Progress Software, offers you a few free goodies to download, including a neat *Web Jump Start Kit*, which allows you to harness Visual Basic for building Web applications, and the *Jump Start Kit*, which eases your transition from Visual Basic 3.0 to 4.0.

Figure 887.1 Crescent home page.

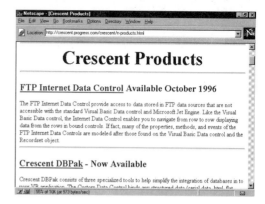

Figure 887.2 Product information.

CYPRESS ENABLE: BASIC SCRIPTING FOR APPLICATIONS

http://www.cypressinc.com/

Cypress Enable: Basic Scripting for Applications is a Visual Basic and VBScript compatible Basic Scripting Language you can use to embed scripts into software applications. With *Enable*, you can add scripting language functionality to your applications or Web pages to automate complex tasks. You can also create scripts for launching and manipulating other applications via OLE automation based on external DLLs. *Enable* is a complete programming language and is available under Microsoft Windows 3.1, Windows 96, Windows NT, MIPS, MacOS, UNIX, and DOS. The product is available in both 16- and 32-bit versions. Check it out.

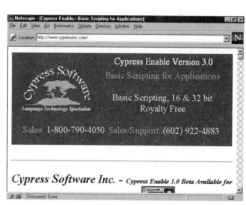

Figure 888.1 Cypress Enable.

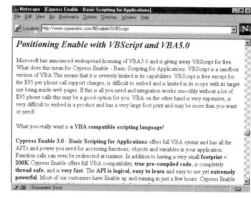

Figure 888.2 Product details.

DYLAN'S VISUAL BASIC HOME PAGE

http://www.wam.umd.edu/~dylan/vb.html

That's right. Dylan has hung up his guitar in favor of becoming a Visual Basic programmer and guru. He has quit touring and quit recording, and now devotes himself full-time to the maintenance of this excellent Web page and its impressive array of Visual Basic tools and references. Well, actually, it is not *that* Dylan. This site was created and is maintained by Dylan Greene. At this site, Dylan provides excellent links, as well as some useful proprietary local resources that include homegrown tools and libraries for milking every last ounce of speed and power from the Visual Basic environment. A stop at Dylan's Visual Basic Home Page is a good idea for any serious Visual Basic developer.

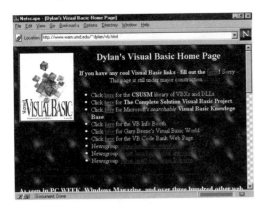
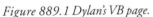

Figure 889.1 Dylan's VB page.

Figure 889.2 The Webmaster in concert?

ED'S VB INFO AND RESOURCE PAGE

http://www.tiac.net:80/users/efields/

Ed Fields' site has some stuff the other typical Visual Basic sites don't. I am talking about unique Visual Basic source code and custom controls—*content*—not just links. What a concept! In addition to the Visual Basic content, you will also find an excellent set of links as well. The links are not just for Web sites but also for Gopher sites, FTP sites, mailing lists, newsgroups, and more. The site also features several excellent archives of Visual Basic tools and utilities. And, you will find links to terrific on-line references and tutorials. Many thanks to Ed Fields of Proctor Associates for an excellent contribution.

Figure 890 Ed's page.

ENTISOFT TOOLS

http://home.navisoft.com/entisoft/

Tools save time and programming. Lots of tools can save even more. *Entisoft Tools* is an OLE automation server-based library containing over 1,000 routines for string manipulation, text processing, data storage, mathematical processes, and more. The library runs with Visual Basic and Microsoft Office. Visit this Web site for complete details on the library. While you are there, check out another neat product, *Entisoft Units*, a measurement conversion calculator for Microsoft Windows and function library for Microsoft Office and Visual Basic. Entisoft invites registered users of *Entisoft Tools* to download system patches and additional documentation. Many a Visual Basic programmer has found *Entisoft Tools* a valuable resource. Perhaps you will, too.

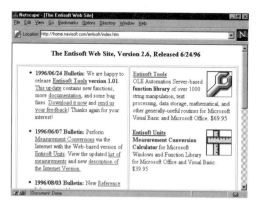

Figure 891.1 The Entisoft Web site.

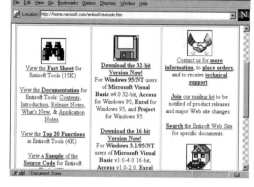

Figure 891.2 Entisoft Tools information.

IDEAL ENGINEERING

http://Mindlink.BC.CA/David_Bailey/

David Bailey's Ideal Engineering develops and markets DXF (Drawing Exchange Format) programming libraries for Windows developers. Bailey's most popular product is *DXF-IN for Visual Basic*—a library which lets you easily add DXF viewing and printing capabilities to your VB projects using a stock VB picture control. End users can then zoom in and out, and pan and print true high-resolution vector images. Bailey invites you to download a demo. There are other products as well. For example, the *TurboDXF* library empowers you to create your own DXF files with VB or Delphi. Do yourself a favor and check out the cool tools at Ideal Engineering.

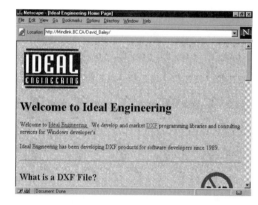

Figure 892.1 Ideal Engineering.

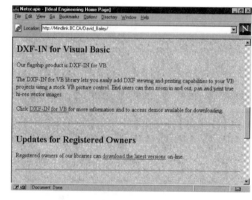

Figure 892.2 Product information.

AI CAFE C/C++ CGI HTML HTTP JAVA J++ PERL VBSCRIPT VRML WIN32 WINSOCK 11001101001011110011011100110101010001100110010101

IMAGEFX

http://www.imagefx.com/

ImageFX is a producer of multimedia, special effects, and imaging software, as well as custom controls for Visual Basic. Tools and controls include *PlanetFX* (lets you add professional, studio-quality effects to Web pages and Internet applications), *FXTools* (custom controls that add stunning special effects to individual multimedia elements like images, text, and shapes), *FXPic* (fast image decompression and color-mapping), *FractalFX* (fast image compression and decompression), and *VectorFX* (a 32-bit ActiveX control that displays a range of images with special effects!). Visit the Web pages for more information, including awesome on-line demos.

Figure 893.1 ImageFX.

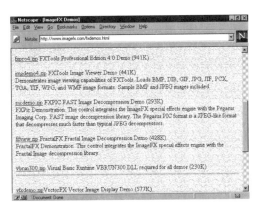

Figure 893.2 Downloadable demos.

AI CAFE C/C++ CGI HTML HTTP JAVA J++ PERL VBSCRIPT VRML WIN32 WINSOCK 11001101001011110011011100110101010001100110010101

INFINICOM'S VISUAL BASIC PROJECT

http://www.vbproj.com/

The Visual Basic Project was started by Gregory S. Youngblood as a way of helping others combine tips, tricks, and programming techniques into finished Visual Basic programs. The idea is to learn to program with Visual Basic in the very best manner possible—in other words, to learn from the good examples of elegantly crafted code. The examples you will find at this site are complete programs, rather than just code snippets, and illustrate exactly how to put (or is it *pull?*) everything together. The Visual Basic Project also contains links to many other useful Visual Basic pages on the Web and forms a good launching pad for all Visual Basic-oriented Web quests.

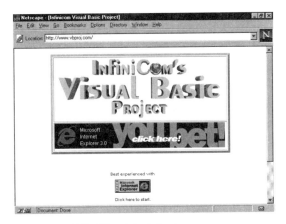

Figure 894 The Visual Basic Project.

895

JOSE'S VISUAL BASIC WORLD

http://www.citilink.com/~jgarrick/vbasic/

This page emphasizes the latest and the best. "The programming I'm doing now is for 32-bit VB4," writes Jose. "If you're still doing 16-bit programming you're on your own to make things work." Jose doesn't waste time talking antiques. But he has some great resources at this site. Check out Jose's Top 10 Programming Sins—Jose's personal list of programming techniques and mistakes that should be avoided "like the proverbial plague." Then, learn how to activate an application with the *WindowClass* name, how to make words from numbers, how to make dates less annoying to contend with in Visual Basic programs, and how to work with a secured Access database using VB. Very good stuff. Thanks, Jose.

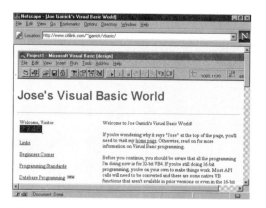

Figure 895.1 Jose's Web site.

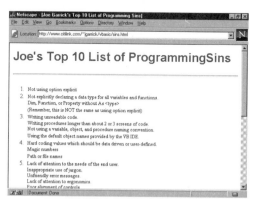

Figure 895.2 The top programming sins.

896

JZ'S ACCESS-VB PAGE

http://www.voicenet.com/~zaums/

JZ is a Microsoft-certified Visual Basic trainer. "After several years of teaching both Microsoft Access and Visual Basic," writes JZ, "I decided to write and maintain these pages as a resource for my students as well as anyone looking for information about these products. The content of these pages is derived from questions, both simple and complex, that my students have asked in these courses. I hope that you find them useful." JZ is actually John Robert Zaums. In addition to questions (and answers) about Visual Basic and Access, the site features are also questions (and answers) related to Windows, Open Database Connectivity (ODBC), MAPI (mail application program interface), and OLE. This site is a terrific resource.

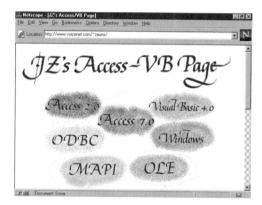

Figure 896.1 JZ's page.

Figure 896.2 Visual Basic information.

SCOTT MADIGAN'S VISUAL BASIC EMPORIUM

http://w3.one.net/~smadigan/vb/

This site is basically just one more set of Visual Basic links and I'd not list it here save for one thing—Scott Madigan's great freeware code snippets which are available for download. This code includes a form template and an HTML link parsing routine. The form template is really great for anyone (and that means everyone) who gets tired of re-creating the same menu items over and over again. And, the HTML link parsing routine is neat. This little module pulls links from HTML pages and adds them to two list-boxes. In creating this module, Scott has made judicious use of form and component object variables. So, making the module run with any form should be a matter of just changing the form names in the declare statements. Go for it.

Figure 897.1 Scott Madigan's Emporium.

Figure 897.2 Code snippets.

MARQUIS COMPUTING

http://www.marquistools.com/

Marquis Computing provides debugging, optimization, error-handling, performance-analysis, quality-control, and copy-protection tools for Visual Basic. Their most popular products are *VB/FailSafe* and *VB/Code Review*. The first, *VB/FailSafe,* is the premier debugging, optimization and performance analysis package for Visual Basic. In essence, it empowers you to create "crash-proof" Visual Basic applications by automatically intercepting and coding errors by class, project, module, procedure, and line number. Second, *VB/FailSafe* writes log files for later debugging and quality assurance, shows calls leading to the error, and provides over 75 data points to help you spot platform problems fast. Visit this Web site for more information.

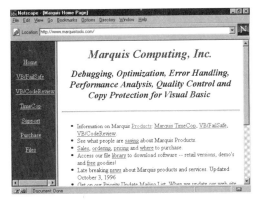

Figure 898.1 Marquis home page.

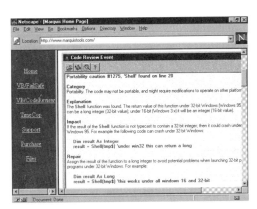

Figure 898.2 VB/CodeReview.

MULTIMEDIA TOOLS FOR WINDOWS PROFESSIONALS

http://www.mediarch.com/

Media Architects provides ActiveX controls for Windows developers working with Visual Basic or Delphi. Whether you are developing applications for the Web or in your favorite development environment (such as Visual Basic or Delphi), Media Architects delivers. At their great Web site, they don't just talk about and describe their controls. They put them in action, letting the controls work right on your machine via the Web. If you like what you see on-line, Media Architects invites you to download a full-blown trial version. Other products you will encounter include *ImageKnife* (professional image handling), *VideoPlay* (digital video and play & load control), and *MediaKnife* (multimedia integration). Visit this site and check out all three.

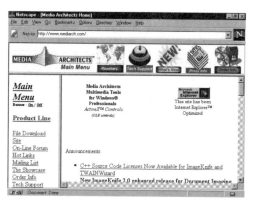

Figure 899.1 Media Architects.

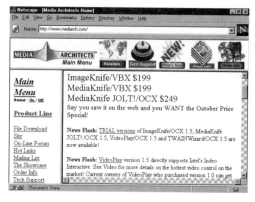

Figure 899.2 Product information.

MICROSOFT VISUAL BASIC SCRIPTING EDITION

http://www.microsoft.com/vbscript/

Microsoft Visual Basic Scripting Edition revolutionizes *active* content development for the Internet. VBScript is a high-performance scripting language designed to create active on-line content on the Web. VBScript lets developers link and automate a wide variety of objects in Web pages, including ActiveX Controls and applets created using Java. Visit this site and download Microsoft Internet Explorer 3.0, VBScript, a list of frequently asked VBScript questions, as well as documentation, tools, and samples. What else do you get from these pages? How about great VBScript sample applications that create active content? Very cool.

Figure 900.1 The VBScript Web site.

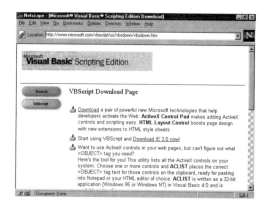

Figure 900.2 Download it now!

AI CAFÉ C/C++ CGI HTML HTTP JAVA J++ PERL VBSCRIPT VRML WIN32 WINSOCK 1100110100101111001101110011010101000110011001001101

MYSTIC RIVER SOFTWARE

http://www.mysticriver.com/

OK, so not everyone is using Windows. Every once in a while, you need to write code for use on multiple platforms. Mystic River Software provides embeddable scripting environments for multi-platform, client/server, and Internet applications to independent software vendors (ISVs) and corporate developers. Mystic River is best known for *SBL* (a multiplatform scripting language you can embed in applications to provide programming capability). SBL is Mystic River's widely used Visual Basic compatible embeddable scripting technology. Now, through an alliance with Microsoft, they are offering the *Visual Basic Applications (VBA) Edition 5.0* development environment with ActiveX controls. Both *VBA* and *SBL* integrate seamlessly into your applications. Mystic River provides high-quality products and outstanding technical support. Find out more by visiting the Mystic River Web site.

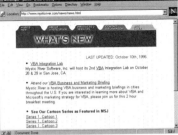

Figure 901.1 Mystic River's Web site. *Figure 901.2 What's new.*   *Figure 901.3 Products.*

AI CAFÉ C/C++ CGI HTML HTTP JAVA J++ PERL VBSCRIPT VRML WIN32 WINSOCK 1100110100101111001101110011010101000110011001001101

OUTRIDER SYSTEMS

http://www.outrider.com/

You don't have time to mess around. You want the best, most efficient custom controls available and you want them now. Outrider Systems' ActiveX custom controls are for use with Visual Basic, VBScript, Visual C++, and any other software that supports ActiveX or OCX components. Outrider has been in business since 1991 providing custom applications and component software to businesses and individuals around the world. Over the years, Outrider Systems has been a leader in the development of reference and data-entry applications. In 1991, Outrider was selected by Microsoft to design and develop the *SpinButton* control for Visual Basic 2.0. In 1995, with the introduction of OLE Controls (now called ActiveX Controls), Outrider ported *SpinButton* control to the OCX for inclusion with Microsoft Visual Basic 4.0. Visit this Web site for more information.

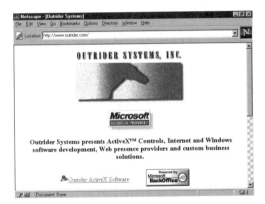
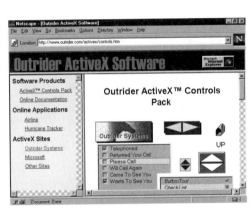

Figure 902.1 The Outrider Web site.   *Figure 902.2 Product information.*

1001 PROGRAMMING RESOURCES

1001100110001010101100111011011110101110111110001101 AI CAFÉ C/C++ CGI HTML HTTP JAVA J++ PERL VBSCRIPT VRML WIN32 WINSOCK

903

ROMY-TEK: VISUAL BASIC TOOLS

http://www.his.com/~romytek/

Download some excellent demo shareware. Visit this site and check out some cool Visual Basic tools. For example, *Multilingual Resource Builder (MuRBi)* helps you translate your Visual Basic 4.0 applications for use by non-English speaking users in minutes. You can translate your applications to any number of languages you need, and have them instantly available. *Visual Bridge* is another excellent product that lets your Visual Basic programs work with data generated by Access. *Visual Bridge* is an add-in module that transforms Access form files to a format Visual Basic can use. The resulting file contains a lookalike version of the form previously created in Access. Excellent.

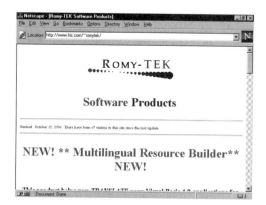

Figure 903.1 The Romy-TEK Web site.

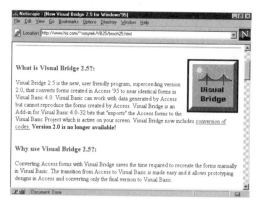

Figure 903.2 Visual Bridge.

904

SAX BASIC ENGINE

http://www.saxsoft.com/product/ssbasic.htm

Changes? I hate changes—especially source-code changes. Luckily, *Sax Basic Engine* gives you an unbeatable, royalty-free way to tailor your Visual Basic applications for individual clients without having to change your source code. *Sax Basic Engine* includes 32-bit and 16-bit OCXs and a 16-bit VBX to give you all the programming power you need. The Basic-like syntax and commands of *Sax Basic Engine's* scripting language mean that there's very little learning curve for you or your users. Just drag the custom control onto an application's form and you'll be able to talk to and control your own applications, as well as every major Windows application, including Word, Excel and Access. The engine includes an object browser that gives your users access to everything they need to know about your application's macro language. Check it out.

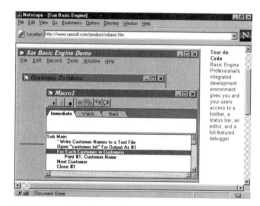

Figure 904.1 A sample engine screen.

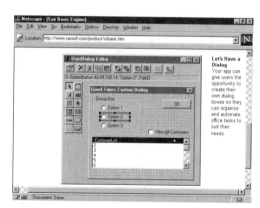

Figure 904.2 And another.

AI CAFÉ C/C++ CGI HTML HTTP JAVA J++ PERL VBSCRIPT VRML WIN32 WINSOCK 1100110100101111001101110011010101000110011001001

SAX COMM OBJECTS

http://www.saxsoft.com/product/sscomm.htm

Are your applications having trouble communicating? Communicating over a modem, that is. *Sax Comm Objects* is a custom control that provides all the VBX and OCX power you need to add serial-communications capabilities to your Windows-based applications. Simply plug in *Sax Comm Objects* to streamline your application and the control will provide your application with the communication tools it needs. *Sax Comm Objects* support most popular file transfer protocols, including X/Y/ZModem, Kermit, and CompuServe B+. *Sax Comm Objects'* built-in terminal emulation lets you create Windows front-ends for character-based programs such as those from *UNIX* systems or from older on-line services. *Sax Comm Objects* is 100% compatible with the Windows *comm* driver, including Windows 95's ability to detect modem types automatically.

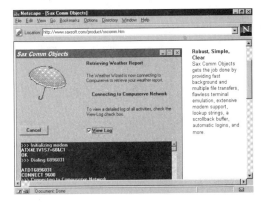

Figure 905.1 Comm Objects screen.

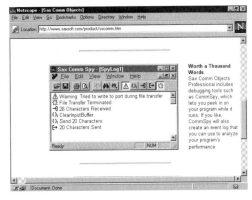

Figure 905.2 And another.

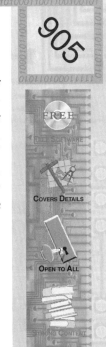

905

AI CAFÉ C/C++ CGI HTML HTTP JAVA J++ PERL VBSCRIPT VRML WIN32 WINSOCK 1100110100101111001101110011010101000110011001001

SHERIDAN SOFTWARE SYSTEMS

http://www.shersoft.com/

Download shareware from the people who helped start it all. Sheridan Software Systems is a leading manufacturer of development and productivity tools, as well as reusable components for Visual Basic developers. Founded in 1991, at the start of the visual-development revolution, their first products were components developed for and marketed by Microsoft as part of the *Professional Toolpack for Visual Basic*. Today, on an OEM basis, they continue to supply many of the components included in *Microsoft's Visual Basic Professional* and *Enterprise* editions, as well as in their *Visual ToolPack for Visual C++*. Sheridan's latest product is *WinAPI Oblets*, which presents the Windows API as OLE Automation Servers.

906

Figure 906.1 Sheridan home page.

Figure 906.2 Latest news.

Figure 906.3 Product information.

PAUL TREFFERS'S VB HOME PAGE

http://www.xs4all.nl/~treffers/

This outstanding site comes from Paul Treffers, a Visual Basic programming guru *par excellence*, who lives in Leiden, in the Netherlands. The coolest aspect of this site is the "VB Code Corner," which includes tons of great Visual Basic functions that you won't find anyplace else, as well as a full Visual Basic 4.0 application for URL filtering that scans HTML documents. As a bonus, this site also contains a lot of good links and some good information on AS/400 development. Take a break now and visit Netherlands by way of this outstanding Web site.

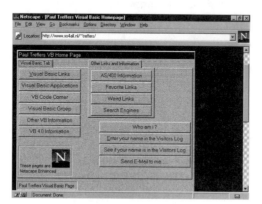

Figure 907.1 Treffers's VB home page.

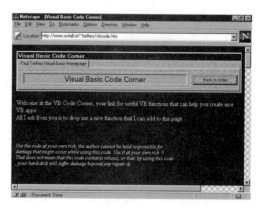

Figure 907.2 Code Corner.

TVOBJECTS

http://www.tvobjects.com/

Applet and Web page creation made easy. TVObjects is the developer and publisher of *VBnet* and *Applet Designer*. These are two tools for Visual Basic developers who want to leverage their skills to create robust Web applications and great Java applets. *Applet Designer* makes it easy to build secure, cross-platform Java applets using Visual Basic design skills. In short, you get all the power of Java without all the complex coding tasks. Equally simple to use, *VBnet* helps you migrate your entire Visual Basic project to the Web, bringing your application design, custom controls, code, and data to the Web's cross-platform environment with a minimum of fuss and muss. Let *VBnet* and *Applet Designer* do your work for you.

Figure 908.1 TVObjects home page.

Figure 908.2 Design sample applets.

VB CODE MASTER FROM TELETECH

http://www.teletech-systems.com/cdmstr.htm

VB Code Master is a breakthrough add-in for Visual Basic that gives you the professional programming features you've always wanted. *VB Code Master's* unique code browser lets you see your entire project in a single window. The browser presents all files, procedures, and even variables in one easy to navigate form. Double-click your mouse on any object in the browser to access the object immediately. *VB Code Master's* advanced printing engine produces easy to read code listings. Also, its advanced searching functions let you locate a module or variable everywhere it is used. In addition, a custom VBA/OLE 2 compatible macro engine can execute any Visual Basic command, and has complete knowledge of all objects. Visit this site for more information.

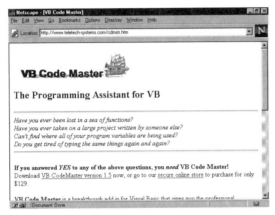

Figure 909 VB Code Master Web site.

VIEWPOINT SOFTWARE SOLUTIONS

http://www.ViewpointUSA.com/

If you are writing Visual Basic applications that must communicate with a large number of serial ports, you have found the right site! Viewpoint Software Solutions provides a host of great Visual Basic tools, including *MultiCom/VB*, which lets you break the Windows serial-communications bottleneck and access up to 96 serial (RS-232 or RS-422) ports using Visual Basic. And, this is in addition to the COM ports available in DOS and Windows. *MultiCom/VB* smashes the Windows limitation of access to only eight serial ports. In addition, you can program each *MultiCom* channel individually for baud rate (50 - 15,200 baud), handshake protocol, data bits, stop bits, and parity. Visit this Web site for more information.

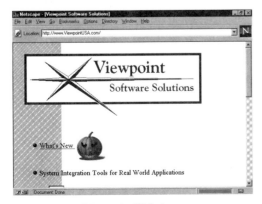

Figure 910.1 Viewpoint Web site.

Figure 910.2 MultiCom/VB details.

VISION SOFTWARE

http://www.vision-soft.com/

If only documentating, defining the requirements, and planning for code reuse was easy. Well, now maybe it is. Vision Software provides Visual Basic-related software tools that automate development of strategic client/server applications, dramatically increase business process re-engineering (BPR) productivity, and are strategically layered with existing mainstream technology. Their most popular and important product is *Vision StoryBoard*, the world's first tool for visually commenting and documenting applications. *Vision StoryBoard* captures design specifications and requirements and then generates "point-in-time" project documentation and training materials for Visual Basic applications. Visit this Web site for more information, including case-studies and on-line demos.

Figure 911.1 Vision Software Web site.

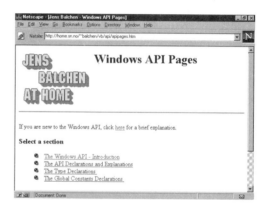

Figure 911.2 Technical support.

VISUAL BASIC BEGINNER'S CORNER

http://home.sn.no/~balchen/vb/novice/novice.htm

The Visual Basic Beginner's Corner comes to you courtesy of Jens Balchen. At this site, you get the answers to fundamental questions like: What is Visual Basic? How can I get started? Jens provides an absolutely splendid introduction to the Windows Applications Programming Interface (API) that addresses API declarations and explanations, type declarations, and global constants declarations in detail. "The Windows API is the backbone of Windows," explains Jens. "Without it, the typical Windows standard wouldn't exist. No matter what language you use, the API is an essential part of your program." Jens is right and the tutorial is excellent.

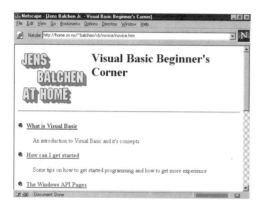

Figure 912.1 Balchen's beginner's corner.

Figure 912.2 Windows API information.

FREQUENTLY ASKED VISUAL BASIC QUESTIONS

http://puta.gurunet.org/vb

This list of frequently asked Visual Basic questions started as a compilation of answers to questions that popped up frequently in the Usenet newsgroup *comp.lang.basic.visual.* The document eventually outgrew the text file format, which is why it became (briefly) outdated some time after Visual Basic 4.0 was released. But be of good cheer. At this site, you can now read a complete up-to-date revamp of the questions rendered in HTML. The list of frequently asked questions is so up-to-date it even includes discussion of Version 5.0, provides resources for VBScript, and offers code for CGI programming. You will also find lots of "newbie" stuff and discussion of advanced, arcane VB voodoo for experienced programmers. Check it out.

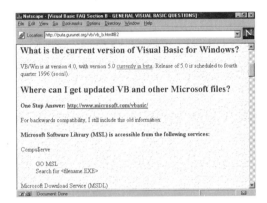
Figure 913.1 Questions and answers.

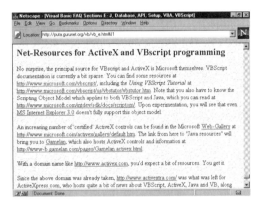
Figure 913.2 VBScript information.

VISUAL BASIC INFORMATION FROM MICROSOFT

http://www.microsoft.com/vbasic/

At this site, you will find in-depth technical articles, tips and tricks, data-sheets, performance-analysis reports, and more related to Microsoft's Visual Basic. This site is the official Visual Basic Web site, direct from Microsoft. In addition to the "Tip of the Week" and expert tutorials on 16- to 32-bit migration, the site includes lots of free software, including an upgrade patch for the *Apex Data Grid* (*DBGrid* control) and the *Application Performance Explorer,* Internet ActiveX controls, a powerful 32-bit tab container control, a remote automation diagnostic wizard, unsupported MAPI DLLs for use with Visual Basic, and the latest release of the *Visual Basic Code Profiler.* Remember, it's their product—visit Microsoft for the specifics.

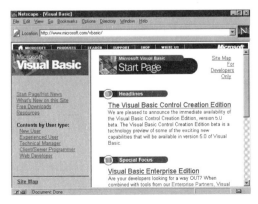
Figure 914.1 Visual Basic Web site at Microsoft.

Figure 914.2 Enterprise Edition.

AI CAFÉ C/C++ CGI HTML HTTP JAVA J++ PERL VBSCRIPT VRML WIN32 WINSOCK

VISUAL BASIC ONLINE: RESELLERS OF VISUAL BASIC SOFTWARE

http://codd.com/vbonline/

Visual Basic Online is a reference listing of custom controls and other Visual Basic productivity tools. Each product listing contains an overview, price, author name, and where possible, a full description of the product's features and how to use them. The site also features hyperlinks to the sites of related software publishers and consultants. A list of commercial and shareware distributors worldwide who deal in Visual Basic add-ons will soon be available at this site. While you are there, treat yourself to a copy of the informative *Visual Basic Online Magazine*, a zine that is witty, entertaining, and packed with useful technical knowledge.

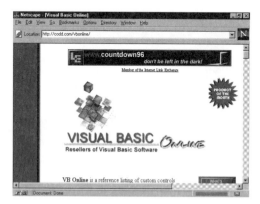

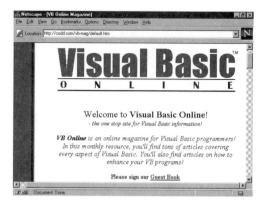

Figure 915.1 Visual Basic Online.

Figure 915.2 The zine.

AI CAFÉ C/C++ CGI HTML HTTP JAVA J++ PERL VBSCRIPT VRML WIN32 WINSOCK

THE PHIL WEBER HOME PAGE

http://www.teleport.com/~pweber/

Phil Weber is the self-appointed funny-man of Visual Basic programming. This Web site is very humorous and entertaining. But along with being funny, Phil also knows his Visual Basic programming. And, the page is packed with his custom Visual Basic tips, tricks, and workarounds. You will learn how to create Windows 95 shell links, prompt the user for a directory in Windows 95, access secured databases from Visual Basic 4.0, use *CompactDatabase* with password-protected databases, cancel *AddNew* or *Edit* without leaving the current record, fix data control errors 3020 and 3246, and save yourself in dozens of other ways. Visit this site for a few good jokes and for more good code examples.

Figure 916.1 Phil Weber's home page.   *Figure 916.2 Phil's VB tips.*

Figure 916.3 Win95 shell links.

AI CAFÉ C/C++ CGI HTML HTTP JAVA J++ PERL VBSCRIPT VRML WIN32 WINSOCK 1100110100101111001101110011010101000110011001100100101

1001 WINDOWS 95 KEYBOARD SHORTCUTS

http://www.zdnet.com/pccomp/1001tips/index.html

Most programmers are good typists—it comes with the territory. Because your hands are already on the keyboard, one of the simplest ways to boost your productivity is take advantage of keyboard shortcuts built into the operating system. With the right key combinations at your fingertips, you'll never have to search for an elusive feature again. It is worth teaching your old fingers some new moves in order to take advantage of a slew of new features. That's why PC Computing has assembled this exclusive and comprehensive collection of 1,001 keyboard shortcuts. It is a one-stop reference guide through the powerful world of Windows 95. And it can save you a lot of time.

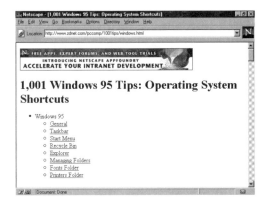

Figure 917.1 Cool shortcuts.

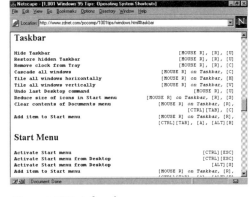

Figure 917.2 A few shortcuts.

AI CAFÉ C/C++ CGI HTML HTTP JAVA J++ PERL VBSCRIPT VRML WIN32 WINSOCK 1100110100101111001101110011010101000110011001100100101

AKSOFT SHAREWARE FOR WINDOWS

http://www.aksoft.com/

Programmers make extensive use of ZIP files to store data in a compressed format. And now there's a new company in the ZIP game. AKSoft has big plans for the future but, for now, they have only one truly exceptional piece of shareware to offer Windows users. The product is called *EasyZIP Self-Extractor Pro*, a program that generates self-extracting archives from existing ZIP files. *EasyZIP Self-Extractor Pro* is capable of building 16- and 32-bit archives and it supports long file names. It works in the background after execution and, if you ask it to, will automatically delete the originals of all archived files. Also, the archive will display a progress bar while files are extracted, so users will know how long the extraction will take. And one more thing: It all comes bundled in an intuitive, easy-to-use, Wizard interface. Go for a download today.

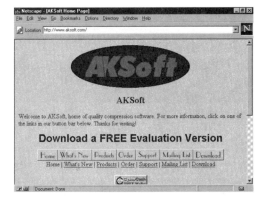

Figure 918.1 AKSoft Home page.

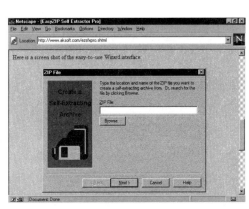

Figure 918.2 EasyZIP wizard screen.

919 *AMF SHAREWARE FOR WINDOWS*

http://www.execpc.com/~amfsoft/windows.html

AMF offers a wide range of proprietary Windows shareware you can download from this site. You will find a number of programs here. The one I like best is called *Elbow Grease*, a Program Manager enhancement that features a 40 launch-button toolbar with large buttons, resource monitors for memory and disk space, a system clock, a perpetual calendar to the year 9000, and an appointment book and to-do list to schedule events until the year 9000. The shareware also includes drag-and-drop file managing launching capability, a few built-in games, and more. Download this shareware today and then let's set a date to get together in, oh, the year 8098. We can celebrate the 6,200th anniversary of the Spanish-American War. Visit this site for more information and some other cool programs.

Figure 919 The AMF Web site.

920 *WINDOWS 95 ANNOYANCES*

http://www.creativelement.com/win95ann/

Windows 95 has bugs? What bugs? This Web page is just a good read, along with being a great clearinghouse of "known" and "unknown" (or should we say *unrecognized?*) Windows 95 bugs. The annoyances started, according to the Webmaster, with the pre-release of Win95. "Microsoft released a beta version to about 400,000 people, calling it the largest beta program in history. The problem was that this pre-release program was engineered for publicity, and not to find bugs. I personally submitted over fifty bugs that Microsoft *never* fixed." You can find a list of the fifty bugs at this site, along with hundreds of other bugs submitted by users around the world. Luckily, the site is filled with workarounds.

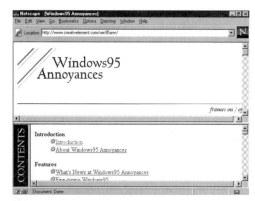

Figure 920.1 Windows Annoyances.

Figure 920.2 Getting rid of the Inbox icon.

AI CAFÉ C/C++ CGI HTML HTTP JAVA J++ PERL VBSCRIPT VRML WIN32 WINSOCK 1100110100101110011011100110101010001100110010101

ANTI-HYPE WINDOWS 95

http://www.xso.com/current/mshype.htm

You've got to keep telling yourself: *It's just an operating system.* "We thought with all the hoopla surrounding the release of Windows 95, that all the "netizens" (citizens of the net) out there need a reality check. With that in mind, we present the Windows 95 Anti-Hype Home Page." So write the Webmasters. Check out the updated slogans for Windows 95: Plug and *PRAY* Operating System. Yesterday's Technology Tomorrow! Windows 95: OS/2 for DOS! The Biggest Thing Until Windows 95.1! Windows 95—It Sucks Less. Windows 95—Does The Same Thing But Looks Prettier. Brings 70's DOS Technology into the 21st Century! Even Faster than Microsoft Word 6!

Figure 921.1 Anti-Hype home page.   *Figure 921.2 Things Windows 95 can't do.*

AI CAFÉ C/C++ CGI HTML HTTP JAVA J++ PERL VBSCRIPT VRML WIN32 WINSOCK 1100110100101110011011100110101010001100110010101

BAKLAVA SPRITE TOOLKIT FOR JAVA APPLETS (SHAREWARE)

http://www.boutell.com/baklava/

Baklava is an excellent sprite graphics library for Java programmers. Baklava's sprites (graphical objects) can only appear inside a Baklava "playfield." To provide an environment for your sprites, you must create a Baklava playfield object and add it to your Java applet. Then, you can create as many sprite objects as you like within the playfield. Baklava sprites can be told what direction to move in and how fast to travel (in pixels per second) without further intervention from the programmer, until something interesting happens, such as a collision. The 30-day evaluation version of the shareware is not "crippled" in any way, however, it does "expire" at the end of the trial period. Visit this site and download your copy, with documentation, today.

Figure 922 The Baklava Web site.

BARRY95/VISUAL GUIDE TO WINDOWS 95 PPP/SLIP INSTALLATION

http://www.users.interport.net/~barry/

This site is packed with information about Windows 95. One of the highlights of Barry's great collection of tools, links, and resources is his Visual Guide to Windows 95 PPP/SLIP Installation. This useful guide walks you step by step through the intricacies of installing the dialup adapter, installing network support for TCP/IP, installing SLIP and dialup scripting capability, creating and configuring an Internet dialup connection, and using Microsoft's dial-up scripting tool. The instructions are concise and to-the-point and, as the title *Visual Guide* would have you believe, are illustrated with detailed screens that *show* you exactly what to do. This is a very worthwhile contribution from our man Barry. Check it out.

Figure 923.1 Barry95.

Figure 923.2 Dialup adapter.

Figure 923.3 Installing TCP/IP.

BASTA.COM: WINDOWS 95/NT SHAREWARE

http://www.basta.com/

Basta offers lots of excellent, home-grown shareware you can download from this site. Let's see. What do we have here? Say, how would you like to view, capture, and integrate icons of other programs for use in your own software's menus? *Exlcon 1.5* lets you capture these icons and save them as bitmaps you can later incorporate in other documents and images. Another neat piece of shareware is *Filo 1.5*, which lets you modify the time, date, and attribute properties of selected files and folders. It is particularly useful for modifying sets of files based on their existing attributes. Another useful bit of shareware is *Horas 1.5*, which lets you create several clocks corresponding to different time zones. There's lots more. Visit the Basta Web site today and download these programs and more.

Figure 924.1 Basta.com.

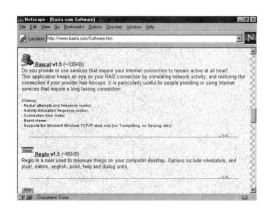
Figure 924.2 A few selections.

BENJAMIN'S SHAREWARE & FREEWARE FOR WINDOWS 95

http://ourworld.compuserve.com/homepages/benjab/

Benjamin Bourderon is the crafter of some elegant and useful shareware and freeware programs for Windows 95. On the freeware side of the fence, check out *Magic Desktop 1.1*, which received a 3-star rating from ZDNet and is an ideal utility for showing or hiding your desktop icons. Another neat piece of freeware is *QuickDisk 1.10*, with which you can quickly display the exact amount of your free disk space. On the shareware side of the fence, you will want to download *Catalog 1.51*, Windows 95 software that lets you catalog a hard drive, a floppy, an optical drive, a ZIP drive, or a CD-ROM. This site makes all these programs available for download, so go get 'em!

Figure 925.1 Benjamin's home page.

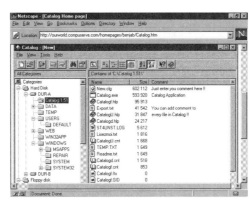

Figure 925.2 Catalog screen.

BJORN'S WINDOWS 95 PAGE

http://www.users.wineasy.se/bjornt/win95.html

Our man Bjorn provides news, must-have utilities and tools, expert tips and tricks, cool software, and workarounds for common Windows 95 problems. The site includes an extensive on-line driver manual for Windows 95, a neat "Tip of the Day," a tutorial on running DOS games under Windows 95, a collection of Windows 95 "stumper" questions (with answers), and links to cool stuff such as *Windows 95 User Magazine*, detailed instructions on how to upgrade your PC to Windows 95, and cool tools and utilities authored by Andrew Schulman. When you are done with the technical stuff, click on the hyperlinks to Bjorn's girlfriend's lipstick page.

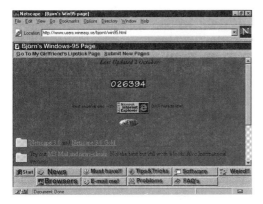

Figure 926.1 Bjorn's Windows 95 Page.

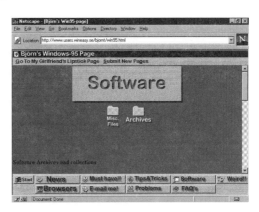

Figure 926.2 Cool software.

BRIAN'S WINDOWS 95 WEB PAGE

http://www.cfanet.com/bmoore/

Brian's Windows 95 Web Page is beautifully designed, Java-enhanced, and includes many updates and add-ons for Windows 95. At this site, you will find service-packs, browser updates, new utilities, and many other additions to Windows 95. You will also find links to many downloadable browsers, graphics programs, and games. Check out Brian's "Must-Have" applications which include *Winhack* (for configuring several hidden options in Windows 95), *McAfee's Virus Scan*, good old *Winzip*, and something called *Magic Folders* which lets you make any folders and files within those folders completely invisible to others but instantly accessible to yourself. These programs are great—visit this site for more information.

Figure 927.1 Brian's Windows 95 Web Page.

Figure 927.2 Windows 95 updates.

CAMELLIA SHAREWARE & FREEWARE FOR WINDOWS NT

http://www.halcyon.com/camellia/

Camellia offers some great shareware and freeware, including a robust batch job server for Windows NT. At this site, you will also find another nice item, *Autostart*, a Windows NT service that will run a batch file when a Windows NT server or workstation boots. The program places the batch file's output (including errors) in a log file. You may also want to download *CompressMail*, software that lets users compress one or more files or directories into a single Compressed Mail Attachment (CMA) file, which you can then send via e-mail. The CMA file automatically restores when the e-mail recipient "activates" (double-clicks) the e-mail attachment. This is all cool stuff and the price is right—Free.

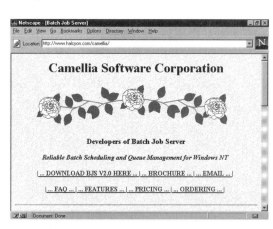

Figure 928 Camellia Software.

AI CAFÉ C/C++ CGI HTML HTTP JAVA J++ PERL VBSCRIPT VRML WIN32 WINSOCK 11001101001011110011011100110101010001100110010101

CANYON SHAREWARE FOR WINDOWS

http://www.canyonsw.com/

The Canyon Web site offers three outstanding, well-reviewed pieces of shareware for Windows 95, NT, and 3.1. The shareware programs are *Drag and File*, *Drag and Zip*, and *Drag and View*. The first, *Drag and File*, lets you kiss your file manager good-bye, easily copy, move or delete files across multiple directories and drives, display and select the contents of multiple driver and directories (including zipped files), hide or display duplicate files, associate data files to multiple applications, and more. The software includes a customizable toolbar, network support, an integrated virus scanner, file filters offering powerful selection criteria (based on date and file size ranges), and more. The other applications are just as cool. Visit this site and download them *now*.

Figure 929.1 Canyon Software.

Figure 929.2 Drag and View details.

AI CAFÉ C/C++ CGI HTML HTTP JAVA J++ PERL VBSCRIPT VRML WIN32 WINSOCK 11001101001011110011011100110101010001100110010101

BOB CERELLI'S WINDOWS 95 PAGE

http://www.halcyon.com/cerelli/

Bob Cerelli provides fantastic hints, tips, and tools to help you install, configure, and maintain Windows 95. You will find tools and techniques for configuring Windows 95 for TCP/IP LANs, *WinChat*, dial-up scripting, and more. The site also discusses using the system monitor, sending and receiving Internet mail using Exchange, editing the Windows 95 registry, adding local or networked printers, and more. The site features tips and related utilities to automate Windows 95 installation (and INF files), and configuring the MSDOS.SYS file. This site is a great place to find answers to your Windows 95 questions. Thanks, Bob.

Figure 930.1 Bob Cerelli's Web page.

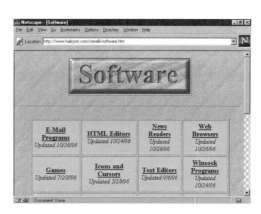

Figure 930.2 Software options.

Frank Condron's World O'Windows

http://www.conitech.com/windows/win95.html

Visit this Web site for driver upgrade information and links related to more than 750 different drivers! Plus, you get hundreds of freeware and shareware drivers available for immediate download, along with an automatic form for requesting other drivers you will receive via e-mail. If you write drivers yourself, you may be interested in surveying the extensive bulletin board of driver requests from Windows 95 developers, managers, and users around the world. Perhaps you've got, or are capable of building, what someone else needs. You should also access Frank's technical tips and his information pages, which address everything from animated cursors to moving to a new hard drive.

Figure 931.1 Condron's World.

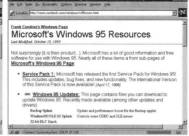
Figure 931.2 Late breaking.

Figure 931.3 Driver suppliers.

Cryptext for Windows (Freeware)

http://www.pcug.org.au/~nipayne/

Cryptext is a freeware program for Windows 95 and Windows NT 4.0 that performs strong file encryption. The program uses a 160-bit key (does Washington D.C. know?). When you install *Cryptext*, it adds "Encrypt" and "Decrypt" items to the context menu Windows 95 displays when you right click your mouse on a file or directory within the Explorer. When you encrypt or decrypt files, *Cryptext* takes your password and uses a one-way hash function to generate a 160-bit key from the password. The software uses this 160-bit key to encrypt or decrypt the files. All of this adds up to substantial security for you, your data, and your computer. Protect your privacy with *Cryptext*, which you can download from this Web site.

Figure 932.1 The Cryptext home page.

Figure 932.2 Easy installation.

CSOCK: C++ SOCKETING LIBRARY SHAREWARE

http://junior.apk.net/~tri/csock/

CSOCK is a shareware socket library for Windows NT and Windows 95. The software lets you easily implement TCP/IP networking into your games and applications without the rote work normally required by the C sockets API. *CSOCK* makes use of the newer C++ standards (templates, exception handling, and the new casting operators) to simplify the work of creating a sockets-based application. With respect to exception handling, the shareware automatically provides a descriptive string as to the cause of most problems, and thus saves you a lot of redundant coding. The shareware also features run-time linking with the sockets API, which lets you write applications that can use TCP/IP but don't *rely* on it. Grab a copy of *CSOCK* and get to work.

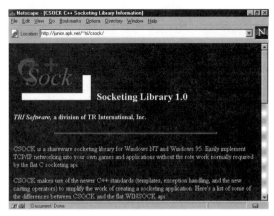

Figure 933 CSOCK.

CUTEFTP FOR WINDOWS (SHAREWARE)

http://www.cuteftp.com/

Are you responsible for a network on which "newbies" occasionally try to engage in FTP file transfers? Are you getting sick of the calls for technical support? Check out *CuteFTP*, a Windows-based Internet application that lets novice users utilize FTP capabilities without having to know all the details of the protocol itself. The software simplifies FTP by offering a user-friendly, graphical interface instead of cumbersome command-line details. One of the strongest features of *CuteFTP* is its ability to gather all available information about files and directory structures of a remote system and present it to the user in an easy to use, file-manager-like browsing screen. Download *CuteFTP* and test-drive it with some newbies.

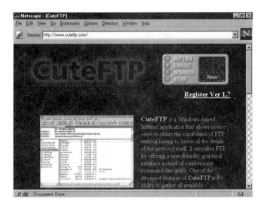

Figure 934.1 The CuteFTP Web site.

Figure 934.2 CuteFTP awards.

CUTTER'S WINDOWS 95 CROSSROADS

http://www.io.com/~kgk/win95.html

At this site, you will find links to Windows 95 usergroups, newsgroups, the *Microsoft Winnews* back issues, Windows 95 Web pages, and more. Visit this site for late-breaking information and rumors from the Microsoft Windows 95 development team, too hot to be published on the official Microsoft Web page. Visit Cutter's for outstanding shareware and freeware tools that enhance Windows 95, customizing it to meet your and your user's unique needs. And, turn to these pages for detailed programming references and help pages related to Visual Basic, Visual C++, and other development environments. This all comes courtesy of Keith Kalet. Thanks, Keith.

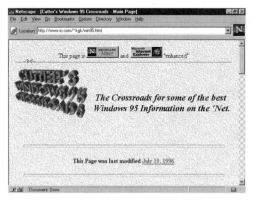

Figure 935.1 The Cutter Web site.

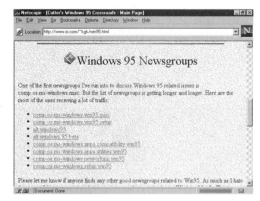

Figure 935.2 Windows 95 newsgroups.

DEVELOPERS ONLY/MICROSOFT

http://www.microsoft.com/DEVONLY/

Microsoft's *Developer's Only* Web site features tips, white papers, technical support, and demos and tools that professional programmers can download for applications and resources related to Windows 95. This Web site puts you in touch with Microsoft, its third-party partners and resources, and other developers just like yourself. Want to learn about the latest changes down deep in the innards of Windows 95? Want to discover how to design a fully-enabled ActiveX Web site? Interested in getting the low-down on Microsoft's ongoing, integrated development strategy? What about a chance to network with Microsoft technical gurus. Get it all right here.

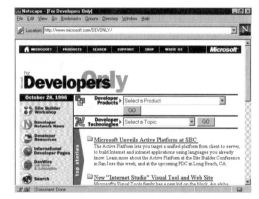

Figure 936.1 Developers Only.

Figure 936.2 International pages.

AI CAFÉ C/C++ CGI HTML HTTP JAVA J++ PERL VBSCRIPT VRML WIN32 WINSOCK 11001101001011110011011100110101010001100100101

DESKTOP PUBLISHING FREEWARE FOR WINDOWS 95

http://www.serif.com/

Serif, a leading publisher of desktop publishing applications for Windows, offers a number of outstanding products as freeware, which you can download from this Web site. Check out *PagePlus Intro 95* for Windows 95. *PagePlus Intro 95* features built-in word processing and logo creation. You can work from scratch or use one of many page wizards for newsletters, business cards memos, and more. Other freeware you will encounter includes *DrawPlus Intro* for Windows 3.1 and Windows 95, along with carefully selected collections of TrueType fonts and clipart. It is all free and waiting for you.

Figure 937 The Serif home page.

AI CAFÉ C/C++ CGI HTML HTTP JAVA J++ PERL VBSCRIPT VRML WIN32 WINSOCK 11001101001011110011011100110101010001100100101

DIR3D SHAREWARE FOR WINDOWS FROM REGNOC SOFTWARE

http://www.regnoc.com/

DIR3D is an alternative to the Windows NT File Manager and Windows 95 Explorer applications. *DIR3D* provides all of the same functions, but uses a three-dimensional user interface to give you the illusion that you are flying around the inside of your hard disk or network directory. *DIR3D* uses the *OpenGL* graphics libraries available with the 32-bit versions of Windows to render the 3-D images in real-time, creating and updating your virtual world as you manipulate files and directories. The site also provides sound effects and music that increase the realism of this completely different perspective on the contents of your hard drive. This is wild. Do a download and check it out.

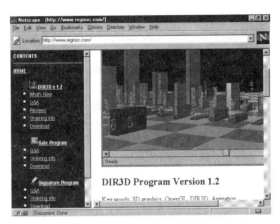

Figure 938 The DIR3D Web site.

939

EASY EDIT FOR WINDOWS 95 — TEXT EDITOR SHAREWARE

http://www.pcisys.net/~jason/easy.html

Easy Edit for Windows 95 is first-rate shareware and, as its name implies, is an easy-to-use text editor that features built-in HTML functions. *Easy Edit* includes a built-in spell checker, a multiple document edit capability, HTML tags, and an intuitive tool bar. *Easy Edit* can also print text into a "booklet" format to conserve paper. In short, *Easy Edit* is not just another HTML editor—it is a great supplement for Windows 95. Download *Easy Edit for Windows 95* and try it on for size. If you like it, continue using the program and just pay a modest $20 registration fee which includes technical support and upgrades.

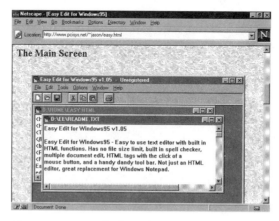

Figure 939 Easy Edit for Windows 95 screen.

940

E-CHECK SHAREWARE FOR WINDOWS 95

http://king.cc.ntu.edu/tw/~b3701246/ECheck.htm

E-Check is an excellent shareware application with which you can check your POP3 e-mail accounts for new mail. The software supports all the features you need: multiple-accounts, model-dialup, MIME, and low network loading. This shareware lets you check up to ten servers. *E-Check* includes a built-in viewer, customizable animation and sound for new-mail notification, and supports hot keys, pop-up menus, tray icons, and dockable buttons. This is a robust, uniquely intuitive product that can simplify many of your e-mail management tasks. Check out this Web site for more information.

Figure 940 E-Check's home page.

EUDORA PRO 3.0 FREE TRIAL AND EUDORA LIGHT FREEWARE

http://www.eudora.com/

Eudora is the #1 electronic-mail application on the Internet, with an estimated 10 million users. Now, you can download *Eudora Pro 3.0* as shareware on a thirty-day trial basis. Also, you can download the freeware *Eudora Light*. Between the two, however, I recommend *Eudora Pro* which has a slew of new features and an expanded set of configuration options. *Eudora Pro* is the undisputed "best product" among all the available Internet e-mail packages. The freeware *Eudora Light* is also a very strong, very robust program. In fact, it is so great that many users just don't bother to take the time to try out the commercial version. And that is a pity, for as excellent as *Eudora Light* is, *Eudora Pro 3.0* is ten times better. Do yourself a favor and download *Eudora Pro 3.0* today.

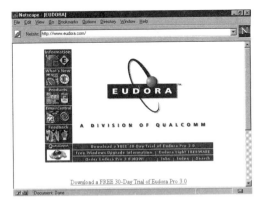

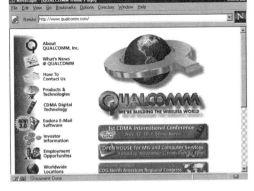

Figure 941.1 The Eudora Web site.

Figure 941.2 Eudora is a Qualcomm product.

FIRASE'S WINDOWS SHAREWARE

http://members.aol.com/felhasan/index.htm

FirasE's offers some excellent shareware for Windows. One application I find particularly appealing is *AddLink* for Windows 95 and Windows NT 4.x, which lets users easily add links, or shortcuts, to any folder in their Start Menu. *AddLink* greatly simplifies the process of having programs start up when Windows starts. In short, you just use *AddLink* to add any program to the Start menu's StartUp folder. After that, the program will automatically run every time Windows starts. Another nice program is *Hot Corners*, a utility that lets you activate a screen saver, or prevent the screen saver's activation simply by moving your mouse cursor to a user-defined corner of the screen. Visit this site and download these and other goodies.

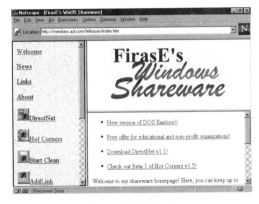

Figure 942.1 The FirasE' Web site.

Figure 942.2 Another great app.

FLASHPOINT SHAREWARE FOR WINDOWS

http://members.aol.com/flashptdev/html/index.html

Like most programmers, you probably make extensive use of ZIP files to store your data in a compressed format. FlashPoint offers two excellent pieces of shareware for Windows users and developers: *UnZIP95* and *ZIP* Navigator. *UnZIP95* is billed as the first "completely simple" solution for managing existing ZIP file archives under Microsoft Windows 95 Explorer. *UnZIP95* is a fully-integrated extension featuring custom ZIP file icons, context menus, and property sheet dialogs for viewing, expanding, testing, and managing any standard *ZIP* archive with only a few mouse clicks. *ZIP Navigator* provides a similar suite for Windows 3.x, and includes *WinSFX* for creating self-extracting Windows (not DOS) archives. Both are available in full shareware versions for your evaluation.

Figure 943.1 The FlashPoint Web site.

F-PROT ANTI-VIRUS SHAREWARE DEMO FROM DATA FELLOWS

http://www.datafellows.fi/

F-PROT is a leading anti-virus and data-security toolkit from Data Fellows. There are versions of the software available for DOS, Windows 95, Windows 3.x, OS/2, and Novell NetWare. *F-PROT* includes everything you need to protect your files against viruses, including the new Word-specific macro viruses. You can select appropriate methods you want to use within your organization or you can use them all for maximum security. The product includes a rule-based scanner to detect previously unknown viruses. It also includes a check-summing program which, in addition to detecting, is also able to disinfect previously unknown viruses. Visit this site for the shareware demo and check it out.

Figure 944.1 The Data Fellows Web site.

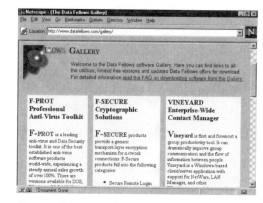

Figure 944.2 Download F-PROT and other demos.

AI CAFÉ C/C++ CGI HTML HTTP JAVA J++ PERL VBSCRIPT VRML WIN32 WINSOCK 1100110100101111001101110011010101000110011001001010

FTP 2000 SHAREWARE FOR WIN95

http://www.qoi.com/cgi-local/qoi.cgi?pg=Ftp2

This site features an excellent Windows 95 FTP client. The software features a built-in remote editor, a built-in HTML editor, a smooth drag-and-drop interface, and a site manager for keeping track of cool FTP sites. The client program lets you cancel uploads and downloads without stopping the entire program. It also lets you sort directory lists by name, size, type, or dates just by clicking on a column header. *FTP 2000* can also pull fire wall and proxy information from the system registry or, if you choose, you may specify custom firewall and proxy parameters. In all, this is first rate stuff. Visit this site and download a copy of *FTP 2000*.

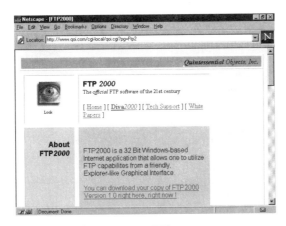

Figure 945 The FTP 2000 Web site.

AI CAFÉ C/C++ CGI HTML HTTP JAVA J++ PERL VBSCRIPT VRML WIN32 WINSOCK 1100110100101111001101110011010101000110011001001010

FTP EXPLORER FOR WINDOWS (SHAREWARE)

http://www.ftpx.com/

FTP Explorer is a 32-bit file transfer protocol client for Windows 95 and NT 4.0 that looks and acts very much like the Windows Explorer. *FTP Explorer* is extremely simple to operate and makes moving files between the Internet and your computer as simple as local file manipulation. Several features of *FTP Explorer* make it stand head and shoulders above most other FTP programs that are currently available. This shareware lets you download or upload files to one or more servers while browsing and selecting files to transfer on another. Can't connect? Not to worry. *FTP Explorer* will automatically retry if the connection attempt fails. Download the *FTP Explorer* and try it on for size.

Figure 946.1 FTP Explorer home page.

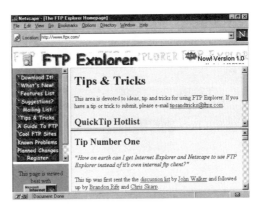

Figure 946.2 FTP Explorer tips and tricks.

947

FUNDUC SHAREWARE FOR WINDOWS

http://home.sprynet.com/sprynet/funduc/

Funduc has several excellent pieces of Windows shareware that you can download from this site. To start, *Search and Replace* for Windows, Windows 95, and NT is a fast and easy to use text search (*grep*) and replace utility. The program can search through multiple files (specified by one or more masks) for a string and can also replace it with another string. The software can also search subdirectories and perform case sensitive or unsensitive searches. Additional shareware offerings include *Directory Toolkit* for Windows 95/NT, *HexView*, a Windows 95/NT hexadecimal viewer, and a utility that automatically loads the contents of any INI file into the Windows 95/NT registry. The *Directory Toolkit* compares (and synchronizes) files in two directories. We are talking about a *very* useful tool. Visit this site and check it out.

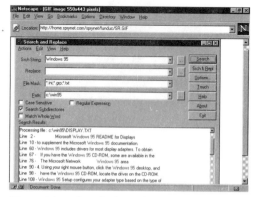

Figure 947.1 the Funduc Software Web site.

Figure 947.2 Search & Replace screenshot.

948

GALT WINDOWS SHAREWARE ZONE

http://www.galttech.com/

Visit the Galt Windows Shareware Zone for hundreds of great Windows shareware and freeware programs. To start, check out *ScreenPix*, which lets you use your own JPEG, GIB, or BMP images in a slide-show screen-saver. Or, download *DeskView32*, which provides instant access to all items on your Windows 95 desktop without minimizing your current applications. Also, grab yourself a beautiful waterfalls screen saver. Or, grab a utility that lets you turn your company logo (BMP) into a screen saver. Then, take *Grouper*, a fantastic file organizer and launcher for Windows 95. Before you leave, check out *Powerstrip* (a tiny program that does it all: clock dialer, CD, calc, alarms, you name it). You will not find a more comprehensive Windows shareware/freeware anywhere on the Web. This is a site for your bookmark file.

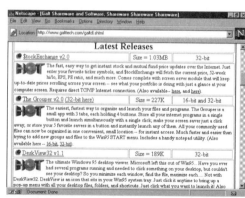

Figure 948.1 Galt Windows Shareware Zone.

Figure 948.2 The latest and hottest shareware.

AI CAFÉ C/C++ CGI HTML HTTP JAVA J++ PERL VBSCRIPT VRML WIN32 WINSOCK 1100110100101110011011100110101010001100110010101

GIF CONSTRUCTION SET SHAREWARE FOR WINDOWS

http://www.mindworkshop.com/alchemy/gifcon.html

GIF Construction Set for Windows is a powerful collection of tools to work with multiple-block GIF files. The software lets you assemble GIF files containing image blocks, plain text blocks, comment blocks, and control blocks. It also includes facilities to manage palettes and merge multiple GIF files. Among its other functions, *GIF Construction Set for Windows* can create wide-palette GIF files that support more than 256 colors, generate sophisticated special-effect text titles, create looping animation GIF files for Netscape-enhanced Web pages, and create animated text banners. Take this shareware out for a test drive and see how you like it.

Figure 949 GIF Construction Set for Windows.

AI CAFÉ C/C++ CGI HTML HTTP JAVA J++ PERL VBSCRIPT VRML WIN32 WINSOCK 1100110100101110011011100110101010001100110010101

GR DISK UTILITY FOR WINDOWS 95

http://mini.net/cgi-bin/sax?2347

Need to format a disk using Windows 95? Instead of using Explorer, try the *GR Disk Utility*, which this site offers as shareware. Using an attractive, tabbed-dialog interface, this 32-bit utility lets you format diskettes in several capacities, including the Microsoft Distributed Media Format (*.dmf*) of 1.68Mb as well as 1.72Mb. You can also use the software to format disks in your choice of reador write access, speed-optimized mode, or standard MS-DOS mode. The *GR Disk Utility* can also format hard disks. The software includes diskette copying tools, and tools that let you check the boot sector of your diskette or hard drive for viruses and then recreate a new save boot. The author is Roberto Grassi, of Italy, who also offers the *GRBack* back-up facility for Windows 95. Bravisimo!

Figure 950 An ugly page with GREAT shareware.

DYLAN GREENE'S WINDOWS 95 PAGES

http://www.dylan95.com/

Yes, this is the same Dylan Greene who brings you the excellent Visual Basic page referenced in site 889. This excellent site, based on software devised by Mr. Greene himself, comes in three flavors: Frames & JavaScript, Frames & Java, and Tables. Tables is the least interesting but loads the fastest. Greene's coverage of programming resources related to Visual C++ and Visual Basic programming for Windows 95 contains the best information at this site. Greene's list of tools, resources, and tutorials is extensive. If you bookmark only one Windows 95 Web page, Dylan Greene's is the one to which you should keep coming back. From this site, you can get anywhere—I mean anywhere. Dylan has more than 1,000 (categorized and annotated) links!

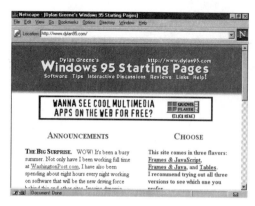

Figure 951.1 Dylan Greene's Windows 95 Pages.

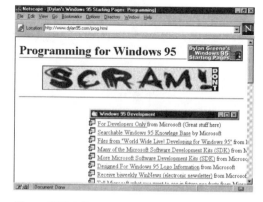

Figure 951.2 Programming resources.

HEX WORKSHOP SHAREWARE FOR WINDOWS

http://ourworld.compuserve.com/homepages/breakpoint/

The *Hex Workshop* shareware is a fully-functional professional hexadecimal editor. This program and disk editor runs under Windows 3.1, Windows 95, and Windows NT. *Hex Workshop* was designed by programmers for programmers and does not double as a text editor. Both the 16-bit and 32-bit versions are available. The program has gotten great reviews. "*Hex Workshop* is a Win95 programmer's dream," says *Windows Sources* magazine. With *Hex Workshop*, you can edit multiple files of unlimited size, edit both logical disks and raw fixed disks, print high-quality customized hex dumps, find and replace Hex or ASCII values, calculate checksums for all or part of a file, and much more. Cool.

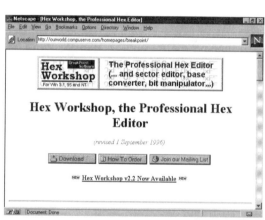

Figure 952 The Hex Workshop Web site.

AI CAFÉ C/C++ CGI HTML HTTP JAVA J++ PERL VBSCRIPT VRML WIN32 WINSOCK 1100110100101111001101110011010101000110011001001001

HUTCH'S WINDOWS 95 PAGE

http://www.nidlink.com/~hutch/win95.html

Starsky is a Mac-head, so Hutch will be all alone with Windows 95 if you don't pay him a visit. One of the best aspects of Hutch's cyberspace precinct is the very good PPP/SLIP settings help he provides for Windows 95 users, which include a fantastic how-to list as well as a list of frequently asked questions, along with details on configuring TCP/IP for Windows 95, and a detailed tutorial on Internet file sharing with Windows 95. Hutch is an internationalist! He provides a great set of links to Windows 95 shareware/freeware archives around the globe, offering local download sites for those in the United States, Germany, Japan, Taiwan, South America, and Australia. Thanks, Hutch.

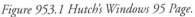

Figure 953.1 Hutch's Windows 95 Page.

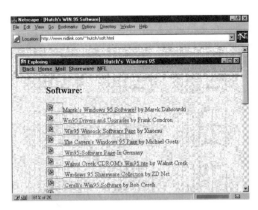

Figure 953.2 Software resources.

AI CAFÉ C/C++ CGI HTML HTTP JAVA J++ PERL VBSCRIPT VRML WIN32 WINSOCK 1100110100101111001101110011010101000110011001001001

iBLAST: E-MAIL BROADCASTING SHAREWARE

http://www.compuaid.baremetal.com/iblast.html

iBlast is, according to its author, "a true 32-bit mailing-list manager/sender for Windows 95 and NT 3.51 or better." The software lets you work with an unlimited number of lists, and unlimited recipients per list. It supports text importing of messages and features the easiest, most-intuitive interface of any mailing-list software. The *iBlast* shareware is a product of CompuAid—an outfit based in Aurora, Colorado. Visit this site and download the fully functional shareware version of *iBlast*, unzip it, run *Setup.exe*, and you are good to go! If you like the shareware, the registration fee is a more than reasonable at $20. And, that includes upgrades. I think the author keeps a mailing list of some kind .

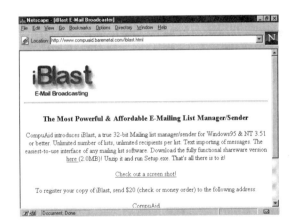

Figure 954 The iBlast Web site.

955

INTEGRA SHAREWARE FOR WINDOWS

http://members.aol.com/integracmp/index.htm

Integra Computing offers some of the finest scheduling, timekeeping, and billing software available. *Chronilist* has nearly everything anyone would want in a scheduler, including an intuitive interface, pop-up alarms, a handy phone book, and scheduling for up to 50 people. *Client Tracks* begins with all the scheduling power of *Chronilist* and then adds a fully integrated client database. *BillPower* combines timekeeping, billing, and the most popular accounting functions into a single program. And, *Integra Office* combines into a single program all the features found in both *Client Tracks* and *BillPower*. These programs are ideal for independent computer programmer and consultants.

Figure 955.1 Integra Computing.

956

KERNEL TOYS FOR WIN95

http://www.microsoft.com/windows/software/krnltoy.htm

The Windows 95 kernel team got of jealous of the attention the shell team has been getting from its *PowerToys*, so they decided to make their own Web page. Mind you, the kernel folks aren't experts at intuitive user interfaces, so don't expect to see jumping icons and friendly things to click on. (These guys still do their taxes in hexadecimal.) If, however, you are a power user, you will want to try these toys out. But remember, there's no lifeguard on duty. These things are unsupported. Swim at your own risk. That being said, the *Kernel Toy Set* includes a conventional memory tracker, a keyboard remap, a process watcher, a time-zone editor, and other cool stuff.

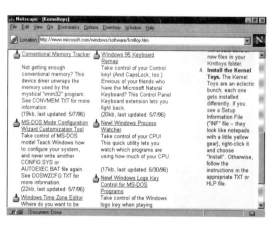

Figure 956 Kernel Toys.

AI CAFÉ C/C++ CGI HTML HTTP JAVA J++ PERL VBSCRIPT VRML WIN32 WINSOCK 1100110100101110011011100110101010001100110010010

LEESOFT'S SHAREWARE FOR WINDOWS

http://www.sliceoflife.com/official/leesoft/

LeeSoft offers several neat shareware products, but the very best of them is *Scratch Pad Version 2.0*, a full-featured editor (and more!) for Windows 95. More, you say? That's right. When you are Web surfing, you can use *Scratch Pad's* auto capture feature to quickly save data from Web pages. You start *Scratch Pad*, turn on its auto-capture feature, and begin surfing with your favorite Web browser. When you find information that you want to keep, just copy it to the Windows Clipboard. *Scratch Pad*, in turn, adds the item to your current document. *Scratch Pad* also includes tools designed to make it easy to cut and paste from one application to another. Visit this site, download *Scratchpad*, and try it out for yourself.

Figure 957 The LeeSoft Web site.

AI CAFÉ C/C++ CGI HTML HTTP JAVA J++ PERL VBSCRIPT VRML WIN32 WINSOCK 1100110100101110011011100110101010001100110010010

LIFESAVER SHAREWARE FOR WINDOWS 95

http://members.aol.com/aeroblade/index.html

LifeSaver, its author tells us, "is a Windows 95 configuration file backup and restore utility. It can be used to recover from problems due to corrupt configuration files or changes to configuration files which cannot be undone." *LifeSaver* can backup and restore up to seven different configuration files (including the registry) and can run from the command line with scheduling programs such as *System Agent*. *Lifesaver* can change default options based on system configuration, save up to two backups, restore system files from the command prompt (DOS) mode with a self-generating batch file, and can safely restore the registry files from Windows. The best part is that you can download it from this site. Go get it!

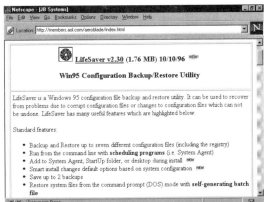

Figure 958 LifeSaver home page.

Angela Lilleystone's Windows 95 Information

http://www.cs.umb.edu/~alilley/win.html

Angela Lilleystone provides an excellent set of resources related to Windows 95 and NT. Visit this site for tips and tricks, technical support, tools, and utilities. The site is particularly strong when it comes to information about Windows 95 OEM Service Release 2 (OSR 2), a Fall '95 update to Windows 95 that adds support for new and emerging hardware. Because most of the new functionality of OSR 2 is applicable only to new hardware devices, OSR 2 is only available on new PCs, and will later be included in the "Memphis" release of Windows 95 (see details on Memphis at this Web site). Resources related directly to OSR 2 are scant, but they are all found at this site.

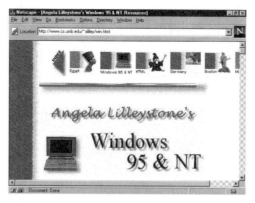

Figure 959.1 The Angela Lilleystone Web site.

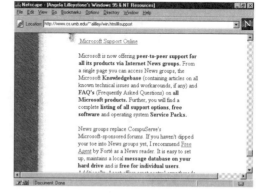

Figure 959.2 Tech support information.

Marek's Win95/Internet Resources

http://md.simplenet.com/

This site is "the place" for the best Windows 95 and Internet-related resources. You will find an outstanding, carefully reviewed collection of 32-bit shareware and freeware. Visit this site for networking and internetworking applications, desktop applications, graphics utilities, browsers, browser plug-ins, HTML editors, mail and news readers, chat clients, and more. You will also find expert tips and tricks, first-class technical white papers and other support, newsgroup connections, electronic news about Windows and related topics, and much more. The site is routinely updated several times a week, so check back every week or so for new stuff.

Figure 960.1 Marek's Web site.

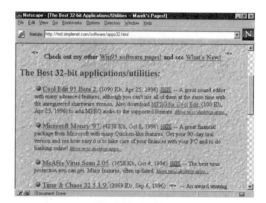

Figure 960.2 32-bit applications/utilities.

AI CAFÉ C/C++ CGI HTML HTTP JAVA J++ PERL VBSCRIPT VRML WIN32 WINSOCK 11001101001011110011011100110101010001100110010010

MICHAEL'S WINDOWS 95 FREQUENTLY ASKED QUESTIONS

http://ourworld.compuserve.com/homepages/mschoebel/faqwin95.htm

What is *EBIOS.VXD*? How do I change a folder's default settings? How do I change the drive letter of my CD-ROM? What is the *SmartCan* directory? My icons suddenly turned black. What now? What are **.GID* files? Why is my computer sometimes so slow? Why doesn't dial-up networking remember my password anymore? How do I invoke the Easter Egg? How do I resize the taskbar? Does Windows 95 work with a Dual-Pentium System? How can I create a new StartUp logo for Windows 95? How do I move the taskbar? How do I delete those shortcuts? Windows 95 reports less memory than I have. Why? Visit this site and get the answers to all these questions and more.

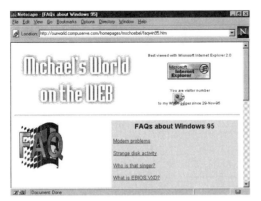

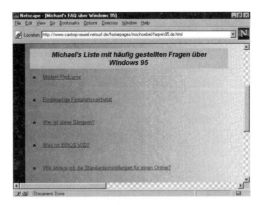

Figure 961.1 In English.   *Figure 961.2 Und Deutsch.*

AI CAFÉ C/C++ CGI HTML HTTP JAVA J++ PERL VBSCRIPT VRML WIN32 WINSOCK 11001101001011110011011100110101010001100110010010

MIDSTREAM SHAREWARE FOR WINDOWS

http://207.176.40.21/

Midstream offers two excellent pieces of shareware for Windows users. At this site, you will find programs such as *BusinessCards for Windows*, a robust Windows *cardfile* replacement available in both 16-bit and 32-bit flavors. *BusinessCards for Windows* was a ZDNet Editor's Best Pick in January 1996. It was also an America Online "Editor's Featured Shareware Selection" and has been officially noted as "Superior Software" by *Windows Magazine*. You will also find *007 for Win32* provides unique security solutions for both Windows 95 and NT and allows you to password protect your most sensitive programs. *007 for Win32* was recently afforded the honor of being "Shareware of the Day" for PC World On-Line. Visit this site for more information.

Figure 962 Midstream home page.

MINUET SHAREWARE FOR WINDOWS

http://ourworld.compuserve.com/homepages/minuet/

The best piece of shareware you will find at this site is *Minuet Fetch,* an easy to use address information system with complete searching and retrieving capabilities. Although at first glance *Minuet Fetch* appears to be a simple address book, the shareware houses powerful search and relational capabilities. In addition to storing and retrieving addresses and phone numbers, the shareware tracks client/sales referrals, prints useful information in concise reports, creates an automatic backup of the main data file, houses a built-in network capability, can work with subsets of information, and is available in versions for Windows 3.1, 95, and NT. Visit this site and go for a download of this excellent professional tool.

Figure 963 The Minuet home page.

MOAL C SHAREWARE COMPILER FOR WINDOWS

http://www.moal.com/mc/

MOAL C is a share compiler that overcomes many of standard C/C++'s limitations. To start, *MOAL C* provides safety. Even if you are careless in your programming, crashing a *MOAL C* program is a rarity. So, you can relax a little. The software also offers debugging advantages. The software's smart compiler and run-time checks work together to give you diagnostics that pinpoint errors. *MOAL C* also offers sophisticated memory management and metadata capabilities. In fact, every space has associated metadata which you can access at any time. Thus, many routine tasks, such as looping through the elements in a space or adding a new element at the end of a space, are greatly simplified. Check out *MOAL C* and see how it can make your programming life easy.

Figure 964 MOAL C home page.

AI Café C/C++ CGI HTML HTTP Java J++ Perl VBScript VRML Win32 Winsock 11001101001011110011011100110101010001100110010101

More Space 95—Shareware

http://members.aol.com/MoreSpc95/index.htm

Contact Plus Corporation presents an excellent bit of shareware called *More Space 95*. This software, they write, "is designed for Windows 95 and will help you free up valuable hard disk space by locating duplicate files and file/folder hogs." The program fully supports long file names. In addition, the software will display duplicate files that are in the Windows search path so that you can delete the appropriate duplicate file. You can delete the files directly or you can send the files to the Windows 95 Recycle Bin, from which you can purge the files later. The program also displays file hogs—listing the culprits by number of sub-folders, number of files, and percent of the free hard disk they consume. Try out this shareware today.

Figure 965 Contact Plus Corporation's home page.

AI Café C/C++ CGI HTML HTTP Java J++ Perl VBScript VRML Win32 Winsock 11001101001011110011011100110101010001100110010101

MS Word Macro Virus Protection Tool from Microsoft

http://www.microsoft.com/msword/freestuff/mvtool/mvtool2.htm

Microsoft has developed a tool which installs a set of protective macros that detect suspicious Word files and alert users to the potential risk of opening files with macros. When alerted, users are given the choice of opening the file without executing the macros, opening the file as is, or canceling the file open operation. Opening the file without macros ensures that macro viruses are not transmitted, but still lets the user view the content of the document. The tool also contains an updated version of the scanning code for the *Concept* virus (also known as the *Word Prak Macro* virus). You can use this scanning code to examine your hard disk for Word files that contain the *Concept* virus. Arm yourself appropriately. Visit this site for a free download.

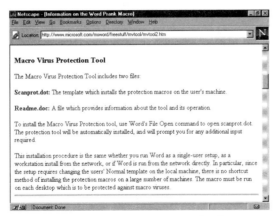

Figure 966 Macro Virus Protection Tool information.

NOTIFYMAIL SHAREWARE FOR WINDOWS

http://www.notifymail.com/

NotifyMail is a new mail notifier that works in cooperation with your mail-server to notify you immediately when new mail arrives. The software is not an active checker like many e-mail clients (such as *Eudora* and *Z-mail*), but rather it is a passive client that "listens" for a cue from the server (a finger connection) when new mail arrives. *NotifyMail* is shareware for Windows (with a version also available for the *MacOS*). Upon receiving the finger connection, *NotifyMail* will either pop-up a dialog box, play a sound, or display a floating mailbox window—based on your preference. As a passive listener on a socket, the beauty of *NotifyMail* is that the software takes up virtually no CPU cycles, unless the server is notifying it. Visit this site for a free download today.

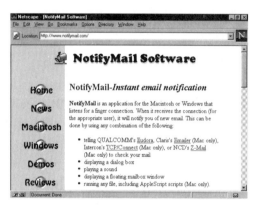

Figure 967.1 The NotifyMail Web site.

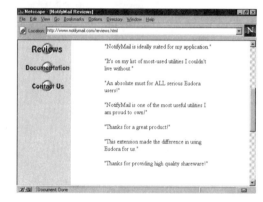

Figure 967.2 Reviews of the software.

ONEDIR PRO SHAREWARE FOR WINDOWS 95

http://www.crl.com/~scrappy/OneDIR/

OneDIR Pro is a complete, high-quality, color, DIR command replacement for Windows 95 and DOS. The software provides many powerful and unique features not available in many other DIR replacements, such as support for long file names and customization of file extensions and colors. "Every effort has been made to make *OneDIR Pro* the best DOS DIR replacement available anywhere," writes its author proudly. "Don't be fooled by similar utilities. *OneDIR Pro* blows away the competition." And, you can't beat the price. If you like the shareware and decide to continue using it, you are expected to fork over the grand sum of $5! Check it out.

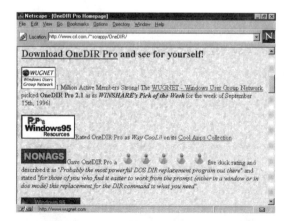

Figure 968 Some rave reviews.

AI CAFÉ C/C++ CGI HTML HTTP JAVA J++ PERL VBSCRIPT VRML WIN32 WINSOCK 110011010010111100110111001101010100011001100100101

OPEN SESAME FOR NT—SHAREWARE

http://www.csm.co.at/OPSEDOCS/index.htm

Open Sesame is a full-featured proxy (mediates traffic between protected data and the Internet) and caching server written especially to make life easier for the network administrator working with Windows NT. The software features DNS forwarding, a native FTP proxy, HTTP caching, POP3 proxy, RealAudio 2.0 proxy, telnet proxy, TCP mapped links, automatic dialing on demand, easy configuration and administration, and a large collection of logging capabilities. The site invites you to download the demo shareware which has the same features as the full product, but it expires after 30 days. You can also view full documentation on-line or download the documentation. Check out *Open Sesame*. It could be just what you are looking for.

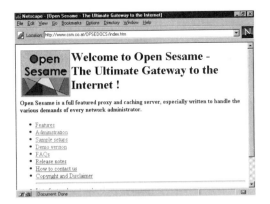

Figure 969.1 The Open Sesame Web site.

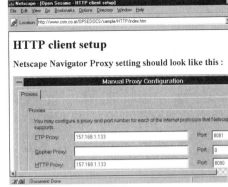

Figure 969.2 Detailed set-up information.

AI CAFÉ C/C++ CGI HTML HTTP JAVA J++ PERL VBSCRIPT VRML WIN32 WINSOCK 110011010010111100110111001101010100011001100100101

PEERSYNC PEER-TO-PEER SYNCHRONIZATION SHAREWARE

http://www.genesysweb.com/peersync/

PeerSync is a file transfer utility that synchronizes (allows simultaneous, real-time updating of all like-minded files across a network), copies, and compresses files and folders. The operation's source and target can be on the same drive, two drives in the same computer, or remote sources linked via a direct connect cable, LAN, WAN, or dial-up remote access. If your system can "see" the drives, this utility offers a very powerful set of features for coordinating and synchronizing files and folders. This is fantastic if you are a network administrator and you want to replicate a program installation over multiple computers spread out across the country on your WAN. Do yourself a favor and grab a copy of *PeerSync*.

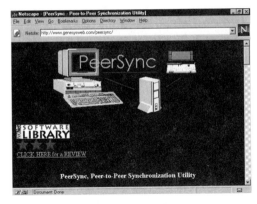

Figure 970.1 The PeerSync Web site.

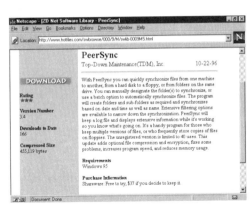

Figure 970.2 A great review from Ziff-Davis.

971

PERL FOR WIN32 FREQUENTLY ASKED QUESTIONS

http://www.perl.hip.com/PerlFAQ.htm

What are the UNIX and Win32 differences with regard to Perl? What functions are unsupported in Perl for Win32? How do I make my Perl script executable from the command line? Why doesn't the UNIX #! notation work with my Perl script on NT? Why isn't function (insert the UNIX system call of choice here) available with my Perl script on NT? How do I tell if a bug is specific to the Win32 port? How do I report a bug? Why can't I treat sockets as file handles? What happened to DBM support? How does the OLE automation stuff work? How do I use NT registry extensions? Is there a way to print to *stdout* in binary mode? Visit this excellent Perl reference for the answers to these questions and many more.

Figure 971 Perl for Win32 FAQ.

972

PIRCH INTERNET RELAY CHAT CLIENT FOR WINDOWS (SHAREWARE)

http://www.bcpl.lib.md.us/~frappa/pirch.html

PIRCH is a shareware IRC (Internet Relay Chat) client for Microsoft Windows 3.x, Window 95, and Windows NT. The software is available in both 16- and 32-bit versions. The shareware features an easy to use interface, supports all IRC2 commands, allows multiple server connections, supports user-definable aliases and variables, and supports CTCP (Client to Client Protocols). You can, if necessary, disable CTCP. The shareware also supports DCC (Direct Client to Client) commands for file trans-fers and secure private chats. Visit this site and download the shareware. I think that you will find that this software is right up your alley.

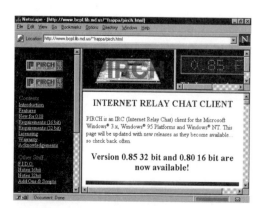

Figure 972.1 The Pirch Web site.

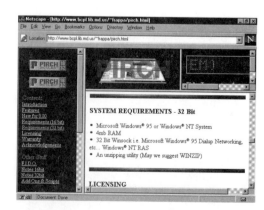

Figure 972.2 32-bit requirements.

AI CAFÉ C/C++ CGI HTML HTTP JAVA J++ PERL VBSCRIPT VRML WIN32 WINSOCK 1100110100101110011011100110101010001100110010010\

PLASMATECH SOFTWARE: INSTALLATION PACKAGER SHAREWARE

http://nemesis.com.au/Plasmatk/INDEX.HTM

Installation Packager is a 32-bit Windows 95, NT 3.51, and NT 4.0 application that takes your existing product installation files and merges them into a single executable. When users download your product, they simply double-click on the single *.EXE* and your installation is extracted and executed. When your setup has completed, the software deletes the setup files. *Installation Packager* provides interactive and command-line interfaces, so you can quickly configure your project and incorporate it into your product's automated build. *Installation Packager* is compatible with existing installation programs such as *Install Shield, Microsoft Setup* and just about all other setup programs. Visit this site for more information.

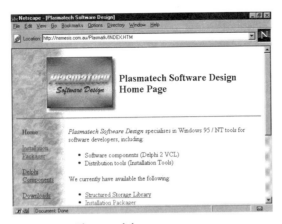

Figure 973 Plasmatech home page.

AI CAFÉ C/C++ CGI HTML HTTP JAVA J++ PERL VBSCRIPT VRML WIN32 WINSOCK 1100110100101110011011100110101010001100110010010\

POP'S WINDOWS 95 RESOURCES PAGE

http://www.clearlight.com/~visanu/win95.html

Pop updates his Windows 95 Resources Page every day of the week with new resources and tools. At this site, you will find cool software programs, trial versions of new applications, as well as shareware and freeware programs you can download. The programs you will encounter include: *Automate 96, Expression 32-Bit Calculator, Microsoft NetShow, WordScribe Lite, PolyView, HomeSite, PSA Cards 3.0,* and *Almanac.* You also get daily news, views, and reviews, along with industry gossip, press releases from Microsoft and other major players, and more. This all comes to us from our gracious hosts, Clearlight Communications. Check it out.

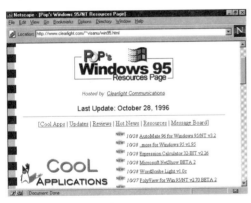

Figure 974.1 Pop's place.

Figure 974.2 NetPC news.

975

PROCESS SOFTWARE'S WINDOWS 95 PAGE & FTP SITE

http://www.process.com/win95/

This site contains great information and resources for Windows 95. You will find everything from the most rudimentary aspects of Windows 95 (installation and startup) to advanced programming hints and tips and tools. A particularly strong collection of tools and programs is available via FTP. The available programs include a math browser that understands *Multi-CD (.MCD)* files, a TCP/IP dialing daemon for 32-bit Windows, an FTP server for Windows 95, as well as global chat IRC clients for Windows 95 and NT. In addition, you will find a *32-bit Finger, Whois, CCSO Ph, Name Server Lookup*, and *ICMP Pinger* for Windows 95. Access all this and more at the Process Windows 95 Web site.

Figure 975.1 Process's Windows 95 page.

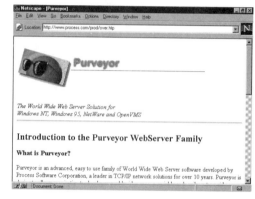

Figure 975.2 You also get Process product information.

976

RAY'S WIN95 SUPPORT, UPGRADES, AND FIXES

http://www.gc.net/rwclements/

This Web site contains a wealth of resources for the Windows 95 user. You will find links to many of the latest software upgrades, updates, and patches from software developers. You'll find links to numerous hardware manufacturers where you can find the latest device drivers. And in addition, this site contains an extensive listing of other Windows 95 sites and Internet search engines. Visit this site for links and information related to *Microsoft Image Composer, Windows 95 PowerToys*, the latest update to *First Aid95*, the freeware 32-bit *NetManage WebSurfer 5.0 for Windows 95*, and much more. This site comes courtesy of Ray Clements. Thanks, Ray.

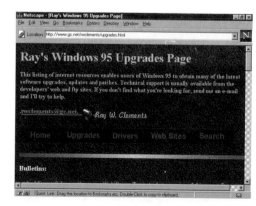

Figure 976.1 Ray's upgrades.

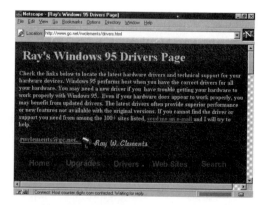

Figure 976.2 Ray's drivers.

AI CAFÉ C/C++ CGI HTML HTTP JAVA J++ PERL VBSCRIPT VRML WIN32 WINSOCK 11001101001011100110111001101010100011001100100101

THE REGISTRATION WIZARD CONTROVERSY

http://www.ora.com/centers/windows/regwiz.html

The Registration Wizard for Windows 95 is a controversial item. It surreptitiously collects information on applications (both Microsoft and non-Microsoft) that users have installed on their hard disks, and send this information back to Microsoft via the Microsoft Network (MSN) during the registration process. The name of this process is "Product Inventory." It is a feature of *PRODINV.DLL,* included with Windows 95. Ralph Nader's Consumer Project on Technology even issued a formal warning to President Clinton "to prevent federal agencies from installing Windows 95 until the information gathering features of the Registration Wizard are modified." Visit this Web site for more information.

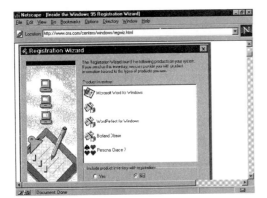

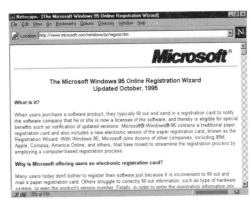

Figure 977.1 The relevant screen.　　　　*Figure 977.2 Microsoft's response.*

AI CAFÉ C/C++ CGI HTML HTTP JAVA J++ PERL VBSCRIPT VRML WIN32 WINSOCK 11001101001011100110111001101010100011001100100101

RFTP FTP CLIENT FOR WINDOWS 95 & NT 4.0 (SHAREWARE)

http://www.primenet.com/~roessler/RFtp.html

RFtp is a GUI-based FTP client available for both Windows 95 and Windows NT 4.0. While incorporating the load-time and footprint of an applet, *RFtp* retains the features and functionality of a full-sized application. *RFtp's* graphical view of remote systems uses familiar icons and context menus. It also saves a list of visited sites and user settings in the system registry (no INI files!). The shareware supports both anonymous and user-name/password logins, the PINGing of arbitrary URLs, and passive-mode transfers required to accommodate firewalls. Another nice touch: the software assigns downloads and uploads its own thread, so the interface remains responsive. Visit this site and download a copy of *RFtp* today.

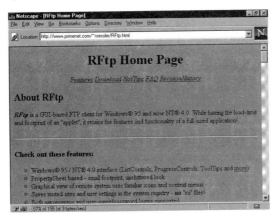

Figure 978 RFtp home page.

ROUTE 95: WINDOWS 95 ON THE INFORMATION SUPERHIGHWAY

http://www.scott.net/~gtaylor/route95/

This excellent Web site is a clearinghouse of information on Windows 95. Of special interest is the excellent font library you will find at this site. As the Webmaster, Geof Taylor, writes: "I am always on the lookout for new fonts. Call it a hobby, obsession, or whatever you will. Here are some goodies I have found on the 'net'." Also, be sure to check out the group of pages entitled "Keystrokes: Do You Ignore Your Keyboard for Your Mouse?" Learn why a point and a click is not always the fastest way to get where you want to go in Windows 95. And, be sure to read and benefit from Geof's great list of updated tips for customizing Windows 95. Thanks, Geof. Stay on the lookout.

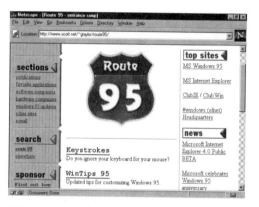

Figure 979.1 Thumb a ride on Route 95.

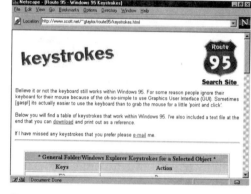

Figure 979.2 Keystrokes!

SAHALIE SOFTWARE: SHAREWARE FOR WINDOWS

http://www.cyber-dyne.com/~sahalie/

Want some hot shareware. Sahalie Software offers three quality shareware products for Windows. *Crowd Control* is a great tool for managing multiple users of your Windows 95 computer. Each user has his or her own Desktop, Start Menu, Programs folder, and other Windows 95 folders. In addition, you can place restrictions on users to control the use of the computer and minimize the risk that other users will accidentally delete important files or change configuration settings. *MAPI Message Pad* is a first-rate telephone message system for Windows 95, Windows for Workgroups, and Windows NT. And, *Reference Bank* is a legal research and work product retrieval system for attorneys. Visit this site and download each of them.

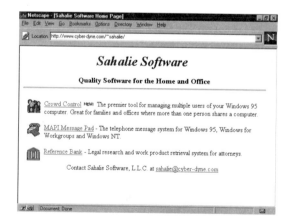

Figure 980 Sahalie home page.

AI CAFÉ C/C++ CGI HTML HTTP JAVA J++ PERL VBSCRIPT VRML WIN32 WINSOCK 1100110100101111001101110011010101000110011001001001

RODNEY SAVARD SHAREWARE FOR WINDOWS

http://www.owt.com/users/rsavard/software.html

Rodney Savard offers a range of excellent shareware for Windows. You will find a number of items at this site but my favorite is *Crypt-o-Text*, an extremely useful and intuitive program that lets you encrypt and decyprt e-mail messages and other small text files with a password. In this way, you can ensure that only your intended recipient (the person knowing the password) can decrypt the e-mail message and read it. I should note that this software is just as secure and robust as PGP but is much easier to use. *Crypt-o-Text* is available in both 16-bit and 32-bit versions. Visit this site for a download and start securing your on-line privacy today!

Figure 981 Savard Software.

AI CAFÉ C/C++ CGI HTML HTTP JAVA J++ PERL VBSCRIPT VRML WIN32 WINSOCK 11001101001011110011011100110101010001100110010010

SERV-U FTP SERVER FOR WINDOWS (SHAREWARE)

http://www.cat-soft.com/

Cat Soft brings you *Serv-U*, a robust, full-featured shareware FTP server for Windows in all its various flavors (3.1, 3.11, Win95, and NT). The shareware offers a simple setup, yet it is powerful, very stable, and has extensive security features. Available in both 16- and 32-bit versions, *Serv-U* supports multiple simultaneous users and transfers, supports links like those in UNIX, supports the resume option, supports multi-homed IP server sites (that support two or more domain names), and can run invisibly with no user access to the program. The shareware also includes a time-out feature that clears connections automatically when they become idle or hung. And, the software is fast. In short, *Serv-U* is well worth a test drive. Try it out today.

Figure 982.1 Cat Soft home page.

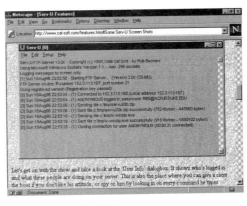

Figure 982.2 Serv-U screen.

SMARTDRAW SHAREWARE FOR WINDOWS

http://www.smartdraw.com/

SmartDraw is shareware for Windows that lets anyone draw great looking flowcharts, diagrams, and other business graphics. Its ease of use makes it particularly suitable for users who need to create professional quality drawings quickly and simply, without having to invest time learning to use a complex application. *SmartDraw* includes more than 1,500 pre-drawn shapes and symbols that you simply drag onto your drawing. It also features instant formatting and tools with which to transfer drawings to your word processor. *SmartDraw* has won considerable recognition and has gotten rave reviews in most leading computing magazines, including *PC Magazine, PC world, Windows Magazine,* and *Windows Sources.* Visit this site for more information.

Figure 983 SmartDraw home page.

SMARTT SOFTWARE LONG FILE NAME UTILITY (SHAREWARE)

http://ourworld.compuserve.com/hmepages/Smartt_Software/

LFNsNow (long file names now) adds long file name support and powerful file-management capabilities to the Open and Save as common dialogs of Windows 3.x programs running under Windows 95 or NT 4.0. With *LFNsNow* nearly all of your old Windows 3.x programs can open and save files using long file names. A right-mouse click in a dialog box supported by *LFNsNow* brings up a file context menu with options for *cut, copy, paste, delete, read me, properties, most recently used files, most recently used directories,* and so on. This makes it easy to perform file-management functions when opening or saving files, rather than having to launch Explorer. It also makes it quick and easy to open a recently used file or to switch to a recently used directory. Visit this site for a download today.

Figure 984 Smartt Software home page.

AI CAFÉ C/C++ CGI HTML HTTP JAVA J++ PERL VBSCRIPT VRML WIN32 WINSOCK 110011010010111100110111001101010001100110010010

SNADBOY'S TOP DESK FREEWARE FOR WINDOWS

http://www.snadboy.com/index.shtml

How often have you had one or more applications running that have completely covered the desktop just when you needed to access some object (such as the Recycle Bin or the Internet icon) that was hidden on the desktop? Rather than continue to endure this frustration, it is time that you downloaded *TopDesk* (for Windows 95/NT 4.0). The software adds an icon to the system area of the taskbar that gives you complete access to everything on the desktop—system objects and files, and even the Display Properties dialog. And, best of all, *TopDesk* is freeware! The generous author of this great utility is Dan Schless, who is also the proprietor of SnadBoy Software. Visit the SnadBoy Web site and download *TopDesk*.

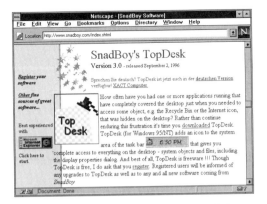

Figure 985.1 SnadBoy home page in English

Figure 985.2 And German.

AI CAFÉ C/C++ CGI HTML HTTP JAVA J++ PERL VBSCRIPT VRML WIN32 WINSOCK 110011010010111100110111001101010001100110010010

TECHWEB/TECHHELPER WINDOWS 95 TIPS

http://www.techweb.com/helper/wintips/wintips.html

The TechWeb/TechHelper Web site is chock full of tools, tutorials, and lists of frequently asked questions supplying information to developers and administrators working with Windows 95. At this site, you will find hundreds of tips and resources related to installation, customization, optimization, communications, hardware, the Windows 95 Registry, the Windows 95 MS-DOS prompt, installing and uninstalling Windows applications, input devices, printing, SCSI devices, video upgrades, and more. You even get "tips from the Top," authored by Peter Norton, John Woram, Jim Boyce, Bill Jones, Karen Kenworthy, and other honchos. TechWeb/TechHelper Windows 95 Tips is an outstanding source for hints and tips and tools you won't find anyplace else on the Web.

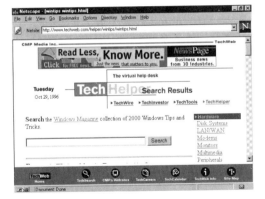

Figure 986.1 TechHelper Windows resources.

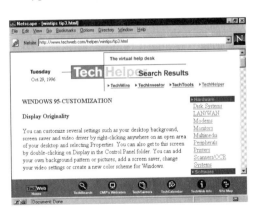

Figure 986.2 Windows 95 customization information.

TextPad: Shareware Text Editor for Windows

http://www.textpad.com/

TextPad is shareware designed to provide the power and functionality to satisfy the most demanding text-editing requirements (including huge files). The software is Windows hosted, and comes in 16- and 32-bit versions. The 32-bit edition can edit files up to the limits of virtual memory, and it will work with Windows 95, Windows NT, and Windows 3.1 with Win32 extensions. *TextPad* has been implemented according to the Windows 95 user-interface guidelines, and in-context help is available for all commands. The software's support for the multiple document interface lets you edit multiple files simultaneously, with up to two views of each file. Visit this Web site and take *TextPad* for a test drive.

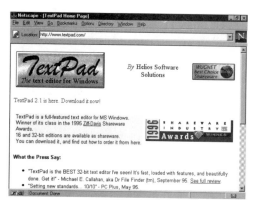

Figure 987.1 TextPad home page.

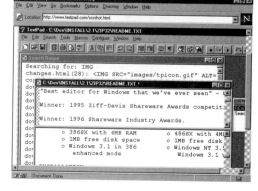

Figure 987.2 Text Pad screen shot.

ThunderBYTE Anti-Virus Shareware

http://www.thunderbyte.com/

ThunderBYTE Anti-Virus (TBAV) is a comprehensive toolkit designed to protect computers against, and to recover from, viruses. *ThunderBYTE* strives to achieve the highest standards in computer security and anti-virus software for millions of users around the world. Come to this Web site to download versions of *TBAV* for Windows 95, Windows 3.x, DOS, networks, and Microsoft Exchange. "We invite you to download an evaluation version of our software with no obligation," they write, "other than to remove the software at the end of your 30-day trial period if it does not meet your needs or expectations." Why not give *TBAV* a try?

Figure 988 The ThunderBYTE Web site.

AI CAFÉ C/C++ CGI HTML HTTP JAVA J++ PERL VBSCRIPT VRML WIN32 WINSOCK 11001101001011110011011100110101010001100110010101

TIPS & TWEAKS FOR WINDOWS 95

http://www.gate.net/~jsharit/windows_95/win95tips_and_tweaks.html

Are you trying to fine-tune Windows 95? "I have found these tips and tweaks to be useful to me," writes the Webmaster. "It is the way my personal system is set up, and I think the choices are rational and reasoned. There is a ton of excellent freeware and shareware software available. I have included links to what I personally feel are the best applications and utilities." But, most importantly, he provides great power-user tips related to desktop operations, general operations using Explorer, and solving such problems as recovering from a system crash, how do restart windows 95 *without* a full warm boot, and how to deal with Word crashes related to recognized problems in OLE32, and more.

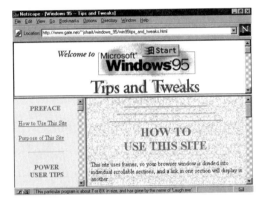

Figure 989.1 Tips and Tweaks.

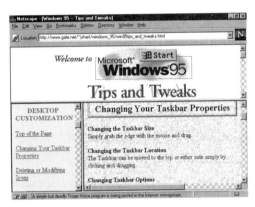

Figure 989.2 Changing Taskbar properties.

AI CAFÉ C/C++ CGI HTML HTTP JAVA J++ PERL VBSCRIPT VRML WIN32 WINSOCK 11001101001011110011011100110101010001100110010101

TRICKS & TIPS FOR WINDOWS

http://www.cris.com/~Jpdel/

This site features great power-user hints, tips, and strategies for Windows. An example? You ask. OK. Want to learn to reboot Windows 95 a little faster? "By now you have figured out that you can't just shut off the power on '95 and walk," writes our guru. "Well, next time you need to reboot, try this: Click Start and choose Shutdown. When the dialog box pops up, select the Restart computer option. (Nothing different so far, right?) Well now, *hold down the SHIFT key* and click OK. This action now lets the computer Warm Boot instead of going through the Power-On Self-Test." And you've just saved yourself a few minutes. Visit this site for other hints and tricks just like this. Good stuff.

Figure 990.1 Tricks and tips.

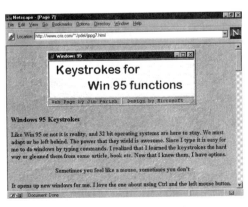

Figure 990.2 Keystrokes for Win95 functions.

ULTRAEDIT SHAREWARE TEXT EDITOR FOR WINDOWS

http://www.idmcomp.com/

Are you still trying to decide which text editor to use? Consider Ian D. Mead's *UltraEdit,* an editor with a 16-bit version for Windows 3.x and a 32-bit version for Windows 95 and Windows NT. There is no limit on size of file you edit. In addition, column-mode editing (specifying specific column widths, colors, and other attributes) is supported. The product includes a 100,000 word spell-checker along with a hexadecimal editor that allows editing of any binary file. The program also incorporates a syntax highlighting tool. *UltraEdit* has received praise from *PC Magazine, Window Sources,* and other publications. Try the shareware out for 45 days and, if you like it, register for the small fee of $30. This entitles you to technical support and free upgrades.

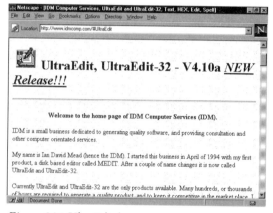

Figure 991 UltraEdit home page.

VISUAL DIFF AND MERGE SHAREWARE FOR WINDOWS

http://ng.netgate.net/~alan/vdifmrg.html

Visual Diff and Merge is a software developer's tool for finding and displaying the differences between two versions of a source file and for merging separate changes made to copies of the same source during concurrent development. The shareware is meant to be useful by itself, or in conjunction with a software configuration-management tool which can automatically detect conflicting source file changes during a "check-in" or related application. The software's graphical user's interface uses color and symbols to distinguish changes by type or origin, and this use of color allows the merge interface to display all text in a single window instead of utilizing three or more windows as do some merge tools. Visit this site and download this shareware. Give it a try. It's an excellent tool.

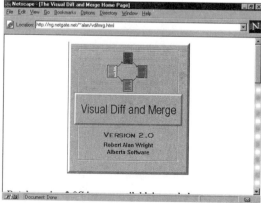

Figure 992 Visual Diff and Merge home page.

AI CAFÉ C/C++ CGI HTML HTTP JAVA J++ PERL VBSCRIPT VRML WIN32 WINSOCK 1100110100101111001101110011010101000110011001001001

WEBSENSE FOR NT SHAREWARE

http://www.netpart.com/websense/

Worried about employee productivity now that your Internet connection is up and running? Do you need to restrict access to undesirable Internet sites? *WebSENSE* gives you the tools you need to implement your own corporate Internet access policy. *WebSENSE* is a serious Internet screening mechanism that lets corporations define and enforce Internet access privileges by "screen-out sites" deemed inappropriate for business use. *WebSENSE* lets you define and enforce Internet access privileges, protect against potential legal liabilities, ensure employee productivity, and (perhaps most importantly) control network bandwidth. Visit this site and download a copy of *WebSENSE*.

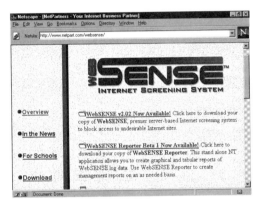
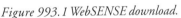

Figure 993.1 WebSENSE download.

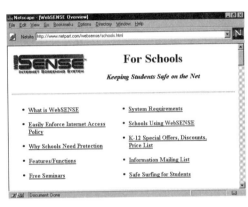

Figure 993.2 A special version for schools.

AI CAFÉ C/C++ CGI HTML HTTP JAVA J++ PERL VBSCRIPT VRML WIN32 WINSOCK 1100110100101111001101110011010101000110011001001001

LEE WILKINSON'S WINDOWS 95 INFORMATION

http://www.innotts.co.uk/~leewilko/index.html

Lee Wilkinson's Web site contains lots of good stuff for Windows 95. To start, check out his tutorial on setting up TCP/IP in conjunction with Windows 95. Then, download his automated PPP login scripts for Windows 95. You will also find links to downloads for dozens of other great 32-bit freeware and shareware applications related to network connectivity, the Internet, spreadsheet operations, printing, database management, and other tasks. Wilkinson is an uncompromising Windows 95 advocate and an unflinching technical expert who dares you challenge him with technical queries about the operating system. Think of a hard one and then test him.

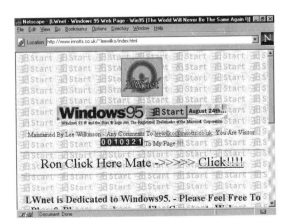

Figure 994 Lee's Win95 home page.

WIN.32BIT.COM: SOFTWARE ARCHIVE

http://www.32bit.com/newhomepage/

At this site, you will find dozens of great examples of Windows 95 shareware and freeware that you can download. To start, check out *$tockExchange32*, which is a fast, easy way to get up-to-date stock and mutual fund data from the Internet. Or, download the *AVIGIF Collection of Graphics*, which includes animated letters (with morph effect) in both AVI and GIF formats. Or, you may want to download and test-drive *CoffeCup*, which many consider to be the coolest HTML editor available anywhere on the Web. Another nice choice is *Deletor*, a program which recursively deletes all the files in your system matching specified patterns. Be careful how you use this one! Visit this site for more information.

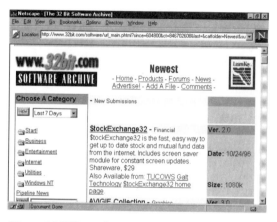

Figure 995 Win.32bit.Com.

WINDOWS95.COM: FANTASTIC SHAREWARE

http://www.windows95.com/

At 28.8 kbps, this site takes absolutely *forever* to load, but once it does you have a marvelous collection of resources related to Windows 95. The site includes a terrific archive of "newbie" information, tools, and links. You'll also find extensive resources related to Internet TCP/IP connectivity, 32-bit hardware drivers, Windows 95 tutorials, and more. Be sure to check out the 32-bit shareware archive, where you will find imaging and OCR (optical character recognition) tools, mail client utilities, calculators and conversion tools, and communications tools, along with some great personal information managers. You will also find cool startup and shutdown screens, printer utilities, shell enhancements, and WAV tools. A great resource collection.

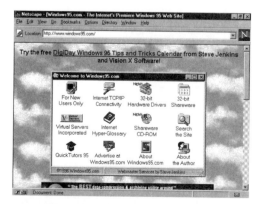

Figure 996.1 Windows95.com.

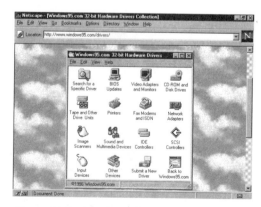

Figure 996.2 Hardware driver collection.

AI CAFÉ C/C++ CGI HTML HTTP JAVA J++ PERL VBSCRIPT VRML WIN32 WINSOCK 11001101001011110011011100110101010001100110010010

WINDOWS CGI 1.3A INTERFACE

http://website.ora.com/wsdocs/32demo/windows-cgi.html

This document is an informal CGI (common gateway interface) specification geared specifically to Windows 95 and Windows NT. The document is intended for both CGI programmers and server implementers. *Version 1.3a* documents the *Authenticated Password* variable, which is "current practice," and a new variable *Document Root* which was recently added. In addition, the description of the authentication variables has been changed in this document to reflect current practice. Servers pass these variables through the CGI interface regardless of whether or not the server has used the variables for authentication. This "pass-through authentication" is used by the majority of existing Windows CGI applications. Read the specification for more details.

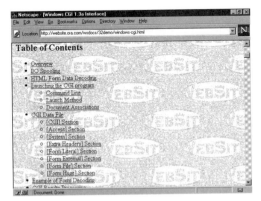

Figure 997.1 Table of Contents.

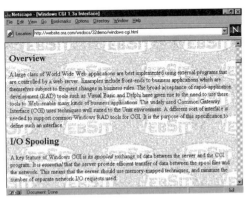

Figure 997.2 Overview.

AI CAFÉ C/C++ CGI HTML HTTP JAVA J++ PERL VBSCRIPT VRML WIN32 WINSOCK 11001101001011110011011100110101010001100110010010

WINPACK32 DELUXE SHAREWARE FOR WINDOWS

http://www.retrospect.com/

WinPack32 Deluxe is shareware published by Retrospect that implements the new 32-bit version of the classic *WinPack* archival and extraction program. *WinPack32 Deluxe* supports Zip, Gzip, Arj, Lharc, Tar, *UNIX* Compress (with LZW option), UUEncode, XXEncode. Binhex 4.0, Mime, and Base 64. You can create and extract files using any of these formats. The software's features include the ability to view any file type within an archive, archive conversion, a built-in self-extractor, drag-and-drop, recursive processing of subdirectories, multipart archive support, disk spanning, self-extracting disk spans, and zip encryption and decryption. Visit this site for a free download and try out the *WinPack32* shareware today.

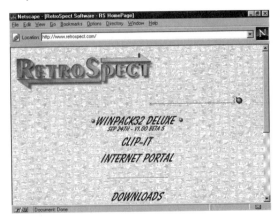

Figure 998 Retrospect home page.

999

WINZIP SHAREWARE FOR WINDOWS 95

http://www.winzip.com/

Uncompressed files simply consume too much disk space. So, compress them. For most users, *WinZip* software needs little introduction. As you may know, *WinZip* blends the convenience of the Windows environment with the convenience of ZIP files. Now, the new *WinZip Wizards* make unzipping files easier than ever. *WinZip* features built-in support for popular Internet file formats, including TAR, Gzip, *UNIX* compress, UUEncode, Binhex, MIME, ARJ, LZH, and ARC files. Also, *WinZip* provides an interface to most virus scanners. *WinZip* also supports long file names, and drag-and-drop operations with the Windows 95 Explorer. *WinZip* keeps getting better and better. Visit this site and check out the latest edition. In short, this is must-have software.

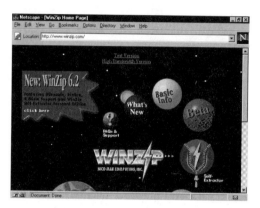

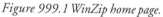

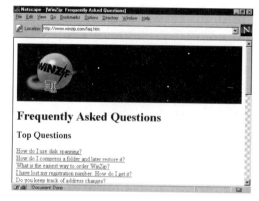

Figure 999.1 WinZip home page.

Figure 999.2 WinZip FAQ.

1000

#WINDOWS OPS: WINDOWS 95 INTERNET RELAY CHAT

http://www.windows95.org/

Are you looking for someone who can answer difficult Windows 95 questions? Try *#Windows Ops*. They are a group of people who started this IRC (Internet relay chat) channel to help users who were in the beta program with technical problems. Today, their focus is on providing general help and pointers to the right place to which users should turn for information. "We aren't paid and we are not Microsoft," they write, "so if we don't answer a question, or don't know, please have respect and thank us for what we did try to do to help you. . . . We try to do a good job and maintain the quality of information and support on a daily basis . . ." Start your IRC software and connect to *#Windows Ops*. You will be glad you did.

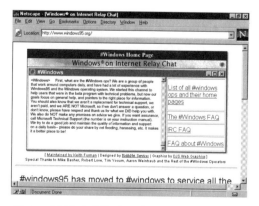

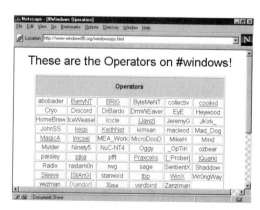

Figure 1000.1 #Windows home page.

Figure 1000.2 #Windows Ops.

AI CAFE C/C++ CGI HTML HTTP JAVA J++ PERL VBSCRIPT VRML WIN32 WINSOCK 1100110100101111001101110011010101000110011001010

ZEUS FOR WINDOWS TEXT EDITOR (SHAREWARE)

http://ourworld.compuserve.com/homepages/jussi/

As a programmer, do you realize that you spend most of your time editing? At last, this site features the "programmer's text editor" we've all been looking for. *Zeus for Windows* is a powerful text editor specifically designed for software developers working with Windows 3.x, Windows 95, and Windows NT. The *Zeus* text editor offers all the features of an IDE (Integrated Development Environment) with the added benefit of providing a powerful text editor that supports the *Brief, Epsilon, WordStar,* and *Emacs* keyboard mappings! The editor also includes color highlighting for C/C++, Java, Pascal, Clipper, COBOL, SQL, and FORTRAN! And, the editor includes built-in DOS command line support. Visit this site and download *Zeus* and try it for thirty days. I think you will like it.

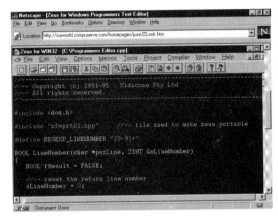

Figure 1001 A Zeus screen.

ADDITIONAL WINDOWS 3.1, NT, AND WINDOWS 95 RESOURCES

Framegrabber SDK/Win 3.1 & NT
http://wheat.symgrp.com/symgrp/datx/sdkframe.html

Setting Up VI POSIX Editor for Windows NT 3.1
http://198.105.232.5/Support/KBSL/bussys/winnt/Q108581.htm

Targeting both Windows 95/NT and Windows 3.1
http://www.solutionsoft.com/w9531.htm

Programming controls / tools for Windows 3.1, 95 & NT
http://204.50.46.33/b_search.htm

C and C++ for Windows (en DOS)
http://comcol.nl/eng/siecw_a.htm

The NeuroSolutions Demo
http://www.nd.com/demo/demo.htm

The HTML3 Table Model
http://www.dtseng.com/sig/rsm/specs/HTML_3.0/html30_table_model.htm

Survey of VR and VRML Systems
http://cybernet.snu.ac.kr/~cyber/vrml/VR_system.html

Index

ABOUT THE AUTHOR

Edward J. Renehan, Jr. is married to Christa Renehan. They have two children: William James Renehan (born 1987) and Katherine Eleanor Renehan (born 1991). Renehan is the author of many books—some related to American history, others related to technology, the Internet, and finance. In the 1970s, Renehan worked as a musician and recorded with Pete Seeger for Folkways Records. He also served on the Board of Directors of the Hudson River Sloop Clearwater, a nonprofit effort in environmental education.

Beginning in 1980, Renehan worked in publishing in New York City for fourteen years (holding positions at John Wiley & Sons, St. Martin's Press, Macmillan Publishing, and K-III/Newbridge) before moving to Rhode Island in 1994. At Macmillan Book Clubs (later named Newbridge Communications, a subsidiary of K-III Holdings), Renehan served as Director of Computer Publishing Programs and in that capacity oversaw the launch of Newbridge's Web site: *http://www.booksonline.com*. Renehan's books and CD-ROMs have been published by Crown/Random House, Springer-Verlag, Chelsea Green, Jamsa Press, and (soon) HarperCollins.

E-mail: *ejren@earthlink.net*

Web: *http://members.aol.com/EJRen/EJRen.html*

ABOUT TRIGGERHILL'S I'M SO HAPPY, C.D.
. . . a computer user's best friend®

From the start, Jamsa Press has been committed to being *a computer user's best friend*. With that in mind, Kris and Debbie designated their five-year-old Dalmatian, Happy, as the company logo. At Jamsa Press, we go to great efforts to make our products easy to understand and use. We design each product with the user in mind.

When Happy is not posing for catalog photos or book covers, he volunteers for therapy work at local hospitals. Happy completed his first obedience title as the number eight Dalmatian in the United States. Currently working on his next title, he is now ranked the number six Dalmatian. On a normal day, however, you can find Happy either sitting behind Kris in his chair as he writes, or laying beside Debbie's desk. Each day, Happy reminds us of our goal to be *a computer user's best friend*.